THE R[illegible]BOOK OF T[illegible]CITY

The Byzantine world contained many important cities throughout its empire. Although it was not 'urban' in the sense of the word today, its cities played a far more fundamental role than those of its European neighbors. This book, through a collection of twenty-four chapters, discusses aspects of, and different approaches to, Byzantine urbanism from the early to late Byzantine periods. It provides both a chronological and thematic perspective to the study of Byzantine cities, bringing together literary, documentary, and archival sources with archaeological results, material culture, art, and architecture, resulting in a rich synthesis of the variety of regional and sub-regional transformations of Byzantine urban landscapes.

Organised into four sections, this book covers: *Theory and Historiography*, *Geography and Economy*, *Architecture and the Built Environment*, and *Daily Life and Material Culture*. It includes more specialised accounts that address the centripetal role of Constantinople and its broader influence across the empire. Such new perspectives help to challenge the historiographical balance between 'margins and metropolis,' and also to include geographical areas often regarded as peripheral, like the coastal urban centers of the Byzantine Mediterranean as well as cities on islands, such as Crete, Cyprus, and Sicily which have more recently yielded well-excavated and stratigraphically sound urban sites.

The Routledge Handbook of the Byzantine City provides both an overview and detailed study of the Byzantine city to specialist scholars, students, and enthusiasts alike and, therefore, will appeal to all those interested in Byzantine urbanism and society, as well as those studying medieval society in general.

Nikolas Bakirtzis is an Associate Professor at The Cyprus Institute in Nicosia, Cyprus. His research focuses on Byzantine monasticism, medieval cities and fortifications, and the island landscapes of the Byzantine, medieval, and early modern Mediterranean. As the Director of the Andreas Pittas Art Characterization Labs, he leads research on the materiality of medieval and early modern art enhanced through the use of advanced digital and analytical methods. His work has received support from the European Commission, the Cyprus Research and Innovation Foundation, the Princeton Seeger Center for Hellenic Studies, the A.G. Leventis Foundation, and the Getty Research Institute.

Luca Zavagno is an Associate Professor of Byzantine Studies at Bilkent University, Turkey. He is the author of many articles and books on the early medieval and Byzantine Mediterranean. His research focuses on Byzantine urbanism and medieval Mediterranean insularity. He has been awarded the Dumbarton Oaks Summer Fellowship twice (in 2011 and 2016) as well as the prestigious Stanley Seeger Fellowship of the Hellenic Studies Center at Princeton University (2012), the Newton Mobility Grant (2018), and he has been twice a fellowship at Center for Advanced Studies 'Migration and Mobility in Late Antiquity and the Early Middle Ages' at the University of Tübingen, Germany (2022 and 2023).

ROUTLEDGE HISTORY HANDBOOKS

THE ROUTLEDGE HANDBOOK OF THE MONGOLS AND CENTRAL-EASTERN EUROPE
Edited by Alexander V. Maiorov and Roman Hautala

THE ROUTLEDGE HANDBOOK OF MEDIEVAL RURAL LIFE
Edited by Miriam Müller

THE ROUTLEDGE HANDBOOK OF EAST CENTRAL AND EASTERN EUROPE IN THE MIDDLE AGES, 500-1300
Edited by Florin Curta

THE ROUTLEDGE HANDBOOK ON IDENTITY IN BYZANTIUM
Edited by Michael Edward Stewart, David Alan Parnell, and Conor Whately

THE ROUTLEDGE HANDBOOK OF MEMORY ACTIVISM
Edited by Yifat Gutman and Jenny Wüstenberg

THE ROUTLEDGE HANDBOOK OF TAXATION IN MEDIEVAL EUROPE
Edited by Denis Menjot, Mathieu Caesar, Florent Garnier and Pere Verdés Pijuan

THE ROUTLEDGE HANDBOOK OF THE BYZANTINE CITY
From Justinian to Mehmet II (ca. 500 – ca. 1500)
Edited by Nikolas Bakirtzis and Luca Zavagno

For more information about this series, please visit: https://www.routledge.com/Routledge-History-Handbooks/book-series/RHISTHAND

THE ROUTLEDGE HANDBOOK OF THE BYZANTINE CITY

From Justinian to Mehmet II (ca. 500 – ca. 1500)

Edited by Nikolas Bakirtzis and Luca Zavagno

Routledge
Taylor & Francis Group
LONDON AND NEW YORK

Designed cover image: Jerusalem on the Madaba Map. Madaba, Jordan.
Eyal Bartov/Alamy Stock Photo 2BC6KRR.

First published 2024
by Routledge
4 Park Square, Milton Park, Abingdon, Oxon OX14 4RN

and by Routledge
605 Third Avenue, New York, NY 10158

Routledge is an imprint of the Taylor & Francis Group, an informa business

British Library Cataloguing-in-Publication Data
A catalogue record for this book is available from the British Library

Library of Congress Cataloging-in-Publication Data
Names: Bakirtzis, Nikolas, editor, author. | Zavagno, Luca, editor, author.
Title: The Routledge handbook of the Byzantine city : from Justinian to Mehmet II (ca. 500 - ca.1500) / edited by Nikolas Bakirtzis and Luca Zavagno.
Description: New York : Routledge, 2024. | Series: Routledge history handbooks | Includes bibliographical references and index. |
Identifiers: LCCN 2023032081 (print) | LCCN 2023032082 (ebook) | ISBN 9780367196790 (hardback) | ISBN 9781032603568 (paperback) | ISBN 9780429203923 (ebook)
Subjects: LCSH: City and town life--Byzantine Empire--History. | Urbanization--Byzantine Empire--History. | Cities and towns--Byzantine Empire--History. | Cities and towns, Medieval--Byzantine Empire. | City planning--Byzantine Empire--History. | Byzantine Empire--Social life and customs. | Byzantine Empire--Social conditions.
Classification: LCC DF531 .R678 2024 (print) | LCC DF531 (ebook) | DDC 949.5/02--dc23/eng/20230826
LC record available at https://lccn.loc.gov/2023032081
LC ebook record available at https://lccn.loc.gov/2023032082

ISBN: 978-0-367-19679-0 (hbk)
ISBN: 978-1-032-60356-8 (pbk)
ISBN: 978-0-429-20392-3 (ebk)

DOI: 10.4324/9780429203923

CONTENTS

FIGURES AND TABLES

Figures

Tables

CONTRIBUTORS

Nikolas Bakirtzis is an Associate Professor at The Cyprus Institute in Nicosia, Cyprus. His research focuses on Byzantine monasticism, medieval cities and fortifications, and the island landscapes of the Byzantine, medieval, and early modern Mediterranean. As the Director of the Andreas Pittas Art Characterization Labs, he leads research on the materiality of medieval and early modern art enhanced through the use of advanced digital and analytical methods. His work has received support, among others, from the European Commission, the Cyprus Research and Innovation Foundation, the Princeton Seeger Center for Hellenic Studies, the A.G. Leventis Foundation, and the Getty Research Institute.

Luca Zavagno is an Associate Professor of Byzantine Studies at Bilkent University. Dr Zavagno is the author of many articles and books on the early medieval and Byzantine Mediterranean. His research focuses on Byzantine Urbanism and medieval Mediterranean insularity. He was also twice awarded the Dumbarton Oaks Summer Fellowship (2011 and 2016) as well as the prestigious Stanley Seeger Fellowship of the Hellenic Studies Center at Princeton University (2012), the Newton Mobility Grant (2018), and a Fellow at Center for Advanced Studies 'Migration and Mobility in Late Antiquity and the Early Middle Ages' at the University of Tübingen (2022).

* * *

Jenny P. Albani holds a diploma in architecture from the National Technical University, Athens, and a Ph.D. in the history of art from Vienna University. She received scholarships from the Hellenic State Scholarship Foundation, the Stiftung FVS, the Katholische Frauenbewegung Österreichs, and the German Academic Exchange Service. Albani was a research fellow at the Institute of Art History of the National Technical University, Athens, an exhibition curator at the Hellenic Ministry of Culture and Sports, and a teaching associate at the Hellenic Open University. She participated in excavation projects in Greece and Egypt and authored several book reviews, papers, and books on Byzantine art and architecture history, iconology, and museology. Her research focuses on the cult and iconography of transvestite female saints, eschatology in art, and cross-cultural exchanges in the Eastern

Mediterranean. She is the co-editor (with Ioanna Christoforaki) of the recently published collective volume *Πάντα ῥεῖ. Change in Thirteenth-Century Byzantine Architecture, Art, and Material Culture* (*Byzantioς. Studies in Byzantine History and Civilization, 20*) (Turnhout, 2022). Albani is currently the President of the Friends of the Herakleidon Museum Non-Profit Cultural Association and a member of the Administrative Board of the Association for the Dissemination of Greek Letters.

Mabi Angar studied Art History (M.A.) and Byzantine Studies (M.A.) at the Free University Berlin and Princeton University. She received her Ph.D. in 2012 at the University of Cologne, where she taught Byzantine art and cultural history from 2006 to 2022 at the Department of Byzantine Studies. In her dissertation she examined Byzantine head reliquaries and their afterlife in the West following the Latin Conquest of Constantinople in 1204. Her latest research project was dedicated to the urban development and identity of the Genoese settlement Pera/Galata, situated across Constantinople. Her teaching and publications deal with the material culture of the Eastern Mediterranean, the topography of Constantinople, and modern perceptions of Byzantium. Mabi Angar initiated and co-organized international academic formats in Cologne, Florence, and Istanbul. She has received grants from prestigious institutions such as the German Academic Scholarship Foundation, the Harvard University Center for Italian Renaissance Studies – Villa I Tatti, the Koç University Research Center for Anatolian Civilizations, and the Federal Ministry of Education and Research.

Suna Çağaptay is an Associate Professor of Art History and Archaeology at Muğla Sıtkı Koçman University. She works on late Byzantine, Early Ottoman, Crusader, and principality-period architecture and city-making practices in the Eastern Mediterranean, in particular, the circulation and translation of Byzantine and Latin architectural techniques and forms in Islamic contexts and the afterlives of the ancient cities. She is the recipient of numerous fellowships and research grants, among them the Dumbarton Oaks, Aga Khan Islamic Art and Architecture at MIT, ANAMED, Barakat, SOAS, and the Getty Foundation. From 2017 to 2022, she worked as a Research Associate for 'The Impact of the Ancient City,' a project based in the Faculty of Classics at the University of Cambridge, funded by the European Research Council. Her publications include The First Ottoman Capital: The Religious, Architectural and Social History of Bursa (London, 2020), as well as numerous book chapters and articles. She also co-edited a volume (with E. Key Fowden, E. Coghill-Zychowicz, and L. Blanke titled *Cities as Palimpsests? Responses to Antiquity in Eastern Mediterranean Urbanism* (Oxford, 2022)).

Maria Cristina Carile is an Associate Professor of History of Byzantine Art (L-ART/01 History of Medieval Art) at the Department of Cultural Heritage of the University of Bologna. Since 2003, she has conducted her research working in international research centers specialised in Late Antique and Byzantine culture. Between 2005 and 2008, she was an Honorary Research Fellow at the Centre for Byzantine, Ottoman and Modern Greek Studies, University of Birmingham (UK), where she worked with the Director Leslie Brubaker. In 2006–2007, she was the recipient of a Junior Fellowship at the RCAC-Research Center for Anatolian Civilizations, Koç University, Istanbul (TR). In 2009, she received an Onassis Fellowship from the Alexander S. Onassis Public Benefit Foundation, Athens. Between 2008 and 2015, she was enrolled as a Research Fellow in the Department of Cultural Heritage of the University of Bologna, where she worked with Luigi Canetti and Alessandro

Volpe. There, between 2015 and 2018, she held the position of Senior Assistant Professor (fixed-term) in L-ART/01 History of medieval Art. Currently, her research focuses on the artistic culture and the circulation of visual communication codes in the Late Antique and Byzantine Mediterranean, particularly in the Adriatic and Aegean Sea. She has presented her research at national and international conferences, scientific lectures, and seminars (UK, France, Serbia, Turkey, Russia, Iran, USA).

Enrico Cirelli is a Professor in Archaeology of medieval Europe at the Department of History and Civilizations, Alma Mater Studiorum – University of Bologna. His main research areas cover late Roman and medieval urbanism, fortified settlements, monasteries, archaeology of productions, and material culture. He directs archaeological excavations and surveys in Italy and Croatia and participates in other international research projects in Spain, Albania, Palestine, Jordan, Libya, Tunisia, and Algeria. His book *'Ravenna: archeologia di una città' has got the Ottone d'Assia and Riccardo Francovich prize* (2008). His last two books focused on material culture and the economy of the early Medieval Mediterranean Sea, as paired with a new research project on amphorae, glass, and marble trade.

Michael J. Decker specialises in the economic and social history and archaeology of the eastern Mediterranean of the 5th–12th centuries. He has been an Andrew Mellon Postdoctoral Fellow (Rice University) and the recipient of a Fulbright Research Fellowship. His publications include *The Sasanian Empire at War* (Westholme, 2022); *The Byzantine Dark Ages, The Byzantine Art of War, and Life and Society in Byzantine Cappadocia* (w/J. Eric Cooper). Decker is currently Maroulis Professor of Byzantine History and Orthodox Religion at the University of South Florida, where he has taught and researched since 2004.

Andrei Gandila is an Associate Professor of Roman History and Director of Ancient and medieval Studies at the University of Alabama in Huntsville (USA), where he teaches a range of courses on Roman, Late Antique, and early medieval civilization. He is a former Junior Fellow at the Dumbarton Oaks Center for Byzantine Studies, a graduate of the Eric P. Newman Graduate Seminar in Numismatics sponsored by the American Numismatic Society, and the recipient of a research grant from the Medieval Academy of America. His research and publications span Roman-barbarian interaction and identity formation, borderlands and cross-cultural exchange, and the economic history of the Mediterranean world, with a specific focus on monetary circulation. His numerous publications include a monograph, *Cultural Encounters on Byzantium's Northern Frontier, c. AD 500-700: Coins, Artifacts and History* (Cambridge, 2018), as well as articles in journals such as *Byzantinische Zeitschrift*, *Dumbarton Oaks Papers*, *Journal of Late Antiquity*, *Revue Numismatique*, and *Numismatic Chronicle*.

Elisabetta Giorgi is a research fellow in Methodologies of Archaeological Research at the University of Siena. She is the director of the archaeological fieldwork projects on the Roman and Late Antique settlement of Vignale (Tuscany) and co-director of the excavations in the Early Byzantine District of Gortys (Crete).

Her main research interests are the water management connected to the transformations of the ancient Mediterranean cities in the Late Antiquity and Early Byzantine age, the urban and suburban landscapes in times of transition, the excavation of daily life contexts, as well as the public archaeology and the interaction between research and the heritage community. Her most recent monograph is *Archeologia dell'acqua a Gortina di Creta in età protobizantina* (Oxford, 2016).

Matthew Harpster is the Director of the Koç University Mustafa V. Koç Maritime Archaeology Research Center at Koç University in Istanbul, Turkey. He received his Ph.D. from Texas A&M University and has held teaching and research posts at the Massachusetts Institute of Technology, Eastern Mediterranean University, and the University of Birmingham. He recently completed a long-term project that demonstrated the value of decoupling the maritime archaeological dataset in the Mediterranean from text-based narratives and interpretive practices, published as *Reconstructing a Maritime Past* (London-NewYork, 2023). He is presently pursuing a project that restudies the maritime underclass in the ancient Mediterranean with postcolonial and postmodern theories about contemporary mobile and migratory communities. His other research interests include maritime cultural landscapes and the history of maritime archaeological thought, and he has conducted fieldwork in Iran, Cyprus, Turkey, Italy, and Morocco.

Michael R. Jones is an Assistant Professor at the Department of Archaeology and History of Art at Koç University, Mustafa V. Koç Center for Maritime Archaeology. He is a maritime archaeologist whose research focuses on the development of shipbuilding and maritime trade in the late antique and medieval eastern Mediterranean. He has participated in a number of archaeological research projects in Turkey, including the excavation and study of eight Byzantine shipwrecks from the Theodosian Harbor site in the Yenikapı neighborhood of Istanbul since 2005, archaeological surveys of late antique coastal sites and underwater remains on the Rough Cilician coast of Turkey near Boğsak/Dana Island (Silifke, Mersin province) and Urla (Izmir province), and the post-excavation study of the hull remains and cargo of the Late Byzantine Çamaltı Burnu shipwreck from the Sea of Marmara.

Ioli Kalavrezou has been the Dumbarton Oaks Professor of Byzantine Art History at the Department of History of Art and Architecture at Harvard University, having earlier taught at UCLA and at the Ludwig Maximilian University in Munich. She has served as Chair of the department for six years and is also a Senior Fellow at Dumbarton Oaks. She is a member of the Executive Committee and Senior Research Associate at Dumbarton Oaks. She also serves as a Trustee at the Cyprus Institute in Nicosia.

Her research focuses on political and ideological history, for example, the relationship between Church and State and the use of King David in imperial propaganda, especially in manuscript illustrations. These questions led her to investigate the visual evidence ranging from monumental wall paintings and mosaics to objects carved in ivory and steatite, icons, and manuscripts. Another topic of special research interest has been the cult of the Virgin Mary. Everyday life and private devotion have also been at the center of her research interests, as published in her book on *Byzantine Icons in Steatite* (Wien, 1985). The sun imagery in the person of the emperor is her most recent project. She also delved into the study of the role and place of women in Byzantine society, which led to a large exhibition at Harvard entitled Byzantine Women and their World.

Nikolaos Karydis is a practicing Architect and Senior Lecturer at the University of Kent specializing in the fields of Architectural History, Urban Design, and Conservation. He studied

Architecture at the National Technical University of Athens, and Building Conservation at the University of Bath. The doctoral thesis he carried out in Bath from 2006 to 2009 was distinguished with the 2010 R.I.B.A. President's Commendation and resulted in his book on Early Byzantine vaulted construction. From 2010 to 2012, Karydis was Assistant Professor of Architecture in the Rome Studies Program of the University of Notre Dame. In 2012, he moved to Kent where he founded and directs the MSc Program in Architectural Conservation. He has recently published a new graphic reconstruction of Justinian's church of the Holy Apostles (2019), as well as two articles retracing the phases of construction of the churches of St. John and St. Mary at Ephesos (2016 and 2019, respectively). Karydis has also published on other topics, including vernacular architecture, the revival of Classical Architecture in nineteenth-century Athens, and the discovery of Byzantine architecture in nineteenth-century England. He is currently working on a book retracing the development of Ripa Grande, the lost river port of early modern Rome.

Tonia Kiousopoulou is a Professor of Byzantine History in the History and Archaeology Department at the National and Kapodistrian University of Athens. Her research focuses on the social history during the late Byzantine period. She has published several books like: *Ο θεσμός της οικογένειας στην Ήπειρο κατά τον 13ο αιώνα* (Athens, 1990) (*The Family Institution in Epirus during the 13th Century*); *Χρόνος και ηλικίες στη βυζαντινή κοινωνία. Η κλίμακα των ηλικιών από τα αγιολογικά κείμενα της μέσης εποχής (7ος-11ος αι.)* (Athens, 1997) (*Time and Ages in Byzantine Society through the Hagiography of the Middle Byzantine Period*); *Βασιλεύς ή Οικονόμος: Πολιτική εξουσία και ιδεολογία πριν την Άλωση* (Athens, 2007) (*Emperor or Manager: Power and Political Ideology in Byzantium before the Fall*]; and, *Οι 'αόρατες' βυζαντινές πόλεις στον ελλαδικό χώρο (13ος-15ος αιώνας)* (Athens, 2013) (*The Invisible Byzantine Cities in the Greek Area 13th–15th Centuries*).

Athanasios Koutoupas is a PhD candidate at The Cyprus Institute. He received his degree from the Department of Theology of the Theological School of Aristotle at the University of Thessaloniki. He received a Master's degree specializing in Religious Studies from the same department, and he also holds a Master's degree in the History of Hellenistic and Roman times from the Center for Hellenistic Studies of Bibliotheca Alexandrina. He collaborates with Société Archéologique d'Alexandrie on various projects. His main research interest focuses on religion, history, and archaeology, especially in the Graeco-Roman and Early Christian eras in the Eastern Mediterranean. During his studies, he had the chance to participate in numerous projects, allowing him to become increasingly engaged in the practical application of technology in studying, analyzing, and disseminating archaeological material and sources. He is co-editor of the *Cultural Exchanges in the Eastern Mediterranean* (Newcastle upon Tyne: Cambridge Scholars Publishing, 2022).

Ian Randall received his Ph.D. from Brown University in 2018 and is currently a postdoctoral research fellow with the Database of Religious History at the University of British Columbia. A Byzantine archaeologist who specialises in identity construction and foodways, he excavates at the site of Kourion in the Republic of Cyprus and at the site of Vlochos in western Thessaly. He has a chapter in *The Archaeology of Medieval Islamic Frontiers* (University Press of Colorado, 2019) on conceptualizing the Byzantine-Islamic maritime frontier and is currently working on a project exploring the heterochronic perceptions of material life in early medieval port societies.

Helen Saradi specialises in Byzantine and Late Antique studies. Her research and publications span Byzantine urbanism and related historical, archaeological, and literary issues, especially the rhetoric of the Byzantine city and the deeds of private transactions and pertaining social topics. She is the author of three monographs: *The Byzantine City in the Sixth Century: Literary Images and Historical Reality* (Athens, 2006); *Il sistema notarile bizantino (VI-XV secolo)* (Milan, 1999); *Le notariat byzantin du IXe au XVe siècles* (Athens, 1991). She is the author of 80 articles.

Professor Saradi taught at Universities in Greece and Canada and lectured at graduate-faculty seminars of many academic institutions, including Dumbarton Oaks, Mac Master University, Simon Fraser, University of Athens, of Thessaloniki, School of Law and Center of Byzantine Studies, Exeter College, Oxford, King's College, London, École des Hautes Études en Sciences Sociales, and Paris. She was awarded Summer Fellowships from Dumbarton Oaks and grants from the Research Council of Canada. Her teaching included classical and Byzantine history, civilization, and literature. She also held many high academic administrative positions.

Ufuk Serin currently is an Associate Professor of architecture at the Middle East Technical University (METU). After graduating from the Department of Architecture at METU, she obtained her MS in Cultural Heritage Conservation at the same university. She received her Doctoral Degree in Early Christian Art and Archaeology from the Pontificio Istituto di Archeologia Cristiana (PIAC), Vatican City. She has been the recipient of doctoral and postdoctoral research grants and fellowships from distinguished institutions, such as the Alexander S. Onassis Foundation, Dumbarton Oaks Research Library and Collection (Harvard University), Fiat International and Koç Foundation, Kunsthistorisches Institut in Florenz/Max-Planck-Institut, the University of California at Los Angeles (UCLA)/Cotsen Institute of Archaeology in association with the School for Advanced Research (SAR), and the Italian Academy for Advanced Studies in America of Columbia University. She has decades of professional experience in archaeological field survey and excavation. She coordinated the Turkish component of the partnership in the Byzantium-Early Islam Project (BYZeIS) of the Euromed Heritage III Program, funded by the European Commission. Her research interests mainly cover Late Antique and Byzantine architecture and urbanism, Early Christian and medieval archaeology, combined with studies in archaeological conservation, contested heritage, and the interpretation and presentation of heritage sites.

Myrto Veikou is an Assistant Professor of Byzantine Archaeology at the Department of History and Archaeology, University of Patras. She is also researcher for the Department of Linguistics and Philology, Uppsala University (Research Program 'Retracing Connections – Byzantine Storyworlds in Greek, Arabic, Georgian, and Old Slavonic (c. 950–c. 1100)' and research collaborator for the Austrian Academy of Sciences (Project 'Medieval Smyrna/Izmir: The Transformation of a City and its Hinterland from Byzantine to Ottoman Times [MESMY]'). She studied History and Archaeology (BA – University of Athens) and further specialised in Byzantine History, Archaeology, Philology, and Literary Studies (M.Phil. – University of Birmingham; MA – University of Paris I – Sorbonne; PhD – University of Athens; PhD – Uppsala University). Her first Ph.D. thesis in Byzantine Archaeology was published in 2012 (*Byzantine Epirus: A topography of transformation. Settlements from the 7th to the 12th Centuries in Southern Epirus and Aetoloacarnania, Greece, the*

Medieval Mediterranean 95 (Leiden, 2012). Her second Ph.D. thesis in Byzantine Philology and Literary Studies will be published within 2023 (*Spatial Paths to Holiness – Literary 'Lived Spaces' in Eleventh-Century Byzantine Saints' Lives, Studia Byzantina Upsaliensia* 22 [Uppsala, 2023). She has been teaching Byzantine history and archaeology since 2007, as well as Byzantine philology and literary studies since 2017.

Joanita Vroom is a Professor of the Archaeology of medieval and early modern Eurasia at the Faculty of Archaeology, Leiden University (NL), specializing in Medieval and Post-Medieval archaeology in the eastern Mediterranean and the Near East (including the Byzantine, Islamic, Crusader, and Ottoman periods). She takes a particular interest in the socio-economic (production and distribution) and cultural aspects (cuisine and eating habits) of material culture (including ceramics) in these societies. She is the series editor of the *Medieval and Post-Medieval Mediterranean Archaeology Series* (MPMAS) at Brepols Publishers (Turnhout).

Earlier she published *After Antiquity: Ceramics and Society in the Aegean from the 7th to the 20th Century A.C.* (Leiden, 2003), *Byzantine to Modern Pottery in the Aegean: An Introduction and Field Guide* (Utrecht, 2005; Turnhout, 2014, *Medieval and Post-Medieval Ceramics in the Eastern Mediterranean: Fact and Fiction* (MPMAS 1; Turnhout, 2015), *Medieval MasterChef: Archaeological and Historical Perspectives on Eastern Cuisine and Western Foodways* (MPMAS 2; Turnhout, 2017), *Feeding the Byzantine City: The Archaeology of Consumption in the Eastern Mediterranean* (MPMAS 5, Turnhout, 2023), as well as many book chapters and articles in academic journals.

INTRODUCING THE BYZANTINE CITY, ITS HISTORIES, IDEAS AND REALITIES[1]

Nikolas Bakirtzis and Luca Zavagno

"The emperor wise in all things was not unaware of why the Roman cities are sickening - and indeed the majority have already died and passed away."[2] Writing on the eve of the catastrophic Fourth Crusade, the newly appointed Metropolitan of Athens, Michael Choniates (brother of the more famous chronicler and historian Niketas), seem to utter a nostalgic lamentation of the fate of the once-prosperous urban centers that had once showcased the political, social, cultural, and economic preeminence of the Eastern Roman Empire.[3] Michael's point of view was shaped by his education in Constantinople where he spent most of his formative years under the tutorship of another famous intellectual, Eusthatios of Thessaloniki, who also lamented the fate of his native city sieged and conquered by the Normans in 1185.[4] When Choniates found himself leading the Church of the city of Athens, which he had idealised as the epitome of Classical antiquity, philosophical and moral, he reflected on the realities he encountered while showing concern for the fading legacy of ancient cities and the related socioeconomic transitions in the Byzantine Empire.[5]

One can only sympathise with Michael, who grew up in the town of Chonai developed in the shadow of a fortress, which inherited the functions of the nearby ancient city of Kolossai (where Saint Paul preached), to eventually find his way to the capital.[6] Chonai was a fortified outpost on the frontier with the Seljuk Sultanate as well as an important center along Anatolian pilgrimage routes. It boasted an important cult site dedicated to Archangel Michael, whose *panegyris* (a fair that reminds us of similar gatherings in Euchaita and Ephesos) periodically turned the quiet fortified settlement into a bustling commercial and economic hub benefitting the broader region.[7] In a sense, Michael's words could be ideally paired with the verses of his brother Niketas (who became the interlocutor in Umberto Eco's famous fictional *Baudolino*) lamenting the loss of Constantinople: "O City, City, eye of all cities, universal boast, supramundane wonder, wet nurse of churches [...]."[8] Niketas' words of ominous praise echo the devastation of Constantinople as the Franks and the Venetians destroyed and looted the wealth and glory of the empire's capital. All was irredeemably lost for Byzantium.

DOI: 10.4324/9780429203923-1

On the one hand, the abovementioned passages, rhetorically fictional (Michael's) and dramatically real (Niketas'), echo their understanding of the trajectory as well as the central role of Byzantine cities. A once-powerful empire that looked like a mosaic carpet dotted with urban sites from which the socio-cultural, political, religious, and administrative life pulsed along with its provinces, to a transformed and in-transition empire, organised around nuclei of provincial urban life in the form of castles until its demise in 1204, and the continuing resilience of fortified cities in the fragmented political and economic realities of the late Byzantine period until the arrival of the Ottomans and beyond.[9] On the other hand, it's important to highlight the juxtaposition that emerges from the Choniates brothers' writings between the "reality" of the Byzantine city and its "idea and ideal," often expressed in relation to Classical stereotypes and *topoi* used by contemporary sources.[10]

The rationale and content of the present volume address the history and the realities of the Byzantine city proposing a multifaceted overview of the Byzantine urban phenomenon rather than singling out the trajectories and development of specific sites and regions. In doing this, the different contributions deliberately move away from the "exceptional," which Constantinople represented as the "Queen of Cities" and rather delve into an epistemology of Byzantine urbanism and urbanites across space (the provinces and regions constituting the empire) and time (as represented by the traditional periodization: early, middle, and late Byzantine era). As this book is about the Byzantine city, its definition can raise all sorts of primary questions: what does one mean by Byzantine? Should this be regarded as having a preeminent political, military, and administrative meaning? And therefore, shall we Byzantinists dedicate our attention simply to those times (long or short) in which a city was part of the Byzantine Empire? Or should it be regarded as one of those "phases" in a *longue durée* of the history of a site in an interrupted dialogue with other moments of city life? Could a city be regarded (at least partially) Byzantine also when it was part of the cultural and religious sphere of Roman-Christian influence (like, for example, in Amalfi and Comacchio in early medieval Italy or later Prousa-Bursa in the Ottoman era)?[11] Partially stemming from this, is Byzantine an adjective that entailed the same functional, urbanistic, and architectural heuristics across more than a thousand-year? In other words, could we define the urban phenomenon and its ontological characteristic in the same way across the Byzantine millennium? Or did Byzantine cities simply occur and recur – and therefore experience ebbs and flows, golden ages followed by an inevitable decline, or, rather, their transformations captured in a timeless snapshot? Finally, should the Byzantine city be realistically interpreted as a layered palimpsest in order to "avoid imposing distinctions that satisfy our own assumptions about historical periodization and cultural practice, but which bear little relation to the experience of ancient, medieval, or early modern persons?"[12]

In order to answer at least some of those questions, it is important to alert readers to what they will not find in this volume, for although broad in its geographical perspective, it is not intended to be a catalog of "Byzantine" cities organised geographically. In fact, previous scholarly contributions on the issue of Byzantine urbanism mainly centered on the historical trajectories of single provincial sites selected mainly on the very basis of their Classical heritage or political/military importance.[13] Far from it, the contributions included in this volume are arranged around selected and rather "transversal" themes, which, in our opinion, will help the reader to move beyond the abovementioned chronological barriers imposed by the changing fate of cities. These should also help to avoid a rather traditional taxonomical dissection of the urban phenomenon along clear-cut political, economic, administrative, and military interpretative lines. The absence of dedicated chapters focusing entirely on one or more of those aspects might be surprising at first; however, we did envisage a full incorporation of these within diachronic and interdisciplinary frameworks that address both the imaginary and the perceived, the ideal and the pragmatic, the monumental and the socio-cultural flows of life as they characterised the Byzantine urban experience. Moreover, chapters focused on the urban economy or administrative structures would have fallen short as fully fledged narratives of those changes would be inevitably required to relate them to the complex transformations of the imperial super-structure at large. Rather, this volume proposes to interject these very changes through the examination of their architectural, material, built, and visual manifestations as they presented themselves in regional and sub-regional incarnations across the Byzantine Mediterranean.

For instance, three relatively recent contributions breathe new life into issues of Byzantine urbanism, although limited in geographical (Andrea De Giorgi and Asa Eger's volume on Antioch in the *longue durée* from the Classical to the Ottoman era) and chronological (Henry Dey's book on the post-Roman City as focused on the seventh to tenth century period and Kiousopoulou's work focusing on the thirteenth and fifteenth centuries).[14] The first presents us with a compelling overview of the history of the third most populous and wealthiest city in the whole Imperial and Late Antique Mediterranean as relying on both literary sources and – above all – archeological evidence. The authors not only stressed the impossibility of writing a conclusive biography of a city that remained vibrant, dynamic, and densely inhabited from its foundation (in the fourth century BCE) to the contemporary era[15]; in fact, they also scrutinise Antioch's uninterrupted history as revolving around four themes that repeated themselves from period to period: resilience, conquest, cosmopolitanism, and foundation and legacy.[16] They allow the author to sketch a picture of a city, capable of surviving disasters and in a constant and incessant dialogue with its past; a city whose archeology proves the restructuring and reshaping of buildings and spaces, urban narratives and memories for "its medieval and [...] modern incarnations, consciously expressed, remembered, and etched into the buildings and walls themselves. This constant awareness of Antioch's history was for some periods a longing for the past, for others a legitimizing of its importance in the present."[17] In showcasing Antioch as a *de facto* urban palimpsest in a diachronic superposition (physical and metaphorical) of thematically linked socio-cultural, religious, and political layers, the authors echoed another recent analytical and interdisciplinary effort to read the history of cities (in particular those of the eastern Mediterranean as 'multi-synchronic' entities) both as we walk through their jumbled present, and as we penetrate the formations and transformations of their past.[18]

Of course, the long continuity of major urban centers like the capital of Constantinople and Thessaloniki, among other examples, present instructive examples to probe inquiries related to the resilience mechanisms that allowed their societies to transition, adopt to and navigate through major political and economic changes during the so-called dark ages.[19] Key urban functions and institutions helped to anchor social, economic, and cultural life, which now relied on the ability of Byzantine authorities to control space and to offer protection through the construction and more importantly the maintenance of fortification works.[20]

Henry Dey's work attempts to stress the resilience of urban lifestyle and the centrality of fabric and architecture to the political and social life of cities in the Medieval period and beyond. The Byzantine Empire certainly survived by hinging on a diminished number of urban sites in comparison to the Late Antique era, and we should take it as natural that cities can survive or die as entities linked to administrative, military, religious, and macro-economy needs of larger polities.[21] In light of this, Dey concludes that "the ideological resonance and practical function of monumental topography never entirely disappear even in tumultuous periods [as it] had a visual, concrete, and paradigmatic implications. [In particular] the fact that civil and ecclesiastical office holders continued to imagine the execution of their public mandates, display of authority within the backdrop of the Late Roman city and its spectators."[22] As Leslie Brubaker has recently shown, the very fact that literary sources made this background more visible in Medieval Constantinople (where ceremonial processions dictated the political and religious tempo of city life) does not exclude that a similar socio-cultural, religious, and ceremonial apparatus remained central to the urban life and fabric elsewhere across the empire.[23] Processions and ceremonies as staged along the main porticoed streets and city squares could have funerary, memorial, or celebratory meanings; nevertheless, they characterised the sensorial and spatial interactions between the city dwellers and the urban fabric and architecture. In this light, archeology has recently paired with the Byzantine literary sources to help us conceptualise the processional routes and the diverse functional types of the peripatetic urban ceremonies staged in both Medieval Constantinople as well as in provincial cities like eleventh-century Thebes.[24]

Indeed, we can now document a previously unsuspected resilience of urban street grids in different cities across the empire like Gortyn in Crete, Naples, Syracuse, Ephesos, Cherson, and Amorium.[25] This is not to deny that – as Tzivikis concludes – cities went through dramatic changes across centuries, but rather to stress that the Byzantine urban space – as a distinctive analytical category and a lived space – bore the fruits of a constant and transformative negotiation between the various elements of urban societies.[26] It is not by chance that Tzivikis writes with the city of Amorium in mind. Located almost at the center of the Anatolian plateau, Amorium developed from a backwater Late Antique town to an impressive provincial capital and military (thematic) and religious center. It provides us with one of the best examples of Byzantine urban archeology as well as an interesting case of resilient urban life reaching out to the late eleventh century when the city was abandoned.[27] In fact, the physical changes in the urbanscape of Amorium over the duration of almost seven centuries reflect the history of the empire as "it also had been transformed: in the seventh and eighth centuries it stood as a major fortress city against the frequent Arab invasions of Anatolia, but by the second half of the tenth century it [....] served as an important supply base on the route to the frontier in northern Syria. Had it survived the transition to Seljuk rule, it may have developed into an Ottoman and later modern Turkish city as did Iconium or Ankara."[28]

Amorium points to the importance of addressing the regional diversity of Byzantine urban life as well as carefully navigating through what has been hastily labeled as the ruralization, militarization, and decline of the city in the so-called Dark Ages of Byzantium. Sailing through these problematic centuries should get us to the safe haven of the revival of Byzantine urbanism in the tenth-to-twelfth-century period.[29] In fact, over the entirety of the Byzantine millennium, cities remained nuclei of intensification of human landscape and contact points between stable micro-ecology and ever-changing macro-economies at the Mediterranean scale. In light of these changes, they acquired new prevalent functionalities shaped by urban planning, fabric, and infrastructure.[30] In the end, it was the reality of the fragmentation of the Late Antique Mediterranean exchange system followed by the catastrophic loss of large swath of the Late Roman imperial provinces (Syria, Egypt, and North Africa) and a dramatic military and administrative reorganization, which led to the creation of new urban entities like Monemvasia (as well as Kastoria, Dazimon, Nafpaktos, and Mystras) and the transformation and restructuring of ancient ones around new urbanistic, functional, and fortification priorities too often simply defined as "castralization" (like in Corinth, Abdera-Polystylon, Nicaea, Serres, Veroia, Athens, Syracuse, and Catania to name some examples).[31]

This latter point can be explicated when we indeed examine the historical trajectories of Monemvasia, a city *de facto* re-founded as centered on a massive rocky outcrop along the eastern coast of the southern Peloponnese in the late seventh century.[32] As Kalligas asserts, "the existence of a port and other installations predating the founding of Monemvasia determined the planning of the new city with three components: the bridge surrounded by the parts of the port, the Upper City and the Lower City."[33] The latter were enclosed by two separate sets of walls, a layout that reminds us of Amorium, as well as Ephesus.[34] Monemvasia was indeed ontologically defined by its harbor (as strategically located along the so-called Trunk Route linking the Aegean to Constantinople[35]) and its role as a natural outlet for the agricultural produce of its hinterland as well as a convenient hub for the Byzantine fleet; so, it was not simply its fortified urban landscape to characterise and connotate the urban life of Monemvasia. The peculiar role of socio-political elites bound to Constantinople, but also capable of exploiting the commercial opportunities offered by its strategic location and benefitting from tax exemptions on land properties, led to the creation of a dense urban landscape with windy roads crisscrossing the rocky outcrop and small squares focusing on religious buildings and possibly monastic institutions.[36] As the Upper city fulfilled the main political, administrative, and religious functions of the city, the resilience of a mercantile elite led to nurturing a sense of local identity even recognised by the central government as local *archontes* ruled the city.[37]

The archontate of Monemvasia, which seems to have been developing from the tenth century on should remind us of similar governmental structures, which betray the ability on the part of Byzantium to navigate through the interstices of Mediterranean politics in the *longue durée*; we indeed find *archontes* (as well as duchies) appearing in the so-called coastal-insular Byzantine *koine* both in the distant provinces like the Balearics (till the early tenth century) as well as in cities like Late Antique Palermo and Medieval Dyrrachium and Trabzon.[38] The history of Monemvasia reveals a city that pierced through the historiographical barriers of the Dark Ages and the collapse of the Empire post-1204. The archetypical merchant city dominated by a group of families vying for political prominence, Monemvasia reminds us of Amalfi (as well as Comacchio) and Venice; the preeminence of fortifications reminds us of thematic capitals like Ankara and Attalea (present Antalya); the fluidity of local administrative structures puts it in the same league as Zadar, Butrint, and Cagliari.[39] Finally, the resilience of Monemvasia at the socio-political and economic levels is exemplary of the historical trajectories of Byzantium from the eleventh century onward, in particular in the post-1204 period. In this respect, it allows us to catch a glimpse of the development of Byzantine cities during a period when the empire shrank around the Aegean and became more integrated into the commercial networks of the West and its monetary systems.[40] Jonathan Shea has suggested that contrary of its Western counterparts, Monemvasia, as well as other cities like Thessaloniki, Ioannina, Thebes, Arta, and Corinth, show us how the Byzantine city profited from the fragmentation of the empire as well as from their own pre-1204 realities.[41] Late Byzantine urban developments were driven by economically vibrant communities and were defined by fortification architecture, which became a defining aspect of the very experience and cultural identity of the Byzantine city.[42]

The work of Tonia Kiousopoulou looks at the last centuries of Byzantium through its cities, thus highlighting their central role through the arrival of the Ottomans and beyond.[43]

More importantly, she focuses on the realities of fortified cities and towns attempting to understand the socioeconomic and cultural drivers of their organization, planning, development, and relation with their rural surroundings. The analysis of urban topographies is used as a methodological mirror to shed light on the daily lives of their societies and inhabitants. Thus, the multifaceted experience of Byzantine cities is best explored through the synthetic study of variable aspects of urban life. The critical treatment of textual and material evidence can contribute to a more nuanced understanding of the realities and the development of local urban identities was already in progress from the tenth century on, as shown for instance in sigillographic evidence and in the revival of literary genres like the *enkomia* and *ekphraseis*.[44] These aimed at promoting and projecting new "urban" narratives and identities on the part of the Late Byzantine urban elites engaging with the expansion of the Ottoman Turks and, above all, vis-à-vis an Empire no more regarded as a unifying point of reference.[45] Indeed, contrary to Amorium, Monemvasia did not vanish with "the arrival of the Turks" as the Aegean remained at the nexus of political, economic, and socio-cultural interactions among Venice, Genoa, Latins, Turkic *beyliks*, and (later) the rising Ottoman power from the thirteenth century onward.[46]

As Byzantine urbanism remained constantly engaged in a dialogue with a cumbersome Roman past and the ever-changing Mediterranean-oriented present, Amorium and Monemvasia reveal two possible outcomes of a large spectrum of regional incarnations (and changes) of the Byzantine idea, functions, planning, and aesthetic of the city. Indeed, as Decker cogently remarks, Byzantine cities may fail or resurge, but as Decker remarks: "the question remains what exactly we make of the fabric of these cities [...] and what these [...] tell us of forms of public, private, and sacred spaces, and economic activity as well as civic and social life."[47] Following the end of the Byzantine state, it is important to consider the legacy of Byzantine urbanism both in relation to the growth of Ottoman power and in relation to its influence in the making of national narratives in the nineteenth and twentieth centuries. The foundations of the Ottoman state were largely set following the capture and control of key cities like Prousa, Andrianoupolis, and Thessaloniki, while the fall of Constantinople and its transformation into the Ottoman capital shaped the ambitions of the new empire.[48] Centuries later, the remnants of Byzantine cities, whether religious monuments or fortification walls, helped the construction of heritage traditions aimed to integrate Byzantine heritage into national narratives, such as in the case of Thessaloniki.[49]

As already mentioned, the aim of the volume is not simply to move and locate a set of urban pieces across the chessboard of Byzantine provinces, but rather to describe their socioeconomic, political, and cultural continuities and discontinuities against the strategic, tactical, and expedient challenges in the different periods of Byzantine history. These stem from the various attack and defense moves chosen by the players, as a hierarchy of pieces is constantly changed and adapted to development of the battlefield. It would therefore make less sense to focus on the range of movements of – let's say – the bishop or any pawns, than to analyze and present snapshots of the chessboard during different times of the game. In fact, the contributions of this volume present the reader with four grand diachronic snapshots of Byzantine urbanism from an interdisciplinary perspective.

The first part focuses on the historiography of Byzantine cities, and therefore of the way, Byzantinists have embraced the trajectories of the urban phenomenon, as well as the ways in which the Byzantine city has been theorised and conceived. Luca Zavagno's Historiography of the Byzantine Cities examines how Byzantinists have only slowly moved away from a long debate that has often been framed within the opposition between "continuists" and "discontinuists."[50] Zavagno points out how this juxtaposition must be regarded as largely ineffectual, for it is not conducive to effectively analyzing the causes and effects of the transition of urban sites in terms of social structures, planning, and fabric. He also shows how new methodologies have enormously contributed to an all-encompassing analysis of the urban in Byzantium. In the following chapter (Theorizing the Byzantine City), Myrto Veikou sheds light on the changing ideas of the city and urbanity in pace with social transformation, as she also tries to examine the reasons behind the lack of Byzantine clear definitions of a city. In doing so, and by examining an important source like the middle Byzantine *Parastaseis Syntomoi Chronikai*, Veikou points to the importance of memories as constitutive of urban space and the history of urbanism (in Byzantium and beyond). Memories are constructed through the relation between city narratives and the materiality of the urban places. Indeed, the material aspects of the city and the various ways of exploring it lie at the heart of Michael Decker's chapter on the Methodologies of Byzantine Urban Studies, for it explores the exciting possibilities offered by new technological (digital and virtual) tools as well as the opportunities presented by ecological, paleo-climatical, archeozoological, and paleo-epidemiology approaches to better survey urban spaces and settlement patterns.

In addition, literary and documentary sources are of central relevance to our understanding of Byzantine cities as discussed in Helen Saradi's and Tonia Kiousopoulou's contributions. Saradi proposes an overview of the different forms in which the scanty literary sources had been presenting Byzantine cities pointing to the fact that the "factual" is often distorted by rhetoric and fiction. Nevertheless, she concludes that ambiguities aside, the terms used and their frequency in sources reflect urban change such as in the decline of Late Antique cities between the seventh and the twelfth centuries and the growth of Byzantine urbanism post-1204, as cities flourished, and many became regional centers for competing dynasts and rivals. Focusing on the last two centuries of the Byzantine state (the thirteenth and the fourteenth), Kiousopoulou stresses the narrative sources' ambivalence regarding urban topography, public and private spaces, and planning with regard to cities like Ioannina, Arta, and Serres. She concludes that Byzantine authors can be deceitful sources of information for they often described cities along with urban ideals with references to walls, residences, churches, and charitable institutions being the necessary attributes of the emperor's or despot's power.

The regional focus of Kiousopoulou's contribution is in tune with the second rationale of this volume, which addresses the fate of the Byzantine city through a comparison between different regions of Byzantium and the broader Mediterranean world within the framework of structured economic systems driven by production and exchange. In this light, the second, and larger, part of the volume focuses on expanding and enriching the geopolitical scope of the debate on the Byzantine city. The part entitled "Geographies of the Byzantine City" encompasses both "traditional" regional areas as well as those too often regarded as simply marginal to the trajectories of the heartland of Byzantine urbanism, for example the so-called insular-coastal *koine* and continental Italy.[51] However, as already mentioned, a counterthrust to the centripetal gravity of Constantinople permeates most of the volume's contributions. In this vein, Andrea Gandila focuses on the Black Sea at large (from Lazica to the Danube) as he examines the role of the sea in unifying cultural micro-regions that betray distinctive elements of diversity and commonality; his essay dwells upon these in a comparative perspective using coins and their distributive patterns of circulation to reveal the vibrant urban network crisscrossing the Black Sea in the sixth century and beyond. Moving to the other constitutive region of the so-called Byzantine heartland (Asia Minor),

Ufuk Serin's chapter proposes a more "traditional" overview of the urban developments in Anatolia. Her survey looks at the main urban sites in the region from a diachronic perspective, while considering the challenges of urban archeology in the Eastern Mediterranean. Archeological sites often remain neglected, submerged by densely built contemporary buildings. In the end, she concludes that Byzantine urban heritage can remain politically sensitive, if not vulnerable, in regions where – contrary to Greece or the Balkans – there are no continuing cultural, religious, or linguistic links with Byzantium.

The last three contributions of the part address issues related to the multifaceted influence of Byzantium on changes experienced by urban structures, fabric, planning, and sociopolitical organization in territories that were not continuously part of Byzantine control and its influence. Luca Zavagno examines the urban trajectories of large Byzantine islands of the Empire; Enrico Cirelli analyzes the urbanisms of "Byzantine Italies"[52] by comparing some of the urban sites along the Byzantine (and Lombard) Adriatic coast. Indeed, his overview focuses mainly on Ravenna, the capital of the exarchate until it fell to the Lombards in 751, and then follows the trajectories of the cities of the so-called Pentapolis and Apulia (Otranto).

Finally, Ian Randall's attention is drawn to a region that was lost to Byzantium from the mid-seventh century, namely Syria and Palestine: by looking at their smooth transition from Byzantine to Islamic rule, one can indeed realise that political and military events did not always cause catastrophic changes to the urban social life and fabric. Indeed, in this case, urban archeology and material culture not only point to continuities of city life but also provide us with comparative perspectives to better grasp the economic resilience (as centered around commercial-artisanal functions) of the urban landscape boasted by Byzantine cities like Amorium, Gortyn. Cherson or Ephesus (in the Dark Ages) and Athens, Thebes, Corinth, Nicaea, and Pergamon (in the Middle to Late Byzantine periods).[53]

The focus on archeology and urban cityscapes characterises the third and fourth parts of the volume, where an array of contributions explore the dialogue between the archeology of people and the archeology of monuments as well as between material culture and literary sources.[54] Part III is dedicated to architecture and urban spaces, for it proposes an overarching approach to the changing functional role of different Byzantine cities across time and alerts the reader to the diverse and complex spatial, topographical, and monumental consequences of change. Nikolas Bakirtzis centers on the multifaceted role of urban fortifications in the diverse experience of cities in Byzantium, moving beyond their defensive purposes. His essay shows how in cities like Thessaloniki, Ankara, Christoupolis, and Monemvasia, among numerous other examples, the aesthetic, iconographic, and spatial aspects of fortified enclosures, as perceived and experienced by the local population, became an essential part of civic culture and came to denote self-assurance and civic pride. Walls could, however, be visible as well as psychological and ideological barriers; in this light, Nikos Karydes examines the importance of ecclesiastical buildings as dotting the urban landscape and marking the city skyline. His focus on the important Constantinopolitan church of Saints Sergius and Bacchus allows him to draw a comparative picture of the evolution of religious architecture (with a focus on the domes as they punctuated the skyline of many Byzantine cities) and their importance as reference points for residential, economic, socio-political, and cultural functions of urban lives.

Elisabetta Giorgi's essay focuses on the archeology of water to offer insights into the Byzantine urban landscape and social fabric. In Gortyn, in particular, archeological work has shown how water was collected, stored, and redistributed within single parceled properties.

Within this organizational scheme of urban islets, communities relied less on the existing Roman and Byzantine monumental structures and networks as water distribution and availability were more localised and/or privatised. In a rather similar vein, exploring the relation between the city and its waters, Michael Jones and Matthew Harpster examine the economic (commercial and artisanal) and social centrality of harbors in coastal cities like Constantinople and Amalfi. The shipwrecks discovered at the Yenikapi excavations (the former harbor of Julian in Constantinople) provide us with unique glimpses of the Mediterranean maritime networks connected with the Byzantine capital. The key study of Amalfi sheds light on the importance of adopting strategies other than military conflicts or religious conversions across the Byzantine maritime frontiers. Evidently, Amalfitan merchants seem to have relied on cooperation and economic interests transcending traditional political and cultural boundaries.

Beyond commercial, productive, organizational, and public service infrastructures, the long urban traditions of Byzantine cities were characterised by aspects of a residual monumentality, which laid at the very center of the social, political, administrative, and religious life. Maria Cristina Carile's essay examines the architectural landscape and fabric of the Byzantine city in the framework of the modern discourse on monumentality. In time, the Byzantine city changed in its basic structures reflecting in its social transformations the expression of monumentality; for instance, it abandoned the grandeur of Classical amenities and acquired numerous churches, which defined the social and cultural experiences of urban societies. Nevertheless, although ancient buildings often did not survive and were replaced by new ones, they were still considered the most prominent urban features well thus contributing to a sense of monumentality, which persisted through space and time. Chiming with Carile's conclusions, Suna Çağaptay introduces the reader to the importance of Byzantine urbanism in molding and shaping the later Ottoman urban idea, landscape, and fabric. By focusing on Bursa (the Byzantine Prousa) on the north-western fringes of the Anatolian plateau, her contribution explores the spatial and visual strategies of Ottoman city-making and architectural enterprises, often relying on pre-existing urban and spatial configurations. A comparable perspective is offered by Thanasis Koutoupas whose essay discusses the fate of the Mediterranean metropolis of Alexandria as it transitioned between Byzantine and Arab control in 641. This is an instructive example of an important city, the transition and transformation of which after the end of antiquity took place in a neighboring yet competing and different to Byzantium socioeconomic and political context.

The last and final part of the volume moves from discussions of monumental landscapes to more focused approaches to the different socioeconomic actors who lived and operated in the urban physical world. Secular architectural structures, religious buildings, fortifications, residential areas, infrastructures serving the primary needs of the population (like aqueducts or fountains), as well as houses and private and public spaces shaped urban perceptions, the experience, and the socioeconomic and cultural lives of urban communities. They constituted integral elements of urban landscapes and through their use "they propose [an ever-changing] reality as a composite of humans and things, kitted together in an infinitely convoluted mesh [of] relations between them which create the physical world."[55] Visual representations and material expressions as well as daily cultural interactions were central to the socio-political life of a Byzantine city. Ioli Kalavrezou discusses the perception and the related experience of art in Byzantine cities. Her essay looks at what was understood as art by city inhabitants and what it meant in the daily experience of their urban environments.

As art, architecture, and culture can tell us a lot about the socioeconomic life of the city, relics (and saints' bodies) can similarly provide us with hints on their ritual and processional use.[56] Relics could coalesce political meanings, supernatural protection, and religious connotations as their veneration (peripatetic through ceremonies and processions or static in churches and monasteries) helped to sanction and express local urban identities.[57] These, on the one hand, contributed to the creation of distinctive images of the city – as Jenny Albani stresses – mirrored in topographic motifs or personifications in public and private contexts and speak of meanings and perceptions they could convey to their contemporary viewers. On the other hand, they could also find expression in the social life of the suburbs of the Byzantine city. Moreover, as Mabi Angar pans out, this distinctiveness abetted western communities to look for immediate internal and external recognition. A distinguishable quarter of its own right, like in the case of the suburban quarter of Pera-Galata in Constantinople, developed as a specific spatial entity with particular features, including religious buildings, specialised commercial and artisan functions, and even a peculiar soundscape, enhanced by the bell towers of its churches. The latter point is relatable to the last two contributions of the part, where Joanita Vroom investigates the role of ceramics to illuminate the activities of production, trade, consumption, and cultural interaction in Byzantine cities and towns. Focusing her attention on Constantinople in the centuries before the Fourth Crusade, she uses ceramic evidence (as both vessels for trade as well as fine and table wares) to look at the Byzantine capital as a parasitic-consumption-oriented city. She nevertheless revises this role for the city in light of the centrality of Constantinople within an interregional network of production and distribution, which was based around the Aegean but could reach out to the Western (Sicily and the Tyrrhenian Sea) and the Eastern (Cyprus and the Levant) Mediterranean.

In tune with a conclusion to this introduction to the volume, our last assertion allows us to view the Byzantine city not simply through the established historiographic labels (*polis* vs. *kastron*) or by following the extensive and varied types of literary sources documenting different definitions of urban entities across the long Byzantine millennium. Building on existing work and by making generous use and reference to material culture, archeology, architecture (secular, military, and ecclesiastical), and arts, the contributors of this volume revisit a wide array of theories, ideas, fabrics, and textures of the Byzantine urban phenomenon. Moreover, the present collection of essays also attempts to explore the changing perceptions, practices, and experiences of the inhabitants of the cities of Byzantium. Of course, this collective effort does not aspire to provide a complete and final overview of Byzantine cities. For instance, some regions remain untouched, and a full-fledged analysis of the "economics of the urban" is not presented in the volume. This is only a step forward as we remain positive to have moved beyond the duplicitous and seemingly inescapable contradictions the Choniates brothers may have forced upon us. Roman cities and their legacies were not moribund corpses, and the Queen of cities was not the only light of urban splendor until Mehmet II blew its enduring shine off as the last move in a nostalgic "candle-waltz." The centuries between Late Antiquity and the beginning of the Ottoman era included endless geopolitical, territorial, administrative, military, cultural, socioeconomic, and religious transitions and transformations across and beyond the world of Byzantium. One should indeed talk of interacting worlds, which led to different and transforming traditions, ideals, and interpretations of the physical experience and the imaginary and spiritual perceptions of Byzantine cities. After all, to paraphrase Baudolino, the hero of Umberto Eco's homonymous novel, when he bids farewell to Nicetas Choniates in Constantinople, what scholars aim at is not to simply record the truth, but to be able to seek the great history, where little (urban) truths can be challenged and altered in order to allow the greater truth to emerge.

Notes

1 Pages 1 to 5 of this chapter were written by Luca Zavagno and pages 6 to 10 by Nikolas Bakirtzis.
2 *Michaelis Choniatae Epistulae*, CFHB 41 (ed.), F. Kolovou (Berlin, 2001), 67–70.
3 P. Magdalino, *The Empire of Manuel Komnenos 1143-1180* (Aldershot, 1993), 172–173. On Michael Choniates in Athens see A. Kaldellis, *The Christian Parthenon. Classicism and Pilgrimage in Byzantine Athens* (Cambridge, 2009), 145–162.
4 J. Melville Jones, *Eusthatios of Thessaloniki. The Capture of Thessaloniki* (Canberra, 1988).
5 Kaldellis, *The Christian Parthenon*, 145,
6 C. Foss, "Choniai", in *The Oxford Dictionary of Byzantium, 3 vols.* (Oxford, 1991), I, 427
7 P. Thonemann, *The Maeander Valley: A Historical Geography from Antiquity to Byzantium* (Cambridge, 2011), 128–129. On the origins and development of the Byzantine panegyris see Sp. Vryonis Jr., "The Panegyris of the Byzantine Saint: A Study in the Nature of a Medieval Institution, Its Origins and Fate", in *The Byzantine Saint*, ed. S. Hackel (Sobornost, 1981), 196–227.
8 H. Magoulias, *Annals. O City of Byzantium, Annals of Niketas Choniates* (London, 1984), 317.
9 L. Zavagno, *The Byzantine City from Heraclius to the Fourth Crusade, 610–1204: Urban Life after Antiquity (New Approaches to Byzantine History and Culture)* (London-New York, 2021).
10 N. Tzivikis, "Moving beyond the Invisible Cities of Byzantium". EJPCA 10 (2020): 325–334.
11 See Zavagno's Chapter 8 and Çağaptay's Chapter 16 in this volume.
12 E.K. Fowden, S. Çağaptay, E. Zychowicz-Coghill, and L. Blanke, *Cities as Palimpsests? Responses to Antiquity in Eastern Mediterranean Urbanism* (Oxford, 2022).
13 Without any pretension of being exhaustive, one can cite the works of Clive Foss on different cities of Byzantine Asia Minor (C. Foss, *Nicaea. A Byzantine Capital and Its Praises* (New York, 1996)), C. Foss, *Byzantine and Turkish Sardis* (Cambridge, 1980), C. Foss, *Ephesus after Antiquity: A Late Antique, Byzantine and Turkish City* (Cambridge, 1979), Klaus Rheidt on Pergamon (K. Rheidt, *Die Statgrabung 2. Die Byzantinische Wohnstadt (AvP 15, 2)* (Berlin, 2001), Charambolos Bouras on Athens (C. Bouras, *Byzantine Athens. 10th-12th Centuries* (London-New York, 2010)), Chris Lightfoot on Amorium (C. and M. Lightfoot, *Amorium: A Byzantine City in Anatolia* (Istanbul, 2006)), Haris A. Kalligas on Monemvasia (H. Kalligas, *Monemvasia. A Byzantine City State* (London-New York, 2010), and John Haldon, Hugh Elton on Euchaita, and John Newhart on Euchaita (J. Haldon, H. Elton, and J. Newhard, *Archaeology and Urban Settlement in Late Roman and Byzantine Anatolia Euchaïta- Avkat- Beyözü and Its Environment* (Cambridge, 2018)).
14 H.W. Dey, *The Afterlife of the Roman City Architecture and Ceremony in Late Antiquity and the Early Middle Ages* (Cambridge, 2015); A. De Giorgi and A. Eger, *Antioch. A History* (London-New York, 2021); T. Kiousopoulou, Οι «αόρατες» βυζαντινές πόλεις στο Ελλαδικό χώρο (13ος-15ος αιώνας) (Athens, 2013).
15 De Giorgi and Eger, *Antioch*, 8.
16 Id., 9–12.
17 Id., 12.
18 E. K. Fowden, S. Çağaptay, E. Zychowicz-Coghill, and L. Blanke "Historical distance, physical presence and the living past of cities." In *Cities as Palimpsests?*, 7.
19 S. Ćurčić, *Architecture in the Balkans. From Diocletian to Süleymanthe the Great* (New Haven and London, 2010), 184–208, 267–94, 350–82; R. G. Ousterhout, *Eastern Medieval Architecture* (New York, 2019), 137–72.
20 N. Bakirtzis, "The Practice, Perception and Experience of Byzantine Fortification," in *The Byzantine World*, ed. P. Stephenson (London-New York, 2010), 352–371.
21 P. Arthur, "Alcune considerazioni sulla natura delle città byzantine," in *Le Città italiane fra la Tarda Antichità e l'Alto Medioevo. Atti del Convegno (Ravenna, 26–28 Febbraio 2004)*, ed. A. Augenti (Florence, 2006), 27–36; E. Zanini, "Macro-Economy, micro-ecology, and the fate of urbanized landscape in Late Antique and early Byzantine Crete," in *Change and Resilience. The Occupation of Mediterranean Islands in Late Antiquity*, ed. M. Cau Ontiveros and C. Mas Florit (Providence, 2019), 139–161.

22 Dey, *The Afterlife*, 127; 137.
23 L. Brubaker, "Dancing in the streets of Constantinople." *Culture & History Digital Journal* 11/2 (2022) e014. https://doi.org/10.3989/chdj.2022.014 retrieved on 1.9.2023.
24 L. Brubaker, "Space, Place and Culture. Processions across the Mediterranean," in *Cross-Cultural Interaction between Byzantium and the West, 1204–1669. Whose Mediterranean Is It Anyway? Papers from the Forty-Eighth Spring Symposium of Byzantine Studies, Milton Keynes, 28th–30th March 2015*, ed. A. Lymberopoulou (London-New York, 2018), 219–235.
25 F. Curta, "Postcards from Maurilia or the historiography of the dark-age cities of Byzantium." *EJPCA* 6 (2016): 89–110.
26 N. Tzivikis, "Amorium and the Ever-Changing Urban Space," in *Space and Communities in Byzantine Anatolia. Papers from the Fifth International Sevgi Gönül Byzantine Studies Symposium, Istanbul, 24–26 June 2019*, eds. N. D. Kontogiannis and T. B. Uyar (Istanbul, 2021), 215.
27 M. Decker, *The Byzantine Dark Ages* (London-New York, 2016), 108–113.
28 C. Lightfoot, "Amorium," in *The Archaeology of Byzantine Anatolia: From the End of Late Antiquity until the Coming of the Turks*, ed. P. Niehwöner (Oxford, 2017), 341.
29 J. Haldon, "Production, Distribution, and Demand in the Byzantine World, c.660–840," in *The Long Eighth Century: Production, Distribution and Demand*, ed. I. L. Hansen and C. Wickham (Leiden, 2000), 231–232.
30 Ch. Bouras, "Aspects of the Byzantine City. Eighth-Fifteenth Centuries," in *The Economic History of Byzantium from the Seventh through the Fifteenth Century*, 3 vols, ed. A. Laiou (Washington, 2002), 497–528; Id., "Πολεοδομικά των μεσοβυζαντινών και υστεροβυζαντινών πόλεων," DChAE 20 (1998099), 89–98.
31 C. Wickham, *Framing the Early Middle Ages. Europe and the Mediterranean ca.400–ca. 800* (Oxford, 2005), 626–635; Ousterhout, *Eastern Medieval Architecture*, 333–351; Ch. Bouras, "Byzantine Cities in Greece," in *Heaven and Earth. Cities and Countryside in Byzantine Greece*, ed. J. Albani and E. Chalkia (Athens, 2013), 45–73; Bakirtzis, "Byzantine Fortification," 352–356.
32 H. Kalligas, "Monemvasia. Seventh-Fifteenth Centuries," in *The Economic History of Byzantium from the Seventh through the Fifteenth Century*, 3 vols, ed. A. Laiou (Washington, 2002), 863–881.
33 H. Kalligas, *Monemvasia. A Byzantine City State* (London-New York, 2010), 100.
34 Kontogiannis, *Byzantine Fortifications*, 179.
35 M. McCormick, *Origins of European Economy. Communications and Commerce AD 300–900* (Cambridge Mass., 2001), 235; 504–505.
36 Kalligas, Monemvasia, 24–25.
37 Id., 23–27.
38 On the Byzantine koine as encompassing liminal coastal spaces as well as insular communities promoting social contact and cultural interchange see M. Veikou, "Mediterranean Byzantine Ports and Harbors in the Complex Interplay between environment and Society. Spatial, Socio-Economic and Cultural Considerations Based on Archeological Evidence from Greece, Cyprus and Asia Minor," in *Harbours and Maritime Networks as Complex Adaptive Systems*, ed. J. Preiser Kapeller and F. Daim (Mainz, 2015), 51 and P. Arthur, "From Italy to the Aegean and Back – Notes on the Archaeology of Byzantine Maritime Trade," in *Harbours and Maritime Networks as Complex Adaptive Systems*, ed. J. Preiser Kapeller and F. Daim (Mainz, 2015), 339–340.
39 L. Zavagno, "'No Island is an Island': The Byzantine Mediterranean in The Early Middle Ages (600s-850s)." *The Legends. Journal of European History Studies* 2 (2020), 57–80.
40 A. Laiou and C. Morrisson, *The Byzantine Economy* (Cambridge, 2007), 166–248.
41 J. Shea, *The Late Byzantine City: Social, Economic, and Institutional Profile*. PhD Thesis, University of Birmingham (2009).
42 Ćurčić, *Architecture in the Balkans*, 528–594; Bouras, "Byzantine Cities", 64–71; N. Bakirtzis, "Τα τείχη των βυζαντινών πόλεων: Αισθητική, ιδεολογίες και συμβολισμοί," in *Οι βυζαντινές πόλεις (8ος-15ος αιώνας). Προοπτικές της έρευνας και νέες ερμηνευτικές προσεγγίσεις*, ed. T. Kiousopolou (Rethymnon, 2012), 139–158.
43 T. Kiousopoulou, Οι «αόρατες» βυζαντινές πόλεις στο Ελλαδικό χώρο (13ος-15ος αιώνας) (Athens, 2013)
44 C. Sode, "The Formulation of Urban Identity on Byzantine seals", in *Seals. Making and Marking Connections Across the Medieval World*, ed. B. M. Bedo-Rezak (Leeds, 2018), 149–165; H.

G. Saradi, "The Byzantine cities (8th-15th Centuries): Old Approaches and New Directions", in *Οι βυζαντινές πόλεις (8ος-15ος αιώνας) Προοπτικές της έρευνας και νέες ερμηνευτικές προσεγγίσεις*, ed. T. Kiousopoulou (Athens, 2012), 25–46.

45 Saradi, "The Byzantine cities," 44–45.

46 J. Harris, C. Holmes, and E. Russel, *Byzantines, Latins, and Turks in the Eastern Mediterranean World after 1150 (*Oxford, 2012); R. Shukurov, *The Byzantine Turks, 1204–1461* (Leiden, 2016); M. Balard, "Latins in the Aegean and the Balkans (1300–1400)," in *The Cambridge History of the Byzantine Empire c.500–1492*, ed. J. Shepard (Cambridge, 2019), 729–880.

47 Decker, *The Byzantine Dark Ages*, 121.

48 Ćurčić, *Architecture in the Balkans*, 703–766; C. Kafescioğlu, *Constantinopolis/Istanbul, Cultural Encounter, Imperial Vision, and the Construction of the Ottoman Capital* (University Park, 2009); S. Çağaptay, *The First Capital of the Ottoman Empire: The Religious, Architectural, and Social History of Bursa* (London and New York, 2021).

49 N. Bakirtzis, "Perceptions, Histories and Urban Realities of Thessaloniki's Layered Past", in *Cities as Palimpsests? Responses to Antiquity in Eastern Mediterranean Urbanism*, ed. E. K. Fowden, S. Çağaptay, E. Zychowicz-Coghill, and L. Blanke, (Oxford, 2022), 199–221.

50 The origins of these debates date back to the 1950s and are epitomised by two contributions: A. Kazdhan, "Vizantiiskie goroda v VII–XI vv." *Sovetskaya Arkheologiya* 21 (1954): 164–188 and G. Ostrogorsky, "Byzantine cities in the early Middle Ages." *DOP* 13 (1959): 45–66. See also Curta, "Postcards," 93–100.

51 Wickham, *Framing*, 26–31.

52 E. Zanini, Le *Italie Bizantine. Territorio, insediamenti ed economia nella provincia bizantina d'Italia (VI–VIII secolo)* (Bari, 1998).

53 On the concept of "smooth transition", see A. Walmsley, *Early Islamic Syria. An archaeological assessment* (London, 2007),

54 E. Zanini, "Macro-Economy," 165–169.

55 D. Deliyannis, H. Dey, and P. Squatriti, *Fifty Early Medieval things. Materials of Cultures in Late Antiquity and the Early Middle Ages* (Ithaca, 2019), 9.

56 E. Zanini, "Cost, value and wealth redistribution: micro- and macroeconomy in Early Byzantine evergetism." *EJPCA* 11(2021), 137–162.

57 H. Klein, "Sacred Things and Holy Bodies. Collecting Relics from Late Antiquity to the Early Renaissance." In *Treasures of Heaven: Saints, Relics, and Devotion in Medieval Europe*, ed. M. Bagnoli, J. Robinson, H. A. Klein, and C. G. Mann (Baltimore and London, 2010), pp. 55–69.

PART I

Theory and Historiography

1
THE BYZANTINE CITY AND ITS HISTORIOGRAPHY

Luca Zavagno

The debate on the trajectories of the city, its structural changes, and its political, administrative, socio-cultural, religious, and economic transformations during the Byzantine millennium has been one of the recurring themes of Byzantine historiography.[1] Obviously, this has a lot to do with the continuous importance of Greco-Roman centers in the Late Antique and Byzantine era.[2] Indeed, "the classical city, the *polis* or *civitas*, had held during the Roman period a central role both in the social and economic structure of Mediterranean society, as well as in the administrative machinery of the [Byzantine] empire."[3] However, and moving from the common premise of an empire which remained (at least until the sixth century) a mosaic of cities,[4] Byzantinists have been arguing on the way to characterise the role and appearance of the city, as well as the essence of urban life, during the centuries often tragically labeled as the *grande brèche* (seventh-to-ninth centuries) or the "Pirennian Mediterranean divide."[5]

Indeed, an inescapable issue reveals when defining and describing the changes experienced by post-sixth-century (or better post-Late Antiquity) urbanism: a conundrum that overlaps with more general issues of periodization concerning the Byzantine era.[6] Is the seventh-century break not as useful a marker for analyzing the study of urban economics and social development (as the same applied later to the eleventh century)?[7] Or shall we regard the beginning of that century as the real take-off of "Byzantine" urbanism (as well as history)?[8] Should we focus on the eighth century as the ending of the long Late Antiquity of an Empire that would not die?[9] Did urban settlement pattern dramatically change all over the territories of the empire between the eighth and tenth centuries (the so-called Dark Ages of Byzantium[10]) due to decreasing demand, ruralization, demographic downsizing, relocation of the army and fiscal machinery, demonetization, and insecurity leading to fortification (*kastra*) as primary considerations in a definition of urban?[11] And if so, can we safely conclude that "the successor of the Dark Ages centers (the Byzantine urbanism of eleventh and twelfth century) owed little to the Classical polis"?[12] Or on the contrary, one should reflect that the city changed little in the ninth and tenth centuries if one regards it simply as a ceremonial stage for political, religious, and cultural life (and the seat of provincial representatives of ecclesiastical institutions).[13] Should one be encouraged to consider the changing nature of socially and economically influencing urban elites when pitting the life

DOI: 10.4324/9780429203923-3

in those cities reconquered by Byzantium in the tenth-to-early twelfth century (in particular along the eastern frontier) against the "old" thematic centers?[14] And, finally, what after the Fourth Crusade? Is a comparison with the trajectories of urbanism in the West (particularly the maritime and mercantile self-ruling city-states of the Italian peninsula) helping to explain the socio-economic structures of the post-1204 Byzantine city?[15] Or should one delve into the increasing importance of political identity and humanistic cultural values in Palaeologan urban life?[16]

As a preliminary caveat, I should alert the reader that answers to all the abovementioned questions will not be found in the present contribution. Indeed, its scope and length will not allow such an in-depth analysis of the trajectories of Byzantine urbanism in the over 1000 years of its history. What this chapter aims for instead is to offer an overview of the most important historiographic contributions on the Byzantine city as they encompass a wide methodological and disciplinary array of scholarly expertise: from history to archeology, from literature to hagiography, from material culture to legal studies. The main idea behind this chapter is nevertheless to avoid a simplistic evolutionary and chronological survey (starting from the Late Antiquity and ending with the mid-fifteenth century); rather, I would like to present and arrange the scholarly contributions to Byzantine urban studies around problematic issues like geography and environment, definition and terminology, city-countryside, and methodology. As these categories are not sufficient to encase the almost endless bibliography on the field, I am positive they will help me to present the main historiographical trends and deconstruct the (often) overlapping approaches and standpoints presented in each scholarly contribution.

In the light of the last assertion, one could be surprised (or rather dismayed) by realizing that the starting point of this historiographical voyage is the rather famous juxtaposition between "continuists" and "discontinuists" as focused on the period between Late Antiquity and the early Middle Ages. This debate was first staged in the 1950s and had as its main actors: Alexander Kazdhan, George Ostrogorsky, Speros Vryonis Jr., and Eric Kirsten.[17] On the one hand, "continuists" stressed that cities did survive physically after Late Antiquity; that, while they may have shrunk and often have been confined to their citadels as a result of constant enemy harassment, they nevertheless retained their role as centers of commercial activity, petty commodity production, and administration). On the other hand, the "discontinuists" argued for a total collapse of the antique urban organization and of social and economic life.[18] As both parties relied mainly on literary sources and numismatic evidence, the issue of continuity vs. discontinuity has continued to frame the debate on Byzantine urbanism for almost five decades as it resurfaced in the work of Dietrich Claude, Cyril Mango, Clive Foss, Wolfram Liebeschuetz, Frank Trombley, Helen Saradi, John Haldon, and Wolfram Brandes (to quote just a few).[19]

The increased importance of archeology and material culture and, more important, the "re-discovery" of the ideological roots of this debate[20] have contributed to regarding such a juxtaposition as increasingly ineffective and simply unproductive to any efforts to analyze the causes and effects of the transition of urban sites in terms of social structures, planning.[21] This, in turn, has also allowed a full reassessment of the "other" apposition with functional and terminological implication: *polis* vs. *kastron*[22] (Figure 1.1). For instance, Mark Whittow and Jim Crow have both stressed the importance of a regional (and micro-regional) approach in making the latter opposition less clear-cut.[23] Whittow, in particular, has enhanced the issue stemming from a quest for a real watershed between a supposed "Golden Age" of Byzantine urbanism and later periods as he also stressed that

Figure 1.1 Ankara [Turkey] – the so-called Byzantine *kastron* (kale)

cities remained the conceptual building blocks of Byzantine spatial geography as they were the creations of rich and powerful elites.[24] The latter conclusion not only clearly contrasts with the idea of villages as pillars of the Byzantine fiscal system, but it also resonates with the assertions that any general theory of Byzantine city could be tainted by one exception too many for diversity is perhaps the most distinguishing feature of Byzantine urbanism.[25]

As Dagron concludes: "continuity? Discontinuity? It matters little. Whether they survived or disappeared, cities changed [...] in appearance, in function, and in the definition."[26]

In my opinion, two important considerations have helped Byzantine historiography to veer away from the dichotomies I have just mentioned. The first is methodological, for the need for an interdisciplinary approach that brings together historians and archeologists has grown more and more urgent since Clive Foss' contributions to single Byzantine cities of Asia Minor (like Ephesos, Sardis, and Nicaea).[27] Although historians and archeologists are often in disagreement as to whether documentary or archeological criteria are more important, their dialogue has helped to frame the debate on urbanism around political/institutional and economic perspectives.[28]

This is not to assert that these two approaches had not been pursued before, but rather to admit, they were often following a rather independent course. In the past, indeed, historians have embraced the political framing to explain the post-Roman decline of the socio-cultural, economic, and political urban elites: the *curiales* (the main government and politically independent body of the city with its tax-raising powers).[29] When available, archeology and material culture were harnessed to literary and documentary evidence in order to create an evolutionary model to interpret changes to urban structures and fabric as mainly based on literary and documentary evidence.[30]

One can trace back the birth of such an approach to A.H.M. Jones' contributions and, in particular, his book on the cities of eastern Roman provinces.[31] According to Jones, the *curiae* lay at the heart of the Greco-Roman heyday of the *polis*; from the fourth and fifth century, it fell prey to two enemies: the growing imperial administration and the formation of a powerful class of landowners as members of the imperial nobility and based in large countryside villas. This led to the loss of independence culminating in the abolition of the *curiales* in the reign of Justinian.[32] In a rather similar vein and a few decades later, Liebeschuetz (following up on Kazdhan and Ostrogorsky) used numismatic and epigraphic evidence as paired with papyri and legal texts to stress the deep bond between the aristocratic civic elites sitting in the *curiae* and the monumental structure of the city.[33] When the first started disappearing, the second was irredeemably lost, ushering urban life into the socio-economic, political, and economic Dark Ages.[34] In tune with the above-mentioned "discontinuist" narrative, indeed, Liebeschuetz concluded that the distinctive classical city as "filled with public monuments erected through aristocratic munificence and paid for expensive amenities and entertainment [...] created a suitable backdrop to civilised life."[35] In this light, demonumentalization was regarded as tantamount to a diminished vitality of the urban social fabric and its economic functions, as from the sixth century onward, the fate of the city was now in the hands of a new ruling class: the so-called *potentiores*.[36] The latter constituted a new macro-class made of civic, military, and religious authorities (often with the bishops at their head) and characterised essentially by the ownership of locally entrenched social and economic power mainly based on extra-urban landed properties.[37]

A refinement to the approach proposed by Liebeschuetz (and still in tune with the political framing mentioned above) was proposed by Whittow, who indeed objected to a purely institutional interpretation of the problem of urban-based elites' transformation.[38] Whittow not only stressed the importance of the new key political actors as not bringing about the socio-cultural collapse of any post-Roman cities but also used a wide array of hagiographical sources, material evidence, and archeology (buildings, liturgical vessels, silver objects, and coins) to conclude that "the disappearance of the *curiales,* far from being a disaster, was part of the process which the landowning elites adapted to new circumstances and embraced the new Christian world."

In fact, and premised upon the "watershed moment" represented by the abovementioned contributions of Foss, Byzantine urban archeology was drastically improving in terms of geographical scope as well as methodology when Whittow wrote his contribution.[39] Stratigraphically aware excavations, extensive or intensive urban surveys, ceramics, coins, inscriptions, seals, and metalworks are essential to assess the developments of urban economy, socio-cultural life, and political-administrative identity as well and military functions as reflected in the diversity of regional urban forms, fabric, and townscape. In this sense, the increasing importance of archeology was entailed by the syntheses of Wolfram Brandes and (more recently) Philipp Niewöhner on Anatolian urbanism and Florin Curta on the cities of the southern Balkans.[40] As I will return to the issue of regional surveys of Byzantine urbanism in a few moments, I would like to stress here how better and better published archeology encouraged scholars like John Haldon, Michael Hendy, and Wickham to stress an economic (and fiscal) functional definition of the city; [41] this not to diminish the "ongoing dialectic between economic activities and administrative centrality [for] rare were indeed economic centers that just grow without imperial intervention."[42]

In particular, Haldon, while recognizing the importance or regional patterns of urban development, stresses both the increasing role of the countryside in the socio-economic life of the empire (with the village becoming the main source of rent and tax extraction) and the drastic alterations to the form of the state as linked with the restructuring of tax collecting mechanism and the ways army was paid and supplied (thematic system).[43] In Haldon's perspective, shrinking (in size and population) cities were now bound to the needs of the state and the Church (as a new elite of service emerged and defensive functions gained the pride of place). "It is no accident that during the later tenth, and especially in the eleventh and twelfth centuries, as towns become much more important economically, they begin to play a central role in political developments."[44] For Wickham, the importance of an archeologically based economic interpretation rested upon urban-oriented elites underpinning levels of local demand, production, and distribution, which provided political and ideological coherence to a less monumental urban fabric. The fragmentation of the Mediterranean system of exchange, the enduring economic (and socio-political) pull of Constantinople, and the reorganization of provincial urban elites along state and church-driven lines took their tolls on many provincial cities.[45] Nevertheless, they remained central to the Byzantine exchange and political networks until the tenth century, when the Aegean Sea and its urban centers (Corinth, Athens, Thebes, and Thessaloniki) became the main economic engine of the empire.[46]

Other scholars also helped to recognise the importance of embracing interconnected methodological and interpretative framings as resting on an honest dialogue between literary and documentary sources. Three good examples are represented by the contributions of Eric Ivison, Lopez Quiroga, and Enrico Zanini, as they all focus on interpreting the changes of Byzantine urbanism in the passage from Late Antiquity to the Early Middle Ages. Indeed, Ivison assesses the role and economic impact of urban fortifications as built between the ninth and eleventh centuries; in his opinion, defense (as well as ecclesiastical buildings) stemmed from defensive needs as well as from the ideological and imperial commitment. Indeed, Ivison concludes that "actions of Byzantine state saved cities from abandonment, and the presence of state apparatus transformed the [economic and political] character and functions of most provincial cities."[47]

Lopez Quiroga (who co-organised the important session on Byzantine cities at the 23rd International Byzantine Congress held in Belgrade in 2016) stresses the importance of Christianization in molding the post-Roman urban socio-economic and structural landscape.[48] He also compares specifically regional outcomes of urbanism in the West and East to conclude that the archeological record does not allow to talk of any break or abandonment but rather of an adaptation transforming classical urban areas in "Byzantine cities." In fact, he questions the latter definition for terminology owes to the political contexts leading scholars to define material evidence, encouraging us to look for regional outcomes when characterizing the early Medieval cities.[49]

Finally, Zanini also questions the terminological and semantic aspect of the word city in defining a new conceptual model of post-sixth-century Byzantine city. This allows him to describe both the new characteristics and old features of Byzantine urbanism: small, fortified, Christian, and imperial centers.[50] In a sense, one of the best excavated examples of such a city is offered by Justiniana Prima. This was an imperial sponsored urban endeavor in the province of Illyricum which, although lasting only one century, reflected the new concept of the polis as elaborated in the Justinianic era built on a strategic mound, well-defended, boasting a clear division of public, private, and economic spaces (zoning), and deeply enmeshed in the micro-ecology of the basin of the river Leskovac[51] In this light, it is not by chance that Zanini uses archeology and material culture to look at cities and their transformation in terms of constant dialogue between the micro-ecologies of single urban sites and the Mediterranean (imperial) macro-economy.[52] On the one hand, this interpretative framework allows casting aside the notions of decline (and continuity) as intensification and abatement were regarded as better interpretative frameworks for bringing together documentary and archeological evidence. [53] As Whittow concludes, "as far as cities are concerned, one cannot sustain that the city retained continuous appearance, but on the other hand, textual and archeological evidence proved that sites were not deserted, and that bishopric lists show that cities remained the conceptual building blocks of spatial geography."[54]

On the other hand, such a framework helps us to better grapple with regional diversity and individual urban profile from a micro-regional perspective.[55] It is not by chance that Ivison and Zanini have been involved in the excavations of two of the best published Byzantine urban sites: Amorium in Anatolia (Figure 1.2) and Gortyn in Crete. As the results of almost 30 years of archeology in Amorium have shown the dangers of stating the demise of urbanism in the absence of good archeology, we have become aware of the need for a more attentive reading of the literary sources in light of the archeological evidence to propose new paradigms to the changes of Byzantine urbanism.[56] As excavations in Amorium revealed a rather dense, economically active, and functionally multifaceted urban site defined by its state as inland economic capital,[57] urban archeology in Gortyn shed light on both urbanism at the so-called periphery of the empire and the importance of the micro-ecological dimension.[58] This, in turn, has also allowed us to move from an archeology of monuments to an archeology of people as centered on the production, supply, and distribution networks of water and bread.[59] In particular, the multifaceted relationship among the water system, the built landscape, and the inhabitants has been interpreted as an indicator of population levels, density, and occupation of the urban landscape and the political status and power of new "private" individuals presiding over the management and location of the distributive outlets.[60]

The latter approach has twofold merit: the first one has to do with a true "bottom-up" interpretation of the urban lifestyle as also reflected in the use of *spolia* on fortifications

Figure 1.2 Amorium [Turkey] – The so-called enclosure (eighth-to-ninth centuries)

and buildings. For instance, Brian Ward-Perkins has stressed the concurrence of ideological and pragmatic decisions in the re-use of architectural and artistic elements as embedded in plain sight on the facades of Late Antique monuments.[61] As even the conversion and re-use of pagan temples into churches was mainly premised on a similar decisional spectrum (i.e., ranging between functional and conceptual motivations), Ward-Perkins concludes that looking at the uses of *spolia* and re-use and transformation of buildings allow us to fully grasp with a large-scale development rather than piecemeal privatization, chaotic squatting, and unchecked encroachment of public spaces.[62] In fact, the latter conclusions echoed the author's skepticism toward the archeological evidence available for the Byzantine empire at the beginning of the twenty-first century and ideally paired with a comparison with the work of Hugh Kennedy on the apparent collapse of the uniform and magnificent appearance of the post-Roman cities of Syria and Palestine as instead caused by continuing (indeed, apparently growing) commercial pressure on public spaces (as enhanced by wooden installations and stools) and therefore pointing to a remarkable economic urban vitality in the seventh and eighth centuries.[63]

There is no space here to dwell upon the so-called smooth transition of Syro-Palestinian urbanism during and post-Islamic conquest as recently reassessed by Alan Walmsley and Avni (the latter substantially revisiting Kennedy's argument).[64] Rather it is worth noticing that Ward-Perkins' comparative remarks encourage us to explore different regional "incarnations" of the Byzantine city: "describing the cities of the empire is like describing a moving target made up of different parts, all traveling in roughly the same direction, but at very different speeds and with different individual trajectories."[65] This in turn pairs with the need to be on the lookout for the "real Byzantine" city as literary images and perceptions often stemmed from a Constantinopolitan cultural milieu and they keep the researchers of Byzantine urbanism from facing a range of issues that the historical and archeological record present.[66] For instance, while recognizing the pervasive presence of cities in Byzantine literary and hagiographical sources, she admits to the fact that the urban image was distorted due to the overlapping of the Christian "Medieval" perceptions on the traditional picture of the Graeco-Roman *polis*; moreover, she acknowledges the fact that most of these texts were written in Constantinople and for a Constantinopolitan audience and therefore project a rather distorted picture of urban lifestyle and expectations.[67]

To address such an unbalance, Nikos Tsivikis urges Byzantinists to overcome the almost traumatic relationship they often have with "the City" (i.e. Constantinople) and advocates for "the need to encounter real Byzantine towns (facing a range of issues that the historical and [above all] archeological record presents to the researcher of Byzantine urbanism." [68] Indeed, Tsivikis has the advantage of writing with the results of the excavations in both a large provincial capital (Amorium) and a smaller town (Messene) in mind. In this light, one can, however, trace the importance of the archeological and architectural reality on the (urban) ground in the works of Nicholas Bakirtzis. Indeed, his analysis of visual language, practices, and perceptions of urban fortifications (primarily those of Thessaloniki) premised on the importance of moving beyond a simplistic idea of urban walls as hastily built in response to increased needs of security.[69]

This is not to deny that fortifications as built between the fifth and seventh centuries (like those documented at Justiniana Prima, Nicaea, Syracuse, Amorium, Ankara, Ephesos, Salamis-Constantia, and Gortyn, to quote just a few) contained and protected urban life (Figure 1.3)[70]; but rather to tip the balance of the abovementioned evolutionary approach simply leading from the classical *polis* to the Byzantine medieval *kastron*. As enhanced by the large use of spolia and inscriptions on their façades, urban fortifications betrayed an aesthetic value matching with a large array of socio-economic, religious, cultural, and political meanings. Only when all these are fully considered in their physical and metaphysical intentions can one indeed fully grasp the relationship of the inhabitants to the fortifications as part of their daily life since walls were a real backdrop, notional and symbolically defining every dimension of the urban life.[71]

As the latter assertion seems in tune both with the abovementioned archeology of people and a true search of the reality on the ground, one can see how urban archeology and analysis of material culture have been contributing to new approaches and theorizations as alternatives to the traditional notion of Byzantine urbanism reflected in the terminology of literary and documentary sources. In this sense, in the past, Kazdhan (for the period seventh to the tenth century) and, as will be seen, more recently Saradi and Kiousopoulou have addressed the complex issue of defining a changing urban life through the use of primary sources across the whole Byzantine millennium (including chronicles, military treatises, hagiographies, *ekphrasis*, and *enkomia*).[72] However useful, this approach has proved rather inconclusive as even on issues like urban identity traditionally addressed through Constantinopolitan eyes, the need for an interdisciplinary approach has been clearly set forth. One can mention here the compelling contribution of Claudia Sode, who addressed the question of cities as developing urban identity, city consciousness as based upon military and economic power, and the existence of local cult as expressed through seals and sealing practices.[73] Sode, in turn, ties the development of a true city self-identity from the tenth

Figure 1.3 Nicaea [Turkey] – View of the Byzantine city and the lake

century onward to monuments and particular sites (including churches), and her analysis of sigillographic evidence ideally pairs with that of Hendrik Dey assessing the ideological continuity of the pragmatic functions of monumental urban topography.[74]

Dey's ingenious characterization of the afterlife of the Roman city is indeed based on a compelling overview of urban archeology across different regions (within and beyond the imperial borders). In a sense, Dey's analysis allows us to tie together the importance of a multidisciplinary (but geographically adjusted) approach, the adherence to urban city life on the part of the elites (with regional characterizations), the resilience of urban landscape and fabric as the stage for public power ceremonies orchestrated by city-based urban elites. The latter point interjects with the role played by religious and secular imperial elites, the changes of the fiscal superstructure, as well as the importance of considering city-countryside relations.[75]

As for the first point, one can only be reminded that "allowing archeology to illustrate the narrative deriving from written sources is one way, but archeologists and textual historians have come to recognise the relation between text, and material culture is more complex and more enriching."[76] As I am returning here to a methodological issue I have addressed already, it is important to stress its relevance to the second point Dey drives home. Indeed, Curta has pointed out the economic importance of cities as centers of surplus appropriation, social differentiation/hierarchies, and concentration of population in the period between the seventh and the ninth centuries. They as all were reflected by the diminished but important role played by street-grid and the presence of church buildings (as pairing with monetarization and centrality of different Byzantine cities in the regional and inter-regional ceramic productive and distributive networks).[77] By analyzing the urban archeology in Amorium, Naples, Cherson, Butrint, Corinth, and Thessaloniki, Curta assesses the role of central places as different from the urban precursors and later incarnations of Byzantine urbanism.[78] In fact, as he is ideally looking at the "other" side of the same coin, Dey stresses the processional-ceremonial functionality of cities/central places.[79]

Dey's interpretative framework includes a large array of sites which (in line with Curta) encourages us to move beyond the "traditional" geography of Byzantine urbanism as limited to the Aegean and the Anatolian plateau (the two regions adding up to what Wickham defined as the Byzantine hinterland);[80] moreover, it stresses the ability to maintain and refurbish the ceremonial armature as serving the needs of local, imperial, and ecclesiastical elites. Although delving into the model Constantinople ("the City" in miniature) represented for most provincial cities (thematic capital or else), Dey concludes that any urban sites remained "the indispensable venue for public ceremony, the obvious place to communicate and connect with the largest possible audience, whence the constant stress on the convergence of the population."[81] In my opinion, this could lead to reassessing the concept of retrenchment of urbanism in terms of political, administrative, military, and religious functions and ruralization of urban lifestyle in the Dark Ages and even before.[82] Moreover, it could help to nuance the gap between the so-called existential crisis of Byzantine urbanism in the seventh-to-ninth-century period and the expansion of a city-based economy from the eleventh century on.[83]

This is not to deny that villages replaced cities as pillars of the fiscal system and Byzantine state (in terms of collection of taxes and redistribution of resources at a local, regional, and supra-regional level)[84]; it is rather important to assess that the decline of traditional aristocracies and their militarization as paired with the increasing socio-economic pull of Constantinople and the increased role of the army should be foisted on different urban patterns of wealth investments at a regional level and paired with a change in the "evergetic" tools regarded as more expedient and convenient in socio-political and economic terms.[85] Institutions of power seem to have continued to reside (at least in some) cities, and local elites remained urban-oriented as cities could develop according to diverse different regional settlement patterns. If some scholars have attempted to create a taxonomy of urban settlements: "the "ruralised" cities (with prominent marks of ruralization), the "city on island" (with the antique urban tissue broken up in small separate communities), the "transferred" or "shifted" city (transferred to a naturally fortified location), the "fortress" city (withdrawn on a *kastron)* and the "continuous" cities (cities in which urban location and urban life continued."[86]

As Niewöhner has pointed out, these urban types should, however, be contextualised in a city-countryside dialogue in a sort of *longue durée* encompassing the Late Antique, Byzantine, and early Ottoman era.[87] Although writing with Anatolian urbanism in mind, Niewöhner addresses the fate of cities like Miletos and Aizanoi as stemming from the changes in structural relations between the urban spaces and their rural hinterland. He indeed concludes that "what worked to the disadvantage of the cities and traditional elites could instead be an advantage for the state (ever-increasing income) and the inhabitants of the countryside."[88] Therefore, and as the focus of scholarly attention is diverted from the Dark Ages, a reassessment of the concept of ruralization (or *rus in urbe*) can be proposed here.[89] Indeed, on the one hand, we are encouraged to recognise a real hiatus in Anatolian urbanism as brought in by the arrival of the Seljuks and Turkmens in the late eleventh century[90]; on the other hand, and as already hinted at in the case of the relationship between the macro-imperial structure and micro-ecology of Gortyn as explored by Zanini, scholars like Tzvikis and Vionis have proved the importance of contextualizing issues like definition and categorization of cities within the framework of a changing settlement pattern at large (and beyond Anatolia).

In particular, Tzvikis cuts a wide swath as he focuses on the results of the excavations at the Peloponnesian city of Messene in the early and Middle Byzantine periods. In his contributions which stem from the quest of the "real" Byzantine city, he questions the process of ruralization as often labeled simply as a sign of the decadence of urbanism and urban lifestyle.[91] As he encourages us to focus on the perceptions of changing city (a perspective in tune with the archeology of people), Tzvikis brings to our attention the materiality of the city as embodied by the structures of water caption and redistribution as well as tools like water mills, as he sees them not as a sign of "a decadence of aesthetic architectural choices, a clear process of re-organizing production and favoring productive installations rather than investing in prestige and status monuments."[92] In a similar vein, by investigating the transformation of the urbanism at Sagalassos, as well the changing sacred settlements in Cyprus and above all in Beotia, Vionis draws attention to demonumentalization and re-monumentalization of cities. These were mainly driven by the changing patterns of investment of wealth on the part of local elites whose ethics and vision were now imbued in Christianity.[93] The emergence of bishops as main reference points for local politics, organization of public power, and religious practices pairs with the abovementioned resilience of the ceremonial and processional stages at the city-level and with their centrality in the new macro-class of *potentiores*. This had clear consequences not only for the fabric and lifestyle of cities, but it also rippled across the economic function as well as ways of expressing urban identity and memory of the urban past. In turn, this is in tune with a theorization of urban sites as central places within a hierarchy of second and third ranks settlements dotting an agricultural area as pertaining (economically, legally, and in terms of property-relations) to the city as exploited by the urban-based elites.[94]

It would only be too simple to mention the changing patterns of evergetism as churches and monasteries continuously acted as a catalyst for elites' patronage and donation; they were often but not necessarily often encased in the newly fortified urban couture, as ecclesiastical buildings, bishop residences paired with *extra-moenia* funerary and memorial monuments celebrating the supernatural powers of local saints and martyrs. As these *de facto* acted as new supernatural protectors and paraded a new ideology and identity of cities, their visibility in the urban landscape could also entail a deliberate ideological connection with the past (like in the very case of the conversion of pagan temples in Aphrodisias (Caria), Syracuse and Agrigento, and Athens).[95] Although this gradual process took its cue from the Late Antique era, its validity and consequences impinged upon the Middle Byzantine period, when the new perception of urban planning and, more importantly, a new concept of monumentality were revealed as no longer connected to administration (or the military) but rather to production and commerce.[96]

Indeed, and as this historiographic is now approaching its last stage, it is worth noting how a sort of augmented reality of urban processes of changes could be traced when examining the trajectories cities followed across the diverse regional and subregional "ecologies." When studying them, it is, however, clear that the scholarly interest has only partially moved away from the seventh- to tenth-century period. One can think here of Veikou's compelling contributions on the use of archeology in determining changes in the Byzantine use of urban spaces (like encroachment and subdivisions) as leading to spatial transformations. As these point to economic diversity rather than a decline in the so-called Dark Ages, they cut a wide swath as occurrences like the abandonment of agricultural lands or urban demographic collapse could also be connected to climatic change around 700.[97] For instance, the importance of Medieval environment and climate is paramount in Haldon's analysis of urban archeology for the Byzantine Anatolian site of Euchaita (tod. Avkat) on the north-Anatolian plateau.[98]

Here the trajectories of a little Late Roman village developing into an important Byzantine strategic and pilgrimage site between the seventh and ninth centuries are analyzed not only through the lenses of a reorganization of the urban settlement pattern in Anatolia as reflecting the different impact of hostile activity in different areas of the plateau and the reorganization of administrative and military state machinery. Rather, one should consider a high degree of local, functional variations in the forms and characteristics of early and Middle Byzantine urban settlements as foisted by geomorphological, environmental, and climate factors.[99] As a less stable climate gave way to a more fluctuating warm-to-wet period (as shown by palynological and dendrochronological evidence), it combined with other political, military, and epidemic factors (the recurring waves of the so-called Justinian plague) in producing dramatic (but locally nuanced) changes in the agricultural regime and demography.[100] As a result, Haldon concludes that "the shifts on patterns of urban settlement again heavily nuanced by subregion within Anatolia must also reflect the availability of human resources, the demands of local and interregional markets, and thus, level of production."[101]

The publication of the extensive and multidisciplinary survey of Euchaita, therefore, has helped to sharpen the focus on a site which on a par with others (like Ephesos) never became a thematic capital and for which, nevertheless, the available material and literary evidence does not allow to support the view of a rarified urban life.[102] Rather, and building upon new methodologies and modes of archeological investigative surveys, it encourages us to delve into the functional diversification (alternatives) of regional and subregional Byzantine urban trajectories.[103] It is indeed when moving away from the Byzantine heartland that multifunctional alternatives can be better documented by urban archeology. The examples of Comacchio and Amalfi are maybe the best ones as similar paths of development could also be shown for the Venetian lagoons and even Cyprus.[104] As I will return to the issue of urbanism of Byzantine islands (and coastal peripheries) in a later chapter, I will simply mention here the Sorrentine peninsula and its peculiar geomorphology and micro-climate. Indeed, the backbone of the peninsula (the Lattari Mountain) functioned as a steep, rugged backstage to the little island-like settlements often developing astride impetuous rivers.[105] This helps to explain the planning and fabric of the Amalfitan conurbation boasting a hierarchy of polycentric settlements acting as a good reminder of the importance of considering functional as well as ideological modifications to the Classic or Late Antique conception of urbanism.[106]

This frame of reference should allow me to finally pierce through the perceived barrier of the Dark Ages of Byzantium and present the reader with the contributions of those (indeed, a few scholars) who have tried to examine the changes to the urban fabric and landscape in the period between the eleventh and the fifteenth centuries. Although I have made scattered references to their works, I would like to mention in the same breath Florin Curta, Andreas Külzer, Charalambos Bouras, Tonia Kiousopoulou, Michael Angold, Jonathan Shea, Jean-Claude Cheynet, and Alan Harvey.[107] This is not to diminish the importance of scholarly monographs on single (and better excavated) urban sites (like Butrint, Athens, Pergamon, or Ephesos);[108] rather, my idea is to give the pride of place to those scholars who have attempted an all-encompassing overview of the so-called Late Byzantine city.

First and foremost, one should admit to the catastrophic effects of the Fourth Crusade (and its aftermath) in terms of territorial losses, sharing of fiscal resources, and a crisis of legitimization as the inheritance of Byzantium was now divided among three (and later two) political courts and capital cities: Trabzon, Nicaea, and Arta (adding to Thessaloniki and, of course, Constantinople). This paired with the political, military, and economic impact of the arrival of "foreign" powers on the Eastern Mediterranean stage: the Normans and the Seljuks already in the eleventh century, the Venetians and the Genoese in the twelfth century, the "Franks," the Catalans, and Turkic *Beyliks* in the thirteenth century, with the Ottomans on the rampage from the mid-fourteenth century on.[109]

Second, and as a partial consequence of the Turkish penetration in Asia Minor and the establishment of a rather organised frontier, the attention of urban historiography has centered on the Aegean basin.[110] For instance, Angold has stressed the quick "recovery" of urban life in Greece as owing to the peculiarity of the local, thematic system (more functional to keep the territories recovered from the Slavs from the ninth century on). More importantly, this urban revival was driven by the economic resurgence of local elites as less subservient to the needs of the Constantinopolitan court.[111] Indeed, both material and literary evidence for urban economic expansion is rather permeant for well-excavated Greek cities like Corinth, Thebes, Monemvasia, Mystras, and Athens. As Harvey concludes: "this [the urban expansion] has been linked to the increase in agricultural productivity in the eleventh and twelfth century with the economic stimulus given by needs of wealthy landowners, ecclesiastical hierarchy and state officials (in larger towns) supplemented by the demands of Italian merchants." [112] As Harvey postulates a strong interrelation between the city and the countryside, Bouras examines the organic development of urban fabric, planning, infrastructures, and residential and commercial/artisanal building characterizing some of the abovementioned sites. As a result, and in tune with the later analysis of Shea, the diversity of urban regional trajectories comes forth, although molded by a similar preeminence of capital investment on the part of local aristocracies in specialised artisanal neighborhoods or commercial harbors.[113]

Third, one should stress the possibility of pairing a better published material culture (and archeological excavations) with a wider array of documentary and literary sources, which allow us to highlight the relationship between the increased urban economic prosperity and the development of local socio-political identities as enhanced by the weakening fiscal and administrative pull of the central Byzantine state over local *archontes*.[114] Indeed, the Late Byzantine (Palaiologan) city (i.e., after 1204) no longer experiences the imperial ideological gravity-pull of a central court as locally based elites foisted a new politically self-determined urban identity.[115] The political, administrative, military, and religious preeminence of aristocratic families whose sources of wealth premised not only on the "traditional" landholdings but also on their active participation in the new role of post-1204 Aegean cities as productive and commercial centers is vividly exemplified by Monemvasia (Figure 1.4).[116] As Shea concludes, it represented "the archetypal merchant city [...] dominated by a group of families jockeying for position: sometimes acting in concert and sometimes acting against one another."[117] An affluent city whose elites have strong commercial and political links both with Byzantium as well as Venice and the Anatolian Seljuks, the city emerged as a powerful stronghold defined mainly by its fortifications enclosing both an upper quarter

Figure 1.4 Monemvasia [Greece]

inhabited by the religious and secular governing elites and a second lower residential area; as churches dotted an urban landscape and fabric developing along windy roads connecting residential buildings, cisterns, and bath-houses.[118] It was the local harbor and its preeminence along inter- and intra-Mediterranean shipping routes which defined Monemvasia as a substantial *emporium*: through it that the agricultural products of the hinterlands were commercialised in local and "international" markets.[119]

Finally, one should consider that Monemvasia (as well as other important excavated sites for the Late Byzantine period like Thessaloniki, Corinth, Pergamon, and Mystras) confronts us with a "real" city in the post-1204 Byzantine empire.[120] Indeed, the latter remained centered around the capital and its ideological rituals evoking the claim to imperial power and retained a cultural prestige as well as a religious influence; nevertheless, the presence of foreign potentates carving new (feudal and not) polities within the former body of the empire and the involvement of members of Palaiologan elites with Italians and others (including the Ottomans) diluted the political, administrative, and territorial coherence of the Byzantine state.[121] This, in turn, echoed in the rather abovementioned "independent" developments of single urban entities. It would be only too easy to mention Thessaloniki, which became more important than Constantinople in terms of cultural and intellectual influence. Nevertheless, urban archeology in cities like Pergamon and Corinth provides us with evidence of both the role of central (imperial) authorities in devising residential patterns, defensive outlook, and urban planning as local churches had a limited impact on the urban landscape and were built under the influence of western models. In other words, as Buchwald asserts, the Late Byzantine city fabric "reflects a generally applied approach to the reconstruction of at least some medieval Byzantine cities; an approach that appears to be based upon a conscious revival of earlier forms parallel revivals are well known in the visual arts and in literature."[122]

The latter assertion is highly revealing for Late Byzantine hagiographies, ekphrasis, and *enkomia* (laudatory text) allow us to appreciate both the perception and representation of the Palaiologan literary imagery of urban lifestyle and sociality. Literary sources, indeed, point to both the urban self-determined political ideology (*patris*) of a new elite as well as a topography foisted upon the religious festivities and prayers represented in post-tenth-century hagiographies.[123] Here we should stress the centrality of the new "urbanites" (the *astoi*/bourgeois) and the respective unification of urban spaces (and neighborhoods) as physically contained by walls which are celebrated in terms of aesthetic as well as embodying the spiritual and moral collectiveness.[124] How this new idea and imagery of city and their functional embodiments in urban fabric and landscape would have developed (along "Italian" mercantile city lines?) is a good question to be asked at the end of this historiographical overview. But once again, it is the reality on the historical ground that needs to be confronted, for as the cities of Byzantium fell to the Ottomans, they came to function under a completely different system although still vibrant and Byzantine to their core.[125]

To conclude, this chapter has tried to present the reader less with an exhaustive anthology of the most relevant contributions than with some thematic issues in the historiography of Byzantine urbanism and its developments along the Byzantine millennium. The main idea behind the chapter was to show how we have come to abandon the traditional juxtapositions and dichotomies (continuity/discontinuity, *polis/kastron*, and literary sources/archeological evidence) as well as the idea of conceptualizing and categorizing the Byzantine city according to fixed models. The history of Byzantine city has been recently emerging as more organic and "real" (and as a result, moving away from "the City" as established on its special privileges, rights, and socio-economic advantages). Indeed, urban planning, forms, meanings, and functions are constantly adjusted to new needs and requirements dictated by changes at the Mediterranean scale, imperial level, and micro-ecological (regional and subregional) stages. Archeology and material culture have shed new light on all these and helped us refine and bridge the gaps between the "usual" chronological indicators (Dark Ages, eleventh century, and post-1204); however, they should not be considered the "end of Byzantine city's history." There is indeed more to do than continuing exploring single urban sites through new surveying techniques and technologically advanced stratigraphic methods of inquiry (important as this task remains).[126] What we need is an interdisciplinary and methodologically inclusive approach that will bring together old and scholarly expertise to grapple with the hundreds of separate decisions made by different agents at different times, which all define the complexity of an urban environment.[127]

Notes

1 This even though chapters specifically dedicated to the issue of Byzantine cities and urbanism appear in the *Oxford History of Byzantium* (C. Foss, "Life in Cities and Countryside," in C. Mango (ed.), *The Oxford History of Byzantium* (Oxford, 2001), 71–96), *The Economic History of Byzantium* (G. Dagron, "The Urban Economy. Seventh to Twelfth Century," in A. Laiou (Ed.), *The Economic History of Byzantium From the Seventh through the Fifteenth Century* (Washington, DC, 2002), 389–455 and C. Bouras, "Aspects of the Byzantine City. Eighth to Fifteenth-Century," in *The Economic History of Byzantium*, 483–579) as well as in the *Palgrave Atlas of Byzantine History* (J. Haldon, *Palgrave Atlas of Byzantine History* (New York, 2010); similar chapters are, however, missing from recent edited volumes like *The Cambridge History of Byzantine Empire* (J. Shepard, *The Cambridge History of the Byzantine Empire* (Cambridge, 2009), *A Companion to Byzantium* (L. James, *A Companion to Byzantium* (Chichister, 2010), and *The Byzantine World* (P. Stephenson, *The Byzantine World* (London-New York, 2010).

2 For the Late Antique period, see, for instance, the remarkable and recent contribution by Luke Lavan on urban public spaces (L. Lavan, *Public Space in the Late Antique City (2 Vols.): PART 1: Streets, Processions, Fora, Agorai, Macella, Shops. PART 2: Sites, Buildings, Dates* (Leiden, 2020).

3 J. Haldon, "Euchaïta: From Late Roman and Byzantine Town to Ottoman Village," in J. Haldon, H. Elton, and J. Newhard (eds.), *Archaeology and Urban Settlement in Late Roman and Byzantine Anatolia Euchaïta- Avkat- Beyözü and Its Environment* (Cambridge, 2018), 241.

4 E. Zanini, "Urban Ideal and Urban planning in Byzantine cities," in L. Lavan (ed.). *Theory and Practice in Late Antique Archaeology* (Leiden, 2014), 196.
5 D. A. Zakythinos, "La grande breche dans la tradition historique de l' hellenisme du septième au neuvième siecle," *Charistirion eis Orlandon,* v. III (Athina 1966), 300–327.
6. L. James, "Byzantium: A Very, Very Short Introduction," in L. James (ed.), *A Companion to Byzantium* (Chichester, 2010), 2–3.
7 Dagron, "The Urban Economy, 396; L. Grig, "Cities in the 'long' Late Antiquity, 2000–2012 - A Survey Essay." *Urban History* 40/3 (2013), 556.
8 M. Whittow, *The Making of Orthodox Byzantium* (Oxford, 1996).
9 L. Grig, "Cities in the 'long' Late Antiquity, 2000–2012 – A Survey Essay." *Urban History* 40/3 (2013): 554–567. J. Haldon, *The Empire that would not Die: the Paradox of Eastern Roman Survival, 640–740* (*Cambridge*, 2016).
10 M. Decker, *The Byzantine Dark Ages* (London, 2016).
11 W. Treadgold, A History of Byzantine State and Society (Stanford, 1997), 402–413; A. Laiou and C. Morrisson, *The Byzantine Economy* (Cambridge, 2007), 41–57; P. Sarris, "Economics Trade and "Feudalism," in L. James, *A Companion,* 25; R. Ousterhout, *Eastern Medieval Architecture. The Building traditions in Byzantium and Neighboring Lands* (Oxford, 2019), 333–352; J. Howard Johnston, "Authority and Control in the Interior of Asia Minor, Seventh-Ninth Centuries," in A. Delattre, M. Legendre & P. Sijpestejin (eds.), *Authority and Control in the Countryside. From Antiquity to Islam in the Mediterranean and Near East (Sixth-Tenth Century)* (Leiden, 2019), 128–171.
12 Decker, *The Byzantine,* 121–122.
13 H. W. Dey, *The Afterlife of the Roman City Architecture and Ceremony in Late Antiquity and the Early Middle Ages* (Cambridge, 2015), 138–145.
14 J. C. Cheynet, "La société urbaine." *TM* 21(2), 449–482.
15 J. Harvey, *Economic expansion in the Byzantine Empire 900-1200* (Cambridge, 1989), 222–242;. J. Shea, *The Late Byzantine City: Social, Economic, and Institutional Profile.* Unpublished Ph.D Thesis, University of Birmingham, 2009.
16 T. Kiousopoulou, "«Αστοί» και «αγροίκοι» κατά την ύστερη, βυζαντινή εποχή," in T. Kiousopoulou (ed.), *Οι βυζαντινές πόλεις (8ος-15ος αιώνας) Προοπτικές της έρευνας και νέες ερμηνευτικές προσεγγίσεις* (Athens, 2012) 253–262; H. G. Saradi, "The City in Byzantine Hagiography," in S. Efthymiades (ed.), *The Ashgate Research Companion to Byzantine Hagiography. Volume II: Genres and Contexts* (London: 2014), pp. 438–52. See also the abovementioned authors' contributions in the present volume.
17 A. Kazdhan, "Vizantiiskie goroda v VII–XI vv." *Sovetskaya Arkheologiya* 21 (1954), 164–188; E. Kirsten, "Die Byzantinische Stadt," In *Berichte zum XI. Internationalen Byzantinisten-Kongreß München.* Bd. I, V, 3, S. 45, (Munchen 1958), 1–53; G. Ostrogorsky, "Byzantine cities in the early Middle Ages." *DOP* 13 (1959), 45–66; S. Vryonis jr, "Problems in History of Byzantine Anatolia." *Tarih Araştırmaları Dergisi* 1(1), (1964), 113–132.
18 L. Zavagno, "'The unbearable transience of the city': Urban spaces in the Byzantine world in the transition from Late Antiquity to the Early Middle Ages (ca. 550-ca. 800 A.D.)," In S. Feist (ed.), *Transforming Sacred Spaces. New Approaches to Byzantine Ecclesiastical Architecture from the Transitional Period. Proceedings of the International Colloquium held at the Ludwig-Maximilians-Universität München, May 2014* (Wiesbaden, 2020), 18–19.
19 D. Claude, *Die Byzantiische Stadt im 6. Jahrhundert* (Munich, 1969); C. Foss, Archaeology and the "Twenty Cities" of Byzantine Asia." AJA 81/4 (1977), 469–486; C. Mango, *Byzantium: The Empire of New Rome* (Oxford, 1980), 60–87; W. Brandes, *Die Stadt Kleinasiens im 7. Und 8. Jahrundert* (Berlin, 1989); F. Trombley, "Byzantine 'Dark Age" Cities in Comparative Context," in M. Anastos (ed.), *To Ellinikon. Studies in honor of Speros Vryonis Jr.* (New York, 1993), 429–449; J. Haldon, "The Idea of Town in the Byzantine empire," in G. P. Brogiolo and B. Ward-Perkins (eds.), *The Idea and Ideal of the Town between Late Antiquity and the Early Middle Ages (Transformation of the Roman World, 4)* (Leiden, 1999), 1–23; J. H. W. G. Liebeschuetz, *Decline and Fall of the Roman City* (Oxford, 2001); H. Saradi, *The Byzantine City in the Sixth Century: Literary Images and Historical Reality* (Athens, 2006).
20 F. Curta, "Postcards from Maurilia or the Historiography of the Dark-Age Cities of Byzantium." *EJPCA* 6 (2016), 89–110.
21 J. Haldon, "Social transformation in the 6th-9th ct East," in L. Lavan (ed.), Local Economies? Production and Exchange of Inland Regions in Late Antiquity (Leiden, 2006), 607.

22 W. Müller-Wiener, "Von der Polis zum Kastron. Wandlungen der Stadt im Agaische Raum von der Antike zum Mittelalter." Gymnasium 9 (1986), 435–74; A. Dunn," The Transition from *polis* to *kastron* in the Balkans (III-VII cc.): General and Regional Perspectives." *BMGS* 18(1994), 61–80; A. Vionis, "Sacred Townscapes in Late Antique Greece: Christianisation and Economic Diversity in the Aegean."*JMA* 30.2 (2017), 141–165.
23 J. Crow, "Alexios Komnenos and Kastamon: Castles and Settlement in Middle Byzantine Paphlagonia," in M. Mullet and D. Smith (eds), *Alexios I Komnenos. Papers of the Second Byzantine International Colloquium, 14–16 April 1989* (Belfast, 1996), 12–37; M. Whittow, "When did the Ancient World End In the Büyük Menderes? New Long-Term Narratives for Regional History," in A. Çevik and M. Keçis (eds.), *Mentesegullati Tarihi 25–27 Nisan 2012- Mugla* (Istanbul, 2013), 35–53.
24 Whittow, "When did the Ancient World End," 52–56.
25 H. Buchwald, "Byzantine Town Planning. Does it Really Exist?" In M. Grünbart et al. (eds.), *Material Culture and Well-Being in Byzantium (400-1453). Proceedings of the International Conference (Cambridge, 8–10 September 2001)* (Wien, 2007), 57–58.
26 Dagron, "The Urban Economy," 400; see also V. Prigent, "The Mobilisation of Fiscal Resources in the Byzantine Empire (Eighth to Eleventh Centuries)," In J. Hudson and A. Rodríguez (eds.), *Diverging Paths? The Shapes of Power and Institutions in Medieval Christendom and Islam* (Leiden, 2014), 182–229.
27 C. Foss, *Ephesus After Antiquity: a late Antique, Byzantine and Turkish City* (Cambridge, 1979); C. Foss, Byzantine and Turkish Sardis (Cambridge, 1980); C. Foss, *Nicaea. A Byzantine Capital and Its Praises* (New York, 1996).
28 C. Wickham, *Framing the Early Middle Ages, Europe and the Mediterranean, 400–800* (Cambridge, 2005), 591.
29 A. Zuiderhoek, *The End of the Ancient City?* (Cambridge, 2016), 167–185.
30 Saradi, *The Byzantine City*, 49–118.
31 A. H. M. Jones, *Cities of the Eastern Roman Provinces* (Oxford, 1937).
32 M. Whittow, "Ruling the Late Roman and Early Byzantine City: A Continuous History." *Past and Present* 129 (1990), 29.
33 Liebeschuetz, *Decline and Fall, 29–104.*
34 Decker, *The Byzantine*, 118–122.
35 B. Ward Perkins, "The Cities," in A. Cameron (ed.), *The Cambridge Ancient History Vol. 13: Late Empire, A.D.* (Cambridge, 2008), 377.
36 Kirsten, *Die Byzantinische*, 7.
37 E. Zanini, "Coming to the End: Early Byzantine Cities after the mid-6th Century", in *Proceedings of the 23rd International Congress of Byzantine Studies (Belgrade, 22–27 August 2016)* (Belgrade, 2016), 137–139.
38 Whittow, "Ruling the Late Roman and Early Byzantine City: A Continuous History."
39 M. Decker, "The Current Status of Byzantine Archaeology." *History Compass* 16(9) (2018), 1–8.
40 F. Curta, *Southestern Europe in the Middle Ages* (Cambridge, 2006). P. Niewöhner. "Urbanism," In P. Niewöhner (ed.), *The Archaeology of Byzantine Anatolia From the End of Late Antiquity until the Coming of the Turks* (Oxford, 2016), 33–59.
41 M. Hendy, *Studies in the Byzantine Monetary Economy c.300–1450* (Cambridge, 1985), 69–117.
42 Wickham, *Framing*, 594.
43 Haldon, *Palgrave Atlas*, 68–81.
44 Haldon, "Social transformation", 633.
45 Wickham, *Framing*, 626–35.
46 C. Wickham, "The Mediterranean around 800: On the Brink of the Second Trade Cycle." *DOP* 58, 161–174.
47 E. Ivison, "Urban Renewal and Imperial Revival 730–1025." *BF* XXVI (2001), 43.
48 J. L. Quiroga, "Early Byzantine Landscapes in the Southwest and Southeast Mediterranean," in S. Marjanović-Dušanić (ed.), *Proceedings of the 23rd International Congress of Byzantine Studies (Belgrade, 22–27 August 2016)*. Plenary Papers (Belgrade, 2016), 69–105.
49 Id., 94.
50 Zanini, "Urban Ideal," 214–215.
51 V. Ivaniševiç, Caričin Grad (Justinianan prima): A New-Discovered city for a 'New" society," *Proceedings of the 23rd International Congress*, 107–126.

52 E. Zanini, "Macro-Economy, Micro-Ecology, and the Fate of Urbanized Landscape in Late Antique and Early Byzantine Crete," in M. Cau Ontiveros & C. Mas Florit (eds.), *Change and Resilience. The Occupation of Mediterranean Islands in Late Antiquity* (Providence, 2019), 139–161.
53 J. Crow, "Conclusions," in *Proceedings of the 23rd International Congress*, 141; A. Eger, Re-Mapping Medieval Antioch: Urban Transformations from the Early Islamic to the Middle Byzantine Periods." *DOP* 67 (2013), 96–97; G. Avni," From Polis to Madina Revisited- Urban Change in Byzantine and Early Islamic Palestine." *JRAS* 3 (2011), 328–329.
54 M. Whittow, "When did the Ancient World End," 43.
55 P. Horden and N. Purcell, *The Corrupting Sea. A Study in Mediterranean History* (Oxford, 2000), 89–122. Here, one should mention the ongoing *Tabula Imperii Byzantinii* project (https://tib.oeaw.ac.at/ retrieved on 1 July 2022) as it carries out "a systematic research in the historical geography of the Byzantine Empire Including but not limited to its urban spaces), from the beginning of the 4th century to the mid-15th century." Indeed, it is important to stress the invaluable contribution this project brings to a bibliographical updated catalogue of the main urban and urban-like sites across different regions of the empire in a diachronic perspective.
56 H. G. Saradi, "The Byzantine cities (8th–15th Centuries): Old Approaches and New Directions", in Οι βυζαντινές πόλεις, 32–33; Day, *The Afterlife*, 201–202.
57 E. Ivison, "Amorium in the Byzantine Dark Ages (seventh to ninth centuries)," in J. Henning (ed.), *Post-Roman Towns, Trade and Settlement in Europe and Byzantium. Vol. 2 Byzantium, Pliska, and the Balkans* (Berlin, 2012), 25–59. Decker, The Byzantine, 109; Curta, "Postcards," 96–98.
58 Zanini, "Macro-Economy," 158.
59 E. Zanini, "Appunti per una 'archeologia del pane' nel Mediterraneo tardo antico," in G. Archetti (ed.), *La Civiltà del Pane. Storia, Tecniche e simboli dal Mediterraneo all'Atlantico*. (Spoleto, 2015), 373–394.
60 E. Giorgi, *Archeologia dell'acqua a Gortina in età proto-bizantina* (Oxford, 2017).
61 B. Ward Perkins, "Re-using the architectural legacy of the past, entre idéologie et pragmatisme," in *The Idea and Ideal of the Town*. 225–259.
62 Ward-Perkins, "Re-using," 243.
63 B. Ward-Perkins, "Urban survival and urban transformation in the Eastern Mediterranean," in G. P. Brogiolo (ed.), *Città altomedievali nel Mediterraneo occidentale* (Mantua, 1996), 149. H. Kennedy, "From Polis to Madina: Urban Change in Late Antique and Early Islamic Syria." *PP* 106 (1985), 1–29.
64 A. Walmsley, *Early Islamic Syria* (London, 2007), 71–112; Avni, "From Polis to Madina Revisited."
65 Ward Perkins, "The Cities," 410.
66 N. Tzvikis, "Moving beyond the Invisible Cities of Byzantium." *EJPCA* 10 (2020), 333–334.
67 Saradi, "The City," 419–422; Saradi, "The Byzantine cities," 40.
68 Tzvikis, "Moving," 333.
69 N. Barkirtzis, "The Practice, Perception and Experience of Byzantine Fortification," in P. Stephenson (ed.), *The Byzantine World* (London-New York, 2010), 352–376; N. Bakirtzis, "The Visual Language of Fortification Facades: The Walls of Thessaloniki." *Mnhmeio & Periballon (Monument and Environment)* 9 (2005), 15–32.
70 See, for instance, C. Foss and D. Winfield, *Byzantine Fortifications: An Introduction* (Pretoria 1986) J. Crow, "Fortifications," in P. Niewöhner (ed.), *The Archaeology of Byzantine Anatolia From the End of Late Antiquity until the Coming of the Turks* (Oxford, 2016), 90–108.
71 N. Bakirtzis, "The Practice," 66–68. See also the author's contribution in the present volume.
72 Kazdhan, "Polis and kastron in Theophanes and in some other Historical Texts," in *Ευψυχία. Mélanges offerts à Hélène Ahrweiler*, 2 vols. (Paris, 1998), II, 345–360; T. Kiousopoulou, "«Αστοί» και «αγροίκοι»" in Οι βυζαντινές πόλεις; Saradi, "The Byzantine cities," 38–44.
73 C. Sode, "The Formulation of Urban Identity on Byzantine Seals", in B. M. Bedo-Rezak (ed.), *Seals. Making and Marking Connections Across the Medieval World* (Leeds, 2018), 149–165.
74 Id., 158–159; Day, *The Afterlife*, 127–128.
75 C. Wickham, *Medieval Europe. From the Breakup of the Western Roman Empire to the Reformation* (Yale, 2016), 43–60.
76 J. Crow, "Archaeology," in *A Companion to Byzantium*, 291.
77 Curta, "Postcards", 96–103.
78 Id., 106.
79 Here I should alert the reader to the effect that Dey wrote his compelling monography one year before the appearance of Curta's article.

80 See, for instance, Hendy, *Studies* and Haldon, *Palgrave*. For a definition of the Byzantine heartland, see Wickham, *Framing*, 29.
81 Dey, *The Afterlife*, 212.
82 I. Jacobs, "The Creation of Late Antique City. Constantinople and Asia Minor during the 'Theodosian Renaissance." *Byzantion* 82 (2012), 113.
83 Harvey, *Economic expansion*, 222–225.
84 J. Haldon, "Euchaïta: From Late Roman and Byzantine Town to Ottoman Village," in J. Haldon, H. Elton, and J. Newhard (eds), *Archaeology and Urban Settlement in Late Roman and Byzantine Anatolia Euchaïta- Avkat- Beyözü and Its Environment* (Oxford, 2018), 210.
85 E. Zanini, "Cost, Value and Wealth Redistribution: Micro- and Macroeconomy in Early Byzantine Evergetism." *EJPCA* 11(2021), 137–162.
86 J. Haldon, "Social transformation," 613.
87 P. Niewöhner, "The End of the Byzantine City in Anatolia. The Case of Miletus," in E. Gruber, M. Popović, M. Scheutz, and H. Weigl (eds.), *Städte im lateinischen Westen und im griechischen Osten zwischen Spätantike und Früher Neuzeit Topographie – Recht – Religion* (Wien, 2016), 63–77. See also Niewöhner, "Urbanism."
88 Niewöhner, "The End," 76.
89 Horden and Purcell, *The Corrupting*, 90–108.
90 Dey, *The Afterlife*, 209–210.
91 N. Tsivikis, "Πού πάνε οι πόλεις, όταν εξαφανίζονται; Ο οικισμός της πρώιμης και μέσης βυζαντινής Μεσσήνης," in *Οι βυζαντινές πόλεις*. 48–71; N. Tvikis, "Messene and the Changing Urban Life and Material Culture of an Early Byzantine City in the Western Peloponnese (4th-7th Century)," in B. Böhlendorf-Arslan and R. Schick (eds), *Transformations of City and Countryside in the Byzantine Period* (Mainz, 2020), 39–54.
92 Tvikis, "Messene," 53.
93 Vionis, "Sacred Townscapes"; see also, A. Vionis "Understanding Settlements in Byzantine Greece. New Data and new Approaches from Beotia, Sixth to Thirteenth Centuries." *DOP* 71, 127–173 and A. Vionis, "Settled and Sacred Landscapes of Cyprus: Church and Landscape in the Xeros Valley during the Early Byzantine period," in M. Horster, D. Nicolaou and S. Rogge (eds.), *Church Building in Cyprus (4th to 7th Centuries): A Mirror of Intercultural Contacts in the Eastern Mediterranean* (Münster, 2018), 45–70.
94 J. Koder, "The Urban Character of the Early Byzantine Empire: Some Reflections on a Settlmente Geographical Approach to the Topic," In *The 17th International Byzantine Congress. Major Papers. Dumbarton Oaks/Georgetown University. Washington D.C. August 3–8, 1986* (New York, 1986), 156–189. See also J. Koder, "Land use and Settlement. Theoretical Approaches," in J. Haldon (Ed.), *General Issues in the Study of Medieval Logistics, Sources, Problems and Methodologies* (Leiden, 2006), 159–183, and S. Cosentino, "Trasformazioni Economiche ed Egemonie Sociali nelle città dell'oriente Mediterraneano tra antichità e Medioevo", in M.C. Parello and M. S. Rizzo (eds.), *Paesaggi Urbani Tardoantichi. Casi a Confronto. Atti delle Giornate Gegoriane VIII edizione (29–30 Novembre 2014)* (Bari, 2016), 9–16.
95 W. Perkins, "Reusing," 233–8; H. Saradi, "The Use of Ancient Spolia in Byzantine Monuments: The Archaeological and Literary Evidence." *International Journal of the Classical Tradition*, 3/4 (Spring, 1997), 395–423; R. Cormack, "Byzantine Aphrodisias Changing the Symbolic Map of a City. *Proceedings of the Cambridge Philological Society, New Series*, No. 36 (216) (1990), 26–41; B. Caseau, "Sacred Landscape," In G. Bowersock, P. Brown and O. Grabar (eds.), *Late Antiquity: A Guide to the Post Classical World* (Cambridge Mass, 1999), 21–59.
96 Vionis,"Sacred Townscapes," 156.
97 M. Veikou, "Encroachment, Subdivision, and Expansion: A Cultural Interpretation of Byzantine Spatial Transformation (6th-9th Century)," in B. Böhlendorf-Arslan and R. Schick (eds), *Transformations of City and Countryside in the Byzantine Period* (Mainz, 2020), 25–28.
98 J. Haldon, "Euchaïta: From Late Roman and Byzantine Town to Ottoman Village," in J. Haldon, H. Elton, and J. Newhard (eds.), *Archaeology and Urban Settlement in Late Roman and Byzantine Anatolia Euchaïta- Avkat- Beyözü and Its Environment* (Cambridge, 2018), 210–256; see also. J. Haldon et al., "The Climate and Environment of Byzantine Anatolia: Integrating Science, History, and Archaeology." *Journal of Interdisciplinary History* 45/2 (2014), 113–161.
99 Id., 246.

100 A. Izdbesky, *A Rural Economy in Transition: Asia Minor from Late Antiquity Into the Early Middle Ages*. (Warsaw, 2013); L. Mordechai and M. Eisenberg, "The Justinianic Plague: An Interdisciplinary Review." *BMGS*, 43 (2019), 156–180.
101 Haldon, *The Empire that Would not Die*, 232.
102 See above ftn. 84.
103 Veikou, "Encroachment," 35.
104 The peculiarities of urbanism on islands and coastal sites will be examined in a dedicated chapter in the present volume.
105 D. Abulafia, "Islands in Context 400–1000," in M. Cau Ontiveros & C. Mas Florit (eds.), *Change and Resilience. The Occupation of Mediterranean Islands in Late Antiquity* (Providence, 2019), 287–288.
106 G. P. Brogiolo, *Le Origini della Città Medievale* (Mantova, 2011), 76–79.
107 Curta, *Southestern Europe*, -28; C. Bouras, "Aspects of the Byzantine City. Eighth to Fifteenth-century," in *The Economic History of Byzantium*, 483–579; Kiousopoulou, *Οι βυζαντινές πόλεις*; -M. Angold, "The Shaping of the Medieval Byzantine 'City." *BF* 25 (1985), 1–37; Shea, *The Late*; Cheynet, "La Société"; Harvey, *Economic expansion*. A. Külzer, "Harbor Cities as Interfaces of Maritime and Terrestrial Communication Systems in Late Antique and Medieval Western Anatolia," In N. D. Kontogiannis and T. B. Uyar (eds.), *Space and Communities in Byzantine Anatolia. Papers from the Fifth International Sevgi Gönül Byzantine Studies Symposium, İstanbul, 24–26 June 2019* (İstanbul, 2021), 95–109.
108 See, for instance, the short surveys of single urban sites in *The Economic History of Byzantium* as well as the compelling catalogue of urban sites in Anatolia (Niewöhner, *The Byzantine Archaeology*), and Greece (J. Albani and E. Chalkia, *Heaven on Hearth. Cities and Coutryside in Byzantine Greece* (Athens, 2013) with further bibliography on all the mentioned sites (for Butrint, see S. Kamani, "Butrint in the mid-Byzantine period: a new interpretation." *BMGS* 35:2 (2011), 115–133 and R. Hodges, "A 'god-guarded' city? The 'new' medieval town of Butrint. *BMGS* 39/2 (2015), 191–218.
109 Sarris, *Byzantium*, 114–27.
110 A. Beihammer, *Byzantium and the Emergence of Muslim-Turkish Anatolia, ca. 1040–1130* (London, 2102).
111 Angold, "The Shaping," 8–11.
112 Harvey, *Economic Expansion*.
113 Bouras, "Aspects", 515–520.
114 Shea, *The Late*, 301–312; on the arch*ontes*, see M. Angold, "Archons and Dynasts: Local Aristocracies and the Cities of the Later Byzantine Empire," in M. Angold (ed.), *The Byzantine Aristocracy IX to XIII Centuries* (Oxford, 1984), 236–253.
115 Saradi, "The Byzantine cities," 44–45.
116 H. Kalligas, *Monemvasia. A Byzantine City State* (London-New York, 2010).
117 Shea, *The Late*, 296. See also A. Cameron, *Byzantine Matters* (Princeton, 2014), 34.
118 Kalligas, *Monemvasia*, 100–150.
119 Sarris, *Byzantium*, 114–115.
120 For Thessaloniki, Corinth, and Mystras, see the single chapters dedicated to each of these cities in Albani and Chaldia, *Heaven on Earth*; for Pergamon, see W. Radt, *Pergamon. Geschichte und Bauten,Funde und Erforschung einer antiken Metropole* (Köln 1988); K. Rheidt, *Die Stadtgrabung. Die byzantinische Wohnstadt. Altertümer von Pergamon 15/2* (Berlin 1991); T. Otten, "Das Byzantinische Pergamon. Ein Überblick zu Forschungsstand und Quellenlage," In F. Daim and J. Drauschke (eds.), *Byzanz –das Römerreich im Mittelalter Teil 2, 2 Schauplätze* (Mainz, 2010), 1–21.
121 Cameron, *Byzantine Matters*, 42.
122 Buchwald, "Byzantine Town," 70.
123 Saradi, "The Byzantine cities," 42–45; see also Saradi's chapter in the current volume.
124 Kiousopoulou, "«Αστοί» και «αγροίκοι»."
125 Shea, *The Late*, 312. See, for instance, the two examples of Nicaea and Bursa/Prusa (Cagpatay in the present volume).
126 Decker, "The Current Status."
127 D. Favro, *The Urban Image of Augustan Rome* (Cambridge, 2008), 8.

2

THEORIZING BYZANTINE URBANITY

The City Constituting Memory, Memory Constituting the City

Myrto Veikou

Theorizing the Byzantine city is quite a challenging call for two main reasons. The first is that one reasonably expects the ideas of the city and urbanity to have changed meaning many times in pace with social transformation, during the empire's eleven centuries of existence. The second reason is the lack of Byzantine definitions of a city. Byzantine texts are often vague around such a definition, as if taking it for granted, and they can also be confusing, when different terms (ἄστυ, πόλις, κάστρον, κωμόπολις, πολίχνιον, πόλισμα, φρούριον and καστέλλι) are often used alternatively for urban settlements and even for the same settlement during the same period of time.[1] This lack of clear definition has had a great impact upon contemporary research. On one hand, due to developments known as 'the Spatial Turn' which are discussed below, historical and archaeological research of cities has been intensive during the last few decades as compared to earlier times.[2] On the other hand, the main obstacle to the investigation of Byzantine urbanity has been the absence of a Byzantine-proper documented theoretical discourse on the city and architecture.[3] This absence appears paradoxal because urbanity appears, through archaeology and texts, as a central feature of Byzantine cultures.[4] It is not uncommon, for example, in narrative texts that a city's name is its only mentioned attribute.[5] Most often this attribute is not accompanied by any physical descriptions or explanations, as if the name alone served as adequate understatement of its meaning to the Byzantine audience or readers.[6] The Byzantine capital sometimes didn't even 'need' a name – it could be simply referred to as *The City* (ἡ Πόλις).[7] Most probably, the meaning of cities needed not be explained in the texts, because it went without saying.

However, theoretical questions around past conceptions of urbanism and urbanity seek answers to be provided by modern historians and archaeologists. For example, what are the criteria today on the basis of which modern scholars should distinguish between the cities and other kinds of Byzantine settlements? What is the characteristic thing that distinguished cities from other settlements in Byzantine conceptions of habitation? Were Byzantine distinctions necessarily clear or were there 'grey areas' in-between their categories of settlement, as nowadays?[8] Was it perhaps the very structure of cities that did not allow – or at least stimulate – the formation of a Byzantine urban theory?[9] Or is this theoretical perception of

DOI: 10.4324/9780429203923-4

urbanity simply latent or elusive in the Byzantine texts, and shreds of it can potentially be reconstructed?

This study defends this latter possibility by means of presenting ways in which critical spatial perspectives allow revealing meanings of Byzantine urbanity. It does not attempt another reconstruction of the idea and ideal of city in Byzantium; instead, it rather aims to provide researchers with a guide around the history of the concepts and the variety of theoretical devices for approaching the concept of urbanity. It is structured in two sections, the second of which (Part III) comprises a case study which exemplifies one such device. The material for this study is a Byzantine narrative text dated approximately at a threshold between the Byzantine capital's late-antique and medieval periods: it is the 8th-century compendium of texts known as *Parastaseis Syntomoi Chronikai.*[10] For the sake of clarity and consistency, the case study is preceded by: (a) a strictly theoretical section comprising a concise outline of approaches to city and urbanity in urban studies (Part I), which allows explaining and contextualizing (b) various ways through which the theoretical question of urbanity has been so far addressed in Byzantine studies (Part II).

(Re-)Theorizing the City and Urbanity in a Historical Context

Defining the Urban

The city and the idea of urbanity, as an intangible socio-cultural quality evoked by city life, are quite old. They date back to ancient Greece, where the city (*polis*) was the main political unit and the polis' inhabitants (the *asteiotes*), developed not only sophisticated political agency and social behaviour but also cultivated manners, refine verbal expression and tolerance in comparison to the so-perceived uncultivated and clumsy manners of the rural population.[11]

Both concepts (the city and the idea of urbanity) have experienced a new zenith research-wise with the rise of modern urban sociology at the wake of the 20th century, and, ever since, the city as a particular spatial formation has been constituting a remarkable and highly contested topic within the field of social sciences.[12] The main challenge has been to conceptualise the constitution of the city as a scientific object of knowledge and its main objectives are, first of all, to conceptualise the city as a particular space-structuring form of sociation and, secondly, to identify and qualify some features of this spatial form.[13] Although efforts to define the urban have existed within academia and practice, definitions of the urban have not been universally agreed or accepted. To give an example from policy and practice: the United Nations does not use a single, globally accepted definition of the urban.[14] Rather, the estimated rate of global urbanization reflects a mix of country-specific definitions based upon one (or more) of the following criteria:

- administrative areas designated as urban;
- any place with a municipality;
- a population threshold (globally ranging from 200 to 20,000 inhabitants);
- some combination of thresholds in terms of population, number of dwellings, economic activity profile, population density or even a minimum number of prescribed services such as a secondary school, grid connection, health centre, or telephone service. Ultimately, definitions of the urban are as many as there are member states. To further complicate matters, these definitions change over time as countries re-assess their different contexts.[15]

Furthermore, academic perspectives have pinpointed more inadequacies of practical criteria for the definition of the city: they escape to acknowledge the socio-cultural dimension.[16] As Allen J. Scott and Michael Storper argued, 'a viable urban theory should enable us to distinguish between dynamics of social life that are intrinsically urban from those that are more properly seen as lying outside the strict sphere of the urban'.[17] So, while the urban offers a range of observable and measurable characteristics in its spatial dimensions (such as the density of built form), its other dimensions can be (and often are) subject to social construction.[18]

Theorizing the Urban: Space and Time

Definition interrelates with available theory and personal perspective. In urban studies, while paradigm shifts have been abounding from structuralist to cultural turns and from political economy to phenomenology, the concept – or the idea – of urbanity (as broadly referred to the way the spaces of a city are receptive to people) is still contested.[19] Two opposing strands of sociological theories on urbanity, structural and cultural, offer different interpretations on its relation to time, place and space.[20] Both strands can be associated with the late-20th-century developments in urban sociology known as the Spatial Turn:

> 'Space matters,' not for the trivial and self-evident reason that everything occurs in space, but because where events unfold is integral to how they take shape. (…) Space is not simply a passive reflection of social and cultural trends, but an active participant, i.e., geography is constitutive as well as representative. Those who relegate geography to epiphenomenal status do so at their own risk, depriving themselves of a critically important instrument with which to gain insight into the contingent logics of human affairs. By now this argument has been made clear a sufficiently large number of times that space has become indispensable across the social sciences and humanities. In this light, the spatial turn is irreversible.[21]

For many around the world and in practically every discipline, the Spatial Turn has meant a turn to urban studies as well.[22] The phenomenon had started in a great city, Paris, in the 1960s, through the seminal works of Henri Lefebvre and Michel Foucault suggesting that the organization of (urban) space was central to the structure and functioning of capitalism as a coherent whole.[23] Through the study of the 'city', social theory repositioned the understanding of space from given to be produced, calling attention to its role in the construction and transformation of social life and its deeply power-laden nature.[24] Lying somewhere between structuralism and post-structuralism, urban theories by Lefevre, Foucault, and Michel de Certeau suggested that indicators for urbanity can be explained through capitalist structures and processes while also putting emphasis on culture and behaviour.[25]

The latter emphasis has been largely developed by the postmodern cultural approaches which are manifold: what unifies them is their criticism of hegemonic Western theories on urbanity centred on political economy.[26] Under the influence of developments in social anthropology, such structural approaches have been considered deficient when it comes to capturing social and material realities of millions of urban dwellers around the world in everyday life.[27] Helmut Berking and Martina Löw introduced the existence of an 'Intrinsic Logic of Cities', a theory marked by the idea that each city bears its very own kind of urban culture, which expresses itself locally through interactions of the built environment with people's perceptions and with symbolisms as well as with institutional structures.[28]

When it comes specifically to historical research, critical spatial thinking was inevitably inserted as a result of the Spatial Turn's process of 'reassertion of space in social theory'.[29] However, its integration to the field has been a rather long, slow and painful undertaking, mainly because transdisciplinary observations of lived time in all its multitude of expressions have been traditionally conceived as not only different but also competitive to equivalent observations of lived space.[30] Although there are deep parallels between the temporal-historical and spatial-geographical perspectives, the two also had (until the Spatial Turn) unequal scientific recognition: Edward Soja observes that there is no term like 'historian' to describe:

> the all-encompassing spatializer, the person who believes not just that space matters but that it is a vital existential force shaping our lives, an influential aspect of everything that ever was, is, or will be, a transdisciplinary way of looking at and interpreting the world that is as insightful and revealing as that of the historian. For me, what is true for the historical applies also to the spatial and I have devoted my academic career to advocating this critical comparability.[31]

Soja has not only shown beyond doubt that the sociospatial dialectic allows seeing not only how social processes shape and explain geographies but also even more so how geographies shape and explain social processes and social action. He successfully combined the temporal-historical and spatial-geographical perspectives in a single approach: his trialectics of spatiality-historicality-sociality and the associated recognition of urban spatial causality bring back into the contemporary discourse what Lefebvre and Foucault had called for in the late 1960s.[32] Followed by David Harvey in 2010, they have made clear that, also in historical approaches, spatial thinking remains central to the production of knowledge thus, here too, the epistemological power of a critical spatial perspective deserves to be drawn out.[33]

Contemporary research on the same line of thought tends to be all the more critical towards clear definitions and theoretical boundaries, thus offering ample possibilities for sensitive onlooks upon Byzantine spatial formations.[34] For example, first of all, contemporary urban theory acknowledges for the 'grey lines' between categories, when it comes to individual, often hybrid, spatial formations between urban and rural. Such is, for example, the new spatial model of re-urbanity, proposed by Claude Lacour and Sylvette Puissant, which focuses on intermediate zones, especially medium-sized and small-sized areas, which witness particular sociospatial dynamics.[35] Their proposed theoretical approach qualifies for updating the analysis of the structuring and the functioning of these areas which are searching for an identity. Secondly, William Whyte returns to the idea of the ancient Greek agora in his work *City: Rediscovering the Center*.[36] By investigating the meaning of the space of the city-centre from the perspective of a simple itinerant, he shows that the city reasserts its most ancient function as a place where people come together face-to-face. A third opportunity, exemplified in this study, refers to conceptualizations of the city and urbanity through local oral historical narratives which allow constructing collective memory and work as a constitutive element of urban identity.

Theorizations of Byzantine Urbanity

The idea of urbanity during the Middle Ages, conceived with the meaning of an urban culture comprising both economic and civic culture and being the source of a city's vitality, can already be traced in the work of Henri Pirenne, *Les Villes du Moyen Age*.[37] The idea has been extensively elaborated in later publications including Albrecht Classen's collective volume *Urban Space in the Middle Ages and the Early Modern Age*, published in 2009, from which Byzantium is missing.[38]

In Byzantine studies, Helen Saradi, by her big range of publications, deserves to be regarded as the actual specialist in the history of cities from the 4th to the 15th century. Her work employs a traditional approach. This perspective allows her to construct historical narratives about Byzantine cities on the grounds of positivist evaluations of mainly not only textual but also iconographic and archaeological evidence.[39] If some theoretical aspects of her earlier work (e.g. an attachment to evolutionary or evaluative metanarratives in understanding urbanity)[40] are not very productive today, her explicit systematization of available knowledge on Byzantine cities, during the last three decades, constitutes a diachronic contribution to research on urbanity.[41] Furthermore, albeit intended to meet an aspiration for historical 'reality', Saradi's sensitive approach reveals instead the yet underexplored multidimensionality of Byzantine urban spaces and ends up generating many more questions than it provides 'definite' answers.[42]

Luca Zavagno's work *Cities in Transition*, published in 2009, has been a turning point for research on Byzantine urbanity.[43] Despite the evolutionary nuance of the term 'transition' in the title, his comparative close-reading of the archaeological record is detached from any effort to direct the historical narrative towards earlier stereotypes and metanarratives about the Byzantine city (such as decline, demise, dissolution, etc.).[44] Instead, Zavagno opens up the discussion on the meanings of urbanism by foregrounding a diversity of parameters: urban planning and topography, landscape, density, resources, networks. His approach diverts from the older structuralist attempts to produce a single story of the Byzantine city and it foregrounds, instead, regionalization as a crucial element in the delineation of possible trajectories of Byzantine urbanism.[45] The regional and sub-regional differentiations, revealed by his comparative method, allow proposing different models of development for the cities of the Byzantine empire, which should be measured against each other to understand how different local needs produced different multifunctional answers to similar problems.[46]

Enrico Zanini approached Byzantine urbanity from a structuralist perspective in 2003.[47] He explores the Byzantine urban ideal in the 6th century by specifically considering the 'new' cities of this period; his main argument is that these new foundations better reflect this ideal, since they were detached from antique cities' traditional structures.[48] In this enquiry, Zanini's principle criterium for the definition of these settlements is urban planning and especially a set of infrastructures as well as natural and architectural features, guided by 6th-century texts some of which are – as he admits himself – ambiguous on the issue.[49] In particular, he forwards architectural features which: (a) allow sustaining large population (e.g. running water, aqueducts, cisterns); (b) allow population to maintain practices which connects it with late antique elements of urbanity (baths, public buildings, churches); (c) refer to what he names 'archaeology of power' (residences for public authorities – secular, religious and military – natural defence, fortification walls).[50] His interpretation attributes four qualities to the 6th-century city: based on size ('small'), physical form and military role ('fortified'), culture ('Christian') and political role ('imperial').[51] In 2016, Zanini employed a different strategy by applying a critical reading of the archaeological record, thus producing an interpretation of post-6th-century Byzantine cities deriving from a dialogue among several different epistemological dimensions.[52] This new approach acknowledges issues of complexity and variation of settlements understood as Byzantine 'urban' contexts. It also allows 'confronting' some contemporary critical debates. Such debates refer, for example: continuity or discontinuity between ancient and late antique/early Byzantine city; cultural change (e.g. Christianization), political change (e.g. militarization and urban space as a power device); regional diversity; progressive or radical transformation; dynamics between city and countryside.

In 2016, Jorge López Quiroga looked upon the late antique city by employing the concept of landscape and discarding the narratives of decline and collapse in favour of a much more chronologically and geographically nuanced picture. His discourse relies on the importance of regional, indeed local, specificity, great diversity and complexity as fundamental for the study of the Early Byzantine occupation forms.[53] Quiroga's analysis allows considering the transformation of Byzantine urban landscapes within the context of their contemporary landscape developments in the entire Southern Mediterranean. This 'holistic' approach reveals common transformation parameters within this vast region, in the longue durée. Some of these are the following: the Christianization of the urban topography; the dismantling process of the Roman classical city; the reduction, restoration or new construction of the city walls, particularly, but not exclusively, in border areas.[54]

Ine Jacobs has looked upon Early Byzantine performances of urban public space by its users and, in particular, on issues of aesthetic maintenance, aesthetic improvisation and encroachment.[55] Apart from the obvious gain from shedding light upon the 'real' everyday Byzantine urban life, a great virtue of Jacobs' approach is her focus upon social/spatial practices and the lived experience of public space (Figure 2.1). By developing the archaeological evidence into a historical narrative which respects anthropological concerns, she brings the discussion of continuity/discontinuity and social-cultural change in the Byzantine cities to a more down-to-earth basis and on more realistic grounds without depriving it from its complexity and diversity.

The clearest example of a theoretical perspective bringing together the spatial-geographical and the temporal-historical approach is offered by Tonia Kioussopoulou who has addressed questions around Byzantine urbanity in two monographs and an edited volume published between 2007 and 2013.[56] Kioussopoulou seems to originally draw her analytical tools from a structuralist theoretical framework by means of using Fernand Braudel's criteria for her definition of a (Byzantine) settlement as city.[57] As she writes, these criteria are the division of labour in it as opposed to the division of labour in the countryside, the development of the settlement, the control it exercises onto its surrounding natural environment and its coexistence with other smaller or bigger settlements.[58] However, her interpretations of Byzantine sources and her theoretical approach to the urban phenomenon, as manifested in her works, reveal a profound integration of theoretical tools drawn from poststructuralist geographers of the Spatial Turn. First of all, through the study of the Late Byzantine city, Kioussopoulou demonstrates the role of space in the construction and transformation of social life and its deeply power-laden nature.[59] Second, by means of a thorough reconstruction of a map of the 15th-century Byzantine capital, she exemplifies a method of turning urban space into a hermeneutical tool for political and social phenomena (Figure 2.2).[60] Third, she addresses the problem of definition of the Byzantine city by encouraging theoretical plurality and without hesitating to develop interpretations of the archaeological record.[61] Last but not least, she provides an answer to the question of how much can the urban phenomenon serve as key for the interpretation of Byzantine society, during the period 1261–1453, by means of scrutinizing the interrelations among urban space and the social groups residing in it, the relations among those groups and the central

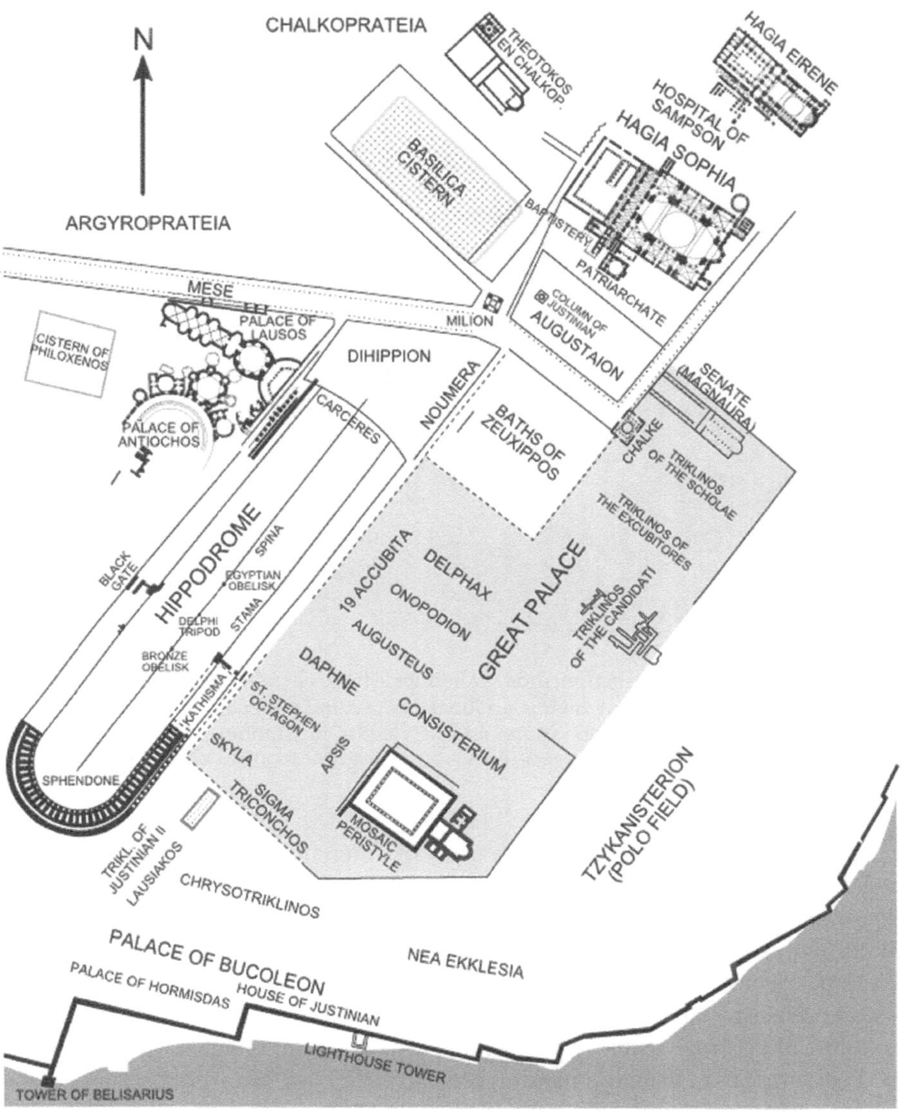

Figure 2.1 Construction of urban memory: The imperial district of Constantinople with the original placing of the Obelisk of Theodosius in the middle of the Hippodrome. Plan of the imperial district of Byzantine Constantinople, with approximate locations of its main buildings

power agents, as well as the connections between cities and countryside.[62] The result of her enquiry is the emergence of the city as a spatial formation inextricable from political and social interconnections, based upon economic relations, and their ensuing cultural conception of a Byzantine urban identity.

When it comes to literary studies, Charis Messis and Paolo Odorico's edited volume on ekphraseis of cities has a clear focus on urbanity. It contributes to the idea of the city as a renewable resource for the political, religious and aesthetic imagination, both in Byzantium

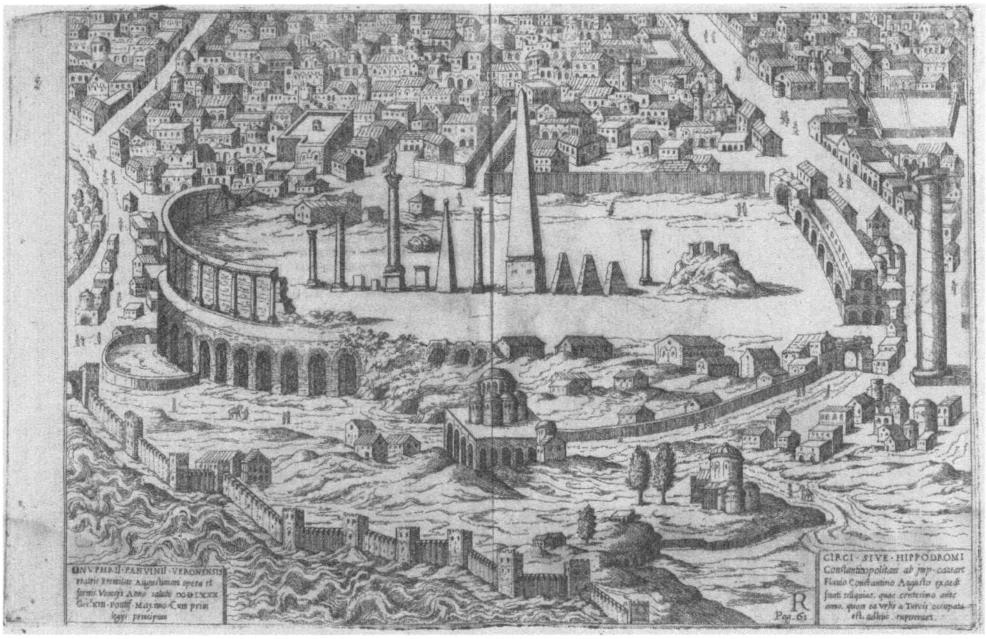

Figure 2.2 Preservation of urban memory: The Obelisk of Theodosius still standing in the middle of the Hippodrome which is no longer in use, in late medieval Constantinople/Istanbul. Engraving of the Hippodrome and its vicinity in Istanbul, Dated to 1580, by Onofrio Panvinio (*De Ludis Circensibus*, Venice: Giovanni Baptista Ciotti, 1600, I, 48)

and beyond.[63] The volume offers a big variety of different approaches which cannot be discussed as a single contribution. However, if considered a whole, in Emmanuel Bourbouhakis's words, 'this variety allow understanding how and why cities remained iconic fixtures in Byzantium, touchstones of experience in an era long (and perhaps wrongly) associated with urban decline'.[64]

A comprehensive literature review on theoretical approaches towards the Byzantine cities is unfortunately impossible to fit the limited space of this chapter. This section can inevitably do no more than display a handful of approaches which are either competitive to each other or at centre-stage today in archaeology, history and literary studies. This review must be concluded by the mention of two exemplary works separated by exactly twenty years of scholarship yet adopting similar approaches to the Byzantine capital. These are, first, the conference proceedings edited by Cyril Mango and Gilbert Dagron in 1995 with the title 'Constantinople and its Hinterland' and, second, those edited by Paul Magdalino and Nina Ergin with the title 'Istanbul and Water'.[65] The open-minded and inclusive scope of the two collective volumes does not allow the reader to be 'trapped' within invented boundary-lines in settlement. Constantinople is, instead, considered only one, inseparable, part of a wide system of settlement functioning by means of the maritime element. The two volumes succeed in promoting the discussion of Byzantine urbanism in terms of sociospatial dynamics and in a dialectic to the non-urban, while also acknowledging the city as a particular space-structuring form of sociation.

Memory Narrates the City: A Critical Spatial Interpretation of the *Parastaseis Syntomoi Chronikai*

Oral History, Collective Memory and Local Identity

A good example of literary text written in the city and about the city, hence reflecting Byzantine urbanity, is the *Parastaseis Syntomoi Chronikai (*hereafter *Parastaseis*).[66] Dating to the 8th or the 9th century, this work has been notably difficult to categorise.[67] It consists of a collection of short comments on the theme of Constantinopolitan topography and monuments, particularly statues, and making reference to non-existent or anachronistic sources. It is anonymous and, even if it was put together by a single final editor, its composition seems to be a collective endeavour of a group of authors unknown from other sources.[68] As for its purpose, many suggestions have come forward over the years. Cyril Mango has proposed that it was a 'kind of tourist's guidebook to the curiosities of Constantinople'.[69] Gilbert Dagron has, instead, characterised this collection of texts as belonging to a genre named 'patriotic literature' (patriographie).[70] Averil Cameron and Judith Herrin argued that the work's incompleteness and repetitiveness are arguments for dismissing the interpretation as a 'guidebook'.[71] Instead they understand Parastaseis as a 'dossier of information', a sort of lay 'research text'.[72] None of these solutions is regarded as entirely satisfactory.[73] Alexander Kazhdan has considered it as a folklore comic text aiming for political and entertaining parody.[74] On the contrary, Paolo Odorico has taken it very seriously: he provides a link between the *Parastaseis* and historiography and suggests that the text was a 'dossier preparé pour servir du recueil historique'.[75] However, this doesn't go without fragmenting the text: Odorico attributes chapters 27–89 to an anthology compiled by a certain Theodore that combines disparate texts about Constantinople, and he suggests that those were brought together with the original *Parastaseis* (chapters 1–26) in a manuscript with the aim of producing a historical chronicle.[76]

Dagron, as well as Cameron and Herrin, has observed a set of interesting traits in the text: anonymity, orality, and a very idiosyncratic and inconsistent historicity.[77] I here also add three more: a strong sense of embodiment, a strong sense of kinaesthetic and sensorial experience, and a deep focus on space. I argue that all six traits point to a different interpretation of text: as an instrument for the construction of collective memory and, through that, urban identity. This construction is achieved by means of performing urban space and placemaking.[78]

To begin with anonymity, Dagron wonders whether it is accidental or deliberate.[79] He considers it as a trait which allows the author to appear omnipresent and in control of space, 'exactly as a guide does'.[80] The anonymous narration in which the narrator manifests himself interchangeably as 'I', or as 'we', not only creates a sense of collectivity but it also implies authority.[81] This way of narrating also points to secondary orality.[82] This orality is extensively implied within the text as a condition upon which the composition is grounded, and it often manifests itself through the phrases 'they said' or 'it is said' (ἔλεγον, λέγεται).[83] Cameron and Herrin observe that:

> Much of their <authors'> work depended not on written records but on hearsay; thus the frequent 'they say' or 'it is said', and hence too the difference of opinion about certain monuments. The first-person entries and the references to unspecified people who

have told the author certain things all point to personal activity, in an atmosphere in which books were not objects of daily and familiar use.[84]

Instead of a library, the source of the text – i.e. the acquisition by the composer of orally transmitted traditional stories about the city – appears to be connected with 'walking in the city'. Walking is a spatial practice which largely involves an embodiment that produces kinaesthetic and sensorial experiences.[85] Visuality, in particular, dominates the *Parastaseis* by means of constant descriptions of visual images and of using terms such as 'spectacle' (θέαμα, throughout), 'viewed' and 'admiring' (ἰδέσθαι, καθορῶνται, θαυμάζων).[86] Other senses, such as hearing (sounds or discussions), come into the narration occasionally, as in the much-discussed story about the Kynegion and a deadly statue.[87]

A surprising feature of the *Parastaseis* (if considered a 'patriotic' text) is that narration often takes a break from the stories about statues and wonders of the city, in order to tell stories about spaces of the capital – as if space, too, constitutes an identity element per se. This strong focus on space is manifested in the text in two ways. First of all, it is shown by means of many detailed descriptions of spaces, which occasionally seem to have no apparent function.[88] Indicatively, in the story about a statue at St Mamas, the authors inform the reader that there once stood a terrifying bridge with about twelve arches and vaults for a very big river used to pour down at that point, especially, 'as they say', in the month of February.[89] Second, it is demonstrated through the authors' decision to register several (and, sometimes, even contradictory) old stories and details about spaces of the capital (even more so in the case of spaces which no longer existed).[90] That is how we learn, for example, among other things: that regarding the bridge at St Mamas (mentioned above), some said that a dragon lived in it and that a certain descendant of a Roman Caesar fell in love with the place, built it up and lived there and erected a temple to Zeus[91]; that the fort of Serapion used to be called Rhegion and was held by the Persians[92]; that Xerolophos was a place associated with pagan spectacles, sacrifices, divination and astronomy[93]; that in Exakionion, there was a large bath, in which many were endangered because they said they had not heard a prophecy[94]; and that at the Proteichisma, there was once a gate built by Carus.[95]

This brings us to the last trait of the text that is of interest to the present discussion, namely the authors' historical 'awareness'.[96] Averil Cameron and Judith Herrin have extensively analysed this inconsistency in the text's references to historical persons and events.[97] Odorico tried to resolve this problems by 'rationalizing' and fragmenting the text, seeking a strict and clear-cut structure which would reveal the intention behind it and its function.[98] Historical credibility was a main concern of the authors as seen from many chapters concluding with phrases such as the following: 'These things can be seen up to the present day by those who wish to examine what we have written with philosophy and effort'.[99] However, historical consistency is not a priority as seen in their citation of several different versions of the story about the city's foundation, at different parts of the text.[100] Historical consistency must have been discarded so as to compromise another primary concern of the authors: I think that this concern was to understand the ways in which the pagan remains (material and immaterial) are integrated in a Christian city.[101]

To conclude, the traits discussed above as well as certain key words spread throughout the text – such as 'people must know' (δέον γιγνώσκειν)[102] and 'most people say' (ἐμφέρεται εἰς τοὺς πολλοὺς) –[103] suggest, I argue, another interpretation of the *Parastaseis*. In specific, this text can be understood as an effort to construct collective memory – and, through that, discuss the meaning of local urban identity – in 8th–9th-century Constantinople. The authors' way to achieve that is to register orally transmitted stories of places and monuments in the capital, because this is their way of conceiving urbanity and performing their own urban identities.[104] The concept of oral history(-ies) is found in the *Parastaseis* within the element of narration: the verb 'ἱστόρησε' is often used throughout the text with the meaning of narrating (a place, an image, a statue).[105] What Cameron and Herrin refer to as 'hearsay' (in the passage cited above) is nothing but the local oral histories which 'narrate the city' or rather 'narrate the many cities within the city' experienced by the narrators.[106]

The City Constituting Memory, Memory Constituting the City

Memories are inseparable from places, because the process of memory construction is based upon spatial experience.[107] The sort of itinerary performed by the authors of the *Parastaseis* in the city, which comprises a documentation of local oral history about the city as communicated by its citizens, is a spatial practice allowing to construct the authors' local and urban identities. Dagron insightfully attributed the authors in a model of Byzantine scholars which he names 'The Philosophers in the Street' (Les Philosophes dans la rue).[108] The content of this identity is determined by their own political agency: they use the urban space in such a way as to perform their personal idea of urbanity. This idea can be defined as alternative and 'unofficial', as compared to the authorities' official establishment of power relations in the capital through urban planning.[109] Furthermore, this political agency – and the communication of the final narrative – constructs collective memory about the city, thus constituting the city (Figure 2.3).

Figure 2.3 Preservation and reconstruction of urban memory: Istanbul, Sultanahmet Square, the Obelisk of Theodosius as integrated in the modern city planning

In this narrated trajectory, the authors seem to connect their notions of urbanity with things that they consistently look for and register: first, spaces, and, second, particular objects – statues, inscriptions, crosses, even unusual things (such as bones of ancient giant men)[110] – which work as markers to signify the spaces as places. It has been enigmatic for modern scholars why the authors have included in this placemaking process statues which must have not existed (thus been visible) at the given places during these centuries. They were, obviously, engaged into a very particular sort of itinerant symbolic placemaking by means of an embodied experience of both present and imaginary urban space.

The choice of focus on statues – often shown as having supernatural and prophetic powers – has also puzzled scholarship.[111] What is the connection between stories about antique statues – many of which should not even been there, when the text was composed – and urbanity in the 8th or 9th century? Liz James has suggested that classical statues in Byzantium were, like Christian images, an essential source of power that could be employed to their own advantage by those with the knowledge of the correct procedures.[112] Ancient statues provided a visible link between the past and the present: having been made and set up, statues had a long and active life, changing in meaning and significance throughout it.[113] The oral narratives about them, written down by the authors of the *Parastaseis*, refer to inhabitants' experiences of monuments in the city. These monuments provoke shifting interpretations as their original significations are often either lost or transformed with time.[114] Similarly, in the *Parastaseis*, the ancient statues and old inscriptions work to achieve a placemaking which signifies a new notion of urbanity. They have a power which is hidden but they can still be prophetic: hence, they still not only reflect and represent an urban content but they also convey the message that the urban is now something different than in old times but connected to that. A particular phrase, used in the narration about the emperor Justinian I (527–565) distributing statues around the city, offers a good example of this conception: 'These statues Justinian distributed around the city when he built the Great Church with faith and effort. Those who know the foregoing find a good number of them if they go round the city and look for them'.[115] Oral history, in this case, makes the difference from contemporary 'official' historical narratives. Namely, the correlation between the statue and urbanity has gone down to the authors of the *Parastaseis* through the citizens' orally transmitted collective memory. In this collective memory, statues are equally important landmarks of the city life, as the inscriptions and the crosses, even if no one can remember exactly why (Figure 2.4).

Paroma Chatterjee has interpreted the text as an attempt to construe the cityscape of Constantinople as a space where known and unknown quantities coexist.[116] She contends that the *Parastaseis* imagines the topography of Constantinople as one composed of nodes of the unknown and that these unknown spaces and monuments articulated the city's links to its ancient – if forgotten – past and thus played a critical role as markers of urban and historical continuity. She argues that ancient statues were associated with the longevity of the Byzantine Empire in a way that holy icons were not, because the former had never been subjected to the atrocities and debates regarding their validity that the latter had during Iconoclasm. She defines this mechanism as follows:

> The emphasis of the *Parastaseis* is on the process of– and, indeed, the importance of – viewing public monuments, even if they remain indecipherable and unknowable to their viewers. (…) Although the sculptures range from Christian figures to ancient exemplars to monumental crucifixes, they are all assumed, in the final analysis, to

Figure 2.4 Continuity or Fade of Urban Memory: Istanbul, Sultanahmet Square, the Obelisk of Theodosius in the contemporary every-day urban life

> be invested with meaning and accessible to interpretation, no matter how ambiguous they appear. They may be read in diverse ways by diverse audiences, but they always yield a message, or several messages, depending on the audience's horizon of expectations.[117]

The persistence of this 'patriotic' agency in the Byzantine capital is revealed by the fact that the *Parastaseis* circulated until at least the 10th century, since a part of it was reproduced in the *Patria Konstantinoupoleos*.[118] In fact, the *Patria* can also be regarded as a text with a similar orientation: it integrates older narratives on the city so as to reproduce the 'historicity' of a 'Byzantine Constantinopolitan local identity' and its patriotic ideology.[119] However, *Patria* seems to be a work based upon oral history but diverts from its limitations: according to Albrecht Berger, it was a more systematic written compendium of widespread dissemination.[120] However, the close connection between 'homeland' and urbanity is detected until the twilight of the Byzantine society. As discussed by Kioussopoulou, the urban patriotism displayed by many Paleologan authors consisted of cultural elements and it had a political content. Urban identity – as distinguished from the rural one – consisted, first, of the glorious past of their city-homeland and, second, by their education while the unifying point of reference between the two was always the emperor.[121]

To conclude, neither interpretation of the *Parastaseis* – as a guidebook or as a history book – appears convincing. I here argued that the text's main focus on three things – space, memory and the city – as well as its six particular traits discussed above (anonymity, orality, idiosyncratic and inconsistent historicity, sense of embodiment, sense of kinaesthetic and sensorial experience, deep and ever-present focus on space) encourage its understanding as a 'memory book' helping to constitute urban identity in the Byzantine capital through a practice of symbolic placemaking. Just like a modern historian working with oral history, its authors employed this practice in order to write down the citizens' oral stories about the city, which constituted the notion of urbanity for them.

The *Parastaseis* helps modern scholarship theorise the city and urbanity because of its affinity to oral history. The memories of the cities are part of their history precisely because the way, in which memories are constituted in urban space, is part of the history of urbanism.[122] These memories are constructed through the relation between materialities of particular places and symbolic markings of urban space by the narrators.[123] The memories of urban space, in particular, represent the many different ways in which memory narrates the city. Oral historical narratives recite cities in many different ways. In that way, they prove that cities cannot be represented by a single normative picture or explained through a single, all-encompassing, historical narrative.

Notes

1 A. P. Kazhdan, "Polis and Kastron in Theophanes and in Some Other Historical Texts", *Εὐψυχία. Mélanges offerts à Hélène Arhweiler*, v. II (Paris: Éditions de la Sorbonne, 1998), 345–360; M. Veikou, *Byzantine Epirus, A Topography of Transformation, Settlements of the Seventh-Twelfth Centuries in Southern Epirus and Aetoloacarnania, Greece* (Leiden – New York, NY: Brill NV, 2012), 335. See also: W. Brandes, "Byzantine Cities in the Seventh and Eighth Centuries – Different Sources, Different Histories?", in G. P. Brogiolo & B. Ward-Perkins (eds), *The Idea and Ideal of Town between Late Antiquity and the Early Middle Ages, The Transformation of the Roman World 4* (Leiden: Brill, 1999), 25–29; W. Brandes & J. F. Haldon, "Towns, Tax and Transformation: State, Cities and Their Hinterlands in the East Roman World, C. 500–800", in G. P. Brogiolo, N. Gauthier & N. Christie (eds), *Towns and Their Territories between the Late Antiquity and the Early Middle Ages, The Transformation of the Roman World 9* (Leiden: Brill, 2000), 141–172; G. Dagron, "The Urban Economy, Seventh-Twelfth Centuries", in A. Laiou (ed), *The Economic History of Byzantium, from the Seventh through the Fifteenth Century*, I (Washington, DC: Dumbarton Oaks, 2002), 400–405; J. F. Haldon, "The Idea of the Town in the Byzantine Empire", in Brogiolo, Ward-Perkins (eds), *The Idea and Ideal of Town*, 10–23; T. Kioussopoulou, *Οι αόρατες βυζαντινές πόλεις στον ελλαδικό χώρο (13ος-15ος αιώνας)* (Athens: Polis, 2013), 19–20; M. Veikou, "Urban or Rural? Theoretical Remarks on the Settlement Patterns in Byzantine Epirus (7th–11th centuries)", *Byzantinische Zeitschrift* 103:1 (2010), 171–193.

2 For discussions of the state of art during the 20th century, see: H. G. Saradi, *The Byzantine City in the Sixth Century. Literary Images and Historical Reality* (Athens: Society of Messenian Archeological Studies, 2006), 13–45; Eadem, "The Byzantine Cities (8th–15th Centuries): Old Approaches and New Directions", in T. Kioussopoulou (ed), *Οι βυζαντινές πόλεις 8ος-15ος αιώνας. Προοπτικές της έρευνας και νέες ερμηνευτικές προσεγγίσεις* (Rethymno: Publications of the Faculty of Arts/University of Crete, 2012), 31–45; C. Bouras, "Μεσοβυζαντινές και υστεροβυζαντινές πόλεις από την σκοπιά της πολεοδομίας και της αρχιτεκτονικής", in Kioussopoulou (ed), *Οι βυζαντινές πόλεις*, 2–4.

3 P. Oraiopoulos, *Ο νεοελληνικός λόγος για την αρχιτεκτονική και την πόλη. Το χωρικό μοντέλο της ελληνικής Ανατολής* (Athens: ESTIA, 1998); Kioussopoulou, *Οι αόρατες βυζαντινές πόλεις*, 19.

4 Kioussopoulou, *Οι αόρατες βυζαντινές πόλεις*, 15–17; H. Saradi, "Towns and Cities", in E. Jeffreys, J. Haldon & R. Cormack (eds), *The Oxford Handbook of Byzantine Studies* (Oxford – New York, NY: Oxford University Press, 2008), 317; Eadem, "The City in Byzantine Hagiography", in S. Efthymiadis (ed), *The Ashgate Research Companion to Byzantine Hagiography, Vol. II: Genres and Contexts* (Ashgate: Farnham, 2014), 419–452; T. Tanoulas, "Αναζητώντας την αντίληψη του αστικού χώρου στο Βυζάντιο", in Kioussopoulou (ed), *Οι βυζαντινές πόλεις*, 18–24.

5 Cities' names in Byzantine hagiographical texts, for instance, the described settlement-features are extremely limited and form part of the setting of the plot. See, for example, the comparative discussion on the "Life of Lazaros from Mount Galesion and the Life of St Symeon the New

Theologian", in M. Veikou, *Spatial Paths to Holiness – Literary 'Lived Spaces' in Eleventh-Century Byzantine Saints' Lives* (Uppsala: Studia Byzantina Upsaliensia 22, in press), Chapter 4.

6 Indicatively: *Life of Lazarus from Mount Galesion* (BHG 979) §9, 15, 25, edition by H. Delehaye, *Acta Sanctorum Novembris collecta digesta illustrata*, a, III (Brussels: s.n., 1910, dig. rep. Cambridge: Chadwyck-Healey, 2002). English translation by R. P. H. Greenfield, *The Life of Lazaros of Mt. Galesion: An Eleventh-Century Pillar Saint, Introduction, Translation, and Notes*, Byzantine Saints' Lives in Translation (Washington, DC: Dumbarton Oaks Research Library and Collection, 2000), 86, 93, 109.

7 D. J. Georgacas, "The Names of Constantinople", *Transactions and Proceedings of the American Philological Association* 78 (1947), 358–366.

8 For an elaboration of this question, see M. Veikou, "'Rural Towns' and 'In-between Spaces'. Settlement Patterns in Byzantine Epirus (7th–11th Centuries) in an Interdisciplinary Approach", *Archeologia Medievale* 36 (2009), 43–54; Eadem, "Urban or Rural?"; Eadem, "Byzantine Histories, Settlement Stories: Kastra, "Isles of Refuge", and "Unspecified Settlements" as In-between or Third Spaces", in Kioussopoulou (ed), *Οι βυζαντινές πόλεις*, 159–206.

9 Kioussopoulou, *Οι αόρατες βυζαντινές πόλεις*, 19; See also Bouras, "Μεσοβυζαντινές και υστεροβυζαντινές πόλεις", 10.

10 *Parastaseis Syntomoi Chronikai*, ed. tr. A. Cameron & J. Herrin, *Constantinople in the Early Eighth Century: The Parastaseis Syntomoi Chronikai* (Leiden: Brill, 1984), 56–165 (hereafter *Parastaseis Syntomoi Chronikai*).

11 B. Knoop, "Urbanity through Time, Space and Place", *Proceedings of the CIST 2020 – Population, Temps, Territoires | Population, Time, Territories | Población, tiempo, territories*, Paris, 18–20 November 2020, 574–577, Open access online publication at https://cist2020.sciencesconf.org/319785/document (last accessed on 21-04-2021), 574.

12 D. Iossifova, C. N. H. Doll & A. Gasparatos, "Defining the Urban: Why Do We Need Definitions?", in D. Iossifova, C. Doll & A. Gasparatos (eds), *Defining the Urban: Interdisciplinary and Professional Perspectives* (London: Routledge, 2017), 1–7; R. E. Toulson, "Theorizing the City: Recent Research in Urban Anthropology", *Reviews in Anthropology* 44:1 (2015), 28–42.

13 H. Berking, "The Distinctiveness of Cities", *Urban Research & Practice* 5:3 (2012), 316–324.

14 *World Urbanization Prospects: The 2014 Revision, Highlights* (New York, NY: United Nations Department of Economic and Social Affairs, Population Division, 2014).

15 Iossifova, Doll & Gasparatos, "Defining the Urban", 3–4.

16 C. R. Tittle, "Urbanity: Influences of Urbanness, Structure, and Culture", *Social Science Research* 30 (2001), 313–335.

17 A. J. Scott & M. Storper, "The Nature of Cities: The Scope and Limits of Urban Theory", *International Journal of Urban and Regional Research* 39:1 (2015), 12.

18 Iossifova, Doll & Gasparatos, "Defining the Urban", 4; T. van Dijk & A. van der Valk, "Shades of Urbanity: Diverging Statistical Definitions", Paper at the *ENHR 2007 International Conference 'Sustainable Urban Areas'*, Rotterdam, 25–28 June 2007, Online publication at https://www.researchgate.net/publication/40103012_Shades_of_urbanity_diverging_statistical_definitions.

19 D. Vieira de Aguiar, "What Is Urbanity About?", in Y. O. Kim, H. T. Park & K. W. Seo (eds), *Proceedings of the Ninth International Space Syntax Symposium* (Seoul: Sejong University, 2013), ch. 086, Online publication at http://sss9sejong.or.kr/paperpdf/ussecp/SSS9_2013_REF086_P.pdf (last accessed on 21-04-2021).

20 Knoop, "Urbanity", 574–577.

21 B. Warf & S. Arias, "Introduction", in B. Warf & S. Arias (eds), *The Spatial Turn, Interdisciplinary Perspectives* (London – New York, NY: Routledge, 2009), 10.

22 E. W. Soja, "Taking Space Personally", in Warf & Arias (eds), *The Spatial Turn*, 23.

23 M. Foucault, *The Archaeology of Knowledge* (New York, NY: Pantheon, 1972); Idem, "Questions on Geography", in C. Gordon (ed), *Power/Knowledge: Selected Interviews and Other Writings, 1972–1977* (London: Harvester Wheatsheaf, 1980); Idem, "Space, Knowledge, and Power", in P. Rabinow (ed), *The Foucault Reader* (New York, NY: Pantheon, 1984); Idem, "Of Other Spaces", tr. J. Miskowiec, *Diacritics* 16:1 (1986) 22–27; H. Lefebvre, *La production de l'espace* (Paris: Anthropos, 1974) English translation by D. Nicholson-Smith, *The Production of Space* (London: Blackwell, 1991); Idem, *Le droit à la ville : Suivi de Espace et politique* (Paris: Anthropos, 1972); Soja, "Taking Space Personally", 17–18.

24 Warf & Arias, "Introduction", 3.
25 See note 23 above; M. De Certeau, *L'invention du quotidien,Vol. 1: Arts de faire'* (1980), English translation by S. Rendall, *The Practice of Everyday Life* (Berkeley, CA: University of California Press, 1984).
26 Knoop, "Urbanity", 576; J. Robinson, "The Urban Now: Theorising Cities beyond the New", *European Journal of Cultural Studies* 16:6 (2013), 659–677.
27 Knoop, "Urbanity", 576; Tittle, "Urbanity"; Robinson, "The Urban Now"; S. M. Low, "The Anthropology of Cities: Imagining and Theorizing the City", *Annual Review of Anthropology* 25:1 (1996), 383–409; Idem, *Theorizing the City: The New Urban Anthropology Reader* (New Brunswick, NJ – London: Rutgers University Press, 1999).
28 H. Berking & M. Löw, "Einleitung", in M. Löw & H. Berking (eds), *Die Eigenlogik der Städte. Neue Wege für die Stadtforschung*, Interdisziplinäre Stadtforschung series 1 (Frankfurt am Main: Campus, 2008), 7–14.
29 Warf & Arias, "Introduction", 1–10.
30 Soja, "Taking Space Personally", 11.
31 Soja, "Taking Space Personally", 11.
32 E. W. Soja, "The Socio-Spatial Dialectic", *Annals of the Association of American Geographers* 70 (1980), 207–225; Idem, *Postmodern Geographies – The Reassertion of Space in Critical Social Theory* (London: Verso, 1989); Idem, *Thirdspace: Journeys to Los Angeles and Other Real-and-Imagined Places* (Oxford: Blackwell, 1996); Idem, *Postmetropolis: Critical Studies of Cities and Regions* (Oxford: Blackwell, 2000); Idem, "Taking Space Personally", 17–22; A. J. Scott & E. W. Soja (eds), *The City – Los Angeles and Urban Theory at the End of the Twentieth Century* (Los Angeles, CA: University of California Press, 1996).
33 D. Harvey, *Géographie et capital: Vers un matérialisme historico-géographique*, Mille Marxismes (Paris: Syllepse, 2010).
34 D. R. Judd, "Theorizing the City", in D. R. Judd & D. Simpson (eds), *City, Revisited: Urban Theory from Chicago, Los Angeles, and New York* (Minneapolis, MN – London: University of Minnesota Press, 2011), 1–20; J. Abu-Lughod, "Grounded Theory Not Abstract Words but Tools of Analysis", *Ibidum*, 21–50.
35 C. Lacour & S. Puissant, "Re-Urbanity: Urbanising the Rural and Ruralising the Urban", *Environment and Planning A* 39 (2007), 728–747.
36 W. H. Whyte, *City: Rediscovering the Center* (Philadelphia, Pa: University of Pennsylvania Press, 2009).
37 H. Pirenne, *Les Villes du Moyen Age, essai d'histoire économique et sociale* (Bruxelles: Maurice Lamertin, 1927). Earlier English translation by F. D. Halsey, *Medieval Cities, Their Origins and the Revival of Trade* (Princeton, N.J.: Princeton University Press, 1925).
38 See A. C. Zijderveld, *A Theory of Urbanity; The Economic and Civic Culture of Cities* (New Brunswick, NJ: Transaction, 1998); A. Classen, "Urban Space in the Middle Ages and the Early Modern Age: Historical, Mental, Cultural, and Social Economic Investigations", in A. Classen (ed), *Urban Space in the Middle Ages and the Early Modern Age* (Berlin: De Gruyter, 2009).
39 Indicatively: E. Saradi, "Space In Byzantine Thought", in S. Ćurčić & E. Hadjitryphonos (eds), *Architecture as Icon: Perception and Representation of Architecture in Byzantine Art, Exhibition at the Princeton University Art Museum: March 6, 2010–June 6, 2010* (New Haven, CT, Connecticut, Yale University Press, 2010), 73–111; Eadem, "The Monuments in the Late Byzantine Ekphraseis of Cities: Searching for Identities", in V. Vavřínek, P. Odorico & V. Drbal (eds), *Ekphrasis – La représentation des monuments dans les littératures byzantine et byzantino-slaves Réalités et imaginaires*, *Byzantinoslavica* LXIX:3 (2011) Supplementum, 179–192.
40 For example, H. Saradi, "The Demise of the Ancient City and the Emergence of the Mediaeval City in the Eastern Roman Empire", *Echos du Monde Classique/Classical Views* XXXII:7 (1988), 365–401; Eadem, "The Dissolution of the Urban Space in the Early Byzantine Centuries: The Evidence of the Imperial Legislation", *Σύμμεικτα* 9:2 (Μνήμη Δ.Α. Ζακυθηνού) (1994), 295–308; Eadem, "The Kallos of the Byzantine City: The Development of a Rhetorical Topos and Historical Reality", *Gesta* 34:1 (1995), 37–56.
41 Saradi, *The Byzantine City in the Sixth Century*, 13–45; Eadem, "Towns and Cities"; Eadem, "The Byzantine Cities".

42 For example, Saradi, *The Byzantine City in the Sixth Century*; Eadem, "The City in Byzantine Hagiography".
43 L. Zavagno, *Cities in Transition: Urbanism in Byzantium between Late Antiquity and the Early Middle Ages (AD 500-900)*, BAR International Series 2030 (Oxford: Archaeopress, 2009).
44 E.g. J. Durliat, *De la ville antique à la ville byzantine: le problème des subsistances* (Rome: École française de Rome, 1990).
45 Zavagno, *Cities in Transition*, 170.
46 Zavagno, *Cities in Transition*, 170–171.
47 E. Zanini, "The Urban Ideal and Urban Planning in Byzantine New Cities of the Sixth Century A.D.", in L. Lavan & W. Bowden (eds), *Theory and Practice in Late Antique Archaeology*, Late Antique Archaeology 1 (Leiden – Boston, MA: Brill, 2003), 196–223.
48 Zanini, "The Urban Ideal", 201.
49 Zanini, "The Urban Ideal", 197–201. Zanini admits that Procopius' use of the term *polis* is inconsistent (198), which is not surprising (see note 1 above).
50 Zanini, "The Urban Ideal", 209–214.
51 Zanini, "The Urban Ideal", 214–220.
52 E. Zanini, "Coming to the End: Early Byzantine Cities after the Mid-6th Century", in *Proceedings of the 23rd International Congress of Byzantine Studies, Belgrade, 22–27 August 2016, Plenary Papers* (Belgrade, 2016), 127–140.
53 J. L. Quiroga, "Early Byzantine Urban Landscapes in the Southwest and Southeast Mediterranean", in *Proceedings of the 23rd International Congress of Byzantine Studies, Belgrade, 22–27 August 2016, Plenary Papers* (Belgrade, 2016), 69.
54 Quiroga, "Early Byzantine Urban Landscapes", 70.
55 I. Jacobs, "Encroachment' in the Eastern Mediterranean between the Fourth and the Seventh Century AD", *Ancient Society* 39 (2009), 203–244; Eadem, *Aesthetic Maintenance of Civic Space: The 'Classical' City from the 4th to the 7th c. AD*, Orientalia Lovaniensia Analecta 193 (Leuven: Peeters, 2013).
56 T. Kioussopoulou, *Βασιλεύς ή οικονόμος, Πολιτική εξουσία και ιδεολογία πριν την άλωση* (Athens: Polis, 2007), English translation by Paul Magdalino, as *Emperor or Manager. Power and political ideology in Byzantium before 1453* (Geneva: La pomme d'or, 2011); Kioussopoulou, *Οι βυζαντινές πόλεις*; T. Kioussopoulou, *Οι αόρατες βυζαντινές πόλεις στον ελλαδικό χώρο (13ος-15ος αιώνας)* (Athens: Polis, 2013).
57 S. Kinser, "Annaliste Paradigm? The Geohistorical Structuralism of Fernand Braudel", *The American Historical Review* 86:1 (Feb. 1981), 63–105.
58 Kioussopoulou, *Οι αόρατες βυζαντινές πόλεις*, 19–20; F. Braudel, *Civilisation matérielle, économie et Capitalisme XVe-XVIIIe siècle. Les Structures du Quotidien*, v. I (Paris : Armand Colin, 1979), 423 ff.
59 Kioussopoulou, *Βασιλεύς ή οικονόμος*; Warf & Arias, "Introduction", 3.
60 Kioussopoulou, *Βασιλεύς ή οικονόμος*.
61 Kioussopoulou, *Οι βυζαντινές πόλεις*.
62 Kioussopoulou, *Οι αόρατες βυζαντινές πόλεις*.
63 P. Odorico & C. Messis (eds), *Villes de toute beauté: L'ekphrasis des cités dans les littératures byzantine et byzantino-slaves. Actes du colloque internationale, Prague, 25–26 novembre 2011*, Dossiers Byzantins 12 (Paris: Centre d'études byzantines, néo-helléniques et sud-est européennes, 2012).
64 E. C. Bourbouhakis, "Review of Paolo Odorico and Charis Messis, eds., Villes de toute beauté: L'ekphrasis des cités dans les littératures byzantine et byzantino-slaves. Actes du colloque internationale, Prague, 25–26 novembre 2011 (Dossiers Byzantins 12.) Paris: Centre d'études byzantines, néo-helléniques et sud-est européennes, 2012", *Speculum* 89:2 (2014), 527–529.
65 C. Mango & G. Dagron (eds), *Constantinople and Its Hinterland, Papers from the Twenty-Seventh Spring Symposium of Byzantine Studies, Oxford, April 1993* (Aldershot: Ashgate, 1995); P. Magdalino & N. Ergin (eds), *Istanbul and Water*, Ancient Near Eastern Studies Supplement 47 (Leuven: Peeters, 2015).
66 See note 10 above.
67 L. James, "'Pray Not to Fall into Temptation and Be on Your Guard': Pagan Statues in Christian Constantinople", *Gesta* 35:1 (1996), 12.

68 Cameron & Herrin (eds), *Constantinople,* 1, 10–17; P. Odorico, "Du recueil à l'invention du texte: le cas des Parastaseis Syntomoi Chronikai", *Byzantinische Zeitschrift* 107:2 (2014), 758–759.
69 C. Mango, "Antique Statuary and the Byzantine Beholder", *DOP* XVII (1963), 60.
70 G. Dagron, *Constantinople imaginaire: études sur le recueil des "Patria"* (Paris: Presses Universitaires de France, 1984), 53–60.
71 Cameron & Herrin (eds), *Constantinople*, 1.
72 Cameron & Herrin (eds), *Constantinople*, 1, 11–15, 53.
73 James, "'Pray Not to Fall into Temptation and Be on Your Guard'", 18.
74 A. Kazhdan, *A History of Byzantine Literature (650-850),* NHRF Institute of Byzantine Research Series 3 (Athens: NHRF, 1999), 308–313.
75 Odorico, "Du recueil à l'invention du texte", 780.
76 Odorico, "Du recueil à l'invention du texte", 755–784.
77 Dagron, *Constantinople imaginaire*, 29–48, 53–60; Cameron & Herrin (eds), *Constantinople*, 34–45.
78 Similar literary strategies are also encountered in the genre of Byzantine ekphrasis, as I have argued elsewhere: M. Veikou, "'Telling Spaces' in Byzantium – Ekphraseis, Place-Making and the 'Thick' Description", in C. Messis, M. Mullett & I. Nilsson (eds), *Telling Stories in Byzantium: Narratological Approaches and Byzantine narration* (Uppsala: Studia Byzantina Upsaliensia 19, 2018), 15–32.
79 Dagron, *Constantinople imaginaire*, 31.
80 Dagron, *Constantinople imaginaire*, 31.
81 Indicatively, *Parastaseis Syntomoi Chronikai*, §59, 28. See also Cameron & Herrin (eds), *Constantinople*, 12–14.
82 C. Messis & S. Papaioannou, "Orality and Textuality (with an Appendix on Byzantine Conceptions)", in S. Papaioannou (ed), *The Oxford Handbook of Byzantine Literature* (Oxford: OUP, 2021), 243.
83 Indicatively, *Parastaseis Syntomoi Chronikai*, §43.6, 44.1. See also discussion by Cameron & Herrin (eds), *Constantinople,* 41–44.
84 Cameron & Herrin (eds), *Constantinople,* 13.
85 The remarkable essay "Walking in the city" by Michel de Certeau is a classic text explaining this issue: M. de Certeau, *The Practice of Everyday Life* (Berkeley, CA: University of California Press, 1984), 91–110.
86 Indicatively, *Parastaseis Syntomoi Chronikai*, §4.20, 41.7–41.8, 44a.7; Dagron, *Constantinople imaginaire*, 40–48.
87 *Parastaseis Syntomoi Chronikai*, §28.
88 Indicatively, *Parastaseis Syntomoi Chronikai* §6, 16, 35, 37, 38, 74.
89 *Parastaseis Syntomoi Chronikai*, §22.1–§22.4, translation by Cameron & Herrin (eds), *Constantinople*, 85.
90 See the relevant discussion by P. Chatterjee, "Viewing the Unknown in Eighth-Century Constantinople", *Gesta* 56:2 (2017), 137–149.
91 *Parastaseis Syntomoi Chronikai*, §22.
92 *Parastaseis Syntomoi Chronikai*, §5c.10–§5c.11.
93 *Parastaseis Syntomoi Chronikai*, §20.
94 *Parastaseis Syntomoi Chronikai*, §21.
95 *Parastaseis Syntomoi Chronikai*, §56.12–§56.13.
96 Dagron, *Constantinople imaginaire*, 29–48.
97 Cameron & Herrin (eds), *Constantinople*, 34–45.
98 Odorico, "Du recueil à l'invention du texte", 773–774, 777–783.
99 Ἅτινα καὶ καθορῶνται σῶα ἕως τῆς σήμερον τοῖς τὰ γεγραμμένα παρ'ἡμῶν μετὰ φιλοσοφίας καὶ πόνου διερευνῶσιν.: *Parastaseis Syntomoi Chronikai* §39.9–§39.11 in Cameron & Herrin (eds), *Constantinople*, 106–107.
100 *Parastaseis Syntomoi Chronikai* §68a, 53, 56; see relevant discussion by Cameron & Herrin (eds), *Constantinople*, 36.
101 See also James, "'Pray Not to Fall into Temptation and Be on Your Guard'".
102 *Parastaseis Syntomoi Chronikai* §1, 16, 66, 68. The expression is translated by Cameron and Herrin as 'Note' (*Constantinople*, 16, 57, 79, 147, 149).

103 *Parastaseis Syntomoi Chronikai* §10.1, translated by Cameron and Herrin as "it is said by the majority" (*Constantinople*, 69).
104 See also Cameron & Herrin (eds), *Constantinople*, 53.
105 Indicatively, *Parastaseis Syntomoi Chronikai*, §45.3.
106 D. Lambropoulou, "Πόλη, μνήμη και προφορική ιστορία", in R. van Buschoten, T. Vervenioti, D. Lambropoulou, M. Mouliou & P. Chantzaroula (eds), *Η μνήμη αφηγείται την πόλη – Προφορική ιστορία και μνήμη του αστικού χώρου* (Athens: Plethron, 2016), 21.
107 S. Trower (ed), *Place, Writing and Voice in Oral History* (New York, NY: Palgrave McMillan, 2011); G. Truc, "Memory of Places and Places of Memory: For a Halbwachsian Socio-Ethnography of Collective Memory", *International Social Science Journal* 203–204 (2011), 147–159.
108 Dagron, *Constantinople imaginaire*, 99–125.
109 S. Westwood & J. Williams (eds), *Imagining Cities: Scripts, Signs and Memories* (London – New York, NY: Routledge, 1997). See also P. Magdalino, "Generic Subversion? The Political Ideology of Urban Myth and Apocalyptic Prophecy", in D. Angelov & M. Saxby (eds), *Power and Subversion in Byzantium: Papers from the Forty-Third Spring Symposium of Byzantine Studies, Birmingham, March 2010* (Farnham: Ashgate, 2013), 208.
110 *Parastaseis Syntomoi Chronikai* §25.
111 Cameron & Herrin (eds), *Constantinople*, 31–34; Kazhdan, *A History of Byzantine Literature*, 312; James, "'Pray Not to Fall into Temptation and Be on Your Guard'". See note 114 for later interpretations.
112 James, "'Pray Not to Fall into Temptation and Be on Your Guard'", 12–20.
113 James, "'Pray Not to Fall into Temptation and Be on Your Guard'", 18.
114 R. S. Nelson & M. Olin (eds), *Monuments and Memory, Made and Unmade* (Chicago, IL: University of Chicago Press, 2003), 205–304; P. Chatterjee, "Viewing the Unknown in Eighth-Century Constantinople", *Gesta* 56:2 (2017), 149; H. Saradi, "The Antiquities in Constructing Byzantine Identity: Literary Tradition versus Aesthetic Appreciation", *Hortus Artium Medievalium* 17 (2011): 95–113; B. Anderson, "Classified Knowledge: The Epistemology of Statuary in the Parastaseis Syntomoi Chronikai", *Byzantine and Modern Greek Studies* 35:1 (2011), 1–19.
115 "Ἄς τινας Ἰουστινιανὸς μερίσας τῇ πόλει τὸν ναὸν τὸν μέγιστον ἀνεγείρει μετὰ πίστεως καὶ πόνου. Οἵ δε πεπειραμένοι τῶν προειρημένων περιερχόμενοι τὴν πόλιν καὶ ζητοῦντες εὑρήσουσιν οὐκ ὀλίγας.": *Parastaseis Syntomoi Chronikai* §11.4.7 in Cameron & Herrin (eds), *Constantinople*, 72.
116 Chatterjee, "Viewing the Unknown", 137–149.
117 Chatterjee, "Viewing the Unknown", 139–140.
118 *Patria Constantinoupoleos*, ed. tr. A. Berger, *Accounts of Medieval Constantinople: The Patria*, Dumbarton Oaks Medieval Library 24 (Cambridge, MA: Harvard University Press, 2013)
119 See I. Nilsson, "Narrative, Theory and Practice", in Papaioannou (ed), *The Oxford Handbook of Byzantine Literature*, 279–280.
120 *Patria*, xvii–xviii.
121 Kioussopoulou, *Οι αόρατες βυζαντινές πόλεις*, 153.
122 Lambropoulou, "Πόλη, μνήμη και προφορική ιστορία", 16.
123 Lambropoulou, "Πόλη, μνήμη και προφορική ιστορία", 16.

3

THE BYZANTINE CITY IN THE LITERARY SOURCES

Helen Saradi

Byzantium inherited a rich literary tradition on cities from the Roman Empire. For centuries, cities were praised in orations on various civic events as marvellous, adorned with spectacular buildings and centres of civic, cultural, economic and religious life.[1] Menander of Laodicea, the 3rd-century teacher of rhetoric, set guidelines for such praises (ἐγκώμιον) and descriptions (ἔκφρασις). Short urban descriptions, often laudatory, were also inserted in histories and biographies to clarify and adorn the account.

In the early Byzantine period, the texts offer us glimpses of urban change, but they rarely analyse its causes, either because almost all the authors wrote from the perspective of the imperial capital and expressed the official view held by the state, or because they intentionally concealed real urban change, attached as they were to an antique image of the city.[2] Another reason for avoiding realistic images of cities is that each literary genre demanded that the writer complies with specific rules dictated by tradition. Historiography, the *patria*, rhetoric, hagiography and later epistolography offer a variety of images of cities, imaginary and symbolic or real.

The 6th Century

By the end of the early Byzantine period, the ancient city underwent profound change in terms of planning, public buildings, civic administration and culture, economic stagnation being evident in the last quarter of the century. Cities, previously responsible for local administration and collecting taxes, had lost revenues to the state and to the provincial administration, the urban landscape had been Christianised, and public space had to a great degree been demonumentalised. Local aristocrats (δυνατοί, πρῶτοι, πρωτεύοντες), together with the bishop, were now responsible for city administration. This administrative system was loose, functioned *ad hoc* and was not institutionalised, in contrast to previous administration by the *boule*.[3]

The sources of the 6th century notice the degradation of urban space, sometimes seen as the consequence of imperial policy. However, most sources retain a rhetorical vocabulary emphasizing urban beauty,[4] seen as a sign of a city's prominence. Sources also preserve an

 DOI: 10.4324/9780429203923-5

antique urban image through reference to local traditions, a trend explained by the attachment to classical models of literature by pagans and Christians.

The first eloquent images of urbanism at the turn of the 6th century are found in the *New History* of the pagan historian Zosimos. Here, while the Western Roman Empire is presented with cities devastated by invaders, depopulated and occupied by barbarians, the Empire of the East possesses numerous and prosperous cities.

Zosimos' accounts of Athens and Constantinople have a symbolic aura inspired by the local tradition. Athens, representing pagan culture, had been twice protected by the goddess Athena and Achilles, during an earthquake (375) and during the attack of the Visigoths (397).[5] The new capital Constantinople was also worthy of divine protection. When the Senate House was burnt in a riot (403), many ancient statues were destroyed in the flames, except for those of Zeus and Athena Lindia, which was interpreted by pagans as the gods' willingness to protect the city.[6]

Zosimos reserved a topographical description only for Constantinople. He refers to Constantine's plan to build his new capital on the site of Troy and then to Byzantium. He describes its superb location and the circuit of the Severan walls. He refers to the temple of Aphrodite and the port of Neorion, the circular forum, the new Constantinian wall,[7] a palace, the adornment of the Severan hippodrome with a temple of the Dioscuri and the Delphic tripod with the statue of Apollo. In the forum of Septimius Severus, renamed by Constantine the 'Augusteon' in honour of his mother, Augusta Helen, Constantine built two temples with statues, one dedicated to Rhea, the Mother of the Gods. Zosimos emphasises Constantinople's Greek roots by stating that the statue of Rhea was set up by the Argonauts at Kyzikos, so distinguishing it from Roman Rhea. He also refers to the transformation of the statue by Constantine into an orant figure, by removing the two lions on both sides of the statue and changing the position of the hands, and so that the statue now protected Constantinople.[8] This account corresponds to the *Patria* of Hesychios of Miletos, according to which Byzas built a temple of Rhea at Byzantium and her statue became the *Tyche* of Constantinople.[9] Thus, Greek and Christian elements merged to form Constantinople's civic identity.

Zosimos draws a picture of Constantinople worthy of a Roman imperial capital. He refers to houses for Roman senators built by Constantine, the city's growing size and the new, larger circuit walls, completed in 439 and 447. He emphasises the busy, jostling life of the capital, and also mentions houses built on poles in the sea that resembled yet another city.

Prophecies predicting the cities' future prosperity, or decline, were part of the civic tradition. With difficulty, Zosimos found a prophecy on ancient Byzantion that foretold its rise to a Roman capital.[10] Thus, he granted Constantinople a civic tradition necessary for the new capital.

From the late 5th century onwards, after the collapse of the Western Roman Empire, historiographers focused on Constantinople's history and local tradition.[11] From the sixth book of the lost *Roman and General History* of the pagan historian Hesychios (written *ca.* 520) is preserved the longest extract on the history of Constantinople, from the city's early years, woven from stories about buildings and statues. This account belongs to the literary genre of the *Patria* of cities, which combines tales of the cities' origin with historical events and prophecies and invests urban monuments with a civic symbolism. Hesychios' account is preserved in a revised form in the 10th-century *Patria* of Constantinople.[12] Zosimos and Hesychios depict Constantinople with a pagan past, which was then Christianised, adorned with imperial buildings and statues and endowed with old civic tradition and Christian symbolism.

The Christian *Chronicle of John Malalas* also follows the tradition of the *Patria* and focuses on cities' foundation myths and tales on urban monuments. To trace a city's origin to a mythical past enhanced its prestige. The greater part of Malalas' Chronicle focuses on Antioch and only in the later part does he turn to Constantinople. The Hellenistic period is presented as a period of great urbanization: new cities were built and small settlements were raised to the status of cities. City foundation included a ritual of purification through sacrifice and the creation of a *Tyche*, after which buildings were constructed and the line of the walls traced out. This antiquarian trend corresponds to the preservation of ornamental facades of buildings that were either inwardly decaying or were assigned to some new use, and of pagan statues preserved in baths, fountains and streets.[13]

Buildings and statues set up by city founders, kings, emperors and local persons, a central theme of Malalas' *Chronicle*, was for centuries a theme in historiography. These were symbols of civic life and many statues were considered civic talismans intended to avert calamities. The Empire of the East emerges fully urbanised, with the memory of urban traditions still alive. Cities appear flourishing and their monuments were eloquent images of civic prosperity. As imperial evergetism was the driving force behind urban development, in the *Chronicle* urban change can be seen in the priorities of Justinian (527–565) in his construction projects. These priorities involved churches and structures with a practical function, such as cisterns, baths or granaries, while interest in civic buildings for public entertainment and buildings adorning the cities clearly diminished. Temples and churches are attested more than other buildings. About 22 temples and 15 churches are mentioned in Antioch and its suburb, Daphne, and over 20 churches in Constantinople. Of the buildings for civic administration references to basilicas are the most numerous. Baths and their decoration are mentioned in various cities – 19 in Antioch – and gates of walls.[14]

In Malalas' *Chronicle*, old urban tradition was fused with the new culture. After Justinian, however, when the Empire was fully Christianised, the mythical origins of cities were replaced with stories from the Christian tradition.[15]

In the early 6th century, orations praising urban benefactors and the cities which received their benefactions continued to be produced.[16] Prokopios of Gaza wrote a panegyric of Anastasios (491–518), Chorikios of Gaza two *enkomia* for Bishop Marcian and for the *dux* Aratios and *archon* Stephanos, and around the middle of the century, Prokopios of Caesarea produced the *Buildings* for Emperor Justinian. While emperors, provincial governors and bishops are eloquently praised in inflated, rhetorical terms for the buildings they had constructed, churches and walls being priorities, the treatise of Julian of Ascalon *On the Laws or Customs of Palestine*, dated to 531–533, regulated building initiatives. Here we have a pragmatic view of cities: the customs and regulations of the Middle East defined the appropriate distance between industrial and residential structures, regulated the construction of gutters and sewers and the planting of trees and vineyards. The aim of these regulations was to prevent annoyance caused by building activities by neighbours, to preserve urban beauty and the right to enjoy the view and light. Some regulations deal with the obligation on the part of owners of apartments in condominium-type of buildings.[17] Stipulations ensuring that new buildings would not deprive residents of the view of mountains and the sea and regulations concerning balconies were influenced by laws of Emperor Zeno (474–475, 476–491) for Constantinople. In 531, Justinian reiterated Zeno's law, this time for all cities.[18] The value of the work of Julian of Ascalon was recognised in Byzantium: it was attached to the *Book of the Eparch* in the 10th century and included in the second book of the *Hexabiblos* of the jurist Harmenopoulos (1345) in Thessaloniki.

Prokopios of Caesarea produced variant descriptions of cities in each of the literary genres in which he wrote: historiography, praise and invective. In his *History of the Wars*, he employs the traditional themes of historiography: distinguished cities are those which were large and populous (μεγάλη τε καὶ πολυάνθρωπος), ranked first in the provinces or in large territories (πρώτη), were ancient (ἀρχαία) and adorned with beautiful buildings. Buildings in Italian cities, such as the Mausoleum of Hadrian at Rome, at the time incorporated in the walls, are praised as symbols of urban life and civic culture. Great cities are distinguished for the strength of their fortifications and for their possession of a theatre and hippodrome.[19]

The *Buildings* is a panegyric to the Emperor Justinian through his construction of buildings in cities and fortifications all over the Empire.[20] Cities and their buildings are praised as beautiful, a theme widely used by orators in the Roman Empire.[21] This cherished urban image is, however, dented, when Prokopios repeatedly refers to buildings in decay on account of the passage of time or neglect. By the 6th century, the city had been transformed and Prokopios was aware of it. He was, however, not interested in analysing its causes and pace in the years before. He does not elaborate on the change in urban monuments or comment on the emergence of the medieval city. He merely mentions the unwillingness or inability of the populace to maintain and restore decaying buildings, while his references to the passage of time are perhaps a nostalgic allusion to the antiquity of urban structures. The author's purpose was restricted to praising the emperor's reconstruction programme, and so Prokopios is confident that the Empire will overcome such urban decline. It is clear that the demands of the literary genre of praise and the official state view of the Empire guided Prokopios in his description of urban renewal.[22]

Prokopios' *Buildings* reveals the priorities of the Justinianic restoration programme and the concept of the city in the 6th century. Fortifications and churches are now the two essential elements of a city. Notably the beginning and the end of Prokopios' work are embedded in religious symbolism. The book begins with the reconstruction and description of Hagia Sophia and other churches of Constantinople and ends with a reference to the Church of the Mother of God in the fortress of Septum on the straits of Gibraltar. Justinian rebuilt this fort, strengthening it with a garrison and endowing it with a church dedicated to the Mother of God, thus bestowing upon her the threshold of the Empire and so making the fort impregnable for the benefit of the whole world.[23]

Prokopios' description of Hagia Sophia is lengthy and with a variety of figures of speech that derive from rhetoric and express a religious spirit.[24] The *ekphrasis* of Hagia Sophia introduces the reader to the capital of the Empire and is intimately connected with the city, thus becoming its symbol. The church, with its imposing height, dominates Constantinople, adorns it and glorifies it. Indeed the entire city can be seen from the church.[25] Later Byzantine church descriptions often maintain this connection between a prominent church and its city.[26]

The two essential elements employed by Prokopios in the praise of churches are their size and their beauty, both defined in rhetoric.[27] Hagia Sophia is praised for its innovative architectural design, the variety of architectural shapes and colours, and for its decoration, including its display of gold adornment. The church's beauty, harmony and magnificence, the splendour of its materials and the abundance of light produce a supreme aesthetic impression and spiritual elevation on Christians.

Prokopios continues with the praise of imperial power. The column in the Augustaeum supporting a statue of a horseman who holds in his left hand the globe surmounted by a cross and who stretches his right hand towards the East symbolised the universal rule of the emperor through the Cross and his power over the Persians.[28] Thus, church and emperor embodied the ecclesiastical and secular power in Constantinople.

Prokopios goes on to describe many churches in Constantinople and its suburbs.[29] In a topographical itinerary through the churches, similar to a *periegesis* of a city, churches are praised for their originality of plan, each church being singled out for some particular feature. For example, while the Church of Blachernai was unusually long, its width was proportionate to length and possessed columns of Parian marble that formed *exedrai* in the centre of the church.[30] Of the Church of the Virgin of Pege, Prokopios describes only the source and its idyllic surrounding.[31] A long description of the beauty of the sea[32] forms an introduction to an *ekphrasis* of the churches on the Golden Horn and on the Sea of Marmara. The sea beautifies Constantinople and provides sailors with shelter, thanks to its many harbours, and the city with riches. The motif of the beauty of Constantinople, due to its maritime location, was established by the court orator Himerios (4th century).[33] Prokopios' linking of his church descriptions with scenes of the sea derives from similar established scenery in *ekphraseis* of pagan temples[34] and from images in ancient philosophy of the sea that refer to the transcendence of the soul.[35] Although Prokopios employs antique literary imagery to describe Constantinople, the essence of his description is entirely Christian. In the *Buildings*, images of churches introduce Constantinople, which is idealised as a sacred city consecrated with churches.

Prokopios continues with brief descriptions of buildings burnt down during the Nika revolt and erected by Justinian in the area stretching from the Palace to the Forum of Constantine. The Senate House at the Augustaeum stood in splendour with its porch of marble columns and vaulted ceiling and adorned with marbles and statues on its roof. Of Palace buildings, Prokopios describes the Chalke Gate, magnificently designed and adorned with mosaics depicting the imperial couple and scenes of victories.[36] The Arkadiane, a court added by Justinian to a public bath outside Constantinople, was a place for promenades by the sea. It possessed columns, shining marble and many statues, including one of Theodora atop of a column.[37] Then follows the description of a cistern designed to secure the city's water supply in summer, of the new palaces of Hieron and Joukoundiane, of two new harbours and of a large hospice.[38]

In strengthening the Empire's defences, Justinian restored city walls, reduced the size of some to make their defence easier, relocated some cities to naturally fortified sites, built forts in passages in areas of strategic importance, and walls to defend large territories, as, for example, at the Isthmus.[39] The relocation of cities to naturally fortified sites brought about new trends in Byzantine urbanism, especially in the Balkans. One example is Diokletianoupolis, in Northern Greece, situated by Lake Kastoria. The city, destroyed by the passage of time and barbarians and long deserted, was moved to the island in the middle of the lake.[40]

Imperial restoration priorities varied depending on the size and importance of each city and of the needs of its urban population. Antioch, one of the great cities of the Empire and celebrated in various texts for its beauty, its pleasure-loving citizens and its classical tradition in letters and the arts, was sacked by the Persians in 540 and subsequently restored by Justinian. Prokopios begins his account with a religious reference. Antioch was called Theoupolis ('City of God'), a Christian name that the city acquired after an earthquake in 528.[41] Prokopios states that Justinian's restoration was intended to make Antioch immensely more beautiful and stronger than it had previously been.[42] While urban beauty has first place in this statement, Prokopios actually begins with a detailed account of the walls, so indicating Justinian's real priorities. The long city wall, which with its twists and turns surrounded uninhabited or sparsely inhabited areas, was reduced, so as to protect only part of the city. This was a measure taken in many cities during the early Byzantine period. The River Orontes, which in the past flowed through the city, was diverted to a new artificial bed near the wall and received new bridges. A formerly precipitous area was levelled off and passages were made for pedestrians, cavalry and wagons. Baths and reservoirs were built there and cisterns in each tower of the wall. To protect the city from flooding, a dam was built in a ravine with sluice-gates that diminished the flow of the water.

The urban area was cleared of the debris of burnt buildings and restored, acquiring stoas, markets, streets dividing up blocks of buildings, water-channels, fountains and sewers, theatres, baths and all the other public buildings that established the prosperity of a city. The emperor also brought artisans and craftsmen to assist the inhabitants in rebuilding their own houses. Thus Antioch became more magnificent (ἐπιφανεστέραν) than it was formerly. Prokopios closes his account in the same religious tone in which he began. He mentions the construction of the Church of the Mother of God, of indescribable beauty and magnificence and of the immense Church of the Archangel Michael with a hospital for the poor and accommodation for strangers.[43]

Engineering work involved in the reconstruction of the walls occupies the longest section of Prokopios' account, the walls being an obvious imperial priority after the sack of the city. Emphasis is also placed on water-based amenities. But there is a mere reference to civic buildings, including baths and theatres which cater to the extravagant, cosmopolitan lifestyle of Antioch's citizens. Antioch, in her restored form, included features appropriate to large cities: strong fortifications, a dam, some public amenities and two churches with charitable institutions.

In the *Buildings*, the new type of city, the city-*kastron*, is also described. This was appropriate in less urbanised areas threatened by barbaric invasions near the frontier zone. Such is the case with Justiniana Prima (Πρώτη Ἰουστινιανή, now Caričin Grad in Serbia), built by Justinian near his birthplace, the village of Taurisium in the province of Dardania. The new city was a notable one (ἐπιφανεστάτη). Justinian's bond with his native city, a theme recurring in city rhetoric, is expressed with his munificence.[44] Prokopios describes Justiniana Prima very briefly mentioning only its basic features. He notes the aqueduct, its many churches, the residences of magistrates, stoas, market-places, fountains, streets, baths and shops and mentions that the city became the seat of the Archbishop of Illyricum.[45] The chief advantage inherent in the location of the city, which is situated on a naturally defended site on a steep hill surrounded on both sides by small rivers, is not mentioned. Prokopios conceals the city's military character, perhaps because it did not adhere to the ideals of Roman urbanism.

Excavations revealed that the city was divided in three sections with three lines of walls possessing 40 towers. On the acropolis were located the episcopal church and the bishop's palace. In the upper city, there was a circular plaza displaying the emperor's statue and surrounded by colonnades with shops, and three churches. In the lower city, there were churches situated along the main street and military compounds. Urban areas lay outside the walls. The aqueduct was 21 km long and a total of 15 churches have been identified.[46] The area around the city was also secured with several forts. This 6th-century structure of a city divided into two or three fortified parts was to become the dominant form of the Byzantine city, the city-*kastron*.

In the *Anecdota*, written as an invective (the rhetorical genre of *psogos*) against Justinian and Theodora, Prokopios refers to the urban crisis caused by Justinian's fiscal measures.

Attorneys were deprived of their rank and, by introducing litigation directly under oath, this class declined. Senators were targeted by Justinian who plundered their properties, and, thus, their decline had obvious consequences for the cities. Doctors and teachers were deprived of public salaries and civic funds were transferred to the fisc. Cities were therefore unable to maintain public buildings or to maintain public lighting, and theatres, hippodromes and circuses were closed. These measures ended the pleasures of life in cities and saddened citizens.[47] The civic funds of all the cities of Greece were appropriated, so as to finance the soldiers who guarded Thermopylae. Consequently, maintenance of public buildings ceased in Greece and even in Athens.[48] Prokopios states that people considered this a new kind of calamity. He does not mention, however, that the process of transfers of civic funds to provincial governors and the imperial treasury had started in the 4th century. Prokopios actually describes the end of a long process of deprivation of the cities of their civic funds.

The military treatise *On Strategy* (*Περὶ Στρατηγίας*) dating to the late 6th century, so-called *Strategikon of Maurice*, explains the priorities of the time involved in building a city to face barbarian invasions. In chapter 10, *On Building a City* (*Περὶ οἰκοδομῆς πόλεως*), the author recommends that, when founding a city, one should consider the location, ensure that the wall would be impregnable and bear in mind water supply, availability of construction materials and production of food in the countryside. In chapter 11, on *The Site for Building a City* (*Ποῦ δεῖ κτίζειν πόλιν*), we are told that new cities, especially if they were close to the border, should be built on steep hills, surrounded by rivers, on maritime promontories or in large rivers connected to the mainland by a narrow strip of land. Such locations were difficult for the enemy to approach. The author states that many, confident that prosperity would remain forever, when they planned large cities, focused on civic adornment, such as gardens and parks, instead of on security. But because of the uncertainty of the times, the author prefers security to a pleasant appearance (τὴν ἀσφάλειαν μᾶλλον τῆς εὐπρεπείας προκρίνοντες), particularly of cities located near the border and so more exposed to the barbarian threat. Large cities could be built on plains, only if they were away from the frontier zone and anyway should be protected by strong walls.[49]

This text reveals the changes in urban planning caused by invasions. In the 6th century, cities in the Balkans were threatened by the Slavs, and in the 7th century, cities in the East were subject to Arab raids. Although in many large cities urban life continued uninterrupted, changes not mentioned in the texts are to be observed in excavations. Buildings were left to decay, public space was encroached upon by industrial and agricultural installations, while population and economic activities declined. Inside the walls, urban space, with its narrow winding streets and agricultural installations, was densely populated. Smaller cities were relocated to fortified sites.[50]

The military form of the new Byzantine city is attested in the use of the term *kastron* as equivalent to the term *polis* in two 6th-century texts, the Justinianic Novel 128 (*a.* 545) (ἐν ταῖς πόλεσιν ἤτοι κάστροις) and John Lydos' *De magistratibus* (…Ῥώμην νέαν δείκνυται καλῶν, κάστρα δὲ καὶ αὐτὴν ἴσα ταῖς ἄλλαις τῶν χωρῶν).[51] This suggests that this new urban form and its accompanying terminology were promoted by 6th-century state policy.[52]

The Middle Byzantine Period

From the 7th century onwards, the terms *kastron* and *polisma* are widely used in texts and indicate radical urban change.[53] Only Constantinople and Thessaloniki continued to be designated 'cities'. In the 10th century when cities begin to recover, the term *asty* reappears and designates provincial cities, while Constantinople is indicated by the terms *basileuousa* and *asty*.

Besides its military role, the medieval city is viewed in the texts from the perspective of the Church and of the emperor. For example, in the *Miracles of St Demetrios* during the Avaro-Slavic attacks from 586 onwards, the Christian concept of Thessaloniki is revealed. While the urban topography of Thessaloniki is mentioned only in passing, the church of St Demetrios and its bishop dominate urban life. The Church's wealth and the silver of the *ciborium* and of the bishop's throne are noted. Thessaloniki was defended by its patron saint: in the attack of 615 St Demetrios appeared in a white garb walking on the wall. The bishop acted as the city's patron, so competing with the members of the upper class and acting as intercessor to the saint. While in 618 the urban elite maintained untrustworthy contact with the Slavs, Bishop John run along the walls manned by citizens, encouraging them to fight. The Byzantine city is now defended by its patron saint and its bishop.[54] In 805, St Andrew on horseback protected Patras from the attacking Slavs.[55]

In the *Parastaseis Syntomoi Chronikai* (*Brief Historical Notes*) (late 8th to early 9th century), Constantinople is described through the legendary stories of its monuments and statues that had the mystical power to predict the future. The text, clearly deriving from the genre of *Patria*, foregrounds emperors with whom buildings and statues are connected. In the late 10th century, when the Byzantine Empire reached its apogee, a medieval version of the *Patria of Constantinople* was composed joining the 6th-century *Patria* of Hesychios with the *Parastaseis*, a narrative (*Diegesis*) on the construction of Hagia Sophia and other accounts of Constantinople's monuments. The landscape of Constantinople, the only city deserving at that time a *Patria*, is experienced through its monuments and churches woven into historical and fictional stories and related to emperors.

In imperial biography and historiography, the landscape of Constantinople was the stage for imperial triumphs. For example, the account of the triumphal entry of Basil I (867–886) in 879 mentions sites and churches of the city.[56] Constantinople is also seen in acts of imperial euergetism. Basil I built or restored numerous churches. His *Life*, allegedly written by his grandson Constantine Porhyrogenitos (r. 945–959), mentions a total of 100 churches and enumerates 31 as restored or newly built. The most renowned of these churches was the Nea Ekklesia (*ca.* 880) in the palace, whose sumptuous decoration is described in a laudatory *ekphrasis*. Basil also built new domestic sections of the Great Palace, the *Kainourgion* and the *Pentakoubouklion*, magnificently decorated with marbles and mosaics depicting the emperor and his family, and his victories and his generals offering him captured cities. He also built houses for the poor and for strangers, hospitals, houses for the elderly and monasteries.[57]

Constantinople's economic activities are the subject of the *Book of the Prefect* (912), which contains regulations for guilds under state supervision. The guild of notaries is mentioned first, followed by 18 guilds of merchants. Regulations refer to the election of members to the guilds, entrance fees, to prevention of illegal competition and to securing of supplies at low prices for the capital's residents. The guilds were located in various porticoes and vaulted markets, most of them concentrated in specific areas.[58]

Byzantine cities began to grow again in the 10th century and in the 11th century, when a middle class is visible in the sources. In the first half of the 12th century, the *Timarion*, a Lucianic dialogue, describes the fair that was taking place in Thessaloniki on the occasion of the feast day of St Demetrios.[59] The description of the festival derives from Heliodoros' *Aithiopika*.[60] It lasted eight days, during which merchants from various parts of the world set up their booths outside the city walls in parallel lines, to sell a wide variety of merchandise. Pilgrims from all over the world came in order to worship the saint. This interest in the fair at Thessaloniki reveals urban economic development.

The urban growth is also reflected in the change in terminology. The classicizing historian Niketas Choniates (1155/1157–1217) in his *Chronike Diegesis* uses the term *polis* for large settlements, instead of *kastron*. For smaller settlements, he employs derivatives of *polis* (*polisma, polismation, polichne* etc.) and *chora, kome, phrourion, eryma, ochyrōma* and *kastron*.[61] A little later, Theodore Skoutariotes (*ca*. 1230–1282) in his *addenda* to the *Chronike Syngraphe* of George Akropolites (1217–1282) writes that small and insignificant settlements were called *phrouria*, rather than cities.[62] He also refers to the multiple lines of walls which defended settlements: tower after tower and successive circular walls. However, the term *kastron* was maintained in demotic literature, to designate urban settlements.[63] The use of the term *polis* by these authors expresses both urban development and the urban ideal promoted by classicizing intellectuals connected with the court.

From the 11th/12th century onwards, Byzantine intellectuals show increasing interest in urban antiquities. The sack of Constantinople by the Latins in 1204 gave the impetus for a lament by Niketas Choniates of the city through its ancient statues with political and cultural symbolism.[64] Statues that had adorned public places for centuries were either melted down for their metal by the Latins or smashed to pieces. Choniates admires the statues as objects of art for their aesthetic value and for stirring powerful emotions to the viewers. In Choniates' passionate description, they symbolise the culture of Constantinople, because they depicted figures from Greek literature and Roman national symbols: the statues of Hera in the Forum of Constantine, of Aphrodite offering Paris the gold apple, which alludes to the Trojan War and to the connection of Constantinople with Troy through Rome, the statue of Herakles by Lysippos in the Hippodrome, the statues of the donkey and its keeper from Nikopolis that commemorated the victory of Augustus at Actium, and the statues of the hyena and the she-wolf which nourished Romulus and Remus, revered monuments of the nation, and the statue of Helen praised in literature for its extravagant beauty. This was a turning point in descriptions of Constantinople. Humanism had opened up new horizons to Byzantine intellectuals and a new view of the Byzantine city was expressed through its classical statuary, now elevated to cultural and national symbols.

The Late Byzantine Period

In the last centuries of Byzantium, references to cities and factual descriptions multiply.[65] This is obviously a sign of urban development triggered by increased trade and the rise of independent despots in cities.[66] After the fall of Constantinople in 1204 and the formation of Latin and Byzantine states on formerly Byzantine territory, cities, threatened by constant war among these states, strengthened their fortifications. The cities that became capitals expanded in population and increased their building activities. The *kastron* of Ioannina in Epiros is a good example. The settlement was perhaps established during the Slavic invasions on a peninsula of Lake Pamvotis with two rocky hills. According to an imperial chrysobull of 1319, the metropolitan Church of the Archangel Michael owned the site (τὸν χῶρον) before the town (πόλισμα) was established and called the Archangel founder of the city (πολιστὴς) and protector (πολιοῦχος), implying that the Church played a decisive role in the establishment of the settlement.[67] In 1082, the Norman Boemund occupied Ioannina and constructed a second acropolis on the southeast hill. After 1204, Michael Doukas, founder of the Despotate of Epiros (1205–1215), settled refugees escaping the Latins in Ioannina and rebuilt the *polidion* in the form of a *kastron*. Civil and ecclesiastical powers were clearly separated: the palace stood on the larger southeast acropolis (κουλᾶς) that included a bath dating to the first half of the 13th century, while the metropolitan church was on the smaller northeast acropolis.[68]

In this new organization of urban space, the acropolis takes the form of a fortified palace-tower, as, for example, in Trebizond, described by Bessarion (1403–1472).[69] The residential area was called the χώρα,[70] in which the central street (μέση), perhaps forming a plaza (πλάτζα), led from the wall to the acropolis.[71] Some cities possessed more than one wall circuit. Servia, built on a steep hill controlling passes from Macedonia to Thessaly between 560 and 630 during the period of Slavic invasions, had three lines of walls, which delineated the acropolis, the upper city and the lower city and so created the impression of three superimposed cities.[72]

Glimpses of a small town are offered in the letters of Ioannes Apokaukos, Metropolitan of Nafpaktos (1199/1200–1232).[73] The fortress (*phrourion*) Nafpaktos, built on a hill rising steeply above the sea, was almost impregnable. Houses were poor, roofed with hay. However, there were some aspects that distinguished Nafpaktos from other towns. The streets, usually muddy elsewhere, here were clean, because they were paved, while fountains provided fresh water, in contrast to the wells found in other cities. The Church of the Theotokos was adorned by the metropolitan with gold and icons. In the town, the bishop's palace was to be distinguished from the humble houses of the residents. It was built entirely in white marble, with marble steps and small columns, so that it resembled a small palace, standing on an elevated site overlooking the sea. A bath constructed in marble stood on a similar site. It was decorated with paintings and flooded with light that entered through the glass windows. The location of the metropolitan's palace symbolised his authority in the town and the conflict between him and Constantine Doukas, brother of the despot of Epiros, points to the symbolism of power in the urban topography. Doukas appropriated the site of the bishop's palace and built a Persian-style house (σουφᾶς). The building was long and stood on a raised platform, while Doukas' throne resembled that of the metropolitan and provoked the ire of the latter.

Documentary sources reveal the introverted layout of urban neighbourhoods. Around a court (αὐλή) with a well, stood houses with porticoes, workshops, a church or monastery, warehouses and an oven. The entrances (εἰσοδοέξοδοι) to the complex resembled to gates.[74]

During this period, political fragmentation, the economic rise of the middle class and the influence of Italian cities created favourable conditions for the development of an independent urban administrative system. Now an antique political vocabulary was employed to designate urban leaders. The 'lords of the senate' (ἄρχοντες τῆς συγκλήτου) and the 'lords of the city' (ἄρχοντες τῆς πολιτείας) probably consisted of members of the upper and of the middle class in the urban councils.[75] These councils appear to convene *ad hoc*, depending on the occasion, and different from one city to another. During this period, privileges, primarily tax exemptions, were also granted by emperors to cities which were placed again under imperial control (Ioannina, Monemvasia, Veroia, Kroia and Rentina). Thus, emperors strengthened their authority.[76]

As interest in cities revived, laudatory descriptions are inserted in various texts, especially orations with a political or a hagiographical content.[77] They follow the models established in rhetorical theory and are written in a highly eloquent style. These city praises are marked by an intense idealization and spirituality, which expressed the authors' humanistic ideas. Such texts may also be seen as a refuge for intellectuals reacting to the collapse of the Byzantine Empire. For example, Nikephoros Choumnos (*ca.* 1250/1255–1327) in his *Συμβουλευτικὸς περὶ δικαιοσύνης* addressed to the inhabitants of Thessaloniki includes a laudatory description of the city. It praises the city's surroundings and the city itself, mentions houses of several storeys and the antiquity and riches of the city itself. It lauds the citizens of the middle and upper classes for their intellectual qualities, piety and the philanthropic disposition towards foreigners. It also exalts the spiritual elevation generated by hymns in churches and monasteries and compares them to hymns of angels and the city to the sky. Finally, the city is praised for the protection it receives from St Demetrios and the miracles performed by his myrrh.[78]

Local courts offered the literati opportunities to deliver orations in praise of their city at festive celebrations. These orations display an endless variety of rhetorical *topoi* with the emphasis on idyllic descriptions of the surrounding natural environment,[79] the supreme moral and learned achievements of the residents, their piety, the city's historic role, all of these formulated in lofty ideas. References to buildings are very brief in such texts, while fortifications and churches continue to be the focal points. Walls are praised for their beauty[80] and strength, churches for their beauty and sublimity.

Seven orations on cities are known from the period after 1204. They praise Nicaea, Constantinople, Trebizond and Corinth, each speech focusing on various aspects of these cities and conveying a different historical message. The *Praise of Nicaea* (*Ἐγκώμιον εἰς τὴν μεγαλόπολιν Νίκαιαν*), capital of the Empire of Nicaea, written in the early 1250s by Theodore II Doukas Laskaris (r. 1254–1258), stands out for its display of the urban ideal. Nicaea is praised in high literary style as the new imperial capital which saved the Empire and the Patriarchate after the fall of Constantinople in 1204. This was achieved through the strength of its walls and the might of its emperor. Now, for the first time, antique monuments are briefly mentioned as important parts of the city: the magnificent material of the walls (τῆς περιφανεστάτης ὕλης), alluding to the antique gates and parts of the walls still standing, and the ancient raised aqueduct, which has provided water up to the time of the author.[81] Images of the beauty of nature complement the sketchy description of the urban topography, walls and churches being the main landmarks. The greatest adornment of the city was its learned inhabitants, who combined the knowledge of ancient letters and science with Christian faith. References to churches and monasteries lead to allegorical images of the divine and of Nicaea as a city of God.[82]

Byzantios or on the imperial great city (*Βυζάντιος ἢ περὶ τῆς βασιλίδος μεγαλοπόλεως*) by Theodore Metochites (1270–1332), written between 1305 and 1311/1312, is a rhetorical masterpiece. It praises Constantinople as the ecumenical Christian capital of the Empire, built on the straits of the Bosporos, a location of supreme beauty and economic importance, and blessed to be eternally renewed.[83] Similar ideas are used to praise Constantinople in a short *enkomion*, whose final section is mutilated, by George Karbones and written probably before 1333.[84]

The city of Trebizond, capital of the Empire of Trebizond, at the north-east end of Anatolia, is praised in a lengthy oration by Bessarion, written around 1436.[85] Bessarion praises the dynasty of the Grand Komnenoi for preserving the freedom of the Empire of Trebizond. Trebizond's Greek roots are developed in a lengthy historical account that connects the city with Athens and attributes to the Trebizondians bravery and philanthropy, qualities of the ancient Athenians.[86] The topographical sketch of the city is factual and lacks rhetorical amplification. Three lines of walls protected the lower city, the upper city and the citadel with the palace. Deep gorges and rivers, spanned by wooden bridges, also secured the city's safety. The commercial area was located outside the walls where merchants from afar sold their merchandise. Bessarion offers the best description we have of a late Byzantine palace. The palace of Trebizond located on the acropolis was so fortified that it itself resembled an acropolis. Bessarion describes the two imperial halls, the one adorned with gold depicting the sky, and on the walls portraits of the Grand Komnenoi and their ancestors, their victories and defeated enemies, and the imperial thrones, a library and a chapel.[87]

In the final century of the Byzantine Empire, the affinities of the Byzantines with the ancient Greeks in terms of letters, culture and ethnic identity are stressed as part of Byzantine national consciousness. Thus, interest in ancient monuments is openly expressed. In the *ekphrasis* of the *kome* Petrina in Lakedaimonia John Eugenikos (*post* 1394 to *post* 1454/1455) describes the idyllic natural environment and the ancient remains nearby.[88] Antiquities in Byzantine cities are mentioned especially in epistles, the literary genre in which personal feelings are expressed. While Theodore Laskaris in his *Praise of Nicaea* only implied to the city's antiquities, in a letter he refers to the ancient ruins of Pergamon with admiration. He takes pride in their splendour and the wisdom of the ancients that they displayed, comparing them favourably to poor contemporary houses.[89] In 1397, Manuel II Palaiologos (1391–1425) mentions in a letter the ancient remains of Pompeiopolis in Pontic Paphlagonia, hardly visible, and admired the size, beauty and art of the stone bridge over the river Amnias.[90]

In 1411, Manuel Chrysoloras (*ca.* 1350–1415), a great humanist and diplomat, composed a *synkrisis* of Rome with Constantinople in the form of a letter addressed from Rome to Emperor John VIII Palaiologos (co-emperor: *ante* 1408, sole emperor: 1425–1448).[91] The antiquities of both cities were damaged by time and had been re-used in other structures. Greek inscriptions proved the affinities of the ancient Romans with the Greeks, an argument of value to John Palaiologos in his efforts to reconcile the Italians with the Byzantines in the face of the advancing Turks. As he surveyed Rome's antiquities, Chrysoloras could visualise scenes of ancient Roman life and admired their beauty and naturalism. Reference to churches, however, is brief. Constantinople is described as the imperial capital. Chrysoloras mentions its excellent location, its harbour, its double wall with its numerous towers, gates and ditches, its many beautiful buildings constructed, with ample use of marble, over the course of centuries, covered and sheltered streets, imperial columns, palaces, theatres, facilities for military exercises, the hippodrome, shipyards, bays, the docks, and towers standing in the middle of the sea, the water supply system with its aqueduct and the underground cisterns, baths and fountains and beautiful suburbs with churches and other buildings. Chrysoloras' more elevated praise is reserved for the wall, its length and strength that offer the city security. A city looks like a city and is called a city primarily on account of its walls and such cities survive for all time (οἰομένη πόλιν τὲ πρώτως ἀπὸ τῶν τειχῶν φαίνεσθαι καὶ καλεῖσθαι καὶ πρὸς τὸν ἅπαντα δὲ χρόνον, οὐ πρὸς τὴν παροῦσαν μόνον ἡλικίαν ταύτας γίνεσθαι).[92] Then follow references to splendid imperial tombs in the Church of the Holy Apostles and in other churches, to the column of Justinian and others to the East. Many statues once existed as is evident from their bases and the inscriptions they display, most of them being in the hippodrome. Chrysoloras himself had seen many others, but these were subsequently removed. He recalls two on which it was believed that silver statues of Theodosios I and Theodosios II once stood. There is also the porphyry column with the cross, statues of seated individuals at crossroads, a statue situated above the source of the river that runs through the city and many more that he had heard of that existed hidden in secret locations. Two of the 12 sculptures on the Golden Gate are mentioned, one depicting Herakles' labours and the other the torture of Prometheus, which clearly symbolise the Empire's distress. Chrysoloras also mentions the splendour of various paintings and mosaics and concludes his description with praise of the Church of Hagia Sophia, as exceeding all human works, and a reference to numerous relics and holy sources of water (ἁγιάσματα).

In concluding, it has been shown that the form in which the literary sources present Byzantine cities over the centuries is usually sketchy, sometimes factual and sometimes distorted by rhetoric. The most elaborate descriptions of cities are found in the 6th century. Rhetorical, historiographical and patridographic texts, adhering to the rules of these literary genres, employ a rhetorical, inflated vocabulary to depict cities and offer fictional accounts that obscure the real picture of the cities in question. Invective, military treatises and, later, epistolography, however, offer factual descriptions. From the 7th to the 12th century, information on cities, except for Constantinople, is limited, a fact which reflects the transformation of urban centres into *kastra* and the decline of the antique form of the city. During the final centuries of Byzantium, the sources on cities, mostly rhetorical, multiply, as cities flourished and many became centres for independent dynasts. As literary sources offer ambiguous images of cities, terminology that defines cities shows urban change more obviously.

Notes

1 On the rhetoric of the city in antiquity, see C. J. Classen, *Die Stadt im Spiegel der Descriptiones und Laudes Urbium in der antiken und mittelalterlichen Literatur bis zum Ende des zwölften Jahrhunderts* (Zürich, New York: Georg Olms, 1986); L. Pernot, *La rhétorique de l'éloge dans le monde gréco-romain. I. Histoire et technique* (Paris: Librairie Générale Française, 1993), 79–82, 178–216 and *passim*; A.-V. Pont, *Orner la cité. Enjeux culturels et politiques du paysage urbain dans l'Asie gréco-romaine* (Paris: De Boccard, 2010).

2 H. Saradi, "Changes of Enduring Consequences in Byzantine Cities: The Allusive Nature of the Texts," *Annual Yearbook of the School of Humanities of the University of Peloponnese*, ed. A. Markantonatos (Athens: Ekdoseis Herodotos), 1 (2016): 81–123.

3 Bibliography on cities in the early Byzantine centuries has been rapidly increasing. General studies: G. P. Brogiolo and B. Ward-Perkins, *The Idea and Ideal of the Town between Late Antiquity and the Early Middle Ages* (Leiden: Brill, 1999); J. Hugo W. G. Liebeschuetz, *Decline and Fall of the Roman City* (Oxford: Oxford University Press, 2001); H. Saradi, *The Byzantine City in the Sixth Century: Literary Images and Historical Reality* (Athens: Society of Messenian Archaeological Studies, 2006); I. Jacobs, *Aesthetic Maintenance of Civic Space. The 'Classical' City from the 4th to the 7th c. AD* (Orientalia Lovaniensia Analecta 193) (Leuven: Peeters, 2013); *The Archaeology of Byzantine Anatolia From the End of Late Antiquity until the Coming of the Turks*, ed. P. Niewöhner (Oxford: Oxford University Press, 2017). A bibliographical survey by P. Magdalino, "Sixty Years of Research on the Byzantine City," in *Städte im lateinischen Westen und im griechischen Osten zwischen Spätantike und Früher Neuzeit. Topographie – Recht – Religion*, eds. E. Gruber, M. Popović, M. Scheutz, and H. Weigl (Vienna: Böhlau, 2016), 45–62.

4 I. Maupai, *Die Macht der Schönheit. Untersuchungen zu einem Aspekt des Selbstverständnisses und der Selbstdorstellung griechischer Städte in der Römischen Kaiserzeit* (Bonn: R. Habelt, 2003); H. Saradi, "The *Kallos* of the Byzantine City: The Development of a Rhetorical *Topos* and Historical Reality," *Gesta* 34, no. 1 (1995): 37–56; eadem, *City*, 49–101.

5 F. Paschoud, *Zosime. Histoire Nouvelle*, I–III (Paris: Belles Lettres, 1979–2000, repr. 2003), IV 18: II/2, p. 278; V 6, 1–2: III/1, p. 12.

6 Ibid., V, 24: III/1, p. 37–38.

7 Ibid., II, 30–37: I, p. 101–08.

8 On the borrowing of characteristics of Virgin Mary from Rhea, see V. Limberis, *Divine Heiress. The Virgin Mary and the Creation of Christian Constantinople* (London, New York: Routledge, 1994).

9 Hesychios, XV, in *Scriptores originum Constantinopolitanarum*, I, ed. T. Preger (Lipsiae: Teubner, 1901 [repr. New York 1975]), 6.
10 *Zosime*, II, 37, 1: I, p. 108.
11 A. Kaldellis, "Constantinople Belated Hegemony," in *Historiography and Space in Late Antiquity*, ed. P. Van Nuffelen (Cambridge: Cambridge University Press, 2019), 14–35.
12 Preger, *Scriptores*, 1, 1–18.
13 P. Niewöhner, "Byzantine Preservation of Ancient Monuments at Miletus in Caria. Christian Antiquarianism in Western Asia Minor," in *Die Weltchronik des Johannes Malalas im Kontext spätantiker Memorialkultur*, eds. J. Borsch, O. Gengler, and M. Meier (Stuttgart: Franz Steiner, 2019), 191–216, 366–72.
14 A. Moffatt, "A Record of Public Buildings and Monuments," in *Studies in John Malalas*, eds. E. Jeffreys, B. Croke, and R. Scott (Sydney: Australian Association for Byzantine Studies, 1990), 87–109; Saradi, *City*, 88–93.
15 A. Busine, "The Conquest of the Past. Pagan and Christian Attitudes towards Civic History," in *Religion and Competition in Antiquity*, eds. D. Engels and P. Van Nuffelen (Brussels: Editions Latomus, 2014), 220–36 at 232–33.
16 Saradi, *City*, 59–68.
17 C. Saliou, *Le Traité d'urbanisme de Julien d'Ascalon (VIe s.). Droit et architecture en Palestine au VIe s., Travaux et mémoires*, monographies, n° 8 (Paris: De Boccard, 1996).
18 *Corpus Juris Civilis*, vol. 2: *Codex Justinianus*, ed. P. Krüger (Berlin: Weidmann, 1877), 8.10.13.
19 Saradi, *City*, 84–88.
20 On the rhetoric of *De Aedificiis*: J. Elsner, "The Rhetoric of Buildings in the *De Aedificiis* of Procopius," in *Art and Text in Byzantine Culture*, ed. L. James (Cambridge: Cambridge University Press, 2007), 33–57; M. Whitby, "Procopius' *Buildings*: A Panegyrical Perspective," *Antiquité Tardive* 8 (2000): 45–57; R. Webb, "Ekphrasis, amplification and persuasion in Prokopios' *Buildings*," *Antiquité Tardive* 8 (2000): 67–71.
21 D. A. Russell and N. G. Wilson, *Menander Rhetor, Edited with Translation and Commentary* (Oxford: Clarendon Press, 1981), 110 (386.21–29), 192 (429.16–17): …*εἶτα τὸ κάλλος τῆς πόλεως· ὡραΐζεται μὲν γὰρ ἡ πόλις κάλλεσιν ἱερῶν καὶ στοῶν καὶ λουτρῶν μεγέθεσιν.*
22 Saradi, "Changes," 101–04, 107.
23 *De Aedificiis*: *Procopii Caesariensis opera omnia*, vol. 4, ed. J. Haury, revised by G. Wirth (Leipzig: Teubner, 1964), VI.7.15–16.
24 Ibid., I.1.20–78. On descriptions of churches, see R. Webb, "The Aesthetics of Sacred Space. Narrative, Metaphor, and Motion in *ekphraseis* of Church Buildings," *Dumbarton Oaks Papers* 53 (1999): 59–74.
25 *De Aedificiis* I.1.27. On this, see H. Saradi, "Beholding the City and the Church: The Early Byzantine *Ekphraseis* and Corresponding Archaeological Evidence," *Deltion tes Christianikes Archaiologikes Etaireias* 24 (2003): 31–36.
26 For example, C. Angelidi, "Un texte patriographique et édifiant: le "Discours Narratif" sur les Hodègoi," *Revue des études byzantines* 52 (1994): 135.24–28.
27 Aristotle, *Nicomachean Ethics*, IV.2.10–11; *Rhetoric* I.9.38–39.
28 *De Aedificiis*, I.2.1–12.
29 Ibid., I.2.13–9.18.
30 Ibid., I.3.3.
31 Ibid., I.3.6–7.
32 Ibid., I.5.
33 A. Colonna, *Himerii declamationes et orationes* (Rome: typis publicae officinae polygraphicae, 1951), Or. 62 (16).
34 A longue description of the sea precedes the *ekphrasis* of the temple of Kyzikos by A. Aristides, ed. B. Keil (Berlin: Weidmann, 1958), ch. 5–8. See also the *Smyrnean Or.* (Or. XXI.5), the *Rodian Or.* (Or. XXV.3–4) and *On the Aegean Sea* (Or. XLIV.16).
35 H. Saradi, "Space in Byzantine Thought," in *Architecture as Icon: Perception and Representation of Architecture in Byzantine Art*, eds. S. Ćurčić and E. Hadjitryphonos, *Exhibition at the Princeton University Art Museum: March 6, 2010–June 6, 2010* (New Haven, CT: Yale University Press, 2010), 73–111 at 74–75.
36 *De Aedificiis*, I.10.

37 Ibid., I.11.1–9.
38 Ibid., I.11.10–27.
39 Ibid., IV.2. 27–28.
40 Ibid., IV.3.1–4; V.4.15–18 (Mokesos in Cappadocia).
41 Ibid, II.10.2; *Ioannis Malalae Chronographia*, ed. Ioannis Thurn (Corpus Fontium Historiae Byzantinae 35) (Berolini: Walter de Gruyter, 2000), 18.29 (p. 371).
42 *De Aedificiis* II.10.2: ... κόσμου τε καὶ ὀχυρώματος ἐνεπλήσατο πολλῷ μείζονος ἢ πρότερον εἶναι ξυνέβαινεν.
43 Ibid., II.10.2–25.
44 Ibid., IV.1.26.
45 Ibid., IV.1.21–25; *Corpus Juris Civilis*, vol. 3, *Novellae*, eds. R. Schöll and G. Kroll (Berlin: Weidmann, 1895), 11 (*a.* 535), 131 (*a.* 545).
46 V. M. Ivanišević, "Une capitale revisitée: Caričin Grad," *Académie des Inscriptions & Belles Lettres, Comptes Rendus* 2017: 93–114, at 104–106, 114 with earlier bibliography.
47 *Historia arcana*: *Procopii Caesariensis opera omnia*, vol. 3, XXVI.1–11.
48 Ibid., XXVI.31–34.
49 G. T. Dennis (ed.), *Three Byzantine Military Treatises. Text, Translation, and Notes* (Washington, DC: Dumbarton Oaks, 1985), 30–33.
50 On the structure of the middle and late Byzantine city, see C. Bouras, "Aspects of the Byzantine City, Eighth–Fifteenth Centuries," in *The Economic History of Byzantium. From the Seventh through the Fifteenth Century*, ed. A. Laiou, vol. 2 (Washington, DC: Dumbarton Oaks Research Library and Collection, 2008), 487–528; P. Magdalino, "Medieval Constantinople: Built Environment and Urban Development," 529–37, and other articles: 602 ff; J. F. Haldon, *Byzantium in the Seventh Century. The Transformation of a Culture* (Cambridge: Cambridge University Press, 1990), 92–124; L. Zavagno, *Cities in Transition: Urbanism in Byzantium between Late Antiquity and the Early Middle Age (AD 500–900)* (BAR Int. Series 2030) (Oxford: Archaeopress, 2000); Niewöhner, *Anatolia*.
51 *Novellae*, 128.20; *Jean le Lydien, Des magistratures de l'état romain. Texte établi, traduit et commenté par Michel Dubuisson, Jacques Schamp* (Paris: Les Belles Lettres, 2006), II, 30.
52 See Saradi, *City*, 96–100; eadem, "The Byzantine Cities (8th–15th Centuries): Old Approaches and New Directions," in *Οι βυζαντινές πόλεις (8ος–15ος αιώνας). Προοπτικές της έρευνας και νέες ερμηνευτικές προσεγγίσεις*, ed. T. Kiousopoulou (Rethymno: Editions of the School of Philosophy of the University of Crete, 2012), 25–45 at 32–33.
53 A. Kazhdan, "*Polis* and *kastron* in Theophanes and in Some Other Historical Texts," in *Ευψυχία. Mélanges offerts à Hélène Ahrweiler*, 2 vols., vol. II (Paris: Editions de la Sorbonne, 1998), 345–60, at 345–50; J. Koder, "Überlegungen zur ländlichen Siedlungsterminologie der Byzantiner, insbesondere zu *chorion*, *kome* und verwandten Termini, *Bulgaria Mediaevalis* 2 (2011) (Studies in Honour of Professor Vassil Gjuzelev): 3–14.
54 H. Saradi, "The City in Byzantine Hagiography," in *The Ashgate Research Companion to Byzantine Hagiography, vol. II: Genres and Contexts*, ed. Stephanos Efthymiadis (Farnham: Ashgate, 2014), 419–52, at 428–29.
55 *Constantine Porphyrogenitus, de administrando imperii*, Greek text edited by G. Moravcsik, English translation by R. J. H. Jenkins (Washington, DC: Dumbarton Oaks Center for Byzantine Studies, 1967), ch. 49. 30–37 (p. 228–30).
56 M. McCormick, *Eternal Victory: Triumphal Rulership in Late Antiquity, Byzantium and the Early Medieval West* (Cambridge, New York, Paris: Cambridge University Press, Editions de la Maison des Sciences de l'Homme, 1986), 154–57, 212–30.
57 I. Ševčenko, ed., *Chronographiae quae Theophanis Continuati nomine fertur, liber quo Vita Basilii imperatoris amplectitur* (Corpus Fontium Historiae Byzantinae, Series Berolinensis 42) (Berlin, Boston, MA: Walter de Gruyter, 2011), ch. 78–93 (p. 264–304), reference to 100 churches: 304.24–25.
58 M. M. Mango, "The Commercial Map of Constantinople," *Dumbarton Oaks Papers* 54 (2000): 189–207.
59 R. Romano, *Pseudo-Luciano, Timarione. Testo critico, introduzione, traduzione, commentario e lessico* (Napoli: Università di Napoli, 1974), 52–59.

60 B. MacDougall, "The festival of Saint Demetrios, the *Timarion*, and the *Aithiopika*," *Byzantine and Modern Greek Studies* 40 (2016): 136–50.

61 A. Kazhdan, "Byzantine Town and Trade as Seen by Niketas Choniates," *Byzantinoslavica* 56, no.1 (1995): 209–18.

62 A. Heisenberg, (ed.), *Georgii Acropolitae Opera*, 2 vols. (Leipzig: Teubner, 1903), corr. P. Wirth (Stuttgart: Teubner, 1978), I, 285.9–11.

63 N. E. Karapidakis, "Οι πόλεις των αρχόντων: Η δυναμική και τα όρια ενός τύπου αστικής ανάπτυξης. Ήπειρος, Αιτωλοακαρνανία, Μοριάς (13ος–16ος αι.)," in *Βυζαντινές πόλεις* 207–24, at 212 ff.

64 N. Choniates, *De Signis*, ed. I. A. van Dieten (Berlin: De Gruyter, 1975), 647–55. On the symbolisms of the text, see H. Saradi, "Perceptions and Literary Interpretations of Statues and the Image of Constantinople," *Byzantiaka* 20 (2000): 38–77, at 66–73; T. Papamastorakis, "Interpreting the *De Signis* of Niketas Choniates", in *Niketas Choniates. A Historian and a Writer*, eds. A. J. Simpson and Stephanos Euthymiades (Geneva: La Pomme d'Or, 2009), 209–24; P. Chatterjee, "Sculptured eloquence and Nicetas Choniates' *De Signis*," *Word and Image: A Journal of Verbal/ Visual Enquiry* 27, no. 4 (2012): 396–406.

65 On cities in the late centuries, see T. Kiousopoulou, *Οι «αόρατες» βυζαντινές πόλεις στον ελλαδικό χώρο (13ος–15ος αιώνας)* (Athens: Πόλις, 2013); A. Konstantakopoulou, *Βυζαντινή Θεσσαλονίκη. Χώρος και ιδεολογία* (Giannena: s. e. 1996); E. Kaltsogianni, S. Kotzabassi, I. Paraskevopoulou, *Η Θεσσαλονίκη στη βυζαντινή λογοτεχνία. Ρητορικά και αγιολογικά κείμενα* (Thessaloniki: Byzantine Research Centre, 2002); Saradi, "Hagiography," 437–42.

66 Karapidakis, "Οι πόλεις των αρχόντων," 215–24.

67 F. Miklosich and J. Müller, *Acta et diplomata monasteriorum et ecclesiarum Orientis*, vol. 5 (Vienna: C. Gerold, 1887), 78. For another example: Efterpi Marki, *Κίτρος. Μια πόλη–κάστρο της βυζαντινής περιφέρειας* (Thessaloniki: Ta tramakia, 2001).

68 M. S. Kordosis, *Τὰ βυζαντινὰ Γιάννενα. Κάστρο (πόλη)-Ξώκαστρο. Κοινωνία-Διοίκηση-Οικονομία* (Athens: s. n. 2002, reprint *Istorikogeographika* 9), 58–74.

69 A. Bryer and D. Winfield, *The Byzantine Monuments and Topography of the Pontos*, 2 vols., I (Washington, DC: Dumbarton Oaks Research Library and Collection, 1985), 184–88.

70 D. A. Zakythinos, *Le Despotat grec de Morée*, vol. 2: *Vie et institutions* (Athens: L'Hellénisme Contemporain, 1953, edition revue et augmentée par C. Maltezou, London: Variorum 1975), 167–68; H. Saranti-Mendelovici, "A propos de la ville de Patras aux 13e–15e siècles," *Revue des études byzantines* 38 (1980): 219–32 at 228–29; Kordosis, *Γιάννενα*, 98–99.

71 Saranti-Mendelovici, "Patras," 230; Kordosis, *Γιάννενα*, 103.

72 *Ioannis Cantacuzeni eximperatoris historiarum libri IV*, eds. L. Schopen and J. Barthold G. Niebuhr (Bonn: E. Weber, 1828–1832), III, 130.

73 V. Katsaros, "Ἀπὸ τὴν καθημερινὴ ζωὴ στὸ «Δεσποτᾶτο» τῆς Ἠπείρου. Ἡ μαρτυρία τοῦ μητροπολίτη Ναυπάκτου Ἰωάννη Ἀποκαύκου," in *Ἡ καθημερινὴ ζωὴ στὸ Βυζάντιο. Τομὲς καὶ συνέχειες στὴν ἑλληνιστικὴ καὶ ρωμαϊκὴ παράδοση*, ed. C. G. Aggelidi (Athens: National Research Foundation, Centre of Byzantine Research, 1989), 631–74 at 642–47.

74 Kiousopoulou, *Οι «αόρατες» βυζαντινές πόλεις*, 62–63, 77–80.

75 A. Kontogiannopoulou, *Local Councils in Byzantine Cities. Tradition and Evolution (13th–15the c.)* (Athens: Academy of Athens – Research Centre for Medieval and Modern Hellenism, 2015).

76 D. Kyritses, "The "Common Chrysobulls" of Cities and the Notion of Property in Late Byzantium," *Byzantina Symmeikta* 13 (1999): 229–45.

77 Konstantakopoulou, *Θεσσαλονίκη*; Kaltsogianni *et al.*, *Θεσσαλονίκη*; Saradi, "Hagiography," 437–42.

78 Konstantakopoulou, *Θεσσαλονίκη*, 149–53 and *passim*; Kaltsogianni *et al.*, *Θεσσαλονίκη*, 36–47.

79 H. Saradi, "Idyllic Nature and Urban Setting: An Ideological Theme with Artistic Style, or Playful Self-Indulgence," in *Villes de toute beauté. L'ekphrasis des cités dans les littératures byzantine et byzantino-slaves. Actes du colloque international, Prague, 25–26 novembre 2011 organisé par l'Institut d'études slaves de l'Académie des Sciences de la République Tchèque et le Centre d'études byzantines, néo-helléniques et sud-est européennes de l'Ecole des Hautes Études en Sciences Sociales*, eds. P. Odorico and C. Messis [Dossiers Byzantins 12] (Paris: De Boccard, 2012), 9–36.

80 N. Mpakirtzis, "Τα τείχη των βυζαντινών πόλεων: Αισθητική, ιδεολογίες και συμβολισμοί," in *Οι βυζαντινές πόλεις* 139–58.

81 A. Tartaglia, *Theodorus II Ducas Lascaris. Opuscula Rhetorica* (Munich, Leipzig: K. G. Saur, 2000), Or. 3, ch. 1.10 (p. 68), 6.234–38 (p. 78).
82 Ibid., ch. 5.204 (p. 76), 7.248 (p. 78). See H. Saradi, "The Monuments in the Late Byzantine *Ekphraseis* of Cities: Searching for Identities," *Byzantinoslavica* 69 (2011): suppl. 3, *Ekphrasis: La représentation des monuments dans les littératures byzantine et byzantino-slaves. Réalités et imaginaires*, 179–92, at 181–82.
83 H. Saradi, "Οι ταυτότητες της Κωνσταντινούπολης στον *Βυζάντιο* του Θεοδώρου Μετοχίτη και τα ιστορικά μηνύματα," in *Cities and Power in Byzantium during the Palaeologan Era (1261–1453)*, ed. A. Kontogiannopoulou (Athens: Academy of Athens, Centre for Medieval and Modern Hellenism, 2018), 19–42.
84 E. Fenster, *Laudes constantinopolitanae* (Munich: Institut für Byzantinistik und Neugriechische Philologie, 1968), 332–36.
85 I. Giarenis, "Η *έκφρασις* του Βησσαρίωνα για την Τραπεζούντα. Η χρονολόγηση του έργου και το εγκώμιο των Μεγαλοκομνηνών αυτοκρατόρων," in *Βησσαρίων εκ Τραπεζούντος του Πόντου. Λόγιος του Βυζαντινού και του Δυτικού Αναγεννησιακού 15ου αιώνα*, eds. I. Ath. Giarenis, A. G. Maras, C. P. Baloglou, and T. Ar. Kyriakides (Thessaloniki: Stamoulis, 2016), 175–208 at 180–87.
86 H. Saradi, "Η *έκφρασις* της Τραπεζούντας από τον Βησσαρίωνα, η αρχαιότης και το ιστορικό μήνυμα," *Byzantinos Domos* 17–18 (2009–10): 33–56.
87 O. Lampsides, "Ὁ «Εἰς Τραπεζοῦντα» Λόγος τοῦ Βησσαρίωνος (κριτικὴ ἔκδοσις)", *Archeion Pontou* 39 (1984): 3–75, palace at 63–65; Saradi, "The Monuments", 190–91.
88 Saradi, "Idyllic Nature," 35–36; eadem, H. Saradi, "The Antiquities in Constructing Byzantine Identity: Literary Tradition versus Aesthetic Appreciation," *Hortus Artium Medievalium* 17 (2011): 95–113, at 106.
89 N. Festa (ed.), *Theodori Ducae Lascaris Epistulae CCVII* (Florence: G. Camesecchi, 1898), Epistle 32, 107–08.
90 G. T. Dennis (ed.), *The Letters of Manuel II Palaeologus. Text, Translation, and Notes* (Corpus Fontium Historiae Byzantinae, Series Washingtonensis VIII) (Washington, DC: Dumbarton Oaks Center for Byzantine Studies, 1977), no. 16.42–46.
91 C. Billò, "Manuele Crisolora, *Confronto tra l'Antica e la Nuova Roma*," *Medioevo greco. Rivista di storia e filologia bizantina* (2000): 1–26.
92 Ibid., 18.18–20 (ch. 45). See G. Dagron, "Manuel Chrysoloras: Constantinople ou Rome," *Byzantinische Forschungen* 12 (1987): 281–88; Saradi, "The Antiquities," 106–08, 112.

4
METHODOLOGIES FOR BYZANTINE URBAN STUDIES*

Michael J. Decker

Introduction

Nearly 70 years after Alexander Kazhdan's influential article 'Vizantiyskie goroda v VII-XI vv', the Byzantine city remains a major focus of investigation.[1] That this remains the case is unsurprising, given the views of Byzantium come mostly from our study of urban-based writers or excavated remains of cities. Our own acculturation has largely taken place within a world of cities. Since Kazhdan wrote, the city has increasingly framed the lived experience of people around the world. In 1950, just over 41 percent of humans lived in urban environments. Today, more than half of us live in cities (over 56 percent). Even if contemporary archaeologists and historians did not grow up in cities, most of them took jobs in academic communities nested within urban spaces, which now have an enormous range of functions. Among these is their serving as centers for gravity of intellectual development through education, through which we perpetuate and transform cultural elements undergirding societies. Our ways of interpreting the world, past and present, and our way of understanding these worlds, are profoundly influenced by our own lived existence as citizens in the strictest sense, as denizens of cities.

Endings and Beginnings

Much has changed since 1959, the prominent Yugoslavian Byzantinist, George Ostrogorsky wrote 'Among the fundamental problems of Byzantine history it would be hard to name one that has been studied less than has that of the cities'.[2] Research since the mid-twentieth century has expanded considerably and debate remains lively. Through recent years, the body of literature devoted to the Byzantine city has grown manifold, including foundational studies on the topography, history, and architecture of Constantinople which stand alongside the analysis of many of the provincial cities of the empire.[3] Scholarly works on early Byzantine Egypt, Palestine, and Syria join studies of various aspects of urban

* This piece is dedicated to the memory of Nick Maroulis, who generously endowed the Chair of History that I occupy at the University of South Florida and whose support of all things good about Hellenism continues to inspire.

DOI: 10.4324/9780429203923-6

settlement in Anatolia, the Balkans, Byzantine Italy, and the islands, all of which offer vistas into the nature of life in Byzantium and its cities.[4] The questions that loom large in all this are as follows: how and why the end came for the ancient city, and, moreover, what does the de-urbanization of many regions mean for our understanding of Byzantine society? If the ancient city, expressed in its organic form in the ancient Greek polis and enlarged, adapted, and sustained by the Romans for over a thousand years, what are we to make of life in the empire as society moved away from these classical forms? Discourse around these questions has dominated and still looms large in much exploration of the urban spaces of the empire, and such debate is likely to persist.

Byzantine urban studies may now draw inspiration from a rich medley of ideas through multiple domains of knowledge. Alongside traditional historical, geographical, and archaeological modes of examination, we now number post-modern, self-reflective, and deconstructive avenues of exploration awareness which can broaden our scope of inquiry. Taken in their totality, the fullness of methods is mere potentiality, as no study has yet to mine them all, nor to amalgamate their gleanings into a holistic perspective that could expose the varieties of life in Byzantine cities. Underlying novel methodologies is the awareness of the great changes in cities of the empire across the sixth to tenth centuries, but equal comprehension that, in many places, of substantial continuity. We must move beyond the rather contentious but ultimately sterile debates staked upon cherished binaries (continuity-decline and decline-transformation and others like them). In order to successfully render a mosaic of Byzantine urbanism, we must focus initially on the individual tesserae in the form of cities, or former cities, and their territories. A useful attitude from which to enhance our understanding of the medieval cities of Byzantium is to adopt at first this sort of regional perspective, a process that relies of course on careful sifting of local materials and a narrow purview. While prior work, such as the magisterial and path-breaking efforts of the *Tabula Imperii Byzantini* (TIB), it seems to me that we must begin with smaller, localised 'regions'.[5]

While the TIB investigators deal with larger geographical areas, often coinciding with the settlement of ancient ethnic groups (e.g. Galatia), my view of a useful 'region' is the scale of a late antique city territory; that is, an area of tens of hundreds of square kilometers. Among the strengths of such regional explorations is the ability to recognise and characterise settlements within local contexts in the first instance, accommodate unique environmental and social conditions peculiar to a given city and its surroundings, and employ useful categorizations of data on a city-by-city basis. In the absence of cities, a regionalized methodology will be determined by factors apart from the notion of an urban central place, but settlement hierarchy is always important in helping us interpret a landscape.

In addition to refining our contextual and spatial delineations of study, we require new analytical perspectives upon which to draw. Recognizing the special characteristic of the Byzantine city, which was neither simply the continuation of the classical polis, is an obvious departure point. Another promising development is a wider appreciation that the Byzantine city was neither a mongrelization of the classical polis, nor something entirely unrelated to urban developments in other places and times in history and prehistory. Reconsidering these basic concepts can help us reorient the study of these important spaces. Following the adoption of new, or sometimes simply different, viewpoints, new methodologies discussed below present themselves with fruitful applications.

Despite a spate of discussion on the topic, scholars continue to struggle with their grasp on and articulation of the essence of the ancient city. The same can be said for Byzantium, where there is a similar lack of consensus. Though this is not the space to attempt an exhaustive study of the topic, a few observations are in order. Many Byzantine cities likely manifest characteristics essential in non-classical Mediterranean contexts. One of these attributes is a relatively short lifespan of particular phases of city organization, something which has yet to be properly acknowledged. This much is evident in the case of Constantinople even apart from the historical record; it is made clear from the fragments of its fabric remaining today. Enduring through its allure as a symbol of Byzantine urbanism and culture is, throughout most of its existence, Constantinople was obviously an outlier. Many cities – most, I would say on a hunch – did not persist through the centuries. During the imperial *resorgimento* that followed on the ashes and grit of the third-century AD crises, urban continuity is broadly assumed, and it should not always be. Instead, significant variety manifests in the fortunes and fates of cities in the lands of the eastern empire. There was considerable urban dynamism, perhaps most easily visible in the less urbanised spaces and especially in marginal regions. On the Anatolian plateau, we have a number of poleis which flourished during the earlier empire, such as Gordion or Aizanoi in Phrygia, the latter of which flowered then faded as old family and euergistic systems on which the city had prospered faded from the scene.[6] Some poleis, like Pepouza, were never large or politically important and simply lost their administrative function at some point between the compilation of Hierocles in the mid-fifth century and George of Cyprus in the seventh, even if life there persisted in some fashion.[7] Similarly Colossae, which was never a major city, gradually morphed into medieval Chonai, with its famous Christian pilgrimage site.

Similar site migrations common throughout history also occurred at Gortyn on Crete, where multi-decade archaeological investigation has yielded considerable data which is now being analyzed with an eye toward some of the problems of Byzantine urbanization,[8] along the Negev Desert settlements, like Mampsis, Oboda, and Eleusis. Others, like Euaria in Phoenice Libanensis, also grew important enough to be accorded the status of polis even though there were villages, like Androna, larger than they.[9]

If this variegated tapestry of cities was thus at the start of late antiquity, are we correct in believing that things should look vastly different in the seventh century, or the twelfth? Different fates and fortunes of cities cannot always be clearly linked with higher level change, and different frameworks will yield an assortment of possibilities. Certainly, through late antiquity and into the early medieval era, cities altered their expressions of civic life and their physical fabrics changed. Sometimes these changes were engendered largely by local or regional forces, while at other times broader environmental, social, or political currents carried the day. Through the vagaries of centuries, some provincial cities remained important administrative, cultural, and political centers (Amorium, Thessalonike), some maintained much of their late antique grid and physical fabric (Thessalonike, Cherson, Naples, Tamatarkha), while others (Butrint, Sagalassos, Hierapolis in Phrygia) developed in cellular fashion, where occupants were rather dispersed over fortified precincts and where life was apparently quite different from the past.[10] In those cases, application of words like 'urbanism' and 'city' cause as many problems as they solve.

Byzantine Cities

In a prominent article, an archaeologist once remarked, 'It is notoriously difficult to agree on a cross-culturally applicable definition of "the" city, but we cannot do without definitions altogether...It is far better to think of "cities" or "a" city, but never of "the" city'.[11] In all likelihood, this scholar did not have in mind a civilization in which there was a settlement of such social, economic, and cultural import as Constantinople, so that it was referred to simply as 'the City'.[12] If the precise nature and articulation of what constitutes Byzantine cities eludes us and generates incessant debate over the nature of the Byzantine city, in this state of affairs, we are not alone. It may come as cold comfort that urban historians and their kindred scholars in sociology, anthropology, and allied disciplines cannot agree on what constitutes a city.[13] Clearly, though, what the city was and meant to the Byzantines was not static but varied through time, space, and among individuals. Categories of different settlements are detectable in the written sources, which themselves are far from straightforward and cannot always be relied upon to offer a clear contemporary picture.[14]

Since the road to Byzantium leads through Rome and Athens, discourse has centered on the nature of the late antique polis and its survival through the traumatic events that gripped the populace in the sixth to eighth centuries.[15] Brandes and Haldon argued that cities could be defined by three functions: first, as market centers, second, as places of administration and the projection of state authority (often denoted by walled enclosures), and third, by the presence of cult, exemplified in Byzantium by the presence of the church.[16] 'By the end of the sixth century the East Roman Empire was becoming increasingly hellenised and de-urbanised' fairly sums up the conclusion; only a handful of cities remained in the Anatolian heartland of the post-Arab conquest landscape of empire.[17] A combination of usurpation of civic authority by the imperial government and the influence of Christianity which created a rival to, and replacement for, old euergetic forms in addition to opposing much of the old ways of civic life, namely pagan civic religion, public festivals and games, and theatrical performances.[18] In addition, exogenous factors like plague and invasion played a role in the demise of the classical polis. Thus, the 'Dark Ages' were the period of the kastron; the time of the polis had faded.

It should be stressed that the full expression of these phenomena was a drawn-out process that began in late antiquity and unfolded over centuries.[19] Moreover, our misapprehension of the organization of Byzantine landscapes and society is not infrequently due to our own assumptions and subsequent misreading of the material and textual evidence and it is unhelpful to work within the simple framework of continuity/discontinuity.[20] What is clear that a careful assessment approaching something akin to reality requires a thorough re-reading of the evidence, both textual and material, and, as has previously been observed by others, new interpretive frameworks. Of special relevance is the need to modify our understanding of 'urban' and 'rural', as well as to get a grip with some precision on what we mean by 'town', 'city', and so forth.

Beyond moving past these simple dichotomies expressed semantically, we may at least refine what we mean when we deploy such categories. To take here, but one example: we would be advised to consider that even in the thriving, large-scale paradigmatic cities of late antique Byzantium exemplified by places like Constantinople, Antioch, Alexandria, and Apamea, elements of what we consider 'ruralization' were, in some ways, a persistent feature. There were fruit trees growing in side streets, courtyards, and abandoned lots.[21] Many citizens engaged in horticulture either to wholly support themselves or supplement their food supply or income. Aqueducts were tapped to supply water to urban gardens. Farms and orchards lay nearby even large settlements, and these were worked by people who lived inside cities and towns. Consequently, there was a great deal of coming and going of farmers, flocks, and produce absent from 'cities' as we often conceive of them.

More recently, prospects drawn of Anglo-Saxon scholarship offer an opportunity to reconsider the framework of discussion. Drawing on models of earlier urban economy derived from the sociological and economic work of Weber, Polanyi, and Pirenne, among others, this approach may help us embed many Byzantine cities within distinctive ecological and economic orders. In these, settlements may prove to be far removed from their ties with the poleis of late antiquity, but part of larger, plastic, and fragile networks established through trade and cultural affinities.[22] Hodges likens Butrint on the Albanian coast with the emporia of the North Sea world, where he was among the first scholars to articulate the 'small world' of trade and exchange and its articulation in Dark Age spaces.[23] It is useful to view settlements like Butrint and a host of others – a garland of them, in fact, that spread around the shores of the Byzantine west, and probably much further to the east, where investigation through his lens has not progressed. These communities maintained long-distance trade interests and exploited their ecological niches (in the case of Butrint fishing grounds and mussel beds). At Butrint, the 'fingerprint' of government or administration is light indeed, traces of a governmental presence are detectable on the Vrina Plain by the city from the ninth century.[24]

Archaeologists have yet to refine their chronologies and classification of the inventory of settlement from explored regions. Thus, the struggle to define the Byzantine city – or more appropriately – Byzantine cities, is not likely to be resolved soon. Due to the extensive space required to unwind the strands, this is not the place to attempt to resolve such longstanding and multi-threaded complexities.

Unfortunately, not much progress has been made in the methodology mapped out by Bouras, some two decades ago. Since these considerations remain valid, it is worth restating them:

- a 'unification of all the surveys of the built evidence (produced either by excavation or by investigation of the surviving buildings) into a single general plan of the situation as it is today
- b reconstruction of the urban fabric during the various periods
- c identification of the functions of rooms and buildings and of land uses; with the assistance of movable finds, emphasis on matters connected with the process of production
- d reciprocal interpretation, where feasible, involving the finds and the written information
- e a study of the growth of each city, settlement, or ekistic unit and interpretation of that growth in historical terms'.[25]

Our approaches could benefit from new perspectives from beyond the horizons of classical and Western medieval scholarships which have heretofore framed the conversation. After all, among the early Byzantine lands must be counted a sizeable portion of the Fertile Crescent, the birthplace of the city. Yet, while urban forms in the Near East through time embody the cycle of 'boom and bust', the cities of the Byzantine Fertile Crescent are somehow to be impervious to such cycles. Closer attention to the Levant in all historic (and prehistoric) periods is a desideratum, as is taking onboard lessons to be learned from the pre-industrial world beyond Europe, or even Eurasia for that matter. Here we would be well advised to apply principles derived from architectural and planning, namely the coordination of buildings and spaces and levels of meaning in the constructed environment.[26]

New interpretive models must consider cities from a range of new perspectives, starting with an approach more rigidly fixed on local and regional environments – something that the emporium framework noted above brings into sharper focus. Central places and network nodes remain fundamental, valid, and vital to our understanding but heretofore underexplored in the Byzantine context. There are other requirements as well – attuning, for example, our explorations with clearer concentration on the essentials of urbanism: the intensification of economic, ideological, and social forms and their repetition through space and time.[27] Moreover, exploration of the productive aspects of Byzantine cities, towns, and other forms of urbanised spaces, however defined, is sorely lacking, attached as we are to notions of the 'consumer' city no different than that of Sombart, Weber, and Finley.[28]

Staying with the theme of amplification of our frame of reference to go beyond the classical polis, it is vital that we engage in critical fashion with the nature of aesthetics and their place in our conception of 'the city'. Not to be dismissed as mere modernist fantasy in which the 'city beautiful' is a reality, an imposed aesthetic informed in part by acculturation, there are multiple, complex reasons for continued appreciation of and fascination with great civic spaces of the classical Mediterranean.[29] Many in 18th- and 19th-century Europe and North America were enamored by what they perceived to be the ancient aesthetic, evidenced in Neoclassicism and Romanticism. For these movements, the beauty of architectural form met the loveliness of nature, illustrated in the paintings as they were in the embrace of the classical city, and continued debates about decay, decline, and transformation demonstrate that the modernist perspective continues to thrive. As many archaeologists in the Mediterranean sail to Byzantium on the seas of classical archaeology, this is unsurprising. There are good reasons, though, to expand our approach, foremost among which is the enrichment of the field that comes from appreciating Byzantine city spaces.[30] One would be remiss not to address this dominant fact – that Byzantine buildings and cities have received nothing like the attention, to mention nothing of the level of appreciation, of their classical predecessors. What follows is something between an appeal to change this situation and potential different ways of seeing, both of which are germane to amplifying the field of urban studies of the Byzantine era.[31]

There can be little argument against broad admiration of the beauty of Graeco-Roman monumental city spaces, even if, to a degree, we recognise our acculturation to appreciate the great temples and fora from the reconstructions of architects, artists, and in movies. There are likely several deeper psychological reasons for our appreciation for these spaces insofar as they appeal both to an intrinsic sense of order in many equated to the good and the appeal of symmetry and certain geometric forms in space. An increasing body of literature supports the view that many essential concepts of beauty are ultimately rooted in the natural world in which humans evolved prior to the emergence of our modern ancestors ca. 150,000 years ago.[32] One likely example is the discovery of Phi, the Pythagorean number of incommensurability, expressed in the irrational number approximately equal to 1.61. This number is also known as the Euclidian Golden Ratio and appears frequently in architectural manifestation, most famously in the Parthenon in Athens, whose façade incorporates the golden rectangle.[33]

Since classical antiquity and especially after the rediscovery of Phi by the Italian friar and mathematician, Luca Pacioli in 1509, the golden ratio has been sought in nature, particularly in anthropometry; the exploration of Le Corbusier is of special significance.[34] Phi has since been studied intensively and manifests in an astonishing array of natural and human contexts, ranging from well-known examples of the Nautilus shell, to phyllotaxis of plants, nucleotide frequencies, and cells.[35] Attempts have been made to link the golden ratio to everything from the rhythm of the human heartbeat and human locomotion to the structure of music.[36] If one objects to the intrusion of biology and psychology in the practice of history, art history, and archaeology, then an argument needs to be made against the application of such knowledge from these domains, since biologically we are more than substantially similar to ancestors who lived hundreds of millennia ago. Moreover, 'the point is that historians habitually think with psychology anyway'.[37]

Aesthetically speaking, then, there is much to explore. Citizens of the empire certainly held strong convictions as to how and why cities were beautiful and what made them so. Two recently active approaches can help us grasp and perhaps even appreciate certain environmental features of Byzantine urbanism. The first is the movement in monument-based studies in aesthetics. Churches are the most frequently investigated architecture in former imperial space. Urban monasteries, though present in the material remains, have also garnered some attention, naturally in the main from an art historical or architectural perspective.[38] In many instances, though, what we know of settlements – and sometimes all we know – are from the remnants of ecclesiastical buildings. At first glance, this may seem limiting, and it does serve to perpetuate some stereotypes that overplay the religious character of the empire.[39] Traditionally churches and monasteries have been the domain of art- and architectural historians, frequently nested within cultural studies. New avenues of exploration of these spaces, especially via archaeoacoustics, have generated exceptional interest among researchers.[40] The acoustic properties of Hagia Sophia, Istanbul, the Acheiropoietos basilica, and Hagia Sophia, Thessaloniki, are among the urban churches explored via their acoustical properties and the study of sensory and emotional experiences of audience participants.[41] Recently Nadine Schibille has examined Hagia Sophia through the aesthetic lens, in an exploration of concepts of space, light, and beauty.[42] The application of these ideas and techniques could be fruitfully applied to many surviving monuments and spaces within the former empire.

The second important area of development which demands much wider application in the study of Byzantine settlements is 3D reconstruction and visualization/virtualization. Few combinations of technologies have more power to generate interest and spark debate than accurately rendered and textured 3D models. Augmented reality is now everywhere, and virtual reality is becoming quite mainstream. In the next decade, developments in these domains will open an entire new field of exploration to Byzantine studies. Public engagement, at a minimum, demands that we consider and take seriously developing scholarly methods whereby these research activities can be credibly peer reviewed and engaged with by the academic community while not losing site of the public appeal and utility that such tools have. While we have yet to attain the promise of visualization many thought on the horizon a decade ago, the capacity to reconstruct medieval monuments and spaces and manipulate them digitally will only grow in importance as the skills and hardware for these applications become ubiquitous. Crowdsourcing of such data sets from tourist scans and photos from cellphones will soon be a commonplace in studying settlements frequented by such individuals.

Cities of the Living

The era of the 'big dig' excavation is over. Contemporary large-scale, stratigraphically controlled, and well-published excavations that promise to shed light on the quilt of middle Byzantine era cities are everywhere absent. Turkey, archaeologically the richest, most diverse, and important archaeological frontier of Byzantium, has little focus on urban archaeology of the medieval empire. The situation is not much better in the Balkan areas where the empire held sway for all or portions of the medieval centuries. While approaches, preparation, research design, and recording have all changed considerably, excavation methodologies have not changed much in their basics since the days of Pitt Rivers and Wheeler, even if we have added to our repertoire approaches employing stepped trenches, probes, slit trenches, shovel-test pits, and the like have been part of the archaeological toolkit for decades.

With the end of large-scale excavation, archaeologists have made two fundamental changes. The first is the pivot to explore past urban space using remote sensing methods, which have quickly come to dominate most research approaches. Closely related are technological advances in ground-based remote sensing, namely ground-penetrating radar, which permits three-dimensional maps of underground archaeological remains.[43] Using powerful software, different building and occupation phases can be visualized and separated into chronologically related 'time slices' based on horizontal and morphological relationships. Geophysical tools have been applied for some time and with good success in some instances on sites with Byzantine era remains.[44] Earth resistance survey, which involves passing a current, and magnetic survey methods are also important in this era of targeted excavation, where funding and time factors limit the areas which can be explored. These methodologies are more common in Northern and Western Europe due to the levels of archeological funding and institutional support.

The digital revolution has finally touched most aspects of archaeological excavation, even if we remain in a period of transition where much processing and recording is still done on paper. Despite their promise, the most powerful of computer-aided tools, such as the identification and processing of ceramic finds using artificial intelligence, for instance, have yet to be realized but progress on deep learning tools of this kind means we are on the threshold of fundamental changes in identifying and classifying recovered materials and labor-intensive portions of archaeology. Application of these technologies will not only permit leaner and more productive field teams, greatly reducing, for instance, the laborious and mundane task of sorting, recording, and recognizing sherds, but also provide much swifter quantification and publication of finds.[45]

Approaches to the infrastructure of the medieval city, the bones of the body social and politic in such spaces, remain underdeveloped in Byzantine studies. The reasons for this are perhaps to be found in the unattractiveness to many scholars of the banal, especially in the effluence of denizens of the city. Nonetheless new methodologies have opened important new perspectives on daily life, especially the health of the inhabitants. While late antique and medieval citizens had access to bathing facilities, they nevertheless hosted parasites which have been commensal in humans for millennia so far in fact we likely coevolved with these organisms.

The ecologies of Byzantium comprised more than the oikos, the city street, and the monastery and went beyond the lichen-covered city wall or sweep of landscape in nested humans from Boeotia to Butrint. This is not to argue, as some would have it, that the city in antiquity or the medieval era is an expression of ecology and essentially epiphenomenal.[46] Byzantine ecologies, like all human ecologies, included spaces seen and unseen, including the world of the microbe. Of pronounced relevance in understanding the daily life of Byzantine people are the host of pathogens that afflicted human beings: viruses, bacteria, fungi, and parasites. Relevant recent studies from the early Roman period indicate that, despite the presence of running water in many public and private buildings, the widespread use of public latrines and relatively frequent bathing, Roman populations hosted a great diversity of endo- and ectoparasites. The heavy parasite load in even, relatively speaking at least, sanitary environments surprises, though less so when one considers that only recently have human societies globally reduced the presence of parasites to any significant degree.

More interesting and important is the commonality of organisms represented and their prevalence. Malaria, caused by five species of *Plasmodium* parasites, was a common scourge of the ancient and medieval worlds, sparing neither poor nor rich; emperor Andronikos Palaiologos (1328–1341) succumbed.[47] Spread principally by the *Anepheles labranchiae labranchiae* mosquito malaria is the greatest killer of humans in history (exceeding aggregate mortality from other disease and warfare) and in much of the Mediterranean malaria was the strongest evolutionary selective force in recent human history, with clear genetic adaptations especially evident in the populations of Sardinia and Sicily.[48]

At Ephesus, analysis of archaeological sediments from a communal public- and private house latrines and runoff from city drains and sewers from the Roman-early Byzantine era (first to sixth century AD) yielded quantities of the common nematodes roundworm (*Ascaris* sp.) and whipworm (*Trichuris trichiura*). Of the two, whipworm was apparently far more common than the two helminths to reside in the local population. A high burden of whipworm can cause serious health problems but there is now good evidence that, due to the long relationship of humans and these common organisms (called pseudo-commensals due to their ubiquity in food and water supplies) that these worms play an important role in regulating the human immune system.[49] The investigations at Ephesus are further important for what investigators did not find. Problems of arguments *ex silentio* aside, the lack of parasite diversity in the Ephesian samples was sufficiently anomalous to require explanation. Possibilities posited by the investigators included that Ephesians cooked their meat more frequently and thoroughly than their northern peers; climatic differences affecting the survival and recovery of helminths; fewer wild animals were consumed; and the use of anti-helminthic medicines prescribed in Galen and other ancient and medieval medicinal texts.[50] One possibility that the authors of the Ephesus study seem not to have considered seriously was that hygienic practices in the city were indeed more effective than in other cities. This is but one example where new methods, more broadly applied, could begin to answer questions with enormous ramifications. The amplification of this sort of work offers us the prospect to gain a greater understanding of life at a basic level and public health in Byzantium with multifarious implications on questions spanning from basic quality of life to demographic trends. The latter need to take center stage in Byzantium if we are to understand more deeply the question of sustainability, or resilience, of cities and model flows of population and assess the knock-on effects of migration with the hinterlands to which cities were by necessity connected as well as the broader networks of the empire as a whole.

Clues to how some of these phenomena can be approached in the early Byzantine era can be partly seen at Sagalassos, one of the best excavated, carefully recorded, and well-published sites of the early Byzantine era, the study of a public latrine affords a view of social change in the city. There, inside the vaulted chamber adjacent to the public 'Imperial Baths' constructed around the time of Hadrian or shortly after (AD 120–165), multiple cores were extracted from stratified deposits. These samples yielded charcoal then subjected both to C14 dating via Accelerator Mass Spectrometry (AMS). Sediments were also subjected to calcium (Ca) analysis. Materials found in the sediments included mammal and fish bones, ceramics, seeds, pollen, and other refuse items.

By the early sixth century, the bath itself, now reduced in size by the closure of the Western women's baths and modification of the caldarium in the men's bath was converted into a service room, had undergone significant alterations and repair.[51] Most relevant for this discussion are the results of sediments from horizon A, dated by AMS to AD 420–600. In this chronological span, the seats had been removed from the latrine and the area was used as a composting site. Animal dung was carried and deposited from ruminant animals, probably sheep, goat, and cattle whose presence in the archaeological record of the early Byzantine period at Sagalassos is well documented.[52] The mingling of broken ceramics, commonly found as dense sherd scatters in ancient tilth known from other archaeological contexts, further supports this view. Lime (mostly calcium oxide CaO) detected in the calcium analysis was periodically scattered on the matrix and incorporated as the dung was turned over during the composting process. The application of lime (and chemically similar ash) is still a common farming practice today; the presence of lime in the compost heap indicates that the inhabitants of the city were following normal farming habits important for the maintenance of soil fertility and productivity and are known in suburban contexts at Sagalassos as well.[53] The use of a repurposed water channel from the bath and the application of lime ensured an efficacious soil amendment capable of fertilizing 1.75–2.25 ha. The application was most likely reserved for intensively cultivated gardens within or near the city walls where increased agricultural activity is in evidence from the fifth century. Thus, another important body of information that emerges from the study of a humble latrine converted to a Byzantine fertilizer heap is a deepening of the local diet, but also the cityscape itself. Pollen and seeds reveal local diet: dill and cumin seeds, favorites in the culinary repertoire of the Roman and late antique world were grown likely locally produced. Olive seeds likely represented imported food, while pollen grains from chestnut (*Castanea*), hazel (*Coyrlus*), walnut (*Juglans*), and plum (*Prunus*) indicate that these trees were grown inside the city.

On the one hand, things were not static for the inhabitants, though, as indicated by the dereliction of the grand 'Imperial Baths', large structural portions of which collapsed in an earthquake of the seventh century. This, and the loss of shops and much of mercantile and manufacturing activity along the main colonnaded thoroughfare, suggests an end of key features of the former ancient city. The unwinding of primary use of public space, as the city gradually gave way to a series of dispersed, nucleated hamlets within the old area of the city, unfolded over the course of the fifth and sixth centuries.[54] On the other hand, people clearly continued to live at Sagalassos and rendered it a different kind of place, one watched over from its kastron. The medieval inhabitants farmed and grazed spaces within and without the city walls (built around 400, enclosing a third of the area of the early imperial era city) and conducted their business and religious ceremonies as had their predecessors.[55] Their story, arguably more difficult to relate than that of their antecedents, is no less worth telling. The community lived on and dispatched a bishop to the Second Council of Nicaea in 787 and the Fourth Council of Constantinople, 869; settlement on the site apparently ended only in the eleventh century, which perhaps marked the end of a millennium and a half of Hellenic influence. To construct the bigger picture and to more fully view some of our deeper questions requires the piecing together of the many small fragments available to us using the best tools at our disposal. For most places in most times of the empire's history, this work has not begun.

Cities of the Dead

Cemetery archaeology in Byzantium is unfortunately underdeveloped and this despite the potential for study of human remains to inform on multiple aspects of life. Discussion of a handful of examples will demonstrate the rich trove of information to be gleaned from careful study of human remains, nearly all of it directly relevant to urban life in some of the least documented areas and periods. While some progress has been made, bioarchaeological investigation of the available material is paltry. Of the 561 cm and burials known from Greece, detailed bioarchaeological methods have been applied in perhaps a score of cases. One city to have portions subjected to such advanced study is Gortyn, which maintained its city status and evidence of seventh- to eighth-century industrial activities and whose citizens undertook the restoration of the Church of St Tito just prior to the year 700.[56] There, study of the contemporary population offers a vivid picture of life for the city inhabitants. The mean age at death for males was 41 years and 34 for females. Among the conditions from which the inhabitants suffered was a high rate (60 percent) of inherited anemia evidenced through cribra orbitalia (evidence of lesions on the skull orbital). This fact is unsurprising, since Mediterranean populations under relentless attack by malaria commonly developed thalassemia (congenital anemia) as a response. Overall, it seems that early Christian populations in Greece suffered from a range of iron and B12 deficiencies or closely related conditions.[57]

At Elaiussa-Sebaste in Cilicia (50 km west of Adana), 116 individuals (sixth to seventh centuries AD) interred in seven separate subterranean vaults. The people buried in these tombs were of higher status. There, as in many Byzantine sites, males and females are found in the record in approximately equal numbers. Despite their presumed wealth, relative to the rest of the population, reasonably high percentages of the population (25 percent of males and 11 percent of females) suffered from chronic health ailments, including periostitic lesions indicating inflammation in tissues around the long bones. Periodontal disease was common, as were degenerative joint diseases (74 percent of males and 50 percent of females) and skeletal lesions associated with poor diet anemia, general infections, and parasite burdens were found in 18 percent of females and 20 percent of males. These numbers imply absolute minima because of the absence of cranial material required for such determinations.[58] All in all, the picture of public health at late antique Elaiussa Sebaste does not differ in crucial ways from what Bourbou explored from populations on Crete.

On Crete Bourbou studied 445 skeletons from six sites (Eleutherna, Kastella, Stylos, Gortyn, Knossos, and Kefali Pediados) ranging in date from the seventh through twelfth centuries. Of these settlements, Kastella and Stylos represent Middle Byzantine period (tenth to thirteenth centuries AD).[59] Not all these sites were cities, of course, though several were. The results are worth revisiting. Mortality among young females (15–34 years old) was due to the hazards of pregnancy and childbirth. Noteworthy is the fact that life expectancy at birth was lower in the middle Byzantine sites (25.55 years at Kastella and 23 years at Stylos) than compared with Gortyn, for example, where life expectancy at birth was 28.63 years.[60] Mean age at death at Gortyn was 41 years for males and 34 years for females (the difference again being mostly attributable to the risks of childbirth).[61] Certainly more investigation is needed, but it seems that life was more difficult and fraught with danger for the average inhabitant of the middle Byzantine city than their earlier ancestors. Insights like these are precious indicators of urban conditions, and much more bioarchaeological work is a desideratum.

Investigation of the diet through stable isotope analysis was instructive but remains in limited use; a much wider application of this suite of tools which measure the ratio of ^{13}C and ^{12}C (carbon) expressed as delta-13-C values (^{15}N and ^{14}N ratios, expressed as delta-15-N values) permit exploration of a whole range of questions regarding diet (for example, the consumption of animal and fish products, and specific kinds of cereal grains as components of the diet) as well as weaning age. Measurement of strontium isotope rations renders possible insights into origins and migration patterns of people in the remote past. Oxygen ratios (expressed as delta-18-O values) permit observation of long-term climate change. Interesting results have been gleaned regarding the diet of throughout isotopic analysis of individuals from sites in Greece ranging in occupation from the sixth to fifteenth centuries AD.[62] Most people, it seemed, relied on the staples of the traditional Mediterranean triad of cereal (mostly wheat and barley), wine, and olive oil. To these staples were sometimes added marine resources, both on the coast and at inland sites, as well as consumption of domesticated animals (mainly pig, sheep/goat, and chickens), as well as the intake of dairy products on a regular basis. Bourbou was also able to determine that in most cases, Byzantine mothers nursed their children later than some contemporary populations, a practice perhaps carried over from Roman era culture.[63]

Advances in ancient DNA studies also can considerably enhance our understanding of a host of questions surrounding the Byzantine city. Ancient DNA (aDNA) has been used to investigate kin groups and trace migrations of multiple groups, and the wider application of these techniques in the context of Byzantine burials could not only reveal relatedness among the inhabitants but also look at specific genetic changes present in local populations. Moreover, the application of aDNA studies to skeletal materials, especially teeth, can offer evidence about various pathogens present and their genetic composition. Ancient DNA studies have only infrequently been applied to Byzantine skeletal remains and there is thus vast potential for its application and a geometric expansion of our knowledge of the populations represented from corpora throughout the Byzantine world.[64]

Even more promising for unraveling the complexities of urban life in Byzantium are recent advances in the so-called omics disciplines (proteomics, metabolomics, among others). The methods on offer in these branches of mass spectrometry and big-data-driven research offer compelling new ways to approach many questions governing our understanding of the Byzantine environment. Few tools promise to revolutionize archaeology in the way that these set of research methods offer. Advances in the field of mass spectrometry, where high-resolution techniques came into wide currency in the 1990s, have led to great leaps in our abilities to detect, categorize, and measure archaeological substances. The study of proteins, complex molecules with unique structures, has been traditionally accomplished through immunoassays, where specific proteins or other substances were detected through the binding of antibodies to antigens. Proteomics offers much more powerful analytic potential, since an entire complement of cellular proteins can be researched through its application. Good examples of specific applications of proteomics in archaeology include the finding of plant residues in ancient containers, but bone, shell, and dental calculus (mineralized microbial biofilm formed on the teeth) have all preserved archaeological proteins.[65]

Metabolomics, the detection and analysis of metabolites produced in the body, is one path of inquiry of relatively recent development that holds considerable promise. Examination of dental calculus has demonstrated that ancient DNA and proteins can be recovered from historic and prehistoric dental calculus.[66] Everything from diet, parasites, the individual and community microbiome, to the presence and bodily response to pathogens can be explored through branches of the 'omics'. Their widespread application in Byzantine archaeology should be the highest priority for researchers in the next decade.[67]

Notes

1 A. P. Kazhdan, "Vizantiyskie goroda v VII-XI vv," *Sovetskaja archeologija*, pp. 164–88, 1954; for a recent analysis and criticism see.

F. Curta, "Postcards from Maurilia, or the historiography of the dark-age cities of Byzantium," *Post-Classical Archaeologies*, vol. 6, pp. 89–110, 2016.

2 G. Ostrogorsky, "Byzantine cities in the Early Middle Ages," *Dumbarton Oaks Papers*, vol. 13, pp. 45–66, 1959, doi: 10.2307/1291128; a note about periodization: I use the terms 'early empire', 'early Byzantium' and 'late antiquity/late antique' to signify the fourth through sixth centuries; the 'Dark Ages' I take to be, based on my earlier writings, to comprise the seventh to ninth centuries, the Middle period of the empire the tenth to twelfth centuries and the late empire to essentially be synonymous with the Palaiologan era at the end of the state across the thirteenth to fifteenth centuries. I am well aware of the problems with such conceptualizations, especially for those (including myself) who can see the value in the 'long late antiquity' continuing in certain places like Sicily and Cyprus into the eighth century: E. James, "The rise and function of the concept "Late Antiquity"," *Journal of Late Antiquity*, vol. 1, no. 1, pp. 20–30, 2008, A. Marcone, "A long late antiquity?: Considerations on a controversial periodization," ibid. pp. 4–19, L. Grig, "Cities in the 'long' Late Antiquity, 2000–2012—a survey essay," *Urban History*, vol. 40, no. 03, pp. 554-566, 2013. Where periodization employed by cited sources differs from that presented above, I note this. Unless otherwise specified, all dates are AD.

3 F. Curta, "Postcards from Maurilia, or the historiography of the dark-age cities of Byzantium," *Post-Classical Archaeologies*, vol. 6, pp. 89–110, 2016, W. Brandes, *Die Städte Kleinasiens im 7. und 8. Jahrhundert*. Berlin: Akademie-Verlag, 1989, W. Brandes and J. Haldon, "Towns, Taxes and Transformation: state, cities and their hinterlands in the East Roman World, ca. 500-800," in *Towns and Their Territories: Between Late Antiquity and the Early Middle Ages*, G. P. Brogiolo, N. Gauthier, and N. Christie Eds.: Brill, 2000, pp. 141–172, M. Veikou, "Space in texts and space as text: a new approach to Byzantine spatial notions," *Scandinavian Journal of Byzantine and Modern Greek Studies*, vol. 2, 2016, M. Veikou, "Settlements in the Greek countryside from 4th to 9th century: forms and patterns," *Antiquité Tardive*, vol. 21, no. 1, pp. 125–133, 2013, M. Veikou, *Byzantine Epirus: A Topography of Transformation. Settlements of the Seventh-Twelfth Centuries in Southern Epirus and Aetoloacarnania, Greece*. Brill, 2012, L. Zavagno, *Cities in Transition: Urbanism in Byzantium Between Late Antiquity and the Early Middle Ages:(AD 500–900)*. Oxford: Archaeopress, 2009, H. Saradi, "The Byzantine City in the Sixth Century: Literary Images and Historical Reality (Athens: Society of Messenian Archaeological Studies)," 2006, J. Henning, *Post-Roman towns, trade and settlement in Europe and Byzantium: v. 1. The heirs of the Roman West*. Berlin, New York: W. de Gruyter, 2007, J. Henning, *Post-Roman towns, trade and settlement in Europe and Byzantium: Vol. 2 v. 2. Byzantium, Pliska, and the Balkans*. Berlin, New York: W. de Gruyter, 2007, L. Zavagno, "La città bizantina tra il V e il IX secolo: le prospettive storiografiche," *Reti Medievali Rivista*, vol. 9, pp. 1–1, 2008, P. Arthur, "Alcune considerazioni sulla natura delle città bizantine," in *Città italiane tra la tarda antichità e l'alto Medioevo: atti del convegno, Ravenna, 26–28 febbraio 2004*. Florence: All'insegna del giglio, 2006, pp. 27–36, L. Zavagno, *The Byzantine City from Heraclius to the Fourth Crusade, 610-1204*. London: Palgrave Macmillan, 2021.

4 I include only a handful of relevant examples, as the literature is too vast to be comprehensively covered here. Constantinople: G. Dagron, "Naissance d'une capitale: Constantinople et ses institutions de 330 à 451," *Bibliothèque byzantine/Etudes*, vol. 7, 1974, W. Müller-Wiener and R. Schiele, *Bildlexikon zur Topographie Istanbuls: Byzantion-Konstantinupolis-Istanbul bis zum Beginn des 17. Jahrhunderts*. Thessalonike: Institute for Balkan Studies, 1977. C. Mango, "Le Developpement urbain de Constantinople (Ive-VII siecles), Travaux et Memories, Monographies 2," ed. Paris: De Boccard, 1985, C. A. Mango, *Studies on Constantinople*. Aldershot: Ashgate, 1993.

C. A. Mango, G. Dagron, and G. Greatrex, Eds. *Constantinople and its hinterland: papers from the Twenty-seventh Spring Symposium of Byzantine Studies, Oxford, April 1993*. Aldershot, Hampshire: Ashgate, 1995, M. Mango, "The commercial map of Constantinople," *Dumbarton Oaks Papers*, vol. 54, pp. 189–207, 2000, P. Magdalino, *Studies on the history and topography of Byzantine Constantinople: Variorum collected studies series*. Aldershot: Ashgate, 2007, K. R. Dark and Ö. Ferudun, *Constantinople: archaeology of a Byzantine megapolis: final report on the Istanbul Rescue Archaeology Project 1998-2004 directed by Ken Dark and Ferudun Özgümüs*: Oxbow Books, 2013. Online. Available: http://swbplus.bsz-bw.de/bsz395186668inh.htm

Materials specified: of contentshttp://swbplus.bsz-bw.de/bsz395186668inh.htm Hours: 20140315160923, K. R. Dark, "Houses, streets and shops in Byzantine Constantinople from the fifth to the twelfth centuries," *Journal of Medieval History*, vol. 30, no. 2, pp. 83–107, 2004; Egypt: R. Alston, *The City in Roman and Byzantine Egypt*. London: Routledge, 2002, G. Majcherek, "Notes on Alexandrian habitat. Roman and Byzantine houses from Kom el-Dikka," *Topoi. Orient-Occident*, vol. 5, no. 1, pp. 133–150, 1995, J. McKenzie and P. R. S. Moorey, *The Architecture of Alexandria and Egypt, c. 300 BC to AD 700*. New Haven: Yale University Press, 2007, W. Kołątaj, G. Majcherek, and E. Parandowska, Eds. *Villa of the Birds: The Excavation and Preservatiopn of the Kom al-Dikka Mosaics*. Cairo: American University in Cairo, 2007, B. Tkaczow, "Alexandrie VIII, Architectural Styles of Ancient Alexandria, Elements of Architectural Decoration from Polish Excavations at Kom el-Dikka (1960–1993)," ed. Warsaw: Polish Centre of Mediterranean Archaeology, University of Warsaw, 2010, G. Majcherek, "Streets and houses of Roman Alexandria revisited," *Antiquity*, vol. 95, no. 379, pp. 1–8, 2021, P. Sheehan, *Babylon of Egypt: The Archaeology of Old Cairo and the Origins of the City (Revised Edition)*. Cairo: American University in Cairo Press, 2010; full bibliography of decades of Polish work in Alexandria can be found here: Alexandria, Kom el-Dikka (uw.edu.pl); much less work has been done on the other cities of Byzantine Egypt, e.g. E. Oren, "A Christian settlement at Ostracine in north Sinai," *Qadmoniot*, vol. 11, pp. 81–87, 1978, D. M. Bailey and P. Grossmann, "The South Church at Hermopolis Magna (Ashmunein): A Preliminary Report," in *Churches Built in Ancient Times: Recent Studies in Early Christian Archaeology. London*, K. S. Painter Ed. London: Society of Antiquaries, 1994, pp. 49–72. – most cities remain unexplored or known only through texts; Palestine: Y. Tsafrir and G. Foerster, "Urbanism at Scythopolis-Bet Shean in the fourth to seventh centuries," *Dumbarton Oaks Papers*, vol. 51, pp. 85–146, 1997, G. Avni, *The Byzantine-Islamic Transition in Palestine: An Archaeological Approach*. Oxford: Oxford University Press, 2014; Syria: a good overview found in C. Foss, "Syria in transition, AD 550–750: an archaeological approach," *Dumbarton Oaks Papers*, vol. 51, pp. 189–269, 1997; Anatolia: P. Niewöhner, *The archaeology of Byzantine Anatolia: From the end of Late Antiquity to the coming of the Turks*. Oxford: Oxford University Press, 2017, C. S. Lightfoot and E. A. Ivison, Eds. *Amorium Reports 3: The Lower City Enclosure Finds Reports and Technical Studies*. Istanbul: Ege Yayinlari, 2012, C. Katsari, C. S. Lightfoot, and A. Özme, *The Amorium Mint and the Coin Finds: Amorium Reports 4*. Akademie Verlag, 2013, E. A. Ivison, "Urban Renewal and Imperial Revival in Byzantium (730–1025)," *Byzantinische Forschungen*, vol. 26, pp. 1–46, 2006, E. A. Ivison, "Amorium in the Byzantine Dark Ages (seventh to ninth centuries)," in *Post-Roman Towns, Trade and Settlement in Europe and Byzantium*, vol. 2, J. Henning Ed., 2007, pp. 25–59, A. Commito, "The cities of southern Asia Minor in the sixth century," in *Asia Minor in the Long Sixth Century: Current Research and Future Directions*, I. Jacobs and H. Elton Eds. Oxford: Oxbow Books, 2019, pp. 109–142; Balkans: A. Dunn, "Stages in the transition from the late antique to the Middle Byzantine urban centre in S. Macedonia and Thrace," in *Aphieroma ston N.G.L. Hammond*, K. Babuskos and N. G. L. Hammond Eds. Thessalonike: Hetaireia Makedonikon Spudon, 1997, A. Dunn, "From polis to kastron in southern Macedonia: Amphipolis, Khrysoupolis, and the Strymon Delta," *Collection de l'Ecole française de Rome*, vol. 105, pp. 399–413, 1999, F. Curta, *The Edinburgh history of the Greeks, c. 500 to 1050: the early Middle Ages*. Edinburgh: Edinburgh University Press, 2011, F. Curta and A. Gandila, "Hoards and Hoarding Patterns in the Early Byzantine Balkans," *Dumbarton Oaks Papers*, vol. 65/66, pp. 45–111, 2011, doi: 10.2307/41933704, A. Dunn, "The transition from polis to kastron in the Balkans (III–VII cc.): general and regional perspectives," *Byzantine and Modern Greek Studies*, vol. 18, no. 1, pp. 60–81, 1994, S. Kamani, "Butrint in the mid-Byzantine period: a new interpretation," ibid.vol. 35, no. 2, pp. 115–133, 2011; Italy: 17, P. Arthur, "Alcune considerazioni sulla natura delle città bizantine," in *Città italiane tra la tarda antichità e l'alto Medioevo: atti del convegno, Ravenna, 26–28 febbraio 2004*. Florence: All'insegna del giglio, 2006, pp. 27–36, E. Zanini, "Le città dell'Italia bizantina: qualche appunto per un'agenda della ricerca," *Reti Medievali Rivista*, vol. 11, 2, pp. 45–66, 2010, P. R. Arthur, *Naples, from Roman town to city-state: an archaeological perspective*. Rome: British School at Rome, 2002; Islands: L. Zavagno, *Cyprus between Late Antiquity and the Early Middle Ages (ca. 600–800): An Island in Transition*. London: Routledge, 2017, L. Zavagno, "At the Edge of Two Empires: The Economy of Cyprus between Late Antiquity and the Early Middle Ages (650s–800s CE)," *Dumbarton Oaks Papers*, vol. 65/66, pp. 121–155, 2011, doi: 10.2307/41933706, L. Arcifa and M. Sgarlata, Eds. *From polis to madina: La trasformazione delle città siciliane tra Tardoantico e Alto Medioevo*. Bari:

Edipuglia, 2020. and now the chapters of S. Cosentino, *A Companion to Byzantine Italy*. Brill, 2021, pp. 360-540.

5 For this (large-scale) regional approach, see the volumes of the *Tabula Imperii Byzantini*: H. Hunger, J. Koder (eds.) *Tabula Imperii Byzantini* (Vienna: Verlag de Österreichischen Akademie der Wissenschaften, 1976–).

6 P. Niewöhner *et al.*, "Bronze Age höyüks, Iron Age hilltop forts, Roman poleis and Byzantine pilgrimage in Germia and its vicinity. 'Connectivity' and a lack of 'definite places' on the central Anatolian high plateau," *Anatolian Studies,* vol. 63, pp. 97–136, 2013.

7 Perhaps due in part to its being the epicenter of the Montanist movement: W. Tabbernee and P. Lampe, *Pepouza and Tymion: The Discovery and Archaeological Exploration of a Lost Ancient City and an Imperial Estate*. Walter de Gruyter, 2008.

8 M. G. Randazzo, "Knossos and Heraklion in the Byzantine-Islamic transition (late 7th–mid-10th century) An archaeological perspective into shifting patterns of settlement ruralisation and urbanisation on medieval Crete," *Journal of Greek Archaeology,* vol. 5, pp. 448–467, 2020, S. Cosentino, "From Gortyn to Heraklion? A Note on Cretan Urbanism During the 8th Century," *Byzantina Symmeikta,* pp. 73–89, 2019.

9 Urban development paralleled intensive agricultural development investment in the region from the Palmyrene to the Red Sea. See M. Decker, *Tilling the Hateful Earth: Agricultural Production and Trade in the Late Antique East*. Oxford: Oxford University Press, 2009.

10 F. Curta, "Postcards from Maurilia, or the historiography of the dark-age cities of Byzantium," *Post-Classical Archaeologies,* vol. 6, pp. 89–110, 2016, L. Zavagno, *Cities in Transition: Urbanism in Byzantium Between Late Antiquity and the Early Middle Ages:(AD 500-900)*. Oxford: Archaeopress, 2009, L. Zavagno, "La città bizantina tra il V e il IX secolo: le prospettive storiografiche," *Reti Medievali Rivista,* vol. 9, pp. 1–1, 2008, R. Hodges, "A 'god-guarded'city? The 'new'medieval town of Butrint," *Byzantine and Modern Greek Studies,* vol. 39, no. 2, pp. 191–218, 2015.

11 G. L. Cowgill, "Origins and development of urbanism: archaeological perspectives," *Annual Review of Anthropology,* vol. 33, pp. 525–549, 2004, p. 526.

12 N. Tsivikis, "Beyond the Invisible Cities of Byzantium," *European Journal of Post-Classical Archaeologies,* vol. 10, pp. 325–334, 2020.

13 H. S. J. Jansen, "Wrestling with the angel: on problems of definition in urban historiography," *Urban History,* vol. 23, no. 3, pp. 277–299, 1996, R. Camagni, "Afterthoughts on urban economic theory and its focus," *Investigaciones Regionales= Journal of Regional Research,* no. 36, pp. 87–105, 2016.

14 H. Saradi, "The kallos of the Byzantine city: the development of a rhetorical topos and historical reality," *Gesta,* vol. 34, no. 1, pp. 37–56, 1995.

15 L. Zavagno, *Cities in Transition: Urbanism in Byzantium Between Late Antiquity and the Early Middle Ages:(AD 500–900)*. Oxford: Archaeopress, 2009, L. Zavagno, "La città bizantina tra il V e il IX secolo: le prospettive storiografiche," *Reti Medievali Rivista,* vol. 9, pp. 1–1, 2008, L. Zavagno, "'A wonderful city of palms and dates': Salamis-Constantia in transition from Late Antiquity to the early Middle Ages (ca. 600–ca. 800 CE)," *Mediterranean Historical Review,* vol. 29, no. 2, pp. 111–138, 2014/07/03 2014, doi: 10.1080/09518967.2014.975566.

16 W. Brandes and J. Haldon, "Towns, Taxes and Transformation: state, cities and their hinterlands in the East Roman World, ca. 500–800," in *Towns and Their Territories: Between Late Antiquity and the Early Middle Ages*, G. P. Brogiolo, N. Gauthier, and N. Christie Eds.: Brill, 2000, pp. 141-172, A. Kazhdan, "Polis and kastron: in Theophanes and in some other historical texts," in *Eupsychia: mélanges offerts à Hélène Ahrweiler*, vol. 2, M. Balard Ed. Paris: Publications de la Sorbonne, 1998, pp. 349–350, J. Haldon, "The idea of the town in the Byzantine empire," in *The idea and ideal of the town between late antiquity and the early middle ages*, G. P. Brogiolo and B. Ward-Perkins Eds. Leiden: Brill, 1999, pp. 1–23.

17 W. Brandes, *Die Städte Kleinasiens im 7. und 8. Jahrhundert*. Berlin: Akademie-Verlag, 1989, 189.

18 A. Leone, *The end of the pagan city: religion, economy, and urbanism in late antique North Africa*. Oxford: Oxford University Press, 2013.

19 J. H. W. G. Liebeschuetz, *The decline and fall of the Roman city*. Oxford: Oxford University Press, 2003.

20 M. Veikou, "Space in texts and space as text: A new approach to Byzantine spatial notions," *Scandinavian Journal of Byzantine and Modern Greek Studies,* vol. 2, 2016, M. Veikou, "Urban or

Rural? Theoretical Remarks on the Settlement Patterns in Byzantine Epirus (7th-11th centuries)," *Byzantinische Zeitschrift,* vol. 103, no. 1, pp. 171–193, 2010; of value, but still presenting difficulties when widely accepted approaches are absent: L. Leontidou, "Postmodernism and the city: Mediterranean versions," *Urban Studies,* vol. 30, no. 6, pp. 949–965, 1993, L. Leontidou, "Alternatives to modernism in (southern) urban theory: Exploring in-between spaces," *International Journal of Urban and Regional Research,* vol. 20, no. 2, pp. 178–195, 1996, L. Leontidou, "On linkages between urbanism and urban restructuring in Mediterranean Europe," in *Tradition in modernity: Southern Europe in question,* C. Kreyder Ed. Madrid: University Complutense, 1998, pp. 85–100, L. Leontidou, "Beyond the borders of Mediterranean Cities: the Mediterranean City in transition," *Quarterly of International Sociology,* vol. 18, no. 3–4, pp. 131–140, 2009.

21 C. Saliou, *Le traité d'urbanisme de Julien d'Ascalon: droit et architecture en Palestine au VIe siècle.* Paris: de Boccard, 1996.

22 D. Skre, "Post-substantivist towns and trade, ad 600–1000," *Means of Exchange: Dealing with Silver in the Viking Age. Aarhus: Aarhus University Press (Kaupang Excavation Project Publication Series, vol. 2, Norske Oldfunn 23),* pp. 327–341, 2008.

23 R. Hodges, "A 'god-guarded'city? The 'new'medieval town of Butrint," *Byzantine and Modern Greek Studies,* vol. 39, no. 2, pp. 191–218, 2015.

24 S. Greenslade and R. Hodges, "The aristocratic oikos on the Vrina Plain, Butrint c. AD 830–1200," ibid.vol. 37, no. 1, pp. 1–19, 2013.

25 C. Bouras, "Aspects of the Byzantine city, eighth-fifteenth centuries," in *The Economic History of Byzantium,* A. Laiou Ed. Washington, D.C.: Dumbarton Oaks, 2002, pp. 497–528, p.500.

26 M. E. Smith, "Form and meaning in the earliest cities: a new approach to ancient urban planning," *Journal of Planning History,* vol. 6, no. 1, pp. 3–47, 2007.

27 G. L. Cowgill, "Origins and development of urbanism: archaeological perspectives," *Annual Review of Anthropology,* vol. 33, pp. 525–549, 2004.

28 W. Sombart, *Der moderne kapitalismus.* Munich: Duncker & Humblot, 1902, 128; M. Weber, D. Martindale, and G. Neuwirth, *The city.* New York: Free Press New York, 1958, p. 68–72; These models are not always carefully considered; for an archaeology of these ideas: M. I. Finley, "The ancient city: from Fustel de Coulanges to Max Weber and beyond," *Comparative Studies in Society and History,* vol. 19, no. 3, pp. 305–327, 1977.

29 G. Kriehn, "The city beautiful," *Municipal Affairs,* vol. 3, pp. 594–601, 1899.

30 M. J. Decker, *The Byzantine Dark Ages.* London: Bloomsbury, 2016.

31 I use the word 'amplifying' here, deliberately avoiding 'escape' or 'overcome' the classical paradigm, which I deem to be deeply rooted and important in the Western cultural tradition and not something negative to be lightly discarded, but a presence to be engaged consciously and creatively considering what comes after.

32 E. Schellekens and P. Goldie, *The aesthetic mind: Philosophy and psychology.* Oxford University Press, 2011, R. Afhami and S. Mohammadi-Zarghan, "The Big Five, aesthetic judgment styles, and art interest," *Europe's Journal of Psychology,* vol. 14, no. 4, p. 764, 2018.

33 P. Hemenway, *Divine Proportion: Phi in Art, Nature, and Science.* New York: Sterling Publishing Company, Inc., 2005.

34 L. Pacioli, *Divina Proportione.* Vienna: C. Graeser, 1889.

35 M. Iosa, G. Morone, and S. Paolucci, "Phi in physiology, psychology and biomechanics: The golden ratio between myth and science," *Biosystems,* vol. 165, pp. 31–39, 2018.

36 R. van Gend, "The Fibonacci sequence and the golden ratio in music," *Notes on Number Theory and Discrete Mathematics,* vol. 20, no. 1, pp. 72–77, 2014.

37 D. L. Smail, *On Deep History and the Brain.* Berkeley: Univ of California Press, 2007, p. 159.

38 U. Peschlow, "Die Johanneskirche des Studios in Istanbul. Bericht über die jüngsten Untersuchungsergebnisse in XVI. Intern. Byzantinistenkongr. (Wien Oktober 1981)," *Jahrbuch der Osterreichischen Byzantinistik Graz, Wien, Koln,* vol. 32, no. 4, 1982, M. S. Pekak, "İstanbul'da Studios Manastırı, H. Ioannes Prodromos Kilisesi I," *Sanat Tarihi Dergisi,* vol. 10, no. 10, pp. 101–121, 2000.

39 A. Cameron, *Byzantine Matters.* Princeton: Princeton University Press, 2014, pp. 87–111.

40 B. V. Pentcheva, "Hagia Sophia and multisensory aesthetics," *Gesta,* vol. 50, no. 2, pp. 93–111, 2011, B. V. Pentcheva and J. S. Abel, "Icons of sound: auralizing the lost voice of Hagia Sophia," *Speculum,* vol. 92, no. S1, pp. S336–S360, 2017, S. E. J. Gerstel, C. Kyriakakis, K. T. Raptis, S.

Antonopoulos, and J. Donahue, "Soundscapes of Byzantium: The Acheiropoietos basilica and the cathedral of Hagia Sophia in Thessaloniki," *hesperia,* vol. 87, no. 1, pp. 177–213, 2018.
41 S. E. J. Gerstel, C. Kyriakakis, K. T. Raptis, S. Antonopoulos, and J. Donahue, "Soundscapes of Byzantium: The Acheiropoietos basilica and the cathedral of Hagia Sophia in Thessaloniki," *hesperia,* vol. 87, no. 1, pp. 177–213, 2018.
42 N. Schibille, *Hagia Sophia and the Byzantine Aesthetic Experience.* Farnham, UK: Routledge, 2016.
43 G. Leucci, G. Di Giacomo, I. Ditaranto, I. Miccoli, and G. Scardozzi, "Integrated Ground-penetrating Radar and Archaeological Surveys in the Ancient City of Hierapolis of Phrygia (Turkey)," *Archaeological Prospection,* vol. 20, no. 4, pp. 285-301, 2013.
44 M. A. Kaya, Y. L. Ekinci, P. Yiğit, and C. S. Lightfoot, "Magnetic investigation at the Amorium archaeological site, Emirdağ, Afyon, Turkey," *J. Balkan Geophys. Soc.,* vol. 10, no. 1, pp. 1–7, 2007, P. Bikoulis, H. Elton, J. F. Haldon, and J. M. L. Newhard, "Above as below: application of multiple survey techniques at a Byzantine church at Avkat," *Landscape Dynamics and Settlement Patterns in Northern Anatolia during the Roman and Byzantine Period,* pp. 101–117, 2015, W. Rabbel *et al.*, "Discovery of a Byzantine Church in Iznik/Nicaea, Turkey: an educational case history of geophysical prospecting with combined methods in urban areas," *Archaeological Prospection,* vol. 22, no. 1, pp. 1–20, 2015.
45 L. Mantovan and L. Nanni, "The computerization of archaeology: survey on artificial intelligence techniques," *SN Computer Science,* vol. 1, no. 5, pp. 1–32, 2020, M. L. Gualandi, G. Gattiglia, and F. Anichini, "An Open System for collection and automatic recognition of pottery through Neural Network Algorithms," *Heritage,* vol. 4, no. 1, pp. 140–159, 2021, W. Sakpere and V. Gallerani, "An intelligent machine-driven perspective to archaeological pottery reassembly," in *Encyclopedia of Information Science and Technology, Fifth Edition*: New York: IGI Global, 2021, pp. 127–137.
46 P. Horden and N. Purcell, *The Corrupting Sea: A Study of Mediterranean History.* Oxford: Wiley-Blackwell, 2000, p. 90.
47 J. Lascaratos and S. Marketos, "The fatal disease of the Byzantine Emperor Andronicus III Palaeologus (1328–1341 AD)," *Journal of the Royal Society of Medicine,* vol. 90, no. 2, pp. 106–109, 1997.
48 The WHO reported 229 million cases of malaria worldwide in 2019; 409,000 people died. Since malaria has burdened human populations since at least 10,000 BP, its significance as a force in human history is obvious. P. W. Hedrick, "Population genetics of malaria resistance in humans," *Heredity,* vol. 107, no. 4, pp. 283–304, 2011.
49 G. A. W. Rook, *The hygiene hypothesis and Darwinian Medicine.* Basel: Birkhäuser, 2009.
50 O. Dubois *et al.*, "Lupin (*Lupinus* spp.) seeds exert anthelmintic activity associated with their alkaloid content," *Scientific Reports,* vol. 9, no. 1, pp. 1–12, 2019, F. Jirsa and V. Winiwarter, "Eingeweidewürmer in Galens Schriften," *Wien Klin Wochenschr,* vol. 122, no. 3, pp. 14–18, 2010.
51 I. Jacobs and M. Waelkens, "From Early Byzantium to the Middle Ages at Sagalassos," *The Long Seventh Century. Continuity and Discontinuity in an Age of Transition Peter Lang, Oxford,* pp. 163-198, 2015.
52 J. Baeten, E. Marinova, V. De Laet, P. Degryse, D. De Vos, and M. Waelkens, "Faecal biomarker and archaeobotanical analyses of sediments from a public latrine shed new light on ruralisation in Sagalassos, Turkey," *Journal of Archaeological Science,* vol. 39, no. 4, pp. 1143–1159, 2012, doi: http://dx.doi.org/10.1016/j.jas.2011.12.019.
53 K. Dirix *et al.*, "Multi-element soil prospection aiding geophysical and archaeological survey on an archaeological site in suburban Sagalassos (SW-Turkey)," ibid.vol. 40, no. 7, pp. 2961–2970, 2013.
54 M. Waelkens, "Sagalassos, Archaeology of," in *Encyclopedia of Global Archaeology (New York),* C. Smith Ed. New York: Springer, 2019, pp. 6434–6443.
55 A. K. Vionis, J. Poblome, B. De Cupere, and M. Waelkens, "A Middle-Late Byzantine pottery assemblage from Sagalassos: typo-chronology and sociocultural interpretation," *Hesperia,* vol. 79, no. 3, pp. 423–464, 2010.
56 L. Zavagno, *Cities in Transition: Urbanism in Byzantium Between Late Antiquity and the Early Middle Ages:(AD 500-900).* Oxford: Archaeopress, 2009.
57 C. Bourbou, *The People of Early Byzantine Eleutherna and Messene: 6th-7th Centuries A.D.: A Bioarchaeological Approach.* Athens: University of Crete, 2004, p. 33; P. W. Hedrick, "Population genetics of malaria resistance in humans," *Heredity,* vol. 107, no. 4, pp. 283–304, 2011.

58 R. R. Paine, R. Vargiu, A. Coppa, C. Morselli, and E. E. Schneider, "A health assessment of high status Christian burials recovered from the Roman–Byzantine archeological site of Elaiussa Sebaste, Turkey," *Homo,* vol. 58, no. 2, pp. 173–190, 2007.
59 C. Bourbou, *Health and disease in Byzantine Crete (7th–12th centuries AD)*. Farnham, UK: Ashgate, 2016, 40.
60 ibid., 40.
61 C. Bourbou, *The people of early Byzantine Eleutherna and Messene: 6th-7th centuries A.D.: a bioarchaeological approach*. Athens: University of Crete, 2004, p. 33.
62 C. Bourbou, *Health and disease in Byzantine Crete (7th–12th Centuries AD)*. Farnham, UK: Ashgate, 2016, p. 144 ff.
63 ibid., p.164.
64 C. Ottoni, F.-X. Ricaut, N. Vanderheyden, N. Brucato, M. Waelkens, and R. Decorte, "Mitochondrial analysis of a Byzantine population reveals the differential impact of multiple historical events in South Anatolia," *European Journal of Human Genetics,* vol. 19, no. 5, pp. 571–576, 2011, M. Rubini, Y. S. Erdal, M. Spigelman, P. Zaio, and H. D. Donoghue, "Paleopathological and molecular study on two cases of ancient childhood leprosy from the Roman and Byzantine Empires," *International Journal of Osteoarchaeology,* vol. 24, no. 5, pp. 570–582, 2014, A. M. Devault *et al.*, "A molecular portrait of maternal sepsis from Byzantine Troy," *Elife,* vol. 6, p. e20983, 2017.
65 J. Hendy, "Ancient protein analysis in archaeology," *Science Advances,* vol. 7, no. 3, p. eabb9314, 2021.
66 I. M. Velsko *et al.*, "The dental calculus metabolome in modern and historic samples," *Metabolomics,* vol. 13, no. 11, pp. 1–17, 2017.
67 I currently lead an interdisciplinary project investigating remains in Byzantine and medieval Italy via proteomics, among other methods.

5

SPATIAL ORGANIZATION IN LATE BYZANTINE CITIES (13TH–14TH CENTURIES)

Tonia Kiousopoulou

If we were to regard the urban space as a carrier of meanings and symbols, it is clear that its organization is interwoven with respective formation of social relations. Thus, city space is by definition organised in a manner corresponding to the needs of the occasional governing bodies and social forces that aim at leaving theirs imprints so as to be established through it as well as to legitimize their existence.

These general principles raise the question of how space was organised in Greek cities during the last centuries of their Byzantine existence. Although, deep down, urban history is the history of individual cities, I will not seek to reconstruct each settlement known from written sources. I will utilize the information available in order to establish, with the requisite abstraction, a typology and to have the social mechanisms that can explain it discharged to the extent possible.

It should be noted here that the research of late Byzantine cities is confronted with, sometimes insurmountable, difficulties. No theory about the city and architecture was developed in Byzantium. The difficulty in "spotting" the cities existing at the period under examination is interwoven with the lack of a theory. Written sources are not always precise as regards the definition of a city. On many occasions, the terms *ἄστυ, πόλις, πολίχνη, κάστρον φρούριον* are indiscriminately used in texts, even when reference is made to the same settlement.[1] On the other hand, the structure of ecclesiastical administration was based on the size of the population in the respective settlement; as such, a metropolitan's or a bishop's see was always a city.[2] However, the population criterion is not necessarily safe in that context. Rarely was a bishop's see abolished, even when the given city's population was reduced. In light of this information, the bibliography available – particularly the studies on historical geography – is not very helpful in searching for and locating urban formations, since it does not usually analyze the criteria on the basis of which it classifies some into the category of cities and others into the category of villages.

Therefore, two separate questions are raised. First, by which criteria does a modern historian distinguish cities from other settlements of the past? Second, what differentiated them in the collective perception of the society he/she studies? Clearly, the answers to both questions are not identical, since settlements have to be examined in their historical dimension, i.e. within a given time and space. For the purposes of the analysis attempted, I have

DOI: 10.4324/9780429203923-7

considered essential the conditions which a settlement must fulfill in order to acquire urban character according to F. Braudel: the division of labor within it and its differentiation from labor in the field, its development, the control it exercises on the natural surroundings, and its co-existence with other smaller or larger settlements.[3] I do not avoid another convention as well: limiting myself to the settlements referred to as cities in the bibliography. Still, the search for the criteria which the Byzantines themselves employed in order to define a city lies under each stage of this review.

Finally, a substantial obstacle in studying late Byzantine cities is the absence of any systematic excavation thereof; that is why there is little available excavated evidence.[4] Written sources, too, are piecemeal. A historian of Byzantium does not have the "luxury" of the extensive records of the contemporary medieval West that have survived. As known, the Byzantine records available lie with the large monasteries and have survived whenever and on account of relating to their history and property. All other Byzantine records, either public or private, have disappeared. Nonetheless, in order to approach the past, the first and decisive step is to put the questions. Despite the lack of sources and various factual information, the questions exist and render us familiar with the late cities, even when it is difficult to answer them.

The Planning of a City

It is known that early cities changed their form on transitioning to the middle age and that any new ones that started being built at the time did not follow the late antiquity planning rules. The spread of Christianity was a phenomenon of decisive importance for the urban web's modification. Already since the 5th century, local bishops were erecting massive ecclesiastical buildings at the cities' centers, without regard for the existing logic of the canvas. These massive buildings that were churches or/and monasteries were creating a novel street layout reality, with irregular streets.[5] At the same time, on many occasions, the residents' daily life commanded use of construction material from older buildings or the occupation of places used for another purpose in the past. The cities' monumental character was thus gradually destroyed; in any case, with the passage of time, it ceased to have a reason of existence.[6] On the other hand, new cities were built at naturally fortified positions. The instructions contained in the Byzantine *Taktika* on how and, more importantly, where should a city be built make no reference to the organization of its space[7]: they rather reflect the central government's will to secure the areas under its jurisdiction from a military point of view. The bibliography available so far, which excluded the application of an all-embracing planning policy and concluded that after the 7th–8th century, city space was organised randomly, relied on the otherwise vague guidelines of the Administration and on emergency war conditions.

In order to build a picture, the minimal archeological data obligate us to have recourse to written sources. First of all, it is important that no written description of any Byzantine city has been saved. Rhetoric texts, the so called *ἐκφράσεις*, which in a way describe the praised city in its entirety, are certainly useful, however, not so much as regards the specific buildings or places which they praise, but mostly as to how their authors perceived the urban landscape and conveyed it through their words. As such, it is necessary to seek the information scattered in narrative or record sources and classify them in order for it to make sense. This approach, however, has the disadvantage that the image of the built-up space that is formed is a static one that does not give out the gradual stages in a city's building history, while, at the same time, the typology sought relies on factual evidence relating to only very few cities of the Paleologian era.

In order to approach the key question, I think that we must begin with a city which acquires urban features during the period under examination. Ioannina was such a city.

Around 1227, the metropolitan of Naupaktos, John Apokaukos, praises the decision of the Michael I Doukas, the Despot of Epirus, to turn *εἰς μόρφωσιν κάστρου* the *πολίδιον* of Ioannina.[8] This decision, which was combined with the settlement of a large number of refugees in Ioannina from other regions of the old Byzantine empire, allows us to investigate which residential elements attributed city features to the existing *πολίδιον*.

Ioannina is a representative example of the limitations set by our sources. John Apokaukos' text does not provide us with any specific information as to whether and how was the city planned. For certain, walls defining its area were erected and the citadel, where the Despot's palace was built, was repaired. The metropolis, which, as has been claimed,[9] was located at the northwestern hill, opposite the citadel, was also founded at the time. Apokaukos admires the compassion of Michael Doukas who provided shelters and land *κατ' ἀξίαν* for the foreigners to stay. Yet, he does not tell us if the plot they received or/and the area where they could settle was determined according to their social background. In any case, the *κατ' ἀξίαν* concession of urban land presupposed a hierarchical sense of space and, therefore, its intentional arrangement, which obviously took place with the citadel as point of reference. In addition, the grand bathhouse that has been excavated[10] near the metropolis' hill and dates to the 13th century is further evidence of an, even rudimentary, planning, since vicinity to the lake facilitated its operation. Anyway, the lake secured the city's water supply, in general.

Subsequent texts of the 14th century, the Chronicle of Ioannina and the Chronicle of the Tocco, quote the *γουλᾶς* and a *πλάτζα* as significant spots. The *γουλᾶς* and its identification have preoccupied the Ioannina researchers on several occasions.[11] In all probability, this was the citadel and, by extension, the Despot's palace.[12] The *πλάτζα* referred to in the Chronicle of the Tocco remains unclear and unidentified.[13] The absence of open public spaces in the form of squares in Byzantine cities would make us think that the Chronicle's author used a word that was in line with his own descriptions. In the Byzantine context, as well as in the context of the text, the Chronicle's *πλάτζα* should probably be identified with the market operating within the walls, near the central gate, according to an opinion.[14] Furthermore, according to the Chronicle of Ioannina, Despot Thomas converted buildings of the metropolis into grain barns and haylofts.[15] I believe that this piece of information makes it reasonable to assume that in order to be used as storehouses, the metropolis' buildings must have been near the *πλάτζα*: this is an assumption supported by the setting up of a local bazaar, the proceeds of which the emperor granted to the Ioannina Metropolis by a chrysobull.[16] It is most likely, therefore, that outside the *γουλᾶς*, probably between the two hills of the citadel and the metropolis, a uniform space was being formed, with religious, commercial, and, whenever necessary, political functions.

Given these facts, both the Despot's decision to give a new image to the *πολίδιον* of Ioannina and the amassing of the basic functions between the two hills – the bathhouse's and the market's existence there – suggest some planning, although we know neither who effected it nor exactly which planning rules were selected and implemented. The choice of the place where the metropolis was erected must not have been random either. In my opinion, the fact that the hill next to the citadel was chosen reveals the sovereign's wish to ensure a balance between the political and the ecclesiastical power, which would also be stamped at a spatial level. The precise planning of the political and ecclesiastical power, as well as the buildable area's organization on the basis of social criteria, per Apokaukos' testimony, were certainly the first steps in upgrading the *πολίδιον* to a city.

The case of Ioannina, which was *ἄστυ μέν ... τῶν πολλῶν διαφέρον*,[17] shows the difficulties encountered in studying the urban space and its evolution. It further shows that the information available makes no effective contribution to the discussion among archeologists and architecture historians regarding the broadly acceptable position that Byzantine cities of the middle and late ages were not a product of planning.[18] Evidently, the morphology of the land had an impact on the settlements that were built at naturally fortified places, on hillsides, such as Didymoteichon, Servia, or Mystras. It has been observed that drawing horizontal and vertical roads was not easy in those cities, which is why buildings were more loosely planned.[19] Nonetheless, we note that in Mystras, which is the best kept late Byzantine settlement, the roads follow the contour lines. Finally, space organization laid down rules, which determined who and where would one settle, depending on the power held. From that point of view, the conflict between the Metropolitan John Apokaukos with the Despot Theodore Doukas' brother, Constantine, is characteristic. The luxurious construction of the bishop's residence in Naupaktos, which Apokaukos describes in a letter of his to the Metropolitan of Thessaloniki, was built at a high city point.[20] Constantine Doukas opted to build his palace near the bishop's residence, thus causing Apokaukos' wrath, who accused him of removing marbles and doors from the bishop's residence. Apokaukos describes Constantine's palace as resembling a *σουφᾶς*.[21] The form of *σουφᾶς* is attributed to Arabic architecture,[22] but I have the impression that here the Metropolitan uses the word just mockingly. The detailed and scornful description of the building shows that Apokaukos was furious not only about the stealing of the marbles and other construction materials from the bishop's residence but mostly about the tangible questioning of his power, as this was imprinted on the city area.

Ioannina belongs to that group of settlements whose functioning was upgraded from the end of the middle ages onward. Of the cities that interest us, Didymoteichon, Servia, Mystras, Christoupoli, and Rentina belong to the same group.[23] Their upgrading falls in the context of the defense strategy that had been drawn up by the central or/and regional authority and they constitute examples of a castle's rearrangement into an organised settlement. In reality, that is, these cities were developed through the population's settlement around the original core, which was the citadel, and the organization of any activities, as planned according to the residents' needs, outside such citadel, within a space defined by a new wall.

At the same time, there is the group of cities which already existed since the earlier periods and which maintained some of their early features, obviously adjusted. Adrianople, Serres, and Berroia belong to that group. All laid on plains and were the largest ones in terms of size. In addition, they are praised by texts about their residents' number[24] and they had evidenced commercial activity. Cities of the Thracian shore, Ainos, Selymbria, Kallipolis, Polystylon (former Abdera) and Herakleia, which were ports, too, also existed since the early times.

From the above, it is deduced that the urban set-up of the late cities, particularly of the "new" ones, was not haphazard, and that, at any rate, they were arranged with reference to the citadel, where the local ruler's seat and the bishop's residence were found. Their planning conveys the sense of space and the residents' needs; something which, after all, becomes apparent, once we attempt to "explore" their interior.

Centers-Routes-Neighborhoods

Modern architectural theory, which defines urban space by means of existing centers, routes, and quarters can be used as guiding thread in "exploring" a city. In order for the elements in question – centers, routes, and quarters – to be studied in historical terms, it is not only necessary for them to be located in the period under examination but also, mostly, to trace the dynamics of their formation in conjunction with existing social needs.

The narrative sources lay emphasis on the walls protecting the cities. The land and its habitants were surrounded by walls, which separated an organised settlement from the country. In other words, they were rendering it a geographical, social and administrative or/and military entity, for controlling which the occasional government appointed a lord who enjoyed its trust.

All cities were walled. In fact, some of them had more than one line of walls. The importance and grandeur of a city was imprinted on the walls' construction, strength, as well as on their aesthetics.[25] For that matter, walls are the first and almost the single element described in greater detail compared to other features thereof. From an archeological point of view, walls mark the boundaries and define the area surrounded. Furthermore, until today, they constitute the most visible remnants of the cities that concern us and indicate the area which they covered. For instance, it is estimated that the lower city of Servia covered an area of about 75,000 square meters and the upper city an area of 20,000 square meters, while the walls of Ioannina enclosed an area of 190,000 square meters.[26]

The citadel constituted one of the centers of the late, larger, or less populated cities, as was associated with administrative and military operations. Traces of a maybe two-storey building, with a double water cistern, which according to H. Kalligas was a public one (possibly the seat of the administration), [27] are found in the so-called upper city of Monemvasia, while there is evidence that the *γουλᾶς*, where the Despot resided, in Ioannina was also turned into the residents' assembly area.[28] In addition, S. Ćurčić has noted that the form of "citadels-palaces", which included large residential complexes, became general in the 14th century.[29]

Certainly the metropolis, which constituted the city's religious center, was of great importance to a city's identity. Already since the early age, the metropolis in Serres was located on the central road, [30] while in Berroia, in the middle period, it was moved further south from the position it held before.[31] In Monemvasia, the metropolitan church of Elkomenos Christos had been erected at the juncture of two main axes. In later settlements, such as Servia, Mystras, or Rentina, the metropolis had been built to the side, adjoining the walls.[32]

Finally, the cities' economic center was the market. In Serres, the existence of the gate of *Φόρος* points to an entire quarter, which perhaps also spread outside the walls,[33] whereat, later on, at the end of the 14th century, the Ottomans built the Bezesteni, which survives to these days. Evidently, the *Φόρος* was identified with the *ἐμπόριον*, where *ξενοδοχεῖα* and *ἐργαστήρια* were located.[34] There is evidence of a *Φόρος* also in Berroia.[35] An express reference to *μπορίο*, i.e. trading space, outside the citadel's walls,[36] is also made about Arta, where there were houses, *φράχτες και μουρσία*.[37] In addition, archeological research has located in the lower town of Servia, traces of a cistern and traces of a large edifice which, according to the excavators, laid in the city center. Excavation findings, also from the same area, evidence the existence of shops.[38] Finally, ground floor workshops, attached to the external wall and with a spacing in-between for the rain waters to run out (something which allows them to be identified as forges or potteries), have been excavated in the western section of Rentina.[39]

We observe that in all cities, the main route was the one connecting the citadel, as administrative center, with one of the outer wall gates.[40] Out of the aforementioned cities, the one in respect of which we have a relatively better idea is Serres. The workshops or residences that were transferred from time to time and eventually came in the possession of the Prodromos monastery or of the Athonite monasteries were all near *τῆς βασιλικῆς πόρτας* or along the *βασιλική* road,[41] ending at the gate of *Φόρος*. Next to the gate of *Φόρος* was the *παραπόρτιον*, another gate from which a smaller trade route began, probably crossing the *βασιλική* road.[42] As for the *Βασιλική* gate, which, by an oversight, is identified in a document with the gate of *Φόρος*,[43] it appears that it was connecting the main city to the citadel and laid on its eastern side.[44] In Serres, therefore, the central route was identified with the *βασιλική* road, which connected the gate of *Φόρος* in the northwest to the *Βασιλική* gate in the northeast, passing from the metropolis. In broad lines, the image of Serres was representative of that of other cities in plains. In Berroia, the main road, a remnant of the early times' drawing,[45] ended at the *Βασιλική* gate northwards and, on the southeast, probably at the *Οψικιανή* gate, mentioned by John Cantacuzene, which, much later, remained known as the gate of *Παλαιός Φόρος*.[46] Near the *Βασιλική* gate laid the citadel that was repaired by Stefan Dušan, who, however, started building yet another citadel, on the south part of the city.[47] In Berroia, one can also see the street that was intersecting the main road and which was ending at the exit gate to Western Macedonia.[48]

In Monemvasia, the main road axis laid on the street's extension from the port and was crossing the lower city lengthwise. There was yet another road though, intersecting the one above, which connected the sea gate of the wall to the upper town.[49] Finally, in Ioannina, which was a "new" city, the central road most probably started at the gate in the so-called Thomas's tower[50] and, continuing serpentine, reached the citadel, while passing through the flat area where we have guessed that the *πλάτζα* and the metropolis' buildings were obviously with one branch ending at the metropolis.

If the central route in all cities, both those existing since the early times and the more recent ones, was indeed stretching along the axis connecting one gate of the outer wall to the citadel, then the opinion, which places the merchants' quarter always outside the (external) walls, must be revised. Especially as regards cities with a long trading tradition, the examples of Serres and Berroia render this opinion's revision necessary. However, in order for the drawing of the central route on the axis in question to be confirmed by excavations, we have to look for the existence of other public buildings, too, alongside it. Furthermore, on that central axis and probably near the citadel's walls, we must also look for the bishop's residence, the local bishop's seat. We have seen where the buildings of the Ioannina Metropolis and the bishop's residence in Naupaktos were, in all probability. We also know, again from a John Apokaukos' letter, that in Arta, the river Aracthos that surrounded it on the western, eastern and northern side carried away the bishop's residence and its surrounding edifices,[51] which we therefore assume were located at the bottom of the hill where the metropolis was built.[52] Despite the lack of any clear information on the location of the bishop's residence in the other cities under review and since space was primarily organised on the basis of political power, as well as according to social criteria, it is certain that the local bishops had an interest in imposing their presence also at the level of space, through churches and their residences.

Churches and monasteries were scattered within the cities. The layout of urban religious institutions is an issue requiring archeological investigation. Some churches or monasteries' *katholika* survive and have been studied to a large extent. Yet, the tracing of others too, which are dormant, and, above all, their mapping, in conjunction with their founders' identity, would provide us with information as to the way in which, apart from the secular one, the local religious authority also interfered with the urban space's arrangement.

According to the Life of Saint Theodora, Despot Michael II Doukas founded two monasteries in Arta, which he dedicated to the Virgin Mary, thus wishing to expiate his marital infidelities.[53] Saint Theodora herself retired to the monastery of Saint George, which eventually took her name and there she engaged in extensive charitable work. Moreover, John Apokaukos expressed his admiration for the fact that Despot Theodore Doukas turned the monastery of Blacherna into a nunnery and installed in it nuns, many of whom were aristocratic refugees from Constantinople, while he dispersed the monks living there, *ταῖς ἐν τῇ πόλει … ἑτέραις μοναῖς*.[54] In fact, Apokaukos states that he was staying at the Peribleptos monastery, where the synod of the local bishops was also meeting. Therefore, at least four monasteries were operating in Arta, while two other large institutions, Blacherna and Kato Panagia, were at a very close distance to the city. In truth, apart from those monasteries' existence, we know nothing about them from the texts. It is, however, interesting that the written sources stress that the establishment of monasteries, both in the capital of their state and in its surroundings, was a fundamental constituent of the Doukas' policy; something, which in my mind, at least, reflects the importance attributed to this construction practice by the despots themselves.

One of the monasteries built by Michael II was perhaps Paregoritissa. The size and sumptuousness of its surviving *katholikon* shows that this was a great monastery, which, regardless of the marital infidelity founding legend, was particularly important for the despots' power, as evidenced by the care shown for the church by Michael Doukas, Nikephoros Doukas and his wife, Anna Paleologina, and their son Thomas, successively.

Researchers agree that Paregoritissa laid at the outskirts of the city,[55] although Arta's urban area is not clearly defined. Compared to its contemporary cities, Arta had the particularity not to be surrounded by walls erected in the Byzantine era.[56] The ancient Ambrakia wall was still standing, certain parts of which were repaired by Michael II. One of the sections repaired was the one connecting the castle to the metropolis' hill in the northwest. Looking at Arta's topographical plan, we observe that Paregoritissa lies at the exact opposite position to the castle and at the other end of a line that proceeds eastwards from the metropolis and which could consist in an imaginary boundary, running in parallel to the ancient wall. In other words, if the metropolis is a fixed spot in the city's perimeter, which begins at the castle, it appears that the Paregoritissa was erected on the specific ground, not only because there would have been an open space available at a prominent position, as has been claimed,[57] but also in order to become *the other* fixed landmark, which moreover bore the Doukas' imprint. Although it is possible that a religious building pre-existed there, which the Doukas family extended,[58] my theory is that the Despot founded the Paregoritissa in order to demarcate the city as an area under his jurisdiction, both for symbolical and for practical reasons. As for the latter, I am of the opinion that in a city with heavy trade activity, as Arta was in the 13th century, demarcation was essential, in order for tariffs to be secured, first and foremost. Its couple of ports in the Amvracian gulf, those of Salaora and Kopraina, wherefrom the farming products of the broader area were being moved, were indeed at a small distance; yet, the *μουρσία*, the warehouses referred to in the Chronicle of the Tocco, and information from other written sources suggest that part of the merchandise was stored and traded inside the city.[59] Of course, there is no indication that the monastery that was erected on the specific spot had any connection with controlling overland trade or the merchants arriving in Arta, in general; nonetheless, its layout must have had a symbolical meaning as regards the city's boundaries. Both the Kato Panagia monastery and Blacherna, which lie at an equal distance to Arta, on either side of the Arachthos river, performed the purpose of a landmark with a rather military character.[60]

In Mystras, a careful observation of its topography shows that an imaginary line connects the three churches of Saint Demetrios, Hodegetria, and Peribleptos and that this line appears to have been the eastern boundary of the city. As known, Saint Demetrios was the metropolis, while the Saints Theodoroi and Hodegetria that were built as *katholika* laid at the northern corner of the wall. The Brontochio monastery, which was eventually founded, adjoins the walls, same as the metropolis buildings. M. Chatzidakis has noted that "*one would say that the second enclosure of Mystras that had Aphentiko as its NW border, the Metropolis on the NE and the Peribleptos on the SE, was made in order to protect these three monasteries*".[61] I think that the nearly simultaneous construction of the Metropolis and Brontochio, at the imperial wish, and their position allows us to claim that these religious establishments were built as landmarks demarcating the newly founded settlement and sanctifying the place.

Therefore, as regards the function and position of urban monasteries, we note that in the cities that were clearly demarcated by pre-existing walls, such as Serres or Berroia, the, usually private, small monasteries were integrated in the urban web, while in cities where, for various reasons, the political authority needed to demarcate its jurisdiction, such as in Arta or in Mystras, apart from the smaller monasteries also encountered also within the cities, large "state" religious institutions were erected on their perimeter, in order to define it.

In the cities we know of, there were quarters; however, it is not always clear if there were spatial differentiations corresponding to social differentiations. John Cantacuzenus comments that families of *ἀρίστων* lived together with the multitude in Servia, at the first level, near the landing.[62] Moreover, the same quotes the *ἔξω συνοικία* of Didymoteichon[63] and the surrounding the *ἄκραν* city of Adrianople.[64] Cohabitation of all social groups at the lower town of Adrianople facilitated the *δῆμος*, when it rebelled against Cantacuzenus' supporters, to pillage the houses of *δυνατών*.[65] If we take into account the signs that Berroian archonts resided in the northern part of Berroia, at the Skoronychos neighborhood, and if we recall John Apokaukos' testimony about the *κατ' ἀξίαν* allocation of shelters to the Ioannina foreigners, we have to consider that, very likely, in the cities under review, there were neighborhoods where the establishment of powerful families was denser. In Berroia, John Chortasmenos states that the archonts were forced to move and cohabitate with the lower classes upon arrival of the Ottomans.[66]

As regards handicraft activities, concentrating some of those in specific areas corresponded to their needs in natural resources, mainly in water. Many of the watermills in Serres were located *εἰς τὸν διερχόμενον ποταμὸν πλησίον τοῦ μεγάλου πύργου, πλησίον τοῦ παραπορτίου*,[67] while in Berroia, there is evidence of two mills, near the *Βασιλική* gate, which was next to the *Βασιλικός* river (today's Tripotamos).[68] In addition, archeological investigation in the northwestern part of Berroia, near the *Βασιλικός* river, revealed remnants of workshops – potteries, in fact.[69] Outside Serres, where several of the estates bought by Cantacuzenus were found,[70] was the *Κεραμαρία* location, the name of which invokes pottery workshops. Moreover, apart from the documents' references to *κεραμάρια*, archeological findings evidence the existence of glazed pottery even inside the city.[71]

It is reasonable that where given handicraft activities, such as mills or potteries, were concentrated, the respective professional groups were also settled there.

Public and Private Space

By all means, the concept of city contains its residents' ability to communicate. This fundamental condition dictates the presence of public spaces, i.e. spaces meant for residents to gather. Information from written sources suggests that churches, their interior or precinct, were the place where residents would gather to celebrate, protest or meet.[72] For instance, the Ioannina metropolis is described as a closed public space, where residents would convene.[73] It would have to be investigated though if also the smaller neighborhood churches, given the cities' size, had a similar "political" use, as the residents' basic social life must have been evolving at a neighborhood level. In any case, there is no evidence of any other public spaces in the late cities and there were definitely no open spaces, designed for residents to congregate.

Most probably by accident, there is no description in any text of any regular collective activity of the residents in the cities under study; not even of any events, which, no doubt, would have been organised on the occasion of religious feasts.[74] The rally of Cantacuzenus's entourage and senators to cheer for him at his coronation[75] took place on an extraordinary occasion, which was certainly not typical of the Didymoteichon residents' social life and did not presuppose a special venue to be available. Besides, Cantacuzenus himself states that *πάντες παρῆσαν ἐκείνου τῇ οἰκίᾳ, ὅσοι διέτριβον ἐν Διδυμοτείχῳ τότε*. Same applies as regards the *ντζούστρα* and the *τορνεμές*, the aristocracy's games, the custom of which was imported from Constantinople by those who followed the Emperor.[76]

The market place turns out to be the public place par excellence. The picture depicted in Arta's Blacherna on the occasion of the procession of the Panagia Hodegetria's icon, regardless of its religious or political co-statements,[77] certainly referred the congregation to the city's commercial activity, as well as to something they were entirely familiar with: that the place where they could get together, trade goods, drink, observe the outside world was the market place. Let us remember that Carlo Tocco, on taking Ioannina, went out to the *πλάτζα* in order to meet the archonts, the *ἐντίμους* and all the residents of the *χώρα*.[78]

Urban construction was dense, particularly in cities that had spread on hills. In the *ἐκφράσεις*, the close proximity of the praised city's buildings is extolled as one of its advantages.[79] Accordingly densely built appear to be the cities when depicted; something which, I believe, reflects the Byzantines' idea of urban space: a space enclosed, withdrawn and, therefore, safe.

For the authors of the praising *ἐκφράσεις*, the city was its residents.[80] That explains why the element which these intellectuals chiefly stress was the residences, the size of which added grandeur to the city. It is also worth noting that, as the *ἐκφράσεις* make reference to the many and tall houses, in the cities' depictions, the walls appear to be encircling only churches[81] and houses. The houses' architecture was interconnected to the lack of public spaces and introvertive character of the late cities. In spite of the rearrangements suffered over the centuries, the surviving houses of Mystras maintain the fortificatory form they had in the first place. After all, they were aristocratic residences, similar of which existed in other cities, too.[82]

The building complexes registered in Thessaloniki,[83] Serres, and Berroia, also referred to above, are representative of the urban social life. In the records of the Athonite monasteries, as regards Thessaloniki, and of the Prodromos monastery, as regards Serres, a number of *αὐλές* are described, which became part of the respective monasteries' property.

These complexes were built in cities where the ground morphology allowed it, mostly in those lying in plains. Normally, they had a courtyard with a well at their center and a *πολύκοινον εἰσοέξοδον*. At a time, the right to use the common entrance-exit was the subject-matter of sale or concession.[84] The buildings were workshops, occasionally *ἐνοικιακά*, and more often residences. In one instance, there was an oven (*μαγκιπεῖον*) in operation at a courtyard, while in another, there was a wine-press.[85] *Αυλές* are also registered in Thessaloniki and Raidestos, much earlier than the period under review.[86] Although our sources' sample is very small, it is almost certain that the registered instances were not isolated and that *αυλές* were not found solely in the three abovementioned cities. For instance, building complexes of such structure appear to be also found in Monemvasia.[87]

Regardless of their destiny over the years, according to their original use, the edifices of the smaller of those residential groups were most probably meant for housing inter-related families, chiefly parents with their married children.[88] Furthermore, the increase in urban population, even when it was circumstantial, on account of natural disasters or military events in the surrounding countryside, created additional needs for residences and, therefore, dictated the construction of houses with more than one storey or the construction of new ones, where there was space available. This is, after all, why property owners were (reportedly) extending existing constructions or building new ones in the courtyards they held.

We can imagine that these building complexes were equivalent to building blocks or even, in the case of large ones, to entire neighborhoods, with a church as focal point. We have said that it is not possible to calculate the area they covered in each city. In studying the individual elements of these building groups, I form the opinion that the *αὐλές* covered a large, if not the largest part of the area built, precisely because they balanced the lack of open public spaces and provided the contact opportunities that residents require by definition. Without cancelling the late cities' introvertive character, or rather precisely on account thereof, living inside the same *αὐλή*, nurtured in the residents a sense of extended privacy, which replaced the limited opportunities for social life in open public spaces.

Cities' space in Byzantium, from the middle age onward, was enclosed and introvertive. The walls encircling it made the residents secure, at the same time as restricting their movement. Its introversion and narrowness reflected the emperor-subjects political relationship, as shaped after the 7th century. The absence of horizontal social relations excluded the formation of open public spaces and the construction of public buildings, because people had no need for such. Only churches and their precinct were assembly areas for the residents.

Although the sovereign-subjects vertical relationship gradually fainted, it never was really questioned during the 13th and 14th centuries, despite the social changes. In light of that, the narrative sources' silence regarding urban topography makes sense. The authors of the texts, which we use as source of information in the course of our tour in the Greek cities, "viewed" and, therefore, described the city which they needed; i.e. a city ordered around the central government's representative. The citadel, where the *κεφαλή* was seated, constituted the administrative center and was a symbol of the emperor's or despot's power. After all, the rule exercised in the province by the ruling social class was secured through its relationship with Constantinople. Therefore, the intellectuals described only what fitted with the idea of a city formed by walls, residences, churches and, where existing, charitable institutions, as proof of the imperial charity. In their praises, they also described in great detail and all the more lyrically[89] the natural environment, of which cities were a part.

Notes

This chapter is based entirely on the book Tonia Kiousopoulou, *Οι «αόρατες» βυζαντινές πόλεις στον ελλαδικό χώρο (13ος-15ος αιώνας)*, Athens 2013, where most of the bibliography is.

1 Kazhdan (1998: 345–360).
2 Pitsakis (2011: 501–517).
3 Braudel (1979: 423 ff).
4 Bouras (2012: 1–14).
5 Lavvas (2001: 29–39).
6 Saradi (2006); Saradi (2012: 25–46); Tsivikis (2012: 47–71); Tsigonaki (2012: 73–100).
7 G. T. Dennis, *Three Byzantine Military Treatises*, Dumbarton Oaks Texts, Washington 1985., 30–32: *Περὶ οἰκοδομῆς πόλεως. Δεῖ δὲ μέλλοντας πόλεις κτίζειν πρῶτον μὲν κατασκοπῆσαι τὸ χωρίον, εἰ τὸ μέλλον ἐπ' αὐτὸ κτίζεσθαι τεῖχος ἀνεπιβούλευτον ἔσται ποτὲ τοῖς πολιορκοῦσι διὰ τὴν τοῦ χωρίου θέσιν.*
8 Papadopoulos-Kerameus (1889: 454).
9 Vranousis (1968: 27).
10 *Αρχαιολογικό Δελτίο* 1983: 245–249 (Olga Gratziou).
11 Kordosis (2003: 88 ff).
12 Vranousis (1968: 23).
13 *Cronaca dei Tocco*, v. 1582.
14 Roghoti-Kyriopoulou (1987: 15).
15 Vranousis (1962: §10).
16 MM V, 82: *τὰ ἐξ αὐτῶν εἰσοδήματα, καθὼς πωλοῦνται εἰς τὴν χώραν.*
17 MM V, 78.
18 Bouras (2002: 508–509).
19 See *ibid*, and Bouras (1998: 89–97).
20 Bees (1971–1979: 122): *μὴ κακίζεις καὶ τοὺς τῶν ἡμετέρων καταλυμάτων μαρμαρίνους ἀναβαθμοὺς καὶ τὰ μαρμαρόστρωτα ὕπαιθρα, διὰ τὴν ὑψηλότοπον ἵδρυσιν τὴν ὄψιν τῶν ὁρώντων πρὸς τὴν ὑποκειμένην θάλασσαν ἀκοντίζοντα καὶ τῆς τῶν φυτῶν εὐώδεσι σκιαζόμενα.*
21 Papadopoulos-Kerameus (1907: 244–248): *Τούτου γοῦν τὴν ἔκτασιν καθ' ἓν τῶν ἄκρων παρατεμόμενος, καὶ τῷ τμήματι τούτῳ χῶμα ἐπιστοιβάσας καὶ τοῦ λοιποῦ πρασαναςπάσας ἐδάφους, λίθοις τε τὸ χῶμα διαλαβὼν ὡς μὴ πρὸς τὸ υποβεβηκὸς καταρῇ, κιγκλίδας ἄνω τούτου τοῦ διαστήματος ἐστήσατο στοιχηδὸν και σχῆμα ἐπισκοπικοῦ θρόνου, ὅ δὴ κοινῶς καλεῖται στασίδιον, διὰ τούτων ἐκαινουργήσατο, ὡς ἀριστᾷ μὲν αὐτὸς ἐν μετεώρῳ ... τὸ δὲ ὑποβεβηκὸς καὶ τὸ πρόσγειον εἰς δίαιταν εἰς ἀκρόασιν τοῖς τὴν τύχην ταπεινοτέροις ἀπένειμεν.*
22 Apokaukos himself assures: *Οἰκίας ὄνομα περσικῆς ο σουφᾶς ... καὶ τοῦτο τὸ σχῆμα καλοῦσι Πέρσαι σουφᾶν.* Relevantly, see Katsaros (1989: 646–647).
23 About Rentina, see Moutsopoulos (2001 and 2002).
24 Cf. about Berroia: Cant. III, 120: *οὐδενὸς γὰρ τῶν ὅσα πόλιν εὐδαίμονα ποιεῖ ἐνδεῖ. διὰ τὸ μεγάλην εἶναι καὶ πολλοὺς τοὺς ἐνοικοῦντας ἔχειν, οὐ δημώδη μόνον ὄχλον ἀλλὰ καὶ στρατιώτας καὶ οὐκ ὀλίγους τῶν συγκλητικῶν.* Regarding Adrianople: Cant. II, 405: *τῶν ἐν Θράκῃ πόλεων μείζω καὶ ἀναγκαιοτέραν οὖσαν*, while as regards Philippopolis: Cant. II, 406: *πόλις θαυμασία καὶ μεγάλη.* In respect of Serres: Greg. II, 746: *τὸ μέγα καὶ θαυμαστὸν ἄστυ.*
25 N. Bakirtzis (2012: 139–158).
26 About Servia, see Evgenidou (1988: 20). Regarding Ioannina, see Kordosis (2003: 100).
27 Kalligas (2002: 881). Walls of a building with a balcony inside the citadel survive in Arta: relevantly, see Papadopoulou (2002: 113).
28 *Cronaca dei Tocco*, v. 1242: *Οἱ γιαννινιῶται οἱ ἄρχοντες, μικροί τε και μεγάλοι,/εἰς τὸν γουλᾶν ἀνέβησαν καὶ ὥρθωσαν ἐτοῦτοι.*
29 Ćurčić (1999: 37 ff).
30 A *ἔκφρασις* of the Serres metropolis that was written around mid-14th century by Theodore Pediasimos survives. See Diovouniotis (1921: 167–174, esp. 171–174). The text describes the church's interior. As regards the surrounding area, which is of greater interest to us here, it is noted: *Αὐλή τις ἔστιν μέσον εἰληφυῖα χῶρον τῆς πόλεως καὶ ἐν αὐτῇ φρέαρ ὡραῖόν τι κατεσκεύασται ... Καὶ τὴν αὐλὴν περίστῳον διαδέχεται ἐπί πολὺ μῆκος ἐκτεταμένον ... Ἑκκαίδεκα δ' ἀναβαθμοὶ τὴν ἔξοδον τοῦ νεὼ τῷ βουλομένῳ διεξιέναι διδόασι.*
31 Karagianni (2010: 94).

32 Bouras (1998: 92).
33 Odorico (1998: 633–648) views the expression *ἐργαστήρια εἰς τὸ ἐμπόριον τῶν Σερρῶν εἰς τὴν λεγομένην Κλοποτίτζαν τρία* (Kout., 52, 86) as an indication of the market's spreading outside the walls.
34 Benou, 156.
35 Chom. 25.
36 In the *Cronaca dei Tocco*, v. 367 et seq., the expression tells us that the market was outside the citadel walls: *εἰς τὸ κάστρο καὶ εἰς τὸ μποριό, φεύγοντας οἱ ἀνθρῶποι, / ὅτι ἐρήμωσαν πολλὰ μέχρι καὶ ἐς τὲς πόρτες*. See also the *Cronaca dei Tocco*, v. 361: *καὶ κονταρὲς ἐδώκασιν μέσα εἰς τὸ μπορίο/ μ' ἐκείνους ὅπου ηὕρηκαν ἔξω ἀπὲ τὸ κάστρο*. See also Papadopoulou (2002: 19), where it is claimed that Arta's market was developed along an external road reaching the castle's gate.
37 *Cronaca dei Tocco*, v. 2555.
38 Evgenidou (1988: 15–22).
39 Moutsopoulos 2002.
40 Apart from the other cities, the central road of Kastoria is also located on that axis, see Drakopoulou (1997).
41 Benou, 138: *τὸ ἐργαστήριον ὅπερ ἐστι πλησίον ... καὶ ἑτέρου ἐργαστηρίου τοῦ Κρικέλα καὶ τῆς βασιλικῆς ὁδοῦ τῆς διαιρούσης τὸ εἰρημένον ἐργαστήριον καὶ ἄντικρυς τῆς πόρτης τοῦ Παλαιολόγου κῦρ Ἀλεξίου.*
42 Benou, 375.
43 Benou, no. 67: *τῆς βασιλικῆς πόρτας, τῆς ἐπιλεγομένης τοῦ Φόρου.*
44 P. Papageorgiou (1894: 244). See also Karagianni (2010: 207).
45 Papazotos (1994: 71ff).
46 Papazotos (1994: 76), where also the reference to the adjacent church of Panagia Pantanassa or Palioforitissa. See also Karagianni (2010: 112).
47 Papazotos (1994: 71).
48 Papazotos (1994: 75).
49 Kalligas, (2002: 882).
50 It has been noted (Kordosis 2003: 83), where bibliography can also be found, that the gate walled by Thomas's tower lies on the axis of the castle's main gate, which supports the assumption that this was the main gate of the outer walls.
51 Papadopoulos-Kerameus (1909: 24).
52 Kordosis (2011: 181).
53 Job, Life of Saint Theodora, *PG* 127, v. 904–908. See also Papadopoulou (2002: 138).
54 Papadopoulos-Kerameus (1909: 18).
55 Kordosis (2011: 213).
56 Papadopoulou (2002: 18–19).
57 Tsouris (1992: 495–503, esp. 502).
58 Orlandos (1963: 24–25); L. Theis, *Die Arkitektur der Panagia Paregoretissa in Arta/Epirus*, Hakkert, Amsterdam, Dumbarton Oaks 1990.
59 Kordosis (2011: 236 ff).
60 From that point of view, it is significative that Despot Thomas had camped at Blacherna in order to repel the Franks. On the Despot's movements, see relevantly, Kordosis (2011: 199–200).
61 Chatzidakis (1987: 123–124).
62 Cant. III, 130, 133.
63 Cant. II, 195, 288.
64 Cant. III, 243. On the position of the citadel, at the edge of the city, see Asdracha (1976: 142).
65 Cant. II, 176.
66 Chortasmenos, 88–89, 168–170: *ἀντὶ δὲ τοῦ συζῆν ἀνδράσιν ἀρετῇ καὶ σοφίᾳ κεκοσμημένοις βαρβάροις ὁμιλεῖν ἀναγκαζόμενοι καὶ ... σκαπανέων ὁμιληταὶ καθεστῶτες.*
67 Benou, 375.
68 Kravari (1989: 66).
69 Karagianni (2010: 113).
70 Bat. II, αρ. 80.
71 Karagianni (2010: 208).
72 More generally, see Kioussopoulou (1993: 279–287). In Thessaloniki, a court is summoned inside the metropolis, in which senators and archonts of the *πολιτεία* participate (Bat. II, αρ. 144). It is

also known that Patriarch Athanasios I was disappointed by the unseemly behavior exhibited by the faithful in the capital's churches.

73 Cf. the *Cronaca dei Tocco*, v. 1350: *Αὔριο 'ς τὴν μητρόπολιν σύναξις θέλει γίνῃ.*

74 The single express reference which I have detected is in the Life of Elizabeth, which contains a description of the seven-day feast in Herakleia, Thrace, with litanies in tribute to the blessed Glykeria: see F. Halkin, "Sainte Élisabeth d'Héraclée, abesse à Constantinople", *Analecta Bollandiana* 91, 1973: 353–354.

75 Cant. II, 166.

76 Greg. I, 482–483.

77 Acheimastou-Potamianou (1981: 4–14).

78 *Cronaca dei Tocco*, v. 1581–1584: *καὶ ἀπεκεῖ ἐστράφηκεν, ἐπέζευσεν 'ς τὴν χώραν./ Καὶ γύρω τὴν ἐγύρισεν 'ς τὴν πλάτζαν εἰς τὴν μέσην,/ καὶ ἄρχισεν νὰ ἐρωτᾷ, νὰ ἰδῇ, νὰ ἐγνωρίσῃ/ τοὺς ἄρχοντες τοὺς ἔντιμους τοὺς ἅπαντας τῆς χώρας.*

79 Bouras (1998: 97 n. 100).

80 Tanoulas (2012: 22–23).

81 Saradi (2009: 98–131, esp. 106–109).

82 Bouras (1983: 1–26); Kalligas (2002: 881).

83 Zivojinović (1993: 465–474).

84 Cf. Esphig. 74–75; Benou, 140.

85 Kout. 52: *καὶ πηγάδιον μετὰ ἰδιοπεριορίστου καὶ μονομεροῦς αὐλῆς, εἰς ἣν* [courtyard] *ἐστι καὶ ἀνώγαιον … ἔχων ἐντὸς ὀσπήτια δύο, ἔκτισα καὶ ἕτερον ὀσπήτιον, ἔχων ἐντὸς λινὸν κτιστὸν ὅπερ ἔταξα εἰς βαγενάριον.*

86 Regarding Thessaloniki, see Papachryssanthou (1984: 254–267).

87 Kalligas (2002: 881).

88 The parents-children cohabitation in the same *αυλή* is presented more clearly in sale deeds from Thessaloniki: Indicatively see Chil., no. 30.

89 Saradi (2012: 9–36).

PART II

Geographies of the Byzantine City

6

CITIES ON THE BLACK SEA COAST AND THE CIRCUMPONTIC EXCHANGE NETWORK (c. 500–700)*

Andrei Gandila

> Il y a eu, au cours des siècles, en ce qui concerne la Mer Noire, plus d'analogies, un plus grand nombre de liens d'interdépendance d'un littoral à l'autre que l'on ne serait tenté de le supposer à première vue. Bien des circonstances s'éclairent par ce fond commun d'intérêts et d'aspirations que révèle l'histoire «pontique» considérée comme un tout.
>
> *G. Brătianu, Mer Noire, 36*

Introduction

From his permanent exile at Tomis, Ovid painted the Black Sea region in bleak tones, a savage and frigid place at the end of the world.[1] An unwelcoming backwater under the Principate, the Black Sea gained central importance in Late Antiquity when the focal point of the empire shifted to Constantinople. Although Pontus Euxinus was far from being a "Byzantine lake", sea lanes and roads now converged upon the Byzantine capital. Stakes in the Pontic region became so high that Procopius feared a Persian seaborne invasion should Byzantium lose control of the sea.[2] Such an invasion never materialized, but Byzantine efforts in the region and the growing significance of the Black Sea brought important cultural changes. In the sixth century, its centrality became paramount. War with Persia concentrated in Lazica, the west-Pontic region was refortified to secure the capital and the strategic significance of Crimea increased as Byzantium grappled with the danger posed by Hunnic and Turkic tribes. Meanwhile, during years of peace, Byzantine harbor cities flourished

* I would like to express my gratitude to a number of colleagues who have provided assistance at various stages of this project. Florin Curta and Andrei Opaiţ offered comments on early drafts and supplied publications from Turkey, Bulgaria and Crimea at a time when libraries in the United States were closed due to the pandemic; Zeliha Demirel Gökalp provided access to unpublished material from Turkey; Stoyan Mihaylov shared information from his unpublished dissertation and Canan Özbil offered details about the Byzantine coins in the Çorum museum. I would also like to thank David Hill, the Francis D. Campbell Librarian at the American Numismatic Society for his assistance and the Humanities Center at the University of Alabama in Huntsville for funding my research trip to New York.

DOI: 10.4324/9780429203923-9

in the shadow of Constantinople and sustained a fragile but intricate web of settlements whose main capillaries crisscrossed the Black Sea.

The history of the Byzantine Pontus as a cultural unit of analysis is yet to be written. The pioneering work of Gheorghe Brătianu in the 1940s when the Black Sea was engulfed in the flames of war was not continued and for decades the study of this region remained dominated by fragmentation.[3] This type of insularity was driven by political circumstances during the Cold War and by the daunting linguistic barrier which remains a serious problem to this day.[4] The present study is an attempt to explore connections and developments in the Pontic region during the transition from antiquity to the middle ages. It will focus primarily on the coin evidence and its associations with the archaeological material pertaining to the Black Sea world in the sixth and seventh centuries. What were the local particularities and what brought together distant cities around the Black Sea? What type of traffic dominated the Black Sea network and what kind of mechanisms drove the circulation of people and goods? How can coins help us understand the level of cultural and economic integration achieved in the Pontic region? These are the main questions addressed in the following pages with the goal of highlighting the wider economic, administrative and political contours of the centuries marking the end of antiquity in the Byzantine world.

The Administrative Geography of the Black Sea Region

The Black Sea embraced more than 4,000 km of coastline and accommodated dozens of towns, documented by the chief sixth-century sources, the latest compilation of the *Periplus Ponti Euxini* and the *Synekdemos* of Hierokles (Figure 6.1). The western and southern shores were controlled by Byzantium, its nine provinces belonging to the Dioceses of Thracia and Pontus, respectively. Byzantine interests extended to the northern Black Sea region, where the cities of Cherson and Bosphorus were the main bastions in a world dominated by barbarian tribes controlling the steppe. Justinian in particular used a mixture of diplomacy and direct intervention to maintain a fragile balance of power in the region and the same strategy was employed on the eastern Black Sea coast controlled by Lazica and its satellite kingdoms on the southern foothills of the Caucasus.[5] Despite the ever-changing political landscape, the archaeological and numismatic evidence reveals the existence of important connections between all these regions and the development of a culture which blended martial and Christian characteristics as well as common features of daily life, which will be the focus of the next sections.

The sixth-century provinces of the western Black Sea coast belonged to the Thracian Diocese, a region still struggling with the legacy of a disastrous fifth century in the Balkans. Justinian responded to the challenge of securing the Danube frontier by creating an atypical administrative unit. The Black Sea provinces of Scythia and Moesia II were joined with Cyprus, Caria and the Cyclades in *quaestura exercitus*, with the seat at Odessos on the coast.[6] Its main purpose was to supply the fortresses defending the Danube frontier in a region where the impoverished local economy could no longer support the large number of troops stationed there. The *quaestura* was a purely maritime district and relied on the sea to transport annonary goods from the Aegean to the Black Sea coast, via Constantinople. Private commerce flourished in the shadow of state-directed traffic and ensured that the entire Black Sea network would be supplied with local and imported goods. Underwater surveys off the western coast in Bulgaria have revealed a concentration of ships dating to this time – mostly carrying amphorae – and the connection to *quaestura* is unavoidable.[7]

Figure 6.1 Towns mentioned in the text and additional settlements around the Black Sea where early Byzantine coins have been found: 1. Halmyris, 2. Noviodunum, 3. Dinogetia, 4. Troesmis, 5. Carsium, 6. Capidava, 7. Sacidava, 8. Mangalia, 9. Creas, 10. Dionyssopolis, 11. Deultum, 12. Chernomorets, 13. Urdoviza, 14. Çorum, 15. Amisos, 16. Neocaesarea, 17. Kerasous, 18. Satala, 19. Apsarus, 20. Kotiaion, 21. Dranda; 22. Sochi; 23. Il'ich, 24. Mangup, 25. Bolhrad, 26. Vynohradne, 27. Parutyne, 28. Ochakiv, 29. Zatoka, 30. Vylkove

The Byzantine cities on the Thracian coast display certain similarities with the Pontic cities in Northern Turkey. The cities of Thracia were not as large and impressive as the metropoleis of Greece in Illyricum, just as the coastal towns of Pontus were never as rich or developed as the venerable urban centers of the Asian Diocese. Much like Sinope, Amastris and Trapezus in Pontus, the cities of the western Black Sea coast were important gateways for the circulation of people, goods and ideas coming from the wider Byzantine world. Geographical as well as historical coordinates going back to the Greek colonization determined the density of settlements on the Balkan coast. South of the Danube Delta cities like Argamum, Histria, Tomis and Callatis served a central role in the economic and cultural life of the province, as well as ensuring the proper supply of the Danube frontier. Further south, the bay of Burgas presents us with the highest concentration of urban centers in the Black Sea region with Mesembria, Anchialos and Sozopolis dominating a web of coastal settlements which occupied almost every single isthmus protruding into the sea.[8] With large-scale agriculture all but collapsing in many regions, sixth-century cities in the Eastern Balkans relied more than ever on their Black Sea connection.[9]

If the cities of the Black Sea coast in Romania and Bulgaria have been studied extensively, the coastal provinces of the Diocese of Pontus for a long time remained a *terra incognita* for systematic archaeological research. The magisterial survey conducted by Bryer and Winfield as well as more recent studies have established that almost half of the number of settlements in Pontus are located on the Black Sea coast.[10] Despite this fact, no administrative capital was established in a coastal city. This is true of the Black Sea region in general. The case of Tomis, capital of Scythia is an exception. Marcianopolis, rather than Odessos, was the capital of Moesia II, although Odessos became the seat of *quaestura exercitus*. Similarly, Adrianople, the important city on *via militaris*, was chosen as the capital of Haemimontus, rather than a major coastal city like Mesembria or Anchialos. The same principle applies in the Diocese of Pontus where important harbors like Sinope or Trapezus were not chosen to serve as administrative capitals. Instead, most provincial centers – Claudiopolis, Amaseia and Neocaesarea – were strung like beads on the trunk road linking Nicomedia in Bithynia with Theodosiopolis in Armenia.

Contemporary historians themselves largely neglected coastal Pontus because the imperial hotspots lay elsewhere during the sixth and seventh centuries. We are best informed about administrative initiatives. Justinian carried out an administrative reform c. 535 in order to increase the efficiency of the local leadership. Paphlagonia and Honorias, the latter a province created by Theodosius II, were unified under the name Paphlagonia, while much of Pontus Polemoniacus became part of Armenia I. Crucially, the separation of civil and military power was abolished and the governor was now responsible for the administration of justice, taxation, command of all troops, and the fight against banditry. We know that the bishop of Hadrianopolis in Honorias received edicts from Justinian against banditry, which may have been one of the reasons behind the emperor's administrative reform in Pontus.[11] Because bandits moved to other provinces, Justinian abolished the previous reforms c. 548 and the vicariate of the whole Pontic diocese was reinstated.[12] Insecurity in the hinterland would have increased the value of communication and transport via the Black Sea. In addition, Northern Anatolia had to cope with a rugged terrain and few natural resources, which enhanced the role of the sea as an essential component to the region's economic life, as well as to its integration in the Byzantine world.

Moving to the eastern Black Sea region, Byzantium pursued the venerable Roman goal of controlling the coast from Trapezus to Pityus. The stakes were particularly high in sixth-century Transcaucasia where the control of the mountain passes had enormous strategic value to the rival superpowers, Byzantium and Sasanian Persia. Unsurprisingly, the region became the central focus of the conflict during Justinian's reign and features prominently in the peace treaty recorded by Menander.[13] The rivalry between the two empires and the tendency of local rulers to shift their allegiance with cynical expediency forced Byzantine emperors to pour substantial resources into the eastern Black Sea region. Justinian's legislation reveals the result of his energetic actions: the pacification of the Tzani, the integration of the Lazi multiethnic confederation into the Byzantine orbit, and the successful fortification of the entire area.[14] Following previous administrative arrangements, the fortified towns of Pityus and Sebastopolis on the Abasgian coast remained attached to Pontus Polemoniacus, while in Lazica proper Justinian founded the formidable city of Petra and brought the neighboring coastal towns in the Byzantine cultural sphere. As a result, within two generations, Christianity became official religion in Lazica and a wider adoption of Byzantine material culture followed.[15]

Finally, the northern Black Sea coast lay outside Byzantium's direct control, but the absence of provinces here should not be interpreted as lack of interest in this strategic region. The Crimean Peninsula was on the edge of Byzantium, hundreds of kilometers away from the nearest fortified border, but was far from being a remote place.[16] Cherson, a sizeable city of c. 30 ha, made obvious efforts to emulate the Byzantine culture of Constantinople, while Byzantine rulers themselves had strong reasons to invest in a bridgehead on the northern Black Sea coast. Cherson, Bosphorus and the smaller fortified settlements in Byzantine Crimea acted as gateways to the steppe world, extending the economic and cultural reach of the empire. Crucially, maintaining a north-Pontic outpost would help the Byzantines learn about changes in the dynamic of power in the barbarian world, assist allies in the region and conduct an efficient Realpolitik in *barbaricum*.

According to Procopius, the fortifications of Cherson were renewed under Justinian, but significant measures were also taken under his successor, Justin II (565–578), when the walls of the city were probably strengthened in response to the expansion of Turkic groups into Crimea.[17] Under his reign, Cherson became the residence of a dux and his responsibilities included the supervision of the garrisons on the south coast, as well as the impressive fortifications in Crimea erected with the help of Chersonite builders and Byzantine engineers.[18] Around 590, the duke's area of influence reached as far as Bosphorus, which had been devastated by the Turks shortly before, in the 570s. The Byzantines had a longstanding interest in eastern Crimea and Bosphorus features prominently in the Byzantine diplomatic and military struggle to gain complete control of the peninsula.[19] After the city walls were reinforced at Justinian's order, Bosphorus became an important Byzantine port which supervised a nexus of commercial and strategic roads leading to the North Caucasus, the Caspian steppes and the Turkish khanate.[20]

The Circulation of Goods in the Black Sea Network

It is a well-established fact that sea travel in antiquity was faster than land routes and heavier cargoes could be loaded on ships. For instance, the sea crossing from the region of the modern Burgas gulf to Constantinople lasted one day compared to at least four by land.[21] From Trapezus to the Danube Delta, it would take nine days and a similar trip was expected if sailing from Lazica or Abasgia to a port on the western coast. Travel by land would have taken much longer, about 25 days from Constantinople to Theodosiopolis, and banditry, which was an endemic problem in sixth-century Pontus, would have increased the preference for sea lanes.[22] Two types of cargoes circulated in the Black Sea network: official ships related to *annona militaris* and private commerce in luxury products. At the same time, the circulation of people and goods took place at a local, regional and inter-regional level in the Black Sea world. Distinguishing between the different types of traffic is notoriously difficult as the archaeological evidence is rarely unequivocal. At the very least, we should attempt to discern a number of patterns of supply in the circumpontic network.

Although the Black Sea world was home to populations embracing different cultural traditions, there are important elements of standardization in the urban landscape; these are most closely connected with the powerful military-religious binary promoted during the long sixth century when Byzantium controlled the Black Sea basin. The encroachment of formerly public urban spaces by houses, workshops and agricultural installations is a constant feature of the urban history of the *spätere Spätantike*, along with a concern with expanding and rebuilding city defenses.[23] The largest and most important Pontic cities were not spared, and as a result, the distinction between the classical cities on the coast and the smaller provincial towns began to fade as the urban fabric itself was undergoing significant changes. The military and religious dimension comes to the fore against this background of transformation and downscaling. This reality brings together cities across the Black Sea region (and elsewhere), while the material culture itself reveals a distinctive "pontic" flavor in what concerns local tastes and preferences as well as the ability to procure goods of daily use. The following discussion is only a quick foray into a daunting list of archaeological questions.

The Christian basilica dominates the urban landscape on the western Black Sea coast and its architecture incorporates a number of standard features. A few examples serve to illustrate this point. The sixth-century church of St. Nicholas at Salmydessos, the only important coastal settlement in Europa, has capitals with analogies at Odessos and Amastris and imitates styles fashionable in Constantinople.[24] Further north in Haemimontus, at Sozopolis, a city which boasted two ports, we find the church of St. George built in the sixth century, if not later, whose northern wall was adjacent to a contemporary storage building, perhaps also belonging to the church complex.[25] Close to Sozopolis, in the fortress of Akra archaeologists have found the remains of an altar made of fine marble imported from Constantinople, as well as fragments of marble columns associated with a large church.[26] Across the Burgas bay, at Mesembria, archaeologists have uncovered several monumental churches including an impressive metropolitan cathedral named St. Sophia.[27] In Moesia II, Odessos, the seat of *quaestura exercitus*, and its immediate hinterland offers an impressive religious landscape where archaeologists documented the remains of 16 basilicas, many rebuilt in the sixth century, some of them having beautiful mosaic floors and expensive internal marble decoration.[28] At Tomis, in Scythia, six churches from the sixth century are known to date and the last known bishop of Tomis was Valentinianus (550–553), who corresponded with Pope Vigilius.[29] Finally, at Histria, the episcopal basilica was the most monumental edifice of the sixth-century city during a time of general agglomeration and ruralization of the town with crowded and poorly built structures.[30] Almost in all cases, the building materials and the architectural decorations were imported and this was common practice across the Black Sea. It is likely that itinerant sculptors and craftsmen from Constantinople traveled along the coast to work on church projects.[31]

In the southern and eastern Black Sea region church activity was equally prominent. Sheltered from the dramatic events unfolding in Anatolia, Amastris remained an important port in the seventh century when three important Christian basilicas decorated with fine Proconnesian marble capitals were functional.[32] East of Amastris, close to Kytoros an Early Byzantine church was found at the center of what may have been a monastic community.[33] Inland at Hadrianopolis, a small but important city with access to the trunk road leading to the eastern frontier, developed into a religious center, with basilicas, a monastery and a convent associated with St. Alypius the Stylite.[34] The main roads also passed by Neoklaudiopolis where a martyrium was excavated and Euchaita, famous for the cult of St. Theodore the Recruit, and eventually reached Tzanica, pacified by Justinian.[35] The emperor built fortresses, churches and roads in Tzanica, a program with a pronounced military character, Christianity being just a means of "civilizing" the warlike Tzani.[36] In Lazica and the small Caucasian kingdoms on the Black Sea coast religion was also used as a diplomatic and political tool. Archaeological research suggests that Christianization was carried inland from the coast.[37] Church building was intensified as illustrated by complexes excavated at Petra, Dranda, Sebastopolis and Pityus, to name a few.[38] The church in Petra was a three-nave basilica with a narthex and a floor covered with a mosaic, while the sixth-century church excavated at Dranda, close to Sebastopolis, boasted columns and capitals made of imported Proconnesian marble.[39] Even more spectacular evidence comes from Tsandripsh, on the Abasgian coast north of Pityus, where an impressive marbled basilica with tombs under the floor was identified with the temple built by Justinian for the Abasgians.[40]

In Crimea and the north-Pontic region, the military and religious dimension of urban life is particularly striking. The sixth century was a time of frantic church building in the port city of Cherson, although the dating of such monuments is sometimes ambiguous.[41] This included several church complexes decorated with sumptuous mosaics and marble fixtures, following architectural styles from Constantinople.[42] The office of the bishop of Cherson in the sixth century also extended to the mountain region of Crimea, dominated by the great basilica with baptistery at Mangup whose early phase dates to this period, and with some certainty beyond.[43] Evidence in this regard comes from Il'ich, across the strait of Kerch. Here the local military barracks protecting Byzantine interests in the Taman peninsula housed a small Christian chapel featuring the image of a hand in a blessing gesture and Byzantine activity in the settlement included a glass workshop of the Syrian school.[44]

In what concerns the intersection of cultural influences in the Black Sea world, the western coast remains the best studied region. Large port cities like Tomis, Odessos, Anchialos and Mesembria were major hubs coordinating the economic integration of their provinces in the Byzantine network of communication and trade.[45] Early Byzantine Tomis, the capital of Scythia, has been the subject of important archaeological research. Epigraphic, numismatic and sphragistic evidence reveals the presence of wine sellers from Egypt, traders from western Asia Minor, as well as the circulation of coins from the Western and Eastern Mediterranean.[46] The city probably became the main entrepôt where *annona* goods were unloaded for their distribution on the Lower Danube frontier. The most spectacular find documenting the activity of the harbor is the mosaic-floored edifice with vaulted storerooms excavated in the last century. The rich material found there includes not only the typical combination of LRA 1 and LRA 2 containers but also amphorae from Africa and the Eastern Mediterranean which brought a variety of resins from Asia Minor, Somalia and Arabia, as well as Christian lamps from North Africa and the Aegean world.[47] In 599, when Tomis was besieged by the Avars and the khan offered an Easter truce and sent food to the beleaguered city, it was still possible to repay the khan's unexpected benevolence with exotic condiments coming from India.[48]

To a great extent, the situation at Tomis is a good cultural mirror of the west-Pontic coast. We note a healthy variety of amphora types in the sixth century and this may have something to do with the region's privileged position as the recipient of regular state-directed *annona* shipments.[49] The publication of several fully quantified assemblages from well-recorded sequences of pottery on Early Byzantine sites in the Northeastern Balkans confirms the role of the state in the economic life of the region.[50] Large quantities of amphora-borne comestibles were imported from outside the Pontic region and transported in LRA 1 and LRA 2 containers, used for wine and olive oil, respectively. Cretan amphorae circulated especially in the second half of the sixth century with examples recorded in the western and northern Pontic regions, while LRA 4 wine amphorae from Gaza increased their presence in the sixth century in the northeastern Balkans.[51] On the other hand, Pontic amphorae and tableware became rare in Scythia and Moesia II after the mid-fifth century.[52] The maritime provinces of the Thracian diocese were flooded with Phocaean LRC wares, the vast majority from the third phase of production, c. 470–580. The supply of fine wares has been tentatively attributed to a community of merchants from Anatolia operating in the large cities of the western Black Sea coast, but their activity could have also flourished in the shadow of state-directed traffic.[53] Phocaean LRC were supplemented by a more modest volume of imported African fine ceramics; sixth-century ARS types Hayes 87, 94, 99 and 104 reached not only larger towns like Ibida, Tropaeum and Histria but also smaller fortresses like Akra, Capidava and Halmyris.[54]

Comparatively less is known from the rugged region of coastal Turkey. In Late Antiquity towns on the southern Black Sea coast adapted their economy and trade patterns to meet the needs of Constantinople.[55] Although the region was not particularly rich in exportable resources, some are known to have circulated outside the coastal provinces; these include hazelnut oil from Amastris, red earth (*sinoper*) from Sinope, alum from Koloneia, salt and copper from Paphlagonia, timber, oil, wine, as well as processed fish for which the Black Sea region was famous.[56] We are best informed about Sinope and its hinterland. Sinope was a center for the production of roof tiles which it perhaps exported via cabotage to neighboring provinces, but it became more widely known for its olive oil.[57] In the sixth century the local economy added oil exports to its wines, which Sinope exported in the Black Sea network and especially further south to Syria.[58] Indeed, the role of Sinopean amphorae in the Black Sea decreased from the fourth to the seventh century. Amphora type D Snp I found with coins of Justinian and Justin II and securely dated to the sixth century is less well attested in the Black Sea region compared to earlier variants, with some finds reported on the eastern coast at Apsarus, Mangup in Crimea, and on a shipwreck heading to the western coast or perhaps Crimea.[59]

The decline of amphora production in the Pontic region or at least its redirection toward more distant markets in Syria-Palestine was part of a wider phenomenon. Similar to the situation noted on the western coast, Phocaean wares flooded the Pontic market, their dominance coinciding with a sharp decline in the production and distribution of Pontic Red Slip Ware.[60] The scale of production of standardized LRC may have something to do with the state-directed shipments which eventually pushed other competing types out of the market. Likewise, the decline of the Sinopean carrot-amphora can be traced back to the fifth century but may have something to do with the growing presence of LRA 1 and LRA 2 amphorae in the Black Sea, carrying oil and wine, respectively, and commonly associated with *annona* shipments sent to frontier regions.[61] Although attested unevenly in northern Anatolia, their popularity is confirmed by the production of imitations, perhaps from

Amastris, found during excavations at Pompeiopolis, and the general influence of LRA 1 on the development of the type D carrot-amphora at Sinope.[62]

Due to its location on an isthmus in Paphlagonia Sinope became the main connection between the southern coast and the Byzantine possessions in Crimea. It is not a coincidence that Tiberius II (578–582) chose Sinope as the starting point of a diplomatic mission to the lands north of the Black Sea aimed to enlist the help of the Turks in the war against Persia.[63] From both an economic and a political standpoint, Crimea was well connected to the Byzantine world. Byzantium controlled the strategic cities of Cherson and Bosphorus, as well as important fortresses like Mangup and Sudak in Crimea and Il'ich, across the Kerch strait, on the Taman peninsula. Settlements varying in size and importance as well as cemeteries such as the ones excavated at Suuk-Su and Chufut-Kale illustrate the degree to which the entire region came under the cultural influence of Byzantium, a process coordinated by appointed dukes whose names we know from seals and inscriptions.[64] From an economic perspective, Cherson and Bosphorus remained major centers for the production of salted fish and fish sauce, the growth of this industry being well-documented in the sixth century. The size of the cisterns and salting vats excavated in Cherson suggests that production was geared towards export, Constantinople and other cities on the coast perhaps being the main destination.[65]

The study of local and imported ceramics provides additional evidence. On the northern coast of the Black Sea, Phocaean LRC and Eastern Mediterranean amphorae are well represented in the second half of the sixth century and the beginning of the next and testify to a growing local demand for oil, wine and resin, which doesn't seem to have changed much by mid-seventh century when Pope Martin wrote from his exile.[66] At Cherson, amphorae from Africa, Crete, and the Levant, together with ARS and LRC finewares, continued to supply the city well into the seventh century.[67] A similar dating was proposed for the material excavated at Mangup, where the ceramic assemblage boasts an assortment of goods and containers: Pontic carrot-shaped amphorae, including types Zeest 96/97 and 100, Phocaean and African Red Slip fine ware and glass vessels, some of them imported. A *pentanummium* (⅛ follis) of Justinian, which circulated in Crimea throughout the sixth and seventh century, secures the dating of the complex.[68] At the eastern end of the peninsula, the strategic city of Bosphorus was equally connected to the Black Sea network. As the production of Pontic Red Slip wares declined, LRC came to dominate the fine pottery market in the sixth-to-early seventh century along with Late Roman Pontic Burnished Ware (LRPB), exclusive to the Black Sea network and probably produced somewhere in northeastern Turkey.[69] Mediterranean trade amphorae type LRA 1 and LRA 2 are also attested, which explains the creation of local imitations in the north-Pontic region. There was considerable demand for wine in Bosphorus, Tyritake and elsewhere in the region as testified by the presence of Palestinian LRA 5 found both in Crimea and the Taman peninsula and especially Colchian amphorae of much larger capacity shipped from the eastern Black Sea coast.[70]

Through Justinian's imperial efforts the eastern Black Sea coast in Lazica and Abasgia was included more firmly in the Byzantine cultural sphere after several fortresses and towns were rebuilt and fortified.[71] Abasgia became the entry point for Byzantine goods channeled further north across the Caucasus, where they became an index of social status.[72] Agathias described the Lazi as wealthy because they had access to the Black Sea trade network and archaeology offers some confirmation.[73] Following a long tradition, Colchian amphorae, some transporting petroleum (*naphtha*), as well as so-called pseudo-colchian amphorae circulated widely in the Black Sea region although they remain exotic finds in ceramic assemblages from the western coast.[74] Amphora material collected from the vaults of the Byzantine church in Dranda and from other settlements in Abasgia, in conjunction with the numismatic evidence discussed below, reveals strong connections to the Black Sea network. Many of the amphorae found here were Pontic while others were Aegean/Mediterranean imports widely known around the Black Sea, including LRA 1, LRA 2 and LRA 5 amphorae. The material from Abasgia is complemented by finds from Apsaros and Petra in Lazica, where imported pottery as well as Byzantine coins have been found.[75] Sixth-century imperial seals, as well as gold coin hoards found at Petra, Pityus and Archaeopolis document the presence of high officials in Lazica and confirm Byzantine involvement in local culture.[76]

Along with amphorae and fine ware, lamps are among the best studied "international" items circulating in the Mediterranean world. The body of finds from the western Black Sea region shows a remarkable degree of similarity and points to frequent contact between the cities dotting the coastline, as well as evidencing the efficiency of the road network bringing such goods to inland towns and frontier fortresses. The lamps collected from towns such as Akra, Deultum and Anchialos in the Burgas bay in Haemimontus are strikingly similar to the ones found further north on the coast at Tomis and Histria and on the Lower Danube.[77] Some designs were local "Danubian" creations, while other lamps were imports.[78] Lamps produced in Asia Minor circulated widely in the Thracian diocese, the most popular being a sixth-century design with globules on the shoulder, evolving from an earlier model. Initially imported via the Black Sea, these lamps started to be imitated locally with a workshop documented at Halmyris in northern Scythia.[79] The traffic of lamps designed in Asia Minor to the Balkans was reciprocated with several Danubian models becoming popular in the south-Pontic region. The ceramic material from Northern Turkey is only beginning to receive proper attention from archaeologists, but the finds from Hadrianopolis which include Danubian lamps with the handle in the shape of a cross or human faces suggest that these types could have been imported more widely in the Pontic diocese through the mediation of Constantinople, where such lamps are relatively common (Hayes, type 11).[80] Lamps designed in the Balkans were also brought to Crimea via the Black Sea, at Cherson, for further distribution inland.[81] The demand must have been considerable (to the extent that oil was available) since the Chersonite created their own molds in order to mass produce imitations of the Danubian design with cross-shaped handle.[82]

Indeed, Christian lamps seem to have been particularly popular in the Black Sea world. Initially they were imported from North Africa in the fourth and fifth centuries, such finds being ubiquitous in the circumpontic region, but later they were imitated locally, with possible workshops identified at Tomis, Odessos and Durostorum.[83] Religious lamps included models imported from Palestine, sometimes connected with the presence of a Jewish community, as seems to be the case at Cherson where such lamps have been found in the proximity of the local synagogue.[84] Similar lamps with Judaic motifs found in the Balkans appear to be local imitations.[85] Finally, a special category of lamps circulating in the Black Sea region in the sixth and seventh centuries are bronze chandeliers usually connected with the Christian liturgy. Such expensive lamps produced in the Eastern Mediterranean and probably ordered by local churches have been found in Crimea and the Thracian Diocese, having arrived in the region on ships carrying *annona* goods or through the strong network of churches in the Byzantine world.[86]

The Monetary Economy of the Black Sea Region

General Observations

Despite their official function as a medium of exchange, bronze coins have been seldom used as an instrument for measuring levels of communication and economic contact in the Black Sea region. Instead, the discussion is based almost exclusively on the distribution of Byzantine amphorae, fine ceramics, and the study of shipwrecks, as well as on information drawn from literary accounts. Because coins, as official economic instruments, are more standardized and more abundant than any other archaeological artifact the discussion must begin with a series of methodological observations. The most obvious one pertains to the collection and publication of coin finds. There are 8,500 bronze coins from *quaestura exercitus* in the northeastern Balkans and c. 12,000 total in the Diocese of Thracia including single finds and hoards.[87] By comparison, we rely on fewer than 1,000 coins from the coastal provinces of the Pontic diocese and in fact all the published coins from Asia Minor do not equal the number of finds from the Thracian diocese alone. In addition, no bronze coin hoards are so far known from the coastal provinces of Pontus[88]; in sharp contrast, some 35 hoards are known from the coastal provinces of Thracia and this cannot be only a function of heightened insecurity on the Lower Danube frontier.[89] Despite this marked imbalance between the two Black Sea regions, the large number of finds from Sardis suggests that it is premature to draw any conclusions from the existing evidence in Anatolia until site finds are published with more regularity.[90] For the time being we should concentrate on a few general remarks.

In the Northeastern Balkans, Moesia II and Scythia display strikingly similar circulation patterns with the coin flow touching the two regions in very similar ways, a reality mirrored by the archaeological evidence discussed in the previous section. No doubt this is due to the administrative unification of the two provinces under the auspices of *quaestura exercitus*. The strategic geography is also similar as both provinces had access to the Black Sea, while at the same time being in charge of a frontier sector on the Lower Danube. Another particularity of the Balkan provinces is the superior number of coins resulting from systematic excavations. Although museum collections from Bulgaria and Romania are published with regularity, the evidence from Northern Turkey relies more heavily on such samples. Aside from the inability to place the numismatic evidence in a proper archaeological context, we must grapple with the reality that many coins in museum collections do not have a secure provenance and their local origin should be accepted only with a degree of caution.

At the moment we rely on a larger corpus of published coins from the interior of the Pontic provinces, rather than the coast. This is not always explained by neglect in the study of coastal settlements. In Honorias, the publication of finds is more substantial in the regions of Claudiopolis and Hadrianopolis than at Tios on the coast. In neighboring Paphlagonia, the Early Byzantine coins in the museum of Çorum are more numerous than the well-published coins from Amastris and Sinope combined, although both settlements were strategically and economically important harbor towns on the Black Sea coast. Finally, moving east to Hellenopontus, we learn about an abundance of Early Byzantine coins at Amaseia, the administrative capital of the province, but we have comparably little information from Amisos on the coast. Unfortunately, we are far less informed about the situation in Pontus Polemoniacus/Armenia I with very few coins published so far from Neocaesarea, Satala and Theodosiopolis.[91] We know virtually nothing about the finds from Trapezus, an important supply base for the eastern campaigns and a focus of reconstruction during Justinian's age.[92]

Chronological Patterns of Circulation

The first half of the sixth century marks important efforts of reconstruction and reorganization in the Black Sea provinces. In numismatic terms, this covers the four decades between the reforms of Anastasius (498) and Justinian (538), an age of remarkable monetary stability and a time when the Black Sea network itself entered its final phase of expansion. The coinage of Anastasius is more abundant in Pontus than in Thracia, with a few notable exceptions. For instance, at Claudiopolis the dossier of finds is particularly thin for the reigns of Anastasius and Justin I, perhaps reflecting the state of uncertainty that prompted Justinian's provincial reform in Honorias (Table 6.1).[93] Further east, at Amaseia coin circulation is very robust in the first half of the sixth century.[94] As the chief town of Hellenopontus, Amaseia seems to have enjoyed a vibrant monetary economy perhaps enhanced by the Black Sea connection and the proximity to Sinope, a major harbor placed in a privileged central location of the Black Sea network. Unsurprisingly, Sinope displays a similar circulation pattern for these decades (Table 6.2).[95] We find some variation in the western Black Sea region as well where towns from the interior, rather than the coast, such as Tropaeum, Odurtsi and Shumen boast a stronger monetary activity during this phase (Table 6.1). Overall, we cannot be sure if the higher frequency of coins from Anastasius in Pontus compared to Thracia can be attributed to disruptions caused by political events such as the revolt of Vitalianus, but the numbers quickly pick up in the Balkans and surpass Pontus in the first decade of Justinian's reign before the reform of 538.[96] If Thracia and Pontus enjoyed similar levels of monetization during this stage, the imbalance is more pronounced in Cherson where the majority of the Early Byzantine coins found in the city are ¼ and especially ⅛ folles issued between 498 and 538 (Table 6.3).[97] A hoard comprised 55 ⅛ folles of Justin I found near the north wall at Pityus in Abkhazia may have been brought from Cherson as well, via the

Table 6.1 Percentage of bronze coins by reign in landlocked towns

Emperor	*Scythia*			*Moesia*		*Honorias*	*Paphl.*	*Hellenop.*
	Ibida	*Tropaeum*	*Odurtsi*	*Shumen*	*Silistra*	*Claudiopolis*	*Çorum*	*Amaseia*
Anastasius (498–518)	4.11	7.63	8.28	5.13	7.80	7.53	8.52	11.98
Justin I (518–527)	6.85	12.21	11.72	16.03	11.48	1.08	10.80	13.77
Justinian (527–565)	42.47	43.13	40.69	46.79	25.42	19.35	19.32	26.05
Justin II (565–578)	36.99	32.44	33.79	22.44	33.67	24.73	19.89	13.17
Tiberius II (578–582)	1.37	1.53	2.76	2.24	2.45	4.30	4.55	0.90
Maurice (582–602)	5.48	2.67	2.07	4.49	11.37	15.05	16.48	11.98
Phocas (602–610)	0.00	0.38	0.69	0.96	3.79	5.38	9.66	7.78
Heraclius (610–641)	2.74	0.00	0.00	0.96	2.90	19.35	7.95	11.98
Constans II (641–668)	0.00	0.00	0.00	0.64	0.89	3.23	2.27	1.80
Constantine IV (668–685)	0.00	0.00	0.00	0.32	0.22	0.00	0.57	0.30
Justinian II (685–711)	0.00	0.00	0.00	0.00	0.00	0.00	0.00	0.30
(Number of coins)	*(73)*	*(262)*	*(145)*	*(312)*	*(897)*	*(93)*	*(176)*	*(334)*

Table 6.2 Percentage of bronze coins by reign in coastal towns

Emperor	*Scythia*				*Moesia*	*Haemim.*	*Bithynia*	*Paphl.*	*Lazica*
	Argamum	*Histria*	*Tomis*	*Akra*	*Odessos*	*Agathopolis*	*Nicomedia*	*Sinope*	*Pityus*
Anastasius (498–518)	2.38	4.68	5.44	7.23	14.75	3.31	12.21	6.10	9.84
Justin I (518–527)	6.34	6.61	8.89	8.43	8.20	13.81	11.45	17.07	29.51
Justinian (527–565)	38.09	29.75	26.86	21.69	33.61	37.57	20.61	19.51	39.34
Justin II (565–578)	26.98	32.51	27.40	24.10	23.77	35.36	19.08	17.07	6.56
Tiberius II (578–582)	2.38	4.41	2.72	3.61	4.51	1.66	1.53	6.10	0.00
Maurice (582–602)	15.87	17.36	16.33	20.48	8.61	1.66	17.56	6.10	9.84
Phocas (602–610)	4.76	4.13	8.17	3.61	2.05	4.42	6.11	6.10	0.00
Heraclius (610–641)	3.17	0.55	3.27	10.84	4.51	1.66	8.40	9.76	4.92
Constans II (641–668)	0	0.00	0.54	0.00	0.00	0.55	2.29	1.22	0.00
Constantine IV (668–685)	0	0.00	0.00	0.00	0.00	0.00	0.00	8.54	0.00
Justinian II (685–711)	0	0.00	0.36	0.00	0.00	0.00	0.76	2.44	0.00
(Number of coins)	*(126)*	*(363)*	*(551)*	*(83)*	*(244)*	*(181)*	*(131)*	*(82)*	*(61)*

Black Sea, as part of the economic contact between the eastern Black Sea coast and Crimea documented by the circulation of amphorae discussed in the previous section.[98]

Justinian's reform saw the introduction of a large follis struck on an impressive weight standard not seen in the Mediterranean world since the days of the Roman sestertius. This coincides with an increased traffic of goods and people arriving from the reconquered provinces in Africa and Italy. The large coins of Justinian were more popular in the Black Sea region than elsewhere in the Mediterranean world, although exceptions can be noted.[99] Much activity of reconstruction in the Black Sea region has been traditionally attributed to Justinian, following Procopius, although in the Balkans archaeologists prefer to date it more generally to the age starting with the rule of Anastasius.[100] The relative uniformity of the monetary economy in the Black Sea world was broken in the second half of Justinian's reign and was never restored. There are c. 30% more coins from 542 to 550 in Pontic cities compared to Thracia but c. 60% fewer coins from 550 to 565. What explains this fluctuation? In Northern Turkey, the reason behind the superior volume of currency from 542 to 550 could be the substantial influx of coins minted in Antioch, 16% compared to 5% in Thracia. In the last stage of Justinian's reign (550–565), the western Black Sea market was flooded with *decanummia* (¼ follis) issued by Constantinople and the Propontic mints.[101] These are particularly common finds in coastal cities like Tomis, Agathopolis, and Akra but also in towns and fortresses further inland like Ibida and Odurtsi (Tables 6.4 and 6.5).[102] Such coins are far less common in the Pontic diocese; surprisingly, this includes the city of Nicomedia, where massive quantities of ¼ folles were minted during Justinian's reign.[103]

Table 6.3 Percentage of bronze coins by reign in the Black Sea region

Emperor	*Scythia*	*Moesia*	*Haemim.*	*Bith.*	*Hon.*	*Hellenop.*	*Paphl.*	*Lazica*	*Crimea*	*C-ple*
Anastasius (498–518)	6.24	8.39	3.88	15.06	5.88	12.31	6.73	11.56	13.39	5.86
Justin I (518–527)	10.44	13.40	11.64	9.64	4.20	14.15	12.50	17.59	13.11	24.37
Justinian (527–565)	30.86	31.87	35.82	16.27	21.85	27.08	19.55	32.16	67.21	6.26
Justin II (565–578)	31.59	31.55	26.57	21.69	20.17	13.23	18.27	10.55	0.82	10.65
Tiberius II (578–582)	2.37	2.22	0.90	4.82	0.84	0.92	4.49	1.51	0.00	1.33
Maurice (582–602)	11.81	6.47	6.27	16.87	12.61	12.31	14.42	13.07	3.55	3.06
Phocas (602–610)	4.02	3.28	6.57	4.82	4.20	6.15	8.33	4.02	0.27	8.39
Heraclius (610–641)	2.25	2.52	2.69	8.43	25.21	11.69	9.29	6.03	0.27	8.12
Constans II (641–668)	0.24	0.24	3.58	1.81	3.36	1.54	2.88	3.52	0.82	21.84
Constantine IV (668–685)	0.09	0.04	2.09	0.00	1.68	0.31	2.88	0.00	0.27	5.46
Justinian II (685–711)	0.09	0.00	0.00	0.60	0.00	0.31	0.64	0.00	0.27	4.66

Table 6.4 Percentage of bronze coins by denomination in coastal towns

Denomination	*Scythia*				*Moesia*	*Haemim.*	*Bithynia*	*Paphl.*	*Lazica*
	Argamum	*Histria*	*Tomis*	*Akra*	*Odessos*	*Agathopolis*	*Nicomedia*	*Sinope*	*Pityus*
Follis	45.67	50.58	35.10	48.89	68.36	15.17	79.26	66.67	54.84
¾ Follis	0.00	0.00	0.00	0.00	1.17	0.00	0.00	0.00	1.61
½ Follis	32.28	36.66	36.75	41.11	24.22	8.99	14.07	19.75	20.97
16 Nummi	0.00	0.00	0.18	0.00	0.00	0.00	0.00	1.23	0.00
¼ Follis	17.32	6.03	14.99	10.00	2.34	17.98	1.48	8.64	3.23
⅛ Follis	4.72	6.73	12.98	0.00	3.91	57.87	5.19	3.70	19.35

Table 6.5 Percentage of bronze coins by denomination in landlocked towns

Denomination	*Scythia*			*Moesia*		*Honorias*	*Paphl.*	*Hellenop.*
	Ibida	*Tropaeum*	*Odurtsi*	*Shumen*	*Silistra*	*Claudiopolis*	*Çorum*	*Amaseia*
Follis	27.63	51.53	37.67	67.00	50.45	79.82	81.67	79.94
¾ Follis	0.00	0.00	0.68	0.34	0.22	0.00	1.11	0.00
½ Follis	23.68	26.34	40.41	25.93	31.57	16.51	13.33	19.16
16 Nummi	0.00	0.76	0.00	0.34	1.01	0.00	0.00	0.00
¼ Follis	26.32	15.65	12.33	5.72	8.65	1.83	2.78	0.60
⅛ Follis	22.37	5.73	8.90	0.67	8.09	1.83	1.11	0.30

During the last decades of the sixth century political events led to further divergence from the common pattern of coin circulation in the Black Sea world. The process underway since the later part of Justinian's reign accelerated under Justin II. The coins of this emperor account for only c. 25% in Pontus versus c. 45% in Thracia. It is not an accident that this high volume of fresh coin coincides with the heyday of state support in *quaestura exercitus*. The massive influx of Thessalonican ½ folles sent to the frontier provinces as payment to soldiers is responsible for this stark difference and is only partly offset by the superior flow of coinage from Antioch in northern Anatolia. Through commerce some of Thessalonica's coinage also penetrated the Pontic market with finds recorded on the coast at Amastris, Sinope and Nicomedia but also inland at Nicaea, Claudiopolis, Çorum and Theodosiopolis (Tables 6.6 and 6.7).[104] Yet, the coinage of Justin II seems to be less abundant moving eastward in the coastal provinces from Bithynia to Lazica and generally as one moves away from the Danube frontier (Table 6.3). Justin II's work of fortification is rarely mentioned in literary accounts, but the emperor's decision to stop sending subsidies to barbarians during the decade of relative peace before the outbreak of the war with Persia probably led to efforts to strengthen defenses. Epigraphic evidence from Crimea suggests that the emperor saw the northern frontier as particularly vulnerable during an age when the Avars were on the rise and the relations of power in the nomadic world were becoming highly volatile.[105]

The high frequency of later sixth-century hoards lost in the Eastern Balkans confirms the climate of instability on the frontier, which did not spare even coastal cities.[106] The crisis deepened under Maurice. The emperor spent the 580s fighting the Persians and the next decade struggling with the Avars in the Balkans and both conflicts left their mark on the monetary economy of coastal Thracia and Pontus. Hoards from cities such as Histria, Varna, Tropaeum and Zaldapa, as well as archaeological evidence of destruction confirm the devastation brought by Avaro-Slavic invasions known from written accounts.[107] In some Black Sea towns this accelerated the process of ruralization. Under Maurice, one-third of the coinage in Pontus was supplied by Antioch, while in the Eastern Balkans its contribution does not surpass 6% on average. This is compensated by the continuous influx of Thessalonican ½ folles accounting for c. 25% of the coinage introduced on the western Black Sea market under Maurice (Table 6.8). More significantly, both in Thracia and Pontus the second decade of his reign saw a disruption of the influx

Table 6.6 Percentage of bronze coins by mint in coastal towns

Mint	*Scythia*				*Moesia*	*Haemim.*	*Bithynia*	*Paphl.*	*Lazica*
	Argamum	*Histria*	*Tomis*	*Akra*	*Odessos*	*Agathopolis*	*Nicomedia*	*Sinope*	*Pityus*
Constantinople	54.54	61.49	63.88	53.57	62.90	57.69	60.90	65.43	78.43
Nicomedia	23.14	16.46	14.83	19.05	17.34	19.87	20.30	14.81	9.80
Cyzicus	9.09	4.97	6.08	8.33	9.68	7.69	3.76	4.94	0.00
Thessalonica	12.39	11.18	11.60	14.29	4.84	3.21	2.26	2.47	5.88
Antioch	0	5.28	3.04	3.57	5.24	9.62	12.78	9.88	3.92
Cherson	0	0.00	0.00	1.19	0.00	0.00	0.00	1.23	0.00
Rome	0	0.00	0.00	0.00	0.00	0.64	0.00	1.23	0.00
Carthage	0.82	0.62	0.38	0.00	0.00	1.28	0.00	0.00	1.96
Alexandria	0	0.00	0.19	0.00	0.00	0.00	0.00	0.00	0.00

Table 6.7 Percentage of bronze coins by mint in landlocked towns

Mint	*Scythia*			*Moesia*		*Honorias*	*Paphl.*	*Hellenop.*
	Ibida	*Tropaeum*	*Odurtsi*	*Shumen*	*Silistra*	*Claudiopolis*	*Çorum*	*Amaseia*
Constantinople	65.75	66.80	63.57	67.22	54.10	45.65	48.26	56.82
Nicomedia	15.07	13.13	16.43	16.72	17.40	21.74	22.67	16.88
Cyzicus	4.11	5.79	5.71	6.69	7.97	10.87	8.14	5.52
Thessalonica	5.48	8.88	10.00	4.68	14.14	1.09	1.16	0.00
Antioch	6.85	5.02	2.86	4.68	5.05	18.48	19.77	20.45
Cherson	0.00	0.00	0.00	0.00	0.00	0.00	0.00	0.32
Rome	0.00	0.00	0.00	0.00	0.45	1.09	0.00	0.00
Carthage	2.74	0.39	1.43	0.00	0.34	1.09	0.00	0.00
Alexandria	0.00	0.00	0.00	0.00	0.56	0.00	0.00	0.00

of fresh coin released in circulation, as many towns around the Black Sea were supplied with only a quarter of the coinage received in the 580s. The situation already noted in the Balkans corroborated now with evidence from Anatolia confirms that the Empire experienced a deep financial crisis in the last decade of the sixth century when mint output dropped significantly.[108] It is not clear whether commerce and communication in the Black Sea were affected but it would not be surprising if the volume of transactions overall suffered during this crisis.[109] To be sure, this did not bring a collapse of the Black Sea network. At Tomis many of the low-value coins found in the mosaic edifice with vaulted storerooms date from the last quarter of the sixth century and the economic function of the harbor appears to have continued at least until the second decade of the seventh century.[110]

The seventh century marks the end of the Early Byzantine phase in many cities from Thracia, while others, like Mesembria and Anchialos had to cope with the new reality of a contracting Byzantine world, being robbed of their safety and forced to become focal points in the empire's first line of defense against the Bulgarian Kingdom.[111] Equally, the situation became dramatic in parts of Asia Minor where the Persians sacked provincial centers and threatened Constantinople itself. The state of chaos further isolated the mountainous region of Pontus. Changes in coin circulation in the Black Sea world are particularly revealing and can help us understand a century marked by profound cultural

Table 6.8 Percentage of bronze coins by mint in the Black Sea region

Mint	*Scythia*	*Moesia*	*Haemim.*	*Bith.*	*Hon.*	*Hellenop.*	*Paphl.*	*Lazica*	*Crimea*	*C-ple*
Constantinople	61.79	59.78	65.99	57.39	53.51	56.63	54.52	60.66	44.05	89.13
Nicomedia	14.52	13.77	17.17	17.61	19.30	16.83	19.73	10.38	2.38	6.38
Cyzicus	5.28	9.72	5.39	3.98	9.65	5.50	6.69	4.37	0.00	1.63
Thessalonica	13.84	11.20	4.04	3.41	0.88	0.00	2.34	4.92	0.00	1.25
Antioch	3.61	5.00	6.40	17.61	14.91	20.71	16.05	13.66	2.38	1.50
Cherson	0.12	0.00	0.00	0.00	0.00	0.32	0.33	2.73	50.00	0.00
Rome	0.09	0.11	0.34	0.00	0.88	0.00	0.33	0.00	0.00	0.00
Carthage	0.59	0.32	0.67	0.00	0.88	0.00	0.00	2.73	0.00	0.13
Alexandria	0.15	0.11	0.00	0.00	0.00	0.00	0.00	0.55	1.19	0.00

change in the larger Mediterranean world. In Thracia, 83% of the coins from Heraclius are dated between 610 and 616. Given his long reign (610–641) and the archaeological evidence of destruction in some cities and frontier fortresses it seemed reasonable to conclude that a major moment of discontinuity occurred c. 615.[112] A similar scenario was suggested by Clive Foss in his classic study concerning the end of antiquity in Asia Minor.[113] However, the numismatic argument can be misleading. Cities on the Black Sea coast in Northern Turkey were obviously not affected by the Avaro-Slavic invasions and were likely bypassed by the Persian offensive whose main target was Constantinople and the large cities of Anatolia. Yet, the issues from 610 to 616 still account for 73% of the coins from Heraclius. Although the situation is slightly better compared to the western Black Sea coast, it still points to a common problem and that cannot be attributed to any particular invasion.

A possible answer is provided by the finds from the capital. In Constantinople, 53% of the coins minted under Heraclius date from 610 to 616.[114] Essentially, we are dealing with two problems. The first is a major monetary crisis marked by a significantly reduced minting activity, which started under Maurice, as we have seen. This is evident in the fact that half the number of coins from a 31-year reign date to the first 6 years.[115] The second problem is the chronological structure of the finds from 616 to 641 in Constantinople, the overwhelming majority dating from the last decade of Heraclius' reign with a peak in 639–640 when the emperor celebrated his *tricennalia*. There are no such finds in towns from the western Black Sea coast with only one coin known from the region of Silistra on the Danube.[116] Such late coins are attested in settlements from three different provinces of the southern Black Sea coast, at Amaseia, Hadrianopolis, Claudiopolis, Nicomedia and Sinope, but percentagewise they are far less well represented than what we see in Constantinople.[117] Based on the current evidence it appears that a major monetary break in the Balkans occurred only in the 630s when coins, although minted in sufficient quantity as reflected by finds from the capital, never reached locations on the western Black Sea coast. The monetary economy was contracting and becoming insular and Byzantine towns, if they survived the upheavals of the seventh century, either abandoned economic exchanges mediated by money or simply used the existing monetary stock from the previous decades.

The crisis was never fully overcome, in part because of dramatic political events in the early decades of the seventh century – the last Persian war, the rise of Islam, and the Avaro-Slavic takeover in the Balkans. Pontic cities, especially former provincial capitals such as Claudiopolis, Amaseia and Nicomedia, but also harbor cities like Sinope, continued to receive coinage in the second half of the seventh century with the latest bronze coins being issues of Tiberius III and Justinian II from Sinope, Nicomedia and Amaseia; their number remains far more modest than what we see at Sardis, at least until Constantine IV, and certainly compared to Amorium where the percentage of late seventh-century to early eighth-century coins rivals the one from Saraçhane and Kalenderhane in Constantinople.[118] Provincial towns in Pontus display similar patterns. At Hadrianopolis, the bulk of the Early Byzantine coinage found in the *domus*, Bath A and Church C dates to the seventh century; this may either reflect the nature of the complexes excavated, or simply the monetary profile of settlements that maintained some significance throughout the seventh century compared to those that faded into obscurity during the reign of Heraclius.[119] Further east, in Paphlagonia, Pompeiopolis boasts the highest concentration of mid and late seventh-century coinage, owing to its role as a military center against the Arab advance.[120] Such coins are very well represented at Sinope, a city enjoying the highest percentage of seventh-century coins from all surveyed sites in the Black Sea region (Table 6.4). By contrast, on the western coast, later seventh-century bronze coins appear only sporadically on several points on the Danube and in large towns such as Tomis, Callatis and Mesembria where Byzantium maintained a foothold, while finds of gold coins are generally connected to imperial diplomatic and military efforts to restore some semblance of control in the Balkans.[121] The crisis also reached Crimea where the local "*pentanummium* economy" all but collapsed in the seventh century. There are, however, important elements of continuity; the city mint remained operational, stamping Heraclian countermarks on older issues and minting coinage as late as the reign of Constans II.[122]

Mints and Denominations

There are good reasons for including mints and denominations among the parameters used to evaluate the monetary economy of the Black Sea region. Mintmarks can provide information about connections established with the wider Byzantine world as well as precious clues regarding the official mechanisms for the distribution of coinage, while denominations can open a window into daily market transactions, whose scale and frequency are reflected in the range and frequency of folles and fractions circulating locally.

The mint of Constantinople dominates the coin assemblage in every town of the western Black Sea region, usually covering more than 50% of the finds. The same consistency applies to the Propontic mints of Nicomedia and Cyzicus, whose contribution averages a combined c. 20% in most settlements (Tables 6.6 and 6.7). Thessalonica is the only mint showing clear signs of consignment for the frontier region, the chief destination for its ½ folles issued in large quantities in the second half of the sixth century.[123] In the Pontic diocese the mint of Constantinople played a similar role, which is not surprising (Table 6.8). It is the activity of the Propontic mints that require special consideration. Although Cyzicus and Nicomedia were located in Hellespontus and Bithynia, respectively, their contribution to the circulating medium in Pontus is not particularly significant. The collection of the Kocaeli museum in İzmit (Nicomedia) indicates that the local mint supplied only 20% of the coinage circulating locally, while coins minted at Nicomedia represent c. 17% of the finds in the Pontic diocese.[124] The activity of the Propontic mints was probably correlated with the needs of the central mint in Constantinople and followed a centralized strategy of distributing coinage to certain provinces, distance being a secondary concern. The concentration of coinage from Nicomedia in distant towns, such as the case of Gerasa in Arabia under Justin II suggests a much more complex function played by the Propontic mints, which awaits further study.[125]

One wonders if Antioch was tasked to supply coinage in a similar fashion. Iconographic and metrological studies suggest that the Syrian mint enjoyed a certain degree of autonomy.[126] It is notable that in several major towns of the Pontic diocese Antioch is the second most important mint after Constantinople. It is unlikely that Antioch was required to dispatch fresh coinage by consignment to Pontic cities like Sinope and Amastris. It is more probable that such coins arrived on the coast on ships coming from the Aegean and the Eastern Mediterranean. Sixth-century Synopean amphorae Type D carrying olive oil are more common in the Eastern Mediterranean and inland in Syria-Palestine than in the Black Sea region and this might offer one explanation for the number of coins minted in Antioch found in northern Turkey.[127] The massive quantity of Levantine LRA 4 and LRA 5 containers found inland in places like Pompeiopolis suggests a two-way traffic of goods between the two regions.[128] Overland routes could have been used as well, with even more frequency, as Antioch's coinage was very influential in landlocked cities of the Pontic diocese and especially on the eastern frontier, at Melitene where the Syrian mint is dominant, a pattern which extends further north to Lazica (Table 6.7).[129] By contrast, in the eastern Balkans the mint of Antioch accounts for less than 5% of the finds. Written accounts inform us that Maurice transferred the army from the east to face the challenge mounted by the Avars in the last decade of the century.[130] At Tropaeum, a hoard found in a tower included an unusual number of coins minted at Antioch. Their presence allowed the editors to speculate that the small purse belonged to a soldier transferred from the east.[131] A similar interpretation can be suggested for the rare Sasanian drachms found at Axiopolis on the Danube frontier, which may reflect traffic from the eastern Black Sea region and the Transcaucasus where these coins are common.[132]

In addition to the common mints, less than a hundred coins from "exotic" mints have been found in the Thracian diocese and while they represent a mere 1% of the finds, their presence in the region indicates some type of long-distance contact with Italy and North Africa (Table 6.8). This need not be direct contact and at least some of these coins are likely to have been brought through the mediation of centers in Illyricum where western goods and coins are more common.[133] Among these mints rarely seen in towns from the western Black Sea region, Carthage is the most common and the circulation of North African ceramics could have brought some coinage on the western Black Sea coast.[134] As the sixth century saw renewed imperial efforts in the West it is very difficult to distinguish between the circulation of goods and the movement of people, especially soldiers from Justinian's multiethnic armies who served in North Africa and Italy. Several coins from Rome and Ravenna have been found in the Northeastern Balkans, as well as coins issued by mobile military mints labeled *Moneta Militaris Imitativa* by W. Hahn.[135] On the other hand, the coins from Alexandria, which include a rare 33-nummia piece found at Tomis, may be connected with the regular supply of Egyptian grain, which also brought "Coptic" bronze lamps and St. Menas flasks to the region.[136] Several Alexandrian *dodecanummia* were part of a hoard found on the Danube frontier at Topalu, its eastern flavor being confirmed by a significant number of coins from Antioch.[137] Finds from this militarized environment are more likely to reflect the movement of soldiers, some returning home after having served in the Eastern Mediterranean.[138] This interpretation might not be equally convincing for the coins minted at Alexandria found in Abasgia, on the eastern Black Sea coast, where the ceramic material discussed in the previous section reveals commercial ties to the Mediterranean world.[139]

Western coins are rare in the coastal provinces of Pontus. Only one coin from Carthage is known, from the region of Claudiopolis, although several more pieces are recorded in the museums of Niğde and Kayseri from Capadoccia, in the southern part of the Pontic diocese. Although still of marginal significance to the circulating pool, the coins of Carthage are more common in Lazica where "military" issues are also known and could indicate that currency minted in the Western Mediterranean was brought by soldiers. A coin from Rome found at Sinope may be connected with the circulation of Sinopean amphorae type C as far as the Italian coast.[140] Among the exotic mints we can also include Cherson, whose city coinage sometimes reached towns across the Black Sea, such as Akra, Sinope, Amaseia as well as locations on the frontier such as Lazica and the Lower Danube (Table 6.6).[141] Additional finds are recorded in the north-Pontic area, as well as further inland on the Dniepr and as far north as Tambov in Russia, evidencing Cherson's economic and cultural connections in the northern *barbaricum*.[142]

Table 6.9 Percentage of bronze coins by denomination in the Black Sea region

Denomination	*Scythia*	*Moesia*	*Haemim.*	*Bith.*	*Hon.*	*Hellenop.*	*Paphl.*	*Lazica*	*Crimea*	*C-ple*
Follis	44.50	62.75	36.10	78.83	77.27	80.00	77.53	69.19	10.59	28.07
¾ Follis	0.12	0.11	0.00	0.00	0.00	0.00	0.63	0.51	0.00	0.38
½ Follis	37.73	27.89	15.47	14.60	17.42	19.10	15.19	16.67	0.00	18.05
16 Nummi	0.38	0.59	0.57	0.00	0.00	0.00	0.32	0.51	0.00	0.00
¼ Follis	10.08	5.98	14.33	1.46	3.79	0.60	4.43	2.02	36.47	14.29
⅛ Follis	7.19	2.69	33.52	5.11	1.52	0.30	1.90	11.11	52.94	39.22

As far as denominations are concerned the most striking feature is the prevalence of the follis in northern Turkey, accounting for more than three-quarters of the published coins (Table 6.9). Such an overwhelming reliance on the follis is unusual even for small military settlements on the Danube frontier which did not benefit from the large volume of transactions typical of urban markets; in a small fortress like Capidava the frequency of the follis remained under 50%.[143] Indeed, the frequency of low denominations remains the most reliable indicator for the health of local exchanges. The best example is Constantinople itself, although the published samples were collected from religious rather than economic complexes.[144] The large urban market was dominated by low-value coinage; the small module coinage of Anastasius from 498 to 512 remained in circulation, while ⅛ folles issued by his successors are very abundant. In fact, more than 50% of the catalogue is comprised small change. The follis sits at c. 28% and half of those are small folles of Constans II having the weight of a sixth-century ¼ follis. A similar situation can be found at Cherson in Crimea. The city mint specialised in the production of *pentanummia* until the last decades of the century, while most of the coins issued by other Byzantine mints found in the city are also low-value coins which probably arrived through trade, evidenced by the ceramic material discussed in the previous section (Table 6.9).[145] In addition, site finds and especially hoards indicate that older coinage of comparable weight, including Greek, Bosporan, Roman and Late Roman issues, continued to circulate into the seventh century side-by-side with contemporary Byzantine issues.[146]

When looking at such discrepancies we should remember the fact that many of the Early Byzantine coins from Pontus were not found during controlled archaeological excavations. Many are stray finds with unclear provenance and some may reflect collecting habits rather than being an accurate reflection of the ancient coin pool. However, we should not be too quick to attribute the scarcity of lower denominations to the nature of museum collections alone. Excavation coins from the Pontic diocese, at Hadrianopolis, Neocaesarea and Tyana have not yielded more substantial numbers of low-value coins, although the sample is sometimes too small to inspire any confidence.[147] Hoard evidence from the Aegean and the Black Sea world as well as securely dated assemblages indicate that Late Roman coinage continued to be used as small change well into the sixth century. Despite this fact, in the Eastern Balkans Early Byzantine small denominations are also present, or even dominant in cities such as Ibida and Agathopolis (Table 6.5). Notwithstanding local variations, on many sites in Thracia, whether urban or military, small change comprised ¼ and ⅛ folles accounts for c. 20% of the finds. The same is true for Cherson in Crimea, where such coins are even more common, as well as Pityus in Lazica where early sixth-century ⅛ folles are particularly well represented. This is not the case in the Pontic diocese where Sinope alone breaks the 10% barrier for lower denominations.[148]

Conclusion

Evidence collected from the Black Sea region reveals the existence of a vibrant network in the sixth century. The network itself was established at least two millennia before the age of Justinian and although the trade partners changed along with the cultural fabric of the region a distinctive Pontic identity slowly developed over centuries of contact. The sixth century in the Black Sea was a long one indeed. The great upheavals of the Heraclian age gripped the Black Sea coast with a gentler touch and in many ways the Pontic region weathered the initial storm better than the Mediterranean. In the Balkans, large cities like Odessos were burned and never recovered, while "life in the city" continued in other coastal cities like Tomis and Callatis where the connection to Constantinople was not severed until c. 680.[149] In the bay of Burgas, Anchialos and Mesembria remained important Byzantine outposts visited by Constantine IV and Justinian II.[150] The southern Black Sea coast fared even better. Most cities were not directly affected by the Persian and Arab invasions aiming to conquer Constantinople. The Black Sea shore was at a distance from their main target and did not offer enough potential to justify the risks of raiding so deep into Byzantine territory.[151] A city like Amastris could retain its role as a commercial, naval and ecclesiastical center on the Black Sea coast.[152] Coin evidence indicates that Sinope remained equally connected to Constantinople via the Black Sea. The eastern coast in Lazica also remained under Byzantine control in the seventh century. Ecclesiastical centers were still functional at Sebastopolis and Phasis and Constans II chose to punish monothelite heretics by sending them in exile to this remote corner of the Byzantine world.[153] Crimea was also a place where officials fallen out of favor were sent into exile by sea. The list includes Pope Martin, exiled to Cherson in 655, and emperor Justinian II in 695, the latter at a time when the Khazars were in almost complete control of the peninsula.[154]

At the beginning of the sixth century, however, these major upheavals still lay in the distant future; dozens of cities strung along the shore "like frogs around a pond" prospered under a resurgent Byzantium. The available archaeological evidence, dominated by coins and ceramics, has guided our journey through the Black Sea network of communication, supply and trade. All evidence points to an age of expansion in the first half of the sixth century. Cities were being rebuilt and refortified, connections in the wider Mediterranean world reestablished and state support ramped up in the Empire's peripheral regions. Ships crisscrossed the Black Sea and the road network ensured the swift deployment of troops and the supply of settlements inland. The harbors of Constantinople acted as the main hub for naval traffic in the Black Sea. Ships loaded with annonary goods followed the coastline to the mouths of the Danube, docking in harbors like Anchialos, Odessos and Tomis. They were bringing wine and olive oil from the Aegean, as well as an assortment of fine wares, lamps and perishable goods no longer visible in the archaeological record. They also brought coins minted in the Propontis or in more distant provinces of the Mediterranean.[155] Ships laden with special orders of Proconnesian marble docked in the ports of Abasgia, where Christian communities flourishing under the protection of Byzantium tried to imitate the architectural styles fashionable in the great centers of the Empire. Following the western and eastern coast as well as venturing into the open sea from Sinope, sea lanes converged on the Crimean Peninsula where imported glass, pottery, liturgical lamps and famous Palestinian wine reinforced the social status of the multiethnic elite in Cherson and Bosphorus.

Much of the exchange was mediated by coins and the existence of a monetary economy was a standard feature of cities, towns and even fortresses. Whether stationed on the

Danube frontier, a fort in Lazica or an outpost on the Taman peninsula, soldiers handled Byzantine money on a daily basis. The same money was used with even more frequency in coastal cities where communities were more cosmopolitan and business more diverse. The imported goods available around the Black Sea were not very different and coin circulation followed a similar pattern. Byzantine coins and goods added an "international" flavor to local tastes and cultural traditions which could differ significantly from one region to another. Most importantly, the role of the sea in bringing together these cultural microregions strengthens the observation that the Black Sea, with its distinctive elements of diversity and commonality, deserves to be discussed on its own terms rather than as a mere periphery of the Mediterranean world.

Notes

1 Ovid, *Tristia* V.X.13–14.

2 Procopius, *Bella* 2.28.23.

3 G. I. Brătianu, *La Mer Noire. Des origines à la conquete ottomane* (Munich: Rumänische Akademische Gesellschaft, 1969 [1942]). For a more general history of the Black Sea from antiquity to present day, see C. King, *The Black Sea: A History* (New York: Oxford University Press, 2002). For the prehistoric age, see M. Ivanova, *The Black Sea and the Early Civilizations of Europe, the Near East and Asia* (New York: Cambridge University Press, 2013). For the Black Sea as a historical focus, see E. Özveren, "The Black Sea as A Unit of Analysis," in *Politics of the Black Sea: Dynamics of Cooperation and Conflict*, ed. T. Aybak (London: Tauris, 2001), 61–84; O. Doonan, "The Corrupting Sea and the Hospitable Sea: Some Early Thoughts Towards a Regional History of the Black Sea," in *Koine: Mediterranean Studies in Honor of R. Ross Holloway*, eds. A. Tuck and D. Counts (Oxford: Oxbow Books, 2009), 68–74.

4 Collective volumes focusing on the Black Sea offered a partial solution to this problem; see B. Rémy (ed.), *Pontica I. Recherches sur l'histoire du Pont dans l'Antiquité* (Istanbul: Institut Français d'Études Anatoliennes – Georges Dumézil, 1991); R. Pillinger, A. Pulz, and H. Vetters (eds.), *Die Schwarzmeerküste in der Spätantike und im frühen Mittelalter* (Vienna: Verlag der Österreichischen Akademie der Wissenschaften, 1992); V. Gabrielsen and J. Lund (eds.), *The Black Sea in Antiquity. Regional and Interregional Economic Exchanges* (Aarhus: Aarhus University Press, 2007); D. Kassab Tezgör and N. Inaishvili (eds.), *Patabs I. Production and Trade of Amphorae in the Black Sea* (Istanbul: Institut Français d'Études Anatoliennes – Georges Dumézil, 2010); G. R. Tsetskhladze, S. Atasoy, A. Avram, Ş. Dönmez, and J. Hargrave (eds.), *The Bosporus: Gateway between the Ancient West and East (1st Millennium BC-5th Century AD)* (Oxford: Archaeopress, 2013); G. R. Tsestskhladze (ed.), *The Black Sea, Paphlagonia, Pontus and Phrygia in Antiquity: Aspects of Archaeology and Ancient History* (Oxford: Archaeopress, 2012); F. Karagianni (ed.), *Medieval Ports in North Aegean and the Black Sea: Links to the Maritime Routes of the East* (Thessaloniki: European Centre for Byzantine and Post-Byzantine Monuments, 2013); F. Karagianni (ed.), *40 Medieval City-Ports in North Aegean and the Black Sea: A Cultural Guide* (Thessaloniki: European Centre for Byzantine and Post-Byzantine Monuments, 2014); V. Kozlovskaya (ed.), *The Northern Black Sea in Antiquity: Networks, Connectivity, and Cultural Interactions* (Cambridge: Cambridge University Press, 2017).

5 D. C. Braund, *Georgia in Antiquity: A History of Colchis and Transcaucasian Iberia, 550 BC-AD 562* (Oxford: Clarendon Press, 1994), 274–287.

6 The most detailed treatment of *quaestura exercitus* remains A. Gkoutzioukostas and X. M. Moniaros, *Η περιφερειακή διοικητική αναδιοργάνωση της Βυζαντινής Αυτοκράτορίας από τον Ιουστινιανό Α (527-565): Η περίπτωση της Quaestura Iustiniana Exercitus* (Thessaloniki: Banias, 2009).

7 S. Stanimirov, "Underwater Archaeological Sites from Ancient and Middle Ages along Bulgarian Black Sea Coast – Classification," *Archaeologia Bulgarica* 7, no. 1 (2003): 27, table 6. For the underwater ceramic assemblage, dominated by fifth- and sixth-century material, see I. Hristov, *Mare Ponticum: Coastal Fortresses and Harbour Zones in the Province of Haemimontus 5th-7th Century* (Sofia: Unicart, 2018), 87.

8 Hristov, *Mare Ponticum*; A. Minchev, "Ten Less Investigated Late Antique Fortresses on the Bulgarian Black Sea Coast (4th–early 7th Century AD)," in Karagianni (ed.), *Medieval Ports*, 248–275.

9 On this long debated question, see recently A. Sarantis, "Military Provisioning in the Sixth-Century Balkans," *Journal of Late Antiquity* 12, no. 2 (2019): 329–379; F. Curta, "Coins, Forts and Commercial Exchanges in the Sixth- and Early Seventh-Century Balkans," *Oxford Journal of Archaeology* 36, no. 4 (2017): 439–454.

10 A. Bryer and D. Winfield, *The Byzantine Monuments and Topography of the Pontos* (Washington, DC: Dumbarton Oaks Research Library and Collection, 1985); D. P. Drakoulis, "Regional Transformations and the Settlement Network of the Coastal Pontic Provinces in the Early Byzantine Period," in Tsestskhladze (ed.), *The Black Sea*, 90; M. Ritter, "The End of Late Antiquity in Paphlagonia: Disurbanisation From a Comparative Perspective," in *Landscape Dynamics and Settlement Patterns in Northern Anatolia during the Roman and Byzantine Period*, eds. K. Winther-Jacobsen and L. Summerer (Stuttgart: Franz Steiner Verlag, 2015), 119–133.

11 E. Laflı, C. Lightfoot, and M. Ritter, "Byzantine Coins from Hadrianoupolis in Paphlagonia," *Byzantine and Modern Greek Studies* 40, no. 2 (2016): 191.

12 T. Brüggemann, "Paphlagonia between Goths, Sasanids and Arabs (3rd-8th Centuries AD)," in Tsestskhladze (ed.), *The Black Sea*, 47; Drakoulis, "Regional Transformations," 85–86.

13 Menander (ed. Blockley), fr. 6.1.

14 *Corpus Iuris Civilis*, Novella 28 (535 AD).

15 Iu. N. Voronov, "The Eastern Pontus within the Sphere of Byzantine Political and Cultural Activities, the Sixth-Eighth Centuries," in *XVIIIth International Congress of Byzantine Studies. Selected Papers: Main and Communications, Moscow 1991*, vol. 2, eds. I. Ševčenko, G. G. Litavrin, and W. K. Hanak (Shepherdstown, WV, 1996), 169; W. Seibt, "Westgeorgien (Egrisi, Lazica) in frühchristlicher Zeit," in Pillinger et al. (eds.), *Die Schwarzmeerküste*, 141; Braund, *Georgia in Antiquity*, 282–284.

16 T. Lewit, "The Second Sea: Exchange between the Mediterranean and the Black Sea in Late Antiquity," *Post-Classical Archaeologies* 5 (2015): 165; F. Curta, "The North-Western Region of the Black Sea during the 6th and Early 7th Century AD," *Ancient West & East* 7 (2008): 169–170.

17 A. Aibabin, "Written Sources on Byzantine Ports in the Crimea from the Fourth to Seventh Century," in Karagianni (ed.), *Medieval Ports*, 60; S. Albrecht, "Cherson als Zentralort auf der südwestlichen Krim (6.-10. Jahrhundert)," in *GrenzÜbergänge: Spätrömisch, frühchristlich, frühbyzantinisch als Kategorien der historisch-archäologischen Forschung an der mittleren Donau*, eds. I. Bugarski, O. Heinrich-Tamáska, V. Ivaniševic, and D. Syrbe (Weinstadt: Greiner Verlag, 2016), 362.

18 C. B. Sorochan, "Vizantijskie voennye sily v Krymu VI-VII vv.," *Stratum plus* 6 (2014): 122.

19 Malalas, 18.14.

20 Procopius, *De Aedificiis*, 3.7.10–12. For the archaeological evidence, see I. O. Gavritukhin and M. Kazanski, "Bosporus, the Tetraxite Goths, and the Northern Caucasus Region during the Second Half of the Fifth and the Sixth Centuries," in *Neglected Barbarians*, ed. F. Curta (Turnhout: Brepols, 2008).

21 Hristov, *Mare Ponticum*, 76.

22 Bryer and Winfield, *Byzantine Monuments*, 18.

23 For the challenges faced by the Late Antique city, see recently M. Humphries, *Cities and the Meaning of Late Antiquity* (Lieden: Brill, 2019), with extensive coverage of previous research, although very little is said about cities from the Black Sea region.

24 J. Crow, "Recent Research on the Late Antique Cities of Eastern Thrace (Provincia Europa)," in *The Roman and Late Roman City*, eds. L. Ruseva-Slokoska, R. Teofilov Ivanov, and V. Dinchev (Sofia: Academic Publishing House, 2002), 345–346.

25 Hristov, *Mare Ponticum*, 279–282; N. Chaneva-Dechevska, *Rannohristianskata arhitektura v Balgaria IV-VI v.* (Sofia: Universitetsko izdatelstvo "Sv. Kliment Okhridski", 1999), 235. C. Drazheva, "Gradskite tsentrove po iuzhnoto Balgarsko Chernomorie prez VII-XV vek – posrednitsi mezhdu Balgaria i Vizantia," *Niš i Vizantija* 3 (2005): 225–240.

26 I. Hristov (ed.), *Akra. Exploring the Early Byzantine Fortress on St. Nikola Peninsula Near the Town of Chernomorets*, vol. 1 (Sofia: Unicart, 2013), 66.

27 V. Velkov, "Mesembria zwischen dem 4. und dem 8. Jahrhundert," in Pillinger et al. (eds.), *Die Schwarzmeerküste*, 20; Chaneva-Dechevska, *Rannokhristianskata arkhitektura*, 228–231.
28 A. Minchev, "Varna," in Karagianni (ed.), *40 Medieval City-Ports*, 220. For a detailed description, see Chaneva-Dechevska, *Rannokhristianskata arkhitektura*, 172–182.
29 L. Buzoianu and M. Bărbulescu, *Tomis. Comentariu istoric şi arheologic* (Constanţa: Muzeul de Istorie Naţională şi Arheologie, 2012), 199–201; E. Popescu, "L'église de Tomis au temps du métropolite Valentinian. L'ambassade (l'apocrisiariat) de Constantinople," *Dacia* 51 (2007): 251–255.
30 A. Suceveanu (ed.), *Histria XIII. La basilique épiscopale* (Bucharest: Editura Academiei, 2006); M. Zahariade, *Scythia Minor: A History of a Later Roman Province, 284-681* (Amsterdam: A. M. Hakkert, 2006), 103.
31 Marble for churches was certainly transported on ships; shipwrecks like the one discovered off the coast of Anchialos provide information regarding the origin of the marble as well as its possible destination; see Hristov, *Mare Ponticum*, 95. For marble decorations, see C. Vanderheyde, "The Architectural Decoration of the Early Byzantine Churches on the West Coast of the Black Sea," *Problemi na izkustvoto* 45, no. 2 (2012): 6–9. A large transport of roof tiles was found off the coast of Anchialos, probably from a shipwreck, which points to a vibrant activity of reconstruction; see Hristov, *Mare Ponticum*, 165.
32 L. Zavagno, "Amastris (Paphlagonia): A Study in Byzantine Urban History between Late Antiquity and the Early Middle Ages," in Tsestskhladze (ed.), *The Black Sea*, 276.
33 M. Cassis, "The Cide-Şenpazar Region in the Byzantine Period," in *Kinetic Landscapes: The Cide Archaeological Project: Surveying the Turkish Western Black Sea Region*, eds. B. S. Düring and C. Glatz (Berlin: de Gruyter, 2015), 344–346.
34 Laflı et al., "Byzantine Coins," 189–193.
35 J. Haldon, "Euchaïta," in *The Archaeology of Byzantine Anatolia. From the End of Late Antiquity until de Coming of the Turks*, ed. P. Niewöhner (Oxford: Oxford University Press, 2017), 375–388; T. Bekker-Nielsen, "Neapolis-Neoklaudiopolis: A Roman City in Northern Anatolia," in *Anatolian Metal VI*, ed. Ü. Yalçin (Bochum: Deutsches Bergbau-Museum, 2013), 211.
36 E. E. Intagliata, "Forgotten Borderlands. Northeastern Anatolia in the Sixth Century and Its Potential for Frontier Studies," in *Asia Minor in the Long Sixth Century: Current Research and Future Directions*, eds. I. Jacobs and H. Elton (Oxford: Oxbow, 2019), 79–90. The control of Tzanica allowed easier access to the strategic southeastern coastline between Trapezus in Pontus Polemoniacus and Apsarus in Lazica, for which see S. Mamuladze and E. Kakhidze, "Roman and Byzantine Forts Survey in the Southeastern Black Sea Area," *Pro Georgia* 26 (2016): 29–51.
37 Seibt, "Westgeorgien (Egrisi, Lazica)," 141.
38 L. Khrushkova, *Les monuments chrétiens de la côte orientale de la Mer Noire, Abkhazie, IVe-XIVe siècles* (Turnhout: Brepols, 2006); L. Khrushkova, "The Spread of Christianity in the Eastern Black Sea Littoral (Written and Archaeological Sources)," *Ancient West & East* 6 (2007): 188–219.
39 D. Koshtaria, "The Basilica at Petra (Tsikhisdziri)," in Karagianni (ed.), *Medieval Ports*, 367–376; M. K. Khotelashvili and A. L. Iacobson, "Vizantijskij khram v s. Dranda (Abkhaziia)," *Vizantijskij Vremennik* 45 (1984): 193.
40 L. Khrushkova, "La propagation du christianisme dans un région pontique. La basilique de Candripš, "temple pour les Abasges"," in *Sympozja Kazimierskie: poswiecone kulturze swiata póznego antyku i wczesnego chrzescijanstwa: 5: miejsca swiete w epoce póznego antyku*, eds. B. Iwaszkiewicz-Wronikowskiej and D. Próchniaka (Lublin: Towarzystwo Naukowe Katolickiego Uniwersytetu Lubelskiego, 2005), 405–445. For the church built by Justinian, see Procopius, *Bella*, 8.3.21. Church construction extended further up on the north-eastern coast, to Sochi, for which see L. Khrushkova and D. E. Vasilinenko, "Basilica Lesnoe-1 Near Sochi in the North-Eastern Black Sea Region," in Tsestskhladze (ed.), *The Black Sea*, 141–151.
41 See the comments in L. Khrushkova, "Khristianiske pamiatniki Kryma (sostoianie izuchenija)," *Vizantijskij Vremennik* 63 (2004): 167–194.
42 Lewit, "The Second Sea," 165; A. Plontke Lüning, "Early Byzantine Churches in the South-West of the Crimea," in Tsetskhladze et al. (eds.), *Bosporus*, 261–267; Khrushkova, "Khristianiske pamiatniki Kryma," 188–190.
43 Khrushkova, "Khristianiske pamiatniki Kryma," 177.

44 E. Nikolaeva, "Kreposty VI veka na Bospore Kimmerijskom," in *Bulgaria Pontica Medii Aevi IV-V*, vol. 1, ed. V. Giuzelev (Sofia: Gutenberg, 2003), 60–62 and figs. 15–16.

45 To be sure, ceramic evidence suggests that even smaller coastal fortresses like Carea, Hrisosotira and Urdoviza, often described as "fortified semi-urban settlements", received imported goods and probably had the role of supplying them to the hinterland. See S. Torbatov, "Portus Caria – Caron Limen – Caria – Carea – Creas," in *La Thrace et les sociétés maritimes anciennes. 18-24 September 1994, Sozopol: Proceedings of the International Symposium*, eds. M. Lazarov and C. Angelova (Sozopol: Centre of Underwater Archaeology, 1994), 325–336; Minchev, "Ten Less Investigated," 249; I. Hristov, *Hrisosotira: An Early Byzantine Fortress on the Hrisosotira Peninsula at the Town of Chernomorets, 5th-7th Centuries* (Sofia: Unicart, 2019), 95; Hristov, *Mare Ponticum*, 346. For the terminology, see V. Dinchev, "Classification of the Late Antique Cities in the Dioceses of Thracia and Dacia," *Archaeologia Bulgarica* 3, no. 3 (1999): 41.

46 E. Paraschiv-Grigore, "Sigilii comerciale descoperite la Tomis," *Cercetări Arheologice* 20 (2013): 168; T. Isvoranu and G. Poenaru Bordea, "Monede bizantine de la Tomis şi împrejurimi în colecţia Institutului de Arheologie 'Vasile Pârvan'," in *Simpozion de numismatică dedicat împlinirii a 125 de ani de la proclamarea independenţei României, Chişinău, 24–26 septembrie 2002. Comunicări, studii şi note* (Bucharest: Editura Enciclopedică, 2003), 137–161; I. Barnea, "Relaţiile provinciei Scythia Minor cu Asia Mică, Siria şi Egiptul," *Pontica* 5 (1972): 260–261. A community of North Africans may have resided at Tomis as well, for which see A. Opaiţ, "North African and Spanish Amphorae in Scythia Minor", *Il mar nero: annali di archeologia e storia* 3 (1997–1998): 47–50.

47 The resins were stored in reused LR2 amphorae, which had arrived with *annona* shipments. A. Rădulescu, "Amfore cu inscripţii de la edificiul roman cu mozaic din Tomis," *Pontica* 6 (1973): 193–207; G. Papuc, "Opaiţe de import la Tomis," *Pontica* 9 (1976): 201–206.

48 Th. Sim., 7.13.1–6.

49 G. Kuzmanov, *Rannovizantiyska keramika ot Trakia i Dakia (IV-nachaloto na VII v.)* (Sofia: Izdatelstvo na Balgarskata Akademia na Naukite, 1985), 56–57.

50 I. C. Opriş, *Ceramica romană târzie şi paleobizantinină de la Capidava în contextul descoperirilor de la Dunărea de Jos (sec. IV-VI p. Chr.)* (Bucharest: Editura Enciclopedică, 2003); F. Topoleanu, *Ceramica romană şi romano-bizantină de la Halmyris* (Tulcea: Institutul de Cercetări Eco-Muzeale, 2000); A. Opaiţ, *Local and Imported Ceramics in the Roman Province of Scythia (4th-6th Centuries AD)* (Oxford: BAR, 2004).

51 A. Opaiţ, "On the Local Production and Imports of Wine in the Pontic and Lower Danube Regions (1st Century BC to 7th Century AD)," in *LRCW 5: Late Roman Coarse Wares, Cooking Wares and Amphorae in the Mediterranean: Archaeology and Archaeometry*, ed. D. Dixneuf (Alexandria: Centre d'Études Alexandrines, 2017), 598–599.

52 A sixth-century amphora stamped "Chersonesos" was found at Sucidava on the Lower Danube frontier and Opaiţ B-I amphorae continued to arrive in Scythia; see Opaiţ, *Local and Imported Ceramics*, 106.

53 A. Minchev "The Late Roman Fine Ware Import to the Western Black Sea Coast," in *Ancient Bulgaria. Papers presented to the International Symposium on the Ancient History and Archaeology of Bulgaria, University of Nottingham, 1981*, vol. 1, ed. A. G. Poulter (Nottingham: Department of Classical and Archaeological Studies, 1983), 197; V. Velkov, "Kleinasiaten und Syrer in den Balkangebieten während der Spätantike (IV.-VI. Jh.)," in *Études historiques à l'occasion du XIIe Congrès International des Sciences Historiques – Vienne, Âoût – Septembre 1965*, vol. 2 (Sofia: Éditions de l'Academie Bulgare des Sciences, 1965), 22.

54 M. Mocanu, "Notes on the "African Red Slip Ware" Ceramics in Scythia Minor," *Studia Antiqua et Archaeologica* 18 (2012): 329–332; S. Ivanov, "Import Red-Gloss Ceramics," in Hristov (ed.), *Akra*, 84; K. Domżalski and A. Panaite, "Tropaeum Traiani in the Late Roman Trade Network and Road System: The Evidence of the Long-Distance Import of Fine Pottery," *Novensia* 30 (2019): 109–125.

55 K. Belke, "Transport and Communication," in P. Niewöhner (ed.), *The Archaeology of Byzantine Anatolia*, 37.

56 Drakoulis, "Regional Transformations," 85; Bryer and Winfield, *Byzantine Monuments*, 2–7.

57 G. Csiky, "Sinope in the Early Medieval Economy on the Black Sea Region (Questions and Problems)," *Antaeus* 33 (2015): 326; Cassis, "Cide-Şenpazar Region," 328.

58 O. Doonan, "Industrial Agriculture, Intensification and Collapse in Sinope and its Territory during the Late Roman/Early Byzantine Periods," in Jacobs and Elton (eds.), *Asia Minor*, 181–196. Finds of LRA 4 amphorae from Pompeiopolis indicate that Gaza wine became more popular in the south-Pontic region after Heraclea ceased to play a major role in the Black Sea wine market; see Opaiţ, "On the Local Production," 599–601. Wine continued to be produced in the area around Hadrianopolis, but it may have served only local needs, see E. Laflı, "Archäologische Evidenzen zum Weinanbau im südwestlichen Paphlagonien in römischer und frühbyzantinischer Zeit," in *Die Schätze der Erde. Natürliche Ressourcen in der antiken Welt*, eds. E. Olshausen and V. Sauer (Stuttgart: F. Steiner, 2012), 271.

59 D. Kassab Tezgör, "Le réseau commercial des amphores sinopéennes entre les IIe-IIIe s. et le VIe s. de notre ère, in K. Tezgör and Inaishvili (eds.), *Patabs I*, 172; A. G. Gercen, A. Iu. Zemliakova, V. E. Naumenko, and A. V. Smokotina, "Stratigraficheskie issledovanija na jugo-vostochnom sklone mysa teshkli-burun (Mangup)," *Materialy po Arkheologii, Istorii i Etnografii Tavrii* 12 (2006): 426. For the Early Byzantine shipwrecks discovered off Sinop, see C. Ward, "Four Ships of Late Antiquity in the Black Sea," *Ancient Civilizations from Scythia to Siberia* 16 (2010): 189–198.

60 K. Domżalski, "Late Roman Pottery from Pompeiopolis," in *Pompeiopolis I. Eine zwischenbilanz aus der Metropole Paphlagoniens nach fünf Kampagnen (2006-2010)*, ed. L. Summerer (Langenweissbach: Beier and Beran, 2011), 166.

61 Csiky, "Sinope in the Early Medieval Economy," 330.

62 Opaiţ, "On the Local Production," 594; D. Kassab Tezgör, "Types amphoriques romains tardifs produits simultanément à Demirci près de Sinope et dans d'autres centres de mer Noire," in *PATABS II: Production and Trade of Amphorae in the Black Sea*, eds. C. Tzochev, T. Stoyanov, and A. Bozkova (Sofia: National Institute of Archaeology with Museum, 2011), 200–201. On the other hand, no LRA 1 fragments have been found during a survey in the Cide region, west of Sinope, although Aegean ceramic material is otherwise well represented; see P. Bes, "Roman-Period Finds from the Cide Region," in Winther-Jacobsen and Summerer (eds.), *Landscape Dynamics*, 23–42.

63 Menander (Blockley), fr. 19,1. Sinope was described as a "Crimean entrepôt" at Bryer and Winfield, *Byzantine Monuments*, 92.

64 Albrecht, "Cherson als Zentralort," 362–364; Aibabin, "Written Sources," 60.

65 M. Čechová, "Fish Products and their Trade in Tauric Chersonesos/Byzantine Cherson. The Development of a Traditional Craft from Antiquity to the Middle Ages," in *Detlefsen zum 100. Todestag. Ein Colloquium der Detlefsen-Gesellschaft Glückstadt*, eds. C. Boldt and K.-J. Lorenzen-Schmidt (Borsfleth: Detlefsen-Gesellschaft, 2014), 229–236.

66 Cherson was importing grain, wine and oil from *Ponticae partes;* Martin, "Epistula XVII," *Patrologia Latina*, 87.202–4.

67 A. I. Romanchuk, A. V. Sazanov, and L. V. Sedikova, *Amfory iz kompleksov vizantijskogo Khersona* (Ekaterinburg: Ural'skoe otdelenie Rossijskoj akademii nauk, 1995), 16–45; E. Klenina, "Trade Relations between the Mediterranean and the Black Sea Region in the 3rd-6th Centuries A.D. in the Light of Ceramic Artifacts," in *LRCW3: Late Roman Coarse Wares, Cooking Wares and Amphorae in the Mediterranean. Archaeology and Archaeometry. Comparison between Western and Eastern Mediterranean*, eds. S. Menchelli, S. Santoro, M. Pasquinucci, and G. Guiducci (Oxford: Archaeopress, 2010), 1006–1007; Lewit, "The Second Sea," 158. In the seventh century, Cherson maintained important trade connections in the Black Sea documented by the seals of Byzantine *kommerkiarioi* and the continuous traffic of goods in the harbor, for which see Aibabin, "Written Sources," 61; L. Golofast, "Cherson in the 7th Century AD: The Archaeological Aspect," *Ancient West & East* 2 (2003): 96–115; A. I. Romanchuk, "K istorii Khersona VII v.," *Antichnaia Drevnosty i Srednie Veka* 31 (2000): 92–97.

68 Gercen et al. "Stratigraficheskie issledovanija," 426.

69 For the production and circulation of Pontic Red Slip ware, see recently K. Domżalski, Pontic Red Slip Ware. Typology, Chronology and Distribution of a Major Group of Late Roman Fine Pottery in the Black Sea Region (Warsaw: Institute of Archaeology and Ethnology, 2021).

70 N. F. Fedoseev, K. Domżalski, A. Opaiţ, and A. V. Kulikov, "Post-Justinian Pottery deposit from Pantikapaion-Bosporos: Rescue Excavations at 12, Teatral'naja St. in Kerch, 2006," *Archeologia* 61 (2010): 63–94; A. Smokotina, "Late Roman Amphorae from Tyritake," *Rei Cretiariae Romanae Fautorum Acta* 44 (2016): 715–724.

71 Voronov, "Eastern Pontus," 167–172; Seibt, "Westgeorgien (Egrisi, Lazica)," 137–144.

72 Gavritukhin and Kazanski, "Bosporus," 134–135.

73 Agathias, *Historiae*, 3.5.3.

74 Opaiţ, "On the Local Production," 594; A. Opaiţ and D. Paraschiv, "Rare Amphora Finds in the City and Territory of (L)ibida (1st-6th Centuries AD)," *Rei Cretiariae Romanae Fautorum Acta* 42 (2012): 116, with further comments about the distribution of this type. For pseudo-colchian amphorae, whose production is dated between the fourth and the seventh century, see D. Kassab Tezgör and M. Akkaya, "Les amphores "pseudo-colchidiennes" du Musée de Samsun," *Anatolia Antiqua* 8 (2000): 127–141.

75 Khoshtaria, "Gonio," in Karagianni (ed.), *40 Medieval City-Ports*, 411; N. Inaishvili and N. Vashakidze, "Typology and Chronology of Greek, Roman and Early Byzantine Amphorae from Petra-Tsikhisdziri," in K. Tezgör and Inaishvili (eds.), *Patabs I*, 152. For Dranda, see Khotelashvili and Iacobson, "Vizantijskij khram," 192–206. For Early Byzantine coin finds in Abasgia, see M. Shamba, *Monetnoe obrashchenie na territorii Abkhazii: (V v. do n.e.-XIII v. n.e.)* (Tbilisi: Metsniereba, 1987), 77–81.

76 I. Iashvili and W. Seibt, "Byzantinische Siegel Aus Petra in Westgeorgien," *Studies in Sigillography* 9 (2006): 2–3; M. Ketevan, "Artifacts from Gonio and Tsikhisdziri," in Karagianni (ed.), *Medieval Ports*, 382–383; T. Abramishvili, "Nokalakevskij klad," *Vizantijskij Vremennik* 23 (1963): 158–165.

77 For Scythia, see Topoleanu, *Ceramica romană*, 172–219, with analogies from Dobrudja. For Moesia II, see G. Kuzmanov and A. Minchev, *Antichni lampi. Kolektsiia na RIM Varna* (Sofia: Natsionalen Arheologicheski Institut s Muzey, 2018). For Haemimontus, see Y. Mutafchieva, "Ceramic Oil-Lamps," in Hristov (ed.), *Akra*, 135–151; N. Rusev, "Glineni lampi ot Anhialo (I-VII v.)," *Izvestia na Narodnia Muzey – Burgas* 5 (2015): 88–118; K. Kostova and D. Dobreva "Roman, Late Roman and Early Byzantine Lamps from National Archaeological Reserve 'Deultum-Debelt'," in *Lychnological Acts 2. Trade and Local Production of Lamps from the Prehistory until the Middle Age*, eds. C.-A. Roman and N. Gudea (Zalău/Cluj-Napoca: Mega, 2008), 161–169. For the circulation of lamps in the Eastern Balkans, see recently F. Curta "Shedding Light on a Murky Matter: Remarks on 6th to Early 7th Century Clay Lamps in the Balkans," *Archaeologia Bulgarica* 20, no. 3 (2016): 51–116.

78 Molds for "Danubian" lamps have been found at Kranevo and in the Burgas bay region; see G. Toncheva, "Keramichna rabotilnitsa krai s Kranevo," *Izvestia Balgarskoto Arheologichesko Druzhestvo* 9 (1953): 81–104; I. Boneva, "Glineni lampi ot rimskata epoha i kusnata antichnost ot muzeia v Burgas," *Izvestia na Muzeite ot Yugoiztochna Balgaria* 12 (1989): 47. For dating, see recently P. Dyczek, "A New Way of dating So-Called Byzantine Lamps as Exemplified by Finds from Novae," in *Orbis barbarorum: studia ad archaeologiam Germanorum et Baltorum temporibus Imperii Romani pertinentia Adalberto Nowakowski dedicata*, eds. J. Andrzejowski, C. von Carnap-Bornheim, A. Cieśliński, and B. Kontny (Warsaw: Institute of Archaeology, 2017), 601–610.

79 F. Topoleanu, "Halmyris – un nouveau centre de production de lampes dans le nord de la Dobroudja (IIe-VIIe s. ap. J.-C.)," *Rei Cretariae Romanae Fautorum Acta* 33 (1996): 91–94.

80 G. Dağlı, "Hadrianopolis surları kurtarma kazısında bulunan Roma ve Bizans dönemi kandilleri," MA Thesis, Dokuz Eylül Üniversitesi, 2008, 146–159, no. 208, 210 and 239–240. Epitaphs from Odessos indicate that individuals born in or around Hadrianopolis relocated to the western Black Sea coast, probably for economic reasons; see Velkov, "Kleinasiaten und Syrer," 22. Lamps with cross-shaped handles and handles in the form of human heads were produced in the Northeastern Balkans, for which see Curta "Shedding Light," 85–96. For the lamps found in Constantinople, see J. W. Hayes, *Excavations at Saraçhane in Istanbul. Vol II. The Pottery* (Princeton: Princeton University Press, 1992), 83 and pl. 21–22.

81 L. Chrzanovski and D. Zhuravlev, *Lamps from Chersonesus in the State Historical Museum – Moscow* (Rome: L'Erma di Bretschneider, 1998), 171–174, no. 108–110.

82 D. Zhuravlev, "Lighting Equipment of the Northern Pontic Area in the Roman and Late Roman Periods: Imports and Local Production," in Gabrielsen and Lund (eds.), *The Black Sea in Antiquity*, 230.

83 Imitations often combined motifs drawn from designs developed in North Africa, Syria and the Aegean world; see C. Iconomu, "Descoperiri de tipare de opaiţe la Tomis," *Pontica* 9 (1976):

135–146; A. Rădulescu, "Die locale Herstellung der Beleuchtungsgegenstände – lucernae," *Pontica* 14 (1981): 204–209; Kuzmanov and Minchev, *Antichni lampi*, 253–254; G. Atanasov, "Rannohristyanski pametnitsi ot Dorostol i dorostolska eparhyata (kraia na IV-VII vek)," in *Istoryata na Silistra. I. Antichnyat Durostorum*, eds. R. Teofil Ivanov, G. Atanasov, and P. Donevski (Silistra: Ivrai, 2006), 351. Greece was also a major supplier of such imitations, for which see recently P. Petridis, "The 6th-7th century AD Greek Lamps Phenomenon: An Indication of Regional Identity or a Large-Scale Imitation?," *Εν Σοφίᾳ μαθητεύσαντες. Essays in Byzantine Material Culture and Society in Honour of Sophia Kalopissi-Verti*, eds. C. Diamanti and A. Vassiliou (Oxford: Archaeopress, 2019), 217–226.

84 D. Zhuravlev, "Syro-Palestinian Lamps from Chersonesos and their Derivatives of the Roman and Byzantine Period," *Rei Cretiariae Romanae Fautorum Acta* 42 (2012): 23–32.

85 Mutafchieva, "Ceramic Oil-Lamps," in Hristov (ed.), *Akra*, 40.

86 M. Xanthopoulou, *Les lampes en bronze à l'époque paléochrétienne* (Turnhout: Brepols, 2010), 106, 177, 281; I. Hristov, "Everyday Objects of Metal and Stone," in Hristov (ed.), *Akra*, 68; Kuzmanov and Minchev, *Antichni lampi*, 175–176; Atanasov, "Rannohristyanski pametnitsi ot Dorostol," 348–351.

87 Aside from the detailed catalogues published for individual sites, we can also rely on up-to-date overviews bringing together all the known coin finds from different provinces of the Thracian diocese; see most recently G. Custurea, *Circulația monedei bizantine în Dobrogea (sec. VI-VIII)* (Constanța: Muzeul de Istorie Națională și Arheologie, 2019); S. Mihaylov, "Parichno obrashtenie v provintsia Vtora Mizia 498–681 g.," PhD Dissertation, University of Veliko Turnovo 'St Cyril and St. Methodius', 2018; A. Tenchova, "Monetna tsirkulatsia prez VI-VII vek na dreshna Yugoiztochna Balgaria," Ph.D. Dissertation, National Institute of Archaeology and Museum, Sofia, 2012.

88 Small hoards are known from Tyana further south in the Diocese of Pontus, for which see M. Asolati and C. Crisafulli, "Tyana bizantina: circolazione e tesaurizzazione monetale," in *La Cappadoce Méridionale de la préhistoire à la période byzantine*, eds. D. Beyer, O. Henry, and A. Tibet (Istanbul: Institut Français d'Études Anatoliennes – Georges Dumézil, 2015), 239–246.

89 V. Ivanišević, "Les trésors balcaniques, témoins des invasions et de leurs routes," in *Les trésors monétaires byzantins des Balkans et d'Asie Mineure (491-713)*, eds. C. Morrisson, V. Popović, and V. Ivanišević (Paris: Lethielleux, 2006), 75–93. Several bronze hoards and even more numerous hoards of gold and silver coins are known from the northern and eastern Black Sea regions; see A. Gandila, *Cultural Encounters on Byzantium's Northern Frontier: Coins, Artifacts and History* (Cambridge: Cambridge University Press, 2018), Appendix A, 2.2.

90 Close to c. 1500, Early Byzantine coins, single finds and hoards have come to light in Sardis where the archaeological and numismatic material has been published in exemplary fashion; see H. W. Bell, *Sardis XI, part I, 1910-1914: Coins* (Leiden/Boston: Brill, 1916), 76–95; G. Bates, *Byzantine Coins* (Cambridge, MA: Harvard University Press, 1971); T. V. Buttrey, "Byzantine, Medieval and Modern Coins and Tokens," in T. V. Buttrey, A. Johnson, K. M. MacKenzie, and M. L. Bates, *Greek, Roman, and Islamic Coins from Sardis* (Cambridge: Harvard University Press, 1981), 204–224; J. DeRose Evans, *Coins from the Excavations at Sardis: Their Archaeological and Economic Contexts: Coins from the 1973 to 2013 Excavations* (Cambridge, MA: Harvard University Press, 2018), 225–242.

91 We only know about the Byzantine gold coins from the museum in Samsun, for which see recently K. Oyarçin and Ş. Dervişoğlu, "Samsun Arkeoloji ve Etnografya Müzesi Bizans Dönemi Altın ve Gümüş Sikkeleri," *Arkeoloji ve Senat* 161 (May-August, 2019): 1–14. For the coins from Çorum we rely only on a brief synopsis, for which see Z. Çizmeli Öğün and C. Özbil, "Çorum müzesi sikke koleksiyonunda bulunan antik sikkeler," in *2. Çorum Kazi ve Araştirmalar Sempozyumu: Mayis 2012*, Çorum, ed. Y. Hazırlayan (Çorum: Çorum Valiliği İl Kültür ve Turizm Müdürlüğü, 2012), 169, fig. 5. For Satala we have only fragmentary information, although Byzantine coins seem to be commonly found around the ancient city; see C. S. Lightfoot, "The Coins from Satala," in *Studies in Ancient Coinage from Turkey*, ed. R. Ashton (London: Royal Numismatic Society, 1996), 149. From Theodosiopolis we have very selective information from what appears to be a substantial collection kept at the archaeology museum in Erzurum, for which see H. Özyurt Özcan, "Erzurum Arkeoloji Müzesi'ndeki bizans sikkeleri," *Araştırma Sonuçları Toplantısı* 24, no. 1 (2007): 1–16. For the other coin samples from Northern Turkey, see the notes below.

92 Procopius, *De Aedificiis*, 3.7.1–2. For the economic importance of Trapezus in the sixth and seventh centuries, see recently K. Durak, "The Commercial History of Trebizond and the Region of Pontos from the Seventh to the Eleventh Centuries: An International Emporium," *Mediterranean Historical Review* 36, no. 1 (2021): 5–7.

93 S. Kılıç, "Bolu Arkeoloji Müzesi'ndeki bronz bizans sikkeleri," in *Uluslararası Katılımlı XV. Ortaçağ ve Türk Dönemi Kazıları ve Sanat Tarihi Araştırmaları Sempozyumu, Anadolu Üniversitesi-Eskişehir 19-21 Ekim 2011*, eds. Z. Demirel Gökalp, N. Çöl, Z. Ertuğrul, S. Alp, and H. Yilmazyaşar, vol. 2 (Eskişehir: Anadolu Üniversitesi Yayınları, 2012), 503–510.

94 S. Ireland, *Greek, Roman and Byzantine Coins in the Museum at Amasya* (London: Royal Numismatic Society, 2000), 101–110.

95 J. Casey, *A Catalogue of the Greek, Roman and Byzantine Coins in Sinop Museum (Turkey) and Related Historical and Numismatic Studies* (London: Royal Numismatic Society, 2010), 79–86.

96 The assumption, not always reliable, is that the bulk of the coinage issued by an emperor would arrive in a region during his reign and generally close to the minting date, rather than later through the channels of coin circulation. This hypothesis is more likely to be true in provinces where monetization relied heavily on regular state payments sent to the army and administration.

97 Unfortunately, the detailed catalogues of site finds in Crimea are old publications and we have only sketchy information about more recent excavation finds; see Iu. S. Khrushkol. "Monety iz razkopok v Khersonese v 1946 godu," *Numizmaticheskij Sbornik* 2 (1957): 61–69; A. M. Gilevich, "Monety iz raskopok portovogo rajona Chersonesa v 1963–1964 gg.," *Antichnaja Drevnost' i Srednie Veka* 7 (1971): 62–80; K. V. Golenko, "Monety iz raskopok Gosudarstvennogo Istoricheskogo Muzeja v Khersonese (1958–1969 gg.)," *Sovetskaja Arkheologija* 4 (1972): 211–222; L. N. Belova, "Monety iz raskopok XIX, XXII i XXV kvartalov Khersonesa," *Numizmatika* 5 (1981): 5–43.

98 I. Tsukhishvili and G. Depeyrot, *History and Coin Finds in Georgia: Late Roman and Byzantine Hoards (4th-13th c.)* (Wetteren: Moneta, 2003), 72–73, no. 4.

99 A. Gandila, "Heavy Money, Weightier Problems: The Justinianic Reform of 538 and its Economic Consequences," *Revue Numismatique* 168 (2012): 396–401.

100 Minchev, "Ten Less Investigated," 248–275; A. Suceveanu and A. Barnea, *La Dobroudja romaine* (Bucharest: Editura Enciclopedică, 1991), 170–174.

101 A. Gandila, "Free Market, Black Market, or No Market? Money and *Annona* in the Northeastern Balkans (6th-7th c.)," *Journal of Late Antiquity* 14, no. 2 (2021): 307–308, tables 3 and 4..

102 Isvoranu and Poenaru "Monede bizantine," 156; V. Parushev, "Antichni moneti ot Kaliakra," *Izvestiia na Narodniia Muzei – Varna* 27 (1991): 27–28; I. Iordanov, A. Koichev, and V. Mutafov, "Srednovekovyat Ahtopol VI–XIII v. spored dannite numizmatikata i sfragistika," *Numizmatika i sfragistika* 5, no. 2 (1998): 71, table 3; G. Poenaru Bordea, R. Ocheşeanu, and A. Popeea, *Monnaies byzantines du Musée de Constanța (Roumanie)* (Wetteren: Moneta, 2004), 44–58.

103 S. Karanfil, "Kocaeli müzesi'ndeki bizans sikkeleri," MA Thesis, Anadolu Üniversitesi Sosyal Bilimler Enstitüsü, 2019, 64–70.

104 S. Ireland and S. Ateşoğulları, "The Ancient Coins in Amasra Museum," in Ashton (ed.), *Studies in Ancient Coinage*, 133–134; Casey, *A Catalogue of the Greek*, 81; Karanfil, "Kocaeli müzesi'ndeki," 73; F. Planet, "La circulation monétaire, étude des monnaies byzantines du musée d'Iznik," in *La Bithynie au Moyen Âge*, eds. B. Geyer and J. Lefort (Paris: Lethielleux, 2003), 500; Kılık, "Bolu Arkeoloji Müzesi'ndeki," 507; Özyurt Özcan, "Erzurum Arkeoloji Müzesi'ndeki," 14.

105 Aibabin, "Written Sources," 60. Evidence from Aphrodision on the western coast indicates that the fortress was rebuilt under Justin II; see Minchev, "Ten Less Investigated," 258.

106 F. Curta and A. Gandila, "Hoards and Hoarding Patterns in the Early Byzantine Balkans," *Dumbarton Oaks Papers* 65–66 (2012): 103–105.

107 A. Madgearu, "The Province of Scythia and the Avaro-Slavic Invasions (576–626)," *Balkan Studies* 37, no. 1 (1996): 35–61.

108 A. Gandila, "Money Talks: Financial Crisis and the Fate of the Roman Balkans, c. 582–602," in *Studia romana et mediaevalia europaensia: Miscellanea in honorem annos LXXXV peragentis Professoris emeriti Dan Gh. Teodor oblata*, eds. D. Aparaschivei and G. Bilavschi (Bucharest: Editura Academiei, 2018), 107–139.

109 Some Thessalonican coinage reached Pityus on the Abasgian coast through commerce or with troops transferred from the west; see I. Tsukhishvili, "Bich'vint'is bizant'iuri monet'ebi," in *Didi*

Pit'iunt'i. Arkeologiuri gatkhrebi Bich'vint'ashi, ed. A. Apakidze, vol. 2 (Tbilisi: Mecniereba, 1977), 326.

110 For an overview of the complex, see V. Canarache, *The Mosaic-Floored Edifice of Tomi* (Constanța: Muzeul Regional de Arheologie Dobrogea, 1968); M. Bucovală, *Marele edificiu roman cu mozaic de la Tomis* (Constanța: Muzeul de Istorie Națională și Arheologie, 1986). The latest coin is a follis of Heraclius dated 613–616, for which see P. Bordea et al., *Monnaies byzantines*, 127, no. 985.

111 G. Simeonov, "Harbours on the Western Black Sea Coast and the Byzantine Campaigns against the Avars and Bulgarians from the 6th until the 8th Century," in Karagianni (ed.), *Medieval Ports*, 49–56.

112 Hristov, *Mare Ponticum*, 399–411; A. Madgearu "The End of Town-Life in Scythia Minor," *Oxford Journal of Archaeology* 20, no. 2 (2001): 207–217; O. Bounegru and M. Adumitroaei, "Life (After Town) in Town în Scythia Minor. Interpretări stratigrafice," *Peuce* 3–4 (2005–2006): 259–282.

113 C. Foss, "The Persians in Asia Minor and the End of Antiquity," *The English Historical Review* 90 (1975): 721–747.

114 M. F. Hendy, "The Coins," in *Excavations at Saraçhane in Istanbul*, vol. 1, ed. R. M. Harrison (Princeton: Princeton University Press, 1986), 309–313; M. F. Hendy, "Roman, Byzantine and Latin Coins," in *Kalenderhane in Istanbul. The Excavations*, eds. C. L. Striker and Y. Doğan Kuban (Mainz: Von Zabern, 2007), 219–222.

115 Although a very common situation, it is certainly not the norm everywhere; for instance, in Cyprus, the coinage from the second half of Heraclius' reign is more abundant and the same is true for Caesarea Maritima in Palestine; O. Callot, *Salamine de Chypre. XVI, Les monnaies. Fouilles de la ville 1964–1974* (Paris: de Boccard, 2004), 54–75; J. DeRose Evans, *The Joint Expedition to Caesarea Maritima. Excavation Reports. Volume VI. The Coins and the Hellenistic, Roman, and Byzantine Economy of Palestine* (Boston: American Schools of Oriental Research, 2006), 197–202.

116 E. Oberländer-Târnoveanu, "Monnaies byzantines des VIIe-Xe siècles découvertes à Silistra dans la collection de l'Académicien Péricle Papahagi consevées au Cabinet des Médailles du Musée National d'Histoire de Roumanie," *Cercetări Numismatice* 7 (1996): 119, no. 52.

117 Ireland, *Greek, Roman and Byzantine*, 108–109; Laflı et al., "Byzantine Coins," 198–200; Demirel Gökalp, "Heraclius'un Follisleri: Bolu Arkeoloji Müzesi Örnekleri," in *Anadolu kültürlerinde süreklilik ve değişim: Dr. A. Mine Kadiroğlu'na armağan*, eds. M. Kadiroğlu. A. Ceren Erel, B. İşler, N. Peker, and G. Sağır (Ankara: Rekmay Ltd., 2011), 257–260; K. Oyarçin, "Sikke buluntulari işiğinda Hadrianoupolis kilise c yapisi," in *Uluslararası Geçmişten Günümüze Karabük ve Çevresinde Dini, İlmi ve Kültürel Hayat Sempozyumu*, eds. A. Işik, T. Aydeniz, and I. H. Imamoğlu (Karabük: Karabük Üniversitesi Yayınları, 2019), 447–448; Casey, *A Catalogue of the Greek*, 84–85; Karanfil, "Kocaeli müzesi'ndeki," 85–87.

118 Bates, *Byzantine Coins*, 6–7; Buttrey, "Byzantine, Medieval and Modern," 205–206; Evans, *Coins from the Excavations*, 241–242; C. Lightfoot, "Hellenistic, Roman, and Byzantine Coin Finds, 1987–2006," in C. Katsari, C. S. Lightfoot, and A. Özme, *The Amorium Mint and the Coin Finds* (Berlin: Akademie Verlag, 2012), 170.

119 Laflı et al., "Byzantine Coins," 187–206; Oyarçin, "Sikke buluntulari," 442–451.

120 J. Dalaison and F. Delrieux, "Les monnaies trouvées à Pompeiopolis durant les campagnes de fouilles 2006–2009," in Summerer (ed.), *Pompeiopolis I*, 144–145. The coins were collected from different areas of the site, but the sample remains too small to permit conclusive statistical observations.

121 A. Gandila, "Câteva monede bizantine rare descoperite în Dobrogea și problema influenței bizantine în Balcani în secolul al VII-lea," *Cercetări Numismatice* 17 (2011) [2016]: 53–64; M. Iacob, "Aspecte privind circulația monetară pe teritoriul României în a doua parte a secolului VII p. Chr.," in *Istro-Pontica: Muzeul tulcean la a 50-a aniversare 1950-2000. Omagiu lui Gavrilă Simion la 45 de ani de activitate 1955-2000*, eds. M. Iacob, E. Oberländer-Târnoveanu, and F. Topoleanu (Tulcea: Consiliul Județean, 2000), 485–498; S. Mihaylov, "Seventh-to-Eighth Century Bizantine Coins from Northeastern Bulgaria," *Cultură și Civilizație la Dunărea de Jos* 26 (2008): 77–85; P. Georgiev, "Izgubenoto monetno sakrovishte ot rayona na Varna i negovoto istoriko-arheologichesko znachenie," *Numizmatika, Sfragistika i Epigrafika* 7 (2011): 87–107; see also Morrisson et al., *Les trésors monétaires*, 141–143, no. 36–38.

122 P. Grierson, "The Crimean Countermarks of Heraclius," *Numismatic Chronicle* 6 (1966): 221–224; V. Guruleva, "Coins of Constans II struck in Cherson," in I. Ševčenko et al. (eds.), *Acts. XVIIIth International Congress*, 252–257.
123 A. Gandila, "The Mint of Thessalonica and the Mediterranean Economy in the 6th-7th c," *Revue Belge de Numismatique et de Sigillographie* 164 (2018): 461, fig. 22.
124 Planet, "La circulation monétaire," 500, table 1; Karanfil, "Kocaeli müzesi'ndeki," 169, table 4.
125 A. Bellinger, *Coins from Jerash, 1928-1934* (New York: American Numismatic Society, 1938), 10; T. Marot, *Las monedas del Macellum de Gerasa (Ŷaraš, Jordania): aproximación a la circulación monetaria en la provincia de Arabia* (Madrid: Museo Casa de la Moneda, 1998), 107, table 20.
126 P. Drapelova, "The Mint of Byzantine Antioch (ca 516 – 610 AD): Some Remarks on Trends in Provincial Coinage," in *Essays in Byzantine Material Culture and Society in Honour of Sophia Kalopissi-Verti*, eds. C. Diamanti and A. Vassiliou (Oxford: Archaeopress, 2019), 313–324.
127 Kassab Tezgör, "Le réseau commercial," 171–172; D. Kassab Tezgör and M. Touma, "Amphores exportées de mer Noire en Syrie du Nord," *Anatolia Antiqua* 9 (2001): 105–115.
128 A. Opaiţ, "A Levantine Trade Diaspora at Pompeiopolis?," *Ancient West & East* 20 (2021): 81–97.
129 Z. Demirel Gökalp, *Malatya arkeoloji müzesi bizans sikkeleri kataloğu* (Istanbul: Arkeoloji ve Sanat Yayinlari, 2014), 137; Asolati and Crisafulli, "Tyana bizantina," 256; S. Métivier and V. Prigent, "La circulation monétaire dans la Cappadoce byzantine d'après les collections de musées de Kayseri et de Niğde," in *Mélanges Cécile Morrisson* (Paris: Centre de recherche d'histoire et civilisation de Byzance, 2010), 613–614.
130 Sebeos (ed. Thomson), 18.90; Th. Sim., 5.16.1; Theoph., 267 (AM 6082).
131 I. Bogdan Cătăniciu and G. Poenaru Bordea, "Un mic tezaur de monede bizantine descoperit la Tropaeum Traiani," *Buletinul Societăţii Numismatice Române* 90–91 (1996–1997): 85–95.
132 E. Petac and A. Ionescu, "Some Sassanian Silver Coins Discovered at Axiopolis (Cernavodă, Constanţa County, Romania)," *Iranica Antiqua* 48 (2013): 355–361; M. Tsotselia, *History and Coin Finds in Georgia: Sasanian Coin Finds and Hoards* (Wetteren: Moneta, 2003).
133 For coin distribution, see B. Callegher, "Moneta e scambi nell'Adriatico altomedievale. La costa dalmata nell'area monetaria bizantina," in *Adriatico altomedievale (VI-XI secolo). Scambi, porti, produzioni*, eds. S. Gelichi and C. Negrelli (Venice: Edizioni Ca' Foscari, 2017), 347–374. For ceramic evidence, see R. Auriemma and E. Quiri, "La circulazione delle anfore in Adriatico tra V e VII sec. D.C.," in *Atti III incontro di studio Cer.Am.Is. sulle ceramiche tardoantiche e medievali. "La circolazione delle ceramiche nell'Adriatico tra tarda antichità e altomedioevo" (Venezia, 24-25 giugno 2004)*, eds. S. Gelichi and C. Negrelli (Mantova: SAP Società Archeologica s.r.l., 2007), 31–64; M. Buora, "La ceramica di importazione (sigillata africana e anfore) come indicatore archeologico per il periodo bizantino nell'alto Adriatico," *Quaderni friulani di archaeologia* 15 (2005): 163–167.
134 Opaiţ, "North African and Spanish Amphorae," 47–95; Mocanu, "Notes on the "African Red Slip Ware"," 319–340; Minchev "The Late Roman Fine Ware," 194–201.
135 W. Hahn, *Moneta Imperii Byzantini II: Von Justinus II bis Phocas (565-610)* (Vienna: Verlag der Österreichischen Akademie der Wissenschaften, 1975), 49–51.
136 J.-M. Carrié, "L'institution annonaire de la première à la deuxième Rome: continuité et innovation," in *Nourrir les cités de méditerranée. Antiquité – temps modernes*, eds. B. Marin and C. Virlouvet (Paris: Maisonneuve et Larose, 2003), 169–170; I. Barnea, "Menasampullen auf dem Gebiet Rumäniens," in *Akten des XII. Internationallen Kongresses für Christlische Archäologie*, eds. E. Dassmann, K. Thraede, and J. Engemann (Münster: Aschendorffsche Verlagsbuchhandlung, 1995), 509–514; For bronze lamps, see above note 83. For the 33-nummia coin, see Isvoranu and Poenaru "Monede bizantine," 140, pl. II/13.
137 E. Oberländer-Târnoveanu, *Tezaure monetare bizantine din colecţia Muzeului Naţional de Istorie a României. I. De la Anastasius I la Constantinus al IV-lea (491-685)* (Bucharest: Muzeul Naţional de Istorie a României, 2017), 23–29.
138 A. Madgearu, "Militari "sciţi" şi "daci" în Egipt, Italia şi Palestina în secolele VI-VII," *Studii şi cercetări de istorie veche şi arheologie* 65, no. 1–2 (2014): 49–58.
139 In Abasgia, coins minted at Alexandria have been found at Akhali Atoni and Sebastopolis, for which see Shamba, *Monetnoe obrashchenie*, 80–81.
140 K. Tezgör, "Le réseau commercial," 171.

141 For Lazica, see Gandila, *Cultural Encounters*, Appendix, no. 450. For the Danube frontier, see E. Oberländer-Târnoveanu, "Monede antice şi bizantine descoperite la Troesmis," *Peuce* 8 (1980): 267, no. 72.

142 Gandila, *Cultural Encounters*, Appendix, no. 89, 204 and 299.

143 Gandila, "Free Market, Black Market," 322, table 6.

144 See note 111. The same can be said about other Byzantine metropoleis, such as Carthage and Antioch, where the lowest denomination issued by the local mint dominated the market; see D. Waage, *Antioch-on-the-Orontes, vol. IV, part 2: Greek, Roman, Byzantine and Crusaders' Coins* (Princeton: Princeton University Press, 1952), 148–166; W. E. Metcalf, "The Michigan Finds at Carthage, 1975–79: An Analysis," *Museum Notes* 32 (1987): 78–84.

145 Hoards found in southwestern Crimea confirm the preference for Byzantine ¼ and especially ⅛ folles; see A. N. Korshenko, "Klad pozdnerimskikh i rannevizantijskikh mednykh monet iz Baidarskoi doliny," in *Imperija i polis. Sbornik nauchnykh trudov*, ed. N. A. Alekseenko (Sevastopol': SPD Aref'ev, 2013), 247–266.

146 N. Frolova, "The Question of Continuity in the Classical Bosporus on the Basis of Numismatic Data," *Ancient Civilizations* 5, no. 3 (1999): 179–205; N. A. Alekseenko, "Denezhnoe obrashtenie okrugi vizantijskogo Khersona v VII v.," *Materialy po Arkheologii, Istorii i Etnografii Tavrii* 11 (2005): 437–451. This monetary culture explains why late sixth-century issues minted outside Cherson are rare in Crimea as the minting of smaller denominations all but stopped at Constantinople.

147 Asolati and Crisafulli, "Tyana bizantina," 233–249; B. Özcan, "Fouilles de la nécropole de Niksar (1982–1987). Avec un appendice sur les trouvailles monétaires par Bernard Rémy et Birsel Özcan," in Rémy (ed.), *Pontica I*, 39–59; Laflı et al., "Byzantine Coins," 187–206; Oyarçin, "Sikke buluntulari," 442–451.

148 At Tios two of the five published coins are ¼ folles, but the sample is too small to be statistically relevant; see D. S. Lenger and S. Atasoy, "Tios kazılarında bulunan sikkeler," in *Zonguldak'ta bir antik kent: Tios. 2006-2012 Arkeolojik çalışmaları ve genel değerlendirme*, eds. S. Atasoy and Ş. Yıldırım (Ankara: T.C. Kültür ve Turizm Bakanlığı, 2015), 391–392.

149 G. Custurea and I. Nastasi, "The End of Urban Life on the Dobroudjan Shore of the Black Sea in the 7th Century AD," in Karagianni (ed.), *Medieval Ports*, 320–331; I. Lazarenko, "Numizmatichni danni za datirane opozharyavaneto na Odesos po vremeto na imperator Irakliy," *Izvestia na Narodniia Muzey – Varna* 34–35 (1998–1999): 150–166.

150 Simeonov, "Harbours on the Western Black Sea," 50; V. Giuzelev, "Die mittelalterliche Stadt Mesembria (Nesebăr)," *Bulgarian Historical Review* 6 (1978): 51.

151 T. Brüggemann, "Paphlagonia," 48.

152 Zavagno, "Amastris (Paphlagonia)," 274.

153 B. Martin-Hisard, "La domination Byzantine sur le littoral oriental du Pont Euxin (milieu du VIIe-VIIIe siècles)," *Byzantinobulgarica* 7 (1981):144–146; Khrushkova, "The Spread of Christianity," 191–192.

154 Aibabin, "Written Sources," 61.

155 The association of coins and goods is attested on Early Byzantine shipwrecks, such as Grazel B and Yassı Ada; see C. Morrisson, "Les monnaies byzantines, in "Les épaves de Gruissan," ed. Y. Solier, *Archaeonautica* 3 (1981): 35–52; J. M. Fagerlie, "The Coins," in G. F. Bass and F. H. Van Doorninck, *Yassı Ada. Volume I. A Seventh-Century Byzantine Shipwreck* (College Station: Texas A & M University Press, 1982), 145–154.

7

THE BYZANTINE 'CITY' IN ASIA MINOR*

Ufuk Serin

In loving memory of my father,
M. Necdet Serin

The historical evolution of cities in the Eastern Roman Empire from Classical Antiquity into the Byzantine Middle Ages is recognised as one of the fundamental themes in Byzantine studies. In tandem with a growing interest in Late Antiquity, research into Byzantine urbanism and urban history has gained momentum, especially after the second half of the last century,[1] resulting in an extensive literary corpus, which, as Wolfgang Brandes observed, 'one could scarcely read, let alone master'.[2] Considerable attention has been devoted to the fate of the Classical city and factors underlying its transformation between Late Antiquity and the Early Middle Ages. Many explanations are often invoked to explain this: administrative/institutional, socio-economic, and demographic changes prompted by and accompanying the disintegration of the Roman Empire by the 3rd century, cultural and ideological transformations associated with the rise and spread of Christianity, natural calamities, foreign threats and the consequent militarisation of the empire, as well as the progressive dependence of provincial cities upon Constantinople.[3] The impact of these wide-ranging factors on the urban (and rural) environment has long been debated, frequently diagnosed as an 'urban decline', starting from the second half of the 6th century (if not earlier) and culminating between the 7th and 9th centuries.[4]

The theory of urban 'decline' has inevitably triggered scholarly controversy on the nature of urban 'transformation' and indications of 'decline', the question of the 'continuity' or 'discontinuity' of cities in transition into the Byzantine Middle Ages, and problems centring

* Abbreviations for Journals, Series, and Lexika are from Deutsches Archäologisches Institut (https://www.dainst.org/fileadmin/Media/Website/02_Forschung/Publikationen/Publizieren_am_DAI/Abbreviations.pdf). Abbreviations for Greek (classical and ecclesiastical) and Latin authors and works are from Henry G. Liddell and Robert Scott, *A Greek-English Lexicon. With a Revised Supplement* (Oxford: Clarendon Press, 1996); Geoffrey W. H. Lampe, *A Patristic Greek Lexicon* (Oxford: Clarendon Press, 1961); *Thesaurus Linguae Latinae. Index* (Leipzig: Teubner, 1990). I thank Başak Kalfa-Ataklı for her help with the digitalisation of some images.

DOI: 10.4324/9780429203923-10

around definitions and terminology.[5] This enduring debate, supplemented by growing numbers of archaeological and regional studies, especially after the mid-1970s onwards,[6] has more recently involved larger, territorial concerns, such as the interaction of town and countryside and the diversity and flexibility of settlement types and patterns.[7]

Most of these broader historical concerns await further investigation and certainly are beyond this chapter's remit. The physical structure of cities definitely underwent radical transformation in transition from Antiquity into the Byzantine Middle Ages, closely or more loosely affected by multiple factors in the *long durée*.[8] However, it must also be recognised that what we want to read in such transformation – referred to as the 'Classical' form of cities – that is either a failure or a change in urban life and the cultural display of power, also depends on the academic background and scholarly point of view that may not always be objective.[9]

The Byzantine 'city' embodies a long and complex history of 'tradition and change' in administrative, institutional, socio-economic, spiritual, and military terms and exhibits shifting relations of power, inextricably linked to the rise and diffusion of Christianity and its institutions. The physical transformation of the urban fabric is the most visual aspect of this. The present work focuses on the historical evolution of cities in Byzantine Asia Minor from an archaeological and topographical point of view, with particular emphasis on their physical transformation within the broader developmental trajectories of Byzantine urbanism. Examples of provincial towns, surviving either as purely archaeological sites or uneasily integrated into modern settlements, will be presented to illustrate some key themes (**Figure 7.1**), deliberately glossing over the centripetal role played by Constantinople (Istanbul) to 'tip the historiographical balance' between the Capital and provincial cities.[10]

Following the imprecise, yet generally acknowledged, chronological distinction between Late Antiquity (4th to mid-7th centuries) and the Byzantine period (7th century–1453),[11] the historical evolution of cities in Byzantine Asia Minor falls into four main periods of change and transformation: the Late Antique, or Early Byzantine (4th to mid-7th centuries),[12] the 'Dark Ages' (7th–9th centuries), the Middle Byzantine (mid-9th century–1204) and the Late Byzantine (1204–1453).[13] In these latter centuries, Anatolia was largely controlled by the Turks, and the period post-1261 in particular witnessed no significant developments in terms of (Byzantine) urbanism – no renaissance of existing towns nor establishment of new ones, with the major exception of Trebizond.

For Late Antiquity, Cyril Mango argues that urban centres until the end of the 6th/early 7th centuries divide into two groups: continuations of a Roman city, often with Hellenistic (or earlier) origins, and foundations *ex novo* in Late Antiquity. Most centres of Classical Antiquity, such as Aphrodisias, Ephesus, Iasos, Miletus, Olympus, Pergamum, Priene, Sagalassus, and Sardis, belong in the former group. The second is represented by a smaller number of settlements in Anatolia (and elsewhere). Constantinople – an extant Greco-Roman settlement (Byzantion) enhanced into a vast metropolis in the 4th and 5th centuries – is an exceptional case.[14]

Alongside the administrative, socio-economic, or defensive issues mentioned earlier, the most significant factors in the transformation of the built environment and physical appearance of cities in Late Antiquity were cultural and ideological in nature, associated with the onset of Christianity.[15] This itself did not encompass a new 'model' of urbanism but accelerated a transformation already in progress, as also pointed out by Gilbert Dagron.[16] The major changes to the physical structure of cities in this period are the dissolution of public spaces of Classical Antiquity; abandonment or transformation of pagan temples and

Figure 7.1 Schematic map of modern Turkey, showing the location of sites mentioned in the text

other public buildings no longer serving their original purposes; proliferation of Christian places of worship; and disintegration of the distinction between the *polis* and necropolis, as the Roman prohibition of burying *intra-urbem* faded away with the rise of the cult of saints and relics. Otherwise, before the late 6th/early 7th centuries, no radical change declares itself in the urban structure of Roman cities in Asia Minor regarding (pre-existing) fortifications, street layouts, water supply, and infrastructure.[17]

For the defence systems preceding the so-called Dark Ages, archaeological evidence indicates that the construction of most urban fortifications in Late Roman/Early Byzantine Asia Minor, incorporating or not the renovation of Hellenistic walls, dates between the mid-3rd and early 5th centuries under direct imperial command (Cod. Theod. 15,1,34; Cod. Iust. 8,11,12). This was in response to recurrent raids of the Goths and the Heruli, threatening the climate of peace and stability of Roman rule, and to similar disturbances caused by the Isaurian and Hunnic raids in the southern provinces.[18] The exact dating of some disputed fortifications still awaits elucidation, while the chronology of some 'Early Byzantine' walls is placed into the 6th, or oscillates between the 6th and 7th centuries.[19]

Glimpses from a number of cities in Late Antique Asia Minor demonstrate that the evolution of urban spaces, observable in the forms of abandonment, (selective) maintenance and preservation,[20] continuation of original purpose(s) or adaptive reuse (for new functions at times associated with Christianity), and natural or human destruction, all depending on site-specific factors and dynamics, did not always necessarily follow a similar pattern in the period before the 7th century. Intensive building activity, including not only the construction of churches but also the maintenance and/or renovation of existing street layouts and public buildings, the remodelling and embellishment of colonnaded streets, and the expansion and reorganisation of domestic spaces, indicates that the majority of urban centres in Asia Minor witnessed a period of prosperity in Late Antiquity.[21] In a number of cities, such as Aezani, Aphrodisias, Ephesus, Miletus, Sagalassus, and Sardis, improvements in street layout are worth noting.[22] One of the latest examples of street renovation can be found at Sagalassus, where the north-south colonnaded street saw a major renovation and monumentalisation, referred to as 'one of the last major civic undertakings in the Eastern Mediterranean', in the second quarter of the 6th century.[23] Similarly, the creation of a vaulted street, an impressive urban 'corridor', in the 6th-century settlement on Gemiler Island (Lycia) is remarkable: a rare – most probably 'unique' – example of Byzantine provincial architecture and urbanism (**Figure 7.2**).[24] The opposite is also witnessed in several cases, with spending on streets and urban spaces cut; such a one is Laodicea, which never fully recovered after an earthquake in 494 CE.[25]

Civic and secular buildings largely remained untouched, or were progressively assigned new functions as their former purposes – as venues for athletic events or public entertainment – diminished, being no longer part of the urban socio-cultural fabric.[26] Public baths were gradually abandoned or replaced by private ones.[27] Simultaneously, the dismantling and spoliation of abandoned temples and other public buildings, or their use as quarries for their stones or lime, were common practices.[28] The epigraphic evidence from Side indicates that the theatre was renovated during the 5th or 6th centuries,[29] but the theatres at Olympus and Priene were transformed into sources of lime and marble.[30] At times, spectacle buildings (theatres, amphitheatres, stadia, and hippodromes), large enough to host multiple functions simultaneously, had relatively long and 'particularly diverse Late Antique lives and fates' in the form of fortifications, habitations, cemeteries, or, despite the general Christian disapproval, in keeping up their original purposes.[31]

Figure 7.2 Gemiler Ada (Lycia) [Turkey], the ruins of a vaulted street, also known as the 'corridor'

Textual, epigraphic, and/or archaeological evidence also indicate repair and renovation in public spaces, such as *fora/agorae* and *bouleuteria*, in a number of cities in Asia Minor (e.g. Assus, Aphrodisias, Ephesus, Sagalassus, Side) through the 4th and 5th centuries. Their abandonment, decay, or transformation (sometimes accelerated by natural calamities) appear to have occurred by the mid-5th and in the course of the 6th centuries, if not later.[32] Sometimes, as at Hierapolis or Iasos, the public character of the agora arguably changed earlier, the result of natural calamities, or foreign threats.[33] In contrast is Elaiussa Sebaste, where an imposing, dual-apsed basilica was built within the agora (**Figure 7.3**): a good example of the effects of changing urban policies that involved the transformation of both built-up and open spaces by the mid-5th/6th centuries.[34] The commercial function of the agora was largely taken over, especially in the 6th century, by colonnaded streets flanked by shops (e.g. Sardis), to be in turn replaced with a commercial axis (*foros*) in later Byzantine times.[35]

The 'privatization' and subdivision of urban properties through the insertion of either private dwellings or secondary structures (stalls, shops, workshops, and other installations) in public urban spaces, such as the agora or in the porticoes flanking major streets, were an empire-wide trend, also referred to as 'encroachment' and observable from the 4th century onwards.[36] Similar changes, including the compartmentalisation of large peristyle houses into smaller dwelling units, or their fragmentation through co-ownership, can also be detected.[37] Literary evidence, including imperial legislation, has shown that such transformations, often labelled and archaeologically dismissed in the past as 'squatter' occupations, were not necessarily illegal activities to be interpreted as signs of decay.[38] These urban alterations should rather be seen as the outcome of 'a long and slow process of change',

Figure 7.3 Elaiussa Sebaste [Turkey], dual-apsed basilica within the agora

in close association, besides site-specific factors, with economic needs, natural calamities, changing attitudes towards public and private spaces, or growing demand for accommodation starting earlier than but certainly accelerated by the disturbances caused by Persian and Arab incursions.[39]

Limitations of space prevent a comprehensive review of a number of themes and examples, embracing such as the development of domestic and public spaces (e.g. *praetoriae*, *curiae/bouleuteria*), the establishment of Jewish alongside Christian places of worship (e.g. Andriake, Priene, Sardis), let alone those urban activities difficult to identify architecturally and archaeologically (e.g. street processions) through to the end of Late Antiquity.[40] Other aspects of urban transformation – the conversion of temples into churches (or for other purposes), and the practice of *spolia* and spoliation, both dramatically modifying urban landscapes – have already been investigated in an extensive literary corpus, and so albeit reluctantly will be passed over here.[41]

Christianisation was not 'quick, sudden, and all-embracing'[42] but gradually established itself in the cultural and physical structure of cities through centuries of conflict, divergence, and conciliation. The erection and multiplication of churches is one of the most typical and repeated effects of Christianity on the urban fabric, irrespective of the size and demographic characteristics of the city, or the growing demands of liturgy; economic factors though would have played an important role.[43] This proliferation affects both major and minor urban centres of Classical and Late Antiquity, such as Assus, Cnidus, Ephesus, Hierapolis, Iasos, Laodicea, Sagalassus, Selge, Side, and Xanthus. The medium-sized city of Olympus, of no particular religious importance, remarkably hosts nine churches; all attributed to the second half of the 5th and 6th centuries.[44] The eight churches identified so far in and around Sagalassus also date from the same period.[45] Likewise, the small city of Aperlae, with its reduced population and 'inhospitable setting', was provided with at least six churches, although it is unclear here whether they were all contemporary, or built at different times.[46] The small city of Corycus, with a dozen churches, and many other examples extend the list.[47]

The earlier churches (4th–5th centuries) were more commonly established in extramural or peripheral areas, often along major access routes, within and around cemeteries, or in relatively remote or isolated locations, such as the acropolis. Thereafter church buildings gradually infiltrated the *intra-muros* area, taking over the central core, sometimes using the sites of earlier buildings, but usually not before the 6th century.[48] However, given the challenges in establishing precise chronologies for the majority of Late Antique churches, this pattern of distribution should be viewed more 'as a tendency, not a hard and fast demarcation', as Allison Frantz observes.[49] Different processes of Christianisation existed even in the same region, and underlying motivations differed from place to place.[50]

At Iasos, for example, the location of the churches fits the general pattern discerned. Of the six churches so far identified here,[51] four are located in the area within the Hellenistic city walls, while the other two are extra-mural (**Figure 7.4**). The partially investigated extramural basilica near a Roman mausoleum (the 'Balık Pazarı') and the excavated churches on the acropolis and in the agora are all attributable to the 5th and 6th centuries. The Balık Pazarı basilica was in all probability the earliest (or one of the earlier) Christian sanctuary attributable to the 5th century, while the agora basilica can more securely be dated to Justinian (527–565).[52] The same is so at Sardis: an early Christian neighbourhood was established *ex novo*, centred on Basilica EA in the extra-mural area, known as Pactolus North, to the south of the Roman city; Building D, the presumed city cathedral in a relatively central location within the walls, is attributed to the 6th century.[53] At Miletus, Christian places of worship, namely the church of St. Michael and the Great Church (both within the sites of earlier temples), did not occupy the centre of the Roman city before the mid-6th century.[54]

The 'Christianization' of the central part of the city at an early date looks more common in the West, and in just a few cities in the Eastern Mediterranean, such as Jerash, Jerusalem, and Philippi.[55] However, as Dagron emphasises, an early occupation of the town centre was sometimes followed by a return to the outskirts of the city.[56] In Asia Minor, such a pattern is observed at Laodicea, the site of one of the Seven Churches of Asia and of the renowned Synod of Laodicea. Here, the so-called church of Laodicea, identified as the cathedral, was inserted within the Hellenistic grid layout next to Temple A between the north theatre and *decumanus maximus* to the east of the north (sacred) agora. The major changes to the agora, containing several temples within its perimeter, were initiated by the erection of the cathedral under Constantine the Great (306–337) on the basis of numismatic evidence.[57] The construction of this church seemingly triggered the formation of an early Christian neighbourhood there, involving several other churches. Others located in less central or extra-mural areas appeared a while after, but not later than the 6th century.[58]

The choice of where to build churches might be prompted by site-specific circumstances: the reuse of pre-existing structures, the transformation (or 'purification') of pagan temples, or the conquest of a place with a particular meaning for Christians.[59] The selection or availability of land to be occupied by religious and ecclesiastical buildings also relied on both private donations and acquisitions by the Church.[60] The importance of visibility and

Figure 7.4 Iasos (Caria) [Turkey], site plan, with the location of churches: **1**. The 'Balık Pazarı' basilica; **2**. Basilica on the acropolis; **3-4**. Unexcavated churches; **5**. Basilica within the agora; **6**. Middle/Late Byzantine church outside the East Gate; (**?**) Building (possibly identified as a church) within the 'castle' on the isthmus. Developed by the author, after Marcello Spanu, "The 2012 and 2013 Excavation and Research Campaigns at Iasos." *KST* 36 [2014]: fig. 12

connectivity was also emphasised, especially for Late Antique churches in port cities, such as Aperlea, Olympus, and on coastal Lycia in general, where the sea was the primary medium of communication.[61] Otherwise, the positioning of churches appears to have followed no particular rules, or predetermined urban plan.[62] This new urban development acquired an organic and decentralised character over time with the formation of neighbourhoods around churches and monasteries and broke with the traditional agora-centred pattern of the city.[63] The less regular but still dynamic urban patterning replaced earlier town planning canons, becoming the usual configuration of cities through the Middle Ages, in close association with the economic and military nature of Byzantine society.

With the spread of Christianity and the growing power of bishops in urban administration, replacing the Roman curial elite, bishopric complexes became the new focal centres in Late Antique cities, especially in the 5th and 6th centuries.[64] *Episcopeia*, embracing a range of religious, administrative, private/residential, and, sometimes public and charitable spaces and functions, often are evaluated as if elite or palatial architecture, but less commonly are they investigated in their own right as urban architecture.[65] This failing is partly explained by the dearth of literary and/or archaeological evidence by which to establish precise architectural typologies of episcopal palaces in Asia Minor (and elsewhere).[66]

Attachment to a church and the presence of spaces larger than in ordinary residential buildings are considered the most fundamental criteria for identifying bishopric palaces.[67] A direct or close connection to a church, as exemplified by the bishopric palace of Miletus next to the church of St. Michael (595–605),[68] is found in likely palaces at Aphrodisias, Bargylia, Ephesus,[69] Myra, Olympus, Priene, Side, and Xanthus.[70] Those complexes at Myra, Olympus, and Side were also enclosed within a perimeter wall.[71] A central position within the city might require adaptation to available land and existing buildings; the episcopal complexes located as such generally occupied the sites of previous structures, either a temple or a civic building, as at Aphrodisias Ephesus, Miletus, Olympus, and Priene.[72]

In terms of setting, there is no 'privileged position' for the establishment of bishopric complexes, at least in cities that were the continuation of Roman ones.[73] Bishopric complexes, especially those centrally located, were usually inserted into the existing street pattern, not necessarily occupying particularly significant or 'representational' positions in terms of urban planning;[74] the positioning along one of the major streets, or at the intersection of two (Olympus, Side, Xanthus), was common. The bishopric complex at Side, a rare example accessible by a monumental gateway, was located at the end of a main street, suggesting the ecclesiastical and administrative importance of the complex.[75] Although a central position in the city appears the more frequent (Aphrodisias, Ephesus, Miletus, Olympus, Priene, Xanthus), a marginal location near the city walls can also be observed at Bargylia and Side.[76] Some of these complexes (Miletus, Olympus, Side) extended over large areas, independent of their position in the city, covering multiple *insulae*.[77]

The bishopric palace at Aphrodisias is noteworthy for its date, attributable to the Middle Byzantine period. Here, the so-called Triconch House,[78] a sizeable Late Roman peristyle house, had long been recognised as the bishop's palace. Situated near the temple of Aphrodite, itself transformed in the late 5th/early 6th centuries into a church, the Triconch House was so identified because of its architectural characteristics and proximity to the temple-church, the presumed cathedral of Aphrodisias.[79] However, recent research has shown that this residential building, mainly occupied in the 5th and 6th centuries, was expanded and incorporated only in the last phases of its history (9th–12th centuries) into a larger complex, properly identifiable as a bishopric palace.[80] Future archaeological research may similarly challenge our knowledge about the *episcopeia*;[81] the architectural characteristics used to identify these buildings apply too to other types of civic architecture. Numerous structures in Asia Minor tentatively associated with bishopric palaces still await further investigation and confirmation.[82]

The emergence of *intra mural* burials is one of the most typical characteristics of Late Antique and medieval cities both in the East and the West, in contrast to the Roman city where burials *intra muros* were prohibited.[83] The long-established custom of burying *extra urbem* did not change immediately with the onset of Christianity.[84] The Late Roman emperors continued to promulgate edicts to maintain and regulate the practice of burying *extra urbem*.[85] The only exception made was for the relics of martyrs. These regulations were also incorporated into the codes of the Emperor Justinian, who reformulated the Theodosian code of 381 to broaden the ban on inhumations in all Christian places of worship of apostolic or martyrial character, urban or non-urban.[86] However, a divergence was noted already in the 4th century between legislation and practice, as can be deduced from the edict of 381 (Cod. Theod. 9,17,6), referring to those evading the law by *fallax et arguta sollertia*.[87]

Archaeological evidence indicates that burials *ad sanctos* around the extra-mural basilicas erected over the sepulchres of martyrs began with the spread of Christianity. In the late 4th and 5th centuries, the burgeoning cult of martyrs and relics produced a 'visible shift in the balance accorded to the areas of the living and areas of the death' in most Late Antique cities.[88] As Umberto Fasola and Vincenzo Fiocchi Nicolai argue, this cult – a determinant in engendering the phenomenon of urban burials – not only altered the topography of both intra- and extra-mural areas but also changed the physiognomy of the city of the dead into religious spaces with urban aggregation for the living.[89] The neat distinction between the *polis* and necropolis thus faded away in a reciprocal process through which one infiltrated into the other, although in different ways, so radically modifying the topography of both urban and suburban areas, inside or outside the city walls.

It is difficult to establish when burying *intra muros* became common practice. Although the legal regulations of the 10th century still referred to the ancient ban on burying *intra muros*, archaeological evidence demonstrates that by the 9th century, burials were taking place in and around churches inside or outside the walls.[90] The *novella* 53 by Leon VI (886–912), which explicitly authorised intra-mural burials, clearly shows how this practice had circumvented the law long before.[91] Starting as sporadic or provisional inhumations on the sites of churches, monasteries, or abandoned public monuments *à la recherche d'un peu de sacré*, i.e. on pieces of land whose status would not allow alienation, burials gradually appeared within the walls, creating new forms of division in the urban space between the dead and the living.[92]

Other reasons, such as demographic factors and the changing character of cities in Asia Minor and the Balkans in relation to foreign threats, are also invoked to explain the practice of urban burials. The majority of provincial cities in Asia Minor were still using their extra-urban necropolises in the course of the 6th century, if not later, while new burials began to accumulate by the 4th century around the extra-mural basilicas of martyrial or funerary character.[93] A good example is Sardis, where the Hellenistic and Roman necropolises remained in use through Late Antiquity, while the Christian cemeteries, extending over a large chronological span from the mid-4th–14th centuries, developed around the extra-mural churches.[94] Recent archaeological investigation in several other cities (Amorium, Ephesus, Hierapolis, Nicaea) also shows that no systematic burial took place within the city walls, excepting sporadic interments or loosely organised cemeteries, until the 6th century, or the Middle Byzantine period, when it occurred within and around the intra-mural churches.[95]

Archaeological evidence also indicates that the use of public spaces within the city walls, such as the agora, for burials did not usually take place before the mid-6th century.[96] At Hierapolis, a Middle Byzantine (10th–11th centuries) cemetery was located immediately east of the commercial agora. This cemetery constitutes one of the few examples of the systematic excavation of an entire Byzantine funerary complex.[97] At Nicaea, the theatre, including a church erected within its ruins, was used as a cemetery in the course of the 12th/13th centuries. A similar use of the theatre can also be found at Kelenderis and Sardis.[98] Although the available data enables one to draw a general picture of burial topography in Byzantine Anatolia,[99] further archaeological investigation is needed to determine the relationship among urban settlements, churches, and cemeteries and to better understand patterns of their evolution.

A second group of cities comprises those established *ex novo* in Late Antiquity. Recent archaeological research has indicated that a growing number belong to this group in the Eastern Mediterranean and the Balkans. They vary considerably as to specific circumstances to which they owe their emergence, as well as their evolution, settlement characteristics, and juridical status.[100] Excluding the exceptional case of Constantinople, the best known of this group are Iustiniana Prima/Caričin Grad (Serbia), Resafa/Sergiopolis and Zenobia/Halabiye (Syria), and Dara/Anastasiopolis in northern Mesopotamia (Turkey). These four cities, as revealed either by textual and/or archaeological evidence, were all established mainly in the course of the 6th century, with short life-spans of about a century.[101] Although they were designed on a relatively small scale, they functioned simultaneously as the administrative, defensive, and ecclesiastical centres of their respective regions along the Asian and European borders of the empire.[102] On the one hand, these cities, with their urban layout, infrastructure, planning of public and private areas, and administrative and religious buildings on a monumental scale, can be considered part of the classical urban tradition. However, they also represent, as Enrico Zanini emphasises, a 'conceptual shift from city to defensive city', being endowed with a strongly military aspect.[103]

The oldest (and largest) among these is Dara/Anastasiopolis originally founded by Anastasius (491–518) as a military base on the Byzantine-Sasanian frontier and rebuilt by Justinian. Its foundation and construction phases under both emperors are well documented by written sources.[104] This, combined with archaeological evidence, makes Dara an ideal case-study not only to illuminate the dynamics and parameters involved in the foundation and planning of new cities during Late Antiquity but also to provide insights into the evolution of settlements from *polis* to *kastron* on the eve of the Byzantine Dark Ages.[105]

The natural defensive strength of the site and the availability of water resources were the main parameters for the choice of location for the foundation of this fortified city, comprising three hills through the centre of which flew the River Cordes. The stone for construction was also available from local quarries extending west of the city.[106] The imposing fortifications, surrounded by a moat on the east, followed an irregular line imposed by the challenging topography. Textual evidence indicates that the intra-mural area included public baths, two churches, colonnaded streets, storehouses for grain, cisterns, and other buildings 'with which distinguished cities were embellished' (αἱ ἐπίσημοι τῶν πόλεων ἐγκαλλωπίζονται)).[107] The presence and location of some of these buildings are confirmed by archaeological investigation, indicating that the intra-mural area to the west of the river was reserved for public buildings, the majority of which were seemingly linked by a colonnaded street running parallel to the river.[108] Excavations have also revealed the remains of a *praetorium*, an almost centrally located episcopal complex, and an outer system of defences to the south of the city walls, with suburban structures between these inner and outer sets of fortifications.[109] The well-preserved necropolis, with its variety of burial types, spread west of the city, occupying sections of the local stone quarries there.[110] A general image of such cities as of a rather 'non-classical', but strongly defensive and militarised nature, is given by the written sources of the Late Antique and Middle Byzantine periods.[111] However, recent archaeological investigations at Dara have confirmed that this fortified town, with its public, ecclesiastical, and infrastructural buildings embellishing both its intra-mural area and densely settled suburbs, actually reflects the continuity of the classical urban tradition, including the conventional relationship between a city and its territory.[112]

The destruction or abandonment of monuments, even the 'decline' of entire urban areas, at the end of Late Antiquity, has usually been attributed to Persian and Arab incursions perturbing Asia Minor from the mid-7th to 9th centuries.[113] The physical transformation of cities during this period, also known as the 'Dark Ages', can be readily observed: their urban area shrinks to within reduced circuit walls, or even into fortified hill tops (*kastron*), and certain urban functions are displaced by a more military existence.[114] The 'ruralisation' of towns equally appears a common phenomenon, resulting from the chaotic and unstable conditions of this period.[115] Foreign raids certainly impinged to some degree on urban life and may therefore be a correct explanation for individual cases. However, textual and (often incomplete) archaeological evidence should be assessed with extreme caution and scrutiny and on a regional basis before determining scenarios of urban failure. Furthermore, it is extremely difficult to assess with any accuracy the scale and extent of damage and destruction, attributable either to foreign attacks or natural calamities (e.g. earthquakes and plagues[116]), affecting an entire urban area.[117] The effects of such incidents should not of course be underestimated, but neither one nor the other category should be taken as mainly responsible for an empire-wide catastrophe that took so long to recover from.[118]

The cities on the southern coasts of Anatolia, more exposed to foreign threats from the south and east than the western provinces, appear to have been largely abandoned following the Battle of Phoenix (Finike) under Contans II (641–668), after being ravaged by the Justinianic plague.[119] There is little evidence of building activity in the cities of coastal Lycia in the 7th and 8th centuries. A recovery involving new building activity, especially the construction of churches (within the ruins of earlier buildings), monasteries, and defensive structures, is detected at Xanthus (and other Lycian sites, such as Arycanda/Arif, Gemiler Ada, Myra, or Patara) only from the second half of the 10th through to the end of the 12th centuries.[120]

Moving inland, Sagalassus also fell into decay by the mid-6th century onwards, and around the mid-7th century, the settlement shifted to a newly fortified area (*kastron,* or perhaps an episcopal *kastron*) on the promontory previously occupied by a temple to the south of the erstwhile town centre. This relocation has been associated with the Arab raids. The former urban area appears to have remained loosely inhabited after an earthquake in the early 7th century, with small hamlets dispersed within the ruins of the old city. Archaeological finds and evidence of (re)building activity both on 'Alexander's Hill' and within the temple-church of Apollo Klarios to the west of the lower agora do indicate continuity of occupation in these areas and within the *kastron* not only during the Dark Ages but also from the 10th through to the first half of the 13th centuries.[121] Archaeological evidence, including early medieval pottery assemblages, suggests the presence of a medieval community at Sagalassus. The excavators thus issue a challenge to the long-established model of 'Dark Age' abandonment.[122]

The archaeological evidence at Hierapolis indicates that the main event leading to the collapse of the major monuments of the city was more likely an earthquake in the middle of the 7th century rather than the Persian raids of 616. Whatever the causes of destruction were, Hierapolis, unlike neighbouring Laodicea, does not appear to have been completely abandoned after the 7th century. Although no major public buildings were (re)constructed following these 7th-century events, settlement activity can be detected in sections of the old town, especially on both flanks of 'Frontinus Street' in the 8th century. The area within and around the Roman bath to the south of the commercial agora was occupied by domestic and agricultural production spaces, revealing several different phases of destruction, abandonment, and rebuilding during the Middle Byzantine period on into the 12th century. Small churches were raised within earlier basilicas or public buildings, while burials occupied areas within and around the intra-mural churches.[123] The medieval built-up area to the south of the commercial agora also appears to have been fortified, making use of the Late Antique city walls, at some time during the Byzantine Middle Ages. This wall is compared by the archaeologists to the 'Lower City Enclosure' at Amorium. In the course of the 10th century, this area was largely given over to agricultural installations, indicating a greater ruralisation of the area around the commercial agora, as also witnessed in other parts of Hierapolis.[124]

In western Asia Minor, the area of the theatre at Miletus, including the north agora, bishopric complex, and the Great Church, was incorporated into a fortress in the 7th century, largely excluding the ancient city (**Figure 7.5**).[125] After an interruption in settlement activity attributable to sometime before the 11th century, the last fortified Byzantine settlement, known as the Palatia (Balat), was developed on the theatre hill for defensive reasons associated with the arrival of the Turks from the late 11th century onwards. In this last phase of loosely planned settlement on the hilltop, earlier urban traditions, such as the Hippodamian

Figure 7.5 Miletus [Turkey], 'Theaterkastell'

plan shaping the layout of Roman and Early Byzantine Miletus, appear to have long been forgotten.[126] At Priene, archaeological evidence suggests an 'urban break' between the late 7th and 11th centuries, when the lower city was largely abandoned and settlement was relocated on the acropolis. Numismatic evidence indicates limited reoccupation in the lower city in the 9th/10th centuries, with, however, increased building activity between the late 11th and 13th centuries in sections of the lower city, including the reconstruction and expansion of both Hellenistic lower city walls and the fortifications on the acropolis.[127] At Pergamum, where sections of the lower city are largely obscured by modern settlement, a massive fortification wall was built on the southern slope of the acropolis following the contours of the topography. The construction of this wall is attributed to the mid-7th century. However, the later stages of the Middle Byzantine period at Pergamum have yielded no datable evidence before the second half of the 11th century.[128] Excavations in the area within the 7th-century fortifications have revealed an organically developed Late Byzantine residential quarter, comprising single-storey houses, with several rooms arranged around a courtyard, connected by an irregular pattern of pathways and blind alleys.[129] This residential area is one of the few surviving examples from this period in Asia Minor.

The withdrawal of urban areas onto fortified hills is no doubt attributable to defensive and military factors for the most part, but concrete evidence of such transformation in this period attributable to Persian or Arab attacks is not always forthcoming, even though such are often stated to be responsible.[130] In this context, the corrective case of Ephesus is noteworthy. Here, the seat of administration had already during the 5th century moved from the Upper Agora towards the lower city incorporating the harbour zone: a Late Antique neighbourhood, comprising domestic and production spaces, developed to the south of St. Mary's. This settlement, destroyed by a fire sometime in the 7th century, was shaped by the local topography, had no signs of regular planning, and was characterised by 'rural components'. No archaeological evidence has been found to correlate this destruction with Persian or Arab raids.[131] The factors leading to and the chronology of the construction of the 'Byzantine wall' encircling the core of the urban area around the harbour zone have also undergone a similar reassessment. In the apparent absence of *spolia* used in its construction, this wall is distinguished from numerous other examples erected hastily in the face of hostilities and recycling building material from earlier buildings. It is better interpreted as a 'prestigious building programme for both the display of power and ongoing protection of the city' rather than an immediate response to any specific threat.[132] This wall, traditionally attributed to the 6th/7th centuries, has recently been backdated to the 5th century, more precisely to the time of Theodosius II (408–450).[133] On the other hand, the development of the fortified hill at Ayasoluk that dominates the hinterland and shelters the new ecclesiastical, administrative, and military centre of Ephesus can more reasonably be placed during the late 7th/8th centuries. These latter fortifications differ from the 'Byzantine wall' in the lower city in construction technique and materials and include quantities of *spolia*.[134]

Some Byzantine sites, largely free of modern settlements and systematically investigated through archaeological survey and/or excavations, do offer valuable data to illuminate aspects of Byzantine urbanism during the Dark Ages. For instance, archaeological and numismatic evidence, combined with historical sources, suggest 'urban continuity and change' at Amorium, a Byzantine thematic capital located in Central Anatolia, where the city's history can be traced from the 7th through to the 11th centuries.[135] Here the major structures of the Roman and Late Roman city within the Lower City Walls (LCW), including the Lower City Basilica (LCB) and the city walls themselves (both attributed to the late 5th/early 6th centuries), survived through the Dark Ages and were maintained into the early 9th century, until their final destruction by fire associated with the turbulent events of this period that culminated in the sack of Amorium in 838.[136] The most important urban transformation attributable to the Dark Ages was the construction of an inner citadel on top of the mound known as the Upper City, thus dividing the urban area into two zones: the Upper City and Lower City.[137] The fortification of this area appears to undergo at least two building phases: the first, constructed with abundant quantities of *spolia*, was attributed to the 7th century, while the second is thought to be part of a major reconstruction of the Upper City following the siege of 838.[138] Excavations within and around an Early Byzantine bathhouse in the Lower City have also revealed evidence of domestic and artisanal activity attributable to the Dark Ages. The gradual subdivision of urban spaces into smaller units can also be observed in this bathhouse district.[139] Archaeological evidence also indicates that Amorium remained as the centre of a 'mixed economy', including agricultural and pastoral activities, through the 8th and 9th centuries.[140] A 'major alteration' to the layout of the Lower City occurred in the Middle Byzantine period with the construction of a fortified enclosure (dated ca. 1000) over the ruins of earlier buildings at the centre of the Lower City. The 'Enclosure', together with the rebuilding of the Upper City *kastron* and reoccupation of sections of the city in the 10th and 11th centuries, marks the last phases of the urban transformation at Amorium, turning it into 'an open settlement dominated by the new *kastron* on the Upper City', before the arrival of the Turks in the late 11th century.[141] Thus, the continued use of the LCW and the area they enclosed during the Dark Ages contradicts the general portrayal of towns withdrawing onto fortified hilltops and the 'discontinuity' or abandonment of urban life outside the latter.[142] The urban evolution of Amorium through the Byzantine Middle Ages is a story of survival through transformation, not an urban collapse; a flexible process requiring a range of different interventions – structural maintenance as well as architectural recycling, renovation and reuse, transformation and development of earlier public and private urban spaces, all in response to ever-changing military, defensive, and socio-economic demands.[143]

Archaeological evidence thus suggests a general recovery for those cities which somehow survived the Dark Ages, with or without major interruption from the 8th through to the 12th centuries,[144] until the permanent establishment of the Turkish Principalities in Anatolia. This recovery of settlement and building activity, whose scale and pace differed from one place to another, is often referred to as 'urban revival', despite the increasingly changing characteristics of former centres towards militarisation, ruralisation (with cultivated lands inside urban areas), or relocation in dynamic response to contemporary requirements. However, as is pointed out by Charalambos Bouras, 'the resettling of a site of strategic and productive importance where there was an abundance of building materials does not coincide precisely with the meaning of the term *revival*; these, too, were new towns, without memories or experiences of the old cites on whose ruins they stood'.[145] The general situation of most urban settlements in Middle Byzantine Asia Minor, with their admixture of domestic spaces alongside units of agricultural, artisanal, or industrial production, and all amid the ruins of their former selves, would be better termed survival through transformation rather than a true 'urban revival'.

Those cities, which re-emerged without major interruption from the ruins and with the memory of their Classical past through the Dark Ages into modern times, can be exemplified by Ancyra (Ankara), Nicaea (Iznik), and Trebizond (Trabzon). The latter two in particular – the capitals of the two rival splinter states, the Empires of Nicaea (1204–1261) and Trebizond

(1204–1461) – witnessed the last centuries of Byzantium, after the Fall of Constantinople to the Fourth Crusade in 1204, and the following political and administrative fragmentation of the Byzantine Empire. A time when relatively little evidence survives elsewhere.

With regard to Ancyra, the city fell to the Persians in the first decades of the 7th century and remained continuously under threat from Persian and Arab attacks until the 9th.[146] During this period, the city was incorporated into a new military administration and, in the 8th century, was designated the capital of the Bukellarion Theme.[147] Both literary and archaeological evidence indicate the implementation of considerable modifications in Ancyra during this period as the city shrank into a fortified hill. The citadel (in Turkish *Kale*), sited on the summit of a steep and rocky eminence dominating the city and its hinterland with closely spaced pentagonal towers (**Figure 7.6**), is the most important surviving monument of the Byzantine period in Ankara.[148] It is composed of two ramparts; the construction of the inner circuit has usually been attributed to the middle of the 7th century, while the outer circuit and the 'rebuilding' of the inner are dated to the 9th century.[149] The capture and destruction of Ancyra by the Caliph Mu'tasim in 838, recognised as one of the most important Arab victories in Anatolia, apparently instigated the large-scale construction activity undertaken by Michael III (842–867), as recorded by the inscriptions.[150]

The citadel is distinguished by the quantities of *spolia* used in its ramparts, towers, and bastions. The south and west sides of the inner circuit facing the city, and sections of walls near the gates, include the most significant pieces of *spolia*, such as blocks of marble,

Figure 7.6 Ankara [Turkey], Byzantine fortifications, inner circuit with pentagonal towers, as seen from the southwest

architectural and carved elements, and inscriptions. The differences in construction materials and workmanship between the south and west walls and the east wall of the inner circuit stemmed in all probability from the intention of the builders to present a more regular and precise appearance to those sides of the wall facing the city, so as to impress visitors. The best quality materials, both in terms of strength and decoration, were usually chosen by medieval builders especially when constructing castles and fortifications intended to impress – and intimidate – with their visual might and sense of endurance.[151] Convenience may well have been a consideration here, as marble would have been abundant on the south and west slopes below the citadel where ancient Ankara was located. However, the careful selection of *spolia* in those sections of the citadel facing the city and near the gates went far beyond concerns for structural stability and convenience.

The citadel of Ankara, in its construction technique and materials, finds a close parallel in the fortifications of Nicaea, the major alterations to which are also attributed to Michael III, and precisely to the year 858, by the inscriptions.[152] In the cases of both Ancyra and Nicaea, the medieval builders, aspiring to build, or rebuild, a chain of defences to reflect both strength and aesthetics, appropriated building materials inherited from Antiquity. In the process, they embellished and presented these materials with new forms and meanings in the fortification walls, providing physical and visual access to, and protection for, their respective cities. Of course, their apparent concern for appearance and aesthetics cannot necessarily be interpreted as a desire to establish a connection with the past. Yet, the citadel of Ankara emerges as a Mnemosyne where the fragmented communal memory of the city was inscribed, intentionally or not, in physically recognisable components of the Classical and Early Christian past.[153]

As part of the changing character of cities in the Middle and Late Byzantine periods, the 'beauty' (τὸ κάλλος) of churches and the splendour and strength of fortifications, both often enlivened with abundant *spolia*, became the central elements admired in medieval cities otherwise now deprived of their classical architectural and urban embellishments.[154] The notable effect of city walls on the Byzantine beholder can be discovered, for instance, in the *ekphrasis* of Theodore Metochites (1270–1332), describing the walls of Nicaea[155]:

> ...Who would not be astounded to look upon these walls around her, which draw so much confidence from their construction that the effort of every kind of engine against them is of no use but a wholly vain spending of time on the impossible? ... She, well disposed toward mankind and regularly built, relies on herself and her external circuits, so finely constructed that it is at once a pleasure and a marvel to behold their undeceived foresight, their great unconquerable beauty, their splendid barrier.

The walls of Iznik, originally raised in the late 3rd century, were frequently rebuilt, modified, and strengthened throughout the centuries, with major modifications attributed to Leo III (716–741), Michael III, and the Lascarid emperors (1204–1261).[156] Once again, abundant quantities of *spolia* from earlier buildings were included in the repair and reconstruction of the walls, especially in the 8th- and 9th-centuries interventions.[157] Although praise for individual structures mostly built with *spolia* was not very common in Byzantine literary sources,[158] the fortifications of Nicaea were also admired for 'the most exquisite material and excellent construction' (τῆς περιφανεστάτης ὕλης καὶ ἐξαιρέτου τῆς οἰκοδομῆς) in the *encomion* of Nicaea written by Theodore II Lascaris (1254–1258).[159]

Nicaea was the imperial capital and the seat of the patriarch for almost half a century during the Latin occupation of Constantinople and, according to Clive Foss, 'the city appears more clearly at this time than any other'.[160] The modern town of Iznik, located on the shore of the eponymous lake (formerly Lake Ascania), subsisted from Antiquity through the Byzantine Middle Ages without major interruption, despite the foreign threats and destructive earthquakes.[161] The city still impresses with its imposing fortifications, encircling an urban area built on an orthogonal plan with the *cardo* and *decumanus* leading to the four gates in the city walls. As the meeting place of the First and Seventh Ecumenical Councils in 325 and 787,[162] Nicaea was provided with numerous churches from the Early Christian period through to the first half of the 13th century.[163] The cathedral of St. Sophia, probably built in the second half of the 5th or 6th centuries, was centrally located at the intersection of the *cardo* and *decumanus*, indicating the survival and continued importance of these major streets.[164] The continuity of building activity during the Dark Ages is evidenced by the church of the Dormition, erected around the late 7th/early 8th centuries, as part of the monastery of Hyacint in the south-eastern part of the city.[165] Nicaea witnessed two further periods of church building in the late 11th and first half of the 13th centuries. In the latter (Lascarid) period, besides the renovation of the existing churches, a number of new Christian places of worship, among which are some identified as cemetery churches, were built west of the *cardo*.[166] Lascarid Nicaea, as pointed out by Foss, emerges as an important and populated urban centre by the standards of the time, with imposing fortifications, wide and regular streets, churches, and other buildings, deserving the admiration expressed in the 13th-century *encomia*. The same *encomia*, it should be remembered, depicted an urban environment within an idyllic, almost rural setting, with meadows and trees overshadowing churches and monasteries, as well as cultivated lands and groves within the city walls.[167] Apart from the fact that the beauty of natural surroundings was among the main elements acclaimed in city *encomia*,[168] the portrayal of a ruralised urban environment is not surprising, given that medieval Constantinople too was often described in the written sources as a 'ruralised network of scattered nuclei' with farmlands occupying both urban and suburban areas.[169]

In contrast to Nicaea, the urban layout of medieval Trebizond, largely determined by the topography with defensive advantages endowed by nature, shows an organic development. The city is dominated by a steep and rocky hill flanked by two ravines stretching down to the sea. Anthony Bryer and David Winfield remark that the area west of today's Meydan Parkı, with three parallel streets running east-west, is the only section of Trebizond showing signs of a regular, orthogonal plan. Here, the main street at the centre (Kahramanmaraş Caddesi), also referred to as the 'imperial way' in historical sources, has been identified as the *cardo*; the *Meydan*, which remained the main open space in the city throughout the centuries, being possibly associated with the site of the Classical and Medieval agora.[170] The main areas of habitation were located north of the imperial way between the Lower and Middle City, stretching east-west on the slopes of the acropolis and around the Daphnous harbour. The eastern and western suburbs, with medieval quarters growing up around churches and other landmarks, were divided by the great rock crowned by three sets of fortifications enclosing 'the city proper' (**Figure 7.7**):[171]

> In the city hemmed between the ravines the traveller would probably see huddled houses first... The houses climbed from the Lower City, which spread over the

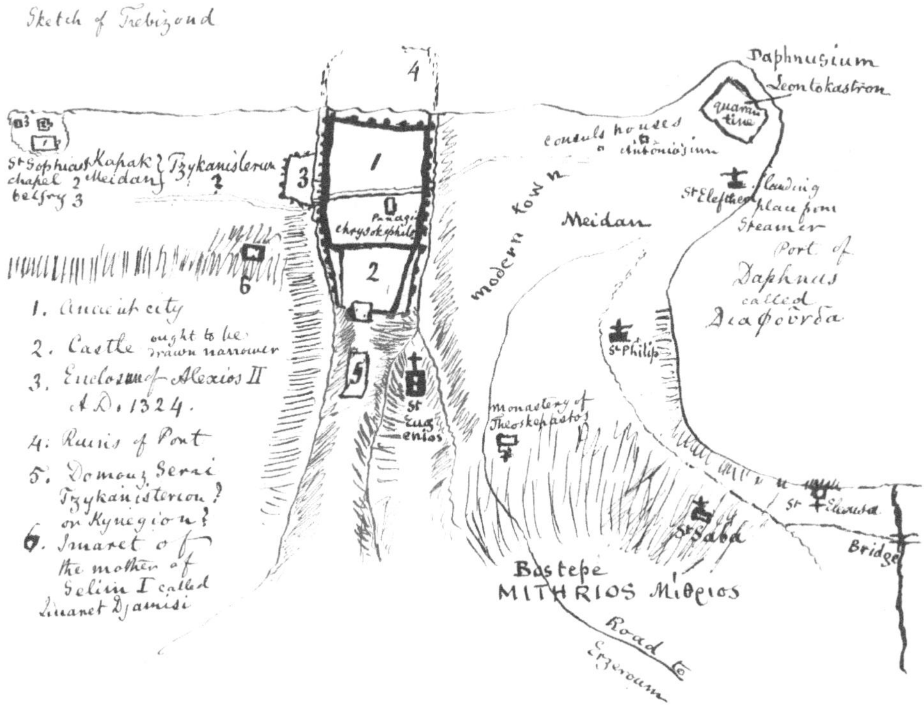

Figure 7.7 Detail from George Finlay's notebook, A.14, double page spread 29, showing (sketch) map of Trebizond, 1850 (George Finlay Personal Papers, British School at Athens; reproduced with the permission of the British School at Athens)

western ravine, to the attenuated Middle City, marked by the dome of the monastery and crowning church of the Chrysokephalos [the city's cathedral], and up to the Citadel where the walls overlooking the ravines finally meet at the grand tower of John IV, newly repaired in 1460. Here stood the golden palace of the Grand Komnenoi, a jumble of halls, barracks, offices, apartments, and chapels around a central square called the Epiphania.

The area east of the rock, including the main commercial and industrial district of Trebizond, was more densely built up than the western suburbs that were largely occupied by fields, orchards, and open spaces. The westernmost limit of this area was marked by the monastic church of Hagia Sophia (Ayasofya Camii) rising from a rural landscape near the shoreline.[172] The selection of this unusual location, far beyond the city walls, for one of the 'great ecclesiastical building projects', was, according to Anthony Eastmond, to remedy a deficit in Trebizond 'as a site for imperial ceremonial' and a desire to alter the 'ritual geography' of the city. With the foundation of Hagia Sophia under Manuel I Grand Komnenos (1238–1263), the functions of coronation and burial, previously incorporated into the centrally located Panagia Chrysokephalos (Ortahisar Fatih Camii), were thus separated, evoking an earlier distinction between the churches of Hagia Sophia and Holy Apostles in Constantinople.[173] Along with the cult church of St. Eugenios (Yeni Cuma Camii), dedicated to the city's patron saint, on the hill overlooking the eastern ravine and a commercial district centring around the *Meydan*, the major churches built, or rebuilt, by the Grand Komnenoi in the course of the 13th century, each fulfilling a specific function (coronation, burial, and cult), defined a new ritual topography, with processional routes extending across the city. The presence and distant location of Hagia Sophia thus enabled imperial ceremonial on a larger and more elaborate scale in the small city of Trebizond, otherwise unsuitable for longer processions.[174]

Besides the above-mentioned fortifications and a number of other defensive structures, numerous churches, chapels, and monasteries (the majority of which were built in 1204–1461), Trebizond was also provided with secular and infrastructure buildings.[175] Some of these edifices, now largely obscured by later urban strata, are better known in the textual evidence.[176] Here, in contrast to the majority of Byzantine cities in Asia Minor, the period of the renewal as exemplified by the built environment starts in the 9th century, when the city became the headquarters of Chaldia Theme and the seat of a *strategos*. The earliest surviving church, St. Anne's, also originates from this period.[177] The period of the Empire of Trebizond is distinguished by large-scale and relatively well recorded building activity: these include the three sets of defences, encircling the Lower City (Aşağı Hisar), Middle City (Ortahisar), referred to as *kastron*, and the Citadel (Yukarı Hisar, or Kale). Literary and epigraphic evidence, as detailed by Bryer and Winfield, indicate that Classical and Byzantine Trebizond was composed of the Middle City (fortified before 257 CE) and the Citadel; the Lower City being enclosed under Alexios II (1297–1330). The Citadel, occupying the acropolis (strongly fortified since Classical times), was an administrative centre associated with the rulers of Trebizond throughout its history and thus displays different stages of masonry. It was adorned with a palace of several different building phases in the period 1204–1460.[178]

The medieval topography of 'dioikicised' Trebizond is complex, and further descriptive attempts here would risk remaining superficial.[179] I shall therefore confine myself to highlighting a few secular buildings that number among the very few surviving, fairly identifiable, examples of their kind from the Late Byzantine period, i.e. the *tzykanisterion*, the imperial polo ground, and the palace of the Grand Komnenoi. The former has tentatively been identified in the area now occupied by the city's football stadium in the western outskirts of the city, a short distance from St. Sophia's.[180] The positioning of this public and imperial open space suggests that it was used for ceremonial activities, deliberately recalling, as Eastmond points out, the Hippodrome of Constantinople 'as a destination during imperial ceremonies'.[181]

The palace of the Grand Komnenoi,[182] whose remnants survive along the west wall of the Citadel overlooking the ravine (**Figure 7.8**), is among the few survivors of Late Byzantine palatial architecture.[183] The main access to the fortress-palace was from the south, strengthened by a tower attributed to John IV (1429–1459), opening into the 'Epiphania', referred to as the 'castle square' in the written sources.[184] It is worth noting that the Epiphania, together with the square of Ano Chora at Mistra, was one of the few public open spaces purposely created as such in this period.[185] The palace complex was the first major secular building programme undertaken by the Trapezuntine rulers immediately after 1204, and a defining monument of imperial ceremonial within the newly established ritual landscape of Trebizond.[186] Analogies to the foundation of Constantinople and the concerns of Constantine the Great can also be found here. Further discussion on these broad topics is beyond the scope of this chapter. Nonetheless, it is worthwhile noting with Eastmond that 'the Grand Komnenoi's buildings were clothed in the local idiom, so rooting their new

Figure 7.8 Trebizond [Turkey], Yukarı Hisar (Kale), remains of the fortress-palace of the Grand Komnenoi, overlooking the western ravine

Constantinople firmly in Trapezuntine soil': this involves a crucial distinction between the two urban foundations.[187]

The above-mentioned survey – several others (e.g. Amastris, Euchaïta) are reluctantly excluded here[188] – indicates that Byzantine cities in Anatolia had their different stories to tell within a more general narrative. Keeping these geographical and chronological diversities in mind, it can be observed that cities had left their Classical past behind by the end of Late Antiquity, undergoing a series of cultural, economic, demographic, and physical changes. This process in the 'Dark Ages' can better be defined as survival through transformation and adaptation; it excludes those towns completely abandoned, or relocated to naturally defendable sites. Multiple reasons have been advanced to interpret this. Foreign raids and natural disasters, powerful earthquakes in particular, certainly played a role, especially when combined with other site-specific factors, in accelerating either large-scale abandonment or urban transformation through reconstruction. Archaeological evidence from numerous sites also proclaims a general recovery of settlement and building activity, albeit not necessarily an indication of true urban 'revival', from the late 9th to 10th centuries until the arrival (1071) and gradual settlement of the Turks in Anatolia. In this wider chronological context, the periods best documented in the majority of Anatolian cities emerge as the 5th–7th centuries of Late Antiquity, and 10th–12th centuries of the Byzantine Middle Ages, with Nicaea, Trebizond, and perhaps a few others providing longer and more coherent stories. The settlements of the Byzantine Middle Ages are also characterised by the ruralisation and deurbanisation of the earlier city fabric, with dispersed nuclei evolving amongst the ruins of the Classical and Late Antique past. The distinction between 'urban' and 'rural' melted away as settlements of a mixed, or intermediary, nature came into being. Attempting to understand these 'new towns' by the standards of their Classical predecessors, or indeed any other, is no longer a viable or fruitful choice. The cities endlessly evolved throughout the centuries in keeping with changing conditions; 'the processes they further, the functions they perform, or the purposes they fulfil' cannot sensibly be evaluated by standards of times gone past, or constrained into narrower definitions. Furthermore:[189]

> No single definition will apply to all its [the city's] manifestations and no single description will cover all its transformations, from the embryonic social nucleus to the complex forms of its maturity and the corporeal disintegration of its old age. The origins of the city are obscure, a large part of its past buried or effaced beyond recovery, and its further prospects are difficult to weigh.

Different stories told, or yet to be told, by individual cities have also been shaped by research priorities and methodologies involved in past archaeological investigations, and the diversity of interpretations and approaches, if not failures, in the challenging process of arriving at an understanding of the past. These factors assuredly apply to Byzantine archaeology. The Late Antique and Byzantine sites and settlements, which typically represent the latest stratigraphic layers at archaeological sites, often remained neglected, or were razed to the ground to access previous periods, usually the Classical.[190] Or they were engulfed by densely built modern settlements. Byzantine cultural heritage can remain politically sensitive, if not vulnerable, in areas of the Eastern Mediterranean where there are no longer cultural, religious, or linguistic links with the Byzantine civilisation, in contrast to the situation in Greece and the Balkans.[191] However, the attention paid in the recent past to Byzantine strata in numerous archaeological excavations (foreign or national) in Turkey (and elsewhere), and a growing number of publications, demonstrates that those 'selective' approaches towards specific areas or periods of the past are hopefully being left behind. Future research enhanced by a multi-disciplinary strategy, free from archaeological subjectivity or political priorities, will continue to challenge and change our current understanding of Byzantine settlements, whether urban, rural, or somewhere 'in between'.

Notes

1 A. P. Kazhdan's "Vizantijskie goroda v VII-XI vekach," *SovA* 21 (1954): 164–183 highly influenced the development of research into Byzantine urbanism. Cf. G. Ostrogorsky, "Byzantine Cities in the Early Middle Ages," *DOP* 13 (1959): 47–48.

2 W. Brandes, "Byzantine Cities in the Seventh and Eighth Centuries – Different Sources, Different Histories?," in *The Idea and Ideal of the Town between Late Antiquity and the Early Middle Ages*, eds. G. P. Brogiolo and B. W. Perkins (Leiden; Boston: Brill, 1999), 57.

3 The bibliography on the transformation of cities (and underlying factors) is exhaustive and cannot be attempted here. For an overview, most recently: Luca Zavagno, *The Byzantine City from Heraclius to the Fourth Crusade, 610-1204. Urban Life after Antiquity* (Cham: Palgrave Macmillan, 2021); and Chapter 1 in this volume.

4 To cite but some: J. Haldon, "Some Considerations on Byzantine Society and Economy in the Seventh Century," *ByzF* 10 (1985): 77–78; H. Saradi-Mendelovici, "The Demise of the Ancient City and the Emergence of the Medieval City in the Eastern Roman Empire," *EchosCl* 32 (1988): 398–400.

5 The definition of the terms 'city' and 'town', and the use(s) of the words *polis* and *kastron* (sometimes used indiscriminately for the same settlement) as seen in the sources of Antiquity and the Middle Ages were as complex and confused/ing to people of the time to understand as they are for modern scholars. On the problems of terminology, among others: J. Haldon, "The Idea of the

Town in the Byzantine Empire," in *The Idea and Ideal of the Town between Late Antiquity and the Early Middle Ages*, eds. G. P. Brogiolo and B. W. Perkins (Leiden; Boston: Brill, 1999), 10–23; and several contributions in the same volume. Cf. L. Zavagno, *Cities in Transition. Urbanism in Byzantium between Late Antiquity and the Early Middle Ages (AD 500–900)* (Oxford: BAR, 2009), 1–8.

6 Clive Foss' seminal publications on Sardis and Ephesus caused a shift of emphasis on archaeological evidence: *Byzantine and Turkish Sardis* (Cambridge, MA: Harvard University Press, 1976); *Ephesus after Antiquity: A Late Antique, Byzantine and Turkish City* (Cambridge; New York: Cambridge University Press, 1979).

7 For the current state of Byzantine archaeology, with thematic and regional studies: M. J. Decker ed., *The Cambridge Handbook to Byzantine Archaeology* (Cambridge: Cambridge University Press [forthcoming]).

8 Cf. A. Cameron, *The Mediterranean World in Late Antiquity AD 395-600* (London; New York: Routledge, 1993), 197.

9 U. Serin, *Early Christian and Byzantine Churches at Iasos in Caria: An Architectural Survey* (Vatican City: PIAC, 2004), 202–204 (with bibliography). Cf. A. Cameron, "Thinking with Byzantium," *Transactions of the Royal Historical Society. Sixth Series* 21 (2011): 42, 47, 54.

10 Imperial capitals, like Rome and Constantinople, better known by historical, textual, and/or archaeological evidence, and seen as more important in their political, economic, and social roles, often dominated scholarly research. Cf. Zavagno, *Cities*, 29.

11 The chronological distinction between Late Antiquity and Byzantium is contentious: Cameron, "Thinking," 43–44. Cf. Mark Whittow, *The Making of Byzantium, 600-1025* (Berkeley, CA; Los Angeles: University of California Press, 1996), 97; J. Shepard ed., *The Cambridge History of the Byzantine Empire c. 500–1492* (Cambridge: Cambridge University Press, 2008), 21–26.

12 Terms such as 'Late Roman', 'Late Antique', 'proto-Byzantine', 'Early Byzantine' or 'Early Christian' may reference identical or different chronological periods in different projects or regions. The same is true of 'Byzantine' and 'Medieval'.

13 For a more elaborate periodisation of the Byzantine Empire: A. P. Kazhdan, "Byzantium, History of," in *The Oxford Dictionary of Byzantium*, vol. 1, ed. A. P. Kazhdan (Oxford; New York: Oxford University Press, 1991), 345–347.

14 C. Mango, *Byzantine Architecture* (Milan: Electra, 1979), 20; J.-P. Sodini, "La création des villes à l'époque byzantine," in *La ville neuve. Une idée de l'Antiquité?*, ed. J.-L. Huot (Paris: Éditions Errance, 1988), 203–204. Cf. I. Jacobs, "The Creation of the Late Antique City. Constantinople and Asia Minor during the 'Theodosian Renaissance'," *Byzantion* 82 (2012): 114–115.

15 Cameron, *Mediterranean*, 157–175; C. Mango, *Byzantium. Empire of New Rome* (London: Weidenfeld and Nicolson, 1980), 228–229; Saradi-Mendelovici, "Demise," 376–377, 388ff.

16 G. Dagron, "Le christianisme dans la ville byzantine," *DOP* 31 (1977): 4. Also: G. Dagron, "La città bizantina", in *Modelli di città. Strutture e funzioni politiche*, ed. P. Rossi (Turin: Einaudi, 1987), 171; J.-M. Spieser, "La christianisation de la ville dans l'Antiquité tardive," *Ktema* 11 (1986): 49; G. C. Wataghin *et al.*, "Topografia della *Civitas christiana* tra IV e VI sec.," in *Early Medieval Towns in the Western Mediterranean. Ravello, 22–24 September 1994*, ed. G. P. Brogiolo (Mantova: Editrice S.A.P., 1996), 35; N. Gauthier, "La topographie chrétienne entre idéologie et pragmatism," in *The Idea and Ideal of the Town between Late Antiquity and the Early Middle Ages*, eds. G. P. Brogiolo and B. W. Perkins (Leiden; Boston: Brill, 1999), 198–203–205, 209. More recently: G. Brands and H.-G. Severin eds., *Die spätantike Stadt und ihre Christianisierung: Symposion vom 14. bis 16. Februar 2000 in Halle/Saale* (Wiesbaden: Reichert, 2003); H. Saradi, *The Byzantine City in the Sixth Century. Literary Images and Historical Reality* (Athens: Society of Messenian Archaeological Studies, 2006), 349–352.

17 Mango, *Byzantine Architecture*, 20.

18 For an overview: Jacobs, "Creation," 117–125, 145–147. J. Crow, "Fortifications," in *The Archaeology of Byzantine Anatolia. From the End of Late Antiquity until the Coming of the Turks*, ed. P. Niewöhner (Oxford: Oxford University Press, 2017), 90–97.

19 Among these are the Early Byzantine walls of Anazarbus, Ephesus, Magnesia (ad Maeandrum), Patara, and Side. On Early Byzantine fortifications in Anatolia: P. Niewöhner, "Byzantinische Stadtmauern in Anatolien. Vom Statussymbol zum Bollwerk gegen die Araber," in *Aktuelle Forschungen zur Konstruktion, Funktion und Semantik antiker Stadtbefestigungen: Kolloquium*

9/10. *Februar 2007 in Istanbul*, eds. J. Lorentzen *et al.* (Istanbul: Ege Yayınları, 2010), 239–260; "The Riddle of the Market Gate: Miletus and the Character and Date of Earlier Byzantine Fortifications in Anatolia," in *Archaeology and the Cities of Asia Minor in Late Antiquity*, eds. O. Dally and C. Ratté (Ann Arbor: Kelsey Museum, 2011), 109–112, 119–122. For a chronological reassessment of the 'Byzantine' walls of Ephesus, Magnesia, and Patara: M. Büyükyolancı, "Patara'nın Doğu Roma (Bizans) Surları," in *Havva İşkan'a Armağan. Lykiarkhissa. Festschrift für Havva İşkan*, eds. E. Dündar, Ş. Aktaş, M. Koçak, and S. Erkoç (Istanbul: Ege Yayınları, 2016), 179–184: "Efes ve Magnesia Bizans Surlarının Yeniden Değerlendirilmesi," in *Geç Antik Çağ'da Lykos Vadisi ve Çevresi. The Lykos Valley and Neigborhood in Late Antiquity*, eds. C. Şimşek and T. Kaçar (Istanbul: Ege Yayınları, 2018), 401–428. For Anazarbus and the southern regions: R. Posamentir, "Anazarbos in Late Antiquity," in *Archaeology and the Cities of Asia Minor in Late Antiquity*, eds. O. Dally and C. Ratté (Ann Arbor: Kelsey Museum, 2011), 221, 224. For Justinian's military establishments in the eastern provinces: Cameron, *Mediterranean*, 104–113, 118–120.

20 For combination of different approaches: E. Öğüş, "Urban Transformations at Aphrodisias in Late Antiquity: Destruction or Intentional Preservation?", in *Reuse and Renovation in Roman Material Culture: Functions, Aesthetics, Interpretations*, eds. D. Ng and M. Swetnam-Burland (Cambridge: Cambridge University Press, 2018), 160–185; P. Niewöhner, "Byzantine Preservation of Ancient Monuments at Miletus in Caria," in *Die Weltchronik des Johannes Malalas in Kontext spätantiker Memorialkultur*, eds. J. Borsch *et al.* (Stuttgart: Franz Steiner Verlag, 2019), 191–216.

21 Anazarbus: Posamentir, "Anazarbos," 215; Aphrodisias: Ö. Dalgıç and A. Sokolicek, "Aphrodisias", in *The Archaeology of Byzantine Anatolia. From the End of Late Antiquity until the Coming of the Turks*, ed. P. Niewöhner (Oxford: Oxford University Press, 2017), 271–272. Olympus: B. Yelda Olcay-Uçkan *et al.* "Olympos'un Roma ve Bizans Dönemi Kent Dokusu", in *Olympos I. 2000-2014 Araştırma Sonuçları*, ed. B. Yelda Olcay-Uçkan (Antalya: AKMED, 2017), 9–30. Sagalassus: J. Poblome *et al.*, "Sagalassos," in *The Archaeology of Byzantine Anatolia. From the End of Late Antiquity until the Coming of the Turks*, ed. P. Niewöhner (Oxford: Oxford University Press, 2017), 303. Sardis: Rautman, "Sardis in Late Antiquity," in *Archaeology and the Cities of Asia Minor in Late Antiquity*, eds. O. Dally and C. Ratté (Ann Arbor: Kelsey Museum, 2011), 23. Side: A. M. Mansel, *Side. 1947–1966 Yılları Kazıları ve Araştırmalarının Sonuçları* (Ankara: TTKY, 1978), 16, 257–291; Ş. Yıldırım, "Side Antik Kentinin Bizans Dönemi Dini Yapıları" (PhD diss., Eskişehir Anadolu Üniversitesi, 2013), 222–233. For southern Asia Minor: A. Commito, "The Cities of Southern Asia Minor in the Sixth Century," in *Asia Minor in the Long Sixth Century. Current Research and Future Directions*, eds. I. Jacobs and H. Elton (Oxford; Philadelphia: Oxbow, 2019), 128–131.

22 Aezani: F. Stroth, "Aezani", in *The Archaeology of Byzantine Anatolia. From the End of Late Antiquity until the Coming of the Turks*, ed. P. Niewöhner (Oxford: Oxford University Press, 2017), 327. Aphrodisias: Dalgıç and Sokolicek, "Aphrodisias," 272–274. Ephesus: S. Ladstätter and A. Pülz, "Ephesus in the Late Roman and Early Byzantine Period: Changes in its Urban Character from the Third to the Seventh Century AD," in *The Transition to Late Antiquity. On the Danube and Beyond*, ed. A. G. Poulter (Oxford: Oxford University Press, 2007), 391–433; S. Ladstätter, "Ephesos from Late Antiquity until the Middle Ages. An Archaeological Introduction," in *Ephesos from Late Antiquity until the Late Middle Ages. Proceedings of the International Conference at the Research Center for Anatolian Civilizations, Koç University, Istanbul 30 November–2 December*, eds. S. Ladstätter and P. Magdalino (Vienna: Verlag, 2019), 11–72; Miletus: P. Niewöhner, "The End of the Byzantine City in Anatolia. The Case of Miletus," in *Städte im lateinischen Westen und im griechischen Osten zwischen Spätantike und Früher Neuzeit. Topographie-Recht-Religion*, eds. E. Gruber *et al.* (Vienna: Böhlau Verlag, 2016), 69; Sardis: Rautman, "Sardis", 11–12.

23 I. Jacobs and M. Waelkens, "Five Centuries of Glory. The North-South Colonnaded Street of Sagalassos in the First and Sixth Century A.D.," *IstMitt* 63 (2013): 233, 236–254. Cf. I. Jacobs, "From Early Byzantium to the Middle Ages at Sagalassos," in *The Long Seventh Century. Continuity and Discontinuity in an Age of Transition*, ed. A. Gnasso *et al.* (Oxford; Bern: Peter Lang, 2015), 167–171.

24 K. Asano, *The Island of St. Nicholas: Excavation and Survey of the Gemiler Island Area, Lycia, Turkey* (Osaka: Osaka University Press, 2010), 128; V. Ruggieri, "L'isola di Gemiler Ada: tessuto urbano, ecclesiastico ed artistico," *RStBiz* 55 (2018): 115.

25 C. Şimşek, "Geç Antik Çağ'da Laodikeia," in *Geç Antik Çağ'da Lykos Vadisi ve Çevresi. The Lykos Valley and Neigborhood in Late Antiquity*, eds. C. Şimşek and T. Kaçar (Istanbul: Ege Yayınları, 2018), 85, 101. For similar modifications at Assus: B. Böhlendorf-Arslan, "The Glorious Sixth Century in Assos: The Unknown Prosperity of a Provincial City in Western Asia Minor," in *Asia Minor in the Long Sixth Century. Current Research and Future Directions*, eds. I. Jacobs and H. Elton (Oxford; Philadelphia: Oxbow, 2019), 230–234.

26 Aphrodisias: K. Welch, "The Stadium at Aphrodisias," *AJA* 102, no. 3 (1998): 547–569. Ephesus: Ladstätter, "Ephesos," 23. Sardis: Foss, *Sardis*, 5–6; Rautman, "Sardis," 22–23. Cf. Saradi, *Byzantine City*, 259–352.

27 A. Berger, *Das Bad in der byzantinischen Zeit* (Münich: Institut für Byzantinistik und Neugriechische Philologie, 1982); Saradi, *Byzantine City*, 325–352.

28 Examples of this practice are numerous. E.g. Hierapolis: F. D'Andria, "The Sanctuary of St. Philip in Hierapolis and the Tombs of Saints in Anatolian Cities," in *Life and Death in Asia Minor in Hellenistic, Roman, and Byzantine Times. Studies in Archaeology and Bioarchaeology*, eds. J. Rasmus Brandt, E. Hagelberg, G. Bjørnstad, and S. Ahrens (Oxford; Philadelphia, PA: Oxbow, 2017), 68–69; C. C. Wenn *et al.*, "Romans, Christians, and Pilgrims at Hierapolis in Phrygia: Changes in Funerary Practices and Mental Processes," in *Life and Death in Asia Minor in Hellenistic, Roman, and Byzantine Times. Studies in Archaeology and Bioarchaeology*, eds. J. Rasmus Brandt, E. Hagelberg, G. Bjørnstad, and S. Ahrens (Oxford; Philadelphia, PA: Oxbow, 2017), 523–524. Sardis: Rautman, "Sardis," 14–15, 22.

29 Yıldırım, "Side," 222–233. Cf. K. Bowes, "Christians in the Amphitheater? The 'Christianization' of Spectacle Buildings and Martyrial Memory," *MEFRM* 126, no. 1 (2014): 108.

30 Olcay-Uçkan *et al.*, "Olympos," 9–30; N. Burkhardt and M. Wilson, "The Late Antique Synagogue in Priene: Its History, Architecture, and Context," *Gephyra* 10 (2013): 179.

31 These buildings might even include entire neighbourhoods, comprising a church or a chapel, as in the theatre-stadium at Aezani: Bowes, "Christians," 101–102, 107, 110; Cf. Saradi, *Byzantine City*, 295–324.

32 L. Lavan, "The Political Topography of the Late Antique City: Activity Spaces in Practice," *Theory and Practice: Theory and Practice in Late Antique Archaeology* eds. L. Lavan and W. Bowden (Leiden; Boston: Brill, 2003), 317–321,324–325, 332; L. Lavan, "Fora and Agorai in Mediterranean Cities during the 4th and 5th c. AD," in *Social and Political Life in Late Antiquity*, eds. W. Bowden *et al.* (Leiden; Boston, MA: Brill, 2006), 195–249; L. Lavan, "The agorai of Sagalassos in Late Antiquity: An Interpretive Study," in *Field Methods and Post-Excavation Techniques in Late Antique Archaeology*, eds. L. Lavan and M. Mulryan (Leiden; Boston, MA: Brill, 2013), 289–353. Assus: Böhlendorf-Arslan, "Assos," 227–228.

33 At Hierapolis, the agora was damaged by an earthquake in the second half of the 4th century and was left outside the late-4th-century fortifications: P. Arthur, "Hierapolis of Phrygia: The Drawn-Out Demise of an Anatolian City," in *Urbes Extinctae. Archaeologies of Abandoned Classical Towns*, eds. N. Christie and A. Augenti (Farnham; Surrey; Burlington, VT: Ashgate, 2012), 278. For Iasos: Serin, *Early Christian*, 19 n.138, 21, 32 (with bibliography).

34 E. E. Schneider, "Spazi di vita, spazi di attività e trasformazioni sociali nella provincia di Cilicia: il caso di Elaiussa Sebaste," *BA on line. Volume Speciale* 1 (2010): 8–10.

35 C. Bouras, "Aspects of the Byzantine City, Eighth-Fifteenth Centuries," in *The Economic History of Byzantium. From the Seventh through the Fifteenth Century*, vol. 2, ed. A. E. Laiou (Washington, D.C.: Dumbarton Oaks Research Library and Collection, 2002), 512; Saradi, *Byzantine City*, 211–235. For the well-explored Byzantine shops at Sardis: J. Stephens Crawford, *The Byzantine Shops at Sardis* (Cambridge, MA; London: Harvard University Press, 1990).

36 H. Saradi, "Privatization and Subdivision of Urban Properties in the Early Byzantine Centuries: Social and Cultural Implications," *BAmSocP* 35, no. 1/2 (1998): 17–43; Saradi, *Byzantine City*, 186–207.

37 Anemurium: Russell, "Anemourion," in *The Economic History of Byzantium. From the Seventh through the Fifteenth Century*, vol. 2, ed. A. E. Laiou (Washington, D.C.: Dumbarton Oaks

Research Library and Collection, 2002), 221–228. Ephesus: Ladstätter, "Ephesos," 29, 35, 37, 55–58; Ladstätter and Pülz, "Ephesus", 402, 406, 419. Hierapolis: P. Arthur *et al.*, "Hierapolis bizantina e turca," in *Hierapolis di Frigia V. Le attività delle campagne di scavo e restauro 2004-2006*, eds. F. D'Andria *et al.* (Istanbul: Ege Yayınları, 2012), 565–583. Sagalassus: Poblome *et al.*, "Sagalassus," 303. For Amorium, below. For an overview: I. Jacobs, "Encroachment in the Eastern Mediterranean between the Fourth and the Seventh Century AD," *AncSoc* 39 (2009): 203–243; Jacobs, "Early Byzantium," 166–167, 173–174.

38 Saradi, "Privatization," 30; Jacobs, "Encroachment," 218–222 (distinctions between squatters and authorized undertakings).

39 Saradi, "Privatization," 22–25, 27–29; cf. Jacobs, "Encroachment," 222–225.

40 L. Lavan, "Late Antique Urban Topography: From Architecture to Human Space," in *Theory and Practice: Theory and Practice in Late Antique Archaeology*, eds. L. Lavan and W. Bowden (Leiden; Boston: Brill, 2003), 181; Lavan, "Political," 325–331. Most recently: Luke Lavan, *Public Space in the Late Antique City*, 2 vols. (Leiden; Boston, MA: Brill, 2020).

41 A selection among the exhaustive sources concerning the fate of temples and the practice of *spolia* is not attempted here.

42 Hanfmann and Buchwald, "Christianity," 192.

43 Serin, *Early Christian*, 200. R. L. Hohlfelder, "Aperlae in Lycia: Ancient Maritime Life beyond the Great Harbors," *CIIre* 12 (2005): 27, attributes such proliferation to 'piety, prosperity and prestige'. Cf. R. M. Rothaus, *Corinth: The First City of Greece. An Urban History of Late Antique Cult and Religion* (Leiden; Boston, MA: Brill, 2000), 95.

44 S. Evcim and G. K. Öztaşkın, "Early Byzantine Churches in Olympos," *Arkeoloji ve Sanat* 161 (2019): 129–162.

45 Poblome *et al.*, "Sagalassos," 302.

46 Hohlfelder, "Apaerlae," 20, 27–28; B. Leadbetter, "Coercion, Resistance and "The Command Economy" in Late Roman Aperlae," in *Violence in Late Antiquity. Perceptions and Practices*, ed. H. A. Drake (London; New York: Routledge 2016), 119–123.

47 Commito, "Cities," 121.

48 Dagron, "Christianisme," 5–6, 11; Saradi-Mendelovici, "Demise," 392; Cf. Gauthier, "Topographie," 205–206; Rothaus, *Corinth*, 99–101.

49 A. Frantz, *The Athenian Agora. Results of Excavations Conducted by the American School of Classical Studies at Athens* XXIV. *Late Antiquity: AD 267-700* (Princeton, NJ: ASCSA, 1988), 73. Several factors – the Early Christians' avoidance of city centres attributable to 'a caution based on insecurity', extra-mural location of martyria and burials *ad sanctos*, use of *res privata* for church building, or the symbolic control of the boundaries of the city – are cited as explanations for the peripheral siting of Early Christian church establishments: Rothaus, *Corinth*, 99–104.

50 R. Sweetman, "Networks and Church Building in the Aegean: Crete, Cyprus, Lycia and the Peloponnese," *BSA* 112 (2017): 31–32; cf. C. Watghin *et al.*, "Topografia," 17, 29. For Anazarbus: S. Hill, *The Early Byzantine Churches of Cilicia and Isauria* (Birmingham: Variorum, 1996), 85–90; Aphrodisias: Ö. Dalgıç, "Early Christian and Byzantine Churches," in *The Aphrodisias Regional Survey*, eds. C. Ratté and P. D. De Stabler (Darmstadt/Mainz: Verlag Philip von Zabern, 2012), 393–395.

51 For possible identification of another church within the castle on the isthmus: A. Viscogliosi, "Il castello di terraferma a Iasos. Indagini 2009," *Bollettino dell'Asscociazone Iasos di Caria* 16 (2010): 25.

52 The two unexcavated intra-mural churches offer no evidence for dating at present: Serin, *Early Christian*, 199. For the positioning of cathedrals and their relationships with Late Antique city walls in the West: C. Wataghin *et al.*, "Topografia," 31. Cf. H. Buchwald, *Churches EA and E at Sardis* (Cambridge, MA; London: Harvard University Press, 2015), 26 n.295.

53 The extra-mural Church EA, with other buildings sited close by, is thought to be the first cathedral and episcopal seat of Sardis before its relocation to intra-mural Church D in the 5th/6th centuries: Buchwald, *Churches*, 26, 59. Building D: N. Karydis, "A Monument of Early Byzantine Sardis: Architectural Analysis and Graphic Reconstruction of Building D," *AnSt* 62 (2012): 117, 133, 137–138.

54 P. Niewöhner, "Miletus," in *The Archaeology of Byzantine Anatolia. From the End of Late Antiquity until the Coming of the Turks*, ed. P. Niewöhner (Oxford: Oxford University Press, 2017),

257–258. The Great Church was hidden behind a Roman *propylaeum* in an attempt to avoid 'altering the traditional aspect of the agora': Niewöhner ("Byzantine Preservation," 196; "The End," 70). For the Byzantine basilicas at Miletus: P. Niewöhner, *Bauwerke in Milet. Teil 11. Die byzantinischen Basiliken von Milet* (Berlin; Boston, MA: De Gruyter, 2016).

55 B. Brenk, "La cristianizzazione della città tardoantica," in *La ciudad en el mundo romano: Actas XIV Congreso Internacional de Arqueológía Clásica. Tarragona, 5-11/9/1993*, vol. 1 (Tarragona: Consejo Superior de Investigaciones Científicas; Institut d'Estudis Catalans, 1994), 129–135.

56 Dagron, "Christianisme," 5–6.

57 Şimşek, "Laodikeia," 93–96, 108, 112.

58 *Ibid.*, 109–110, 112.

59 At Ephesus the positioning of churches was largely determined by the availability of land and pre-existing buildings: Ladstätter, "Ephesos," 41–43. A similar pattern can be found, among many others, at Elaiussa Sebaste (E. Schneider, "Spazi," 9) and Kyaneai (Commito, "Cities," 120).

60 C. Wataghin *et al.*, "Topografia," 36.

61 Evcim and Öztaşkın, "Olympos," 149–150; Hohlfelder, "Aperlae," 28; Sweetman, "Networks," 2, 26–27, 32, 34–35. Cf. P. Horden and N. Purcell, *The Corrupting Sea. A Study of Mediterranean History* (Oxford; Malden, MA: Blackwell, 2000), esp. 440, 443, 460.

62 Dagron, "Christianisme," 5. For a different opinion on the locational 'casualty' in the West: Cantino Wataghin *et al.*, "Topografia," 36.

63 M. Angold, "The Shaping of the Medieval Byzantine City," *ByzF* 10 (1985): 18–19; Dagron ("Christianisme," 4–10; "Città," 172); Saradi-Mendelovici, "Demise," 392–393; Spieser, "Christianisation," 52. For the West: Cantino Wataghin, "Urban Burials," 153–154.

64 W. Müller-Wiener, "Riflessioni sulle caratteristiche dei palazzi episcopali," *FelRav* 125–126 (1983): 104. The presence of a bishopric see became the 'distinctive sign' of a 'city' with the Council of Chalcedon (451): Dagron, "Christianisme," 19–20. For the role of bishops in different contexts in Late Antiquity: C. Rapp, *Holy Bishops in Late Antiquity: the Nature of Christian Leadership in an Age of Transition* (2nd ed.) (Berkeley, CA: University of California Press, 2013).

65 Müller-Wiener, "Riflessioni," 103–104. Cf. B. Ceylan, "*Episkopeia* in Asia Minor," in *Housing in Late Antiquity*, eds. L. Lavan *et al.* (Leiden; Boston, MA: Brill 2007), 169, 171.

66 Müller-Wiener, "Riflessioni," 104, 108; J.-P. Sodini, "Les groupes épiscopaux de la Turquie," in Actes du XIe Congrès International d'Archéologie Chrétienne (Lyon, Vienne, Grenoble, Genève, Aoste 1986) (Rome: École française de Rome; Vatican City: Pontificio Istituto di Archeologia Cristiana, 1989), vol. 1, 417, 419–420. Cf. C. Wataghin *et al.*, "Topografia," 27; Ceylan, "*Episkopeia*," 174. For literary sources: D. Pallas, "Episkopion," in *RBK*, vol. 2 (1971), 335–372.

67 Pallas, "Episkopion," 335; Müller-Wiener, "Riflessioni," 105–108, 145.

68 Müller-Wiener, "Riflessioni," 111. P. Niewöhner, "Der Bischofspalast von Milet. Spätrömisches Peristylhaus und frühbyzantinische Residenz," *AA* 2 (2015): 181–273, dates this building to the first half of the 5th century.

69 The centrally located bishop's palace next to the church of St. Mary was later transferred to the proximity of St. John's on Ayasoluk: Ladstätter, "Ephesos," 58; Ladstätter and Pülz, "Ephesus," 411–413.

70 Müller-Wiener, "Riflessioni," 140, 145; Sodini, "Groupes," 416.

71 E. Akyürek, "Myra. The City of St. Nicholas," in *En Orient et en Occident le culte de Nicolas en Europe (Xe-XXIe siècle). Actes du colloque de Lunéville et Saint-Nicolas-de-Port, 5-7 décembre 2013*, eds. V. Gazeau *et al.* (Paris: Les Éditions du Cerf, 2015), 28; G. K. Öztaşkın, "Olympos Kenti Episkopeion Yapı Topluluğu," in *Olympos I. 200-2004 Araştırma Sonuçları*, ed. B. Yelda Olcay-Uçkan (Antalya: AKMED, 2017), 54; Yıldırım, "Side," 25. For the Patriarchate of Constantinople, with a similar feature: R. Janin, "Le palais patriarcal de Constantinople," *ReByz* 20 (1962): 133.

72 Müller-Wiener, "Riflessioni," 138, 142. The need to adapt to existing structures is obvious in the longitudinal layout of the former bishopric palace at Ephesus built adjacent to the church of St. Mary: Ceylan, "*Episkopeia*," 178–179. Priene: Burkhardt and Wilson, "Synagogue," 179–81. For the cathedral church: S. Westphalen, "The Byzantine Basilica at Priene," *DOP* 54 (2000): 275–280.

73 Sodini, "Groupes," 416. For the role of defensive considerations in a frontier zone such as Caričin Grad: Müller-Wiener "Riflessioni," 139. For Dara, below.
74 Müller-Wiener, "Riflessioni," 139, 145. Cf. C. Wataghin *et al.*, "Topografia," 30–31.
75 Öztaşkın, "Olympos," 53–54; Mansel, *Side*, 267–284; Yıldırım, "Side," 255. For the East Basilica complex (late 5th/early 6th century) at Xanthus, located at the intersection of the *cardo* and *decumanus* and identified as the cathedral: M.-P. Raynaud, *Corpus of the Mosaics of Turkey,* vol. 1. *Lycia. Xanthos.* Part 1. *The East Basilica* (Bursa: Uludağ University Press, 2009), 35.
76 Müller-Wiener, "Riflessioni," 137–138, 142; Sodini, "Groupes," 416. Bargylia: Marina Falla Castelfranchi, "Il complesso ecclesiale di Bargylia," in *Iasos e la Caria. Nuovi studi e ricerche*, ed. R. P. Benoit (Naples: Macchiaroli Editore, 2005), 461–462. For the marginal location of the Church of St. Nicholas and the bishop's palace at Myra: Akyürek, "Myra," 27–28.
77 For Miletus and Olympus: Öztaşkın, "Olympos," 53–54; above n.68. Mansel, *Side*, 282, describes the bishopric complex at Side as 'a city within the city'; Yıldırım, "Side," 253. A recent project of the Austrian Academy of Sciences suggests that a whole 'episcopal district' existed at Side rather than merely an episcopal palace: https://www.oeaw.ac.at/oeai/forschung/altertumswissenschaften/antike-religion/das-bischofsviertel-von-side (accessed July 27, 2022).
78 The apsidal halls, sometimes with a trefoil plan, identified as *triclina*, were recurrent in Late Antique residential architecture: Müller-Wiener, "Riflessioni," 142. The triconch at Aphrodisias is one of the few known examples in a civic architectural context in Asia Minor, together with the *triclinium* of the bishop's palace at Side: M. L. Berenfeld, "The Triconch House and the Predecessors of the Bishop's Palace at Aphrodisias," *AJA* 113, no. 2 (April 2007): 223 n.78; cf. Yıldırım, "Side," 154–162.
79 R. Cormack, "The Temple as the Cathedral," in *Aphrodisias Papers. Recent Work on Architecture and Sculpture*, eds. C. Roueché and K. T. Erim (Ann Arbor, MI: JRA, 1990), 75–88; A. Chaniotis, "The Conversion of the Temple of Aphrodite at Aphrodisias in Context," in *From Temple to Church. Destruction and Renewal of Local Cultic Topography in Late Antiquity* (Leiden; Boston, MA: Brill, 2008), 243–273.
80 Berenfeld, "Triconch House," 224–226.
81 Recent research at Limyra has identified a large bathhouse in the Late Antique building complex formerly associated with the bishop's palace: K. Sewing, "Die Südthermen (ehemals Bishopfspalast) in Limyra. Bauaufnahme und Interpretation," *ÖJh* 84 (2015): 213–257.
82 Assus: Böhlendorf-Arslan, "Assos," 230; Patara: B. Ceylan and O. Erdoğan, "The Architecture and History of the City Basilica of Patara: A Preliminary Report on Four Seasons of Excavations," in *Havva İşkan'a Armağan. Lykiarkhissa. Festschrift für Havva İşkan*, eds. E. Dündar, Ş. Aktaş, M. Koçak, and S. Erkoç (Istanbul: Ege Yayınları, 2016), 208, 210–211.
83 Cic. *leg.* 2, 23, 58 (Law of the Twelve Tables).
84 Cod. Iust. 3, 44, 12. Cf. Gr. Nyss. *Thdr.*; Chrys. *hom. in Mt.* 73.
85 Cod. Theod. 9, 17, 5 (363); Cod. Theod. 9, 17, 6 (381).
86 Cod. Iust. 9, 44, 12; Cod. Iust. 1, 2, 2; Dig. 47, 12, 3.
87 For the interpretation of these codes: Dagron, "Christianisme," 13–14.
88 P. Brown, *The Cult of the Saints. Its Rise and Function in Latin Christianity* (Chicago, IL: University of Chicago Press, 1981), 7–8.
89 U. M. Fasola and V. F. Nicolai, "Le necropoli durante la formazione della città cristiana," in *Actes du XIe Congrès International d'Archéologie Chrétienne (Lyon, Vienne, Grenoble, Genève, Aoste 1986)* (Rome: École française de Rome; Vatican City: Pontificio Istituto di Archeologia Cristiana, 1989), vol. 2, 1157.
90 E. A. Ivison, "Burial and Urbanism at Late Antique and Early Byzantine Corinth," in *Towns in Transition. Urban Evolution in Late Antiquity and the Early Middle Ages*, eds. N. Christie and S. T. Loseby (Aldershot; Hants; Brookfield, VT: Scolar Press, 1996), 102.
91 P. Noailles and A. Dain, *Les novelles de Léon VI le Sage* (Paris: Les Belles Lettres, 1944), 202–205.
92 Dagron, "Christianisme," 11–19.
93 *Ibid.*, 14–15.
94 Hanfmann and Buchwald, "Christianity," 204–210; Buchwald, *Churches*, 153–169; below n.98.
95 Amorium: C. Lightfoot, "Christian Burials in a Pagan Context at Amorium," in *Life and Death in Asia Minor in Hellenistic, Roman, and Byzantine Times. Studies in Archaeology and Bioarchaeology*, eds. J. Rasmus Brandt, E. Hagelberg, G. Bjørnstad, and S. Ahrens (Oxford;

Philadelphia, PA: Oxbow, 2017), 489, 492, 497. Ephesus: M. Steskal, "Reflections on the Mortuary Landscape of Ephesus: The Archaeology of Death in a Roman Metropolis," in *Life and Death in Asia Minor in Hellenistic, Roman, and Byzantine Times. Studies in Archaeology and Bioarchaeology*, eds. J. Rasmus Brandt, E. Hagelberg, G. Bjørnstad, and S. Ahrens (Oxford; Philadelphia, PA: Oxbow, 2017), 476–477; Ladstätter, "Ephesos," 2019, 51, 59; Hierapolis: Wenn *et al.*, "Romans," 513–514, 524–525, 529, 539–542; Nicaea: Ü. Melda Ermiş, "İznik ve Çevresi Bizans Devri Mimari Faaliyetinin Değerlendirilmesi" (PhD diss., University of Istanbul, 2009), 351–364.

96 Ivison, "Burials," 103–104. An earlier exception can be found at Elaiussa Sebaste, where burials within the agora basilica are attributed to the first phase of the church (5th–7th centuries): S. V. Moore, "A Relational Approach to Mortuary Practices within Medieval Byzantine Anatolia" (PhD diss., Newcastle University, 2013), 194.

97 Arthur *et al.*, "Hierapolis bizantina," 573–576.

98 Nicaea: Ermiş, "İznik," 351–364; Kelenderis: L. Zoroğlu, "Kelenderis Nekropolü," *Olba* 3 (2000): 118–119; Sardis: Buchwald, *Churches*, 154; N. D. Cahill ("Sardis 2010," *KST* 33, vol. 4 [2012]: 213; "Sardis 2011," *KST* 34, vol. 2 [2013]: 148).

99 Moore, "Mortuary Practices," 23–33, 56–87.

100 These include cities built, rebuilt or extensively enlarged from the 3rd through to the 6th centuries, in association with factors of security, economy, commerce, connectivity, or pilgrimage: Efthymios Rizos, ed., *New Cities in Late Antiquity. Documents and Archaeology* (Turnhout: Brepols, 2017); E. Zanini, "The Urban Ideal and Urban Planning in Byzantine New Cities of the VI century A.D.," in *Theory and Practice: Theory and Practice in Late Antique Archaeology*, eds. L. Lavan and W. Bowden (Leiden; Boston: Brill, 2003), 201.

101 B. Croke and J. Crow, "Procopius and Dara," *JRS* 73 (1983): 151; Zanini, "Urban," 201–214.

102 Zanini, "Urban," 214–216.

103 *Ibid.*, 209–210, 214, 217.

104 The longest and most detailed account of Dara can be found in Procopius' *Wars* and *Buildings*. For inconsistencies in the *Buildings*: Croke and Crow, "Procopius". Cf. Zanini, "Urban," 203 n.21. For other sources: below n.107.

105 Zanini, "Urban," 217.

106 Defensive suitability, availability of water resources and stone for construction were considered the main prerequisites for the building of fortifies cities in Late Antiquity according to the Greek military manual, known as Περὶ Στρατηγικῆς, or *De Re Strategica* (chaps. 10–12): G. T. Dennis, *Three Byzantine Military Treatises. Text, Translation, and Notes* (Washington, DC: Dumbarton Oaks Research Library and Collection, 1985). On the identification and date of this text: P. Rance, "The Date of the Military Compendium of Syrianus Magister (formerly the Sixth-Century Anonymus Byzantinus)," *ByzZ* 100, no. 2 (2007): 701–737.

107 Evagr. *h.e.* 3, 37. Cf. Jo. Mal. *chron.* 16, 399; Jo. Styl. 90; Zach. Mit. *h.e.* 7, 6. Procopius (*Aed.* 2.1–3) also describes the complex system of water management and hydraulic engineering: Croke and Crow, "Procopius," 150.

108 E. Keser-Kayaalp *et al.*, "Recent Research on Dara/Anastasiopolis," in *New Cities in Late Antiquity. Documents and Archaeology*, ed. E. Rizos (Turnhout: Brepols, 2017), 155.

109 *Ibid.*, 155–168.

110 *Ibid.*, 168–174.

111 E. Rizos, "Introduction," in *New Cities in Late Antiquity. Documents and Archaeology*, ed. E. Rizos (Turnhout: Brepols, 2017), 9–10; above n.107.

112 Keser-Kayaalp *et al.*, "Dara/Anastasiopolis," 175. For the suburbs: Zanini, "Urban," 214.

113 To cite but some: E. W. Brooks, "The Arabs in Asia Minor (641–750) from Arabic Sources," *JHS* 18 (1898): 182–208; H. Ahrweiler, "L'Asie Mineure et les invasions arabes (VIIe-IXe siècles)," *Revue Historique* 227, no. 1 (1962): 1–32; C. Foss, "The Persians in Asia Minor and the End of Antiquity," *English Historical Review* 90, no. 357 (1975): 721–747. Cf. J. Russell, "The Persian Invasions of Syria/Palestine and Asia Minor in the Reign of Heraclius: Archaeological, Numismatic and Epigraphic Evidence," in *The Dark Centuries of Byzantium (7th–9th centuries)* (Athens: National Hellenic Research Foundation, 2001), 57–71.

114 Brandes, "Byzantine Cities," 32. Cf. W. Müller-Wiener, "Von der Polis zum Kastron. Wandlungen der Stadt im A. Raum von der Antike zum Mittelalter," *Gymnasium* 93 (1986): 435–475. For a

critical approach: A. Dunn, "The Transition from Polis to Kastron in the Balkans (III–VII cc.): General and Regional Perspectives," *Byzantine and Modern Greek Studies* 18 (1994): 60–80. For a survey of cities and settlement patterns in this period: W. Brandes, *Die Städte Kleinasiens im 7. und 8. Jahrhundert* (Berlin: Akademie-Verlag, 1989); L. Brubaker and J. Haldon, *Byzantium in the Iconoclast Era, c. 680-850. A History* (Cambridge: Cambridge University Press, 2011), 531–572; M. J. Decker, *The Byzantine Dark Ages* (London; New York: Bloomsbury, 2016), 81ff.

115 Brubaker and Haldon, *Byzantium*, 536. For literary evidence on the changing character and ruralisation of cities: H. Saradi, "The City in Byzantine Hagiography," in *The Ashgate Research Companion to Byzantine Hagiography*, vol. 2. *Genres and Contexts*, ed. S. Efthymiadis (Farnham; Burlington, VT, Ashgate, 2014), 429–432, 442.

116 J. Durliat, "La peste du VIe siècle. Pour un nouvel examen des sources byzantines," in *Hommes et richesses dans l'Empire byzantine*, vol. 1. *IVe-VIIe siècle* (Paris: Lethielleux 1989), 107–119 (underlines the silence of literary sources and the improbable role of the plague on the 'urban crisis'). Cf. D. Ch. Stathakopoulos, *Famine and Pestilence in the Late Roman and Early Byzantine Empire* (London; New York: Routledge, 2004), esp. 110–154; L. K. Little, ed., *Plague and the End of Antiquity. The Pandemic of 541–750* (Cambridge: Cambridge University Press, 2007).

117 The (destructive) effects of earthquakes on buildings and urban areas can be understood to a certain extent through archaeological evidence. Assus: Böhlendorf-Arslan, "Assos," 242–243; Ephesus: Ladstätter, "Ephesos," 6, 16, 21; Ladstätter and Pülz, "Ephesus," 394–398; Laodicea and Miletus: Şimşek, "Laodikeia," 84–85; Niewöhner, "The End," 71. For Hierapolis, below.

118 Serin, *Early Christian*, 203.

119 Hohlfelder, "Aperlae,"13. Cf. C. Foss, "The Lycian Coast in the Byzantine Age," *DOP* 48 (1994): 1–52.

120 J.-P. Sodini, "La Lycie Byzantine," in *Corpus of the Mosaics of Turkey*, vol. 1. *Lycia. Xanthos.* Part 1. *The East Basilica* (Bursa: Uludağ University Press, 2009), 19–21. For the lack of archaeological evidence after the 7th century at Myra and Olympus: Akyürek, "Myra," 23; Olcay-Uçkan, "Olympos," 15. At Patara, the later Byzantine settlement receded into a newly fortified area next to the harbour: Ceylan and Erdoğan, "Architecture," 213–214. Büyükyolancı, "Patara," proposes an earlier date (ca. 400) for the 'Early Byzantine' walls at Patara. Cf. V. Ruggieri, "Patara: due casi di architettura bizantina e la continuità urbana," *OrChrPer* 75 (2009): 322–323 (opts for the 7th century).

121 Jacobs and Waelkens, "Five Centuries," 221, 252; Jacobs, "Early Byzantium," 171ff; Poblome *et al.*, "Sagalassos," 304–311.

122 Jacobs, "Early Byzantium," 191.

123 Arthur, "Hierapolis," 279–287; Arthur *et al.*, "Hierapolis bizantina".

124 Arthur, "Hierapolis," 283, 288.

125 W. Müller-Wiener, "Das Theaterkastell von Milet," in *IstMitt* 17 (1967), 279–290; Niewöhner ("Miletus," 258, 260; "The End," 69–71). Cf. Niewöhner, "Market Gate," 103–122.

126 Niewöhner ("Miletus," 260–263; "The End," 67–69, 71).

127 J. Fildhuth, "Priene," in *The Archaeology of Byzantine Anatolia. From the End of Late Antiquity until the Coming of the Turks*, ed. Philip Niewöhner (Oxford: Oxford University Press, 2017), 252–253.

128 T. Otten, "Pergamon," in *The Archaeology of Byzantine Anatolia. From the End of Late Antiquity until the Coming of the Turks*, ed. P. Niewöhner (Oxford: Oxford University Press, 2017), 228–229. For multiple building phases of Pergamum's fortifications: Manfred Klinkott, *AvP* XVI. *Die Stadtmauren*, I. *Die byzantinischen Befestigungsanlagen von Pergamon mit ihrer Wehr-und Baugeschichte* (Berlin; New York: De Gruyter, 2001).

129 K. Rheidt, "Byzantinische Wohnhäuser des 11. bis 14. Jahrhunderts in Pergamon," *DOP* 44 (1990): 195–204; K. Rheidt, *AvP* XV. *Die Stadtgrabung* 2. *Die byzantinische Wohnstadt* (Berlin; New York: De Gruyter, 1991). Cf. Bouras, "Aspects," 508.

130 Fildhuth, "Priene," 252; Jacobs, "Early Byzantium," 187–188; Niewöhner, "Miletus," 258.

131 Ladstätter, "Ephesos," 28–39.

132 Whatever the reasons for the 7th century destructions at Ephesus were, the earlier urban traditions were completely lost in this period in favour of increasing 'ruralisation' and encroachment on earlier public and private spaces: Ladstätter, "Ephesos," 39, 56–58.

133 Ladstätter, "Ephesos," 40. Cf. Büyükyolancı, "Efes," 403–416. For the traditional 6th/7th century dating: A. Pülz, *Bizans Döneminde Ephesos'un Görünümü*, in *Bizans Döneminde Ephesos* (transl. S. Gün *et al.*), eds. F. Daim and S. Ladstätter (Istanbul: Ege Yayınları, 2011), 63. For the lack of emphasis on the defensive character of fortifications built in the Theodosian period: Niewöhner, "Byzantinische Stadtmauern," 253.

134 Ladstätter, "Ephesos," 58–61.

135 C. Lightfoot ("The Survival of Cities in Byzantine Anatolia: the Case of Amorium," *Byzantion* 68, no. 1 [1998]: 56; "Amorium," in *The Archaeology of Byzantine Anatolia. From the End of Late Antiquity until the Coming of the Turks*, ed. P. Niewöhner (Oxford: Oxford University Press, 2017), 334 341); E. A. Ivison, "Amorium in the Byzantine Dark Ages (Seventh to Ninth Centuries)," in *Millennium-Studien zu Kultur und Geschichte des Ersten Jahrtausends n. Chr. 5/2. Post-Roman Towns, Trade and Settlement in Europe and Byzantium*, vol. 2. *Byzantium, Pliska and the Balkans*, ed. J. Henning (Berlin; New York: De Gruyter, 2007), 27.

136 Ivison, "Amorium," 35–37, 40–41, 49; Lightfoot, "Amorium," 336.

137 Ivison, "Amorium," 41, 43–44; Lightfoot, "Survival," 63–65.

138 Lightfoot, "Amorium," 335.

139 Ivison, "Amorium," 37–38, 44–49.

140 Lightfoot, "Amorium," 337, 341.

141 The reconstruction of LCB as a domed basilica is also attributed to this period: Ivison, "Amorium," 51–55; Lightfoot ("Amorium," 338–341; "Survival," 69).

142 Ivison, "Amorium," 55; Lightfoot ("Amorium," 333; "Survival," 62, 65).

143 Ivision, "Amorium," 54–55.

144 Some of these cities, such as Ancyra/Ankara, Attaleia/Antalya, Nicaea/Iznik, or Pergamum/Bergama, are still densely inhabited.

145 Bouras, "Aspects," 502. For imperial sponsorship of urban 'rebuilding' in strategically important cities: E. A. Ivison, "Urban Renewal and Imperial Revival in Byzantium (730–1025)," *ByzF* 26 (2000): 1–46.

146 For Byzantine Ankara: C. Foss, "Late Antique and Byzantine Ankara," *DOP* 31 (1977): 27–82; U. Peschlow, *Ankara. Die bauarchäologischen Hinterlassenschaften aus römischer und byzantinischer Zeit. Mit einem Beitrag von Wolfram Brandes* (Vienna: Phoibos Verlag, 2015). The section on Byzantine Ankara in this chapter is based upon the works by the author: U. Serin ("Late Antique and Byzantine Ankara: Topography and Architecture," in *Marmoribus Vestita. Miscellanea in onore di Federico Guidobaldi*, eds. O. Brandt and P. Pergola [Vatican City: PIAC 2011], 1257–1280; "Ankara and the Temple of Rome and Augustus in the Late Antique, Byzantine and Turkish Periods," in *Progetto Ancyra. Il tempio di Augusto e Roma ad Ankara,* eds. P. Botteri *et al.* [Trieste: EUT, 2018], 335–377, with earlier bibliography and historical sources).

147 On the development of the military administration in Byzantium: J. Haldon, *Byzantium in the Seventh Century* (Cambridge: Cambridge University Press, 1990), 208–253.

148 For the citadel of Ankara, G. de Jerphanion, "Mélanges d'archéologie anatolienne," *MelBeyrouth* 13 (1928): 144–221, remains fundamental.

149 The emperors Nicephorus I (802–811) and Michael III are thought to be responsible for the 9th-century interventions (for synthesis: Serin, "Ankara," 356 n.123). Cf. Peschlow, *Ankara*, 139–186; A. M. Sitz, "A New Approach to Old Inscriptions in Late Antique Anatolia," *AJA* 123 no. 4 (October 2019): 654 n.68.

150 Serin, "Ankara," 354–356. On the Byzantine concept of 'rebuilding' a city 'from the foundations': Ivison, "Urban Renewal," 5, 7.

151 For an overview: M. Greenhalgh, "Spolia in Fortifications: Turkey, Syria and North Africa", in *Ideologie e Practiche del Reimpiego nell'Alto Medioevo* (XLVI Settimane di Studio del Centro Italiano di Studi sull'Alto Medioevo, XLVI, 1998) (Spoleto: Centro Italiano di Studi sull'Alto Medioevo, 1999), 785–932.

152 C. Foss and D. Winfield, *Byzantine Fortifications. An Introduction* (Pretoria: University of South Africa 1986), 101.

153 U. Serin, "Bizans Ankara'sı ve Kaybolan bir Kültür Mirası: 'St. Clement' Kilisesi," *METU Journal of the Faculty of Architecture* 31, no. 2 (2014): 80.

154 H. Saradi, "The *Kallos* of the Byzantine City: The Development of a Rhetorical *Topos* and Historical Reality," *Gesta* 34, no. 1 (1995): 47.

155 C. Foss and J. Tulchin, *Nicaea: A Byzantine Capital and Its Praises with the Speeches of Theodore Laskaris* (Brookline, MA: Hellenic College Press 1996), 175; Saradi, "*Kallos*," 45–46. Cf. A. Akışık, "Praising a City: Nicaea, Trebizond, and Thessaloniki," *Journal of Turkish Studies* 36 (2011): 5–8.
156 The walls took their final shape in the Lascarid period, with double ramparts and a new moat on the landside, thus presenting a close resemblance to the walls of Constantinople: C. Foss, "The Walls of Iznik 260–1330," in *Iznik throughout History*, eds. I. Akbaygil *et al.* (Istanbul: Türkiye İş Bankası, 2003), 259, assumes that this resemblance was no coincidence, as 'the [new] capital of the empire naturally took on the image of the old ruling city'.
157 Foss, "Walls of Iznik," 249–262; Foss and Tulchin, *Nicaea*, 89–96; Foss and Winfield, *Byzantine Fortifications*, 79–120.
158 Saradi ("*Kallos*," 45–48; "The City," 438).
159 Foss and Tulchin, *Nicaea*, 132–133; H. Saradi, "The Use of Ancient Spolia in Byzantine Monuments: The Archaeological and Literary Evidence," *IntJClTrad* 3, no. 4 (1997): 405–406; Saradi, "The City," 438 n.57.
160 Foss and Tulchin, *Nicaea*, 110–114 (the Patriarchate), 118; U. Peschlow, "The Churches of Nicaea-Iznik," in *Iznik throughout History*, eds. I. Akbaygil *et al.* (Istanbul: Türkiye İş Bankası, 2003), 202.
161 For the lack of archaeological evidence between the late 9th and early 11th centuries: U. Peschlow, "Nicaea," in *The Archaeology of Byzantine Anatolia. From the End of Late Antiquity until the Coming of the Turks*, ed. P. Niewöhner (Oxford: Oxford University Press, 2017), 216.
162 C. J. Hefele and H. Leclerq, *Histoire des Conciles d'après les documents originaux*, vol. 1 (Paris: Letouzey et Ané, 1908), 386–652; *ibid.* vol. 3/2 (Paris 1910), 741–798.
163 These include a submerged basilica discovered not far from the western shore of Lake Iznik.
164 Foss and Tulchin, *Nicaea*, 102.
165 This church temporarily served as the seat of the Patriarch and was also the site of imperial and patriarchal burials: Foss and Tulchin, *Nicaea*, 97–101, 110–111; Peschlow ("Churches," 215; "Nicaea," 210–211).
166 In addition to churches and monasteries archaeologically identifiable, several others are known in the written sources: Foss and Tulchin, *Nicaea*, 97–122; Peschlow ("Churches," 210–218; "Nicaea," 209–215).
167 Foss and Tulchin, *Nicaea*, 116, 120, 142–143, 172–173, 180–181.
168 Saradi, "The City," 437–438.
169 P. Magdalino, "Medieval Constantinople: Built Environment," in *The Economic History of Byzantium. From the Seventh through the Fifteenth Century*, vol. 2, ed. A. E. Laiou (Washington, D.C.: Dumbarton Oaks Research Library and Collection, 2002), 533–534, 536. Cf. A. Bryer, "The Structure of the Late Byzantine Town: *Dioikismos* and the *Mesoi*," in *Continuity and Change in Late Byzantine and Early Ottoman Society*, eds. A. Bryer and H. Lowry (Birmingham: the University of Birmingham, Centre for Byzantine Studies; Washington, DC: Dumbarton Oaks Research Library and Collection, 1986), 271–274.
170 A. Bryer and D. Winfield, *The Byzantine Monuments and Topography of the Pontos*, vol. 1 (Washington, DC: Dumbarton Oaks Research Library and Collection, 1985), 180, 198, 201; A. Eastmond, *Art and Identity in Thirteenth-Century Byzantium. Hagia Sophia and the Empire of Trebizond* (Aldershot; Burlington, VT: Ashgate, 2004), 48.
171 Bryer and Winfield, *Pontos*, 179. For similar description of a typical Late Byzantine town: I. Cantacuzenus, *Historiarum Libri IV. Graece et Latinae*, vol. 3 (Bonn: Impensis Ed. Weberi, 1832), 130–131.
172 Bryer and Winfield, *Pontos*, 178; A. Eastmond, "The Empire of Trebizond," in *Byzantium's Other Empire: Trebizond*, ed. A. Eastmond (Istanbul: ANAMED, 2016), 32.
173 Eastmond, *Art and Identity*, 53–54 n.20.
174 *Ibid.*, 54, 56.
175 Bryer and Winfield, *Pontos*, 195–250.
176 *Ibid.*, 178.
177 *Ibid.*, 182; Eastmond, "Empire," 51.
178 Bryer and Winfield, *Pontos*, 182–195.

179 Bryer, "Structure," 274–279. These cross-cultural influences are encapsulated in the decoration of the church of Hagia Sophia, the best preserved monument of the Trapezuntine Empire: Eastmond, "Empire," 32–33, 55.

180 Bryer and Winfield, *Pontos*, 202; Eastmond, "Empire," 54. In addition to the one enclosed within the precinct of the Great Palace at Constantinople, references to *tyzkanisteria* can be found in the written sources, but are difficult to locate archaeologically: Bouras, "Aspects," 526.

181 Eastmond, *Art and Identity*, 255–256.

182 A detailed description of the citadel-palace complex can be found in Bessarion's (1403–1472) *Encomium* of Trebizond: Bryer and Winfield, *Pontos*, 184–186. Most recently: S. Kennedy, ed., *Two Works on Trebizond. Michael Panaretos, Bessarion* (Cambridge, MA: Harvard University Press, 2019).

183 Bouras, "Aspects," 523–524. Besides the Blachernae Palace in Constantinople, the administrative/palace complex (13th–15th centuries) at Ano Chora in Mistra is among the best preserved examples, more or less contemporary to the Palace of the Trapezuntine emperors: S. Kalopissi-Verti, "Mistra. A Late Byzantine Fortified Settlement," in *Heaven and Earth. Cites and Countryside in Byzantine Greece*, eds. J. Albani and E. Chalkia (Athens: Hellenic Ministry of Culture and Sports; Benaki Museum, 2013), 229.

184 Bryer and Winfield, *Pontos*, 184.

185 Bouras, "Aspects," 513 (Mistra).

186 Eastmond, *Art and Identity*, 54–55.

187 *Ibid*., 55.

188 J. Haldon *et al.*, eds., *Archaeology and Urban Settlement in Late Roman and Byzantine Anatolia. Euchaïta-Avkat-Beyözü and Its Environment* (Cambridge: Cambridge University Press, 2018); Zavagno, *Cities*, 95–151 (Amastris); syntheses in *The Archaeology of Byzantine Anatolia. From the End of Late Antiquity until the Coming of the Turks*, ed. P. Niewöhner (Oxford: Oxford University Press, 2017).

189 L. Mumford, *The City in History. Its Origins, Its Transformations, and Its Prospects* (4th ed.) (London; New York: Penguin Books, 1991), 11. Cf. Bryer, "Structure," 273–274 (*synoikismos/dioikismos*). For the complexities of (individual) urban transformations: A. A. Eger, "(Re)Mapping Medieval Antioch. Urban Transformations from the Early Islamic to the Middle Byzantine Periods," *DOP* 67 (2013): 134.

190 J.-P. Sodini, "La contribution de l'archéologie à la connaissance du monde byzantin (IVe-VIIe siècles)," *DOP* 47 (1993): 139.

191 U. Serin, "Byzantium-Early Islam and Byzantine Cultural Heritage in Turkey," in *Byzantium Early Islam. Cultural Heritage Management: Shared Experience beyond Boundaries*, eds. P. Assimakopoulou-Atzaka *et al.* (Thessaloniki: Hellenic Society for the Protection of the Environment and the Cultural Heritage 2008), 209–239.

8

INSULAR URBANISM IN BYZANTIUM

Luca Zavagno

Introduction: The insular Worlds of Byzantium

Traditionally, islands have not attracted a good deal of attention on the part of Byzantine historiography. [1] In truth, if one leaves aside the pulverized constellation of islets dotting the Aegean basin, which was regarded as part and parcel of the Byzantine heartland in the seventh to ninth century and the real economic pillar of the empire from the tenth century till 1204, the islands of Byzantine Mediterranean have been regarded as mere distant outposts and peripheral worlds.[2] The bigger ones, like Crete, Cyprus, and Sicily, have attracted a good deal of attention, although the latter has often been regarded as a sort of black hole in Byzantine archaeology till a few decades ago; the smallest like Malta or those perceived as too distant from the Constantinopolitan center, like Sardinia or the Balearics, have often been neglected. One must, however, admit that in the past few decades, scholars have slowly moved away from this traditional historiographical approach regarding islands simply as marginal to the political, social, and economic changes the Byzantine heartland was experiencing, from the seventh century until they were recaptured by the gravity of an expanding Empire in the tenth century (Crete and Cyprus) or were lost forever (Sicily, together with Sardinia Malta and the Balearics).[3] Better and better-published archaeology, as well as a refined analysis of the material culture, the ability to pinpoint the chronological markers, and, finally, an attempt to frame islands within a Mediterranean comparative approach, has led to propose a new interpretative models for the economic, political, administrative, and cultural history of the abovementioned Byzantine islands.

Although an all-encompassing alternative to the only existing systematic account on the history of the Byzantine insular world has yet to be produced, scholars like Salvatore Cosentino, Enrico Zanini, and Myrto Veikou have recently tried to re-assess the role of islands in the Byzantine Medieval Mediterranean.[4] Indeed, a preliminary caveat must be made at the onset of this contribution, for the historiographical re-discovery of large Byzantine islands has not entirely hinged on urban archaeology, for often (and with the exception of Kastro Apalirou in Naxos, Gortyn in Crete, and Salamis-Constantia in Cyprus, which however remains inaccessible to archaeologists due to the current political situation on the island) the most important insular cities are still occupied and had sketchy excavations.

DOI: 10.4324/9780429203923-11

Intensive and extensive surveys across the countryside of different islands, as well as a focus on rural villas and ecclesiastical buildings (from the large early Byzantine basilicas on Cyprus and the Balearics to small Medieval rural churches in Sardinia),[5] have helped to assess "settlement transformation in island systems of the Eastern Mediterranean [and] to describe different aspects of its inhabitants' flexibility to 'adjust' to constant changes of power, trade networks, and cultural interactions-usually provoked by the central administration."[6] This, in turn, has allowed redefining the very concept of islands and promotes the alternative notion of "islandness" as describing the political changes, social constructions, and cultural perceptions that characterised insular spaces.[7]

Indeed, it is important to stress the location of insular urban sites along the so-called maritime continuation of the "frontiers" of the Byzantine Empire (and, in particular, the eastern one with the Caliphate).[8] In fact, urban archaeology, rural surveys, and a more punctual and comparative analysis of pottery and coins have led to conclude that islands possibly acted as a third political and economic pole between the Anatolian plateau and the Aegean Sea in the Byzantine Mediterranean, rather than as a marginal area at the border of two conflicting polities (the Byzantine Empire and the Islamic Caliphate).[9] However, more recently, the identification of a wide array of material chronological indicators, like the Sicilian "ceramica a stuoia," as well as globular and ovoidal amphorae, has led scholars like Paul Arthur, Joanita Vroom, and Jonathan Shepard to cut a wide swath as islands reveal as part and parcel of a wide Byzantine maritime *koine*.[10] The latter encompassed liminal coastal spaces as well as insular communities promoting social contact and cultural interchange. [11] As Paolo Delogu concludes, "this area seems to coincide with the territories and the seas on which the Byzantine Empire retained a political and naval rulership."[12] Moreover, it suggested a certain common cultural unity; in fact, the peculiar political-administrative infrastructures (as documented in most of the abovementioned islands and gateway communities like Amalfi and Comacchio) de facto pointed to an other-than-imperial Greco-Roman identity.[13]

In light of the abovementioned details, the present chapter will present the reader with a short overview of some insular urban sites from a comparative perspective: Gortyn, Eleutherna, and Heraklion in Crete, Salamis-Constantia, Kerynia, and Nicosia in Cyprus, Syracuse, and Enna in Sicily, and Cagliari in Sardinia. There are two main reasons for this. First, this selection has a lot to do with expediency as the abovementioned sites are the best excavated and published ones for their respective islands (and in the case of Gortyn for the whole Dark Ages).[14] Unfortunately, urban archaeology is still in its infancies in some islands like the Balearics (where however we have well excavated early Christian basilicas and Roman/Late Antique sites like Pollentia), Corsica (which was nevertheless lost to Byzantium in the seventh century), and Malta (which seems to have boasted a set of small gateway communities).[15] So these islands will not be included in the present chapter.

In fact, and returning to the abovementioned urban sites, in most cases, they also acted as the main political, military, religious, and socio-economic foci of the insular areas they were located in. Nevertheless, in particular for Cyprus, one can document a peculiar transformation to the local urban settlement pattern: this foisted upon a rather fluid response to the variable shear political-military stress endured by the island due to its position at the edge of two empires, as Cyprus capitalized on the lack of a unique and permanent urban catalyst for the main political, military, and religious functions.[16]

As I will return to this in a few moments, I would like to move to the second rationale for my choice of insular sites. Indeed, in my opinion, their historical trajectories testify to the importance of islands (even those located on the western fringes of the empire like the

Balearics and Sardinia) to the political, administrative, and military imperial structures. As partially mentioned, it would be only too easy to dismiss insular spaces as marginal political and administrative spaces, simply fulfilling the role of distant "guardians to the imperial galaxy." This is shown by the repeated imperial efforts to keep and reassert Constantinopolitan rule over insular spaces, although using different and expedient political tactics for only Sicily was elevated to the rank of theme, whereas Sardinia, Cyprus, Crete, and the Balearics were ruled by dukes or *archontes*.[17] As Byzantium left the trouble waters of its Dark Ages, the targets of its expansive territorial policy and military expeditions in the tenth and eleventh centuries were indeed Crete (turned into an Emirate after the invasion of Andalusian Muslim pirates in 820s) and Cyprus, as – after the fall of Syracuse in 878 – it also staged counterattacks from its last outposts in eastern Sicily.[18] The two large eastern Mediterranean islands returned in Byzantine hands in 965 and 969, whereas Sicily was completely lost to the Fatimids with the conquest of Taormina (962), Rametta (965), and Messina (976).[19] Nevertheless, a great expedition to reconquer Sicily was staged by Michael IV, who dispatched the brilliant general George Maniaces to the islands in the early 1040s only to have him accused of high treason and arrested after he successfully took Syracuse back.[20]

Third, one should also look beyond the simple strategic and military value large islands had to Constantinople; indeed, the repeated military expeditions targeting Crete and Sicily resonate with the economic importance not only for the Byzantine fiscal system but also as outposts along the Mediterranean (fragmented) shipping and exchange routes. On the one hand, as Cosentino concludes, in "the seventh and eighth century islands seem to remain an economic space relatively more developed than northern and central Italy, the Balkans or Asia Minor."[21] Indeed, as Wickham recently assessed, islands like Cyprus and Malta seem to have linked the Islamic and Byzantine networks of exchange as enhanced by the pattern of distribution of Byzantine globular amphorae and ceramics as dated to 700–900. In other words, a reassessment of the resilient insular economy bridges the gap between two prosperous "trade cycles" (the Late Antique and the tenth- to eleventh-century ones) that help to propose a model of central and eastern Mediterranean regional, sub-regional, and inter-regional connectivity in the aftermath of the Arab invasion.[22] On the other hand, it seems now clear that if the empire would not die, that also owed to the fact that "the fact that it remained in possession of a strip of islands that connected it from the Cypriot Levant to the Balearics [for] this corridor of islands allowed the Byzantine Empire to continue to operate large-scale movements of men, foodstuffs, and artifacts between Constantinople and its insular ports until the reign of Michael II."[23]

So, large islands boasted a rather sustained economic vitality and socio-cultural resilience as paired with peculiar administrative and governmental structures as well as political expediency on the part of the local elites, which often remained urban-oriented. First, one should resist the temptation of labeling urban life as veering away from the coasts and retrenching in small, fortified outposts, in particular, vis-à-vis the Arab naval raids dated to the seventh and eighth centuries. By using archaeology and material culture, we should follow insular urban trajectories on a rather broad connectivity spectrum swaying like a pendulum between relative isolation from hegemonic political and economic systems to integration into such systems. In this light, and this is the second point I would like to drive home, the following section will indeed also try to use the "limited" territorial scope insular spaces possessed in order to draw a picture of changing urban settlement pattern hierarchy and new urban forms which coexisted next to old, but transforming, urban fabric, landscape, and structures. The key studies I will be presenting here, indeed, could help to better address differences, categories, and problems as they emerge in the archaeological record.

This is not to assert a sort of uniqueness of insular urban culture, stemming from isolation or resulting from specific cultural identity possessed only by islands; or to flaunt the idea that the intensification and abatement or better, the success and failures, functional transformation, structural alteration and demographic changes experienced by of urban entities owed not only to the needs and priorities of central administration and/or to the natural resources of the regions they were located in.[24] Rather by examining the centrality of communications and connectivity in molding the trajectories (sometimes successful, sometimes less) of urbanism in regions often simply demurred as the peripheries of the empire.

"Cities of Islands"

In this section, and as already mentioned, I will be encasing the trajectories of urbanism across different Byzantine islands within the chronological limits of Byzantine and rulership, which in the central Mediterranean (Sicily and Sardinia) came to an end in the tenth century and in the Eastern continued to the late eleventh century (for Cyprus) and the Fourth Crusade (for Crete).[25] I will occasionally refer to "other" examples of Byzantine urban insularity like Naxos in the Aegean as these show similarities not only in terms of urban forms, planning, and functional characteristics but also in their diachronic developments across the Byzantine millennium.

I will start this journey from Crete for its capital – Gortyn – has been the focus of extensive archaeological campaigns which started at the beginning of the nineteenth century and culminated in the past decades (and still ongoing). [26] Although they did not shed light on a minimal part of the Classical and Byzantine urban landscape, they allow concluding that Gortyn remained the main political and religious focus of Byzantine Crete until the late eighth century.[27] Indeed, it preserved a complex social and demographic structure, a vital economic life, and political and religious importance in the seventh and early eighth centuries.[28] This mirrored in an urban landscape, which maintained its coherence in terms of fabric and morphology, although revealing the first traces of a changing type of urbanism (the so-called city of islands model).[29] Indeed, the topography of most of the cities presented in the chapter developed along with multiple foci of settlement and socio-economic activity revolving around built centers of political, military, or religious power. A diversified constellation of centers of population, activities, and functions was therefore not always limited to or contained within imposing walled enceintes.

In the case of Gortyn, "Classic" monumentality (for instance, the orthogonal road-network), indeed, coexisted with artisanal workshops and commercial activities (as documented in the so-called Byzantine Houses) encroaching onto the public space and pointing to the considerable social and economic vitality of the ecclesiastical and administrative elites.[30] The analysis of pottery further enhances the picture I have just outlined: in particular, both locally produced highly decorated painted wares and imported Glazed White Wares (a type of pottery produced in Constantinople from the mid-seventh century onward), together with amphorae of a type found exclusively in the capital in late seventh- and eighth-century contexts, point to the role of the city within the local and medium-distance exchange patterns as well as the consistency of shipping links with the capital.[31] Although a portion of the city (the acropolis) was enclosed by a new set of walls dated to the mid-to-late seventh century, Gortyn preserved a multifunctional image with different foci of settlement (both inside and outside the wall). In fact, a comparison with another well excavated – but smaller in size – Cretan site (Eleutherna) allows Tsigonaki to conclude that "fortification does not signal the shrinking of the city and subsequent decline of the urban space, but rather the demarcation of controlled areas within the city."[32] Indeed, for Eleutherna, located on the northern slope of the Ida mountains, one can document a reorganization and relocation of the administrative and religious functions as pairing with an upgrade of the defensive structures which singled the central plateau out, although the city retained a clear urban character as enhanced by numismatic and sigillographic evidence.[33]

In other words, both in Gortyn and Eleutherna, poorly built, architecturally demonumentalised and demographically diminished, "islands" or "foci" of settlement (made of commercial shops and artisanal workshops with residential housing) seem to have boasted persistent urban economic activity as sitting next to areas where there were concentrations of religious buildings and others where possibly military-administrative state-driven institutions resided. In this light, it is worth mentioning that the lead seals belonging to *kommerkiarioi, archontes, spatharioi, and stratelates*, as well as to a *Vestitor* and *Protonotarios* of the Imperial Treasury yielded both in Gortyn and Knossos (on the northern coast of the island) and dated to the eighth century.[34] They show that the island was integral to both the Byzantine administrative system and its military machinery.[35] The same could be stated for the importance of Gortyn as an ecclesiastical and pilgrimage center. Indeed, one could mention here the Cretan Archbishop Andreas, whose hagiography was compiled in the second half of the eighth century.[36] Once appointed as Metropolitan of Crete (an office he held from 711 to his death in 740), Andreas actively sponsored the promotion of the memorial cult of Saint Titus (the first bishop of the island as ordained by Saint Paul) as well as for the large building activities in Gortyn. This led to the creation of a new iconography appearing on the archbishopric's lead seals as well as the erection of the ecclesiastical complex of Blachernitissa (tod. Hagios Titos) as the area around it seemed to have been in use well into the ninth century.[37] As the image and functions of the Gortynian cityscape were rearranged, it is also worth mentioning the transformation of the water-supply system. This reveals in a set of cisterns dotting the urban landscape and partially replacing the sixth-century aqueduct. Water was collected, stored, and redistributed within single parceled properties, providing us once again with an image of a city of islands where urban communities relied less on the Roman and Byzantine monumental structures or infrastructural networks as water availability was more localised and/or privatised.[38]

The abovementioned evidence seems to hint at a "longer" urban life for Gortyn than previously thought.[39] Nevertheless, on the one hand, the transformations in the appearance and structures of [Cretan cities] seem to have been part of a top-down process. In fact, they demur the widely accepted assumption that Cretan cities were abandoned before the Andalusian pirates' invasion in the 820s.[40] On the other hand, as Cosentino concludes, "the new political framework of the seventh and eighth centuries, which entailed a concentration of military operations in the Balkans and Asia Minor, resulted in an emphasis of the geo-strategic importance of the northern coast of Crete."[41] This, in turn, led to a real redefinition of Cretan urbanism and settlement pattern hierarchy from the mid-eighth century on with the emergence of the coastal harbor of Heraklion as the urban reference point for the whole island.[42] The arrival of the Andalusian pirates only strengthened up the ongoing trend. Eventually, with the return of the island in Byzantine hands in the late tenth century the economic, political, administrative, and religious importance of the northern coast was finalized. Crete became the southern border of the Aegean exchange system, which played a central role in the growth of trade, demographic upturn, increased rural production and intensification of urban activities experienced by Byzantium between the late tenth and the twelfth centuries.[43]

As partially referred to already, rather similar trajectories in terms of urban settlement pattern and hierarchy, as well as changes to urban fabric and landscape, could be surmised for Cyprus, where Salamis-Constantia, located on the eastern coast of the islands, acted as the ecclesiastical and political capital of the island of Cyprus until the mid-ninth century. Although excavations in Salamis-Constantia stopped due to tragic events of 1974, a reassessment of urban archaeology produced till then as well as a poignant comparison with other sites in the Republic of Cyprus where investigations continued and were constantly published (like in Amathus, Paphos, and Polis-Arsinoe) has allowed proposing a multifunctional image with different foci of settlement dated to seventh to ninth century.[44] The city did not simply shrink in size during the passage from late antiquity to the early Middle Ages, and – as seen for Gortyn and Eleutherna – the construction of a new, well-built fortified enceinte in the second half of the seventh century reflected a degree of planning on the part of the local and imperial elites, as well as the availability of resources.[45] The impact of militarization was indeed limited on both insular social fabric and settlement patterns until the mid-eighth century, for in Salamis-Constantia, the construction of the city walls appears to be contemporary to rebuilding works at the basilica of Saint Epiphanius.[46] The basilica continued to function both as a pilgrimage center and as the seat of the Cypriot Autocephalic Archbishopric, thus underlining the continuity of key institutions of the cultural life of the city. Pilgrimage continued to Saint Epiphanius as well as to the Campanopetra church; both were refurbished in the eighth century and indicatively visited by Anastasius Sinaita and Willibald in the early eighth century and by Epiphanius the Monk in the ninth century.[47] Moreover, evidence of a late seventh/early eighth century artisanal/workshop phase of occupation of a former Roman urban villa located not far away from the city's harbor provides evidence of economic activity and continuity as a comparison can be made with the abovementioned structures excavated in Gortyn as well as with area of the city of Polis-Arsinoe (on the northern coast of the islands) which revealed as composed of workshops, roads, and burials dating in the late seventh/early eighth century.[48] Contemporary evidence also comes from Amathus, where workshops and residential buildings were erected around the basilica on the acropolis. Moreover, in Paphos, a number of small houses and simple workshops (frequented during the period 680–780) were also uncovered in the area of the former Roman agora around the Chrysopolitissa church complex (refurbished in the eighth century with a new apse on the axis of the original basilica).[49]

All in all, it is possible to conclude that Salamis-Constantia did not disappear after the Arab raids but managed to adapt to the new political and economic realities in the island and the broader region (Figure 8.1). An appraisal of both numismatic evidence and the distributive pattern of the so-called globular amphorae as manufactured in Cyprus (together with locally made kitchen wares) has revealed that the island was at the epicenter of regional interlocking economies with strong contacts with both Palestine and Umayyad (and later Abbasid and Fatimid) Egypt.[50] Indeed, Cypriot cities other than Salamis-Constantia also provided signs of economic resilience, yet political developments (as exemplified by the famous treaty of 686–686 between the Umayyads and the Byzantines, and the forced transfer of local population to Nea Justinianoupolis in the early eighth century) affected the island and its role in the context of a Byzantine Empire whose control over its southern territories was fading fast.[51]

Figure 8.1 Salamis-Constantia [Cyprus], Basilica of Campanopetra

As a result, although Salamis-Constantia remained the main religious and pilgrimage center of the island and its harbor seemed to have been frequented well into the eleventh century, both literary and archaeological evidence shows that the northern coast of the including sites, like Kerynia and Lapithos-Lambousa, started functioning as a Byzantine military and administrative hub from the ninth century onward.[52] As the Pentadaktylos mountain range acted as a de-facto borderline separating the northern coastline from the fertile Mesaoria plain, the northern harbor of Kerynia (Figure 8.2), which had been fortified most probably in the eighth and ninth centuries, slowly turned into the most important Byzantine city of the island and the *de facto* capital of Cyprus.[53] Its location on the coast was conveniently oriented in relation to their respective centers of Byzantine state authority along the southern coast of Anatolia (in particular Attaleia), as proved by its role in the *reconquista* of the island in 965 and even later.[54] Eventually, and although Pentadaktylos continued to play a key role in the strategic organization of Cyprus as strengthened by a system of fortifications organised around the existence of three key castles, the city of Nicosia emerged in the second half of the eleventh century as the new insular capital. This reflected the increased economic importance of the Mesaoria plain and the transfer of the metropolitan of Cyprus from Salamis-Constantia in the early twelfth century. [55]

So, for both Cyprus and Crete, one can hint at the development of local insular urban centers (and in particular, the capitals) which did not see urbanism disappearing from the coasts; more important ceramics (as well as sigillographic and numismatic evidence) points to complex strategies aiming at reorganizing and adapting local urban settlement patterns

Figure 8.2 Kyrenia [Cyprus]

to the new socio-political, cultural, and military dynamics of an early Medieval "maritime frontier." In fact, the latter should be defined as a contact zone, where insular actors shaped an ever-changing cultural and economic balance at the interface between Mediterranean polities in the early medieval period while at the same time remaining part and parcel of a Byzantine Mediterranean coastal system. This is reflected by the resilience of economic activities as often mirrored by the transformations experienced by the urban landscape, fabric, and planning with fortifications paired with foci of artisanal and commercial activities. Things obviously changed with the return of the two islands in Byzantine hands in the second half of the tenth century, when Crete was part and parcel of the Aegean exchange system and Cyprus, which remained central to the Byzantine efforts to remain relevant in relation to the developments brought by the foundation of Latin States in the Levant and the establishment of the Seljuks in Asia Minor.[56]

Since both Cyprus and Crete boasted frequented urban areas characterised by a fragmented but highly functional landscape and fabric as de facto predicated upon the economic resilience, political and fiscal importance, and ecclesiastical centrality of the so-called Byzantine insular system, it is important to see how urbanism developed on other Byzantine islands, and, in particular, Sicily and Sardinia.

Contrary to Cyprus, Crete, and (as it will be seen) Sardinia, and, as mentioned already, Sicily became a thematic capital and remained central to the Byzantine state mainly because of its importance in supplying Constantinople with grain after the disruption of the Egyptian tax-spine in the 640s.[57] It is also important to note that a drastic improvement in the study and availability of Sicilian material culture (in particular seals, coins, and ceramics), as well as stratigraphically excavated urban sites, has only happened in the past 20 years. This has nonetheless led scholars to produce an all-encompassing picture of the changes in Sicilian urban settlement patterns as well as developments of the local economy (in terms of production, distribution, and consumption). In this light, I will present the reader with two examples of Sicilian urbanism: Syracuse and Enna. The former acted as the religious and political capital of the island until its fall by the hands of the Aghlabids in 878 (and so can be ideally paired with Gortyn and Salamis-Constantia); the latter represents a good example of the changes in the urban settlement pattern as the Byzantine authorities actively sponsored and encouraged the adoption of a new form of urban planning and structure with a defensive penchant vis-à-vis the Arab slow advance toward the eastern coast of the island.[58]

Syracuse acted as the main administrative, political, and military center of the island as well as the seat of the Sicilian Archbishopric from the eighth or ninth century. Although the city reduced in size and was mainly focused on the island of Ortygia, protected by a fortified isthmus, archaeology shows that the main road connecting the two most important quarters of the Roman city (Akradina and Neapolis) were majestically repaved in the second quarter of the seventh century.[59] One can indeed conclude that in Syracuse, although the city shrank, the ancient street grid was (at least partially maintained) until the late ninth century (an occurrence also documented in Gortyn and Salamis-Constantia). Moreover, the Syracuse harbor, as protected by a double-walled enceinte (generically dated to the seventh to eighth century), also continued to be frequented by pilgrims, traders, diplomats, and officials for Syracuse remained a regular hub for travelers from both Constantinople and the Adriatic. One can think here of the famous journey of Willibald, who visited Catania and Syracuse before embarking for Constantinople in the early eighth century, or Gregory Decapolite in the early ninth century.[60]

In Syracuse, churches were actively restored or built from scratch, as shown by the conversion of the Temple of Athena into the city Cathedral sometime in the late seventh century (Figure 8.3). It became the seat of the newly appointed local Archbishop with full jurisdiction over the rest of the Sicilian bishoprics.[61] Furthermore, the sigillographic evidence points to both the provenance of the local *stratēgoi* (mostly eunuchs directly dispatched from the imperial Palace) and the presence in the city of *kommerkiaroi* (in charge of providing Constantinople and the army with grain and other supplies) and *topoireitai* (officers leading elite military corps).[62] This allows us to conclude that Syracuse, with its two main "islands of settlements" (Akradina and Ortygia), had extraordinary importance within the military (and political) Byzantine networks of power which lasted until the city was conquered by the Arabs in 878.

Ease of communication between Constantinople and the island should come as no surprise, for Sicily acted as an economic interface at the intersection of the eastern and western Mediterranean. Indeed, the island lay astride the trunk-route linking the Tyrrhenian with the Aegean and southern Anatolia.[63] Coins and coinage confirm the exceptional economic vitality of Sicily: the mint of Syracuse was the only one issuing gold and bronze coins together with Constantinople in the period under scrutiny, as its output found its way across the Mediterranean and the Balkans as well as central European and Scandinavian trade

Figure 8.3 Syracuse [Sicily], Cathedral

routes. Moreover, the analysis of Sicilian oval lamps, table-wares, and globular amphorae bespeak a double-fold network of connectivity as the eastern coast (centered on the capital Syracuse) slanted toward the southern Adriatic and the Peloponnese, whereas the north-western coast was oriented toward the Tyrrhenian and its main harbors/cities (mainly Rome but also Cagliari and Naples) as well as Muslim north Africa.[64]

Indeed, as Maurici remarks: "Sicily remained a land of cities during the entire Byzantine period" for other examples of resilient Sicilian urbanism can indeed be offered by Palermo (whose harbor remained active and frequented well into the eighth century and beyond as documented by both material and literary evidence) and Catania (whose impressive set of walls accommodated two religious and pilgrimage foci).[65] The latter was also connected to Syracuse (to the south) and Taormina (perching on a rock-spur at the north-easternmost corner of the islands) by the costal Via Pompeia.[66] Although the Sicilian cities shrank in terms of size and population, the coherence of urban landscape and the reorganization of their urban planning and fabric stemmed less from impending Arab naval threats than from the ability of local elites to navigate the changing political, administrative, and military Tyrrhenian flux.[67]

Nevertheless, one should also be reminded that old Classical cities like Agrigento could experience a striking downturn as it turned into a conglomeration of "agro-towns" centered on the fortified acropolis of Girgenti.[68] More important, and in a similar vein with the Cypriot and Cretan example, a territorial reorganization was imposed by the advance of the Aghlabids, leading to a calculated effort on the part of the thematic/imperial government to create a strategic line of defense. This wriggled away from the coast, for it shielded the south-eastern coastal cities. It was centered on inland fortresses and urban-like *kastra*, all dated to the decades that followed the institution of the Sicilian theme. A good example of the former type of settlement is offered by the *kassar* of Castronovo strategically located at the intersection of the main north-south and east-west inland axis crisscrossing the island[69]; on the contrary, newly founded fortified centers like Butera, Ragusa, and Enna offer a good complement with sites like Kerynia in Cyprus, Oxa in Crete (which is not included in the present chapter), and Kastro Apalirou in Naxos. These added up to a new model of urbanism, developed from the seventh century onward across the Byzantine Mediterranean, where pride of place is given to security, fortifications, and strategic control of the hinterland, as reflecting new adaptive strategies in settlement patterns (as seen in the case of Cyprus).

In particular, Kastro Apalirou, located on the small Aegean islet of Naxos, as established in the early Middle Ages, reveals as not simply a walled safe haven built in response to the Arab raids in the Aegean, but rather as an expression of a different kind of functional needs for, as Magdalino remarks: "trade, shipping and human resources of the Aegean world as central to the existence of the empire in the eighth century."[70] Kastro Apalirou is exemplary of a new type of hilltop, fortified, seventh- to eighth-century urbanism, bespeaking scale, complexity, and imperial sponsorship: large walled settlements with a dense urban fabric made up of houses, cisterns but (surprisingly) few religious buildings.[71] Indeed, we are confronted with a new model of urban settlement and landscape that was clearly cutting all ties with the Late Antique urban environment and fabric. Such settlements provided locations where local elites could reside and retain a degree of control over the nearby plains and their landholdings, as indeed can be shown in the case of the Enna, a strategically located and heavily fortified center at the heart of Sicily.[72] Recent archaeological investigations have indeed shed light on Enna's articulated fortified settlement pattern, which included two sets of walls: one protecting the lower town and the other encasing the upper fortress (Castello di Lombardia). Indeed, in Enna, the military function had pride of place, for no bishopric is documented. A great effort was put by the Byzantine authorities into strengthening the local defense vis-à-vis the Aghlabid invasions in the early ninth century.[73] It is, however, worth mentioning that the ceramic evidence yielded in the city all date to the period between the eighth and the tenth centuries and point to a settlement that remained well connected with the insular coastal centers while also assuming a preeminent and strategic role in the military confrontation with the Aghlabids.[74] Enna was nevertheless conquered by the Arabs in 858, and as a consequence, the last remnants of Byzantine territory were put under a huge demographic and strategic pressure with a new "fortification season" buoyed by the creation of defensive *kastra* and *kastellia* along those military roads crisscrossing the Val Demone and gravitating around the "new capital" Taormina (the latter sieged already in 902).[75] Little is known of these as we have scanty archaeological remains even for Taormina itself, and one has to rely mainly on Arab literary sources and toponymic evidence.[76] As Arcifa concludes, the Byzantine presence in the last season of the Arab-Byzantine confrontation was strong enough to delay the fall of the island and "justified the two long sieges of Taormina and Rometta in 962/963 on behalf of the Fatimid army and demonstrated that the defense was entrusted to a well-equipped army as well as the relative ease with which Manuel Phokas, after the landing in 964, conquered Termini and Syracuse."[77]

With the Sicilian diverse cases of urban transformations and settlement pattern change in mind, we can now move to Sardinia, which from the mid-seventh century onward acquired increased importance as bases for a local detachment of the Byzantine Tyrrhenian fleet and following upon the fall of Carthage in 698, the seat of the former African Exarch's fiscal, administrative, and military machinery as well as its mint.[78] Unfortunately, we possess good urban archaeology for only a limited number of Sardinian cities. The scanty evidence has, however, allowed scholars like Galoppini to tentatively conclude that "coastal Sardinian cities maintained a noteworthy vitality well into the eighth century, thanks to their strong [inter-Tyrrhenian] commercial and cultural ties with the Italian peninsula as well as the coastal regions of Africa."[79]

Recent excavations at Cagliari – on the southern coast of the island – have confirmed that the administrative reorganization introduced by Justinian confirmed the city as the religious and political capital of the island as also enhanced by literary evidence.[80] Recently, a sort of duplication of the urban fabric and landscape of Cagliari has been proposed by Martorelli, with the harbor separating two conurbations (eastern and western) in a way that reminds us of Ephesos.[81] The eastern one centered on the well-excavated sanctuary of Saint Saturno, an important pilgrimage church built around the martyrium of the saint. The harbor of Cagliari was central in promoting commercial and artisanal activities as well as intercultural (and interreligious) contacts as heightened by the presence of Greek monastic institutions in the city as well as the Sardinian Archbishops. [82] Indeed, an underwater survey at the harbor has yielded a large number of eighth- to ninth-century globular amphorae as ceramics (like forum and painted wares) also attest to the economic vitality of at least some other areas of the city.[83] Notwithstanding the little urban archaeology available, it seems that the multifunctional role in religious, military, and economic terms played by Cagliari and the importance of its harbor for the Constantinopolitan elites may have translated into an urban landscape characterised by multiple foci of settlements. Although some parts of the city were deserted, others remained frequented as the administrative and episcopal urban cores moved to the west of the Classical city. [84]

So, and as already seen in the case of Sicily, Cyprus, and Crete, the story of Cagliari's resilience points once again to a rather different model of insular urban settlement pattern than a simple and hasty run to the hills and away from a coast threatened by the Muslim advance (in a way that also reminds us of other insular spaces like Cyprus). Of course, not all coastal Sardinian cities survived as centers like Nora or Tharros (although its harbor nevertheless yielded four Islamic seals dated to the mid-eighth century and possible evidence of an Arab incursion) and possibly fell prey to the political and military insecurity brought about by the Arab raids which culminated with the subjugation of Cagliari which was forced to pay the *jizya* in 752.[85] Nevertheless, on the one hand, the continuous Constantinopolitan interest in the fate of the island is exemplified by the famous mid-eighth-century inscription from Turris Libisonis (on the western coast of the island) "celebrating a great victory by the consul and duke Constantinos over the Lombards and other barbarians" as well as the role of Cagliari as the seat of the Byzantine Sardinian governor (whose title however changed from duke to *archon* sometime in the tenth century).[86] On the other hand, recent excavations at the city harbor of Olbia (on the eastern coast of the island) have yielded evidence of continuous commercial activities well into the ninth century (although with a low point in the seventh century), which runs counter to the traditional narrative of an abandonment of the city after a Vandal incursion in the sixth century.[87] Moreover, one should mention Aristànis on the south-western coast of Sardinia. This city was recorded for the first time by the seventh-century Byzantine geographer George of Cyprus, as it boasted a church dedicated to the Virgin (restored in the ninth century); however, some officials bearing Byzantine titles have been documented by sigillographic evidence as stationed in the city already in the sixth century.[88] In conclusion, urban life in Sardinia seems to show previously unsuspected resilience on both the eastern (Olbia) and western coast (Turris Libisonis and Aristhianis), for Cagliari remained the center of political, religious, and administrative life as predicated upon a (loose) but continuous socio-political, fiscal, and military dependence on Byzantium. Indeed, local elites looked to Constantinople as a source of political legitimacy and status while at the same time they were able to perform creative acts of political expediency, betraying their capacity to bend to the military and political pressure of the moment as shown, for instance, by a treaty the local authorities signed with the Arabs in 752/3 or by the abovementioned delegation from Cagliari who visited the Frankish kingdom in 815.[89] Sardinia nevertheless remained at the heart of imperial interest fora Byzantine naval squadron used Sardinia as an operational base. In this light, and notwithstanding the political transition from a duchy to an archontate, it is interesting to notice that Arab sources recognise the fact that Sardinia remained under Byzantine rule and not to have fallen to Islam until the attack from the Taifa of Denia, which took place in 1015.[90]

Conclusions: Urbanism in a Byzantine Mediterranean

This chapter has tried to shed light on the developments of urbanism and the historical trajectories of cities across some of the major islands of the Byzantine Empire. By proposing a comparative survey of some of the most important insular urban sites, it has also tried to overcome three major obstacles which have beleaguered past interpretative approaches to insular urban history. The first one was historiographical as I hope I showed that major islands (and their cities) were not secondary characters on the imperial political, military, and religious stage. Constantinople genuinely continued to pay attention to eastern and western Mediterranean islands and their cities. Obviously, this attentiveness was modulated by the ebbs and flows of Mediterranean politics across the period between the seventh and the eleventh centuries. Indeed, the geopolitical balance was constantly in flux, switching from one sector of the Great Sea to another for Byzantium never had enough resources to focus on more than one front. This notwithstanding, Byzantium managed to keep a close eye on the affairs of Sicily, Sardinia, and Crete (at least until the first half of the ninth century) as it also accepted that Cyprus (mainly owing to its proximity to the Caliphate) became a sort of political and more important economic middle ground between the Byzantine *koine* (as exemplified by the distribution and circulation of globular amphorae in most of the abovementioned cities) and the Islamic system of exchange. As a result, I have debunked the traditional interpretation of insular urbanism as hastily retreating from the coasts of both eastern and western Mediterranean on the eve of the Arab raids, only to resurge with the return of Byzantine power in the eastern basin of the Great Sea from the tenth century on or upon the arrival of the new political actors (the Papacy, Amalfi and Naples, and, above all, the Aghlabids and later the Fatimids) in the central and western half of it.

In this light, it is important to reassess another possible objection to the interpretation I have proposed here, which centered on the survival of insular cities as foisted entirely upon administrative, fiscal, military, and religious lines. In other words, the only "real" city of islands would have been those playing the role of regional (thematic or not) capitals. We are catching two birds with one stone here for countermanding the latter objection allows us to tackle the second of the obstacles I mentioned before: the methodological one. Indeed, very often, the idea of thematic capitals as fading ghosts of Classical urbanism and *de facto* the only insular (quasi)-urban centers has been built upon the scanty literary and documentary sources of the period as well as the interpretative premise of islands as simply peripheral to the political and military imperial core. The drastic improvement of urban archaeology and a refined assessment of material culture (in particular ceramics) has, in fact, allowed us to interpret islands and their cities as *plaque tournantes* along the more fragmented intra and inter-regional Medieval Mediterranean shipping routes.[91] The changes experienced by the urban landscape and settlement patterns reflected the ability on the part of imperial and local secular and ecclesiastical elites to tap into the economic vitality of islands and benefit from their position at the interface of regional systems of exchange.

This was particularly clear in Sicily, divided between two distinct networks of distribution, circulation, and consumption of goods as gravitating toward Constantinople (the eastern one) and the Tyrrhenian Sea (the north-western one). In turn, and upon the Aghlabid invasion, this buoyed the development of a rather complex response with the adoption of a new model of urbanism (in terms of fabric and planning) predicated upon defensive needs for urban sites like Enna and fortresses like Castronovo were meant to protect the access to the eastern coast and the Byzantine cities located along it like Syracuse (until 878), Catania, and Taormina. Nevertheless, and until their fall to the Arabs (but even later), at least some Sicilian cities other than the capital retained urban coherence (in terms of form and planning) and economic resilience, as cursorily seen in the case of Palermo. In this sense, a more rarified density of urban settlement pattern than the one experienced in Sicily, like the one we can document for Sardinia, nevertheless presented us with a similar trajectory.

Although much poorer than the Sicilian counterpart in terms of urban archaeology and material culture, the picture that can be sketched for Sardinia comparably includes both a political and religious center (Cagliari) as well as a gateway communities centered upon frequented (for military or commercial purposes) harbors like Olbia (as well as Aristhianis and, possibly, Turris Libisonis). At the other end of the Mediterranean, Crete and Cyprus also experienced a re-orientation of the urban settlement pattern, which saw the northern coast emerging as the gravitational point of the urban life on both islands. Indeed, in Cyprus, the de-structuring of urban functions was rather more pronounced than in Crete, most probably reflecting the contemporary presence of Byzantine and Arab fiscal, military, and political authorities. However, this did not mean that the former Classical urban centers (like Salamis-Constantia or Gortyn) disappeared, but rather that urban fabric, landscape, and infrastructures responded to new functional needs (as enhanced by the presence of fortifications) as well as economically fragmented and contested Mediterranean (as mirrored by the urban developments in centers like Eleutherna or Polis-Arsinoe).

The latter point is important to introduce the third and final obstacle. This has to do with the traditional chronological partition and the importance of embracing a "diachronic" and fully Mediterranean perspective when examining insular urbanism [92]; this is because islands (and their urban centers) not only boasted a previously unsuspected economic resilience which pierced the barrier of the so-called long eighth century but were also able to navigate (although in regionally nuanced ways) the interstices of a shared Mediterranean.[93] In this light, old periodizations are not useful to fully grasp the complexities of the insular socio-political game and its reflections on the changes experienced by its urban landscapes. In this light, therefore, cities of islands seem to be a good standpoint to fully come to grasp with the idea of a Byzantine "Mediterranean" urbanism which predicated upon the fluidity of the rules of Medieval Mediterranean political game, and on a Byzantine Empire as characterised by a low maintenance variable geometry across the whole early Medieval period;

an empire composed of open cities, gateway communities, and urban centers (as dotting the islands and the coasts of a so-called Byzantine maritime *koine*) in which Byzantium had state, economic, or occasionally ideological interest.[94] They allowed to project political and religious influence and affirmed the geopolitical preeminence of Byzantium across the Mediterranean shipping routes even when a full-fledged political or military control ceased to be possible (like in the case of Sardinia from the tenth century on). For Byzantium understood only too well that the "multiplication of contacts, peaceful and otherwise, demanded the invention of new rules that all the actors in the Mediterranean could accept and share, and that largely survived in the modern period."[95]

Notes

1 See L. Zavagno, "'Islands in the Stream': For a New History of the Large Islands of the Byzantine Mediterranean", *Mediterranean Historical Review* 33:2 (2018), 149–177.

2 E. Malamut, *Les îles de l'Empire byzantin. VIIIe-XIIe siècles* (Paris, 1988); C. Wickham, *Framing the Early Middle Ages. Europe and the Mediterranean (400–800)* (Cambridge, 2005), 29–32.

3 For Crete see E. Zanini, "Macro-Economy, Micro-Ecology, and the Fate of Urbanized Landscape in Late Antique and Early Byzantine Crete", in M. Cau Ontiveros & C. Mas Florit (eds), *Change and Resilience. The Occupation of Mediterranean Islands in Late Antiquity* (Providence, 2019), 139–161; E. Zanini, "Creta in età Protobizantina: un quadro di sintesi regionale", in E. Zanini, P. Pergola & D. Michaelidis (eds), *The Insular System of Byzantine Mediterranean. Archaeology and History* (Oxford, 2013), 173–190; D. Tsougarakis, *Byzantine Crete. From the 5th Century to the Venetian Conquest* (Athens, 1988); for Cyprus see D. Metcalf, *Byzantine Cyprus 491–1191 A.D.* (Nicosia, 2009) and L. Zavagno, *Cyprus between Late Antiquity and the early Middle Ages. An Island in Transition* (London – New York, 2017); for Sicily see A. Nef & V. Prigent, "Per una nuova storia dell'alto medioevo Siciliano", *Storica* (2006), 9–63; S. Valpreda Miceli, *Sikelia 2. La Sicilia dei Bizantini, i Bizantini di Sicilia* (Padova, 2020), and L. Arcifa, "Byzantine Sicily", in S. Cosentino (ed), *A Companion to Byzantine Italy* (Leiden, 2021), 472–494; for Malta see B. Bruno & N.Cutajar, "Byzantine Malta", in *A Companion to Byzantine Italy*, 522–539; for Sardinia see S. Cosentino, "Byzantine Sardinia between West and East. Features of a Regional Culture", *Millennium* 1 (2004), 328–367; P. G. Spanu, "Byzantine Sardinia", in *A Companion to Byzantine Italy*, 496–520; and A. Metcalfe, H. Fernández-Aceves & M. Muresu, *The Making of Medieval Sardinia* (Leiden, 2021); for the Balearics see J. Signes Codoñer, "Bizancio y las islas Baleares en los siglos VIII y IX", in R. Durán Tapia (ed.), *Mallorca y Bizancio* (Palma de Mallorca, 2005), 45–107.

4 Zanini, Pergola, & Michelides, *The Insular System of Byzantine Mediterranean*; M. Veikou, "One Island, three Capitals. Insularity and the Successive Relocations of the Capital of Cyprus from Late Antiquity to the Middle Ages", in S. Rogge & M. Grünbart (eds), *Medieval Cyprus. A place of Cultural Encounters* (Munster, 2015), 353–363; S. Cosentino, "Insularity, Economy and Social Landscape in the Early Byzantine Period", *Rivista di Studi Bizantini e NeoEllenici* 55 (2018), 89–104.

5 See for instance T. Papacostas, "The Economy of Late Antique Cyprus", in M. Decker & S. Kingsley (eds), *Economy and exchange in the East Mediterranean during Late Antiquity : Proceedings of a Conference at Somerville College, Oxford, 29 May 1999* (Oxford, 2001), 107–128; G. Papantoniou & A. Vionis, "Landscape Archaeology and Sacred Space in the Eastern Mediterranean: A Glimpse from Cyprus", *Land* 6 (2017), 1–18; R. Martorelli & R. Coroneo, "Chiese e culti di matrice Bizantina in Sardegna", in *The Insular System of Byzantine Mediterranean*, 47–63; A. Castrorao Barba, "Sicily before the Muslims. The Transformation of the Roman Villas between Late Antiquity and the Early Middle Ages, Fourth to Eighth Centuries CE", *Journal of Transcultural Medieval Studies* 3:1–2 (2016), 145–189; M. Hoerster, D. Nicolaou, & S. Rogge (eds), *Church Building in Cyprus (Fourth to Seventh Century). A Mirror of intercultural contacts in the Eastern Mediterranean* (Münster – New York, 2018); M. Decker, "The current status of Byzantine archaeology", *History Compass* 16(9): 5.

6 Veikou, "One Island, three Capitals", 357.

7 ead., 359; see also G. Varinoğlu, "'Imagine There Is No (Is)land': Conceptualizing Byzantine Islands in Southern Asia Minor", in K. Durak & I. Jevtić (eds), *Identity and the Other in Byzantium.*

Papers from the Fifth International Sevgi Gönül Byzantine Studies Symposium, Istanbul 2019 (Istanbul, 2019), 93–113.

8 T. Lounghis, *Byzantium in the Eastern Mediterranean. Safeguarding East Roman Identity (407–1204)*, (Nicosia, 2010).

9 S. Cosentino, "Mentality, Technology and Commerce: Shipping amongst Mediterranean Islands in Late Antiquity and Beyond", in *The Insular System of Byzantine Mediterranean*, 65–76.

10 P. Arthur, "From Italy to the Aegean and Back Again. Notes on the Archaeology of Byzantine Maritime Trade", in S. Gelichi & R. Hodges (eds), *Da un mare all'altro. Luoghi di scambio nell'Alto Medioevo europeo e mediterraneo Atti del Seminario Internazionale Comacchio, 27–29 Marzo 2009* (Turnhout, 2012), 337–352; J. Vroom, "The Byzantine Web. Pottery and Connectivity between the Southern Adriatic and the Eastern Mediterranean", in S. Gelichi & C. Negrelli (eds), *Adriatico altomedievale (VI–XI secolo). Scambi, porti, produzioni* (Rome, 2017), 285–313. J. Shepard, "Bunkers, Open Cities and Boats in Byzantine Diplomacy", in D. Dzino & K. Perry (eds), *Byzantium, Its Neighbours and Its Cultures* (Leiden, 2017), 1–33.

11 M. Veikou, "Mediterranean Byzantine Ports and Harbors in the Complex Interplay between Environment and Society. Spatial, Socio-Economic and Cultural Considerations Based on Archeological Evidence from Greece, Cyprus and Asia Minor", in J. Preiser Kapeller & F. Daim (eds), *Harbours and Maritime Networks as Complex Adaptive Systems* (Mainz, 2015), 51.

12 P. Delogu, "Questioni di Mare e Costa", in *Da un mare all'altro*, 463.

13 Zavagno, "Islands in the Stream", 159–160, 165.

14 Although curiously, Gortyn does not appear in Decker's compelling overview of Byzantine urban archaeology for the sixth- to tenth-century period (see M. Decker, *The Byzantine Dark Ages* [London, 2016], 81–122).

15 M. Cau Ontiveros & C. Mas Florit, "The Early Byzantine Period in the Balearic Islands", in *The Insular System of Byzantine Mediterranean*, 31–46; M. Riera Rullan, M. Orfila & M. Cau, "Els últims segles de Pollentia", *Bulletí de la Societat Arqueològica Lulliana* 55 (1999), 335–346; M. Orfila, M" E. Chávez & M. A. Cau, "Pollentia and the cities of the Balearic Islands", in L. Abad Casal, S. Keay & S. Ranallo Asensio (eds), *Early Roman Towns in Hispania Tarraconensis. JRA Supplementary Series* (Portsmouth, 2006), 133–145. P. Pergola & D. Istria, "La Corse byzantine (Vie-VIIe) siècles)", in *The Insular System of Byzantine Mediterranean*, 77–86; B. Bruno, *Roman and Byzantine Malta. Trade and economy* (La Valletta, 2009).

16 N. Bakirtzis & L. Zavagno, "Beyond Capitals: Urbanism in Cyprus between Late Antiquity and the Middle Ages (ca.600–ca.1100 CE.)", in S. Esders et al. (eds), *The 8th Century: Patterns of Transition in Economy and Trade throughout the Late Antique, Early Medieval and Islamicate Mediterranean in Multidisciplinary Perspectives* (forthcoming, 2024).

17 Zavagno, "Islands in the Stream", 161–162.

18 As Kaldellis (A. Kaldellis, *Streams of Gold, Rivers of Blood. The Rise and Fall of Byzantium, 955 A.D. to the First Crusade* [Oxford, 2017], 34–42) points out the emperors had repeatedly tried to retake Crete from 843 till the catastrophic failure of the 911 and 949 campaign Constantine Porphyrogennetos '*Book of Ceremonies*' reports on. "Crete [represented] a gap in the imperial defenses that the emperors had to close [especially because it was from there] that the Arabs (sic.) had brought other Aegean islands under their authority." (Kaldellis, *Streams of Gold*, 35). For the Byzantine-Arab warfare in Sicily see A. Nef, "Byzantium and Islam in Southern Italy (7th–11th century)", in *A Companion to Byzantine Italy*, 200–224.

19 Nef, "Byzantium", 215.

20 W. Treadgold, *A History of Byzantine State and Society* (Stanford, 1997), 587–588.

21 Cosentino, "Mentality", 73.

22 C. Wickham, "The Mediterranean around 800: On the Brink of the Second Trade Cycle", *DOP* 58 (2004), 161–174. P. Horden & N. Purcell, "The Mediterranean and the European Economy in the Early Middle Ages", in P. Horden & N. Purcell (eds), *The Boundless Sea. Writing Mediterranean History* (Abingdon – New York, 2020), 136–156.

23 Cosentino, "Insularity", 104.

24 P. Arthur, "Alcune considerazioni sulla natura delle città byzantine", in A. Augenti (ed), *Le Città italiane fra la Tarda Antichità e l'Alto Medioevo. Atti del Convegno (Ravenna, 26–28 Febbraio 2004)* (Firenze, 2006), 27–36.

25 This section is based on two recent contributions of mine as centered on the problesm and perspective of insular urbanism: L. Zavagno, "Salamis-Constantia and the Cypriot early Middle Ages", in L. Summerer & H. Kaba (eds), *The Northern Face of Cyprus* (Istanbul, 2016), 159–177 and L. Zavagno, "Brief Notes on the Byzantine Insular Urbanism in the Eastern Mediterranean between Late Antiquity and the Early Middle Ages (ca. 650 to ca. 800 CE)", *JCS* 21 (2020), 63–76.

26 A. Di Vita, *Gortyn in Crete: Archaeology and History of an Ancient City* (Rome, 2000); J. F. & G. W. M. Harrison, "Gortyn: First City of Roman Crete", *AJA* 107(3) (July 2003), 487–492.

27 I. Baldini et al., "Gortina, Mitropolis e il suo Episcopato nel VII e nell'VIII secolo. Ricerche Preliminari", *SAIA XC*, Serie III, 12 (2012), 280–290.

28 S. Cosentino, "From Gortyn to Heraklion? A Note on Cretan Urbanism during the 8th Century", *Byzantina Symmeikta* 29 (2019), 73–89.

29 My starting points in devising the "city of islands" model came from G. P. Brogiolo, "A proposito dell' organizzazione urbana nell' alto medioevo", *AM. Cultura materiale, insediamenti, territorio* XXXVI (2009), 27–45; see also Wickham, *Framing*, 676–678; J. Crow, "Archaeology", in L. James (ed), *A Companion to Byzantium* (Oxford, 2010), 297–298; and S. Loseby, "Mediterranean City", in P. Rousseau (ed), *A Companion to Late Antiquity* (Oxford, 2009), 152.

30 F. Curta, "Postcards from Maurilia or the Historiography of the Dark-Age Cities of Byzantium", *EJPCA* 6 (2016), 96–98; Zanini, "Macro-Economy", 156–158.

31 J. Vroom, 'Limyra in Lycia: Byzantine/Umayyad Pottery Finds from Excavations in the Eastern Part of the City", in *Céramiques antiques en Lycie (VIIe S. a.C. – VIIe S. p.C). Les produits et les marchés (Études 16)* (Bordeaux, 2007): 252–253; 67; E. C. Portale, "The Sunset of Gortyn: Amphorae in the 7th–8th Centuries CE.", in *Late Roman Coarse Wares, Cooking Wares and Amphorae in the Mediterranean* 4 (Oxford, 2014), 477–490; N. Poulou-Papadimitriou, "The Aegean during the 'Transitional' period of Byzantium: The Archaeological Evidence", in J. Crow & D. Hill (eds), *Naxos and the Byzantine Aegean: Insular Responses to Regional Change* (Athens, 2018), 38–45.

32 C. Tsigonaki, "Crete. A Border at the Sea. Defensive Works and Landscape-Mindscape Changes, Seventh-Eighth Centuries A.D", in *Change and Resilience*, 180.

33 C. Tsigonaki, "Les Villes Crétoises aux VIIe et VIIIe siècles: l'apport des recherches archéologiques à Eleutherna", *SAIA*, LXXXV, Serie III, 7 (2007), 296–297.

34 D. Tzougarakis, *Byzantine Crete: From the 5th Century to the Venetian Conquest* (Athens, 1988), 176–177; Baldini et al., "Gortina", 246.

35 Cosentino, "From Gortyn to Heraklion?", 86.

36 A. Papadopoulos-Kerameus, *Vita Andreae Hierosolimitanis. Ἀνάλεκτα Ἱεροσολυματικῆς σταχυολογίας* V, (BHG 113) (St Petersburg, 1899), 169–179.

37 Baldini et al., "Gortina", 256–276.

38 E. Giorgi, *Archeologia dell'acqua a Gortina in età proto-bizantina* (Oxford, 2017), 90–91.

39 According to Di Vita, life in Gortyn came to an end after a series of destructive earthquakes in the late sixth century (Di Vita, *Gortyn in Crete*, 134–137).

40 Tsigonaki, "Crete", 179–185.

41 Cosentino, "From Gortyn to Heraklion?", 86.

42 M. Randazzo, "Knossos and Heraklion in the Byzantine-Islamic Transition (Late 7th–Mid-10th Century). An Archaeological Perspective into Shifting Patterns of Settlement Ruralisation and Urbanization on Medieval Crete", *JGA* 5 (2020), 460–467.

43 A. Laiou & C. Morrisson, *The Byzantine Economy* (Cambridge, 2007), 90–165.

44 Zavagno, "Salamis-Constantia", 165.

45 S. Öztaner, "Salamis-Constantia Kent Planlamasi Üzerine Yani Arastirmalar: Cardo ve Decumanus", *Anadolu-Anatolia* 36 (2010), 208–210.

46 C. Stewart, *Domes of Heaven: The Domed Basilicas of Cyprus*. Unpublished Ph.D. Thesis, Indiana University, Bloomington (2008), 73.

47 See on this M. McCormick, *Origins of European Economy. Communication and Commerce AD. 300–900* (Cambridge, 2001), 132–133, 894–895.

48 W. Caraher & A. Papalexandrou, "Arsinoe in Late Antiquity and the Middle Ages", in W. A. P. Childs, J. Smith & J. M. Padgett (eds), *City of Gold. The Archaeology of Polis Chrysochous, Cyprus* (Yale, 2012), 266–282.

49 E. Procopiou, Τα μνημεία της πόλης και της επαρχίας Λεμεσού κατά την παλαιοχριστιανική, πρωτοβυζαντινή και μεσοβυζαντινή περίοδο 324-1191", in A. Marangou & T. Kolotas (eds), *Limassol. A Journey to the Past of a City* (Nicosia, 2006), 114.
50 J. Vroom, "The Byzantine Web. Pottery and Connectivity between the Southern Adriatic and the Eastern Mediterranean", in *Adriatico altomedievale*, 288–289; N. Coureas, "Economy", in A. Nicolaou-Konnari & C. Schabel (eds), *Cyprus Society and Culture 1191–1374* (Leiden, 2005), 102–156.
51 Zavagno, "Salamis-Constantia", 164.
52 D. Metcalf, *Byzantine Cyprus 491–1191 A.D.* (Nicosia, 2009), 479–486.
53 J. Scott Petre, *Crusader Castles of Cyprus: the Fortifications under the Lusignans (1191–1489)* (Nicosia, 2012), 231–234.
54 Bakirtzis & Zavagno, "Beyond Capitals", forthcoming (see above endnote 16).
55 T. Papacostas, "Byzantine Nicosia", in D. Michaelides (ed), *Historic Nicosia* (Nicosia, 2012), 85–92.
56 Metcalf, *Byzantine Cyprus*, 536–549.
57 Wickham, *Framing*, 789–794.
58 N. D. Kontogiannis, *Byzantine Fortifications. Protecting the Roman Empire in the East* (Yorkshire-Philadelphia, 2022), 85–87, 141.
59 E. Kislinger, "La città bizantina in Sicilia come centro amministrativo", in M. Congiu et al. (eds), *La Sicilia bizantina: storia, città e territorio: atti del VI convegno di studi* (Caltanissetta, 2010), 151.
60 For a full overview of these and other trips with punctual reference to all the literary and documentary sources see S. Davis-Secord, *Where Three Worlds Met Sicily in the Early Medieval Mediterranean* (Utica, 2017), 29–70.
61 Kislinger, "La città", 154–155.
62 Most of the Sicilian *stratēgoi* were indeed dispatched from the *Cubiculum* (the Imperial bedchamber), one of the most important offices of the central administration (M. Nichanian & V. Prigent, "Les stratèges de Sicile. De la naissance du thème au règne de Léon V", *REB* 61 (2003), 133–898; On the *topotereitai* see V. Prigent, "Note sur le topotèrètès de cite en Italie Méridionale durant les siècles obscurs de Sicile.", *SBS* 9 (2006), 145–158. On the Sicilian *kommerkiarioi* and their role in provisioning the capital see Haldon, *The Empire that would not die*, 260–263 with further bibliography.
63 M. McCormick, *Origins*, 235.
64 P. Arthur, "From Italy to the Aegean", 346–367; E. Vaccaro, "Sicily in the Eighth and Ninth Centuries AD: A Case of Persisting Economic Complexity?" *Al-Masāq* 25:1 (2013), 38; Molinari, "Sicily between the 5th and the 10th Century: Villae, Villages, Towns and beyond. Stability, Expansion or Recession?", in *The Insular System*, 104–105.
65 On Palermo see F. Maurici, *Palermo Araba. Una sintesi dell'evoluzione urbanistica (831–1072)* (Palermo, 2015); V. Prigent, "Palermo in the Eastern Roman Empire", in A. Nef (ed), *A Companion to Medieval Palermo. The History of a Mediterranean City from 600 to 1500* (Leiden, 2018), 7–8; for Catania see M. G. Branciforte, "Continuità e trasformazioni di Catina Romana fra Tardo Antico e l'Alto Medioevo", in L. Arcifa & M. Sgarlata (eds), *From Polis to Madina. La trasformazione delle città siciliane tra Tardoantico e Alto Medioevo* (Bari, 2020), 98–102, with further bibliography.
66 D. Sami, "The Network of Interregional Roads and Harbours", in *A Companion to Byzantine Italy*, 263.
67 L. Arcifa, "Per un nuovo approccio allo studio delle città Siciliane nell'alto-medioevo: Catania e Siracusa fra VIII e IX Secolo", in C. Giuffrida & M. Cassia (eds), *Silenziose Rivoluzioni. La Sicilia dalla Tarda Antichità al Primo Medioevo. Atti dell'Incontro di Studio. Catania-Piazza Armerina, 21–23 Maggio 2015* (Catania-Roma, 2016), 418.
68 On Agrigento see F. Ardizzone, "Trasformazione dello Spazio Pubblico di Agrigento: la Valle dei Templi fra Tardo Antico e Altomedioevo", in *From Polis to Madina*, 253–266 with further bibliography.
69 S. Vassallo, "Il Kastron di Castronovo di Sicilia: fortezza o città mai nata?", in *From Polis to Madina*. 246.
70 P. Magdalino, "The Historical Context of Settlement Change on Naxos in the Early Middle Ages", in J. Crow & D. Hill (eds), *Naxos and the Byzantine Aegean: Insular Responses to Regional Change* (Athens, 2018), 23–24. See also on the Aegean Sea J. Koder, *Aigaion Pelagos (Die*

nördliche Ägäis) Unter Mitarbeit von Peter Soustal und Alice Koder Tabula Imperii Byzantini, 10 (Wien, 1998).

71 Kontogiannis, *Byzantine Fortifications*, 97–98; D. Hill, "Urban Relocation and Settlement Adaptation on Naxos from the Early to Middle Byzantine Periods", in L. Dierksmeier, F. Schön, A.Kouremenos, A. Condit, & V. Palmowski (eds), *European Islands between Isolated and Interconnected Life Worlds: Interdisciplinary Long-Term Perspectives* (Tübingen, 2021), 73–88; D. Hill, K. Ødegård, & H. Roland, "Kastro Apalirou, Naxos: A 7th Century Urban Foundation", in E. Ryzos (eds), *New Cities in Late Antiquity* (Turnhout, 2017), 281–292.

72 M. G. Randazzo, "La Transizione Bizantino-Islamica in Sicilia (VIII–X Secolo): Il Caso di Enna e degli Erei Meridionali", *AM* XLVIII (2021), 127–160; C. Bonanno, L. Guzzardi, & E. Canzonieri, "Da Henna a Qasryannah: i dati di scavo nell'area del castello di Lombardia", in *From Polis to Madina*, 193.

73 Randazzo, "La Transizione Bizantino-Islamica", 128–131.

74 E. Giannitrapani, R. Nicoletti & F. Valbruzzi, "Nuovi dati provenienti dalle indagini archeologiche presso la Rocca di Cerere a Enna: crisi e trasformazione delle strutture urbane in età tardoantica e altomedievale", in *From Polis to Madina*, 182–187.

75 Randazzo, "La Transizione Bizantino-Islamica", 144–149; L. Arcifa & F. Ardizzone, "La Ceramica dipinta di rosso in Sicilia", in E. De Minicis (ed), *Le Ceramiche di Roma e del Lazio in età medievale e moderna. Atti del VI Convegno di Studi "La ceramica dipinta in rosso. I contesti laziali a confront con altre realta italiane" (Segni, 6–7 maggio 2004)* (Rome, 2009), 172–176; F. Muscolino, "Da Tauromenion a Tabarmin. Continuità e trasformazione del Sistema urbano e del territorio", in *From Polis to Madina*, 137–152.

76 Arcifa, "Byzantine Sicily", 489.

77 *ead.*, 490.

78 M. Muresu, *La moneta "indicatore" dell'assetto insediativo della Sardegna bizantina (secoli VI-XI)* (Perugia, 2018), 326–465.

79 L. Galoppini, "Overview of Sardinian History", in M. Hobart (ed), *A Companion to Sardinian History, 500–1500* (Leiden, 2017), 87.

80 P. G. Spanu, *La Sardegna Bizantina fra VI e VII Secolo* (Oristano, 1998), 20.

81 M. Stejskal, "Ephesos and its Harbors: A City in Search of Its Place", in S. Ladstätter, F. Pirson & T. Schmidts (eds), *Harbors and Harbor Cities in the Eastern Mediterranean from Antiquity to the Byzantine Period: Recent Discoveries and Current Approaches* (Istanbul, 2014), 325–338; A. Külzer, "Harbor Cities as Interfaces of Maritime and Terrestrial Communication Systems in Late Antique and Medieval Western Anatolia," in N. D. Kontogiannis and T. B. Uyar (eds), *Space and Communities in Byzantine Anatolia. Papers from the Fifth International Sevgi Gönül Byzantine Studies Symposium, İstanbul, 24–26 June 2019* (Istanbul, 2021), 95–110.

82 R. Martorelli, "L'assetto del "quartiere" portuale nella Cagliari bizantina. Dai dati antichi e attuali alcune ipotesi ricostruttive", in R. Martorelli (ed), *Know the sea to live the sea. Conoscere il mare per vivere il mare Atti del Convegno (Cagliari – Cittadella dei Musei, Aula Coroneo, 7-9 marzo 2019)* (Perugia, 2019), 88.

83 I. Sanna and L. Soro, "Nel Mare della Sardegna centro meridionale fra 700 e 1100 d.C. Un contributo dalla ricerca archaeologica subacquea." in R. Martorelli (ed.), *Settecento-Millecento Storia, Archeologia e Arte nei "secoli bui" del Mediterraneo Dalle fonti scritte, archeologiche ed artistiche alla ricostruzione della vicenda storica. La Sardegna laboratorio di esperienze culturali. Atti I* (Cagliari, 2013), 777-80.

84 Spanu, *La Sardegna Bizantina*, 28.

85 P. G. Spanu, "Iterum est insula quae dicitur Sardinia, in qua plurimas fuisse civitates legimus (Ravennatis Anonymi Cosmographia V, 26). Note sulle città sarde tra la tarda antichità e l'alto medioevo", in A. Augenti (ed), *Le Città Italiane tra la tarda Antichità. Atti del Convegno (Ravenna, 26-28 febbraio 2004)* (Firenze, 2006), 594–597; M. G. Stasolla, "La Sardegna nelle fonti arabe", in P. Corrias & S. Cosentino (eds), Ai Confini dell'Impero. Storia, Arte e Archeologia della Sardegna Bizantina (Cagliari, 2002), 86–87.

86 On the archon of Sardinia see the recent detailed account in L. Gallinari, "Iudex Sardiniae and the Archon Sardanias", in A. Metcalfe, H. Fernández-Aceves & M. Muresu (eds), *The Making of Medieval Sardinia* (Leiden, 2021), 210–213. On the inscription see F. Fiori, *Costantino Hypatos e doux di Sardegna* (Bologna, 2001);

87 R. Martorelli, "Le Città in Sardegna fra tardoantico ed altomedioevo", in S. Angiolillo et al (eds), *Corpora delle antichità della Sardegna – La Sardegna romana e altomedievale. Storia e materiali* (Cagliari, 2017), 265–278.
88 Spanu, *La Sardegna Bizantina*, 60.
89 Zavagno, "Islands in the Stream", 165.
90 Possibly even later then for the Taifa of Denia was defeated one year later. E. Fagnan, *Ibn el-Athir. Annales du Maghreb, et de l'Espagne* (Alger, 1898), 51–52. I am indebted to Dr. Jonathan Jarrett for bringing the passage to my attention.
91 P. Horden & N. Purcell, "The Mediterranean and the European Economy in the Early Middle Ages", in P. Horden & N. Purcell (eds), *The Boundless Sea. Writing Mediterranean History* (Abingdon-New York, 2020), 136–156.
92 D. Valérian, "The Medieval Mediterranean", in P. Horden & S. Kinoshita (eds), *A Companion to Mediterranean History* (Chichester, 2014), 82–87.
93 I. Lysen Hansen & C. Wickham, *The Long Eighth Century (The Transformation of the Roman World 11)* (Leiden, 2000).
94 Shepard, "Bunkers, Open Cities", 19–28.
95 Valérian, "The Medieval", 88–89.

9

THE CITY IN THE BYZANTINE 'ITALIES'

Enrico Cirelli

Introduction

Many cities of Roman tradition disappeared in the Mediterranean Sea in the period between Late Antiquity and the early Middle Ages. Almost a third of the urban settlements were abandoned but more generally the concept of the city itself gradually changed starting from the 4th century. Even if the number of attestations and the level of degradation or decline of these settlements take on different characteristics according to the regions and geographical characteristics, the specifics of these transformations have now been recognise by many researchers who have dealt with the phenomenon[1]: shrinkage of built-up areas, new centres of aggregation, private occupation of public spaces, with homes and workshops, burials in the city, ruralization of the town, birth of decentralized religious centres with various forms, and growth of deposits due to accumulations of organic debris.[2]

In northern Italy, for example, the picture is extremely different, and in *Piemonte*, the collapse of the urban system is almost total,[3] and in *Venetia*, 5 of the 12 cities founded in Roman times just over half survive, other areas in the north-east territories are instead characterised by new proto-urban settlements which in some cases became real cities during the early Middle Ages.[4]

The parameters for the definition of these settlements are extremely variable and not always satisfactory, whether we resort to elements linked to the economic sphere or try to delineate their geographical and social characteristics.[5] Even the use of written sources is not satisfactory if we consider, for example, the variety of terms that each author associates with a settlement within the same work, think of the ambiguity that often occurs between *castrum* and *civitas*.[6]

Only the combination of the various elements and the clarification of the material characteristics is perhaps able to qualify an urban settlement compared to other types of sites. For example, Classe satisfies many of the parameters indicated in the literature as characteristic of a city between the 5th and 8th centuries. According to the scholar, the association of three or four of these parameters would be sufficient to qualify a city: (1) defences, (2) road system, (3) market, (4) mint, (5) legal autonomy, (6) a role as central place, (7) a relatively large/dense population, (8) a diversification in the economic structure, (9) houses of an

DOI: 10.4324/9780429203923-12

urban type (presumed different from those of the rural world), (10) a social differentiation, (11) a complex religious organization, and (12) legal functions.[7] Classe in the 9th century is defined as *civitas*[8] or even *urbs*[9] and should in effect be considered an urban settlement, distinct from Ravenna.[10] The settlement has a paved road trim and a well-organized sewer system; a market and warehouses for the storage of food and commercial products, also raw materials[11]; houses with urban characteristics,[12] funerary areas[13] and impressive religious buildings, one with baptistery and clergy palace, patronized between the beginnings of the 5th and the end of the 6th century the subject of donations and restorations even after the mid-8th century.[14] The settlement is also capable of producing a surplus sufficient to ensure the existence of a substantial proportion of non-peasant workers and part of its population is part of the exarchal army, at least until the early 8th century, with an own regiment (*banda*), at the disposal of the Byzantine *strategos*, the *bandus classensis*, listed together with the *Constantinopolitanus, Firmens, Laetus, Mediolanensi, Veronense*, to oppose the army sent by Justinian II.[15]

Other Adriatic cities show signs of a substantial resilience of urban characteristics, as in the case of Rimini and Ravenna, where the transfer of the imperial seat determined a new and impressive development after the crisis of the 4th century.[16]

Goods of all kinds are poured into the city and the region, evidenced by material sources and described by contemporary written records: in addition to oil for lighting and conservation of food, oriental wines, fish and wheat sauces, fine tableware from Tunisia and southern Turkey, cooking pots and other types of pottery from Palestine and the Aegean, Ravenna and Romagna were reached by huge fluxes of marble[17] and precious tissues, metal artefacts and other several types of materials from the main regions of the Mediterranean regions, from the 5th to the 8th century. The birth of Classe as a new urban settlement is accompanied in this region by an overall seal of the system of cities founded in Roman times[18] and perhaps to other settlements linked above all to economic development and the marketing of salt, such as *Ficucle* (Cervia), seat of a rural episcopal centre as early as the end of the 5th century[19] and *Ad Novas* (Cesenatico),[20] as well as villages with a new productive vocation, such as the settlement of kinsmen that developed near Santarcangelo di Romagna, whose toponym survives until the mid-8th century as *pagus acervolanus*.[21]

Ravenna

At the time of the war between the Byzantines and the Goths, Ravenna was in its maximum monumental phase. Churches, aristocratic residences, bridges, roads and warehouses along the river ports were supplied with goods of all kinds, coming from any area of the Mediterranean Sea and from the most remote regions of the former Roman world. This wealth distinguishes it from other European urban settlements. Ravenna and its economy were growing in an extraordinary way even compared to the many cities that saw a period of rebirth and growth during the Theoderician administration. The absolute peak of investments within the Adriatic city is due not only to the Ostrogothic court but also to the Orthodox bishops of that period, Ecclesius, who patronized some of the most representative buildings of Ravenna: S. Vitale, S. Apollinare *Nuovo* and S. Apollinare *in Classe*, S. Michele *in Africisco* and S. Mary.[22]

Archaeology has shown several times how not only ecclesiastical buildings but also numerous other buildings can be referred to this as moment of architectural prosperity. The reference model for these constructions is clearly Constantinople and the great eastern metropolises, even if the architects and workers more generally were probably enrolled in the Adriatic area.[23]

Procopius recalls in detail the conquest of the city by the Roman army, after five years of war and a long siege, solved without a military confrontation due to the conformation and strength of its natural and artificial defences.[24]

From what emerges in the latest research, Byzantine Ravenna is actually an Ostrogothic achievement and that the military conquest by Justinian's army and the exarchal administration consolidated this cultural climate without however leaving an indelible trace in the Ravenna monuments and despite some commissions which must have been of extraordinary importance around the middle of the 6th century, but which have left no visible trace in the urban landscape.

Civil Monumental Buildings

After the numerous interventions necessary to transform and expand the small Roman town into an imperial seat, started at the beginning of the 5th century with the construction of the city walls delimiting an area five times greater than in the past, other important community works have been commissioned by the King of Goths, both by investing in monumental civil and religious buildings. For example, not only the construction of a new and imposing civil basilica, dedicated to Hercules (Figure 9.1), commissioned by Theodoric, but also the restoration of the city's plumbing system, with new water pipes serving the city and the imperial palace. After the Justinian conquest, the city walls, considered solid and defended, thanks also to its natural resources, did not undergo any restructuring interventions. The *Liber Pontificalis*, however, recalls the construction of a new wall circuit, wanted by Longinus (568–575 AD),[25] to defend the extra-wall religious complex of S. Lorenzo in Cesarea. The fortification of Cesarea is also mentioned by Paolo Diacono, built in the early stages of the Lombard conquest. No archaeological trace remains of the intervention and there is no mention of it even in the 10th-century documentation, when a palace for Emperor Otto was built in the area next to the Benedictine monastery and the funerary chapels enriched by the Saxon kings. According to Agnellus' indications, it is a wooden wall circuit, a 'palocopia',[26] a sort of wooden palisade, preceded by a moat in which the two river courses that surrounded the walls of Ravenna and the complex of S. Lorenzo are channelled.[27] After the middle of the 6th century, the exarch settled in the area of the imperial palace. In the site behind S. Apollinare Nuovo, a set of phases have been also associated with the Byzantine period (Figure 9.2),[28] poorly documented and therefore apparently chronologically crushed into a single group of early medieval structures.[29]

The construction of a corridor that leads to an area in the centre of the courtyard dates back to this phase, to the east of which a rectangular room is identified.[30] It put in direct connection the rooms to the south with the central apsidal hall, crossing the courtyard longitudinally. The dating of these interventions, including a refurbishment of the flooring inside the corridor, which is probably associated with the first floor known for the connected room, was probably built in the 7th century.[31] The hippodrome remained in function at least until the middle of the 7th century. It is mentioned in the *Liber Pontificalis* of Rome, in an episode linked to the capture of a Byzantine officer (*Chartularius*), Mauricius,[32] captured and executed by the exarch of Ravenna, Isacius, in AD 640.[33] In the following centuries, the circus is indicated as a topographical reference in documents of the 10th century, and

Figure 9.1 The Capture of the Golden Hind of Cerinea, by Hercules, part of the marble decoration inside the Theoderician Basilica

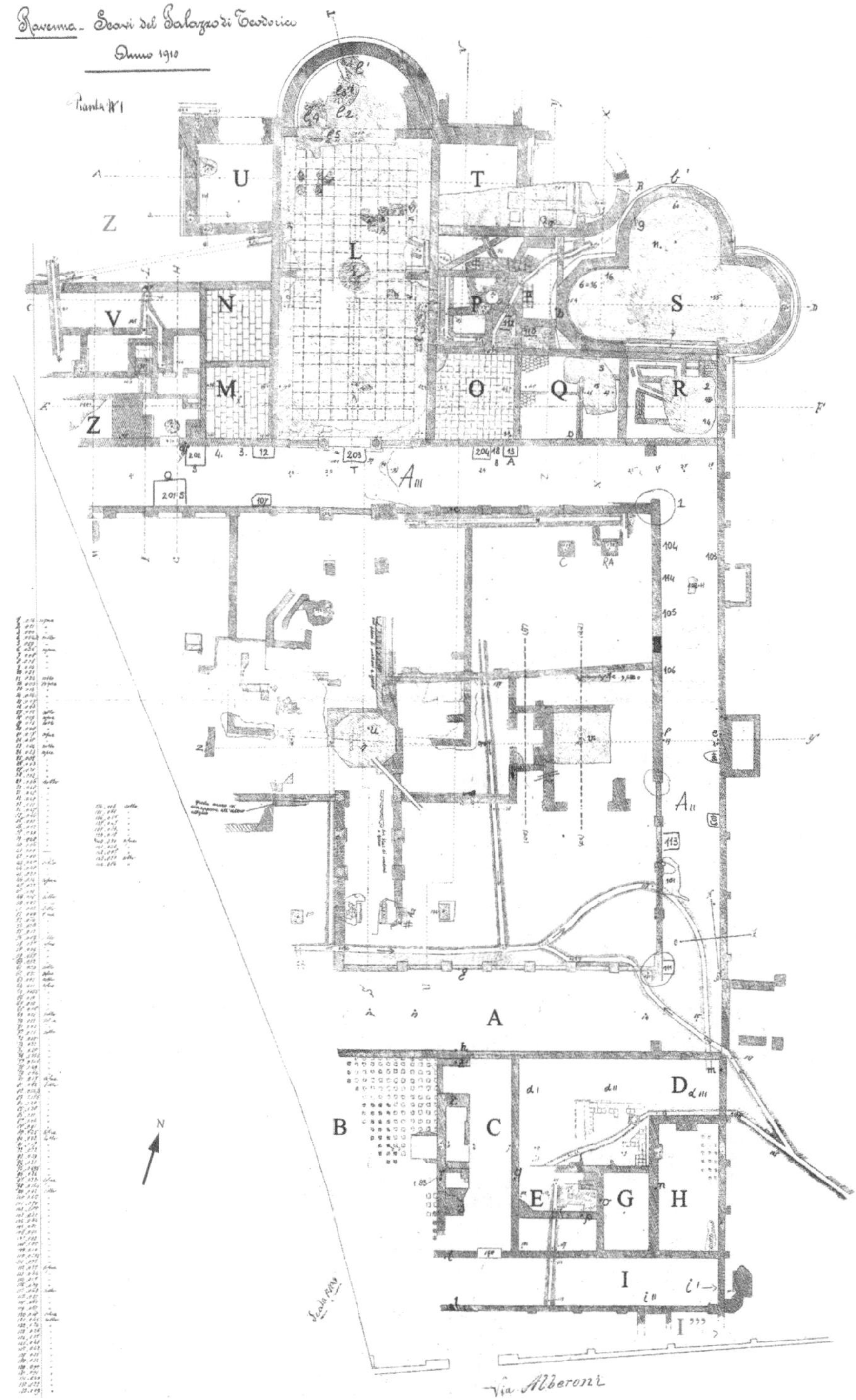

Figure 9.2 The imperial Palace of Ravenna with some Byzantine phases

from its presence, the *regio* where the church of S. Agata Maggiore also takes its name, but in this period the monument is probably already in ruins.[34]

The Bishop Palace

The Bishop Palace of Ravenna is one of the best preserved in the Mediterranean World, but since its date of construction, at the beginning of the 5th century, by the hand of the Bishop Ursus, it was considerably enlarged and enriched also in the following centuries. Immediately after the conquest of the city, Maximian of Pola completed the construction of a tri-apsidal reception room, the so-called tricoli, with the same shapes as the triclinium built by King Theoderic in the imperial palace.[35] Inside the current archbishopric is still preserved the extraordinary ivory chair, donated by the emperor to the bishop of Ravenna, around the middle of the 6th century (Figure 9.3). In the following decades, the mosaic decoration of the archbishop's chapel was also completed,[36] dedicated by Maximian to Andrew, with a representation of Victorious Christ armed to fight and trample the Arian heresy (Figure 9.4). Around AD 540, perhaps patronized by Bishop Vittore, the mosaic cycle of the baths annexed to the bishop's complex was also renewed, also in operation in the Carolingian age and made available to the urban community at least twice a week, according to the testimony of Agnellus.[37]

Ravenna's Bishop Palace had also an *Archivus*, an archive, which kept the registers of the episcopal administration and a *Chimeliarchium*, a sort of Museum-Treasury, which housed the precious assets of the Curia, remembered by Pope Gregory and administered by a high official of the Ravenna clergy.[38]

Infrastructures and Public Buildings

New investments to ensure the functioning of the urban water refurnishing are archaeologically documented in Byzantine/early medieval age. A fragment of an epigraph, found on the floor of the Cathedral, recalls the restoration carried out by the exarch *Smaragdus* who administered the city in the early 7th century, during the government of Emperor Tiberius.[39]

The effectiveness of the water supply system in Ravenna in the 5th century is also demonstrated by the considerable amount of private *thermae* still in use up to the early Middle Ages. In addition to the *balneum* previously mentioned in the episcopal area, used also during the mid-9th century, the *balneum* of the Arian episcope and the heating systems in the southern sector of the Theodoric Palace are also mentioned.[40] Some archaeological excavations have also brought to light a small thermal building in the city centre, perhaps to be connected with a rich *domus*,[41] while in the suburban area, close to the north Gate, an imposing residential complex was discovered, outside the walls and next to the embankments of the *Padenna* river, with thermal spaces and numerous other rooms, of ancient foundation, but restored several times also during the Late Antiquity and early Middle Ages.[42]

Religious Buildings

New ecclesiastical buildings were also planned in the period following the conquest of Ravenna by the Byzantines. The most important enterprises took place during the episcopate of Agnellus (Figure 9.5) and Maximian, while a pause has been recorded at the beginning of the 7th century, probably due to economic and political factors, such as the

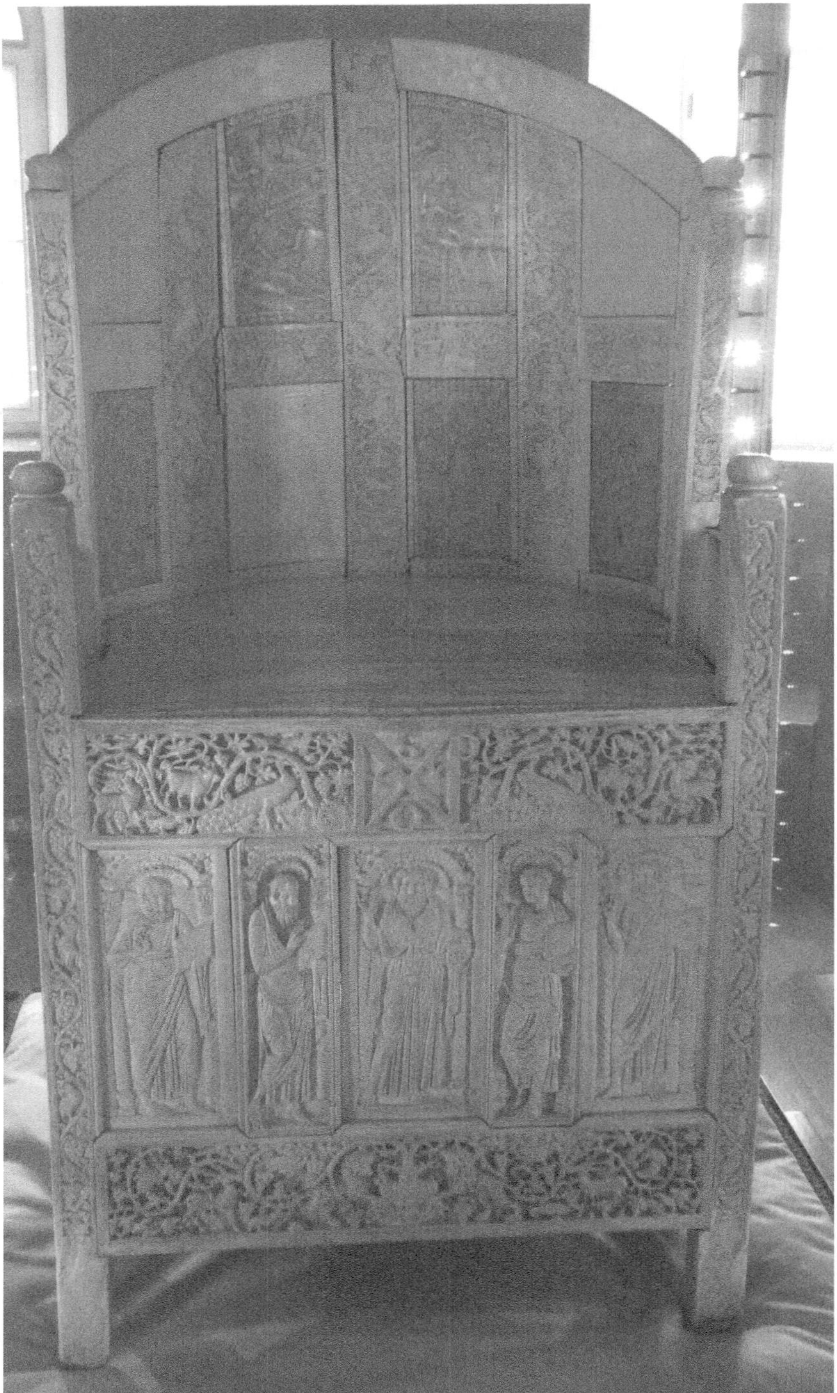

Figure 9.3 The Throne of Maximian (AD 546–555), made with carved ivory panels, Archiepiscopal Museum, Ravenna

Figure 9.4 Polychrome mosaic representing a Christ in Arms, in the Chapel of S. Andrea, Archbishop's Palace of Ravenna

pressure of the Lombards and the antagonism with Rome in the administration of ecclesiastical assets. A second slowdown factor in the construction of new religious buildings was also determined by a large number of existing churches, perhaps now greater than the real needs of the inhabitants of Ravenna

At a time when the economic and political conditions were much more favourable, that is immediately after the conquest of the city by the Byzantines, in AD 540, even if the war

Figure 9.5 Distribution map of the Churches of Ravenna in the Byzantine Period

with the Goths was still ongoing, in the rest of the peninsula, the construction of one of the most prestigious buildings in the early medieval Mediterranean: the basilica of S. Vitale (Figure 9.6).[43] This was probably designed by a Constantinopolitan architect, during the Gothic reign and under the episcopate of Ecclesius and his successor Victor, as evidenced by the monograms engraved on the pulvini, and built by oriental and Adriatic workers who built the coverings in clay pipes, a feature that generally distinguishes a local work performance.[44] The building was finished and dedicated in the early years of Maximian's episcopate (AD 548), under the Byzantine rule. It is a unique building without any comparison in Italy, in some ways similar to the contemporary building dedicated to SS. Sergius and Bacchus in Constantinople[45] and after it a model for several early medieval European constructions. During the same period, the small church of S. Michael *in Africisco* was commissioned by a great banker from Ravenna.[46] The building was built by Giuliano Argentario and Bacauda, later buried in a tower close to the same complex (Figure 9.7).[47]

It is a small square-plan building, derived from Constantinople, with a polygonal apse on the outside and a semi-circular inside, now typical of Ravenna's ecclesiastical architecture. The three aisles were separated by pillars on wide arches, as in the Syrian church of Qalb Laozeh.[48]

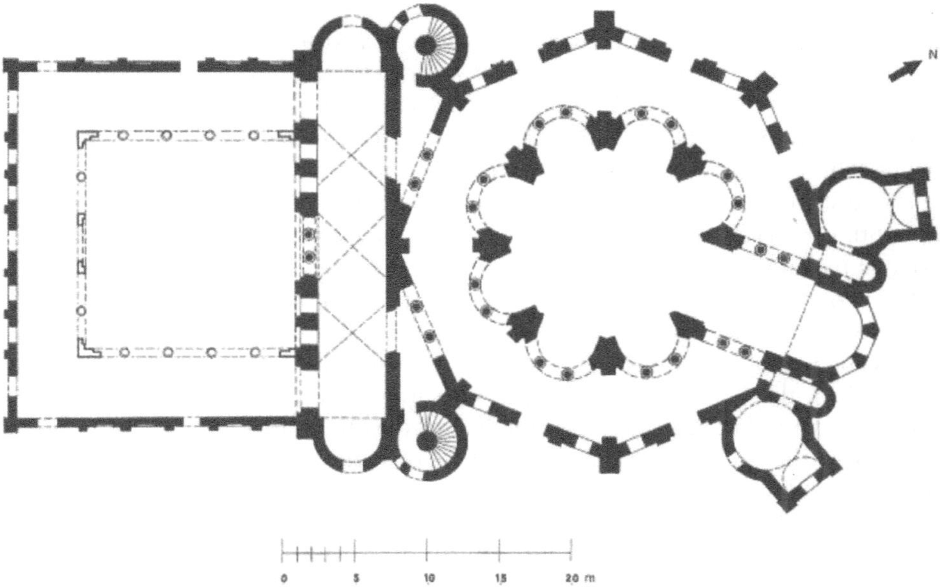

Figure 9.6 S. Vitale, map by Deichmann

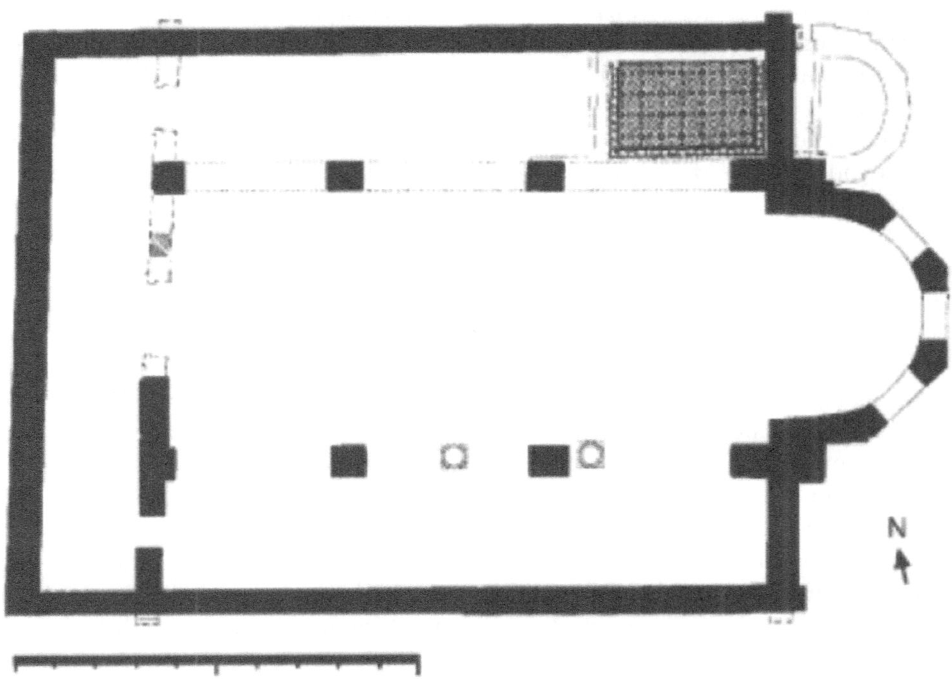

Figure 9.7 S. Michele in Africisco, map by Deichmann

A new church was then built within the ancient urban space, close to the wall circuit, near the *Posterula Zenonis*. This is the church dedicated to Saints Jhon and Paul, where Ravenna's army victory against Byzantines was celebrated in the 8th century (AD 737) (Figure 9.8).[49] Very close to S. Vitale, a few years later bishop Maximian built one of the major and more beautiful Byzantine church, according to contemporary sources and to Agnellus. This new imposing basilica was dedicated to St. Stephan.[50] This Byzantine church has never been found. Damaged by an earthquake in the 13th century and in a state of ruins in the 16th century, it has been supposed to have had a central plan. A similar building, inserted in the monastic enclosure of S. Vitale, is visible in all the representations in modern aerial view of the city in the 16th and 17th centuries. With the construction of this basilica, it must be emphasized that the north-western sector of the city was literally invaded by churches and is configured as the highest religious pole of the settlement. Behind the church of St. Stephan, there were two other funerary shrines.[51] These are two small monasteries commissioned by Maximian in the second half of the 6th century.[52]

Perhaps to the same *patronage* of Bishop Maximian, we owe the construction of the church of St. John *in Marmorato*,[53] in the area of the Coriandro port, outside Porta Anastasia, still not identified by archaeological discoveries, but very important for the idea of a marble warehouse in the imperial city. On the contrary was very well preserved before Second World War the Byzantine church of St. Victor, attested for the first time by a papyrus document in AD 564, possibly of earlier construction (Figure 9.9).[54] It was located in the northern quarter of the city and overlooked a street up on the *Flumen Padennae*. It is a three-nave basilica that has some similarities with S. Michele *in Africisco*, such as the presence of pillars that support the arches separating the aisles.[55]

At the same time, in the northern sector of the city, near the Padenna, the *patricius* Baduario, *praefectus praetorium* at the time of Emperor Justin II (565–578), had a three-nave basilica with an external portico built between AD 575 and AD 577, dedicated to St. John the Baptist.[56]

Finally, a church of uncertain dating is the one partially identified on the edge of a large *domus* found in Via D'Azeglio. It is possible to identify the church with S. *Eufemia ad Arietem* (Figure 9.10).[57]

The church is described by Agnellus in the 9th century, who attributes a restoration due to the outcrop of groundwater to Bishop Martin (ca AD 810).[58] The building is also connected with an episode in the life of the first bishop of Ravenna, Apollinaris, who would have imparted the baptism of a high Roman official, the *tribunus militum* of the city, and of his family members, inside the *domus* within which he was later housed. To the healing of his wife, in a hagiographic text dated by critics between the end of the 6th and 7th centuries.[59] It still remains to be clarified whether the church was built immediately after the abandonment of the Ostrogothic rich house and therefore built around the middle of the 6th century, or whether its construction is not to be referred to a later time, for example between the 7th and 8th century, in the exarchal phase.

Two churches are also linked to Theoderic's *Damnatio Memoriae* in Ravenna and to the conversion of Arian religious buildings into 'orthodox' churches.[60] In the Mausoleum of King Theoderic, for example, a monastic community was established and the important monument was transformed into a small church, dedicated to Mary (*S. Maria que dicitur ad Farum*) with a lighthouse and rectangular buildings, just close to the mausoleum, to facilitate the stopover in the canal port and in the salt warehouses managed by the monastic community. The same happened for the Arian Baptistery transformed

Figure 9.8 End of the 6th-century marble Ambo of Sts John and Paul at Ravenna

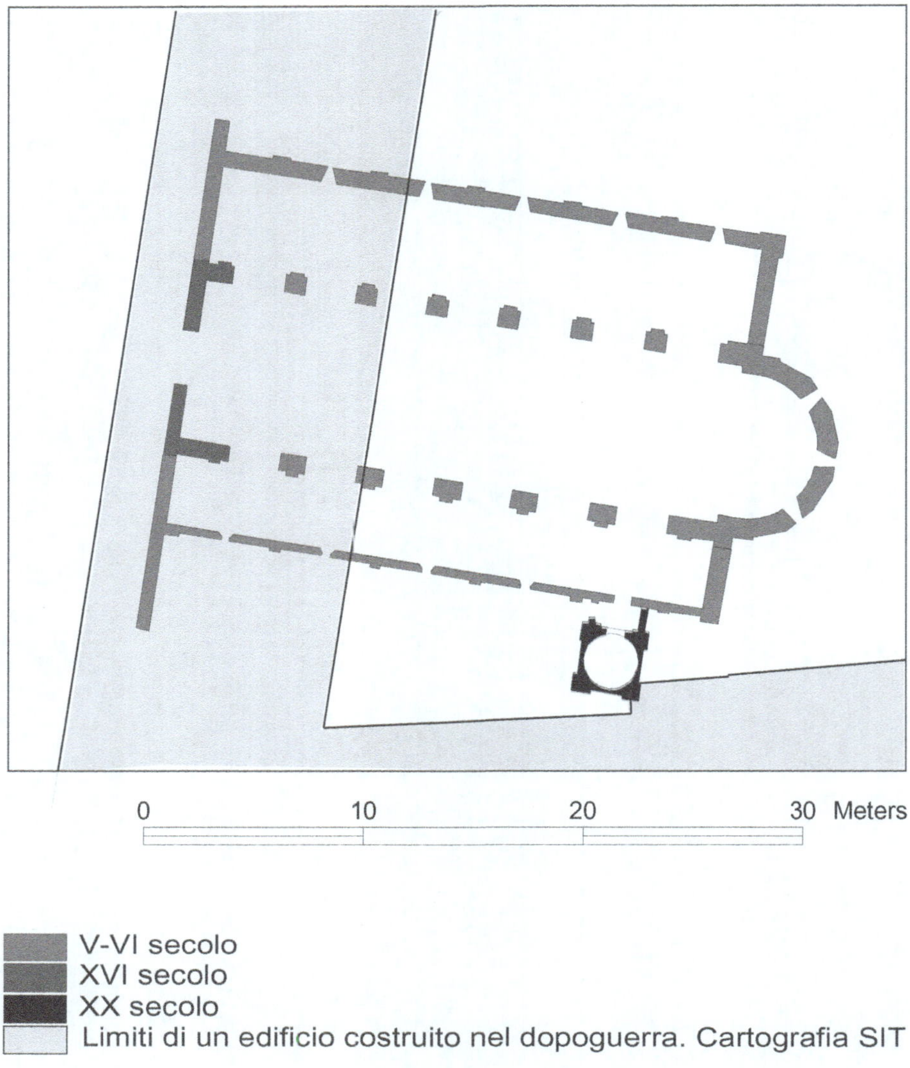

Figure 9.9 S. Vittore, map by the author

under the episcopate of Agnellus, AD 557–570, in the monastic church of S. Maria *in Cosmedin*.[61]

Some important investments dating back to the Byzantine age are also known in the city of Classe and in the extra-urban area, with the construction of the extraordinary basilica of S. Apollinare over the first Ravenna's bishop tomb. The church was patronized by Bishop Ursicinus and then dedicated by Massimian, after the Byzantine military conquest. The building, with polygonal apse on the outside and semi-circular on the inside, is divided into three naves marked by two sets of 12 marble columns. The façade was preceded by a four-sided portico, reduced in the 16th century only on the side facing the church. The building was built entirely with new bricks, such as S. Vitale and S. Michele *in Africisco*.[62]

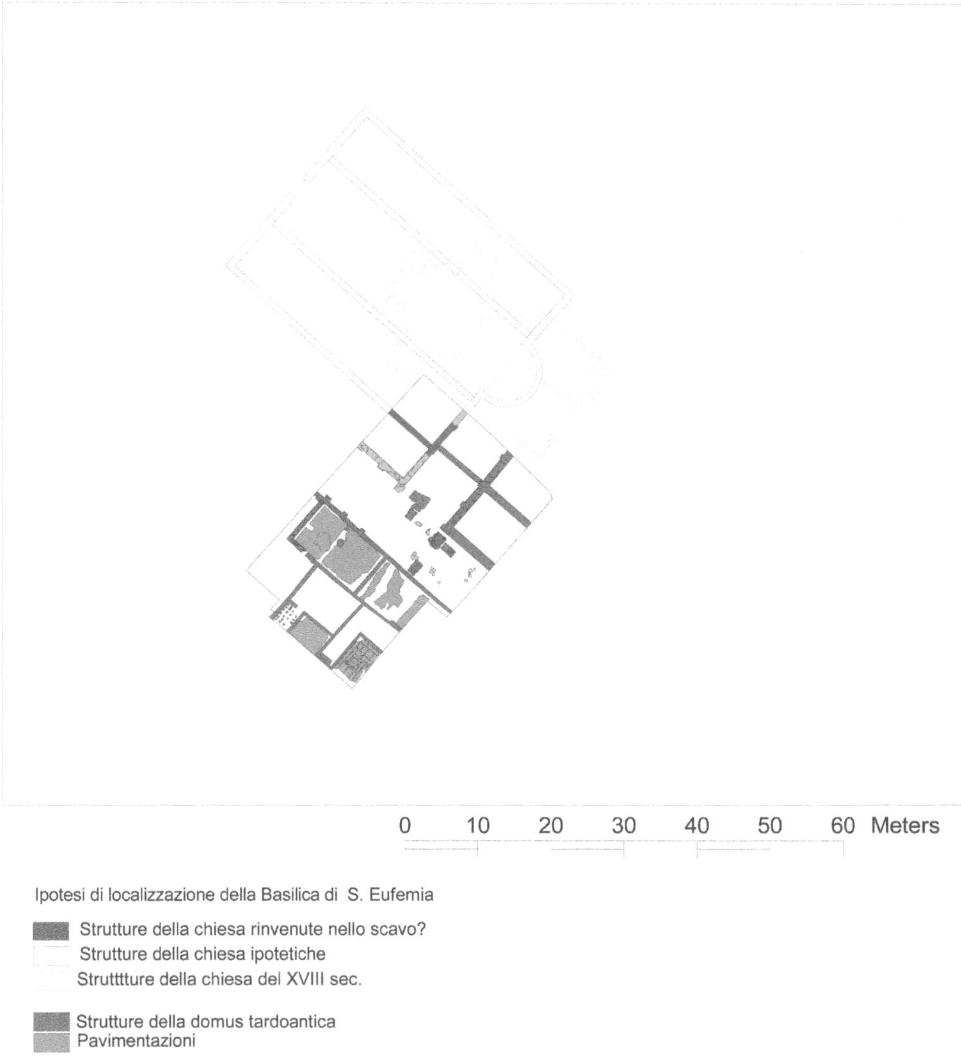

Figure 9.10 S. *Eufemia ad Arietem*, map by the author

The most impressive and monumental building built entirely in the exarchal period is however the basilica of S. Severo *in Classe*. It was built, on behalf of the bishop, in total imitation of the church of S. Apollinare, otherwise though using recycled brick material and extraordinary marbles, coming from different regions of the Mediterranean Sea.[63] The church, a real swansong of Ravenna's monumental building golden age, was built within the city walls of Classe, close to a small mausoleum with a West-oriented apse, that housed the relics of Bishop Severus and his family originally placed on the edge of a private rural house, around the middle of the 4th century (Figure 9.11). From the very beginning, the chapel caused the realization of several burials by the inhabitants of the suburbs of Ravenna and then, from the 5th century onwards, of those of the citizen of Classe. After the construction of the great basilica of S. Severo, at the end of the 6th

Figure 9.11 Aerial view of the St. Rufillo Shrine (4th Century), close to the Basilica of St. Severus at Classe (AD 582 ca)

century, tombs were also buried around the perimeter of the building and the chapel was enlarged and enriched.[64]

Outside the city walls, 6 miles away, perhaps in an area close to a *vicus* or an agricultural center of which there is no archaeological trace actually, a richly decorated church is also built, in Byzantine time, with its own baptistery, the so-called Ca Bianca basilica,[65] possibly to identify with St. Demeter mentioned by Agnellus (Figure 9.12). A second hypothesis is that it is the church of St. Eufemia *ad marem*, remembered for a restoration commissioned by Bishop Maximian, who provided it with a splendid decoration in mosaics. In the archaeological excavations, two very close phases have been identified, the first perhaps dated back to the end of the 5th century, and the second to the mid-6th century.[66]

In addition to the construction of churches and the re-titling of some previous buildings, with the middle of the 6th century, Maximian also transformed and restored some previous buildings, trying to transfer to Ravenna, for example, the relics of prestigious exponents of Christianity, without however particular success, as in the case of the apostle Andrew. On this occasion, however, the original walnut wooden pillars of the building were replaced with columns of precious Proconnesian marble.[67]

In the 7th century, ecclesiastical constructions are less impressive. The religious buildings mentioned for this period are far fewer. Agnellus describes a monastery dedicated to St. Bartholomew in which he himself was abbot and previously governed by Archbishop

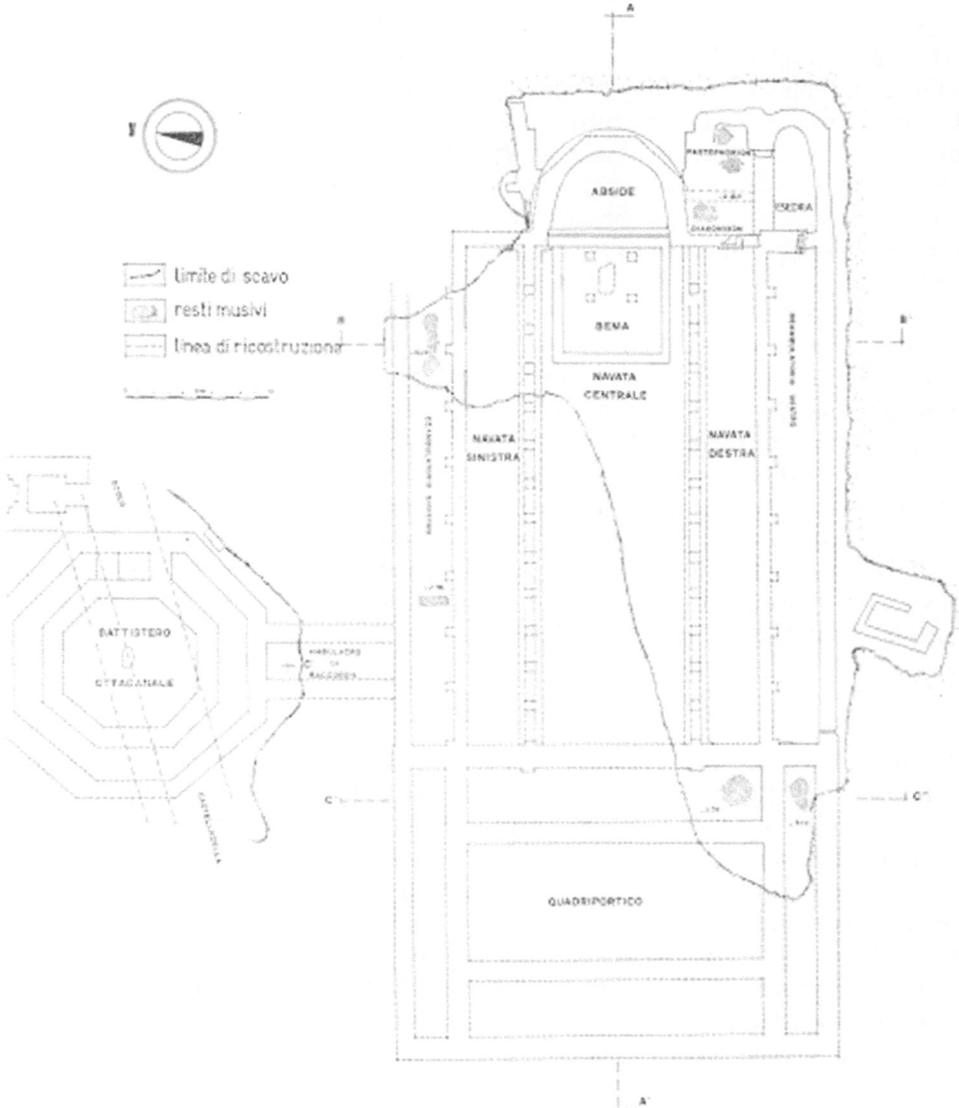

Figure 9.12 Basilica Cà Bianca. Sixth-century church and baptistery found outside classe city walls (2 km by S. Apollinare)

Mauro (AD 642–648), so as to provide an *ante quem* chronology of extreme importance. This *monasterium* stood on the opposite bank to the episcopal complex in that triangle formed by the city walls and the graft of a secondary canal, the Lamises, in the main course of the Padenna, in the space where the Camaldolese monks later built the church of San Romualdo and where the Classense Library is located today.[68] Towards the end of the 7th century, a church was dedicated to St. Theodore by the bishop, close to the imperial palace, and probably facing the monumental bronze gate, the Calchè, as we know from the toponym associated with the building also in medieval documentation, the *monasterium S. Theodori ad Calchi, also called S. Theodori greco in palatio.*[69]

We owe a considerable number of buildings to the patronage of the exarch Theodore. The first is the church dedicated to St. Mary *Ipapanti*[70] and also St. Mary *ad Blachernas*,[71] a church that was located in the suburb of Caesarea, close to the *Wandalaria* Gate, in the south-eastern corner of the city. The exarch Theodore and his wife Agatha were buried inside in AD 687. In the same area, there was also another church linked to the same patron, the church of St. Paul, built on the ruins of a Jewish synagogue, inside the city walls. Unfortunately, no material evidence remains. The only 7th-century religious building whose exact location is known is S. Apollinare *in Veclo*.[72]

Between the 5th and 7th centuries, there is therefore a general trend towards a decrease in the construction of churches. Even apart from the numerical value of this evidence, it is necessary to focus on the different dimensions that the various buildings had. The construction buildings of the first part of the 5th and 6th centuries had to require a considerable economic commitment and have left an indelible trace in the urban fabric. The decline in the construction of ecclesiastical buildings, which is determined in the subsequent period, can be determined by various factors, such as the demographic crisis and at the same time the saturation of spaces for the foundation of new churches within the city. The political crisis and considerable military pressure from the Lombards may also have been influential in this regard. It should be emphasized that the buildings attested for the first time in the 7th century do not return any material evidence.

'Greek' Monasteries in Ravenna

In Byzantine Ravenna, some monastic communities were established for the first time. At least four monasteries are known, but only one certainly housed a congregation of Hellenophonic monks and a *hegumenos*.[73] This is the monastery of S. Maria in Cosmedin,[74] built around the church that reused the Arian Baptistery as an apse.[75] The original shape of the baptistery was characterised by a central octagonal plan, inscribed with four apses oriented at the cardinal points, the one placed to the east of larger dimensions, and probably two doors on the north-west and south-west sides.[76] The building was equipped with a narrow ring ambulatory, with a width of approx. 190 cm, which surrounded it on seven sides. On the east side, the main apse protruded, against which the ambulatory leaned. The three minor apses were incorporated within the annular structure and covered by the only roof of the ambulatory, possibly covered with cross vaults.[77] The date of foundation of the monastery is unclear. It is placed after AD 540, perhaps after the so-called reconciliation which took place in AD 560, but otherwise we have no information. At the same time, the basilica of the Arian bishop was dedicated to St. Theodorus *a vultu*. It is possible that the church was also entrusted to the Hellenistic community, but there is no evidence of this. The term *kosmìdion*, associated with the church, defines a particularly decorated place, 'adorned',[78] but most likely it is a reference to the Constantinopolitan district that bore the same name, where the church of SS. Anargyroi[79] was assigned to the Ravenna monastery by a Hellenistic community. Agricultural properties in the territory of Imola and Forlì are donated to the Ravenna community of St. Mary *in Cosmedin*, and the monastery possibly possessed a vast heritage in the territories of the former exarchate.[80] Other Hellenophonic ensembles could have been present in the city but we have no certain proof. In a passage contained in a series of edifying narratives composed in the 7th century, however, we find traces of the strong political role played by the Byzantine monks. The original Greek text is no longer preserved but a Georgian translation derived from an Arabic text is known.[81] The text describes the events of the pilgrimage of a 'Grecized' oriental monk who goes to Rome with some of his brothers to visit the tomb of Peter and then move to Ravenna where they were received by the exarch Gregory, one of the two we know in the 7th century, they were received right in the Imperial Palace and on that occasion the monk tells of being imprisoned by the Avars and would have been saved only thanks to a miracle. It is therefore perhaps that Gregory who between AD 619 and AD 625 allegedly plotted the assassination of the two Lombard dukes Tasone and Caco rather than the exarch Gregory II, attested in the year 666.[82] The fact of being received by the highest civil authority in Ravenna denotes a privileged position of the Hellenophonic monks in this city, but their properties were then entirely absorbed by the Benedictine communities.

Housing in Byzantine Ravenna

The settlement of the new imperial residence in the 5th century had partially arrested the process of decay and downgrading of urban houses that characterised Ravenna and several Adriatic cities and which continued to occur in the nearby cities of Central and northern Italy.[83] Some buildings are made with ambitious architecture and in stark contrast to the degraded landscape that surrounds them. This is the case of the *domus* in via D'Azeglio, the building identified in via Pier Traversari, and the various complexes that constitute the imperial and the bishops' palace. These new buildings of great prestige, with rich floors (not only mosaics but also marble pavements) and large reception halls, intended for senior imperial officials and members of the city aristocracy, which therefore invests considerable resources, still between the 5th and 7th centuries, in the construction of representative urban residences. Some previously occupied *domus* are also readapted and partially transformed for new housing needs, fragmenting the original units into several small residential units, such as in the *domus* identified in Largo Firenze. However, these are isolated cases limited in time. In fact, more modest houses coexist around them, of which small archaeological trace remains, but which are attested by written documents. For example, thanks to the reading of an early medieval papyrus, we know the existence of arcaded houses, divided into small rooms that overlook courtyards shared with other owners. Reference is made to the well-known 'caenacolata' house, or two floors, registered in a deed of sale dated AD 616–619.[84] The house had 'ahera portici' and service rooms and was flanked by a narrow passage that led to the Padenna, 'androna que perexet usque ad ripa flubii Padennis'. Ortalli believes he can compare this building with a small room identified along the Late Antique Port channel, inside one of the arcades of the warehouses on the Classe settlement, built in reused material and divided by wooden partitions: a small two-storey building with beaten-in clay and a hearth on the ground floor for cooking meals; on the side, there were also other mixed-material buildings destined for handicraft activities. The chronology of this building is fixed around the 7th century, and it is really similar to other early medieval buildings excavated within the same archaeological area. These evidences testify to the transformation of the living spaces of the Roman age, generally closed in on itself with rooms generally arranged in a symmetrical manner. The main nucleus of the house becomes the courtyard, jointly owned with other owners, a structure that perhaps indicates the splitting of the ancient Roman *insulae*.[85] Often in the written documentation of the mid-7th century, open spaces begin to be mentioned: a *horticellum*, with *pistrinum*,[86] probably a private bakery oven, a *domucella* with a small vegetable garden,[87] one *hortus in pergulis exornatus*, facing a public street.[88]

Ravenna is therefore configured as a space where the large public buildings wanted by the new Byzantine administration coexist with the large religious buildings and the residences of the urban aristocracies and the bishop, surrounded by numerous small buildings in perishable material, within a landscape of large cultivated fields, belonging to private citizens and housed within ruins and monuments stripped of the ancient urban layout. The housing fabric also becomes sparser and different areas of the city begin to be occupied by sporadic cemeteries or large funerary spaces close to the main parish churches.

A Different Urban Model

The economic growth of Ravenna and its territory since the beginning of the 5th century and the installation of a large redistribution terminal for Mediterranean trade directed to all of northern Italy, through well-equipped river circuits, are in any case a strong anomaly compared to the framework of other regions bordering the central Adriatic, especially the Marche.[89]

In this area, which is so important for the political dynamics of the entire peninsular order and for the supply of Rome, archaeology has focused above all on issues of abandoned cities, paying less attention to urban transformations. The Marches are characterised in Roman times by a substantial number of cities which according to various scholars entered into crisis at different times and as a result of different traumatic factors, such as the invasions of *Alamanni* and *Jutungi*, invasions of Visigoths, the plague and famine during the 20 years of wars between Romans and Ostrogoths, in the mid-6th century.[90]

The extraordinary network of cities had characterised this territory from the 1st century BC. It had already entered a crisis in the 3rd century and the numerous and subsequent upheavals that crossed it up to the 8th century determined a notable change in the landscape with the birth of new forms of settlement and with the reorganization of the countryside not always linked to the events that characterised the urban centres. These changes, however, are not always to be sought in the geographical characteristics, as is often the case recently, following a deterministic model of human choices, essentially conditioned almost always by nature and by the possibilities offered by the landscape. Settlement choices were also conditioned by cultural factors and the survival or disappearance of many cities in this region was probably influenced by these elements.

Cities in the Pentapolis

This area is generally divided into two different sectors overlooking the central Adriatic, flowing into it after crossing long valleys that branch off from the Apennines, separated by the valley of Musone river, just south of Ancona. This division does not exactly correspond to the division into two regions that characterizes them in Late Antiquity, when the border passed north of Ancona along the Esino river, distinguishing the territory in Piceno (*suburbicarium*) and Flaminia (previously *ager gallicus*), a division still existing during the 'Greek-Gothic' war.[91]

In this region, there were 36 cities: 17 in the north and 19 in the south (Figure 9.13). These are very different settlements in terms of monumentality, demographic consistency and extension of the controlled territory. Abandonments between the 5th and 8th century are

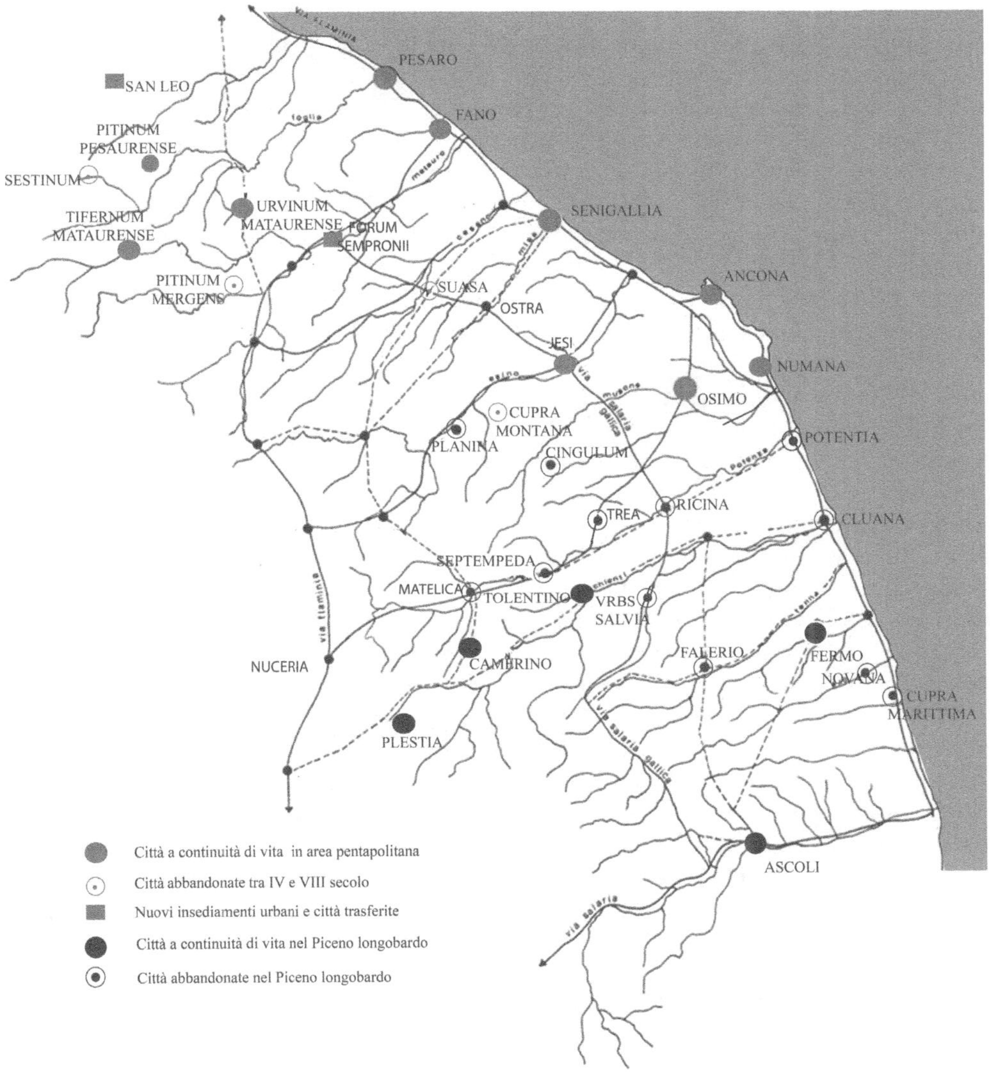

Figure 9.13 Mid-Adriatic early medieval cities (Pentapolis versus Lombard Duchy)

calculated in today's Marche region in about a quarter of the entire settlement system, even if the ways and times of this phenomenon are very different and new archaeological researches are significantly changing the data so far in recent years acquired from the tradition of studies. The town of Potenza, for instance, was considered abandoned until a few years ago following the Visigothic invasions of the early 5th century, while today we know that much of the settlement was occupied with urban features until the 7th century. The site clearly underwent various transformations, such as a sharp contraction of the built-up area, the reoccupation of the monumental area in the *Forum*, with wooden houses, an artisan area and the birth of intramural cemeteries as early as the 6th century. The monumental *Macellum* of the early imperial age was re-occupied by a blacksmith's workshop, in Late Antiquity. Dwellings in perishable materials, in mixed media, were installed within the monumental area, in various quarters of the town and the occupation lasted until the 7th century.[92]

A similar picture is emerging from Suasa, a small town in the Cesano valley, considered by tradition to have been abandoned as early as the 5th century, but where the excavations of the last season of research have shown traces of continuity in the use of urban road systems until the end of 7th century. An area of urban burials has recently been identified, set on stratifications of the 5th century, probably associated with readapted sectors of the large *Domus dei Coiedii*, whose monumental court was reused as a vegetable garden in the early Middle Ages.[93]

The *domus* structures were also replaced by smaller houses and bivouacs.[94] It is probable that more than cities these settlements must have resembled rather agglomerations of houses that emerged from the ruins of the ancient *municipia*.[95] What was lacking, however, above all, is the management of a rural territory that guaranteed its existence in Roman times. The administrative system and the organization of the landscape that had arisen in the early and middle imperial age slowly collapsed and the population of this territory chose different settlement logics. This happened over a long period and perhaps not surprisingly in a different way in the two sectors in which this region is commonly divided. In the northern Marche, which remained under the exarchal administration until the mid-8th century, the cities survived in greater numbers, albeit with the redefinition of spaces, characteristic of all early medieval urban settlements. In fact, if *Sestinum*, *Pitinum Mergens*, *Suasa* and *Cupra montana* were abandoned, perhaps during the 6th century, coastal cities such as Pesaro,[96] Fano, Senigallia, Ancona and Numana survived, but also inland cities such as Jesi, Osimo, Tifernum Mataurense (S. Angelo in Vado)[97] and Urbino, which indeed grew in size and importance, as evidenced by the investigations on the walls of the 6th century[98] and recent archaeological excavations in the *Forum*,[99] increasing its area of jurisdiction within the so-called *Pentapolis montana* and continuing to receive imported goods and pottery until the late 7th century. Closer to the border with the exarchate and perhaps influenced by the economic development that went through this territory between the 5th and 7th centuries, it is also important to point out a case of a new proto-urban foundation. This is the case of San Leo, on the Valmarecchia, a fortified settlement called *civitas* by the Anonymous from Ravenna[100] developed in 5th century and became the seat of an important diocese in the 7th century. Also within this territory another Roman city, *Forum Sempronii* (now Fossombrone), move from the bottom valley to the hill above, probably after AD 560, while part of the ancient city was surrounded by a defensive wall built in the course of the 6th century. Inside the current town, wooden houses and a funeral area were investigated[101] datable to the 7th century, perhaps to be associated with a Christian building built on the heights and outside the city, which helped to attract the town. The dynamics and the chronology of the abandonment of *Pitinum Pisaurese*, where the parish church of San Cassiano in Pitino was built in the 10th century, are unclear. In the area of the ancient Roman city, coins and other materials were found that show a presence up to the 8th–9th century, but no archaeological investigations have been conducted that would allow us to define the forms of occupation at the time.[102] This is in fact the biggest problem facing all urban settlements in the region. Even when it is plausible to determine the continuity of life, it is difficult to indicate the forms of these settlements in the period between the 4th and 9th centuries. Apart from some isolated cases, archaeological investigations are still not very published and often concentrated on the monumental aspects of the settlements. In many cases, groups of tombs or isolated burials placed in association with small houses, on the ruins or even on the rubble of more ancient large *domus*, are reported, as also in the case of Pesaro, in Piazzale Matteotti, where these activities are dated to the 6th–7th century and are located on the edge of roads kept in good condition.[103] The same is also valid for the archaeological area of the Teatro La Fenice, in Senigallia, where the most interesting innovations of recent years come from.[104] Over the looting of a large district of the Roman city, some wooden houses and a cemetery area are set up,[105] currently detached from any religious structure, alongside large areas intended for rural activities, between the 6th and 7th centuries. In this area of the city, frequentations dating back to the 8th century have also been found, thanks to numerous specimens of purified achromatic ceramics of local production and glazed pottery imported from Lazio. In the same layers, there are also examples of soapstone, imported from the Alps.[106]

Outside the Byzantine limes, the phenomenon of the abandonment of cities in the territory conquered by the Lombards is more consistent, in many cases leading to long trajectories of abandonment and decline that began in Late Antiquity.[107]

Cities in Adriatic Lombard Territories

In the territory south of Ancona and Osimo, from the Musone to the Tronto River valley, only Fermo, Camerino, Plestia survived as urban settlements, later abandoned during the Middle Ages and attested as cities still in a diploma from Otto III of 996,[108] Tolentino and Ascoli.[109] Even the maritime cities were gradually abandoned, such as Potentia, Cluana, Cupra Marittima, as well as those of the internal valleys, especially on the border with the Pentapolis: *Planina*, *Cingulum*, *Ricina*, *Trea*, Matelica, *Urbs Salvia, Pausulae, Septumpeda,* Faleria e Novana. It is therefore not risky to underline how the characteristics of the settlement in the Lombard Piceno are distinguished above all by cultural choices with respect to the Byzantine territories, which already in its definition is a territory of cities. Moreover, these are distinctive traits already highlighted by numerous historians. However, it should be noted that this phenomenon of abandonment and more generally of crisis had already been underway in Late Antiquity and Lombards only accentuated the process without causing it, as it happened in other Mediterranean regions.[110]

In this area as well as in the north, the cities had changed considerably, and in recent years, archaeology is increasingly defining the characteristics of these settlements. In addition to the new projects along the Potenza Valley, planned excavations and research are in progress at *Urbs Salvia*[111] and there are many emergency archaeology interventions also in other urban settlements, such as Tolentino and Camerino.[112]

New data are also emerging from the two main urban centers of this territory: Fermo and Ascoli. The city is characterised by large abandoned spaces used as rural zones and in some cases occupied by small funerary areas, since the beginning of the 6th century.[113] Some burials have been found underneath the Caffè Meletti close to the medieval *Palazzo dei Capitani* and other tombs, close to Lungo Castellano (Figure 9.14); large areas, with accumulations of dark layers, found in recent archaeological excavations. The defensive system inherited from the Roman age seems to resist and be maintained even after the Lombard conquest of the city, as evidenced by the case of Porta Romana.[114] The episcopal complex probably dates back to the end of the 5th century, in the same area where the 10th-century cathedral will rise in a decentralized area of the Roman city within the ancient city walls,[115] and that from this moment on, it became a pole of attraction for the urban area. This new pole of aggregation also led to a new road layout which, on the other hand,

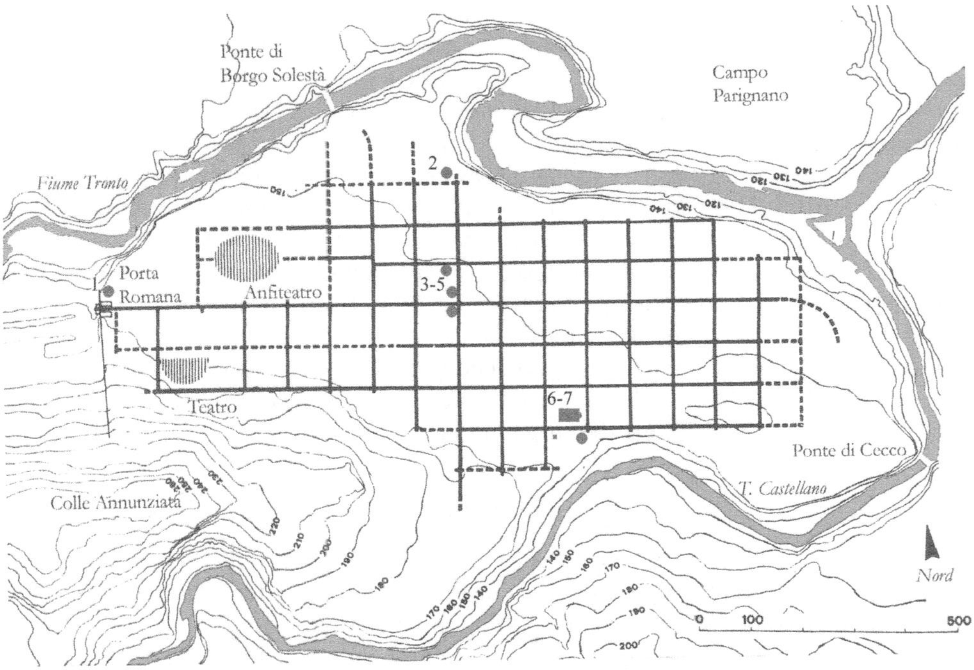

Figure 9.14 Early medieval Ascoli, map by the author

in the rest of the town remains substantially linked to the blocks that had been parcelled out in the Augustan age. There are also homes with the use of perishable materials, inside abandoned Roman buildings and in areas covered by rubble and layers of destruction associated with the phases of conquest of the city in AD 578.[116] The city was ultimately configured like many of the contemporary early medieval cities, becoming a thriving control centre of the territory and as shown by the excavated materials, receiving goods from different areas of the Mediterranean Sea. In spite of the crises and the notable settlement change, the region in any case demonstrates a consistent capacity for receiving various commercial products on a large scale, certainly mediated by the nearby maritime landings and by the valley floor paths, which remained active throughout the Middle Ages. The distribution of imported tableware from Tunisia and transport amphorae from the eastern Mediterranean, North Africa and Sicily, between the second half of the 6th and 7th centuries, is currently similar both in the Lombard Piceno and in the administered territory from the exarch. More uncertain are the data we have for the 8th century, when there are signs of a resumption of amphorae and semi-fine ware circulation in the region, found in various urban and rural archaeological contexts.[117]

Otranto

Compared to other cities observed in the central Adriatic, the topographical development of Otranto after the end of the 5th century goes against the trend, as seen for Ravenna and as it was verified for other centres of the Pentapolis in the same period. The reasons are linked to the settlement, in the small city built on the River Idro, of a large administrative, economic and religious outpost both during the Ostrogothic domination and even later, after the Greek-Gothic war. The city is located on a landing, in an inlet of the Salento coast, on the western shore of the canal of the same name, well connected to Constantinople and the site is placed in control of one of the most important areas of southern Italy in the early Middle Ages. In Roman times, Otranto was the seat of a town hall, with a leading role as a port for the East. Senator Cassiodorus, during the 6th century, describes Otranto as an important textile centre for the processing of purple,[118] and its productive vocation is confirmed a few decades later by Procopius from Caesarea,[119] which underlines its role as a mighty Byzantine fortified city. Otranto becomes a bishop's seat only from the late 6th century.[120]

Formerly the site of flourishing artisan workshops for the processing of wool and linen fabrics, it was enriched by numerous Apulian *mercatores* and *negotiatores*, belonging to the Adriatic port communities and to eastern merchants, among whom was also a thriving local Jewish community dedicated to trade with the Mediterranean Sea. The *Pragmatica sanctio pro petitione Virgilii*, a provision by which Justinian extended his Codification to the Italian Territories (AD 554), testifies how these businessmen were able to sustain, thanks to their income, a tax that was not at all light. Otranto, in these years, became 'Υδρεντὸς': it adopts customs, language, oriental cult and is also the seat of a *Stratigòto*, which represented one of the highest judicial offices in the Byzantine bureaucratic organization chart. During the 7th century, the Salento territories were delimited, to the north, by the so-called *Limitone dei Greci*, a defensive wall built with dry stone and accompanied by fortified turrets which, according to the most accredited historical reconstructions, starting from Otranto crossed the entire territory of Brindisi and Taranto, with the purpose of warding off the Lombard threat.[121]

The city was occupied between AD 680 and 710, and returned under the control of Byzantium in AD 758, taking advantage of the conflict between King Desiderius and Liutprand, Duke of Benevento.[122]

Subsequently, Salento and Calabria are also involved in the administrative reorganization of the territories of the Eastern Empire, with which a new territorial unit was introduced during the reign of Heraclius I (AD 575–641) to replace the ancient districts of Roman memory, such as *Prefectures, Dioceses, Provinces*: Themi, in Greek *θέματα*. Emperor Justinian II (AD 669–711), at the end of the 7th century, organised the Byzantine lands of the South in the Thema of Sicily, also including the Duchy of Calabria of which Otranto was part, while the bishops of the city strongly depended on the Roman Church Administration.[123] In AD 830, Otranto has an iconoclastic bishop[124] and becomes an independent diocese starting from the third quarter of the 9th century.[125] In AD 892, under Leo VI the Wise (AD 866–912), Apulia territories became Thema of Langobardia, corresponding almost to the entire current region, excluding part of the Gargano administrated by Lombards, and distinct from that of Sicily, including other territories taken from the Duchy of Benevento. This huge territory, very productive from an agricultural and commercial point of view, in the following century, became part of the Catapanate of Italy, and 'Υδρεντὸς followed its fate.[126]

The topography of Otranto in the Byzantine age and in the early medieval centuries is still little known. Only through recent archaeological investigations have been identified, in the area called *Collina di San Giovanni* and along the Idro River to the north, as well as in the *Memorie* valley to the south, some cemetery areas, with *arcosolii* and larger environments, and small anchorite cells, referable most likely to the oldest settlements in the area (Figure 9.15). Small rupestrian churches are also attested, such as S. Angelo and S. Nicola,

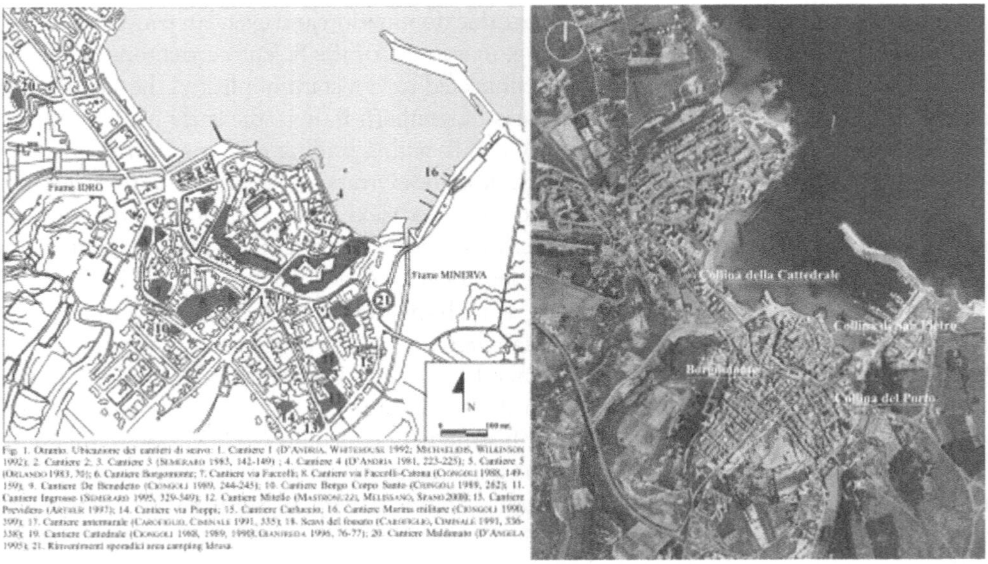

Figure 9.15 Otranto's map, with archaeological discoveries, by De Mitri 2016

of which few remains survive with traces of frescoes (Figure 9.16).[127] Early medieval-Byzantine houses were also identified close to the port area, with a system of urban organization and a new typology of construction method (Figure 9.17). In a quartier called *contrada Maldonato*, near the inhabited area, other archaeological investigations have allowed the discovery of a small funerary church, with pit tombs carved into the rock dating back to between the 6th and 7th centuries. In the area of the altar, a reliquary consisting of two capsules was also discovered, the first, smaller, in silver and the second, larger, in marble in the shape of a sarcophagus, datable to around the 6th century.[128] Few elements of the Byzantine and medieval wall circuit of Otranto are preserved, of which we have information in the useful book *De situ Iapygiae*, written between AD 1510 and 1511, by Antonio de Ferrariis (the Galateo), while a plan of the end of the 16th century reproduces a double wall: the exterior characterised by a thick series of towers; the interior included the castle area and the oldest part of the town.[129] Some elements relating to architectural structures, identified in recent excavations, seem to refer to the path of the outer wall. Other excavations were carried out in the area close to the Spanish walls of the city, where, among other things, moments related to a fortified settlement, developed in the Middle Ages, which returned abundant ceramic and glass material, were highlighted.[130]

As evidence of the strong production vocation, the findings of the fantastic kilns for amphorae and other vascular products from the Mitello shipyard, in the port area, are of extraordinary importance for the Mediterranean High Middle Ages,[131] close to an artisan district that was already active in the 7th century and occupied until the 10th century (Figure 9.18).[132]

The area on which the medieval cathedral stands has also been the subject of archaeological investigations.[133] The existence of a religious building, datable to the 5th century, enriched by a floor mosaic with quadripetal flowers, now preserved in the Diocesan Museum, has been highlighted, and some pit burials with finds from the 6th to 7th centuries have also been identified.[134] The existence of a building preceding the cathedral had already

Figure 9.16 Byzantine paintings of S. Michele in Otranto

Figure 9.17 Sixth-century Byzantine houses in Otranto, via Del Porto, by De Mitri 2016

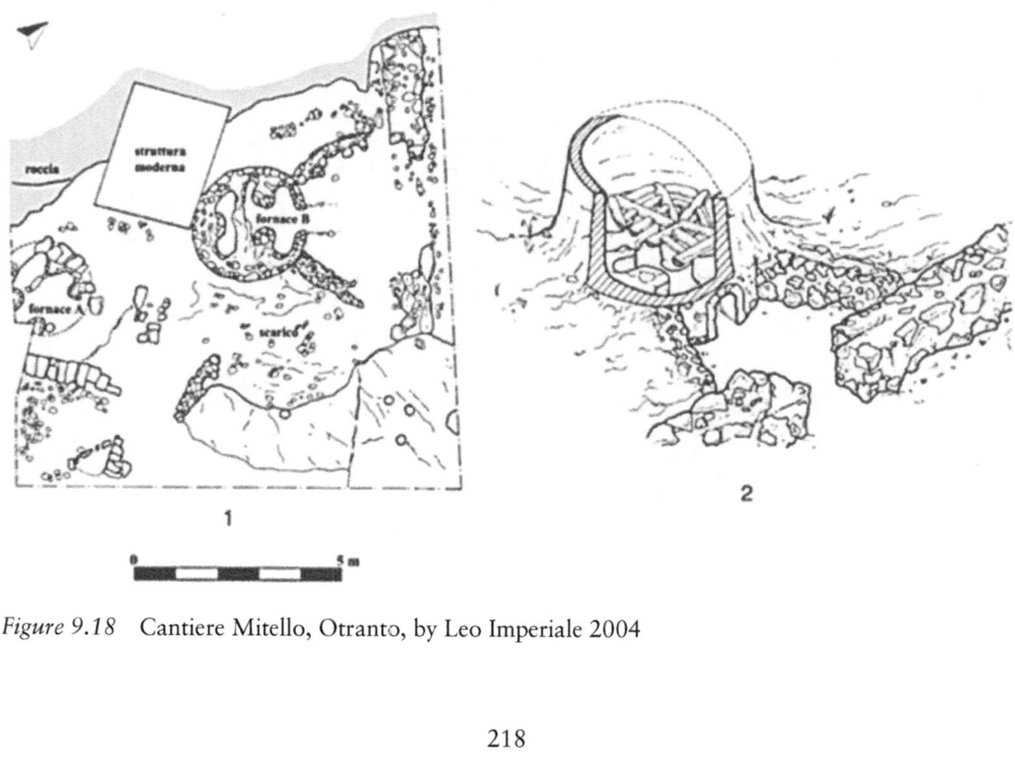

Figure 9.18 Cantiere Mitello, Otranto, by Leo Imperiale 2004

been hypothesized thanks to the *arcosolium* tomb frescoed with crosses, which is located along the staircase leading to the crypt and datable between the 8th and 10th centuries, in relation to the Benevento/Carolingian pictorial world.[135] The church is a very precious jewel of Byzantine religious architecture, and during the Middle Ages, it was dedicated to St. Peter.[136] The ichnographic layout of the building, built in limestone ashlars and tuff blocks, is one of the most extraordinary examples, in Salento, of a Byzantine basilica that appears unchanged and not 'distorted' by the architectural transformations of the following centuries.[137]

The church stands in the centre of the early medieval city, on a small hill, a few meters from the Pelasgians' Bastion which delimits the defensive system of the city to the south-east, overlooking the Mediterranean Sea. Although the presence of a place of worship already in Late Antiquity is plausible, the church is a 'very rare monument of pure early medieval style', built in the 8th century[138] or perhaps after the destruction and depredations of AD 857 due to Muslims' assaults. A new constructive programme is due to Nicephorus Phocas the Elder (AD 830–896), progenitor of the Phoca dynasty, who after having fought and driven back Muslims and Lombards from the South did his utmost in the reorganization of Southern Italy. It is precisely in the context of this reconstruction and re-Bizantization programme of the territory, at the end of the 9th century, when the construction of St. Peter's Basilica in Otranto is chronologically placed. A location that is also confirmed by the architectural style, typical of provincial Byzantine art of the 9th–10th centuries.[139]

The pictorial element is undoubtedly the one that immediately strikes the visitor's eye: the profuse expertise is high, in almost all artist follows the iconic styles of Byzantium to the letter, for a more than admirable result. It is possible that the cycle was pictured by a talented artist of the 12th century, Paolo di Otranto, author of the frescoes of the Eurgetide Monastery, outside Constantinople, from which many monks of the Otranto Greek community of St. Nicholas of Casole came.[140] According to most scholars, the building follows on a reduced scale (Figure 9.19). The model of Santa Sofia of Constantinople: the plan is a Greek cross, with the arms almost the same length (8.38 × 7.98 m); there are two doors: that of the Basileus and that of the people, still walled up; three apses, one central and two lateral, externally decorated with single lancet windows, a mighty central dome, hemispherical, without base (drum), resting directly on four columns describing a perfect square right at the intersection of the arms: everything recalls the magnificent Constantinopolitan Archetype. The columns, both the four central and the four leaning against the walls, are massive and unadorned, with capitals obtained in a single piece and devoid of any plastic ornament: the expertise of the artists dedicated, in this case, to purely geometric solutions, four smooth walls (a prism) with a lot of surface to devote to pictorial decoration. The pulvinus, in the shape of an inverted truncated pyramid, placed between the end of the capitals and the base of the arches, is simply obtained by sculpting the ends of the overlying arches, while still giving impetus to the columns. The round arch dominates everywhere inside the basilica, and given its architectural style, it could not be otherwise. The three apses stand out on the east wall: the central, larger, measures 2.02 m wide, the two lateral 0.96: these are *prothesis* and *diakonikon* intended for the conservation of the Sacred Eucharistic Species, the consecrated Host, to the dressing of the clergy and to the conservation of furnishings and clothing.

In AD 1200, Anthony of Novgorod, a Russian monk and historian, attested that Paul had also frescoed the Baptistery of Santa Sofia, in Constantinople, with depictions of the Baptism of Christ. It is possible that Paul also wanted to pay homage to the hometown of

Figure 9.19 S. Pietro at Otranto

his talent, but admiring the representations that the Basilica holds, we like to imagine it: the Virgin with child in the basin of the central apse, the four evangelists in the pendentives, the triangular bases of the dome, various saints in hieratic pose, such as St. Basil, St. Nicholas, St. Lucia, St. Francis of Paola, St. Leonard, made in the intrados of the arches and on the side walls by various workers in different periods (Figure 9.20). And again, biblical scenes, such as the Tree with the snake and the Shame after sin, and scenes from the life of Christ, such as the Annunciation, the Birth, the Presentation in the Temple, Baptism, the Washing of the feet, the Last Supper, the Apostles, the Deposition from the Cross, the Anastasis, descent into Limbo and Victory over Satan: in short, a pictorial cycle of extraordinary workmanship, which not only guarantees a didactic purpose for the faithful but also makes this monument one of the most shining testimonies, in Southern Italy, of the zeal and artistic, religious and cultural passion that the Byzantines bequeathed to us.

Already the critics, after having ascribed the monument to different periods, highlighted a common architectural matrix, in the 10th century, between S. Pietro, the Cattolica di Stilo (Reggio Calabria) and S. Marco in Rossano (Cosenza).[141] In the Calabrian buildings, however, the internal space is enriched by domes also at the corners and the three apses have equal widths. Generic icnographic comparisons with buildings made in the provincial areas of the Byzantine world and, above all, the examination of the inscriptions painted on the frescoes made it possible to recognise in S. Pietro of Otranto a work of local workers, partly linked to provincial Byzantine models. An alternative dating proposal places it between the end of the 10th century and the beginning of the 11th century.[142]

Figure 9.20 Mid-Byzantine Frescos from S. Pietro at Otranto

Conclusions

After the Justinian conquest and in many ways also in the decades following the Lombard conquest, the Byzantine cities overlooking the Adriatic retain a strong role of conjuncture between eastern Mediterranean Italy and Europe, with maritime commercial control and thanks to the close relationship with the Sicily. Both the documentary evidence and the archaeological materials document a still extremely flourishing and articulated urban life, with multi-ethnic communities and a highly developed civil organization. There are urban archives and magistrates, legal offices and a land registry with staff able to read and write in Latin and Greek, at least up to the Carolingian age. Cities develop with multiple gravitational centres with distinct political-administrative, religious and economic functions. The administrative structures developed around the nucleus of the imperial palace, in the case of Ravenna, starting from the mid-6th century, which constitutes the reference axis of the new early medieval urban plan, overlooking the port area in the case of Otranto around the area of the basilica, expanding the space of the ancient settlement. The religious centre of Ravenna instead develops around the episcope, within the ancient city. The churches will constitute from the second half of the 6th century the main instrument of manifestation and evergetism of the Ravenna urban elites and the religious space will constitute real agglomeration centres within the city landscape, in the areas left free from building and monumental design imperial. The considerable investments and large-scale construction that distinguished the city between the 5th and 7th centuries marked the characteristics of the urban landscape throughout the course of the early Middle Ages. The great buildings of the aristocracies close to the imperial court in Ravenna, such as the *domus* in via D'Azeglio and the large public buildings such as the religious one in Otranto, are the material testimony of an economic power and a manifestation of wealth with few comparisons in the Italian peninsula and in the Mediterranean West of the same centuries. The levels of urbanization and wealth reached at the end of this long century will never be equalled by the city even in the following centuries when it became the reference model of the imperial ideology of early medieval European culture. The shape of these Roman cities takes on a Byzantine imprint already at the beginning of the 6th and will determine their fortune in the following centuries, representing in all respects a golden age, the idealised basis of an identity on which they have still founded the urban communities of these Byzantine Adriatic cities.

Notes

1 S. Gelichi, *La città in Italia tra VI e VIII secolo: riflessioni dopo un trentennio di dibattito archeologico*, in A. Garcia (ed.), *Espacios urbanos en el Occidente mediterraneo (s. VI–VIII)*, Toledo, 2009, p. 65–85.

2 G. P. Brogiolo, *Le origini della città medievale*, Padova, 2011.

3 C. La Rocca, *"Castrum vel potius civitas". Modelli di declino urbano in Italia settentrionale durante l'alto medioevo*, in R. Francovich, G. Noyè (eds.), *La storia dell'alto medioevo italiano (VI-X secolo) alla luce dell'archeologia, Atti del Convegno (Siena 1992)*, Firenze, 1994, p. 545–554, part. p. 550–553.

4 S. Gelichi, *Tra Comacchio e Venezia. Economia, società e insediamenti nell'arco nord adriatico durante l'Alto Medioevo*, in F. Berti, M. Bollini, S. Gelichi and J. Ortalli (eds.), *Genti nel Delta da Spina a Comacchio. Uomini, territorio e culto dall'Antichità all'Alto Medioevo, Catalogo della Mostra (Comacchio, 2006–2007)*, Ferrara, 2007, p. 365–386.

5 P. Arthur, *Naples. From Roman Town to City-State*, Roma, 2002.

6 S. Gelichi, *La città in Italia tra VI e VIII secolo: riflessioni dopo un trentennio di dibattito archeologico*, in A. Garcia (ed.), *Espacios urbanos en el Occidente mediterraneo (s. VI–VIII)*, Toledo, 2009, p. 65–85, part. p. 67–68.
7 M. Biddle, *Towns*, in D. M. Wilson (ed.), *The archaeology of Anglo-Saxon England*, Cambridge, 1976, p. 99–150.
8 *Hist. Lang.*, VI, 44: "Per haec tempora Faroaldus Spolitanorum ductor Classem civitatem Ravennantium invasit".
9 *Hist. Lang.*, III, 13: "Hac etiam tempestate Faroald, primus Spolitanorum dux, cum Langobardorum exercitu Classem invadens, opulentam urbem..."; III, 19: "Huius sane Droctulft, de quo praemisimus, amminiculo saepe Ravennatium milites adversum Langobardos dimicarunt, extructaque classe, Langobardos, qui Classem urbem tenebant, hoc adiuvante pepulerunt".
10 G. Lepore, G. Montevecchi, *Classe (Ravenna), suburbio*, in «Ocnus» 17, 2009, p. 155–157.
11 A. Augenti, E. Cirelli, *Classe: un osservatorio privilegiato per il commercio della Tarda Antichità*, in S. Menchelli, S. Santoro, M. Pasquinucci, G. Guiducci (eds.), *LRCW 3. Late Roman Coarse Wares, Cooking Wares and Amphorae in Mediterranean*, Oxford, 2010, p. 605–615.
12 A. Augenti, E. Cirelli, D. Marino, *Case e magazzini a Classe tra VII e VIII secolo: nuovi dati dal quartiere portuale (scavi 2002–2005)*, in G. Volpe, P. Favia (eds.), *Atti del V Congresso della Società degli Archeologi Medievisti Italiani (Manfredonia-Foggia, 2009)*, 2009, p. 138–144.
13 D. Ferreri, *Sepolture e riti funerari a Classe: una lunga prospettiva diacronica*, in G. Volpe and P. Favia (eds.), *Atti del V Congresso della Società degli Archeologi Medievisti Italiani (Manfredonia-Foggia, 2009)*, 2009, p. 459–464.
14 A. Augenti, F. Boschi, E. Cirelli, *Il sito della basilica petriana a Classe. Dalla diagnostica archeologica allo scavo*, in *Ocnus* 18, 2010, p. 103–116.
15 S. Cosentino, *L'approvvigionamento annonario di Ravenna dal V all'VIII secolo: l'organizzazione e i riflessi socioeconomici*, in *Ravenna da capitale imperiale a capital esarcale, Atti del XVII congresso internazionale di studio sull'alto medioevo (Ravenna, 2004)*, Spoleto, CISAM, 2005, p. 405–434.
16 E. Cirelli, *Ravenna: archeologia di una città*, Firenze, 2008.
17 Y. A. Marano, *Il commercio del marmo nell'Adriatico tardoantico (IV-VI secolo d.C.)*, in S. Collodo, G. L. Fontana (eds.), *Eredità culturali dell'Adriatico. Archeologia, storia, lingua e letteratura*, Roma, 2008, p. 159–174, part. p. 163.
18 A. Augenti, E. Cirelli, *From suburb to port: the rise (and fall) of Classe as a centre of trade and redistribution*, in S. Keay (ed.), *Rome, Portus and the Mediterranean*, Oxford, 2012, p. 205–221.
19 S. Santoro Bianchi, *Un paese d'acque: il territorio cervese nell'antichità*, in O. Maroni, A. Turchini (eds.), *Cervia, natura e storia*, Cervia, 1988, p. 63–117, part. p. 103–104.
20 D. Sami, *Archeologia a Cesenatico. Lo stato delle ricerche e prospettive per il futuro*, in *Studi Romagnoli* LXI (2010), 2011, p. 11–35.
21 *Cod. Bav.*, *Breviarum ecclesiae Ravennatis (Codice Bavaro) secoli VII-X*, a cura di C. Curradi, G. Rabotti, A. Vasina, Roma, 1985, part. p. 34, anni c. 748–769; M. L. Stoppioni, *Romagna sud-orientale e appenninica: imitazioni fittili di ceramiche da mensa e di stoviglie metalliche da portata nella tarda Antichità*, in E. Cirelli, F. Diosono, H. Patterson (eds.), *Le forme della crisi. Produzioni ceramiche e commerci nell'Italia centrale tra romani e longobardi (III-metà VIII sec.), Atti del Convegno di Spoleto (2012)*, Ravenna, 2015, p. 63–74.
22 D. Mauskopf Deliyannis, *Ravenna in Late Antiquity*. Cambridge, 2010, p. 123–124; J. Herrin, *Ravenna. Capital of Empire, Crucible of Europe*, London 2020.
23 E. Russo, *L'architettura di Ravenna paleocristiana*, Venezia 2003.
24 Proc., Bell. Goth., II. 28–29.
25 The date of his death is not known, but it is still attested in 574–575 by a funerary epigraph: *CIL* 11, 00317 = *ILCV* 00622 (add).
26 'Tunc illis temporibus in Cesarea iuxta Ravena (sic) a Longino prefecto palocopiam in modum muri, propter metum gentis, extructa est', in Andrea Agnellus, *Liber Pontificalis Ravennatis Ecclesiae*, in O. Holder Egger (ed.), *Monumenta Germaniae Historica*, *Scriptores Rerum Langobardicarum et Italicarum saec. VI-IX*, Hannoverae 1878, p. 265–391, part. p. 320, by now cit. as *LP*.
27 D. Mauskopf Deliyannis (ed.), *Agnellus Ravennas, Liber pontificalis Ecclesiae Ravennatis,* Thurnout, 2006, p. 369, n. 81.
28 E. Cirelli, *Palazzi e luoghi del potere a Ravenna e nel suo territorio tra tarda Antichità e alto Medioevo (V-X sec.)*, in *Hortus Artium Medievalium* 25, 2019, p. 283–299.

29 G. Ghirardini, *Gli scavi del palazzo di Teodorico a Ravenna*, in *Monumenti Antichi dell'Accademia dei Lincei*, 24, 1917 (1918), p. 737–838, part. p. 742.
30 P. Novara, Palatium, *Le ricerche archeologiche nelle proprietà dei Salesiani attraverso le relazioni di scavo di Gaetano Nave (1911–1915)*, Ravenna, 2001, p. 15.
31 F. Berti, *Mosaici antichi in Italia*, Aemilia, *Ravenna*, Roma, 1976, p. 39.
32 S. Cosentino, *Prosopografia dell'Italia bizantina (493–804)*, Bologna, 2000, *ad vocem Mauricius chartularius*, II, G-O, 356–357.
33 *LP*, 332, "*...et posteaquam decollatus est, levantes caput eius duxerunt eum Ravenna. Videns autem Isacius caput Mauricii, gavisus est et fecit eum ad exemplum multorum in circo ravennate in stipitem poni*". See also S. Cosentino, *L'iscrizione ravennate dell'esarca Isacio e le guerre di Rotari*, in *Atti e Memorie della Deputazione di storia Patria per le Antiche Province Modenesi*, ser. 11a, 15, 1993, p. 23–43, part. p. 34–35.
34 G. Vespignani, *Il Circo di Costantinopoli Nuova Roma*, Spoleto, 2001, p. 98.
35 F. W. Deichmann, *Ravenna. Hauptstadt des spätantiken Abendlandes, Kommentar II/1*, Wiesbaden 1974, p. 197.
36 P. Verzone, *Il Palazzo arcivescovile e l'oratorio di S. Andrea di Ravenna*, in *CARB*, 13, 1966, p. 445–454.
37 Cirelli, *Ravenna..., cit.* (n. 16), p. 77.
38 Greg., *Epist.* IX, 124.
39 *CIL* XI, 11 "...CIPID(ICUS) PIVS FEL(IX) INCI. VICT(OR) A .../... FVISSE AD NECESSARIAM N .../... ACVAEDVCTVM EIVSD(EM) CIVI(TATEM).../...CONSTITVTA SMARAGDVM V...". See also: S. Gelichi, *Il paesaggio urbano tra V e X secolo*, in A. Carile (ed.), *Storia di Ravenna. Dall'età bizantina all'età ottoniana. II. 1. Territorio, economia e società*, Venezia, 1991, p. 153–165, part. p. 159; Cirelli, *Ravenna, cit.* (n. 16), p. 260.
40 Ghirardini, *Gli scavi, cit.* (n. 29), p. 234.
41 V. Manzelli, *Ravenna*, Roma, 2000, p. 126.
42 M. G. Maioli, *Ravenna, via S. Alberto. Impianto termale romano e Impianto termale bizantino*, in L. Prati (ed.), Flumen Aquaeductus. *Nuove scoperte archeologiche dagli scavi per l'acquedotto della Romagna*, Imola, 1988, p. 85-90.
43 F. W. Deichmann, *Studi sulla Ravenna scomparsa*, in *FR*, 103–104, 1972, p. 61–112, part. p. 67–70.
44 E. Cirelli, *Bricks for Ravenna: Materials and the Construction of a Late Antique Imperial Residence*, in S. Cosentino (ed.), *Ravenna and the Traditions of Late Antique and Early Byzantine Craftsmanship,* Berlin, 2020, p. 153–194.
45 R. Krautheimer, *Early Christian and Byzantine architecture,* Suffolk-Wisbech, 1965, p. 161.
46 Cirelli, *Bricks for Ravenna, cit.* (n. 44).
47 *LP*, 329-330, "...in archa saxea non longe ab ipsa arcangeli eclesia infra turem Bacauda requiescit". See also P. Grossmann, *S. Michele in Africisco zu Ravenna*, Mainz 1973.
48 Krautheimer, *Early Christian, cit.* (n. 45), p. 160.
49 Cirelli, *Ravenna, cit.* (n. 16), p. 238.
50 M. Mazzotti, *Ferrettiana, notizie di storia e archeologia ravennate*, in *FR*, 18, 1955, p. 36–48.
51 G. Cortesi, *I principali edifici sacri ravennati in funzione sepolcrale nei secc. V e VI*, in *CARB*, 29, 1982, p. 63–107, part. p. 105.
52 *LP, 192:* 'Ad latera vero ipsius basilice [Maximianus] monasteria parva subiunxit'.
53 P. Novara, *L'ubicazione di un gruppo di chiese ravennati in alcune mappe di età moderna,* in *Studi Romagnoli* 44, p. 61–81.
54 N. Lombardini, *I restauri della chiesa di San Vittore a Ravenna*, in *Ravenna Studi e Ricerche* 5, 1998, p. 75–106.
55 T. Kirova, *La distrutta chiesa di S. Vittore a Ravenna*, in *FR*, 105-106, p. 65–106.
56 Cirelli, *Ravenna, cit.* (n. 16), p. 234.
57 P. Novara, *Storia delle scoperte archeologiche di Ravenna e Classe*, Ravenna, 1998, p. 60–62.
58 *Passio Sancti Apolenaris*, Bibliotheca Hagiographica Latina antiquae et mediae aetatis. Novum Supplementum, edited by H. Fros, Bruxelles 1986 (Subsidia hagiographica 70), p. 623–630. See also: G. Orioli, *La* Passio sancti Apolenaris *secondo il codice metropolitano*, in «Ravenna Studi e Ricerche», 8 (2001), 2002, p. 13–62, part. p. 37–38.
59 I. Baldini Lippolis, *La chiesa di S. Eufemia* ad Arietem, in G. Montevecchi (ed.), *Archeologia urbana a Ravenna,* 2004, p. 71–73.

60 M.C. Carile, E. Cirelli, *Architetture e decoro del complesso vescovile ariano: ipotesi ricostruttive e modelli di riferimento*, in G. Garzia, A. Iannucci, M. Vandini (eds.), *Il patrimonio culturale tra conoscenza, tutela e valorizzazione. Il caso della Piazzetta degli Ariani di Ravenna*, Bologna, p. 97–127.
61 J. Biarne, *L'influence des Monastères sur le paysage urbain en Occident (IVe-VIIe siècles)*, in B. Beaujeard (ed.), *La naissance de la ville chrétienne. Mélanges en hommage à Nancy Gauthier*, Tours 2002, p. 122–134.
62 Cirelli, *Bricks for Ravenna, cit* (n. 44).
63 H. Tůmová *et. al.*, *Late Antique marble trade in the new light of stone artefacts study from the San Severo complex (Ravenna, Italy)*, in Geological Society, London, Special Publications, 416, 2016, p. 1–13.
64 D. Ferreri, *Spazi cimiteriali, pratiche funerarie e identità nella città di Classe*, in *Archeologia Medievale*, 28, 2011, p. 59–74.
65 G. Bovini, *Note sull'edificio paleocristiano di culto rinvenuto nel 1965 a 2 km a sud di S. Apollinare in Classe*, in *FR*, 93, 1966, p. 104–115.
66 '..quam Maximianus pontifex tessellis variis mire ornavit', *LP*, 282.
67 'Eclesiam vero beati Andree apostoli, hic Ravene, cum omni diligencia non longe a regione Herculana, columnas marmoreas suffulsit, ablatasque vetustaa ligneas de nucibus, proconisas decoravit' *LP*, 329.
68 Cirelli, *Ravenna, cit.* (n. 16), p. 106, fig. 87.30.
69 A. Zirardini, *De antiquis sacris Ravennae aedificiis. Liber posthumus*, Ravenna, 1908-1909, p. 138–139.
70 Deichmann, *Studi, cit.* (n. 43), p. 73–74.
71 P. Novara, Ad religionis claustrum construendum. *Monasteri nel medioevo ravennate: storia e archeologia*, Ravenna, 2003, p. 30.
72 Zirardini, *De antiquis, cit.* (n. 69), p. 133–134.
73 J. M. Sansterre, *Monaci e monasteri greci a Ravenna,* in A. Carile (ed.), *Storia di Ravenna, vol. II/2, Dall'età bizantina all'età ottoniana. Ecclesiologia, cultura e arte*, Venezia, 1992, p. 323–329.
74 Deichmann, *Ravenna, cit.* (n. 35), p. 252.
75 E. Cirelli, *Monasteri greci a Ravenna nell'alto Medioevo (VI-X sec.): storia e archeologia,* in F. Marazzi, C. Raimondo (eds.), *Monasteri italo-greci (secoli VII-XII). Una lettura archeologica, Atti del Convegno di Studi in Internazionale (Squillace, 2018)*, Napoli, 2019, p. 15–25.
76 G. Gerola, *Il restauro del battistero ariano di Ravenna*, in H. Glück (ed.), *Studien zur Kunst des Ostens. Josef Strzygowski zum sechzigsten Geburtstage von seinen Freunden und Schülern*, Wien-Hellerau, 1923, p. 112–129.
77 C. Rizzardi, *Il mosaico a Ravenna. Ideologia e arte,* Bologna, 2011, p. 82.
78 D. Mallardo, *Il calendario marmoreo di Napoli,* Roma, 1947, p. 133.
79 C. Loessel Connor, *Saints and Spectacle: Byzantine Mosaics in Their Cultural Setting*, Oxford, 2015, p. 115.
80 A. Vasina, *Per una storia del monachesimo in Emilia Romagna,* in G. Spinelli (ed.), *Monasteri benedettini in Italia,* Milano, 1980, p. 9–15, part. p. 10.
81 G. Garitte, *«Histoire édifiantes» géorgiennes*, in *Byzantion*, XXXVI, 1966, p. 396–423, part. p. 408–410.
82 V. von Falkenhausen, *I rapporti dei ceti dirigenti romani con Costantinopoli dalla fine del V secolo alla fine del VI secolo*, in G. G. Archi (ed.), *Il mondo del diritto all'epoca giustinianea. Caratteri e problematiche*, Ravenna, 1985, p. 90.
83 J. Ortalli, *L'insediamento residenziale urbano nella Cispadana*, in M. Heinzelmann, J. Ortalli (eds.), *Abitare in città. La Cisalpina tra impero e medioevo*, Roma, 2003, p. 95–119, part. p. 114–115.
84 J. O. Tjäder, *Die nichtliterarischen lateinischen Papyri Italiens aus der Zeit 445-700*, Lund-Stockolm, 1954–1982, II, 38–41.
85 J. Ortalli, *L'edilizia abitativa*, in Carile, *Storia di Ravenna, cit.* (n. 27), p. 167–192, part. p. 181.
86 Tjäder, *Die nichtliterarischen, cit.* (n. 84), I, 21.
87 Tjäder, *Die nichtliterarischen, cit.* (n. 84), I, 25.
88 Tjäder, *Die nichtliterarischen, cit.* (n. 84), I, 24.
89 E. Cirelli, E. Giorgi, G. Lepore (eds.), *Economia e Territorio nell'Adriatico centrale*, Oxford, 2019.

90 P. L. Dall'Aglio, *La viabilità nelle Marche tra età romana e primo medioevo*, in E. Menestò (ed.), *Ascoli e le Marche tra tardoantico e altomedioevo, Atti del Convegno di studio (Ascoli Piceno 2002)*, Spoleto, 2004, p. 63–98.
91 S. Bocci, *Le Marche nelle fonti storico-letterarie tra V e VI secolo*, in *Ascoli, cit.* (n. 90), p. 27–61, part. p. 29.
92 F. Carboni, F. M. R. Vermeulen, *Il ruolo della colonia costiera di Potentia nell'ambito delle rotte adriatiche tra IV e VII secolo*, in Cirelli, Giorgi, Lepore, *Economia*, cit. (n. 89), p. 351–358.
93 E. Giorgi, G. Lepore (eds.), *Archeologia nella valle del Cesano da Suasa a Santa Maria in Portuno, Atti del Convegno (Castelleone di Suasa, Corinaldo, San Lorenzo in Campo 2008)*, Bologna, 2010.
94 M. Destro, *L'abbandono delle città interne delle Marche settentrionali tra età romana e altomedioevo*, in *Ascoli*, cit. (n. 90), p. 99–121, part. p. 112.
95 E. Giorgi, *Le Marche tra Tarda Antichità e Alto Medioevo*, in Cirelli, Giorgi, Lepore, *Economia*, cit. (n. 89), p. 20–31.
96 D. Sacco, *Da* Pisaurum *a Pesaro. Lettura archeologica e storico artistica sull'evoluzione del tessuto urbano e dei monumenti*, Urbino, 2013.
97 N. Alfieri, *Le Marche e la fine del mondo antico*, in *Istituzioni e società nell'alto Medioevo marchigiano*, in *Atti e Memorie della Deputazione di Storia Patria delle Marche* 86 (1981), Ancona, 1983, p. 9–34.
98 M. Luni, A. L. Ermeti, *Le mura di Urbino tra tardoantico e Medioevo*, in S. Gelichi (ed.), *Atti del I Congresso nazionale di Archeologia Medievale (Pisa 1997)*, Firenze, 1997, p. 45–50.
99 M. Luni, *Dal* Forum *di* Urvinum Mataurense *alla "Platea magna" di Urbino in età ducale: la Piazza Duca Federico "ritrovata"*, Urbino, 2009.
100 *An. Rav.* IV 33, 19.
101 M. C. Profumo, *Archeologia funeraria e insediamento nelle Marche nei secoli VI e VII*, in L. Paroli (ed.), *L'Italia centro-settentrionale in età longobarda, Atti del Convegno (Ascoli Piceno, 1995)*, Firenze, 1997, p. 55–80, part. p. 60–61.
102 W. Monacchi (ed.), *Storia e archeologia di* Pitinum Pisaurense, San Leo, 1999.
103 G. Baldelli, M. Destro, E. Giorgi, *La* domus *di Piazzale Matteotti a Pesaro*, in *Ocnus* 9–10, 2002, p. 263–267.
104 G. Lepore *et al.*, *Progetto "archeologia urbana a Senigallia" II: le ricerche di via Baroccio e via Gherardi*, in *The Journal of Fasti online* 265, 2012, p. 1–30.
105 M. Salvini, *Area archeologica e Museo La Fenice. Guida*, Senigallia, 2003.
106 E. Cirelli, G. Lepore, M. Silani, *Ceramica e vita quotidiana a Senigallia tra Medioevo ed età moderna: il caso di Via Gherardi*, in *Facta. A Journal of Late Roman, Medieval and Post-medieval Material Culture Studies* 7 (2013), 2016, p. 37–54.
107 Destro, *L'abbandono delle città, cit.* (n. 94), p. 115.
108 *Ottonis II et III diplomata*, edited by T. Sickel, in *Mon. Germ. Hist.*, *Scriptores*, III, Hannoverae 1893.
109 R. Bernacchia, *Territori longobardo-spoletini e territori pentapolitani nelle Marche (secoli VI–VIII)*, in *Ascoli, cit.* (n. 90), p. 273–311, part. Tav. I.
110 E. Migliario, *Sopravvivenza e declino delle città romane dalla provincia Valeria al ducato di Spoleto*, in *Visigoti e Longobardi*, a cura di J. Arce, P. Delogu, Firenze, 2001, p. 239–256.
111 G. M. Fabrini, G. De Marinis, F. Becker, C. H. Delplace, P. Quiri, *Il nuovo volto di* Urbs Salvia*: il Criptoportico, l'area templare, il Foro*, in G. de Marinis, G. Paci, E. Percossi, M. Silvestrini (eds.), *Archeologia nel Maceratese. Nuove acquisizioni*, Macerata 2005.
112 F. Melia, S. Virgili, Camerinum *tra tarda Antichità e alto Medioevo: dati preliminari sugli scavi di emergenza di P.za Cavour*, in Cirelli, Diosono, Patterson, *Le forme della crisi..., cit.* (n. 21), 2015, p. 321–328.
113 D. Ferreri, *Grave Goods and Burial Typologies: Funerary Customs in Ravenna*, in Cosentino, *Ravenna and the Traditions*, *cit* (n. 44), p. 211–258.
114 E. Giorgi, *L'urbanistica di Ascoli Piceno dall'età romana all'altomedioevo*, in *Ascoli, cit.* (n. 90), p. 313–332, part. p. 328.
115 F. Cappelli, *Le origini della cattedrale di* Ausculum. *Aspetti di urbanistica alto-medievale in una città del Picenum*, in Paroli, *L'Italia centro-settentrionale*, *cit.* (n. 101), p. 81–90.
116 E. Giorgi, *L'urbanistica..., cit.* (n. 114), p. 329.

117 E. Cirelli, *Anfore medievali rinvenute a Ravenna e nell'area centro-adriatica (VIII-XII secolo)*, in 'Archeologia Medievale', XLV, 2018, p. 35–46.
118 *Variae* 507–537, Libro I, 2. Cassiodoro, Variarum libri XII, a cura di A.J. Fridh, in Corpus Christianorum Lat., XCVI, 1973, p. 10.
119 *De bello Gothico*, Libro III, 10. Procopio di Cesarea, De bello Gothico, in *Opera omnia*, a cura di J. Haury, II, Leipzig 1905, p. 337
120 F. Lanzoni, *Le diocesi d'Italia dalle origini al principio del secolo VII (an. 604)*, Faenza, 1927, vol. I, p. 317.
121 G. Stranieri, *Un limes bizantino nel Salento? La frontiera bizantino-longobarda nella Puglia meridionale. Realtà e mito del Limitone dei greci*, in *Archeologia Medievale* XXVII, 2000, p. 333–355.
122 T. S. Brown, *Otranto in Medieval History*, in D. Michaelides, D. Wilkinson (eds.), *Excavations at Otranto, I, The Excavations*, Galatina, 1992, p. 25–39.
123 P. F. Kehr, *Italia pontificia*, IX, 1962, p. 408–412
124 V. von Falkenhausen, *La dominazione bizantina nell'Italia meridionale dal IX all'XI secolo*, Bari, 1978.
125 L. Safran, *San Pietro at Otranto. Byzantine Art in South Italy*, Roma, 1992, p. 224–225.
126 Von Falkenhausen, *La dominazione bizantina..., cit.* (n. 124), p. 48–51.
127 G. Uggeri, *Otranto paleocristiana, in Contributi alla storia dell'arte in memoria di Maria Luisa Ferrari*, in *Itinerari* 1, 1979, p. 37–46; C. De Mitri, Hydruntum. *Lo studio della città di Otranto in età romana attraverso l'analisi delle fasi e del materiale ceramico del Cantiere 2*, in Mélanges de l'école Française de Rome. Antiquité, 128.2, 2016 [en ligne].
128 C. D'Angela, *Recenti scoperte paleocristiane ad Otranto*, in *CARB* 42, 1995, p. 275–288.
129 L. Maggiulli, *Otranto. Ricordi*, Lecce, 1893, tav. I.
130 H. Patterson, D. Whitehouse, *Medieval Domestic Pottery*, in F. D'Andria, D. Whitehouse (eds.), *Excavations at Otranto, II, The Finds*, Galatina, 1993, p. 87–195.
131 P. Arthur, M. P. Caggia, G. P. Ciongoli, V. Melissano, H. Patterson, P. Roberts, *Fornaci altomedievali ad Otranto. Nota preliminare*, in *Archeologia Medievale* XIX, 1992, p. 91–122.
132 M. Leo Imperiale, *Otranto, cantiere Mitello: un centro produttivo nel Mediterraneo bizantino. Note attorno ad alcune forme ceramiche di fabbricazione locale*, in S. Patituccci Uggeri (ed.) *La ceramica altomedievale in Italia. Atti del V Congresso di Archeologia Medievale (Roma, 2001)*, Firenze, 2004, p. 327–342.
133 G. P. Ciongoli, *Otranto (Lecce)*, in *Taras* 8, 1988, p. 126–128.
134 D'Angela, *Recenti scoperte..., cit.* (n. 128).
135 M. Falla Castelfranchi, *L'inedita tomba ad arcosolio presso la cripta della cattedrale di Otranto*, in *Vetera Christianorum* 21, 1984, p. 373–380.
136 G. Gianfreda, *Basilica Bizantina di S. Pietro in Otranto – Storia e Arte*, Lecce 2010.
137 V. von Falkenhausen, *S. Pietro nella religiosità bizantina, in Bisanzio, Roma e l'Italia meridionale nell'Alto Medioevo*, XXXIV Settimana di studio del CISAM (1986), Spoleto 1988, II, p. 627–658.
138 C. Diehl, *L'art bizantin dans l'Italie meridionale*", Paris 1894.
139 A. Guillou, *Italie méridionale byzantine ou Byzantines en Italie méridionale?*, in *Byzantion* 44, 1974, p. 152–190, part. p. 181–182; R. Farioli Campanati, *La cultura artistica nelle regioni bizantine d'Italia dal VI all'XI secolo*, in *I Bizantini in Italia (Antica Madre, 5)*, Milano, 1982, p. 137–426, part. p. 240.
140 Safran, *San Pietro..., cit.* (n. 125), p. 430.
141 H. Teodoru, *Eglises cruciformes dans l'Italie méridionale*, *Ephemeris Dacoromana* 5, 1932, p. 22–34; A. Prandi, *Il Salento provincia dell'arte bizantina*, in *L'Oriente cristiano nella storia della civiltà, Atti del Convegno internazionale* (Roma-Firenze 1963), Roma, 1964, p. 671–711.
142 Safran, *San Pietro..., cit.* (n. 125).

10

URBANISM IN SYRIA AND PALESTINE BETWEEN THE 7TH AND 9TH CENTURIES

Ian Randall

The debates around urbanism and the fate of the Byzantine city in Syria-Palestine have, of course, been heavily influenced by the loss of those regions to the Empire in the second quarter of the 7th century and the advent of Islam. Discussion has centered around the 'death' of Classical urbanism and the emergence of what has been termed the prototypical 'Islamic city' complete with narrow, meandering streets, industrial or artisanal quarters, and a general lack, outside the mosque and *suq*, of monumental, public architecture. For those influenced by Classical archaeology, this cannot but seems to be indicative of decay and decline, an erosion of the urban fabric and all the criteria that defined Late Roman *municipia*.[1] In the last few decades, however, many Byzantine and Islamic historians and archaeologists have raised serious questions about the implicit (sometimes explicit) narrative that these transformations, and the abandonment of some settlements, were the result of the Arab conquest.[2] Fueled by excavations at many urban sites across the Middle East, they have challenged the chronology of this move away from the classical Greco-Roman orthogonal city, the root causes of the cessation of most types of monumental public building, and, in some cases, whether this can be called decline at all.[3] What constitutes 'urban' in the Late Roman/Early Islamic Middle East has been largely redefined as a result, and nuanced, intra-regional pictures of urban adaptation, abandonment, and vitality have emerged (Figure 10.1).

In this chapter, I will discuss the major theoretical contributions to the discussion on Late Roman/Early Islamic urbanism in Syria and Palestine from the 7th to the 9th centuries and the recent work that has been done at major urban sites across these regions that has provided the fodder for this debate. Moving city by city will provide not only a picture of the types of transformations occurring and their chronology but will also serve as a catalog of the more recent archaeological interventions and the current paradigmatic understandings of the post-Byzantine city in Syria and Palestine. The interface and interaction of city and countryside have loomed large in recent years, with regional survey and the excavation of small town and village sites coming to the fore, particularly as budgets have tightened, political instability has increased, and ethical and theoretical considerations have prompted a move away from major urban excavations. This is as it should be as there was a serious lacuna in our understanding of how the rural economies of the post-Byzantine Middle East

 DOI: 10.4324/9780429203923-13

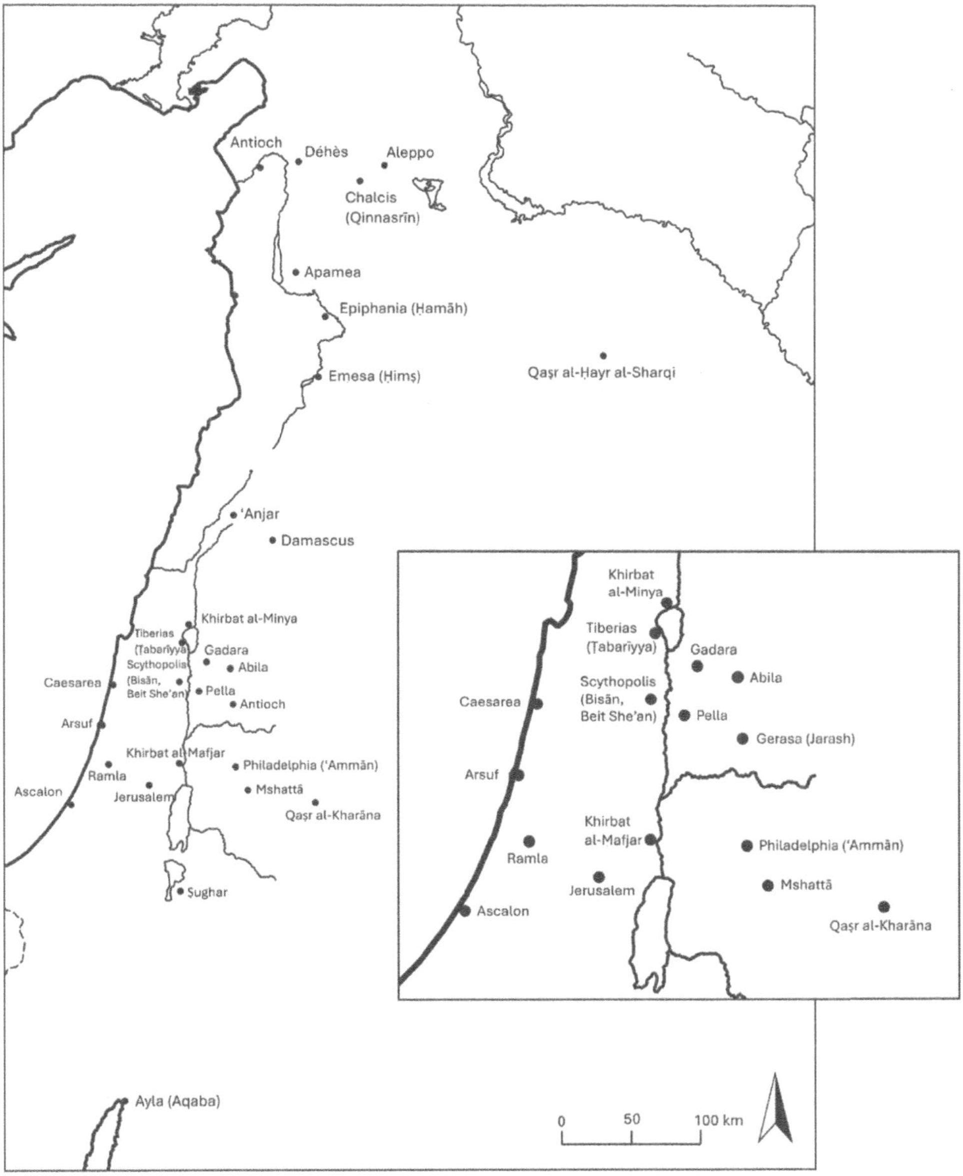

Figure 10.1 Urban sites mentioned in the text

functioned. This work, however, will lie largely outside the scope of this chapter.[4] How one defines a 'city' in this period is one of the principle questions I will be exploring, but for the sake of this volume, I will be following Wickham in focusing on the urban core of sites that were commonly considered to be *civitates* in Late Antiquity and those new Islamic foundations that had significant space set aside for dense, and sizeable, populations.[5]

In a discussion of the changing face of urbanism in Late Roman/Early Islamic Syria and Palestine, it is perhaps useful to start at the end, rather than the beginning, and work backward. The urban characters of contemporary cities like Marrakesh and Baghdad were familiar to Western archaeologists of the late 19th and early 20th centuries, and in them, they saw an apparent civilizational understanding of the city that differed from their own, Classically based model.[6] The Classical city had broad, orthogonal paved streets, to make room for cart traffic, public buildings and infrastructure like aqueducts, theaters, baths, colonnaded porticoes, and basilicas, funded by city elites, and public open spaces for *fora* or *agores.*[7] These were nowhere to be seen in the contemporary Middle Eastern city, which had the features mentioned above, and it was thought that the Arab conquest, which surely must have marked a civilizational sea change, was the culprit. Archaeologically, this seemed to be borne out; in those cities that continued to be occupied from Late Antiquity through the Early Islamic period, houses were subdivided, shops appeared amidst porticoes, streets narrowed, and industrial facilities or housing cropped up in the theater and the agora, or these areas were abandoned entirely.

Writing in the second half of the 20th century on northern Syria, J. Sauvaget did the most to cement the idea that the Arab conquest, and the coming of Islam, had led to the collapse of the Classical city and this idea held sway among many scholars until the late 1980s.[8] In 1985, however, Hugh Kennedy published his seminal article *From Polis to Madina: Urban Change in Late Antique and Early Islamic Syria* and fired a number of shots across the bow of this narrative. He claimed that, based on the archaeological evidence for Syria and Jordan, the decay of the urban fabric could be seen to start roughly a century *before* the coming of Islam, and could be tied, not to conquest and religious change, but to longer term social and administrative shifts in Late Antiquity. The 'Islamic city' of the 7th and 8th centuries was, in many cases, just the continuation of processes that had begun in the 6th century and not completed until the 10th or 11th.[9] Citing evidence from Apamea, Antioch, Gerasa, and many of the sites of the limestone massif, he noted that, after the economic boom of the 4th and 5th centuries, there was little evidence of major investment in public structures. In the 6th century, houses and shops appear in colonnaded streets and theaters, baths shrink, and the repair of earthquake damage is often shoddy at best. The much vaunted rebuilding of Syria by Justinian following the Persian invasion of 540 is, outside of Antioch, archaeologically invisible, and even this urban intervention Kennedy refers to as a 'rearguard action.'[10] The last inscriptions from the villages to the West of Antioch date to 610.[11]

Kennedy pointed to a few factors that he believed had led to this erosion of the urban fabric. For some cities and towns, the simple fall in population attendant on invasion, the Justinianic plague, or major earthquakes could help to explain the archaeological signatures of contraction, abandonment, and lapsed maintenance that appear in the 6th century.[12] While some cities like Damascus, Ḥimṣ, or Aleppo probably increased in population from Late Antiquity to the Early Islamic period, many cities and towns, particularly in the Decapolis, became mere villages or disappeared altogether. Another, possibly more important factor, though, was the shift in how cities were governed in Late Antiquity. City councils, which are the *curia* or *boule*, lost their tax-raising powers over the course of the 5th and 6th centuries and the central government of the Empire largely took over the collection and distribution of funds.[13] With this move toward central control, the city lost its role as the traditional stage on which Roman power politics was enacted by the urban elite. The Christianization of the empire also meant that the church was an attractive alternative for a man of means, and the shift toward patronage of ecclesiastical structures in Late Antiquity is readily apparent. Provincial governors still invested in public infrastructure, but hardly at the level of their curial forebears, and in many cases, the church stepped in to fund those amenities that they considered worthwhile.[14] This did not, as one can easily imagine, involve theaters. The last vestiges of the old urban elite Kennedy believed had fled following the disruptions of the Persian wars of the 6th and early 7th centuries, and then the final Arab conquest of the mid-7th.[15]

Into this space a new, Muslim elite had stepped, with different ideas about the functional requirements of a city. Far more amenable to merchant activity than the apparent indifference of the previous administration, and mindful that the Prophet himself had been involved in commerce, the *suq* became a focus of public concern, as of course did mosques, city walls, and the water supply.[16] Overall, though, no radical transformations to the existing cities of Syria and Palestine were required. Narrowing streets were of little concern given that the pack animal had largely replaced the wheeled cart in terms of commercial transportation. The mosque took over most of those spatial functions related to public gatherings and political grandstanding, and much of the tax revenue stayed local.[17] Nor were Islamic rulers averse to many of the principles that governed the Classical city; new Islamic foundations, like Sāmarrā, Baghdad, and, as will be discussed below, 'Anjar, featured orthogonal plans with public markets, mosques, and palaces seamlessly integrated into the planned whole.[18] Indeed, the 'Islamic city' was just a Late Antique cocktail, with a twist.

In making this argument, Kennedy largely severed the associations between Islam and the perceived decline in the Classical city of 7th-century Syria and Palestine. Hugely influential, his thesis garnered much support, although building on the work of Sauvaget the narrative was still one of a general decline in the urban fabric.[19] It should be noted, though, that he went to great pains to explain that decline did not preclude economic vitality.[20] This 'declinist' view has been met in recent years by those who argue for a continuation of the social and political life of the city in addition to often burgeoning commercial and industrial activity.[21] Revisitations of Kennedy's evidence, and syntheses of new archaeological activity, have built a picture of broad continuity in various parts of Syria and Palestine in terms of dense population centers as viable **political** units, reorienting the discussion around the definition of the city under the Early Islamic state. Alan Walmsley, for example, has pointed to the city, and indeed the town, as the home of Muslim elites, as well as Christian bishops who continued to perform the functions of community leaders.[22] Moreover, rather than seeing the flight of Byzantine elites like Kennedy and Liebeschuetz, he points to the use of Greek in much Early Islamic administration, no doubt plied by former Byzantine officials looking to capitalize on a felicitous job market. There is now considerable evidence that, although local elites became less essential to the central Byzantine administration, they still stayed in their urban contexts and maintained some level of influence in Syria and Palestine.[23]

The Early Islamic administration did shift the loci of these hierarchies, however, with the old Byzantine provincial centers of Antioch, Apamea, and Scythopolis (Bisān), exchanged for Chalcis (Qinnasrīn), Emesa (Ḥimṣ), and Tiberias (Ṭabarīyya), largely to protect them from Byzantine coastal assault.[24] Damascus, as the capital of the new Umayyad caliphate, also grew in importance, and Jerusalem maintained its significance as a religious center. This reorganization would clearly have impacted the urban fabric of these cities, as their political and economic fortunes rose or fell. This type of contextual variability has come to the fore in much recent work, as a more complex picture has emerged of inter-, and even intra-regional responses to economic, political, and social shifts from Late Antiquity through the Early Islamic period. While the differences between the cities of northern and southern Syria had already been noted by Clive Foss in 1997, and indeed by Kennedy himself in formulating his thesis, Gideon Avni's 2011 revisitation of Kennedy's article did much to add further nuance to the overall picture. Pointing out that limited archaeological evidence at the time forced Kennedy's article to rely on historical descriptions, legal documents, and architectural observations, Avni drew on recent, large-scale excavations at major sites throughout Syria and Palestine in noting that the connections between change and long-term decline could not be definitely proven on a wide scale.[25] No archaeological evidence could be found to support massive damage to the urban fabric due to wars or plague, and one even sees an increase in construction in most cities over the course of the period.[26] He instead pushed for an 'Intensification and Abatement' model. That the 6th and 7th centuries saw significant natural disasters and political upheaval could not be denied, but each city responded on their own terms to safeguard their economic and social life. Those cities that were not resilient to such change declined, but overall the manner in which these responses to change manifested on the ground was less a function of external political movements and more a factor of the longer term social and economic processes that Kennedy had begun to highlight.[27]

Further support for the 'continuist' position can be found in Luca Zavagno's broad 2009 synthesis and in Walmsley's 2007 discussion of the Palestinian archaeological material. Zavagno noted that many Syrian cities appeared to maintain significant levels of prosperity until at least the mid-7th century, when more regional differentiation starts to become apparent. In the North, Antioch and Apamea seem to suffer a significant economic downturn, along with much of the limestone massif.[28] This coincided with the general decline of the Mediterranean exchange network around the same time and its collapse into more regional systems of commercial activity.[29] Epiphania, Emesa, and Damascus, however, seem to continue much as before, if not showing signs of expansion and growth. In Palestine, coastal cities like Caesarea, Arsuf, and Ascalon adapted to the changing economic picture of the mid-7th century with varying degrees of success. Caesarea in particular has seen significant excavation over the last few decades and its decline and eventual abandonment in the Fatimid period will be discussed below. The Trans-Jordan also evinces a picture of differentiated growth and abatement. MacAdams pointed to several areas which saw a 'smooth transition' from the Byzantine to Early Islamic period.[30] In the Decapolis, cities like Gerasa, Pella, Gadara, and Abila maintained significant prosperity while the well-irrigated areas of central Jordan supported the continued growth of Philadelphia ('Ammān) well into the 7th and 8th centuries. The southern strip of Jordan also saw continued vitality in the market town of Ṣughar, and Ayla, constructed next to the old Byzantine township, remained occupied and lively until the early 'Abbāsid administration.[31] Jodi Magness' 2003 volume goes a step further in developing the argument for continuity with its focus on the ceramic evidence in Early Islamic Palestine. Highlighting work done at Déhès, Antioch, and Caesarea, she argued that the pottery for these sites, and many others in Palestine, had been dated far too early, and that much of the evidence for urban decline could not be seen until the 8th or more probably the 9th century.[32] This produces a picture of an Early Islamic urban Palestine that maintained significant trade and wide-scale construction in the transition from Byzantine to Umayyad rule.

These then are the general threads of the argument around urbanism in Late Byzantine and Early Islamic Syria and Palestine. Questions of economic prosperity and demographic vitality have vied with concerns around political and institutional change and shifts in building projects by both private and public parties in the move from Byzantine to Early Islamic administration. The construction of *qusur*, desert castles, and *amsar*, created settlements often next to existing cities, has further complicated the issue. I will now shift the resolution to look at the recent archaeological evidence from individual sites that have contributed to this discussion. These include Gerasa (Jarash), Scythopolis (Bisān/Beit She'an), Ramla, Apamea, Caesarea Maritima, Antioch, and Tiberias (Ṭabarīyya). I shall also consider evidence from Antioch, although the continued occupation of this city has severely limited archaeological investigation. With the exception of Ramla, these are all existing urban centers at the beginning of the 7th century, and I have included them in order that a fine-grained examination of the alterations to the physical cityscape might better elucidate the changing face of urbanism in Early Islamic Syria and Palestine.

I will also discuss the site of 'Anjar, and here I should mention the issue of the *qusur*, which, for the purposes of this chapter, I will largely be ignoring. These desert castles have been a source of rigorous debate in Islamic Archaeology. These isolated Umayyad constructions, such as Khirbat al-Minya, Qaṣr al-Ḥayr al-Sharqi, or Khirbat al-Mafjar, are built on the fringes of the desert and feature orthogonally planned baths, reception halls, lodgings, mosques, and imposing walls, towers, and gates, although these latter seem to serve no military function.[33] What are they? Clearly elite residences, they project political power in nearly every aspect of their construction, although their location contrasts sharply with the *dar al-imara*, or governor's palace, often found in the urban core of Early Islamic cities. Hypotheses have been floated that these are rural estates, meeting places for tribal groups that remained essential to Umayyad governance, or strategic outposts meant to safeguard key military and trade routes.[34] Perhaps they are all three. What they lack, however, is evidence of a significant population and thus will not feature in our discussion. The site of 'Anjar, however, while sharing many of the features of the *qusur*, differs in this respect, and thus I will consider it first as an outlier to place alongside the other cities in considering the nature of Early Islamic urbanism.

'Anjar lies at a strategic location, equidistant from Beirut and Damascus, in the southwest corner of the Biqa' valley at the crossroads of important routes between those two cities, the Transjordan and Tiberias, and the Umayyad administrative district, or *jund*, of Ḥimṣ.[35] Sauvaget, writing in 1939, identified the site as having been constructed by the Umayyad caliph al-Walīd I (705–715) and the chronicle of Theophanes states that 'Garis' was built by al-'Abbas ibn al-Walīd in 709–710.[36] Syriac graffiti in a quarry from which some of the stone for the construction comes has also been dated to 714.[37] Excavated by Maurice Chehab between 1953 and 1975, the results remain unpublished apart from a short article from 1963.[38] In 1969, K. A. C. Creswell discussed the ruins at length, and in the 2000s, Barbara Finster further measured and discussed the visible remains.[39] The site was further surveyed in 2017 by A. Santi.[40] R. Hillenbrand's article on the place of 'Anjar in the context of Early Islamic urbanism also remains an important resource.[41]

Consisting of a large rectangular enclosure of 310 × 370 m with four cardinal gates and 40 regularly spaced towers, the site is three times the size of the next largest *qusur*, Qaṣr al-Ḥayr al-Sharqi, with whom and other *qusur* it shares many common features.[42] 'Anjar is divided into four quadrants by a *cardo* and *decumanus*, with a Classical tetrapylon at the intersection. The southwestern and northwestern quadrants show signs of dense habitations, as well as 114 shops.[43] The southeastern quadrant displays a *dar al-imara* and *masjid*. Near the North gate, a bath complex similar to that at Qusair 'Amra can be found, and another small *hammam* is located near the West gate. The five-room *dar al-imara* follows a plan similar to those at Qaṣr al-Kharāna, Khirbat al-Minya, Khirbat al-Mafjar, Qaṣr al-Ḥayr al-Sharqi, and Mshattā.[44] Architectural decoration, similar to that at the aforementioned sites, predominates, including friezes with acanthus tendrils and stylized leaves, rosettes, and pomegranates.[45] There is also a figural decorative program.[46] Remarkably, this 'palace city,' as Hillenbrand calls it, appears to have only been inhabited for about 40 years and was left unfinished at the time of its abandonment.[47]

The purpose behind this new foundation is no less enigmatic than the other *qusur*, perhaps more so. While accepting that 'Anjar could be an alternate capital for a peripatetic Umayyad court, a royal bolt-hole in times of trouble, or a station for crack troops at a strategic location, Hillenbrand argues more vociferously for it to be seen as an attempt to colonize the Syrian countryside by the Umayyad elite.[48] He notes that Roman spolia is replete in the settlement, and that a spring with Roman masonry lies merely 1 km to the North, while a Roman temple is also to be found a scant 3.5 km away. Perhaps this *qusur* was established near an earlier Roman foundation, much like the *amsar* found at various locations in the Umayyad caliphate. We have very little idea what an early *miṣr* looks like; this could be an early experiment, a failed experiment, in a process that was to culminate with 'Abbāsid Baghdad 50 years later.[49]

Santi's 2017 survey of the architecture at the site, however, has suggested a quite different interpretation. Focusing on the mosque of 'Anjar, she noted a number of oddities in its construction. First, the blocks of the *maqsura* appeared to be resting on the pavement, not interrupting them, indicated a secondary chronological relationship.[50] Moreover, column plinths incorporated into the enclosure of the adjacent prayer hall appear to be lying on a level some 12 centimeters below that of the present walking surface, indicating a pre-existing level. This was confirmed by the discovery of two column plinths that had been bisected to allow for the construction of the mosque walls.[51] An additional spoliate column in the courtyard of the palace, matching the plinths incorporated into the mosque and inscribed in Greek with a dedication to the Virgin and a reference to an unidentified church of St. Mary, led Santi to propose that a basilical structure predated the construction of the mosque, possibly the aforementioned church. Other irregularities in the mosque's construction could further be explained by the adaptation of a structure originally oriented to the East.[52] Citing comparanda in the dimensions and construction of other Syrian churches in the region, and textual references to a monastery of 'YNGR' or a settlement known as Gerra in the area, Santi proposes that 'Anjar is not a new foundation at all, but an extensive adaptation of a pre-existing Late Antique settlement.[53] She goes further and suggests that, were this the case, it would provide a reason for the investment of al-Walīd in this site. Under the caliph Umar, the area had been granted to the Banū Kahlan, a part of the Kalbi tribal federation with whom al-Walīd sought to repair relations following the pro-Qaysite policies of his predecessor, 'Abd al-Malik. The grand refurbishment of a settlement the Banū Kahlan may have occupied would have gone a long way toward securing their support. Its subsequent abandonment could also be explained by the violent swing of the last Umayyad caliph against the Kalbi some 40 years later.[54] This compelling interpretation provides a window into the types of political maneuvering that could have played a significant role in the form, and fortunes, of urban environments, pre-existing or otherwise, during the Early Islamic period. Even if the 'palace city' of 'Anjar is a unique case, the imposition or integration of an orthogonal plan into an Islamic city speaks to a contextual, adaptive approach to pre-Islamic forms of urbanism that is mirrored at other sites in Syria and Palestine.

I shall turn now to those cities that entered the 7th century with significant populations, and whose archaeology has contributed to the more recent debates around the nature of Late Antique and Early Islamic urbanism, starting with Jarash. Jarash (Gerasa) of the Decapolis is located in the Gilead of Jordan, some 35 km North of 'Ammān (Philadelphia). Situated in a wide, fertile valley, it was a major urban center throughout the Roman and

Byzantine periods and, after the Islamic conquest of 635, continued to flourish through much of the Early Islamic period. Initially identified for archaeology by the antiquarian Ulrich Jasper Seetzen in 1806, excavations began in 1925 under George Horsfield; a team from the British School joined in 1928 followed by another from Yale under John Crowfoot. The American Schools of Oriental Research took over in 1930, first under Clarence Fisher and then Nelson Glueck, who continued excavations until 1934. These early excavations concentrated on the monumental Roman temples and some Byzantine churches, ignoring the Early Islamic material.[55] In 1975 work was resumed by the University of Turin and in 1982 the Jerash Archaeological Project was formally initiated.[56] Since 2011, the Danish-German Northwest Corner Project has also been working at Jarash in order to comprehensively investigate the entire settlement history of a targeted portion of the site.[57]

A total of 15 Byzantine churches have been identified over the course of the excavations, none of which were damaged at the time of the Arab conquest, and most were still in use in the 8th century and possibly later.[58] Starting in the 6th century we see the changes to the urban fabric that have become familiar: the theaters and agora cease in their original function, monumental public construction tapers away, and shops, industrial facilities, and private residences invade the wide colonnaded streets, including a large ʻAbbāsid pottery kiln North of the *decumanus* constructed in the 9th century. A very early mosque has also been discovered in the oval plaza, which reused a Roman conch for its *mihrab*.[59] Evidence from the hinterland of Jarash points to increased prosperity in the 7th and 8th centuries, indicated by intensified church building, some of which were constructed during the short-lived Persian occupation of the early 7th century and just after the Arab conquest.[60] This building activity corresponds with the increased private construction in the urban core of the city, and recent excavations in the Northwest quarter of the city have confirmed the Byzantine and Umayyad periods as those showing the most growth and economic vitality in the history of Jarash.[61] A large congregational mosque, built near the beginning of the 8th century, was situated near the juncture of the *cardo* and *decumanus*. Interestingly, this mosque was built to accommodate these thoroughfares, which necessitated adaptations to the building in order to maintain the orientation of the *qibla* wall.[62] Further constructions in the city core at this time are also fit into the pre-existing urban fabric; growth and adaptation are the order of the day rather than decline.[63] Only following the devastating earthquake of 749 does Jarash cease to thrive, and reoccupation of abandoned areas occurs during the Ayyubid through Mamluk periods.[64]

In contrast to the picture painted by Kennedy of the city, Caesarea Maritima is another urban center that continues to prosper in the transition from Late Antiquity to the Early Islamic period; significant urban contraction only appears in the later 7th century.[65] Situated on the Palestinian coast, Caesarea was promoted by Justinian and given jurisdiction over the three Palestinian provinces.[66] A bustling port that served as the primary interface between Palestine and the Mediterranean, trade and urban life boomed through much of the Roman and Byzantine periods. Covering 120 hectares at its height, the city featured numerous elite residences in its southern quarter, clustered around the ornate home of the provincial governor, complete with baths, gardens, and large courtyards. A monumental octagonal church above the harbor dominated the skyline, particularly if one approached Caesarea by sea. This church was constructed in the early 6th century and continued in use during the 8th, destroyed only by the 749 earthquake that will become increasingly familiar.[67] The largest city in Byzantine Palestine, Caesarea, also featured a wealthy and extensive hinterland that served the wine trade, of which the city was a major entrepot. The city acted as the base of a Persian governor during the 620s and then fell violently to the Arabs in 640, although no archaeological trace of destruction has been identified from either of these episodes.[68] In the 9th and 10th centuries, Caesarea had shrunk to a mid-sized, though affluent, town and was only abandoned after its destruction by the Mamluks in 1291.

The site was surveyed in the 19th century and intermittent, small-scale excavations took place in the 1950s and 1960s, although any post-Byzantine material only appeared in appendices.[69] The Mission Archeologia Italiana, between 1959 and 1963, excavated outside the city walls and uncovered some early Islamic material, although this did not appear in the final report.[70] A. Negev's excavations of the medieval city in the 1960s and early 1970s only produced a brief discussion of the late pottery.[71] Between 1975 and 1979, E. Netzer's excavations North of the Herodian temple exposed a considerable late Byzantine building, with wide-ranging pottery imports and coins dated to 630–660.[72] The Joint Expedition to Caesarea Maritima (JECM) and the Caesarea Ancient Harbour Excavation Project (CAHEP) have been working since the 1970s, but this has produced only one, small joint exhibition book on the Early Islamic period.[73] Under the co-direction of K. G. Holum, A. Raban, and J. Patrich, the Combined Caesarea Expedition (CCE) has been digging on a large scale on the South shore outside the city walls, on the temple platform, and in the inner harbor since 1989, with far more information emerging on the Early Islamic settlement.[74]

The picture pained by these excavations, and by the pottery in particular, is of a city that thrived from the mid-6th to mid-7th centuries, with wide-scale trade indicated by the sheer quantity and variety of imports.[75] A luxurious bath dating to the late 6th or early 7th century was located to the North of the city among some ancient villas, featuring *opus sectile* floors, and another villa to the North East of the Byzantine city wall displayed polychrome geometric mosaics.[76] The octagonal church also dates to this period, and the CCE has turned up gold belt or scabbard decorations from the 6th or 7th centuries.[77] In the material culture, two distinct phases are apparent in the post-conquest period, the first lasting from 700 to 750, the second from 750 to 950. Material culture change during the first period is minimal from the earlier Byzantine material, and it is only in the second phase that a notable shift to imported glazed wares from Egypt and the ʿAbbāsid heartland appears.[78] In the course of the late 6th through early 8th centuries, there is an increase in private construction in the city that impinges on the colonnaded streets and introduces artisanal and industrial activity into the urban core.[79] This continues as the inhabited area begins its contraction to just around the port in the late 7th century, although given the vibrancy of this building activity a drop in population should not be equated with a loss of prosperity. This contraction is likely the result of the exodus of much of the city's Christian and Samaritan populations and administrative changes within the Islamic state, such as the transfer of the capital of the *Jund Filastin* to Ramla in 715.[80] In the late 8th and 9th centuries, there is a massive change to the urban plan. A new street network is laid down in the contracted area with minimal attention paid to the earlier grid. The inner harbor is filled in and built over and the dwelling units feature a series of rooms with wide courtyards and sophisticated drainage and water supply systems.[81] This street network was then repaved in the 10th century, when Caesarea shows a further uptick in economic vitality.

This complicated picture displays the contextual factors that affected economic and political vitality and their manifestation in the urban fabric during the transition from Byzantine to Early Islamic administration. It also raises questions about the relationship between demographic rise and fall, economic prosperity, and urban status. Another site that challenges these connections and more generalizing models is Scythopolis in the Decapolis.

The major urban center in northern Palestine during the Roman period, Scythopolis, was chosen as the capital of *Palestina Secunda* at the beginning of the 5th century, and by the 6th, it may have had a population of around 30,000.[82] Excavations were begun in the late 1920s by a team from the University of Pennsylvania, with further small-scale work carried out in the 1950s and 1960s by the regional archaeologist N. Zori.[83] More recently, two teams, one from Hebrew University and the other from the Israel Antiquities Authority, undertook large-scale exposures between 1986 and 2002 focusing on the city center. This work exposed a Classical city plan that underwent significant change over the course of the 6th century.[84] Monumental construction largely ceased and the major colonnaded streets were encroached upon by private shops and industry, as we have seen elsewhere.[85] Again, no sign of the Persian or Arab conquests is apparent in the archaeological remains. In 659/660, a large earthquake damaged much of the city and some parts of the civic center appear to have been deserted. By the late 7th century, the old agora and neighboring areas were used as a cemetery, containing 350 cist graves, and significant spoliation of surrounding structures occurs.[86] In some places, alluvium was allowed to fill the city streets.[87] At the same time, there is a large-scale introduction of industry into the altered city fabric, including pottery kilns in the amphitheater, at the edge of the old theater, in the eastern bathhouse, and what appears to be a linen workshop in the western bathhouse.[88] A large *suq* is built in 738 on the ruins of the basilica of Silvanus, with two levels of shops and a monumental entrance gate with mosaic and two framed Arabic inscriptions.[89] This *suq*, and much of the city, was destroyed in the earthquake of 749, although there are signs of significant 'Abbāsid building in the ruins, including a large congregational mosque and substantial private dwellings to the South and East, which now seems to form the civic center.[90] By this time, Scythopolis had shrunk to a mid-sized town, although it appears to have remained economically viable into the 11th century.[91] The varied fortunes of this city cannot be seen as part of a general model of long-term decline, or even continuation. Earthquakes, and no doubt the transfer of the capital of the *Jund al-Urdun* to Tiberias (Ṭabarīyya), all played their role in altering the urban fabric and indeed the nature of urbanism in the Early Islamic period.

Tiberias saw its administrative status enhanced under the Umayyad caliphate and it expanded significantly in population and area during the 8th through 11th centuries. It was also the location of a *miṣr*, one of the Umayyad 'new' cities, often placed next to an existing settlement. Located on the western shore of the Sea of Galilee, Tiberias was well placed to dominate inland Palestine, although why it was chosen over Scythopolis as the capital of the *Jund al-Urdun* is not clear.[92] Work began at the site in 1921 with excavations at the synagogue of Hammat Tiberias, by N. Slouschz, with further broad exposures in the city center in 1954–1956 and 1964–1968 by B. Rabani and A. Durks, respectively, but these excavations remain unpublished. Further excavations were carried out in the 1970s by G. Foerster and the Early Islamic levels were then published by D. Stacy.[93] More recently, work has been conducted between 1994 and 2009 that uncovered two Early Islamic residential quarters and a large church and monastery from the transitional period.[94]

Again, no trace of the Arab conquest appeared in the material culture. A large congregational mosque was established under the Umayyads, as were two dense residential districts, one in the deserted Roman theater and the other to the North of the theater featuring a series of buildings with central courtyards along a narrow street.[95] Both areas remained occupied into the 11th century. An additional Early Islamic district was discovered in the modern town center, although these houses were of poor construction, dating to the 9th and 10th centuries.[96] The colonnaded streets of the city show the usual encroachment by shops during the Umayyad and 'Abbāsid periods, although these could also be earlier.[97] A new, somewhat smaller main street was installed in the 8th or 9th century in the city center with shops and small workshops and both pottery and dyeing production centers are also in evidence.[98] The pace of building to the South of the city wall seems to have quickened in the 9th century, and much of the new housing seems to be designed for the elite.[99] All in all, a considerable building program is apparent at multiple parts of the site, speaking to Tiberias' rise in fortunes and prosperity under both the Umayyads and 'Abbāsids.

A final note on Tiberias relates to the urban expansion outside of the city walls. Timothy Harrison, writing in 1992, observed what he thought was the outline of a traditional *miṣr* in the city plan of Ottoman Tiberias, recorded by the British after the First World War. He postulated that, coupled with the presence of active synagogues and churches in the city at the time of the conquest and later, the new Arab foundations might be indicative of this type of Early Islamic extramural settlement. He located this settlement under the present town of Ṭabarīyya, to the North of the city wall, while speculating that the additional building to the South, in the former Byzantine city, may have been of a more industrial character.

Ramla, another *Jund* capital, has also seen considerable recent excavation, making it another good case in which to consider the role of administrative good fortune in urban transformations in the Early Islamic period. This city, however, was a new foundation, established by the caliph Suleyman II at some point before 715. Likely a *miṣr* foundation, given its proximity to the pre-existing site of Lydda, Ramla is situated on the coastal plain of Palestine, some 15 km from the sea and roughly 40 km North of Jerusalem. Its location placed it on the trunk road from Egypt to Damascus, passing through Gaza and Ṭabarīyya, and trade was clearly an important part of the life of the city.[100] This route was of greater importance in the Islamic period than it had been under the Byzantines, as movement between the capital, Damascus, and the rich province of Egypt took precedence over northern Syria and the hostile border with Byzantium. Archaeological work at the site has, until recently, been mostly limited to rescue excavations by the extent of the modern city. In 1949, digging in the area of the White Mosque, presumably the congregational mosque, by Joseph Kaplan identified the original Umayyad structure.[101] Further, small scale, excavations were undertaken in 1965 by R. Aylon and A. Eitan in the Bar Giora neighborhood and 'elsewhere in the city,' which turned up large amounts of 8th and 9th century material and evidence of kilns, workshops, and drainage systems.[102] In 1973, an elaborate mosaic was uncovered in the southeastern portion of the Old City. This mosaic, dating to the 8th century, displayed a stylized *mihrab*, had passages in Kufic script from the Qur'an, and was located in an elite private dwelling.[103] Between 1990 and 2008, a further 85, poorly published, rescue excavations were also conducted, in addition to multiple soundings near the White Mosque by Avni and Gutfeld.[104]

These excavations, particularly the latter in the vicinity of the congregational mosque, have exposed a steady growth in the population and economic vitality of Ramla from the 8th through the 11th centuries. In addition to numerous private dwellings, Gutfeld and Avni uncovered the remains of two large Umayyad structures of large ashlar construction. A complex water system that was installed in the 'Abbāsid period was also in evidence. The remains of industrial activity, in the form of large quantities of slag, point to the incorporation of workshops into the urban fabric of the 'Abbāsid city.[105] Ramla reached its peak in the 10th and 11th centuries, with considerable growth apparently beginning under the early 'Abbāsids. The placement of gates suggests an orthogonal plan from the beginnings of the site, and later additions included caravanserai, baths, and mosques along wide avenues with large markets.[106] The 749 earthquake appears not to have adversely affected Ramla, and growth and prosperity seem to have gathered momentum despite the shift in administrative focus from Damascus to Baghdad with the 'Abbāsid takeover in 750. Ceramic evidence points to burgeoning trade with the rest of the Arab world throughout this period.[107]

Shifting to the North, a potential counter-example to this type of growth can be seen at the site of Apamea. Located on the banks of the Orontes river, some 100 km from Antioch, Apamea thrived during the Roman period and was still a major urban center around the middle of the 6th century. Much of our information about the Late Antique and Early Islamic levels comes from the excavations of J. Balty in the 1960s and 1970s, although there has been additional work more recently on the Roman city.[108] After a series of devastating earthquakes in the 520s, Apamea was refurbished by Justinian, who added new paving to the main thoroughfares and a tetrapylon at the intersection of the *cardo* and *decumanus*.[109] Apamea was captured and occupied by the Persians on more than one occasion in the late 6th and early 7th centuries, prior to its fall to the Arabs in 636, and this has long been considered a major factor in its subsequent decline, although there is no archaeological evidence to connect these events. The grand colonnaded street of the city was blocked with walls and rubble at some point after the mid-6th century, and the subsequent spaces filled with shops and or residential units. A limekiln and animal troughs re-using ancient sarcophagi also invade this area. These changes were formerly thought to have occurred during the Persian occupation of the city in the late 620s, but Clive Foss has argued that this should be pushed some 30 years later, or more, based on Arab coins found amongst the blocking walls of the street.[110] Similar changes can be seen in the agora, with animal troughs hinting at animal husbandry being practiced in the former city center. Material evidence again suggests a mid-7th century date at the latest. The nearby *nymphaeum* also goes out of use sometime in the 7th century, although a lamp kiln along the *decumanus* appears to go out of use nearly a century earlier.[111] At some point, the grand, 6th-century Atrium church of the city was repaired using considerable amounts of spolia. It not only maintained in use at that time but also found itself the center of a cemetery inserted into the center of the cityscape. At some later time, most of the entrances of the church were blocked up and the structure was subsequently sub-divided by spoliate walls before the edifice is abandoned.[112] The only evidence for dating is a single coin of 575 found associated with the first series of repairs. Many of the graves produced mid-7th- and 8th-century pottery. A small glass factory installed in the atrium of the church produced an 'Abbāsid coin of the 9th century. The main cathedral of Apamea saw similar changes.[113]

The area of the cathedral was dominated by several luxurious Late Antique villas that also changed considerably following the mid-6th century, the date, in most cases, of the latest refurbishments following the original design. Subsequently, colonnades are blocked up, large rooms are subdivided, and industrial and agricultural processing facilities appear. Coins and pottery seem to indicate a 7th-century date for these renovations.[114] Dumping and evidence for animal husbandry can be found in some areas. Later occupation seems limited to the former courtyards and adjoining rooms, with further evidence of animal husbandry and food processing apparent. Wells are dug and rooms advance into the area of the street. The early coin finds associated with these changes date from the 6th or 7th century, but the pottery, and the majority of coin finds in the courtyards, are from the 9th and 10th centuries, pointing to an extended occupation.[115] The drainage system appears to have still been in use in the early 7th century but shows signs of accumulation and blockage thereafter. Although two of these villas showed signs of burning early in their transformations, there was nothing to directly link these events to either the Persian or Arab conquests.

How are we to interpret these changes? While Balty and Foss are consistent in their view that this represents an onset of extreme poverty and decline following the Persian or Arab invasions, this conclusion is not self-evident. Many of the cities previously discussed showed signs of commerce and industry creeping into main thoroughfares in the 6th and 7th centuries, as well as the subdivision of larger buildings into areas devoted to a variety of activities. The consistent ruralization seen at Apamea, however, would seem to indicate a decline in both population and a certain type of prosperity in the transition to the Early Islamic period. On the other hand, the excavations focused on monumental structures in the core of the Byzantine city, a shift in focus for urban activities and population density is not unknown as administrative and economic priorities change on a city-, or region-wide basis.

The primary example of decline cited by Kennedy was the city of Antioch.[116] Situated on the northern coast of Syria, on the banks of the Orontes, Antioch was one of the largest and most important cities of the Roman East. Historical sources seem to indicate a significant loss of status, population, and prosperity over the course of the 6th and early 7th centuries, largely due to a series of catastrophes that befell the city.[117] The findings of the 1932 through 1939 Princeton excavations under J. Lassus seemed to confirm this, and further archaeological work in the urban core has been largely precluded by Antioch's status as a living city.[118] Working along the main colonnaded *cardo* of the city, Lassus documented the now quite familiar blocking off of spaces to produce small shops, industrial and agricultural processing facilities, and the invasion of public space by private constructions and funerary areas.[119] While Lassus placed this activity after the Persian conquest, Kennedy preferred the 6th century, while Magness, in her 2003 reassessment, decided upon the 7th century.[120] The ceramic material from the excavations was published separately, and not linked, thus the chronology relied exclusively on numismatic finds. Asa Eger, in his 2013 further reassessment, focused on the ceramic finds from several of these areas and, while he agreed generally with Magness' chronology, stated that the shops along the *cardo* could have begun as early as the 4th century.[121] He also noted the wide range of imports from across the 7th-century Arab world from the excavations, which portrayed a significant amount of economic vitality.[122] A large number of early 'Abbāsid coins found in the Princeton excavations further speak to continued prosperity, if accompanied by urban contraction. Soundings by Lassus in other parts of the city also produced evidence of building and ceramic production from the 7th through 12th centuries, with intensification starting in the 9th century, further complicating a picture of steady decline from either the 6th or 7th centuries.[123]

I have tried here to give an introduction to the general debates surrounding urbanism in Syria and Palestine from the 7th to the 9th centuries and some of the recent excavation work, where available, that has contributed to our understanding of the transformations in the urban fabric in the transition from Late Antiquity to the Early Islamic period. In so doing, I have chosen those sites that provide a broad overview of the types of growth, adaptation, and abatement that occurred in pre-existing cities and new foundations as well as the specific regional or intra-regional dynamics that contributed to their relative economic, demographic, and political fortunes. The administrative relationship between the Umayyad and 'Abbāsid courts and individual cities, the roles of those cities within their specific regions, the changing face of the urban economic interface with their hinterlands and trade routes following their transfer from a Byzantine to an Islamic 'world system,' all played an important role in determining how they would adapt over the coming centuries in their functional and aesthetic lives as spaces of concentrated social and economic activity. The debate on Late Antique and Early Islamic urbanism, and the fate of the Byzantine city in Syria and Palestine, is just beginning, and to consider these cities' trajectories alongside those that remained within the Empire is a necessary next step.

Notes

1 C. Wickham, *Framing the Early Middle Ages* (Oxford: Oxford University Press, 2005), 591.
2 H. Kennedy, "From *Polis* to *Madina*: Urban Change in Late Antique and Early Islamic Syria," *Past & Present* 106 (1985); C. Foss, "Syria in Transition, A. D. 550–750: An Archaeological Approach," *Dumbarton Oaks Papers* 51 (1997): 189–269; T. Insoll, *The Archaeology of Islam* (Oxford: Blackwell Publishers, 1999); Wickham 2005; L. Zavagno, *Cities in Transition: Urbanism in Byzantium between Late Antiquity and the Early Middle Ages (AD 500–900)*, BAR International Series 2030, v-206 (Oxford: Archaeopress, 2009).
3 J. Magness, *The Archaeology of Early Islamic Settlement in Palestine* (Winona Lake: Eisenbrauns, 2003).
4 I would refer the reader to Magness 2003, Wickham 2005, and A. Walmsley, *Early Islamic Syria – An Archaeological Assessment* (London: Duckworth, 2007), for a synthesis of this material.
5 Wickham, *Framing*, 594.
6 Insoll, *Archaeology*, 202; also see J. L. Abu Lughod, "The Islamic City – Historic Myth, Islamic Essence, and Contemporary Relevance," *International Journal of Middle Eastern Studies* 19 (1987): 155–76, for a synopsis of these earlier approaches.
7 Kennedy, *Polis*¸4.
8 J. Sauvaget, *Alep* (Paris: P. Geuthner, 1941); See G. Avni, ""From Polis to Madina" Revisted – Urban Change in Byzantine and early Islamic Palestine," *Journal of the Royal Asiatic Society* 21, no. 03 (2011) for a list of some of these scholars.
9 Kennedy, *Polis*, 27.
10 Ibid. 6.
11 G. Tchalenko, *Villages antiques de la Syrie du Nord, Le massif du Bélus a l'époque romaine, I-III* (Paris: Geuthner, 1953–58), 426–38; Magness, *Palestine*, 196.
12 Kennedy, *Polis*, 18.
13 Ibid.; Wickham, *Framing*, 596.
14 Kennedy, *Polis*, 19; Wickham, *Framing*, 598.
15 Kennedy, *Polis*, 24.
16 Ibid. 19, 24.
17 Ibid. 21.
18 Ibid. 16.
19 J. Patrich, "Church, State and the Transformation of Palestine – The Byzantine Period (324-640 CE)," in *The Archaeology of Society in the Holy Land*, ed. T. Levy (London: Leicester University Press, 1995), 477; Foss, *Syria*, 1997; J. Liebeschuetz, *Decline and Fall of the Roman City* (Oxford: Oxford University Press, 2001), 12.
20 Kennedy, *Polis*, 17.
21 Magness 2003; Walmsley 2007; G. Avni, ""From Polis to Madina" Revisted – Urban Change in Byzantine and early Islamic Palestine," *Journal of the Royal Asiatic Society* 21, no. 03 (2011): 301–29, *The Byzantine-Islamic Transition in Palestine: An Archaeological Approach* (Oxford: Oxford University Press, 2014); M. Decker, *The Byzantine Dark Ages* (New York: Bloomsbury, 2016), 86.
22 Walmsley, *Syria*, 72.
23 Wickham, *Framing*, 603.
24 Walmsley, *Syria*, 74.
25 Avni, *Revisted*, 326.
26 Ibid. 328.
27 Avni, *Revisited*, 328.
28 Zavagno, *Cities*, 30.
29 Wickham, *Framing*, 621.

30 H. MacAdam, "Settlements and Settlement Pattern in Northern and Central TransJordania, ca. 5500-ca. 750," in *The Byzantine and Early Islamic Near East II. Land Use and Settlement Pattern*, eds. G. R. D. King and A. Cameron (Princeton: Darwin Press, 1994).
31 D. Whitcomb, "Islam and the Socio-Cultural Transition of Palestine – Early Islamic Period (638-1099 CE)," in *The Archaeology of Society in the Holy Land*, ed. T. Levy (London: Leicester University Press, 1995); A. Walmsley, "Production, Exchange, and Regional Trade in the Islamic East Mediterranean: Old Structures, New Systems?" in *The Long Eighth Century*, eds. I. L. Hansen and C. Wickham (Leiden: Brill, 2000), 302–3; Zavagno, *Cities*, 30.
32 Magness 2003.
33 Whitcomb, *Islam*, 491.
34 Ibid.; Insoll, *Archaeology*, 217; Wickham, Framing, 595; Zavagno, *Cities*, 29.
35 A. Santi, "ʿAnjar in the Shadow of the Church? New Insights on an Umayyad Urban Experiment in the Biqāʿ Valley," *Levant* 50 (2018): 267.
36 J. Sauvaget, "Les ruines omeyyades de 'Andjar," *Bulletin du Musée de Beyrouth* 3 (1939): 5–11.
37 R. Hillenbrand, "'Anjar and Early Islamic Urbanism," in *The Idea and the Ideal of the Town between Late Antiquity and the Early Middle Ages*, eds. G. P. Brogiolo and B. Ward-Perkins (Boston: Brill, 1999), 59; Santi, *'Anjar*, 270.
38 M. Chehab, "The Umayyad Palace at 'Anjar," *Ars Orientalis* 5 (1963): 17–25.
39 K. Creswell, *Early Muslim Architecture*, vol. I (Oxford: Clarendon Press, 1969); B. Finster, "Researches in 'Anjar: I. Preliminary report on the architecture of 'Anjar," *Bulletin d'Archéologie et d'Architecture Libanaises* 7 (2003): 209–44, "Vine Ornament and Pomegranates as Palace Decoration in 'Anjar," in *The Iconography of Islamic Art, Studies in Honor of Robert Hillenbrand*, ed. B. O'Kane (Edinburgh: Edinburgh University Press, 2005), 143–62, "Researches in 'Anjar: II. Preliminary Report on the Ornaments of 'Anjar," *Bulletin d'Archéologie et d'Architecture Libanaises* 11 (2007): 143–65, "'Anjar: Spätantik oder Frühislamisch?" in *Residences, Castles, Settlements: Transformation Processes from Late Antiquity to Early Islam in Bilad al-Sham.* Proceedings of the International Conference Held at Damascus, 5–9 November 2006, eds. K. Bartl and M. Abd al-Razzaq (Rahden: Verlag Marie Leidorf, 2008), 229–42.
40 Santi 2018.
41 Hillenbrand 1999.
42 Hillenbrand, *Urbanism*, 61; Finster, *Researches I*, 210; Santi, *'Anjar*, 267.
43 Hillenbrand, *Urbanism*, 62.
44 Ibid. 71.
45 Santi, *'Anjar*, 268; Finster 2005.
46 Finster 2005, 2008.
47 Hillenbrand, *Urbanism*, 62.
48 Ibid. 91.
49 Ibid. 79.
50 Santi,*'Anjar*, 273.
51 Ibid. 276.
52 Santi, *'Anjar*, 277.
53 Ibid. 278.
54 Ibid. 279.
55 C. Kraeling, *Gerasa, City of the Decapolis* (New Haven: American Schools of Oriental Research, 1938); See F. Zayadine (ed.), *Jerash Archaeological Project 1981-1983* I (Amman: Dept. of Antiquities, Hashemite Kingdom of Jordan, 1986) for a discussion of the early excavation history.
56 M. Aubin, "Jerash," in *The Oxford Encyclopedia of Archaeology in the Near East*, vol. I, ed. E. Meyers (Oxford: Oxford University Press, 1997), 215; F. Zayadine, A. Naghawi, and I. 'Oweiss, "The Jerash project for excavation and restoration," in *The Jerash Archaeological Project 1981*-1983, ed. F. Zayadine (Amman: Dept. of Antiquities, Hashemite Kingdom of Jordan, 1986), 7.
57 A. Lichtenberger and R. Raja, "New Archaeological Research in the Northwest Quarter of Jerash and its Implications for the Urban Development of Roman Gerasa," *American Journal of Archaeology* 4, no. 119 (2015).
58 Avni, *Revisited*, 312.
59 Zayadine *et al.*, *Jerash*, 18.
60 Avni, *Revisited*, 314.

61 Lichtenberger and Raja, *Archaeological Research*, 487.
62 A. Walmsley and K. Damgaard, "The Umayyad Congregational Mosque of Jarash and Its Relationship to Early Mosques," *Antiquity* 79 (2005): 362–78.
63 A. Walmsley, L. Blanke, K. Damgaard, A. Mellah, S. McPhillips, I. Simpson, and F. Bessard, "A Mosque, Shops and Bath in Central Jarash: The 2007 Season of the Islamic Jarash Project," *Annual of the Department of Antiquities of Jordan* 52 (2008): 109–37.
64 Lichtenberger and Raja, *Archaeological Research*, 487.
65 Avni, *Revisited*, 317; Kennedy, *Polis*, 23.
66 Avni, *Revisited*, 315.
67 K. Holum, "Caesarea's Temple Hill – The Archaeology of Sacred Space in an Ancient Mediterranean City," *Near Eastern Archaeology* 67 (2004): 184–99.
68 Y. Arnon, *Caesarea Maritima, The Late Periods 700-1291*, BAR International Series 1771 (Oxford: Archaeopress, 2008), 13; Wickham, *Framing*, 622.
69 See Arnon 2008 for excavation history.
70 Arnon, *Caesarea*, 12.
71 A. Negev, *Caesarea* (Tel Aviv: Lewin-Epstein, 1967).
72 L. Levine and E. Netzer (eds.), *Excavations in Caesarea Maritima 1975, 1976, 1979 – Final Report*, Qedem vol. 21 (Jerusalem: The Institute of Archaeology, The Hebrew University of Jerusalem, 1986).
73 K. Holum, R. Hohlfelder, R. Bull, and A. Raban, *King Herod's Dream: Caesarea on the Sea* (New York: Norton, 1988).
74 J. Patrich, D. Reshef, D. Ben Yosef, S. Rotgaizer, S. Pinkas, Z. Bar-Or, H. Van-Dam, and A. Moscu, "The Warehouse Complex and Governor's Palace (areas KK, NN, May 1993-December 1997)," in *Caesarea Papers* II, eds. K. Holum, A. Raban, and J. Patrich (Portsmouth: Journal of Roman Archaeology Supplemental Series, 1999), 82–3; K. Holum, "The Temple Platform: Progress Report on the Excavations," in K. Holum *et al.* (eds.) 1999, 12–34; A. Raban, R. Toueg, S. Yankelevitz, and Y. Arnon, "Land Excavations in the Inner Harbour (1993-1994)," in K. Holum *et al.* (eds.) 1999, 198–224.
75 Y. Arnon, *The International Commercial Activity of Caesarea during the Early Islamic II Period (749-969 CE) According to Ceramic Evidence* (MA Thesis: University of Haifa, 1996), 97–8; A. Raban, "Combined Caesarea Excavations," *Excavations and Surveys in Israel* 17 (1998): 64–6; Magness, *Palestine*, 212.
76 F. Horton Jr., "A Sixth-Century Bath in Caesarea's Suburbs and the Transformation of Bathing Culture in Late Antiquity," in *Caesarea Maritima: A Retrospective after Two Millennia*, eds. A. Raban and K. Holum (Leiden: Brill, 1996), 177–89.
77 Magness, *Palestine*, 211.
78 Arnon, *Caesarea*, 19.
79 Avni, *Revisited*, 318.
80 Ibid. 317.
81 Arnon, *Caesarea*, 19; Avni, *Revisited*, 318.
82 Wickham, *Framing*, 615.
83 Y. Tsafrir and G. Foerster, "Urbanism at Scythopolis – Beth Shean in the Fourth to Seventh Centuries," *Dumbarton Oaks Papers* 51 (1997): 87.
84 Avni, *Revisited*, no. 8.
85 Ibid. 305.
86 Tsafrir and Foerster, *Urbanism*, 138; Avni, *Revisited*, 305.
87 G. Mazor, "Beth Shean: The Hellenistic to Early Islamic Periods: The Israel Antiquities Authority Excavations," in *The New Encyclopedia of Archaeological Excavations in the Holy Land* 5, Supplementary Volume, ed. E. Stern (Jerusalem/Washington, DC: Israel Exploration Society/Biblical Archaeology Society, 2008), 1623–35.
88 Avni, *Revisited*, 305.
89 Tsafrir and Foerster, *Urbanism*, 139 and Figure F; E. Khamis, "Two Wall Mosaic Inscriptions from the Umayyad Market Place at Bet Shean/Baysān," *Bulletin of the School of Oriental and African Studies* 64, no. 2 (2001): 159–76.
90 Avni, *Revisited*, 306.
91 Tsafrir and Foerster, *Urbanism*, 87.
92 T. Harrison, "The Early Umayyad Settlement at Tabariyah: A Case of Yet Another Miṣr?" *Journal of Near Eastern Studies* 51, no. 1 (1992): 52.

93 D. Stacy, *Excavations at Tiberias 1973-1974 – The Early Islamic Period*, IAA Reports 21 (Jerusalem: Israel Antiquities Authority, 2004).
94 Y. Hirschfeld and K. Galor, "New Excavations in Roman, Byzantine, and Early Islamic Tiberias," in *Religion, Ethnicity, and Identity in Ancient Galilee*, eds. J. Zangenberg, H. W. Attridge, and D. B. Martin (Tübingen: Mohr Siebeck, 2007).
95 K. Cytryn-Silverman, "The Umayyad Mosque of Tiberias," *Muqarnas* 26 (2009): 37–61; Avni, *Revisited*, 309.
96 M. Hartal, "Tiberias," *Excavations and Surveys in Israel* 120 (2008).
97 Avni, *Revisited*, 311.
98 Wickham, *Framing*, 618.
99 Avni, *Revisited*, 311.
100 Whitcomb, *Islam*, 493.
101 J. Kaplan, "Excavations at the White Mosque in Ramla," *'Atiqot* 2 (1959): 106–15; Whitcomb, *Islam*, 492.
102 M. Rosen-Ayalon and A. Eitan, *Ramla Excavations: Finds from the VIIIth Century C.E.*, Israel Museum Catalogue (Jerusalem: Israel Museum, 1969).
103 M. Rosen-Ayalon, "The First Mosaic Discovered in Ramla," *Israel Exploration Journal* 26 (1976): 104–19.
104 O. Gutfeld, "Ramla (A and D)," *Excavations and Surveys in Israel* 109 (1999a): 65–8, "Ramla: Excavations to the North of the White Mosque," in *Ramla: The Development of a Town from the Early Islamic to Ottoman Periods*, eds. S. Gibson and F. Vitto (Jerusalem: Israel Antiquities Authority Booklet 4, 1999b), 34–7; G. Avni and O. Gutfeld, "Ramla," in *The New Encyclopedia of Archaeological Excavations in the Holy Land 5*, Supplementary Volume, ed. E. Stern (Jerusalem/Washington, DC: Israel Exploration Society/Biblical Archaeology Society, 2008), 2007–10.
105 O. Gutfeld, "Final Report on the Excavations North of the White Mosque," *Qedem* 51 (2010): 15.
106 Whitcomb, *Islam*, 492.
107 K. Cytryn-Silverman, "The Ceramic Evidence," in O. Gutfeld, "Ramla: Final Report on the Excavations North of the White Mosque," *Qedem* 51 (2010): 97–211.
108 J. C. Balty, "Apamée," in *Apamée de Syrie: Bilan des rescherches archéologiques 1965-1968. Actes de colloque tenu à Bruxelles les 29 et 30 avril 1969,"* ed. J. Balty, Fouilles d'Apamée de Syrie 6 (Brussels: Centre Belge de Recherches Archaéologique in Apamée Syrie, 1969), 20, "Archéologie et témoignages litteraires," in *Apamée de Syrie: Bilan des rescherches archéologiques 1969-1971. Actes de colloque tenu à Bruxelles les 15, 17, et 18 avril 1972,"* eds. J. Balty and J. C. Balty, Fouilles d'Apamée de Syrie 7 (Brussels: Centre Belge de Recherches Archaéologique in Apamée Syrie, 1972), 209–14; C. Finlayson, "New Excavations and a Reexamination of the Great Roman Theater at Apamea, Syria, Seasons 1–3 (2008–2010)," *American Journal of Archaeology* 116, no. 2 (2012): 277–319.
109 Foss, *Syria*, 208.
110 Ibid. 209.
111 Ibid. 210.
112 Ibid. 213.
113 Ibid. 216.
114 Ibid. 218.
115 Ibid. 219.
116 Kennedy, *Polis*, 12.
117 A. Eger, "(Re)Mapping Medieval Antioch: Urban Transformations from the Early Islamic to Crusader Periods," *Dumbarton Oaks Papers* 67 (2013): 95.
118 J. Lassus, "Sondage Prés de la Mosquée Habib en Najjar," in *Antioch-on-the-Orontes, The Excavations of 1932*, vol. 1, ed. G. W. Elderkin (Princeton: Princeton University Press, 1934).
119 Eger, *(Re)Mapping*, 109.
120 Kennedy 1985, Magness 2003.
121 Eger, *(Re)Mapping*, 111.
122 Ibid. 127.
123 Eger 2013.

PART III

Architecture and the Built Environment

11

DOMES IN THE URBAN SKYLINE

The Case of Sts. Sergius and Bacchus and Its Transformations through Time

Nikolaos Karydis

Introduction

The transition from the timber-roof basilica to vaulted church architecture did not just reshape the interiors of churches but also changed the Byzantine cityscape. Byzantine church domes often stood tall, extending above the roofs of adjacent buildings. Viewed from afar, the earliest of these domes must have transformed the skyline of Byzantine cities, taking pride of place among earlier pediments, aqueducts, honorific columns, and fortifications.[1] Domes were to become an increasingly visible element of the skyline in later periods. Grown taller through the progressive extension of their drums, later domes must have stood out in the skyline of medieval cities and monasteries from Armenia to Venice and from Kievan Rus' to the Peloponnese.[2] Their proliferation in Palaiologan Constantinople is reflected in the fifteenth-century representations of the Imperial capital by Hartman Schedell and Cristoforo Buondelmonti.[3] Both panoramas emphasise the city's vaulted churches, depicting Constantinople as an early 'city of domes', prefiguring the iconic skylines of Early Modern Florence, Rome, and Paris.[4]

Viewing Schedell's and Buondelmonti's panoramas, one wonders to what extent the domed skyline of late-Byzantine Constantinople is representative of earlier periods in the city's history, and whether other Byzantine cities had a similar skyline. The emergence of domes as a hallmark of the Byzantine cityscape has not yet been mapped with certainty. Although the introduction of domes in the design of basilicas has often been linked with the reign of Justinian, recent studies challenge this. Take, for instance, the great vaulted basilicas of Ephesos: that of St. John was likely begun shortly before the reign of Justinian[5]; that of St. Mary is probably the product of the Transitional Period, just like St. Nicholas at Myra, the church at Dereağzı, St. Clement in Ankara, and Hagia Sophia in Thessaloniki.[6] If we consider that the great dome of Basilica B at Philippi collapsed shortly after construction, one struggles to find Justinianic domes outside Constantinople.[7] On the other hand, Justinian has been reliably credited with the construction of no less than four major domed churches at the capital: Hagia Sophia, St. Eirene, Sts. Sergius and Bacchus, and the Holy Apostles.[8] These basilicas seem to have transformed the city's skyline with a speed and an intensity that appears not to have occurred elsewhere in the sixth century.

DOI: 10.4324/9780429203923-15

It is tempting to see Justinian's Constantinople as the first true Byzantine 'city of domes', serving as a model for other Byzantine cities. However, a more careful view of the development of Justinian's churches seems to suggest that their impact on the skyline of the capital was not as immediate as one might think. With their shallow curvature and relatively low drums, the original domes of Hagia Sophia and the Holy Apostles would have hardly been visible from surrounding streets, squares, and peristyles. The dome of Hagia Sophia surely became more prominent when it reached its current height following the rebuilding of 558 AD.[9] Originally resembling the first, shallow dome of Hagia Sophia according to Procopius, the sail vaults of the Holy Apostles had been replaced by full hemispherical domes by the tenth century, when Constantine of Rhodes described them in his famous *Ekphrasis*.[10] Therefore, the impact of the domes of the Holy Apostles and Hagia Sophia on the skyline of Constantinople was gradual and became more intense after a modification of these churches' original design.

The above examples illustrate that to fully understand the gradual impact of domes on Constantinople's skyline, it is necessary to examine the earliest domed churches not as 'static' forms but as dynamic palimpsests, which resulted from several modifications of an original design idea. In many cases, this original idea remains elusive. If the original forms and subsequent phases of Hagia Sophia, the Holy Apostles, and St. Eirene have been the object of systematic study, the original phases of Sts. Sergius and Bacchus remain obscure. This chapter contributes to previous efforts to shed light on the initial form of this monument and its transformations through time. As this is the earliest church constructed by Justinian, our attempt to visualise its initial form holds the key to understanding whether the use of domes was part of the Emperor's original vision for Constantinople's skyline. By considering the way in which this original design was modified, the article aims to enhance our understanding of the role of retrofit in the evolution of one of the most significant Early Byzantine churches, and its changing role in the urban skyline.

The Origins of the Church of Sts. Sergius and Bacchus: A Debate

The church of Sts. Sergius and Bacchus at Constantinople has long been considered one of the architectural masterpieces of the time of Justinian, and one of the earliest surviving buildings of this era.[11] Used continuously during the last 15 centuries, this building has been considerably modified while its surroundings have changed radically. Our knowledge of the early history of the church relies mainly on the account of Procopius, which was probably written when the church was a couple of decades old.[12] Information derived from Procopius and other sixth-century records has previously been interpreted with the help of clues in the fabric of the building itself, namely the inscription in the monument's internal frieze and the monograms in the building's capitals.[13] Despite these efforts, the exact date of the construction of the church and its original purpose has been the object of debate between scholars of Byzantine Architecture.[14] In the early 1970s, Cyril Mango provided a convincing interpretation of the date and original role of the building. His crucial findings, recently summarised and expanded upon by Bardill, shed light on the circumstances in which the church was built and interpreted crucial aspects of its design.

Bardill challenged the view of the building as an isolated relic of Justinianic architecture, inviting us to view the current monument firstly as a fragment of a broader initial design, and secondly as an architectural amalgamation of several phases of construction. Our new understanding of the history of the building calls for a revised analysis of its complex and evolving form and structure. The following section looks at the development of the building from its sixth-century origins to its recent restoration from 2003 to 2006. This provides the base for understanding the building's changing architectural form, which is analysed through a historical, constructional, and typological lens.

This approach provides new clues for the form of Justinian's church. So far, all scholars assume that Justinian's church was domed.[15] However, the fact that Procopius's description of the sixth-century church fails to mention a dome has never been discussed. Despite Bardill's recent publication of evidence suggesting that the dome is actually a later structure, the possibility that the original building was not domed has not been considered. Evaluating this evidence from a typological and a constructional point of view, the present chapter proposes a new, alternative model for visualising the nave of Justinian's church of Sts. Sergius and Bacchus as a timber-roofed structure. Before we move on to re-visualise the original form of the church and its transformations over the centuries, a few preliminary words are necessary to review its history.

Sts. Sergius and Bacchus: Historical Overview

The church of Sts. Sergius and Bacchus was built by Justinian after his accession to the throne in 527 AD, and shortly after he and Theodora decided to connect Hormisdas Palace, their original residence, with the Great Imperial Palace nearby. Both the internal inscription and the Imperial monograms on the internal capitals confirm the terminus post quem of 527 AD for the building of the church.[16] Jonathan Bardill's recent analysis of the account of Procopius as well as a lesser known Syriac account attributed to abbot John bar Aphtonia suggests that this terminus post quem should be revised to 532 AD.[17] The petitions of the council of 536 AD suggest that the church was operational at that time and that it formed part of the monastery of 'Sts. Peter and Paul and the holy martyrs Sts. Sergius and Bacchus'.[18] As its name suggests, the monastery also included a church dedicated to Sts. Peter and Paul, which, according to a letter by Justinian to Pope Hormisdas, had been built by Justinian by 519 AD.[19] Procopius provides some indications about the general layout of the two churches: built within the palace of Hormisdas, the two buildings stood side by side, sharing a common atrium and a common narthex.[20] The above evidence suggests that by 536 AD, part of Hormisdas Palace functioned as a monastery, which included the churches of St. Peter and Paul and Sts. Sergius and Bacchus.

Mango's analysis of John of Ephesus' 'Lives of Eastern Saints' sheds light on the conditions in which the church of St. Sergius and Bacchus was built. According to this account, a community of Non-Chalcedonian (i.e. Monophysite) refugees settled in a convent in Hormisdas Palace where they enjoyed the protection and patronage of Theodora.[21] This convent has plausibly been identified as the monastery of 'Sts. Peter and Paul and Sergius and Bacchus', which is mentioned in the petitions of the council of 536. The account of John of Ephesus also refers to a 'martyrs' chapel' where the Non-Chalcedonian congregation would gather. This martyrion may have been the church of Sts. Sergius and Bacchus, but there is no conclusive evidence for this.[22] The association of the church with a Non-Chalcedonian community resident in Constantinople provides useful insights for our analysis of the origins of the design of the church, later in this chapter.

Despite its possible influence in the creation of this church, the presence of a Non-Chalcedonian congregation probably did not last long. By the reign of Justin II (565–574), the policy to integrate Monophysites in the Empire's religious and political structures had changed in favour of a tendency to prosecute the adherents to this doctrine.[23] As

Non-Chalcedonian communities were being expelled from Constantinople, the church of Sts. Sergius and Bacchus must have lost its particular congregation and, with it, the special symbolic meaning it had during Justinian's time.

The development of the monastery of Sts. Sergius and Bacchus and Sts. Peter and Paul during the seventh and eighth centuries is unknown. The tumultuous period of Iconoclasm may have had some impact on the churches of the monastery, but this cannot be determined with certainty.[24] What is certain is that by the mid-ninth century, the church required repair. Indeed, according to the eleventh-century account of John Skylitzes, during the reign of Basil I (867–877), the church was redecorated and repaired at the instigation of Patriarch Ignatius.[25] The Middle Byzantine church of Sts. Sergius and Bacchus was a cosmopolitan monument with a great ceremonial role. In a letter of 880 AD from Pope Julius VIII to Basil I, the Byzantine Emperor is 'thanked for permitting Roman clergy to officiate again in Sts. Sergius and Bacchus, according to ancient custom'.[26] Our only source about liturgy in the church during the Middle Byzantine period is the tenth-century *De Ceremoniis* by Emperor Constantine Porphyrogenitus.[27] The latter describes the ceremonial protocol related to the annual participation of the Emperor to the liturgy of Easter Tuesday. The ceremonial route of the Emperor within the church suggests that the gallery of Sts. Sergius and Bacchus communicated directly with a triclinium within the Emperor's palace.[28]

The degree to which the church maintained its connection with the palace in the following centuries is not certain. What we do know is that it was open to visitors. Indeed, chronicles of Russian pilgrims of the thirteenth and the fourteenth centuries suggest that the church was an important pilgrimage destination.[29] Around this time, the neighbouring church of Sts. Peter and Paul must have fallen into ruin or disuse, as it stops being mentioned in references to the monastery.[30] By the Late Byzantine period, the church of Sts. Sergius and Bacchus was probably the only church within the monastery complex.

The conversion of Sts. Sergius and Bacchus to a mosque after the fall of Constantinople in 1453 is typical of the reorganisation of the city's Byzantine infrastructure by the Ottomans. Sts. Sergius and Bacchus was one of several Byzantine churches that were transformed into a mosque in the times of Beyazit II. Its transformation is attributed to Hüseyin Ağa, who was 'Babüssaade Ağasi' of Sultan Beyazit II.[31] Between 1495 and 1510, the form of the Church and its surroundings underwent a series of modifications that aimed to transform the ancient monastery to a dervish lodge dedicated to the Khalwati (i.e. Halveti) order.

According to the endowment deed related to the mosque, Hüseyin Ağa added a 'straight minaret, a mihrab, a minbar and a mahfîl, embellishing the building with lights and oil lamps'.[32] The courtyard to the west of the church was replaced by a zaviye, a group of cells that, arranged around an atrium, accommodated itinerant Dervishes (Figure 11.1).[33] The building of the turbe (mausoleum) of the founder to the north of the zaviye, and of a hamam, completed the new complex.[34] The church itself underwent serious alteration, mostly focusing on its internal decoration and its entrance. Thus, when Petrus Gyllius visited the monument at the end of the sixteenth century, he could probably not see any mosaic decoration in the interior.[35] It is very probable that changes such as the raising of the floor level up to the height of the ground floor window sills, and the blocking of windows must have also taken place during the same period.[36] At the same time, a six-column portico was added in front of the building's narthex changing the character of the building and shaping the way it is perceived today.[37]

The condition of the monument seems to have deteriorated during the first two centuries after the Ottoman conquest of Constantinople.[38] A serious earthquake in 1648 is reported to have caused damage to the dome.[39] By 1740, the building was in an advanced state of

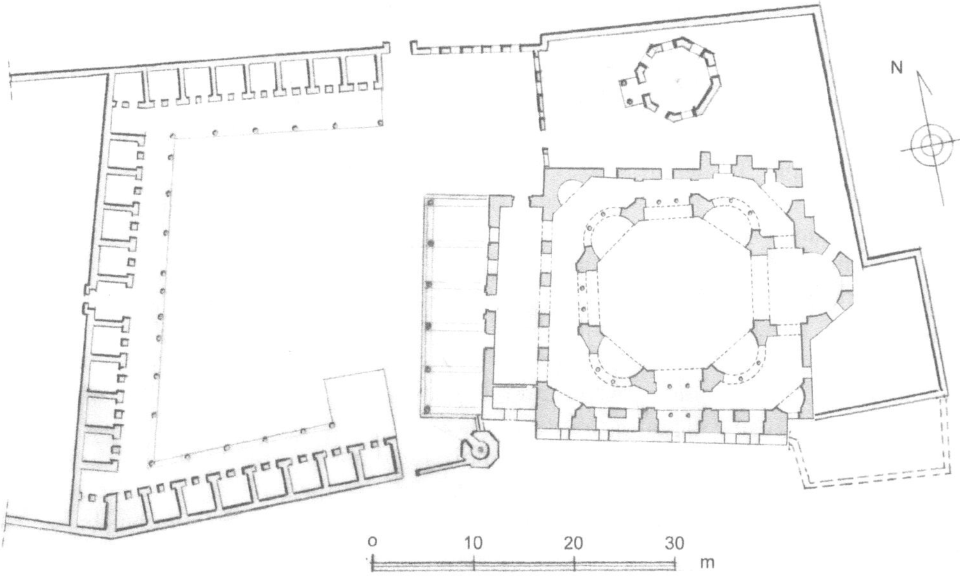

Figure 11.1 Istanbul [Turkey] Küçük Ayasofya Camii (Church of Sts. Sergius and Bacchus) – Schematic site plan

Source: Author's drawing after W. Muller Wiener, 1977.

decay and was repaired by the Grand Vizier Haci Ahmet Pasha. Soon after those works, in 1762, the Grand Vizier Kose Bahir Mustafa Pasha added a Minaret to the south west of the Mosque.[40] A year later, another earthquake made new repairs necessary.[41] The restoration works of the eighteenth century were not able to consolidate the mosque durably. When Paspates studied the building in the 1870s, the latter was almost a ruin. The railway in the European side of Istanbul, which had just been constructed and passed just a few metres south of the Mosque's south wall, caused the monument to shake visibly whenever a train passed, aggravating its cracks and threatening it with collapse.[42]

The urban regeneration of Istanbul during the nineteenth and twentieth centuries had a profound impact on the surroundings of the mosque. The opening of new streets necessitated the demolition of some of the buildings of its complex. It is quite probable that the former church, which by that time was known as 'Kucuk Aya Sofya Camii' (Little Hagia Sophia Mosque), must have seemed somewhat anachronistic to those witnessing the regeneration of the area around it. However, the monument was never abandoned. Indeed, during the Balkan Wars, in 1912, the entire building complex was used as temporary shelter for refugees.[43] It is very probable that it was this constant use and wide popularity that saved the old church from becoming one more victim of urban regeneration and ensured its maintenance after every earthquake, even if this maintenance was minimal and not frequent enough.

During the twentieth century, the character of Kucuk Aya Sofya changed radically. In 1937, the dome's drum was replastered externally. In 1940, the cloister of the zaviye to the west of the mosque was demolished in order to be rebuilt 16 years later. The new cloister had its east side open to the church like the old one. However, this arrangement changed during the 1980s, when a wall blocked access to the mosque from the zaviye. This wall perhaps symbolised the religious community's disapproval of the new use of its western cloister that had started to accommodate tourist shops.[44] Thus, Sts. Sergius and Bacchus, once the heart of a monastery within an Imperial residence, became an introspective monument, disconnected from its surroundings.

The earthquake that hit Istanbul in 1999 brought the building to a critical state of decay. According to a report by the ISCARSAH committee, in 2001, the dome was severely cracked and had lost the shape it had before the earthquake – now being much shallower than before.[45] At the same time, several walls and piers appeared to lean outwards.[46] This deformation is probably due to the combined action of earthquakes, vibrations, water infiltration, and soil settlement due to the rising water table. In 2002, the World Monuments Fund included Sts. Sergius and Bacchus in its annual register of the world's hundred most vulnerable sites.

In 2002, a major restoration project was launched.[47] During the following four years, the foundations of the building were reinforced with micropiles to deal with the problem of uneven settlement, while the intrados of the cracked dome was strengthened with the use of carbon fibre-reinforced resins, and the roof above the dome was releaded.[48] The restoration project also involved significant changes in the interior of the building. Interior decorative elements of the Ottoman period were reinstated, while the Byzantine column shafts, capitals, and bases were cleaned. More importantly, some of the hidden layers of the building, such as the brick structure of the vaults above the central bays of the north and south ambulatories or the traces of an earlier stylobate in the nave, were exposed. The restoration team also decided to reveal the pedestals of the ground floor columns, which until 2002 had been covered by the Ottoman raised floor. This was achieved by lowering the floor level, to the level of the floor during the Byzantine period. This modification not only resulted in the reinstatement of the internal columns in their complete form but also in the reinstatement of the interior's original proportions.[49] These interventions suggest that the aim of the restoration was to reach a compromise between the building's Byzantine character and its new identity from the fifteenth century onwards.

Looking back at the history of Sts. Sergius and Bacchus during the last 1500 years, we realise that this building has remained one of Constantinople's most important public places. The church, its users, and their rituals have all been affected by the religious, political, and social developments that marked the Byzantine and the Ottoman periods. One might ask to what extent these developments shaped the original design of the building and its transformations through time. To understand this, it is necessary to re-examine the building's intriguing architectural form in the light of the recent discoveries regarding the building's history. The following architectural analysis will focus on those aspects of the form of the building that help us to understand its building phases and shed light on some of its lost elements.

The Evolving Architectural Fabric

To understand the transformation of the building's fabric through time, it is necessary to examine its current form. The building consists of an internal octagonal domed core, enveloped by a lower, two-storey ambulatory, preceded by a narthex. Although the exterior gives the impression of a 'spartan', robust structure, the interior is characterised by extensive sophistication and spatial complexity (see Figure 11.2). Eight piers mark the corners of the centralised nave, which is surrounded by alternating rectangular and semicircular niches, or exedras. Each of these niches contains pairs of columns in two stories. While the columns on the ground floor support a horizontal architrave, the ones on the gallery level support

Figure 11.2 Küçük Ayasofya Camii (Church of Sts. Sergius and Bacchus) – Interior (Photograph by Maxim Atayants, 2011)

arches. Alternatively curved and straight, the two-storey arcade is interrupted in the east side of the internal octagon, where the octagonal nave opens freely onto the sanctuary.[50]

The upper part of the building is as complex as its plan. The piers support an alternation of broad arches, above the rectangular niches, and semi-domes above the exedras. These barrel vaults and semi-domes support the octagonal base of the dome. The latter, often characterised as 'a pumpkin dome', is divided into 16 compartments (see Figure 11.3). The compartments above the eight corners of the octagonal base are concave and the eight compartments above the centres of the octagon's north, west, south, and east sides are flat.[51] The vaults of the ambulatory are far simpler: both levels are mainly covered by barrel

Figure 11.3 Küçük Ayasofya Camii (Church of Sts. Sergius and Bacchus) – Cut-away axonometric
Source: Drawing by the author, 2006.

vaults, with the exception of the centre of the south ambulatory, an area covered by three cross vaults. Following this brief description of the church, we will now look at its fabric in more detail in order to highlight those aspects that provide evidence for the constraints of the original design and its modifications over the centuries.

The plan of the church and its irregularities provides valuable clues for the general orientation of the lost surrounding buildings. The main axis of the nave and sanctuary does not align with the centre of the narthex and is not parallel to the south external wall (see Figure 11.4). The central core of the building is rotated at an angle of 3° in relation to its southern and western surrounding walls. The symmetry of the plan is also undermined by the difference in length and thickness between the north and the south walls. Indeed, the north wall is 2.5 m longer than the south one and, in a great part of its length, almost half as thick. The extra thickness of the south wall allows for the creation of a central rectangular niche in the centre of the south ambulatory. These irregularities have been interpreted with reference to the original environment of the church.[52] The church of Sts. Sergius and Bacchus was connected with the pre-existing church of Sts. Peter and Paul to the south and the Palace to the north. These two buildings did not necessarily align. If the narthex and the south wall of Sts. Sergius and Bacchus conformed to the orientation of the church of Sts. Peter and Paul, the octagonal core probably aligned itself with the orientation of the palace.

Investigating the connection between the two churches, Ebersolt and Thiers have interpreted the colonnaded central niche of the south ambulatory of Sts. Sergius and Bacchus

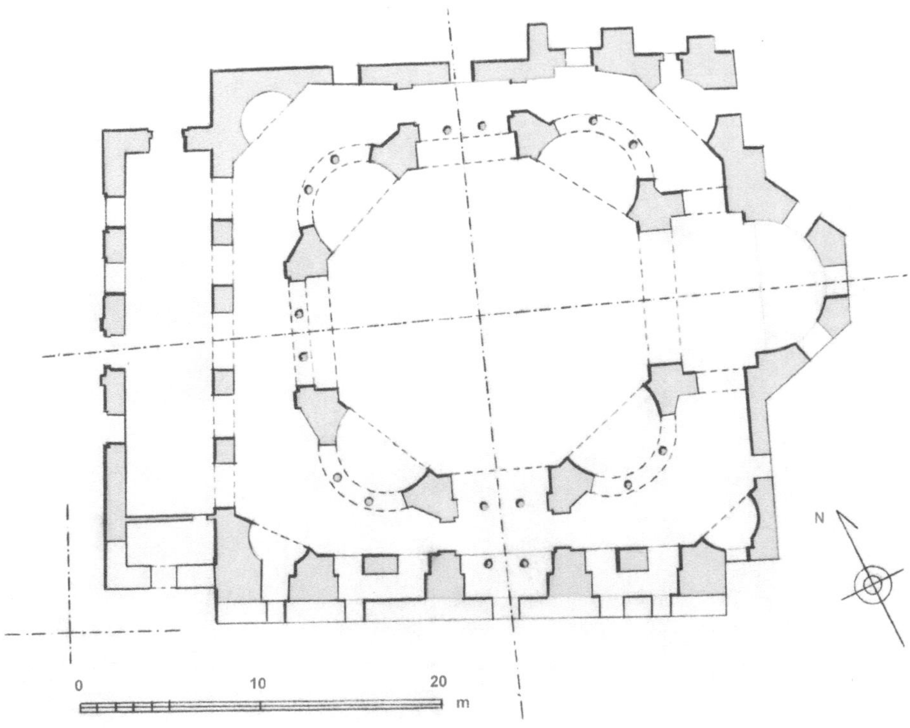

Figure 11.4 Küçük Ayasofya Camii (Church of Sts. Sergius and Bacchus) – Schematic site plan (Karydis's drawing, after the plan published by Thomas Matthews, 1977.)

as a monumental triple gate that ensured the communication with the nearby church of Sts. Peter and Paul (see Figure 11.5).[53] The protruding rectangular fillets in the shafts and the capitals of the columns that screen off this niche indicate that this colonnade contained door frames. The holes of the hinges to which doors were fixed also survive.[54] This detail is likely to be the last remaining trace of a vestibule between the two adjacent churches.

The difference of length between the two churches is probably what caused the current indentation in the southeast corner of the church of Sts. Sergius and Bacchus: the eastern extremity of the church's south wall projects from the thicker mass formed by the two

Figure 11.5 Küçük Ayasofya Camii (Church of Sts. Sergius and Bacchus) – Southern ambulatory (Photograph by Efthymios Rizos, 2014)

monuments' joined walls. This indentation seems to suggest that the south wall of the church has a double thickness because it incorporates parts of the north wall of the church of Sts. Peter and Paul. This seems to be confirmed by the external face of this wall. This includes five vertical sections made of alternating brick and stone masonry bands. This masonry is typical of fifth- and early sixth-century buildings in Constantinople. Distinctive from the later types of wall masonry elsewhere in the building, these parts of the south wall may be the only surviving remains of the church of Sts. Peter and Paul.

The greatest part of the walls consists of many different masonry structures that cannot be easily dated. There is extensive brick masonry, which in certain parts, such as in the east elevation of the church, is interspersed with stone courses (see Figure 11.6). This specific

Figure 11.6 Küçük Ayasofya Camii (Church of Sts. Sergius and Bacchus) – Sanctuary (Photograph published by J. Ebersolt and A. Thiers, 1913)

reinforcement is characteristic of building methods developed during the times of Justinian, and the corresponding parts of the masonry may well be original.[55] In other parts, the bricks are set on thick beds of mortar according to a technique that develops from the sixth century onwards.[56]These sections of wall can plausibly be attributed to the sixth-century church and its repairs from the sixth century through the Middle Byzantine period.

The most important surviving elements of the original design of Justinian's Sergius and Bacchus are found in the interior of the building. Indeed, the internal colonnaded screens constitute some of the best preserved sixth-century structures of this kind in Constantinople.[57] The 'folded' capitals are deeply undercut with foliage and some of them still preserve the monograms of Justinian and Theodora.[58] The entablature consists of an Ionic architrave, an 'egg and dart' band, and a band of acanthus leaves (see Figure 11.7). The latter is surmounted by the frieze with the dedicatory inscription and a Corinthian cornice decorated with floral patterns and modillions. The same artistry is reflected in the smaller scale decoration in the gallery, with its Ionic impost capitals. The inventive, free juxtaposition of classical mouldings is reminiscent of sixth-century churches like Hagia Sophia and St. Eirene at Constantinople while the inscription running along an internal frieze resembles that of the lost church of St. Polyeuktos. This sculptural decoration is typical of sixth-century church architecture in Constantinople. The opulence of this internal sculpture contrasts with the simplicity of the external elevations, which reminds us that the church was originally surrounded by other structures, and was experienced mostly as an interior space.

Figure 11.7 Küçük Ayasofya Camii (Church of Sts. Sergius and Bacchus)

Source: Photograph by Efthymios Rizos, 2014

The interior of the building preserves traces of the fixtures added to it during the Byzantine period. For instance, in the shafts of the columns in the west part of the gallery, there are holes filled with iron or lead, which possibly belonged to metal elements fixed on the columns. According to Constantine Porphyrogenitus, it was at this part of the gallery that the Emperor stood during religious ceremonies.[59] Taking this into account, Ebersolt and Thiers interpreted these details as the stands or hinges of ornate crosses that once decorated the columns of the Emperor's 'tribune'.[60]

The transformation of the church into a mosque had a major impact on its interior. The corners of the piers were enriched with small, engaged semi-columns at the level of the gallery. Most of the interior was covered by a thick layer of white plaster and decorated with calligraphy and ornamental designs of intertwined flowing lines (see Figure 11.3).[61] Painted ornamental bands under cornices or across the dome's groins underline the architectural form, which is still admirable despite the loss of the original wall finishes, such as mosaics and marble revetment. Finally, the insertion of a mihrab and a minbar in the sanctuary provided a new focal point for the visitor of the building.

The external walls also provide valuable clues for the form of the original windows and their transformation during the late Byzantine and the Ottoman periods. Indeed, the north and east elevations preserve the outlines of the large, round arch windows.[62] Most of these windows were partly blocked with masonry infill. The large, triple arched openings of the north elevation, which probably connected the church with the Palace, were blocked with single courses of roughly hewn stones alternating with thin brick bands (see Figure 11.8).

Figure 11.8 Kucuk Ayasofya Camii (Church of Sts. Sergius and Bacchus), View of the north elevation.
Source: Photograph by Io Carydi, 2011

These infills may be earlier than the Ottoman period as similar walls are also encountered in late Byzantine structures.[63] Other windows such as those of the apse were partly blocked with randomly coursed rubble typical of the Ottoman period (see Figure 11.6).[64] Some of the Ottoman windows are rectangular, while others are covered with pointed brick arches. The alternation of these two types of windows, combined with the alternation of the original brick masonry with Ottoman coursed rubble masonry, for instance in the northeast side, gives the exterior of the building a picturesque character.[65]

The Current Dome and the Original Ceiling of Justinian's Church

If the repeated restoration of the walls of Sts. Sergius and Bacchus has never been disputed, the soaring dome that crowns the church tends to be attributed to the times of Justinian and is considered to be an integral part of the original design. However, in his 2017 article, Jonathan Bardill raised the possibility that the dome is not original but a later structure of an unspecified date.[66] Bardill's hypothesis was based on new evidence for the modification of the original roof structure, such as the truncated arches on the dome's drum as well as the crooked and unconventional shape of the dome itself. Showing evidence of large-scale, systematic repairs over the centuries, our above examination of the external walls seems to justify Bardill's point. Vulnerable to earthquakes due to its weight and wide span of approximately 16 m, the original nave ceiling could not have remained unscathed during the catastrophic events that necessitated so many repairs in the lower levels of the structure. Indeed, the following analysis of the form and structure of the dome and its buttresses provides additional reasons for attributing the dome to a later phase.

Let us start with the profile of the dome. As Van Millingen has shown, this consists of three parts, each with a noticeably different radius and curvature (see Figure 11.2).[67] The drum only has a slight inward curve. Above the level of the windows, the curvature of the dome increases sharply to create a transition to a shallow crown. The fact that the arches at the exterior of the drum seem to be interrupted at the same level as the 'bend' in the internal profile suggests that the current dome may have resulted from the modification of an earlier structure.[68]

The unusual, undulated form of the dome has no parallel in Early Byzantine architecture and is also indicative of an element that was adapted to the structure at later date. In this respect, the unusual concave compartments of this dome could serve two purposes. Firstly, they facilitate the adaptation of the dome to the octagonal plan of the base. Secondly, these elements compensate for the absence of suitable support and abutment at the lower levels of the structure.[69] Reinforced by external buttresses at their base, they behave like ribs, reinforcing the dome, and facilitating its construction on top of a load-bearing structure which may not have been originally intended to carry a standard hemispherical dome.

A close examination of the external buttresses of the dome also indicates that these and the dome were added at a later point (see Figure 11.9).[70] These buttresses lie at the level of the drum of the dome, just behind the latter's concave compartments. As Bardill has noted, the truncated arches between these buttresses indicate that the original windows of the dome were larger than the current ones, occupying part of the area of the drum currently blocked by the buttresses. This would suggest that these buttresses constitute a later addition to the structure. The theory that the buttresses are not original is further corroborated by their design and problematic relationship with the rest of the structure. Indeed, each buttress consists of two wall projections. Only one of these lies directly on top of the arches of the gallery, as one would expect.[71] The other transmits loads to the

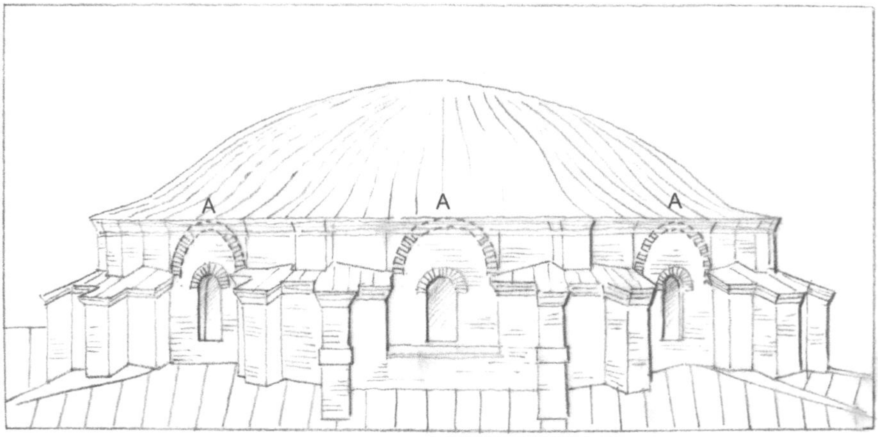

Figure 11.9 Kucuk Ayasofya Camii (Church of Sts. Sergius and Bacchus), Schematic elevation of the dome showing the arch fragments (A) revealed during the building's repair in 2002.

Source: Drawing by the author, based on the elevation published by J. Ebersolt, and A. Thiers, 1913 as well as the information about the arches published by Jonathan Bardill, 2017.

vaults of the gallery, below (see Figure 11.10). This is rather unconventional, as in most Byzantine churches, gallery vaults rarely carry such major loads.[72]

Finally, the way in which the dome 'sits' on the octagonal walls of the nave is also atypical, as it avoids the use of pendentives, which is one of the standard features of vaulted construction in the times of Justinian. The concave compartments are set back from the inner face of the interior wall, creating little 'shelves' above each of the angles of the octagonal walls of the nave (see Figure 11.3).[73] This unusual transition from octagon to dome is more likely to be the result of a later addition than the faithful implementation of the original, sixth-century design.

The above observations suggest that the current dome was not part of the original design. The form of the original ceiling of Justinian's church and the extent to which this was replaced or modified remain enigmatic. Bardill has proposed a reconstruction of this ceiling as a shallow dome on a drum. This reconstruction was based on the evidence for a taller drum (i.e. the truncated arches mentioned above and shown in Figure 11.9), as well as on the comparison with the roughly coeval church of St. Vitale in Ravenna, which also features an octagonal nave surrounded by semicircular niches. Bardill interpreted the concave compartments of the current dome of Sts. Sergius and Bacchus as the result of the modification of an original series of squinches which lay at the base of the drum. These squinches currently survive in San Vitale, where they facilitate the transition from the octagonal walls of the nave to the circular base of the dome. Bardill claims that Justinian's church of Sts. Sergius and Bacchus may also have had a similar dome with a shallower crown. According to Bardill, it was the modification of this original dome, which explains the peculiar form of the current dome.

While Bardill's attribution of the dome to a later phase is compelling, his reconstruction of the original roof is not entirely convincing. This proposal overlooks the important differences between the structure of the church of Sts. Sergius and Bacchus and that of San Vitale. While the domes of the two churches have a similar diameter, the piers of San Vitale are three times as thick as the piers of Sts. Sergius and Bacchus, the maximum thickness of which is barely 2 m. In Ravenna, the dome was abutted by semi-domes (and possibly

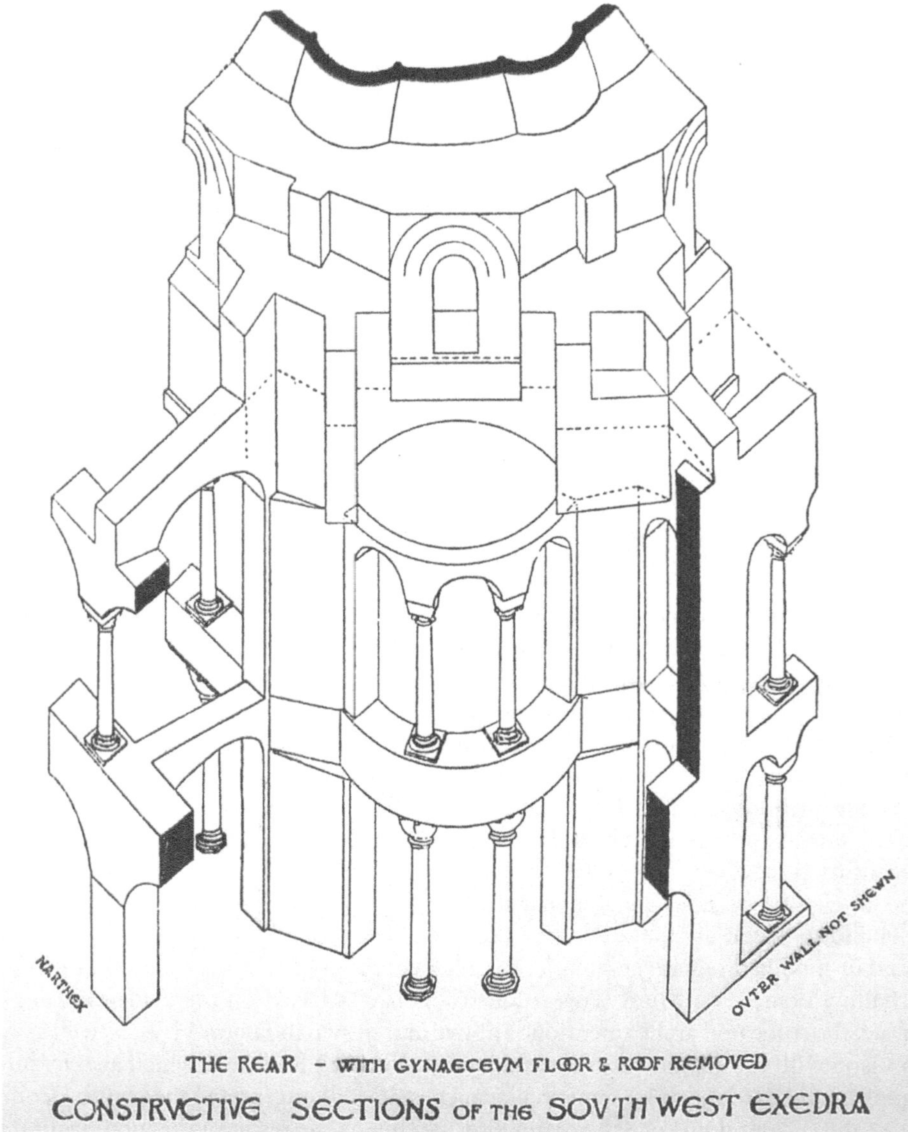

Figure 11.10 Kucuk Ayasofya Camii (Church of Sts. Sergius and Bacchus) – Interpretive axonometric diagram of the load bearing system and buttresses. Drawing published by A. Van Millingen, 1912.

buttresses) throughout its circumference, whereas in Constantinople semi-domes only occur in four points. Despite the similar size of both domes, the load-bearing structure of San Vitale is much better equipped to counteract the lateral thrusts of a dome on a drum, not to mention that the use of hollow terracotta tubes must have reduced the weight and lateral thrusts of the dome. The adoption of a similar hemispherical dome made of standard bricks in the original church of Sts. Sergius and Bacchus would pose serious structural challenges.

These challenges would risk becoming insurmountable in the case of a shallow dome like the one shown in Bardill's recent reconstruction.[74] The massive lateral thrusts of such a large and shallow dome could not have possibly been counteracted by a thin drum without any buttressing, as Bardill proposes. Besides its improbable structure, this reconstruction proposal is also unconventional from a morphological point of view. Despite Rabun Taylor's interesting theory about the first dome of Hagia Sophia, there is no conclusive evidence for the existence of such shallow domes sitting directly on vertical drums during the Early Byzantine period.[75] These observations suggest that despite its thoughtfulness, this reconstruction proposal cannot be considered a plausible basis for visualising the original form of the church.

To come up with a more plausible interpretation of the original structure of the church, it is necessary to re-examine the vaults, paying particular attention to Bardill's evidence regarding different phases of construction. Understanding the way in which the vaults are currently supported is essential to develop hypotheses about the structure that preceded them.

A great dome such as that of Sts. Sergius and Bacchus necessitates suitable supports to carry its increased loads and counteract its lateral thrusts. At first sight, the load-bearing structure of the church does not seem to have been designed to deal with the lateral thrusts of a 16-m dome. Measuring 1/8 of the dome's diameter, the thickness of the piers is one of the smallest ever observed in a Late Antique or Early Byzantine domed structure. In the domed baptisteries of Early Christian Ephesus, for instance, the ratio ranges from 1/3.2 to 1/3.6. Only in Italy do we notice thinner supports. In Santa Costanza, in Rome, the ratio between dome diameter and drum thickness is 1/7 and in San Vitale, the dome measures only 6.7 times the thickness of the piers. The fact that the 'pier thickness' to 'dome width' ratio of Sts. Sergius and Bacchus is even smaller than that of Italian domed buildings seems to be at odds with the increased seismicity of Constantinople. Summarised in Table 11.1, these observations suggest that the piers of Justinian's church of Sts. Sergius and Bacchus are not as thick as the piers of most other Late Antique and Early Byzantine domed structures.[76]

The above observations may indicate that the piers of Sts. Sergius and Bacchus were originally intended to carry a much lighter roof than the current one. For instance, a pyramidal,

Table 11.1 Ratios of dome diameter to pier thickness in domed Late Antique and Early Byzantine structures

Monument	*Approx. thickness of supporting piers or walls in metres (A)*	*Approx. dome diameter in metres (B)*	*Approx. ratio A/B (larger ratios are typical of stronger structures)*
Santa Costanza, Rome	1.65	11.5	1/7
Mausoleum of Diocletian, Split	2.85	13.3	1/4.7
Baptistery, St. John the Theologian at Ephesus	2.6	8.5	1/3.2
Baptistery, St. Mary at Ephesus	2.5	9	1/3.6
San Vitale, Ravenna	2.5	16.7	1/6.7
Sts. Sergius and Bacchus	2	16	1/8

timber roof would be more consistent with the shape of the nave, the lack of pendentives, and the size of the piers than a dome.

A careful re-reading of Procopius's sixth-century description of the church of Sts. Sergius and Bacchus may also provide a useful indication of the nature of the original roof. Procopius states that our church and that of Sts. Peter and Paul differ in *just one* respect: 'the long axis of one of them [ie. Sts. Peter and Paul] is built straight, while in the other church [ie. Sts. Sergius and Bacchus] the columns stand for the most part in a semi-circle'.[77] If the original church of Sts. Sergius and Bacchus had been covered by a 16-m-wide dome, this would have distinguished it markedly from the nearby basilica of Sts. Peter and Paul contradicting Procopius' description.[78] Besides, Procopius never mentions that the church of Sts. Sergius and Bacchus had a dome. One could argue that this is a justifiable omission within an inherently fragmentary account. However, it is worth pointing out that Procopius's account often devotes extensive passages to the domes of coeval structures at Constantinople.[79] These domes were often considered by Procopius as too distinctive and remarkable to overlook, especially in the context of references to the form of Justinian's churches, and comparisons between them. Procopius' silence with regard to the roof of Sts. Sergius and Bacchus may indicate that this was a standard, conventional timber roof.

A pyramidal timber roof would be consistent with the original drum of the building, which as Bardill has shown, was much taller than the current one and included larger windows. Such a thin drum could not have easily carried a dome without buttresses, whereas a lighter timber roof would have been much more compatible with it. We should therefore evaluate the possibility that Justinian's church was a hybrid building. Its nave was surmounted by a timber roof raised on a tall drum with large windows. However, the galleries and aisles of this building were covered with the barrel vaults and groin vaults that still survive today. Recently exposed, the structure of these vaults, consisting of bricks set pitched on their edge is typical of Early Byzantine vaulting practices (Figure 11.11).[80] Known in coeval churches and elsewhere, this combination of vaults and timber roof in the same structure would be typical of a transitional period that is marked by a gradual break with the tradition of the timber-roof basilica, and the slow adoption of vaulted forms.[81]

Conclusion

Looking at the repairs and modifications of the church of Sts. Sergius and Bacchus over the centuries, this chapter highlighted the character of this church as a 'palimpsest' of different phases of construction. Only part of the current building should be attributed to the times of Justinian, its famous dome probably being a later addition. This dome had to be adapted to an octagonal nave which was probably not designed for such a heavy vaulted roof. This helps to explain the peculiar form of the dome and its atypical connection with the walls of the nave and the supports of the gallery. The addition of this new element required the lowering of the drum and the addition of the buttresses that restricted the available space for windows. Shallower than the previous roof of the building, its new dome must have changed radically the character of the church, actually reducing its impact on the skyline of Constantinople.

Considering that the original church of Sts. Sergius and Bacchus may have actually been a timber-roofed, centralised church, we should consider the possibility that this church had very little to do with the emergence of domes in Constantinople's skyline. If the above hypothesis is true, then the interpretation of this church as a precursor to Hagia Sophia

Figure 11.11 Küçük Ayasofya Camii (Church of Sts. Sergius and Bacchus) – View of the Vaults of the South Gallery

Source: Photograph by Efthymios Rizos, 2014

needs to be revised. The original church of Sts. Sergius and Bacchus could have been part of a different sixth-century architectural typology. Its typological affiliation can be deduced by shifting our attention from the current dome of the building, to consider the other elements of its design. This design combines contrasting elements into a harmonious whole. Arched and trabeated colonnades coexist, square and circular niches alternate, and the square outer perimeter encloses an octagonal interior. This marriage of square and octagon is typical of Early Christian Syria.[82] The semicircular exedrae in the interior are reminiscent of the church of St. Polyeuctos at Constantinople, a church that may have also followed eastern design models.[83] Dedicated to two Syrian martyrs, our church seems to have had a strong morphological connection with Syrian martyriums such as that of St. George at Izra. Built in 515 AD, the latter also includes a later dome that has been adapted to an earlier octagonal structure.[84] The centralised character of this monument, the octagonal central space, the extension of this space through diagonal semicircular exedras, and the transition from a square external perimeter to an octagonal core are all encountered in Sts. Sergius and Bacchus. The adoption of these typically Syrian design features in the design of the Constantinopolitan church must have resulted in linking the building, symbolically, to church construction in the southeastern provinces of Byzantium. The possible initial role of the church of Sts. Sergius and Bacchus as a religious centre of Non-Chalcedonian refugees, many of whom came from Syria, justifies the choice of such models in the original design of the church.

The possibility that Justinian's original church of Sts. Sergius and Bacchus was not domed calls for a reconsideration of the Emperor's role in the 'punctuation' of the urban skyline of Constantinople with domes. One of Justinian's first churches may have actually been timber roofed, and the Emperor's later vaulted basilicas were covered by shallow domes, which were co-spherical with the supporting pendentives, and largely invisible from the exterior. This was far from being the prototype of the 'city of domes' depicted in the fifteenth-century panoramas that opened this chapter. The idea of a prominent, visible, 'urban' dome is absent from Justinian's earliest architectural realisations and will only appear as the unintended result of the collapse of the first dome of Hagia Sophia. Twenty feet taller, the replacement dome exposed a much larger part of its curved extrados than that of the original design. We will never know if this increase in height was a conscious attempt to make the new dome more visible or whether it was simply motivated by structural considerations. Whatever the intention was, the second dome of Hagia Sophia wrote a new chapter in the history of Constantinople's urban skyline. It dominated visually the image of the city, ultimately becoming one of the visual embodiments of its public realm. The origin of the 'city of domes' lies probably here, in the response to an accidental event at the last years of Justinian reign.

Notes

1 See H. Buchwald, "Byzantine Town Planning Does It Exist?", in *Material Culture and Well-Being in Byzantium (400–1453)*, eds. M. Grunbart, E. Kislinger, A. Muthesius and D. Stathakopoulos (Viena: Verlag der Österreichische Akademie der Wissenschaften, 2007), 57–74.

2 See R. Krautheimer, *Early Christian and Byzantine Architecture* (Harmondsworth: Penguin, 1965), 345–375.

3 See A. Berger and J. Bardill, "The Representations of Constantinople in Hartmann Schedel's World Chronicle, and Related Pictures", *Byzantine and Modern Greek Studies*, 22, 1998: 2–37; I. Manners, "Constructing the Image of a City: The Representation of Constantinopole in

Christopher Buondelmonti's Liber Insularum Archipelagi", *Annals of the Association of American Geographers* 87/1, 1997: 72–102.

4 For an analysis of the role of domes in the urban skyline of Medieval and Early Modern cities, see S. Kostof, *The City Shaped, Urban Patterns and Meanings through History* (London: Thames and Hudson, 1991), 292–298.

5 For the early phases of St. John at Ephesos, see N. Karydis, "The Evolution of the Church of St. John at Ephesos during the Early Byzantine Period", *Jahreshefte des Österreichischen Archäologischen Institutes in Wien* 84, 2015: 97–128, esp. 120–121.

6 For St. Sophia at Thessaloniki and St. Nicholas at Myra, see S. Feist, *Die byzantinische Sakralarchitektur der Dunklen Jahrhunderte* (Wiesbaden: Reichert, 2019), 94–104, 109–125. For St. Mary at Ephesos, see N. Karydis, "The Development of the Church of St Mary at Ephesos from Late Antiquity to the Dark Ages", *Anatolian Studies* 69, 2019: 175–194. For the church at Dereagzi, see J. Morgastern, "The Church at Deragzi: A Preliminary Report", *Dumbarton Oaks Papers* 22, 1968: 217–225. For St. Clement at Ankara, see G. De Jerphanion, "L'Eglise de Saint-Clément à Angora", in *Mélanges d' Archéologie Anatolienne* (Mélanges de l'Université St. Joseph XIII) (Beyrouth: Université St. Joseph, 1928), 113–143.

7 For the collapse of Basilica B at Philippi, see R. F. Hoddinott, *Early Byzantine Churches in Macedonia and Southern Serbia, A Study of the Origins and Initial Development of East Christian Art* (London: Macmillan, 1963), 189–190 and S. Ćurčić, *Architecture in the Balkans from Diocletian to Suleyman the Magnificent, c. 300–1550* (New Haven: Yale, 2010), 207.

8 Further information about the domes of these monuments and complete bibliographies can be found in: R. Mainstone, *Hagia Sophia: Architecture, Structure and Liturgy of Justinian's Great Church* (London: Thames & Hudson, 1988), 160–165; Urs Peschlow, Die Irenenkirche in Istanbul, Tübingen: E. Wasmuth, 1977, 206, and J. Ebersolt and A. Thiers, *Les Eglises de Constantinople* (Paris: Ernest Leroux, 1913), 19–52.

9 According to the contemporary testimonies of Agathias and Malalas, the first dome of Hagia Sophia had a shallower profile than the one that replaced it, with a height 20 ft inferior to the height of the reconstructed dome. Both accounts have been discussed by Mainstone (*Hagia Sophia*, 90).

10 See Constantine the Rhodian, *Ekphrasis*, line 626, published in L. James, *Constantine of Rhodes, On Constantinople and the Church of the Holy Apostles, with a New Edition of the Greek Text by Ioannis Vassis* (Farnham: Ashgate, 2012), 60–61.

11 According to Thomas Mathews '... students of Architecture have examined the structure of Sts. Sergius and Bacchus countless times recording with various interpretations the subtle alteration of the regular and apsed recesses, the complexity of the design of the sixteen – sided dome, and the treatment of the architectural sculpture. See Mathews, *The Early Churches of Constantinople, Architecture and Liturgy* (University Park and London: The Pennsylvania State University Press, 1977), 42.

12 See Procopius, Buildings, I, iv. 1–7.

13 Indicatively, we should mention the early efforts of Alexandros Paspatis (*Βυζαντιναί Μελέται, Τοπογραφικαί και Ιστορικαί*, Constantinople: Koromilas, 1877) who provided a description of the building's late nineteenth-century urban context as well as a review of its history on the basis of early and middle Byzantine records. The first architectural survey of the church was provided by Alexander Van Millingen in 1912. The following year, Jean Ebersolt and Adolphe Thiers published a lavishly illustrated and more detailed architectural and archaeological survey, accompanied by a graphic reconstruction of Justinian's church and its immediate context. Cf. Ebersolt and Thiers, *Les Eglises de Constantinople*, 36; Alexander Van Millingen, *Byzantine Churches in Constantinople, Their History and Architecture* (London: Macmillan, 1912), 68.

14 C. Mango ("The Church of Saints Sts. Sergius and Bacchus at Constantinople and the Alleged Tradition of octagonal Palatine Churches", *Jarbuch der Osterreichischen Byzantinistik* 21, 1972: 189–193) argued that 'the church of Sts. Sergius and Bacchus was a martyrium specially built for a large Monophysite monastery'. However, R. Krautheimer ("Again Saints Sergius and Bacchus at Constantinople", *Jahrbuch der Österreichischen Byzantinistik* 23, 1974: 251–153, esp. 252) interpreted the building as a palatine chapel and refuted the connection with the Monophysite refugees, as this situation 'would not have arisen before the Council of 536 which condemned the Monophysites and presumably not before early 537 when persecution in the provinces started in earnest'. J. Bardill ("The Church of Sts. Sergius and Bacchus in Constantinople and the

Monophysite Refugees", *Dumbarton Oaks Papers* 54, 2000: 1–11) published evidence supported Mango's argument. This evidence was challenged by B. Croke ("Justinian, Theodora, and the Church of Saints Sergius and Bacchus", *Dumbarton Oaks Papers* 60, 2006: 25–63, esp. 36–40), who claimed that construction of the church of Sts. Sergius and Bacchus was commissioned by Justinian before his accession to the Imperial throne, while he and Theodora were resident in the Palace of Hormisdas. However, Bardill ("The Date, Dedication, and Design of Sts. Sergius and Bacchus in Constantinople", *Journal of Late Antiquity* 10/1, 2017: 62–130.) provided further clarifications and support for his theory, which provides the most plausible interpretation of the date of the church and its original role. See also Mathews, *The Early Churches of Constantinople*, 42–52, and Wolfgang Muller-Wiener, *Bildlexikon Zur Topographie Istanbuls* (Tubingen: Wasmuth, 1977), 65.

15 Most scholars assume that the current dome dates back to the time of Justinian. However, Bardill's recent, hypothetical model of Justinian's church visualises this with a slightly different dome on a drum that seems to be rather atypical from both the morphological and structural points of view. See Bardill, "The Date, Dedication, and Design of Sts. Sergius and Bacchus in Constantinople", 115.

16 According to a legend, Justinian wanted to pay tribute to Sts. Sergius and Bacchus, two Saints who intervened to save his life during the reign of Emperor Anastasius. See J. J. Norwich, *Byzantium, The Early Centuries* (London: Penguin, 1988), 195. According to Ebersolt and Thiers (*Les Eglises de Constantinople*, 23), 'les monogrammes sculptes sur les chapiteaux, la grande inscription conservée dans la nef, indiquent clairement que l'édifice n'a pas été érigé avant le couronnement d' Avril 527'.

17 See Brock, "The Conversations with the Syrian Orthodox under Justinian (532)", *Orientalia Christiana Periodica* 47, 1981: 87–121, esp. 92; Bardill, "The Date, Dedication, and Design of Sts. Sergius and Bacchus in Constantinople", 73.

18 According to Mathews, ("The Early Churches of Constantinople", 47), the Hegoumenos (Abbot) of Sts. Peter and Paul and of the Holy Martyrs Sts. Sergius and Bacchus was present in the Church Council of 536.

19 See Mango, "The Church of Saints Sts. Sergius and Bacchus at Constantinople", 189–193, Mathews, *The Early Churches of Constantinople*, 43 and J. Bardill, "The Church of Sts. Sergius and Bacchus in Constantinople and the Monophysite Refugees", *Dumbarton Oaks Papers* 54, 2000: 1–11.

20 According to Procopius (*Buildings* I.iv.1-7) "these two churches do not face each other, but stand alongside to one another, being at the same time joined to each other; (...) and they share the same entrances ...".

21 According to John of Ephesus, "Theodora had been gathering together persecuted men from all quarters and looking after them, in that they had been placed by her in the palace named Hormisda". See Mango, "The Church of Saints Sts. Sergius and Bacchus at Constantinople", 191.

22 See Mango, "The Church of Saints Sts. Sergius and Bacchus at Constantinople", 192.

23 See Norwich, *Byzantium*, 270.

24 Theophanes Continuatus gives as a vivid account of the fury that led to the destruction of figural decoration in churches and to the abolishment of Icons during the Iconoclast period (eighth to ninth centuries). Throughout every church, the figures of Saints were destroyed, and the forms of beasts and birds were painted in their places. See J. Beckwith, *The Art of Constantinople. An Introduction to Byzantine Art* 330–1453 (London: Phaidon, 1961), 57; Muller-Wiener, *Bildlexikon Zur Topographie Istanbuls*, 65

25 See Beckwith, *The Art of Constantinople*, 63; A. Berger, *Untersuchungen zu den Patria Konstantinupoleos, Poikila Byzantina 8* (Bonn: Habelt, 1988), 568; Bardill, "The Date, Dedication, and Design of Sts. Sergius and Bacchus in Constantinople", 99.

26 See Van Millingen, *Byzantine Churches in Constantinople*, 68; Semavi Eyice, *Istanbul, Petit Guide a Travers les Monuments Byzantins et Turcs* (Istanbul: Istanbul Matbaasi, 1955), 35.

27 For a discussion of Constantine Porphyrogenitus' account of tenth-century Byzantine liturgy and the Emperor's annual visits to the church; see Mathews, *The Early Churches of Constantinople*, 113.

28 See Ebersolt and Thiers, *Les Eglises de Constantinople*, 36.

29 See G. P. Majeska, *Russian Travelers to Constantinople in the Fourteenth and Fifteenth Centuries* (Washington: Dumbarton Oaks, 1984) 38, 164.
30 According to Mathews (*The Early Churches of Constantinople*, 47–50), late Byzantine records omit any reference to Sts. Peter and Paul.
31 See Paspatis, *Βυζαντιναί Μελέται*, 334.
32 The endowment deed is preserved in the Archive of the *Topkapı Palace* Museum: TS.MA.d6977, folio.10b. The deed and the Ottoman history of Sts. Sergius and Bacchus have recently been discussed by İrem Gündüz Polat, *Küçük Ayasofya And The Foundation Of Babüssaade Ağasi Hüseyin Ağa* (MA Diss. Istanbul: Boğaziçi University, 2016), 89.
33 The zaviye is mentioned in the endowment deed: TS.MA.d6977, folio.11a (see Figure 11.1).
34 See Muller-Wiener, *Bildlexikon*, 65.
35 Petrus Gillius or Pierre Gilles visited Constantinople in 1580 and published a description of the city's main monuments, among which Sts. Sergius and Bacchus, in his book *De Constantinopoleos Topographia*. One of his most interesting remarks is that the monument, although used as a mosque was known with its Byzantine name. When it comes to the internal decoration, the sixteenth-century author repeats Procopius' description. See P. Gyllius, *De Constantinoupoleos Topographiae, The Antiquities of Constantinople with a description of its Situation* (London: John Ball, 1729), 117–119.
36 According to Van Millingen (*Byzantine Churches in Constantinople*, 71), all the windows of the church were altered in the Ottoman period.
37 See Gündüz Polat, *Küçük Ayasofya*, 89.
38 See Van Millingen, *Byzantine Churches in Constantinople*, 304.
39 See G. Ozsen and F. Aköz, "Diagnostic Studies on Kucuk Ayasofya Mosque – The Church of Sts. Sergius and Bacchus – in Istanbul" (Paris: ICOMOS International Millenium Congress, 2001), 1.
40 See Muller-Wiener (1977), 66.
41 See Ozsen and Akoz, "Diagnostic Studies on Kucuk Ayasofya Mosque", 1.
42 According to Paspatis, the adjacent railway shakes the entire building causing the dome to crack, while stones and bricks fall from the unrendered walls. Many windows and niches had to be filled in. See Paspatis, *Βυζαντιναί Μελέται*, 334.
43 See Muller-Wiener, *Bildlexikon*, 67.
44 See G. Arun, A. Alkis, H. H. Demirel, R.-D. Duppe, C. Gerstenecker and M. Hovenbitzer, "Determination of Old and New Deformations at Kucuk Aya Sofya Mosque in Istanbul by Photogrammetric Methods and an Attempt of their Interpretation" (Anatalya: CIPA 16th International Symposium, 2003), 2.
45 According to the ISCARSAH committee (2001, 1–2), the main cause for the monument's decay was not the sudden increase of loads during the earthquake, but the exacerbation of soil settlement the latter caused. The cracks of the dome started from the semi-domes of the northeast and southeast 'exedras' and reached about two thirds of the dome's height, passing through the area between the drum's windows and the dome's concave segments. Those cracks went through the entire thickness of the dome's structure, and their thickness reached 1 cm. See Ozsen et al., "Diagnostic Studies", 2.
46 See Arun et al., "Old and New Deformations at Kucuk Aya Sofya Mosque", 4.
47 The restoration of the building was launched by the Istanbul Heritage Fund, in connection with the World's Monument Fund and Yildiz Technical University of Istanbul. The same year, the Department of Civil Engineering of Yildiz University performed a detailed structural survey of the structure and designed and specified the measures that should be taken for the structure's strengthening. The design and supervision of restoration work were carried out by Mehmet Alper and Nilgun Olgun, who completed the project in 2006.
48 The information about the restoration of the building was kindly provided by Nilgun Olgun, conservation architect during my visit to the monument in 2006. For the use of carbon fibre-reinforced resins, cf. A. Cripps, *Fibre-Reinforced Polymer Composites in Construction* (London: CIRIA, 2002), 27; S. Briccoli Bati and T. Rotunno, "Environmental Durability of the Bond between the CFRP Composite Materials and Masonry Structures", in *Historical Constructions 2001. Possibilities of Numerical and Experimental Techniques*, eds. P. Roca and P. Lourenco (Guimaraes: University of Minko, 2001), 39.
49 See Van Millingen, *Byzantine Churches in Constantinople*, 76.

50 The sanctuary lacks subsidiary rooms or chapels, characteristic of later developments of Byzantine architecture. See Mango, "The Church of Saints Sts. Sergius and Bacchus at Constantinople", 51.
51 According to A. Choisy, the groined segments behave like ribs that make the dome less deformable and their edges allow the dome to rest directly on top of the octagonal base. See A. Choisy, *L' Art de Batir Chez les Byzantins* (Paris: Librairie de la Société Anonyme de Publications Périodiques, 1883), 68.
52 See Van Millingen, *Byzantine Churches in Constantinople, Their History and Architecture*, 71.
53 This hypothesis is confirmed by Ebersolt's observation of three great blocked arches on the ground level of the south façade, which are repeated on the first floor. According to the French researcher, the fact that those arches are seen in the interior of the building proves that they were originally open in order to give access to the church of Sts. Peter and Paul. See Ebersolt and Thiers, *Les Eglises de Constantinople*, 36. The same author noticed that the two columns that screen off the central niche of the south wall were cut to receive some kind of doorframe: a flat band runs up the side of the columns and over the capitals, containing holes for fastenings. See Mathews (1977), 45.
54 Mathews follows Ebersolt's observation that the two columns were cut to receive some kind of doorframe. See Mathews (1977), 45.
55 The bonding courses of the original masonry are made of green stone, a local kind of granite which was also used in sixth-century Hagia Sophia. Other stones present in the structure are shelled diatomaceous limestone, travertine, and argillaceous limestone. The stone bonding courses of the 'Justinianic' masonry are made of big, well-dressed rectangular stone blocks about 40 cm thick and up to 80 cm long. Those well-carved blocks of the early Byzantine period betray a level of craftsmanship that is clearly missing in the coursed rubble masonry of the Middle Byzantine and Ottoman repairs. The later masonry typically consists of smaller, roughly hewn stone blocks, approx. 25 cm thick and up to 55 cm long. The original constructional quality was only equalled in the masonry over the arches of the Beyazit portico added to the church at the beginning of the sixteenth century. Similar wall structures are seen in original parts of Hagia Sophia and St. Eirene. See Mathews, *The Early Churches of Constantinople*, 44.
56 This building technique was also used in the tenth-century repairs in Haghia Sophia. The similar parts of the wall of Sts. Sergius and Bacchus are also likely to date to the same period. See Krautheimer, *Early Christian and Byzantine Architecture* (Harmondsworth: Penguin, 1965), 258.
57 The shafts of the columns on the ground floor are made of red synnada marble, whereas those of the gallery are constructed of verd antique marble. The bases and the capitals as well as in the stylobate and the entablature are made of blue-veined, white Proconnesian marble, which was used very often in church construction throughout Late Antiquity and the Early Byzantine period.
58 For the monograms see Swainson "Monograms of the Capitals of S. Sergius at Constantinople", *Byzantinische Zeitschrift* 4, 1895, 106–108, Van Millingen, *Byzantine Churches in Constantinople*, 73, Croke, "Justinian, Theodora, and the Church of Saints Sergius and Bacchus", 49 and Bardill, "The Date, Dedication, and Design of Sts. Sergius and Bacchus in Constantinople", 76.
59 See Constantine Porphyrogenitus, *Book of Ceremonies* I, 11.
60 See Ebersolt and Thiers, *Les Eglises de Constantinople*, 30–31.
61 See Van Millingen, *Byzantine Churches in Constantinople*, 72 (see Figure 11.3).
62 See Mathews, *The Early Churches of Constantinople*, pl. 26.
63 The walls of the Lascarid palace at Nymphaeum also feature this masonry. See H. Buchwald, "Lascarid Architecture", *Jahrbuch der Österreichischen Byzantinistik* 28, 1979: 261–296, esp. 263.
64 For the alteration of the original windows during the Ottoman period, see Van Millingen, *Byzantine Churches in Constantinople* 71 (see Figure 11.6).
65 For the use of a similar masonry in Ottoman buildings, see Mathews, *The Early Churches of Constantinople*, 45.
66 See Bardill "The Date, Dedication, and Design of Sts. Sergius and Bacchus in Constantinople", 105–118.
67 See Van Millingen, *Byzantine Churches in Constantinople*, 78 (see Figure 11.2).
68 See Bardill, "The Date, Dedication, and Design of Sts. Sergius and Bacchus in Constantinople", 56.
69 As we will see in the following paragraphs, the piers of Sts. Sergius and Bacchus are thinner than the piers that usually support domes in Early Byzantine structures. The concave segments of this dome and the external buttresses make up for this.
70 On the buttresses, see Van Millingen, *Byzantine Churches in Constantinople*, 79.

71 According to Ebersolt and Thiers (*Les Eglises de Constantinople*, 32), the buttresses are only partly supported by the arches between the barrel vaults of the gallery.
72 The semi-domes and broad arches below the dram also counteract lateral thrusts, relieving the piers. For the buttressing role of vaulted structures, see G. Croci, *The Conservation and Structural Restoration of Architectural Heritage*, Computational Mechanics Publications, Southampton, 1998, 242.
73 See Van Millingen, *Byzantine Churches in Constantinople*, 77.
74 See Bardill, "The Date, Dedication, and Design of Sts. Sergius and Bacchus in Constantinople", 115.
75 See R. Taylor, "A Literary and Structural Analysis of the First Dome on Justinian's Hagia Sophia, Constantinople", *Journal of the Society of Architectural Historians* 55/1, 1996: 66–78, esp. 72.
76 For a structural survey of the load-bearing structure of the church, see M. Massanas, P. Roca, M. Cervera, and G. Arun, "Structural Analysis of Kucuk Ayasofya Mosque in Istanbul", in *Structural Analysis of Historical Constructions* IV (London: Taylor & Francis, 2005), 679–686, esp. 683.
77 See Procopius, *Buildings* I. iv. 6.
78 Most scholars consider the church of Sts. Peter and Paul as a basilica, due to Procopius' reference to this building's longitudinal shape. Cf. Bardill, "The Date, Dedication, and Design of Sts. Sergius and Bacchus in Constantinople", 81; Procopius, *Buildings*, I. iv. 6.
79 See Procopius, *Buildings* I. iv. 15; viii. 13.
80 The combination of vaults over the ambulatory and timber roof over the nave may appear peculiar but it is also encountered in other Early Byzantine monuments, such as the basilica of St. Mary at Ephesos. See N. Karydis, "The development of the Church of St Mary at Ephesos from late antiquity to the Dark Ages", 175–194, esp. 187–188.
81 For the development of early Byzantine vaulted construction, see N. Karydis, *Early Byzantine Vaulted Construction in the Western Coastal Plains and River Valleys of Asia Minor* (Oxford: Archaeopress, 2011).
82 The best example of this Syrian practice is the Cathedral in Bosra, built in 513, where a huge circle was enveloped within a rectangular niched exterior. See W. MacDonald., *Early Christian & Byzantine Architecture* (New York: Braziller, 1962), 25, pl. 24.
83 See M. Harrison, *A Temple for Byzantium, The Discovery and Excavation of Anicia Juliana's Palace – Church in Istanbul* (London: Harvey Miller, 1989), 65
84 See Walter Karnapp, "Das Kuppelproblem von St. Georg in Ezraa (Syrien)", in *Tortulae: Studien zu altchristlichen und byzantinischen Monumenten*, ed. W. N. Schumacher (Rome: Herder, 1966), 178–186; W. Eugene Kleinbauer, "The Origin and Functions of the Aisled Tetraconch Churches in Syria and Northern Mesopotamia", *Dumbarton Oaks Papers* 27, 1973: 89–114, esp. 108. The octagonal element combined with diagonal niches also occurs in the church in Seleucia-Pieria (unknown date), as well as in the Cathedral of Bosra. Cf. Krautheimer, *Early Christian and Byzantine Architecture*, 105–106; C. Bouras, *History of Architecture* (Athens: Melissa, 1993) 132; H. Buchwald, *Form, Style and Meaning in Byzantine Church Architecture* (Aldershot: Ashgate, 1999), 205.

12

FORTIFICATIONS AND THE MAKING OF THE BYZANTINE CITY[1]

Nikolas Bakirtzis

The theme of transition provides a useful conceptual framework to probe an array of inquiries related to the multifaceted role of fortifications in the evolution of Byzantine cities from the end of Late Antiquity to the fall of Constantinople to the Ottomans in 1453.[2] As cities faced various economic and social challenges that transformed their civic functions and influenced the spatial and cultural experience of their inhabitants, fortification works were not only a product of, but also contributed to these processes. Walls, towers and gates were integral components of the built environment mirroring the economic, social and cultural complexity of cities.[3] Before anything else, the need for protection and control of space was a dynamic factor that shaped cities' development, while providing the necessary conditions for socioeconomic and cultural life. This chapter will try to address aspects of these realities in an attempt to better understand the ways military architecture framed the spatial perception as well as the daily experience of cities in Byzantium.

Through the long history of Byzantium, fortification works outlined and contained urban life.[4] Especially, during periods of volatility and transition, city life was identified with the existence of defensive walls. In Late Antiquity, the increased need for defense, protection and control precipitated the construction of fortifications which effectively shaped the development of urban centers and strengthened the adaptive resilience of Byzantine societies.[5] The topic of the transformation of the ancient *polis* to the Byzantine *kastron* (castle) has received extensive attention in scholarship addressing various aspects of the socioeconomic and political continuities, discontinuities and transitions of cities. In a way, the fact that the *kastron* became synonymous with the presence of a city or town underlines the central role of military architecture in Byzantium.[6] It's important to note that the making of the Byzantine castle-town was the product of a complex transformation which adjusted to, as well as, reflected the particular conditions and characteristics of each case.[7]

In this context, fortifications served a primary role in the making of the Byzantine city. They had an enduring presence in the cityscapes of the Byzantine Empire, whether in the examples of urban centers that retained their spatial footprint through time or in cases where cities shrank in size, moved or were newly built. The long history of urban centers, like Constantinople, Thessaloniki, Nicaea and Nicomedia, to name a few examples, was directly linked with their defensive capacities.[8] Their fortification works did not lose

DOI: 10.4324/9780429203923-16

their role and function over time, thus proving the lasting impact of late Roman military architecture.[9] Responding to a range of political, economic and military challenges facing the empire from the third through the sixth century, the construction of succeeding lines of defenses enclosing the urban fabric of cities became standard practice. These defensive lines utilized moat works, outer and inner walls, towers, gatehouses and citadels to support complex fortification systems, which, of course, received updates and restorations through time.

Urban Continuities, Transitions and Transformations

A typical example of cities with long and uninterrupted use of their late antique fortifications is Thessaloniki, which was founded in 315 BC by Cassander, King of Macedonia, at the tip of the Thermaic Gulf in Northern Greece. Defensive walls were constructed in the third century and mostly in the late fourth to the first half of the fifth century; work that has largely been attributed to Emperor Theodosius I, making extensive reuse of materials from buildings of the ancient city (Figure 12.1).[10] Parts of redundant institutions of the city's pagan past, such as temples, gymnasia and other public buildings, were used in this momentous defensive endeavor.[11] The facades of structures, like the so-called tower of 'Klaudianos', dating from the third century and named after the official mentioned in the past of a Roman inscription displayed on the tower's façade, and the facades of the late fourth-century western land walls bear the visual evidence of displayed spolia.[12] Examples

Figure 12.1 Thessaloniki [Greece]; view of the Western Walls of the city

of the practice can be seen in various parts of the city's fortifications, with the lower western walls being among the most indicative.

It's important to note that the reuse of building material in defensive works was common practice in late Antiquity, which is frequently associated with hasty efforts to erect protective walls in the hope of repelling an imminent raid or attack. What is important in this period is that the construction of fortifications and the related use of spolia happened during times of major socioeconomic and cultural transition related to the Christianization of Empire; cities like Thessaloniki were the central stages of this process. As a result, and not simply as a matter of timing, city authorities and builders utilized the opportunity. As mentioned, unwanted pagan institutions were available to be 'harvested' as building material in order to serve the defensive needs of urban societies. I believe that this was a very important aspect of the complex process of the Christianization of early Byzantine cityscapes. In this context, the material dimension of fortification facades carried important cultural connotations and meaning.

Even though Thessaloniki's population fluctuated and declined in later centuries, its physical size remained the same with the city continuing to be encircled by its late antique walls. The resiliency of Thessalonians against a series of threats and attacks was manifested by their capacity to maintain the city's defenses and thus to sustain control over it. The close affiliation of the city with the presence and permanence of its walls can be attested in the array of dedicatory inscriptions spanning the centuries while marking the work of church and state officials. For example, the inscriptions of Hormisdas, dating from the end of the fourth century, of Andronikos Lapardas and Michael Prosuch, members of the Komnenian court of Thessaloniki in the 1160s, or that of George Apokafkos on behalf of Manuel Palaiologos, governor of the city between 1369 and 1373, are indicative examples of the long tradition of the practice.[13] The walls of Constantinople offer additional examples like the inscriptions commemorating the work of Theophilos (829–842) along the walls of the Marmara Sea were prominently places to the sides of gateways like Değirmen Kapı and the gate of St. Barbara (Figure 12.2). The restorations sponsored by Basil II (976–1025) and Constantine IX (1025–1028), were properly located on the towers of the gates of the Pege and Rhousiou, or Rhegium. Overall, the reuse of building materials as well as the practice of displaying the deeds of emperors and city officials on the facades of walls, towers and gates underscored the long continuity of cities thus strengthening their sense of identity. The city's enclosure was not only its lifeline but also an ark of its memory and past.

Beyond the examples of Thessaloniki, Constantinople and other urban centers which retained their size, the vast majority of cities saw major transformations that ranged from abandonment and decline, to reduction in size and relocation. Over the past decades, archaeological work has been able to offer a nuanced understanding of the complexity of these changes. With little doubt, the spatial transformations of urbanscapes during this period and the making of the Byzantine castle, which effectively became synonymous with city and town, are a fascinating phenomenon which greatly shaped the history of Byzantine urbanism. Of course, regional peculiarities in conjunction with local geographical and socioeconomic conditions affected these developments. Yet, key urban functions depended on the capacity of Byzantine authorities to protect and control space. In this effort, the construction of fortifications and, equally if not more important, the maintenance of defensive enclosures were a critical tool for the Byzantine state. In essence, fortifications enabled the transformations of Byzantine cities.

Figure 12.2 Istanbul [Turkey]; tower bearing the dedicatory inscription of Emperor Theophilos from the sea walls facing the Marmara Sea

There are numerous examples of these processes across the landscapes of Byzantium. Amorion, Ankara, Sardis, Ephesus and Miletus in Asia Minor, Abdera and Maroneia in Thrace, Serres, Veroia and Philippi in Macedonia, Athens in Attica, Corinth and Argos in the Peloponnese, as well as Salamis-Constantia in Cyprus are some indicative cases of cities which gained new defensive walls as they contracted in size.[14] Newly built defenses usually protected easier to defend parts of cities. In Mytilene in the island of Lesbos and in Limenas in Thassos, Byzantine castles developed on the fortified hills that served as the acropoleis of the ancient cities.[15] At Stageira, the birth-place of Aristotle located in the Chalkidike peninsula in Northern Greece, the emergence of a fortified town mentioned in the sources as Livasdias occupied the northern hill of the small peninsula where the ancient city developed.[16] The Byzantine town came into existence through the construction of a strong wall across the peninsula cutting in half the area of ancient Stageira. The transformation of ancient Edessa in Macedonia into the notably smaller middle Byzantine town of Vodena provides another example of the phenomenon.[17]

It's worth mentioning that frequently these new fortified urban formations obtained new names which reflected aspects of their transformation. Instructive examples can be seen at the ancient cities of Abdera and Plotinoupolis in Thrace, which became known as Polystylon, meaning 'having many columns', and Didymoteichon which means 'having twin walls'.[18] Appropriately, these new names demonstrated key aspects of city fortifications. At Polystylon, the extensive use of spoliated columns from the ancient city in the construction of the Byzantine walls became the attribute which gave the castle its name. In the example of Didymoteichon, the name described the fortification system which protected two neighboring hills (Figure 12.3).

Relocating to sites which offered better protection was frequently a preferred choice for city authorities and populations. The abandonment of cities like Diocletianoupolis in Western Macedonia or Comana Pontica in the Ancient Pontus led to the establishment of

Figure 12.3 Didymoteicho [Greece]; view of the eastern walls of the Byzantine Castle

new towns like Kastoria and Dazimon (Tokat) in more defensible sites.[19] Another example is provided by Nikopolis, located in the southwestern part of Epirus. By the end of the ninth century, the city had largely faded with the strategic castle of Naupaktos taking its place as the theme capital and the seat of the metropolitan.[20] In later centuries, the fortified port-town of Anaktoroupolis in Eastern Macedonia was founded on a hill on the Aegean coast in close proximity to the site of ancient Oisime. It's useful to consider how political volatility and insecurity shaped the settlement choices of local populations in the island of Aigina.[21] In the end of the sixth century, the ancient city's acropolis, located at the so-called Kolona hill, became a fortified settlement that continued its life until the end of the ninth century, when local populations moved to the island's interior. Their choice of location at the naturally fortified site of Paliachora mirrored their need for protection away from the coast.[22] In general, the foundation of new towns in inaccessible locations like the examples of Monemvasia in the southern Peloponesos (Figure 12.4), which developed at a key coastal location and Servia, situated to control the Aliakmon river and the natural passage from Western Macedonia to Thessaly, reflects the growing appreciation for naturally protected sites.[23] Instructive examples of such choices were also the Byzantine fortifications of Amastris on the south coast of the Black Sea, Christoupolis in Macedonia, Mystras in the Peloponnese and Berat in Albania.[24]

On the whole, fortifications were instrumental in the organization of urban space, frequently reflecting the divisions of socioeconomic functions and administrative hierarchies.[25] A common organizational scheme was the presence of successive lines of defenses which

Figure 12.4 Monemvasia [Greece]; general view from the Southwest

utilized their natural locations. The position and protection of gates were of key significance as they controlled access to the main street arteries, the commercial thoroughfares, public squares, cathedrals, institutions, residential quarters and every other component of the urban fabric of cities. Fortifications also defined the spatial hierarchies existing within cities reflecting levels of protection and socioeconomic stratification.[26] Walls separated lower from upper towns while access to strong citadels and acropoleis was primarily the privilege of state and church authorities. The castle-towns of Servia, Serres, Redina, Monemvasia and Arta, among numerous others, provide instructive paradigms of the practice.[27] In addition, Veliko T'rnovo in the north part of central Bulgaria offers a very useful example as it was organised in separate fortified parts that adjusted to the geomorphology of the natural site.[28]

Walls and the Cultural Experience of Byzantine Cities

The continuing agency of fortifications in urban life relied on their symbiotic relationship with local societies, which in turn found its expression in cities' cultural life.[29] The experience of the urban-built environment was largely shaped by the presence of protective enclosures and the spatial and conceptual contrasts they drew in daily life. As such, walls separated inside from outside, known from unknown, familiar to hostile, local from foreign, healthy from sick and so on.[30] The daily experience of these separating boundaries reinforced the mystical dimension of fortifications thus adding to their apotropaic function.[31] Seeking divine protection from the enemy was a need embedded in the cultural realities of the Byzantine city. The presence of the symbol of the cross on wall façades and the placement as well as the procession of icons on fortifications strengthened their sacred and *hierotopical* (meaning sacred spatial) roles, keeping evil at bay.[32] The existence of chapels within fortified towers, like the example of a decorated with frescos chapel from the eastern walls of Nicaea and another small chapel from the eastern fortifications of Thessaloniki, points to their use by members of the guard.[33] At the same time, the integration of these chapels within defensive works helped to sanctify the built boundaries of cities. As a result, fortifications were ever-present in the daily experience of the Byzantine city related to both the communal and the private understanding of urban space. In fact, they were an integral part of urban identity.

As mentioned, dedicatory inscriptions announced the patronage of rulers and city authorities.[34] Among the numerous inscriptions from the walls of Thessaloniki, it's worth looking closely at the intriguing placement of a dedicatory inscription at the northeast tip of Thessaloniki's enclosure.[35] Dating from 1336, it commemorates the construction or enlargement of a small gate by Ioannis Chamaetos, who was the military commander of the city's acropolis. According to the carved text, Chamaetos acted under the orders of Anna Palaiologina, wife of Emperor Andronicus III, who assumed the administration of Thessaloniki in 1352 and continued to rule the city until her death in ca.1365. Carved on the inner face of one of the vertical marble jamb of the gate, the inscription was visible only to those passing through the open gate (Figure 12.5). Due to its hidden nature, the inscription initiates an intimate, almost personal relationship with the viewer at the time of crossing this transitional threshold.

In middle-Byzantine Christoupolis, present-day Kavala in Northern Greece, an anonymous inscription still echoes messages from the past. It provides an instructive example of the apotropaic dimension of fortifications in Byzantine life. Located on the north façade of a rectangular tower from the northern curtain of the middle-Byzantine kastron, the inscription reads: 'Oh Tower divinely sustained, God shields you as the most beautiful (*hyperkallos*) of all towers'. [36] The tower was praised for its beauty and protection by God due to its location as it guarded one of the gates into the town (Figure 12.6). Moreover, the *pyrgos* strengthened a site of strategic importance, namely the position where castle defenses met the southern end of the long wall and aqueduct which provided water to the town and controlled the narrow natural passage of the old Via Egnatia at the particular geographical location.[37] The *hyperkallos* tower held the defensive keys for the strategic role of the castle of Christoupolis and as such was the most beautiful of all towers, even though the building's humble scale and construction certainly do not meet the expectations for the inscription's praise.

Comparable messages were carried by inscriptions from the walls of Constantinople.[38] An anonymous prayer can be seen on the façade of a rectangular tower from the land walls of the Byzantine capital. Specifically, it's a two-line brickwork inscription on the western façade of the fourth tower north of the Rhegium, or Rhousiou, gate asking for the protection of Christ against enemies. The tower is located on a natural outcrop and dates from the reign if Leo IV (775–780) or Leo V (813–820).[39] Like at Christoupolis, the inscription provided a timeless apotropaic message echoing the city itself praying for Christ's protection against the forceful attack of enemies. Besides the meaning of its text, the visual presence of the inscription as well as the brickwork cross accompanying it had significant protective connotations.

Praising fortifications in admiration of their strength and beauty was a *topos* in Middle and Late Byzantine literary tradition.[40] The words of rulers, officials and historians reflect aspects of the central position fortifications occupied in the collective imagination and sense of identity of Byzantine societies. Theodore Lascaris offered generous praise for

Figure 12.5 Thessaloniki [Greece]; the Gate of Anna Palaiologina

Nicea's defenses, which were admired by Theodore Metochites for their 'unconquerable beauty'.[41] Niketas Choniates also praised cities for their strong walls and towers.[42] In addition, several other historians, poets and hagiographers like Maximos Planoudes gave similar impressions of Byzantine city fortifications.[43] Indicatively, a tenth-century epigram by John Geometres commemorated the strength and beauty of a tower from the land walls

Figure 12.6 Kavala [Greece]; the *Hyperkallos* tower from the north

of Constantinople: 'To us God gave a tower of strength, a tower of firmness, a tower of life not to be broken, overcoming all the sufferings of life and the assaults and machines of the barbarians, full of all beauties and wonders'.[44] I believe it's clear that the direct association of cities' descriptions with the strength and beauty of fortifications points to the emergence of aesthetic sensibilities related to the need for protection and security.

Religious connotations further attest to this Byzantine experience such as in the famous Akathistos Hymn likening the Theotokos (Mother of God) with an unconquerable fortified wall and an immovable tower, references related to the Theotokos' miraculous interventions and support during sieges and attacks against Constantinople.[45] In general, the imagined active participation of the Theotokos and other saints, like Saint Demetrius, in the defense of cities was part of the collective cultural experience of urban societies. As mentioned, icons and other objects of cult were paraded on top of fortifications, thus strengthening efforts to defend them, while the walls and gates of cities, like the capital Constantinople, were key elements of ceremonial processions.[46] Walls came to represent cities and acquired sacred dimensions associated with their patron saint.[47] For example, seventh-century mosaics in the Basilica of Saint Demetrios show the city's patron saint embracing city and church officials while standing in front the city's walls.[48] The well-known 'Miracles of Saint Demetrios' contain narratives that echo this apotropaic tradition, describing the city's patron fighting on the walls alongside Thessalonians, helping them to repel enemy attacks.[49] Literary descriptions of the city, such as that of Ioannis Kameniatis in 904, described Saint Demetrios as a warrior able to protect the city and secure its survival.[50] These narratives were visualized in artistic representations like the twelfth-century image of the saint defending the city's walls from a silver reliquary from Vatopedi Monastery on Mount Athos.[51] Another example comes from a late sixteenth-century icon from the island of Corfu depicting Saint Demetrius as a mounted warrior in front of the fortified city of Thessaloniki.[52] Overall, fortifications became a staple attribute in representations of cities in Byzantine and post-Byzantine art.

Returning to the example of Christoupolis, it's important to emphasize that the physical location of fortified cities was a key factor that significantly shaped their spatial experience as well as perceptions of their invincible 'beauty'.[53] As it can be witnessed by the visitor to contemporary Kavala, the fortified enclosure developed along the steep edges of the rocky peninsula where the castle-town developed (Figure 12.7).[54] Written sources mention its strategic position and refer to the sense of security projected by the visual impression of its walls.[55] Indicatively, in the Late-Byzantine period, written sources praise its castle without differentiating between the natural and the built aspects of its defenses. Nicephoros Gregoras in the middle of the fourteenth century referred to Kavala's castle as *avaton* (inaccessible), while John Kantakouzenos described it as 'strong by its natural formation'.[56] Clearly, the rocky peninsula was a major asset in Kavala's fortification and as such was the inspiration for the praises of its impregnable beauty. In the case of Servia in west Macedonia, Kantakouzenos describes the town as suspended in the air – a metaphorical reference to its steep natural location.[57] Numerous other examples, such as Monemvasia and Mystras in the Peloponnese, Redina and Gynaikokastro in Macedonia, Berat in Albania, provide further evidence of the phenomenon.[58]

The material aspects of fortifications also carried cultural meaning, especially in the use of spolia. As mentioned in relation to the examples of great cities like Constantinople and Thessaloniki, where the sustained use of late antique defensive enclosures made good use of the availability of earlier building material, the utilization of spolia was widely practiced in the diverse development of Byzantine castle-towns. Using easily obtainable material was certainly not only practical but also carried ideological significance.[59] The visual and decorative dimension of the material fabric of walls and towers was packed with apotropaic meaning and symbolisms which drew from the physical appropriation of cities' past. Continuing earlier practices, construction at the acropolis at Sardis, Ephesos, the Pergamon Acropolis and Chania considered the visual aspects of reused material.[60] In this context, the defenses of

Figure 12.7 Kavala [Greece]; view of the western walls built along the bedrock edges of the peninsula

Ankara and Amastris showcase eclectic collections of reused building materials, which point to the aesthetic and cultural considerations of their masons (Figure 12.8).[61] The middle and late-Byzantine defensive works in Nicaea also point to the continuity of the practice.[62]

Among the extensive use of spoliated material in Byzantine fortifications, it's important to highlight the decorative use of ancient sculpture on walls and towers as it points to the nuanced cultural perception of these remnants of the past as well as to the aesthetic sensibility of patrons and builders.[63] The placement of ancient funerary stelae, parts of statues and reliefs, and sculpture architectural pieces animated the facades of fortifications also serving an apotropaic role while providing evidence of the long continuity of cities.[64] It's worth noting that these relics of the ancient past were accepted as an embedded component of the visual culture of the Byzantine city. Examples from Thessaloniki in the ninth century and Patra in the fifteenth offer instructive examples of the long tradition of the practice.

The placement of a late Hellenistic funerary stele on the façade of a tower from the sea walls of Thessaloniki reflects the aesthetic sensibilities of its builders and patrons.[65] The tower which seems to have been extensively rebuilt in the ninth century was integrated in the sixteenth century into the Ottoman fortress, known as Vardar fort, which protected the city's harbor.[66] During the ninth-century works, the stele was built and placed on the wall façade, almost in the same manner one would hang a portable icon.[67] Part of mullion capital was positioned over the stele thus creatively completing and framing it as a visual composition. It's very likely that the relief depiction of the deceased seated individual and its standing living companion was not necessarily perceived as a pagan image but was

Figure 12.8 Ankara [Turkey]; the western walls of the castle

interpreted and understood within the context of Byzantine iconography as a diachronic remnant of the city's past.

The walls of the castle of Patras preserve one more important example of the decorative use of ancient sculpture on Byzantine fortification façades.[68] Specifically, the south façade of the tower close to the southeastern corner of the castle's enclosure was adorned with a visual synthesis of spoliated sculptural pieces. It's worth mentioning that the building history of the architectural complex dates back to the sixth century with subsequent construction phases following the transformation of the ancient city's acropolis into the Byzantine castle and the structure's continuous use until the middle of the twentieth century.[69] The tower, known as 'Patrinela's tower', reflects this long history with its base and lower part belonging to the sixth century, while its upper part extensively rebuilt in the second quarter of the fifteenth century, a period when the city came under the control of the Palaiologoi Despots of Mystras (Figure 12.9).[70] During this extensive remodeling, the tower's builders composed a sculptural synthesis framed within a rectangular niche, centrally positioned on the building's façade. Parts from two different ancient Roman statues, the torso of a young man and the head of a bearded man, were put together to create a visually striking composition, which in time came to be identified as 'Patrinela', the spirit of which, according to local legends, haunts and continues to protect the castle of Patras.[71] The example of Patrinela highlights both the aesthetic and the apotropaic dimension of fortifications facades in Byzantium. In addition, the selection of ancient sculptural parts, which were readily available to be used in the creation of Patrinela, mirrors the historic and artistic sensibilities of the project's builders and patrons.

Figure 12.9 Patras [Greece]; the tower of Patrinela

In conclusion, it is important to consider that the central role of fortifications in the daily life of Byzantine cities shaped the rise of new cultural values. During the Middle and Late Byzantine periods, the beauty of fortifications emerged as an aesthetic quality that mirrored the increased need for security. As discussed earlier, an inaccessible natural location being the foundation of the strong walls of a castle-town, a well-maintained defensive system and a tall tower guarding a gate were visually recognizable and appreciated. The praise of walls and towers for their impregnable beauty was a literary *topos* in the descriptions of cities.

Similarly, visual representations of cities in art became conflated with the depiction of fortifications and patron saints engaged in their defense. Moreover, it's important to also reflect on the material aspects of fortification works. The reuse of building material, the decorative insertion of spoliated sculpture, brickwork motifs and the placement of dedicatory inscriptions on the facades of defensive works provided a rich material and visual context, which was full of cultural meaning.

Finally, I want to return to the concept of transition in cities and cityscapes and to address the role of fortifications in the experience of Byzantine cities. Defensive enclosures secured continuity and served a critical role in the adaptive resilience of Byzantine societies. Separated from the countryside behind defensive enclosures, cities' organization and layout mirrored their role as administrative centers and hubs of religious, social and economic life. The architecture, organization and topography of fortifications and the enclosed urban fabric consisting of markets, shops, streets and public spaces, monasteries, palaces and private houses framed socioeconomic activity and cultural life; as such they defined the urban experience of citizens and visitors alike. In this context, fortification works were a staple feature and a key element in the making of the Byzantine city.

Notes

1 This chapter brings together ideas from various research projects. I am indebted to the Getty Foundation for its support for the program "Mediterranean Palimpsests: Connecting and the Art and Architectural Histories of Medieval and Early Modern Cities" which allowed me to revisit and expand my interests in Byzantine and medieval cities. My gratitude goes to my co-director, D. Fairchild-Ruggles, for endless discussions and valuable insights on the study of historic cities. My appreciation also goes to Luca Zavagno, my dear partner in the development of the present volume, for persistently urging me to continue my work on the multifaceted role of fortifications in Byzantium. Finally, I want to thank Nicolette Vollero Levy for all her help in the preparation of my essay.

2 An overview of research on Byzantine cities is offered in with, Ch. Bouras, "Aspects of the Byzantine City. Eighth-Fifteenth Centuries," *EHB* (2002), 497–528; H. Saradi, "Towns and Cities," in E. Jeffreys, J. Haldon and R. Cormack (eds.), *Oxford Handbook of Byzantine Studies* (Oxford and New York, 2008), 317–327; Ch. Bouras, "Byzantine Cities in Greece," in J. Albani and E. Chalkia (eds.), *Heaven and Earth. Cities and Countryside in Byzantine Greece* (Athens, 2013), 45–73. See also: A. Kazhdan, "La ville et le village à Byzance au XIe–XIIe siècles," *XIIe Congrès International des études byzantines: Rapport collectif, Ochrid, 1961* (Belgrade, 1964), 31–54; C. Mango, *Byzantium: The Empire of New Rome* (New York, 1980), 60–87; A. Bryer, "The Structure of the Late Byzantine Town: Dioikismos and the Mesoi," in H. W. Lowry and A. Bryer (eds.), *Continuity and Change in Late Byzantine and Early Ottoman Society: Papers given at a Symposium at Dumbarton Oaks in May 1982* (Washington, DC, 1986), 263–279; C. Foss, "Archaeology and the "Twenty Cities" of Byzantine Asia', *AJA* 81 (1977), 469–486. On the development and archaeology of cities in Greece, see the collected studies volumes, T. Kiousopoulou (ed.), *Οι βυζαντινές πόλεις 8ος-15ος αιώνας. Προοπτικές της έρευνας και νέες ερευνητικές προσεγγίσεις,* (Rethymnon, 2012); J. Albani and E. Chalkia (eds.), *Heaven and Earth. Cities and Countryside in Byzantine Greece* (Athens, 2013). Also see the recent work by L. Zavagno, *The Byzantine City from Heraclius to the Fourth Crusade, 610–1204. Urban Life after Antiquity* (Cham, 2021).

3 N. Bakirtzis, "The Practice, Perception and Experience of Byzantine Fortification," in P. Stephenson (ed.), *The Byzantine World* (New York, 2010), 352–371.

4 On Byzantine fortifications, see C. Foss and D. Winfield, *Byzantine Fortifications* (Pretoria, 1986); A. W. Lawrence, "A Skeletal History of Byzantine Fortification," *ABSA* 78 (1983), 171–227; N. Bakirtzis and Ph. Oreopoulos, *An Essay on Byzantine Fortification: Northern Greece Fourth-Fifteenth Centuries* (Athens, 2001); N. D. Kontogiannis, *Byzantine Fortifications: Protecting the Roman Empire in the East* (Barnsley and Havertown, 2022).

5 On the decline, continuity and transformation of Late Antique cities, see E. Kirsten, "Die Byzantinische Stadt," in *Berichte zum XI. Internationalen Byzantinischen-Kongress München 1958*,

vol. 3, (Munich, 1958), 1–48; C. Foss, *Ephesus after Antiquity: A Late Antique, Byzantine, and Turkish City* (Cambridge and New York, 1979); W. Brandes, *Die Städte Kleinasiens Im 7 Und 8 Jahrhundert* (Berlin, 1989), 80–131; J. F. Haldon, *Byzantium in the Seventh Century* (Cambridge, 1990), 93–117; M. Whittow, "Ruling the Early Byzantine City," *Past and Present* 129 (1990), 3–29; J. F. Haldon, "The Idea of the Town in the Byzantine Empire," in G. P. Brogiolo and B. Ward-Perkins (eds.), *The Idea and the Ideal of Town Between Late Antiquity and the Early Middle Ages* (Leiden, 1999), 1–24; M. Whittow, "Recent Research on the Late-Antique City in Asia Minor: The Second Half of the 6th C. Revisited," in L. Lavan and W. Bowden (eds), *Recent Research in Late-Antique Urbanism* (Portsmouth RI, 2001), 137–153; J. H. W. G. Liebeschuetz, *Decline and Fall of the Roman City* (Oxford, 2001), 249–317.

6 W. Müller-Wiener, "Mittelalterliche Befestigungen im südlichen Jonien," *Istanbuler Mitteilungen* 11 (1961), 5–122; A. Dunn, "The Transformation from Polis to Kastron in the Balkans (Iii-Viii Cc): General and Regional Perspectives," *BMGS* 18 (1994), 60–80; A. Kazhdan, "Polis and Kastron in Theophanes and in Some Other Historical Texts," in *Eupsychia: Mélanges offerts à Hélène Ahrweiler*, vol. 2, (Paris, 1998), 345–360; H. Saradi-Mendelovici, "The Demise of the Ancient City and the Emergence of the Mediaeval Eity in the Eastern Roman Empire," *Echos du monde classique/Classical View*, 32 (1988), 365–401; H. Saradi, "The Byzantine Cities (8th-12th centuries): Old Approaches and New Directions," in Kiousopoulou (ed.), *Οι βυζαντινές πόλεις 8ος-15ος αιώνας: Προοπτικές της έρευνας και νέες ερευνητικές προσεγγίσεις* (Rethymnon, 2012), 25–35; Zavagno, *The Byzantine City*, 38–68. On the terms used to describe a city in Byzantine written sources see, N. E. Karapidakis, "Οι πόλεις των αρχόντων: η δυναμική και τα όρια ενός τύπου αστικής ανάπτυξης: Ήπειρος, Αιτωλοακαρνανία, Μοριάς (13ος-15ος αι.)," in Kiousopoulou (ed.), *Οι βυζαντινές πόλεις 8ος-15ος αιώνας: Προοπτικές της έρευνας και νέες ερευνητικές προσεγγίσεις* (Rethymnon, 2012), 209–216.

7 Whittow, "Ruling the Early Byzantine City"; Dunn, "The Transformation from Polis to Kastron in the Balkans (Iii-Viii Cc)"; L. Zavagno, *Cities in Transition: Urbanism in Byzantium between late Antiquity and the early Middle Ages* (AD 500-900) (Oxford, 2009); L. Zavagno, *Byzantine City*, 83–149.

8 Ch. Bouras, "Aspects of the Byzantine City, Eighth-Fifteenth Centuries," 505. On the fortifications of Constantinople, with B. Meyer-Plath and A. M. Schneider, *Die Landmauer von Konstantinopel*, 2 vols, (Berlin, 1938-1943); Müller-Wiener, "Mittelalterliche Befestigungen im südlichen Jonien," 286–323; Space needed between B. C. P. Tsangadas, *The Fortifications and Defense of Constantinople* (Boulder NY, 1980). For Thessaloniki, see O. Tafrali, *Topographie de Thessalonique* (Paris, 1913); J. M. Spieser, *Thessalonique et ses monuments du Ive au Vie siècle: Contribution à L'étude d'une Ville Paléochrétienne* (Paris, 1984); J. M. Spieser, "Les remparts de Thessalonique: À propos d'un livre recent," *Byzantinoslavica* 60 (1999), 557–574; G. Velenis, *Τα τείχη της Θεσσαλονίκης. Από τον Κάσσανδρο ως τον Ηράκλειο* (Thessaloniki 1998); E. Rizos, "The Late-Antique Walls of Thessalonica and their Place in the Development of Eastern Military Architecture," *JRA* 24 (2011), 450–468. On Nicaea, see A. M. Schneider and W. Karnapp, *Die Stadtmauer Von Iznik (Nicaea)* (Berlin, 1938); C. Foss, "The Walls of Iznik 260–1330," in I. Akbaygil, H. İnalcık, and O. Aslanapa (eds.), *Iznik Throughout History* (Istanbul, 2004), 249–262. For Nicomedia: C. Foss, "Nicomedia and Constantinople," in C. A. Mango, G. Dagron, and G. Greatrex (eds.), *Constantinople and its Hinterland: Papers from the Twenty-Seventh Spring Symposium of Byzantine Studies, Oxford, April 1993* (Brookfield, 1995), 181–190.

9 J. Crow, (2001), "Fortifications and Urbanism in Late Antiquity: Thessaloniki and other eastern cities," in L. Lavan, (ed.), *Recent Research on Late Antique Urbanism* (Portsmouth, 2001), 91–107; Ch. Bouras, "Μεσοβυζαντινές και υστεροβυζαντινές πόλεις από την σκοπιά της πολεοδομίας και της αρχιτεκτονικής," in Kiousopoulou (ed.), *Οι βυζαντινές πόλεις 8ος-15ος αιώνας. Προοπτικές της έρευνας και νέες ερευνητικές προσεγγίσεις* (Rethymnon 2012), 6–7; N. Bakirtzis, " The Practice, Perception and Experience of Byzantine Fortification" 353–354.

10 Velenis, *Τείχη*, 17–88; Spieser, "Les remparts de Thessalonique. À propos d'un livre récent," 558–569.

11 N. Bakirtzis, "The Visual Language of Fortification Facades: The Walls of Thessaloniki," *Monument and Environment* 9 (2005), 17–20.

12 Spieser, *Thessalonique et ses monuments,* 64; Velenis, *Τείχη*, 53–54, figure 52.

13 J.-M. Spieser, "Inventaires en vue d'un recueil des inscriptions historiques de Byzance. I. Les inscriptions de Thessalonique," *Travaux et Mémoires* 5 (1973), 151–152, no. 3, 165–166, no. 16 and no. 29, 176–177, no.29.

14 Brandes, *Die Städte Kleinasiens Im 7 Und 8 Jahrhundert*, 82–111; Haldon, *Byzantium in the Seventh Century*, 93–117; W. Brandes, "Byzantine Towns in the Seventh and Eighth Century – Different Sources, Different Histories?," in G. P. Brogiolo. and B. Ward-Perkins (eds.), *The Idea and the Ideal of Town between Late Antiquity and the Early Middle Ages* (Leiden, 1999), 25–57; T. E. Gregory, "Fortification and Urban Design in Early Byzantine Greece," in R. L. Hohlfelder (ed.), *City, Town, and Countryside in the Early Byzantine Era* (New York, 1982), 43–46. For Abdera and Maroneia, see Ch. Bakirtzis, "Byzantine Thrace," in *Thrace* (Athens, 1994), 158–164; for Serres, see A. Xyngopoulos, *'Ερευναι εις τα βυζαντινά μνημεία των Σερρών* (Thessaloniki, 1965), 1–21; on Veroia, see Th. Papazotos, *Η Βέροια και οι ναοί της: Ιστορική και αρχαιολογική σπουδή των μνημείων της πόλης* (Athens, 1994), 37–71; for Philippi, see P. Lemerle, *Philippes et la Macédoine orientale à Pépoque chrétienne et byzantine: recherches d'histoire et d' archéologie*, 2 vols., (Paris, 1945); E. Kourkoutidou-Nikolaidou, "Philippi," in J. Albani and E. Chalkia (eds.), *Heaven and Earth: Cities and Countryside in Byzantine Greece* (Athens, 2013), 94–103; on Athens, see Ch. Bouras, *Βυζαντινή Αθήνα* (Athens, 2010), 29–46 and Ch. Bouras, "Byzantine Athens, 330–1453," in J. Albani and E. Chalkia (eds.), *Heaven and Earth: Cities and Countryside in Byzantine Greece* (Athens, 2013), 169–179; for Corinth, see G. D. R. Sanders, "Corinth", in A. Laiou (ed.), *The Economic History of Byzantium: From the Seventh through the Fifteenth Century*, vol. II (Washington D.C. 2002), 647-654 2002; on Argos see A. Bon, "Les fortresses medievales de la Grece Centrale," *BCH* 61 (1937), 136–139 and A. Vassiliou, "Argos from the Ninth to Fifteenth Centuries," in J. Albani and E. Chalkia (eds.), *Heaven and Earth: Cities and Countryside in Byzantine Greece* (Athens, 2013), 216–223; for Amorium, see E. Ivison, "Amorium in the Byzantine Dark Ages (Seventh to Ninth Centuries)," in J. Henning (ed.), *Post-Roman Towns, Trade and Settlement in Europe and Byzantium* (New York, 2007), 25–59; for Ankara, see C. Foss, "Late Antique and Byzantine Ankara," *DOP* 31 (1977), 27–87; for Sardis, see C. Foss, *Byzantine and Turkish Sardis* (Cambridge MA, 1976); for Ephesus and Miletus, see C. Foss and D. Winfield, *Byzantine Fortifications*, 137–138.

15 S. Dadaki and Ch. Giros, "Αρχαιολογικός χάρτης Θάσου. Βυζαντινοί χρόνοι," *Αρχαιολογικό έργο στη Μακεδονία και τη Θράκη* 5 (1991), 383–397; F. Karagianni, *Οι βυζαντινοι οικισμοί στη Μακεδονία μέσα από τα αρχαιολογικά δεδομένα (4ος-5ος αι.)* (Thessaloniki, 2010), 132–137; V. Petrakos, "Το κάστρο της Μυτιλήνης," *AD* 31 (1976), 152–165.

16 K. Sismanidis, *Ancient Stageira. Birthplace of Aristotle* (Athens 2003), 16, 61–70.

17 A. Chrysostomou, *Αρχαία Έδεσσα* (Edessa, 2008); Karagianni, *Οι βυζαντινοι οικισμοί στη Μακεδονία*, 176–180.

18 On Abdera, see Ch. Bakirtzis, "Byzantine Thrace," 158–161. For Didymoteichon, see R. Ousterhout and Ch. Bakirtzis, *Byzantine and Post-Byzantine Monuments of the Evros/Meriç River Valley* (Thessaloniki, 2007), 86–143; A. I. Gouridis, *Διδυμότειχο. Μια άγνωστη πρωτεύουσα (Didymoteichon* 2008).

19 On Kastoria, see E. Drakopoulou, *Η πόλη της Καστοριάς τη βυζαντινή και μεταβυζαντινή εποχή (12ος-6ος αι.). Ιστορία-Τέχνη-Επιγραφές, Τετράδια βυζαντινής αρχαιολογίας και τέχνης 5* (Athens, 1997).

20 E. Chalkia, "Nikopolis," in J. Albani and E. Chalkia (eds.), *Heaven and Earth: Cities and Countryside in Byzantine Greece* (Athens, 2013), 140–155.

21 Ch. Pennas, *Byzantine Aigina* (Athens, 2005), 12–19, 40–83.

22 N. K. Moutsopoulos, *Η παληαχώρα της Αιγίνης* (Athens, 1962).

23 A. Xyngopoulos, *Τα μνημεία των Σερβίων* (Athens, 1957); D. Evgenidou, "Servia and Moglena: Two Byzantine cities of Macedonia," *Ιστορικογεωγραφικά* 2 (1988), 15-22; K. Andrews, *Castles of the Morea* (Princeton NJ, 1953, reprinted 2006), 192–210; Foss and Winfield, 15–17; N. Bakirtzis, "Τα τείχη των βυζαντινών πόλεων: Αισθητική, ιδεολογίες και συμβολισμοί," in Kiousopoulou (ed.), *Οι βυζαντινές πόλεις 8ος-15ος αιώνας. Προοπτικές της έρευνας και νέες ερευνητικές προσεγγίσεις* (Rethymnon 2012), 141–144.

24 J. Crow and S. Hill, "The Byzantine fortifications of Amastris in Paphlagonia," *AS* 45 (1995), 251-265; K. Tsouris, "Νεάπολις-Χριστούπολη-Καβάλα" Διορθώσεις-προσθήκες-παρατηρήσεις στην οχύρωση και την ύδρευση," *AD* 53 (1998), 387–454; S. Kalopissi-Verti, "Mistra: A Fortified Late Byzantine Settlement," in J. Albani and E. Chalkia (eds.), *Heaven and Earth: Cities and Countryside in Byzantine Greece* (Athens, 2013), 224–228; S. Ćurčić, *Architecture in the Balkans: From Diocletian to Süleyman the Magnificent* (New Haven and London, 2010), 570–571; G. Karaiskaj, "Fortifications of Berat, Albania," in E. Hadjitryphonos and S. Ćurčić, (eds.), *Secular Medieval Architecture in the Balkans 1300–1500 and its Preservation* (Thessaloniki, 1997), 114–115.

25 For a discussion of urban planning in Byzantine cities, Ch. Bouras, "Πολεοδομικά των μεσοβυζαντινών και των υστεροβυζαντινών πόλεων," *DChAE* 20 (1998–1999), 89–98.
26 Bouras, "Aspects of the Byzantine City," 506–508; Bouras, "Byzantine Cities in Greece," 61.
27 D. Evgenidou, "Servia and Moglena: Two Byzantine cities of Macedonia,"; Xyngopoulos, *Έρευναι εις τα βυζαντινά μνημεία*, 1–21; Xyngopoulos, *Τα μνημεία των Σερβίων;* N. K. Moutsopoulos, *Ρεντίνα II: Η οχύρωση και η ύδρευση του οικισμού* (Thessaloniki, 2001); D. Zivas, "Byzantine Fortress of Arta," *Internationales Burgen-Institut Bulletin* 19 (1964), 33–43; B. Papadopoulou, "Art," in J. Albani and E. Chalkia (eds.), *Heaven and Earth: Cities and Countryside in Byzantine Greece* (Athens, 2013), 126–139; H. A. Kalligas, *Monemvasia: A Byzantine City-State* (London and New York, 2010).
28 A summary discussion of the importance of the T'rnovo example, see Ćurčić, *Architecture in the Balkans*, 473–475, with related bibliography.
29 Bakirtzis, "Byzantine Fortification," 358–360.
30 Bakirtzis and Oreopoulos, *An Essay on Byzantine Fortification*, 65–68.
31 For the ideological and symbolic significance of the walls as boundaries between the city and the countryside, see A. Kostantakopoulou, *Βυζαντινή Θεσσαλονίκη: Χώρος και ιδεολογία* (Ioannina, 1996), 15–43.
32 Bakirtzis, "Byzantine Fortification," 361–362.
33 Foss and Winfield, *Byzantine Fortifications*, 87.
34 E. Ivison, "Urban Renewal and Imperial Revival in Byzantium," *ByzF* 26 (2000), 18–25; A. Rhoby, "The Meaning of Inscriptions for the Early and Middle Byzantine Culture. Remarks on the Interaction of Word, Image and Beholder," in *Scrivere e leggere nell'alto medioevo. Spoleto, 28 aprile – 4 maggio 2011 (Settimane di Studio LIX) (*Spoleto, 2012), 741–479; Bakirtzis, "Τα τείχη των βυζαντινών πόλεων," 150–158.
35 Bakirtzis, "Visual Language," 24; Spieser, "Inventaires", 175–176, no. 28.
36 G. Bakalakis, "Πύργος υπέρκαλος," *Προσφορά εις Στίλπωνα Κυριακίδη* (Thessaloniki, 1953), 499–507; Tsouris, "Νεάπολις-Χριστούπολη-Καβάλα", 391; Bakirtzis, "Τα τείχη των βυζαντινών πόλεων," 139–140, 153–157.
37 Known as "Kamares" (meaning arches), the Ottoman aqueduct dating from the rule of Suleiman the Magnificent (1520–1566) replaced earlier structures that both supplied water to the castle and controlled the narrow passage, Tsouris, "Νεάπολις-Χριστούπολη-Καβάλα", 408–416 and M. Lychounas, *Μεσαιωνικό Υδραγωγείο Καβάλας: Καμάρες* (Kavala, 2008).
38 A. Van Millingen, *Byzantine Constantinople: The Walls of the City and Adjoining Historical Sites* (London, 1899), 100; Ivison, "Urban Renewal," 24.
39 Foss and Winfield, *Byzantine Fortifications*, 62.
40 H. Saradi, "Kallos of the Byzantine City: The Development of a Rhetoric Topos and Historic Reality," *Gesta* 34 (1995), 37–56; Bakirtzis, "Visual Language," 27–29.
41 A. Tartaglia, *Theodorus II Ducas Lascaris*, (Munich, 2000), 68–84. C. Foss, *Nicaea: A Byzantine Capital and its Praises* (Brookline MA, 1996), 132–133, 144–145, 174–175.
42 H. J. Magoulias (tr.), *O City of Byzantium: Annals of Niketas Choniates* (Detroit, 1984), 44, 46, 156, 159, 236, 258, 348.
43 L. G. Westerink, "Trois textes inédits sur saint Diomède de Nicée," *Analecta Bollandiana* 84, 1–2 (1966), 182; For an overview of the ways the idea and reality of the city appear in the work of Byzantine hagiographers, Saradi, "The City in Byzantine Hagiography," in S. Euthymiades, *The Ashgate Research Companion to Byzantine Hagiography*, volume II: Genres and Contexts (Surrey, 2014).
44 H. Maguire, "The Beauty of Castles: A Tenth-Century Description of a Tower at Constantinople," in H. Maguire, *Rhetoric, Nature and Magic in Byzantine Art* (Ashgate, 1998).
45 L. M. Peltomaa, *The Image of the Virgin Mary in the Akathistos Hymn* (Leiden, 2001); *G. Papagiannis, Ακάθιστος Ύμνος. Άγνωστες πτυχές της πολύ γνωστού κειμένου. Κριτικές και μετρικές παρατηρήσεις, σχολιασμένη βιβλιογραφία* (Thessaloniki. 2006).
46 Magoulias, *O City of Byzantium*, 209–210; L. Sternbach, *Analecta Avarica* (Krakow, 1900), 104; B. V. Pentcheva, *Icons and Power: The Mother of God in Byzantium* (University Park, 2006), 37–144. On processions in the life of the capital, A. Berger, "Imperial and Ecclesiastical Processions in Constantinople," in N. Necipoğlu (ed.), *Byzantine Constantinople: Monuments, Topography and Everyday Life*, (Leiden, 2001), 73–87.
47 N. Bakirtzis, "Η Θεσσαλονίκη και τα τείχη της: Πτυχές μιας διαχρονικής σχέσης," in D. Pilides and E. Alphas (eds.), *Fortified Cities: Past, Present and Future* (Nicosia, 2012). 84–90.

48 G. A. Soteriou and M. G. Soteriou, *Η Βασιλική του Αγίου Δημητρίου* (Athens, 1952), 193–194, pl. 63–64.
49 P. Lemerle, *Les plus anciens recueils des miracles de saint Démétrius et la pénétration des Slaves dans les Balkans. I. Le Texte* (Paris, 1979-81).
50 G. Böhlig, *Ioannis Caminiatae De expugnatione Thessalonicae* (Berlin, 1973), 8.
51 A. Grabar, "Quelques reliquaires de saint Demetrius et le martyrium du saint à Salonique," DOP 5 (1950), 3–6, Figures 12.1–12.5.
52 P. Vocotopoulos *Εικόνες της Κέρκυρας* (Athens, 1990), 99–100.
53 Foss and Winfield, *Byzantine Fortifications*, 15–17.
54 Tsouris, "Νεάπολις-Χριστούπολη-Καβάλα", 387–418; K. Dakari, A. Bakirtzis and G. Karabasis, *Το παράλιο τείχος της Καβάλας* (Kavala, 2008).
55 D. I. Lazaridis, *Νεάπολις, Χριστούπολις, Καβάλα.* Οδηγός Μουσείου Καβάλας (Athens, 1969), 13–82.
56 L. Schopen, *Ioannis Cantacuzeni Eximperatoris historiarum Libri IV Graece et Latine*, vol. I (Cambridge, 2012), 24; I. Bekker and L. Schopen, *Nicephori Gregorae Byzantina Historia,* vol. III (Cambridge, 2012), VII. 6.
57 Schopen, *Ioannis Cantacuzeni*, vol. III, 130. 12–14.
58 Andrews, *Castles of the Morea*, 192–210; Kalligas, *Monemvasia*; Kalopissi-Verti, "Mistra"; Moutsopoulos, *Ρεντίνα;* A. Tourta, "Gynaikokastro," in E. Hadjitryphonos and S. Ćurčić (eds.), *Secular Medieval Architecture in the Balkans 1300–1500 and its Preservation* (Thessaloniki, 1997), 110–111; Karaiskaj, "Fortifications of Berat," 114–115.
59 For the use of spoliated building material in Byzantine fortifications, see M. Greenhalgh, "Spolia in Fortifications: Turkey, Syria and North Africa," in *Ideologie e pratiche del reimpiego nell'alto Medioevo, Settimane di studi del centro Italiano di Studi sull'alto Medioevo* 46, (Spoleto, 1999), 785–935; N. Bakirtzis, "Τα τείχη," 144–150. On the general use of spolia and the reuse of antiquities in Byzantium, see M. Greenhalgh, *The Survival of Roman Antiquities in the Middle Ages* (London, 1989); M. Greenhalgh, *Marble Past, Monumental Present: Building Antiquities in the Medieval Mediterranean* (Leiden, 2009); B. Brenk, "Spolia from Constantine to Charlemagne: Aesthetics Versus Ideology," *DOP* 41 (1987), 103–109; J. Alchermes, "Spolia in Roman Cities of the late Empire: Legislative rationales and architectural reuse," *DOP* 48 (1994), 167–178; D. Kinney, "Rape or Restitution of the Past? Interpreting spolia," in S. C. Scott (ed.), *The Art of Interpreting* (University Park, 1995), 52–67; H. Saradi, "The Use of Ancient Spolia in Byzantine Monuments: The Archaeological and Literary Evidence," *International Journal of Classical Tradition* 3 (1997), 395–423.
60 Foss and Winfeld, *Byzantine Fortifications*, 131–136, 143–144; Foss, *Sardis*, 57–59; Müller-Wiener, 91–97; Foss, "Byzantine Asia," 480; On Chania, M. G. Andrianakis, "Το έργο της επιστημονικής επιτροπής ανάδειξης βυζαντινού και βενετσιάνικου οχυρωματικού περιβόλου Χανίων," in M. G. Andrianakis and I. Tzachili (eds.), *Αρχαιολογικό έργο Κρήτης 1. Πρακτικά της 1ης συνάντησης, Ρέθυμνο 28-30 Νοεμβρίου 2008* (Rethymnon, 2010).
61 On Ankara, see Foss, "Byzantine Ankara," 79–86. For Amastris, see Crow and Hill, "Byzantine Fortifications of Amastris," 255–260.
62 For the walls of Nicaea, see, Foss, "The walls of Iznik," 249–262.
63 Bakirtzis, "Τα τείχη των βυζαντινών πόλεων," 148–150.
64 Bakirtzis, "Byzantine Fortification," 362–364.
65 Tafrali, *Topographie*,pl. XV, 1
66 E. Marki, "Συμπληρωματικά αρχαιολογικά στοιχεία για το φρούριο Βαρδαρίου Θεσσαλονίκης," *Μακεδονικά* 22 (1982), 144–148.
67 Bakirtzis, "Visual Language," 18.
68 On Patras, see, Andrews, *Castles of the Morea*, 116–129; M. Georgopoulou-Verra, *Το Κάστρο της Πάτρας* (Athens, 2000).
69 A. Moutzali, "Στοιχεία της πολεοδομικής εξέλιξης της Πάτρας," *Αρχαιολογία* 30 (1989), 82–87; A. Moutzali, "Τοπογραφικά *της Μεσαιωνικής Πάτρας*," in V. Katsaros (ed.), *Αντίφωνον, Αφιέρωμα στον καθηγητή Ν.Β. Δρανδάκη* (Thessaloniki, 1994), 132–157.
70 Georgopoulou-Verra, *Το Κάστρο της Πάτρας*, 21, figure 16.
71 Georgopoulou-Verra, *Το Κάστρο της Πάτρας*, 25, figure 20.

13
MONUMENTALITY AND THE BYZANTINE CITY

Maria Cristina Carile

As Melchior Lorichs' panorama of Constantinople shows, in 1559, the former capital of the Byzantine Empire appeared as an enormous expanse of roofs. The only elements that stand out over the roofs were the walls surrounding the whole city, the mosques (among which Hagia Sophia dominated for its dimensions), the tall silhouettes of freestanding columns, and the remains of Valens' aqueduct. Except for the mosques, all these were Byzantine buildings, still easily recognizable in the urban setting.

Yet by the mid-sixteenth century, they had become the outstanding landmarks of the Ottoman capital, their prominence in the city retained until the twentieth century's urban growth. The monuments in the view captured by Lorichs are identified with captions that, at a time, when their original names had been forgotten, just read *antiqua* in order to denote their antiquity. It can be assumed that these ancient monuments dating from the Byzantine past were important to Lorichs, as well as to the artwork's patron, who may have been Sultan Suleyman the Magnificent.[1] Since the panorama aims not to visualize a fantastical imagining of the city, but to produce an accurate reproduction,[2] it can be argued that the Byzantine buildings portrayed here maintained their function as the city's major urban landmarks.

Lorichs' panorama introduces questions that this chapter will aim to answer: how do we define the monumentality of Byzantine cities? Were Byzantine cities perceived as possessing monumentality? Was monumentality intended for Byzantine cities – and particularly for the capital of the empire, Constantinople – or was it an unintentional, organic characteristic that developed through time as a result of the visible architectural features of the buildings or the appearance of the built spaces? These questions first require reflection on the meaning of the term "monumentality" and on the ways it can be applied to the Byzantine city.

Assessing the Problem

In order to investigate the monumentality of the Byzantine city, the city must be considered the subject – just as it has been portrayed in Lorichs' panorama. A city is a spatial unity formed within boundaries by an ensemble of built and natural elements, with components that grow and change through time, both adapting to and shaping the surrounding

 DOI: 10.4324/9780429203923-17

Figure 13.1 Melchior Lorichs (Lorck), *Panorama of Constantinople*, 1559

environment. Its major features are landmarks of the urban setting and their function may have a certain weight in the construction – and perception – of a city's monumentality. Fundamentally, to investigate the monumentality of the Byzantine city, one should consider the natural setting – more specifically, how the built environment copes with or relates to the natural setting. Natural features may shape the built environment, determining the choices of the builders; they can be adapted to the builders' decisions or exploited to augment a building's impact on the viewer. Accordingly, this chapter will reflect on the Byzantine city focusing on Late Antiquity when most Byzantine centres took form. In the long span of the over 1000 years of the Byzantine Empire's history, it will take into consideration not only the capital but also major and provincial cities.

As several Byzantine centres have been built up over their ancient foundations to become modern metropolises of the twenty-first century, this chapter will make use of all the available sources but necessarily rely upon textual and visual evidence, which convey viewers' perceptions and the cities' reception through the time. Archaeological, architectural, and art historical evidence will be considered testimonies for the monumentality of Byzantine cities that, since they now survive as fragmentary remnants of the past, can be understood in their monumental value only by association with texts. In order to understand a city's monumentality, one cannot look solely at the material evidence but should also take into consideration its value for the people who perceived it and received it through time. Lorichs' is a reproduction of the city, an interpretation – though based on observation – through the eyes of the artist, expressing his view and most likely responding to the expectations of the patron. This aspect is of foremost importance as monumentality is something to be perceived/received, a quality recognised and felt by the beholder.

From antiquity to the present, innate in the concept of monumentality is the temporal dimension.[3] A monument was envisioned as having a lasting impact on the environment where it was built and on the people who saw it, who recognised in it the embodiment of the patron who founded it, its function, or the institution that it hosted. Therefore, a monument is a building or a structure meant to contain a memory. However, due to the way it is used at times by the inhabitants of the city or viewed by people, it has a present dimension that entails its perception. Furthermore, its permanence in a changing environment through time lends itself to its repurposing or its reinterpretation by people, the loss of its original significance, and a transformation of its identity. It also entails an interiorization of the monument itself by every individual, who can connect to it personal memories and develop feelings towards it that bring about personal views and a resemantization of the monument. In brief, the future dimension of a monument involves its reception through the time. Therefore, the temporal dimensions of the monument, its past, present, and future, are related to the social system that promotes its construction, perceives it, and receives it in history.[4]

However, when approaching the theme of the city monumentality, one does not deal with any single monument, but with the monumental value of a city, the city itself being a construct of single monuments and natural spaces with certain impacts on viewers. Consequently, investigating its temporal dimension cannot prescind from considering it as a whole, in its monuments' major phases of construction, which shaped its urban setting at major historical periods. Moreover, it should consider the way the city was perceived by its inhabitants or visitors, being the latter Roman citizens or foreigners, as well as its reception by outsiders, even after the end of the Byzantine Empire in 1453. Such temporal dimension, which entails the social value of the city as a monument in itself, will be considered in the following.

Terminology and Scholarly Approach

The term "monumentality" derives from the Latin *monumentum*, itself a derivative from the verb *moneo*, which means not only "to remind, put in mind, bring to one's recollection" but also "to admonish, advise, warn, instruct, teach".[5] As such, *monumentum* is "that which preserves the remembrance of anything, a memorial, a monument".[6] First used to identify a tomb or a memorial linked to an event,[7] the term and its derivative, *monumentality*, came to be used frequently from the eighteenth century onwards and not necessarily in relation to architectural structures. Rather, it was applied in archaeological and art historical research to indicate ancient buildings or objects which possessed strong historical value.

Yet, did Romans and Byzantines have a concept of monumentality? As Alessandra Bravi points out, the statues that adorned the squares and streets of Constantinople were considered *monumenta*, elements recalling the past and carrying social and political value.[8] The Latin word *monumentum* was not necessarily used in relation to a building or an object and could well identify an event or an exemplary act that had to be remembered in the future:[9] this explains the presence of inscriptions to evoke meaningful memories, which, by extension, were associated with the structures themselves. Still, the term monumentality does not exist in Greek or in Latin sources and the idea of monumentality was rendered through passages emphasizing the grandeur of a building or a work of art, its meaning, social significance, and its power – often reflecting the patron's. This is exemplified in the introduction to Procopius' *De Aedificiis*: the author's poem celebrates Justinian's buildings as material manifestations of the patron's power and wealth, which will evoke his memory for centuries to come.[10] Indeed, buildings had a primary role in sixth-century imperial propaganda. Within the text, addressing the various structures erected by Justinian, from churches to bridges and city walls, Procopius outlines their enormous size, the exploitation of manpower, the variety of materials and means used in their construction, their value to the people, and their location within their geographical context.

Perhaps it is because of the absence of the term, "monumentality", in Greek and Latin sources that scholars of Byzantium have never directly approached the theme, particularly the monumentality of the Byzantine city. In the last 20 years, substantial reflection has arisen on the subject, though rarely in relation to the city. Rather monumentality has been considered in relation to specific structures or a building typology in prehistory,[11] Etruscan and Roman architecture,[12] and in comparative studies of Late Antiquity.[13] The early Middle Ages are largely overlooked.[14]

Recent research on monumental constructions has defined several criteria for understanding/detecting monumentality in antiquity and avoiding the risk of superimposing the modern concept of "monumental" to the ancient understanding of the term and old possible concepts regarding monumentality. The major characteristics of monumentality, used to ascertain the monumentality of any particular building or structure according to recent studies, are as follows: its enormous size, which makes a building or structure stand out from the surroundings; its position, as the location of the object could significantly impact the surroundings, becoming a centre, even if it was actually located in a peripheral area; its permanence, that is the time the object has survived, as time is inherent to the function of memory and the "monumental"; the financial investment in its construction, which entails large sums of money, thus intention and expense; and the complexity of the project, involving the technology, artisanal skills, and organizational and logistic efforts to build the structure.[15] Indeed, all these elements arise in the *ekphraseis* of buildings in Procopius' *De aedificiis*. Still, as Felix Levenson underlines, it is particularly difficult to find an objective way to define monumentality and none of the above principles alone "makes a monument monumental", as the concept of monumentality is dependent on subjectivity, that is intention, reception, and perception.[16] As we will see, the Byzantine city included all these characteristics, even though the model developed by Brunke *et al.* did not consider monumental "an object that is *large* in terms of its dimensions but that was formed through the agglomeration of many smaller objects",[17] a definition that would apply to a city.

Constantinople – New Rome and Its Intended Monumentality

From the fifth century onwards, accounts on the foundation of Constantinople mention that Constantine built his capital on the model of Rome.[18] Accordingly, the city had several major structures that duplicated the ones in Rome.[19] Among those were the city walls, the hippodrome, the palace, imperial squares, fountains and porticoes, the Senate House, and churches.[20] Later sources, such as the sixth-century *Chronographia* of John Malalas, also mention the *Regia*, the *Augusteon* square with its statues, and the baths of Zeuxippos.[21] Clearly these buildings were considered the important features of Constantine's capital and were celebrated as such. All together they made the city and, if focused upon separately, each of them was able to convey the grandeur of the emperor and the capital. Each of the buildings mentioned by the sources had a specific function related to military, administrative, or social needs. An imperial city founded in 330 obviously should have had great walls to prevent invasions and attacks; a palace to accommodate the emperor and his court, also responding to the administrative needs of the empire; and a hippodrome, which by the fourth century was considered a hendiadys with the palace, the natural extension of the latter, the meeting place between the emperor and the populace in a cosmic celebration of the *basileia*, pleasing the citizens with games and chariot races.[22] The Senate House offered a gathering space to the political governance of the empire.[23] Constantine's Forum would celebrate the emperor for the centuries to come, until the fall of Constantinople in 1453; so, too, the *Augusteon* square. Both places served to display to the public statues and works of art collected from all around the empire, exhibiting the historical legacy of Byzantium, its classical tradition, and its refinement of governance.[24] In addition to these major structures, the sources mention porticoes, fountains, and the public Baths of Zeuxippos: all these were typical features of the major cities of the empire and were meant to accommodate citizens, providing them with monumental urban ways for walking, water (which was so precious in a city devoid of natural water sources),[25] and a beautiful public bath that retained the strong social and cultural value of the public baths of Rome.[26] Although the actual construction of churches by Constantine is a subject of extensive debate,[27] fifth-century authors attribute to him Hagia Eirene and the church of the Holy Apostles, if not the Great Church of Hagia Sophia,[28] which was completed under Constantius (337–361), as well as several other structures, among which were the city walls. In fact, ascribing to Constantine, the various buildings of the capital became a constant theme in later sources as a way to magnify their construction and their legacy.[29]

All the urban structures mentioned above certainly had a great significance, each had its own function, and together were the most representative elements of the founder's new capital. As such, they were distinguished in the literary texts, but as three-dimensional architecture with imposing dimensions, they possessed enormous visual value for anyone walking in the streets. The walls of Constantinople were marked by doors, foremost among them, Constantine's Golden Gate, which crowned the route of imperial triumphs along the Via Egnatia into the city.[30] Later, Theodosius I probably built a triumphal arch located on the Egnatia, before Constantine's walls, which then was incorporated into Theodosius II's major enceinte, becoming the Golden Gate for the centuries to come.[31] The triumphal way of Constantinople, the *Mese*, lined by two-storey porticoes,[32] linked the Golden Gate to one of most representative squares of the capital, the *Augusteon*, a kind of atrium for the major political centres of the city: the complex formed by the imperial palace and the hippodrome and, from the middle of the fourth century, the religious core with the patriarchate and the cathedrals of Hagia Eirene and Hagia Sophia.[33]

Starting with the Forum of Constantine in the age of Constantine, the *Mese* was dotted with major squares and honorific arches or columns, monuments intended to celebrate the ruling emperor and his dynasty in the eyes of posterity. During the reign of Constantine, another square opened on the *Mese*, close to a building with a courtyard called the *Philadelphion* in the eighth-century *Parastaseis Syntomoi Chronikai*, but originally intended to be the Capitolium.[34] The square, the so-called *Ta Amastrianou* ("the property of the man from Amastris"),[35] was located to the south of the *Mese*, just in front of the Capitolium to the north of the street, where the main road leading to the Golden Gate forked, adding a north-west branch. A semicircular courtyard connected it to a centrally planned building to the south, a fifth-century palace which, around 920, Romanos I Lekapenos (919–944)

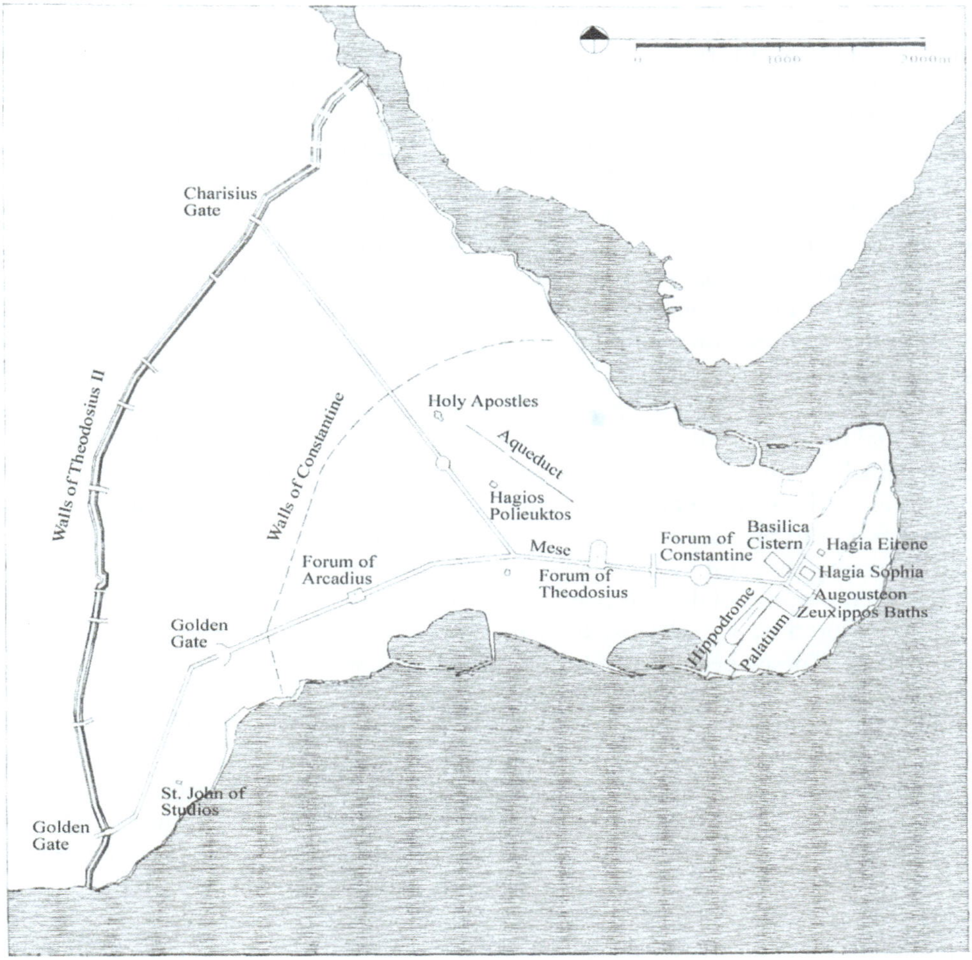

Figure 13.2 Map of Constantinople in late antiquity

converted into the Myrelaion Monastery.[36] Originally, it was decorated with statues and, according to Albrecht Berger, associated with the imperial cult of Helena, just as the Capitolium was associated with Constantine.[37]

Between 380 and 393, Theodosius I transformed an area located between the Forum of Constantine and the *Philadelphion* into another major forum – the so-called *Tauros* or *Forum Tauri* – which he dedicated to himself and his sons.[38] There, a monumental arch and a column celebrated the grandeur of Theodosius and his dynasty.[39] Soon after, in 401–402, his son, Arcadius, built another imperial square further west, on the last stretch of the *Mese* towards the Golden Gate. Just as his father did at the *Tauros*, at its centre Arcadius erected a column with a helical frieze.[40] In the following centuries of Late Antiquity, the process of building imperial squares with honorific monuments continued on the northern branch of the *Mese*, with the Forum of Marcian located not far from the complex of the Holy Apostles, and the Forum of Leo I in the area of the ancient acropolis near Hagia Eirene.[41] Later, after the turmoil of the Nika riot in 532, during Justinian's reconstruction of the

Augusteon, this latter square was turned into another area modelled after the other imperial *fora*, celebrating the ruling emperor with a colossal column supporting a statue.[42] Thus, by the sixth century, Constantinople's urban landscape was dotted with open-air squares monumentalized by lavish architecture expressing the grandeur of the emperors.

Under Constantine, the northern branch of the *Mese* was designed to connect the main street with the *martyrion* of the Holy Apostles, the imperial mausoleum built on one of the highest hills of the city. The martyrion-mausoleum, which was enlarged by Constantius with the construction of a cross-plan church in 356,[43] expanded in grand scale the architectural and conceptual tetrarchic precedent of placing imperial palace, hippodrome, and mausoleum in relation to one another. Starting with the building projects of Maxentius in Rome, these three buildings, each designed to celebrate the imperial power in its private and public spheres in life (palace and hippodrome) and in death (mausoleum), were structurally linked, forming a unity for the major exaltation of the *basileia*.[44] In the new capital of Constantine, they embraced the whole city, dispersed over a vast expanse but nonetheless connected by monumental porticoed streets. Moreover, their location up on the highest hills of the peninsula united them: to anyone looking at the city arriving by boat from the Marmara Sea, they appeared as the tallest structures of all – and this effect increased once Justinian's rebuilt the new churches of the Holy Apostles and Hagia Sophia as enormous buildings topped with lead domes.[45] It is also worth noting that the *fora* of Constantine, Theodosius, and Arcadius were all located upon hills rising above the cityscape. These open-air monuments, which, like windows opening up in the urban landscape, also exhibited ancient and new statuary, formed the settings for monumental columns supporting colossal imperial statues that rose high over the cityscape.[46] As demonstrated by Pelin Yoncaci-Arslan with a fabulous new three-dimensional model of the city and its monumental streets, the columns with their tall statues were a Late-Antique "urban signature", having a long-lasting effect on visitors.[47] In fact, a number of sources celebrate the columns as among the most extraordinary aspects of the city, from the popular traditions recorded in the *Patria* to the tenth-century poetry of Constantine Rhodius, and well after until Melchior Lorichs.[48]

Beside these major urban elements, Constantinople saw the rise of a number of other monumental structures. Starting with the reign of Constantius, the city was christianised with churches that formed a sacred geography visibly manifesting the Christian character of the empire and sanctifying the urban space with their relics. Socrates' claim that, under Theodosius II, Constantinople was turned into a sanctuary is perhaps an exaggeration,[49] but indeed according to the written sources the number of churches built in the first two centuries after the city foundation was very significant. By the time of Justinian, many of these sacred buildings were embellished with domes, further monumentalizing their appearances. Apart from being places of worship, several churches with their relics established processional paths inserted into the crowded liturgical calendars of cities like Constantinople.[50]

Furthermore, in keeping with the typically Roman attitude, the infrastructures of Constantinople were also designed to leave a long-lasting imprint on the city. Overcoming the irregular geography of the capital, Valens (364–378) promoted the construction of a massive aqueduct that brought water from over 250 km away and, between the third and the fourth hill, jutted above the city with its massive, superimposed rows of arches.[51] Later, Theodosius II, in response to the increasing population, completed an innovative and impressive walled enceinte formed by a complex system of fortifications, which made the city impregnable until its fall to the Ottomans in 1453. Its most exposed surfaces hosted monumental towers and gates and showed inscriptions recording the name of emperors responsible for embellishments or repairs through the centuries.[52] The creation of infrastructures, such as the aqueduct and the walls, which entailed enormous expenses in materials and manpower, not only served the practical and basic needs of a city and its populace but also monumentally displayed the philanthropy and grandeur of emperors to inhabitants and visitors. Authors from throughout history never fail to mention the walls of Constantinople. Although a victim of a twentieth-century reconstruction done in a way one might describe as a Disneyworld style, they are considered among the most prominent features of the city. The great import of such infrastructures in terms of a kind of embodied, so to say, physical, and three-dimensional propaganda was well known to Procopius, who celebrates bridges and fortifications that Justinian had built in the provinces.

Moreover, between the fourth and sixth centuries, the emperor and the richest of the élites oversaw the construction of lavish palaces. For instance, these include the Palace of Lausus and Antiochus, later turned into the Church of St. Euphemia[53]; the above-mentioned palace built by "the man from Amastris"; and the palace of Anicia Juliana, who was also responsible for the building of a church – Hagios Polyeuktos – beautiful enough to compete with Justinian's churches.[54] These large and lavish buildings stood out in a cityscape crowded with other smaller houses.

From Imperial Cities to Provincial Towns

In the second half of the fourth century, writing a poem in praise of the major urban centres of the empire, Ausonius celebrates the splendour of Milan by naming its most representative constructions: the palace, the city walls, the hippodrome, the theatre, the temples, the mint, the baths, the colonnades.[55] He was a Gallic intellectual and teacher at the court of Valentinian I (364–375), so he places particular emphasis on the description of Milan as the seat of the western court. The major buildings of Milan praised by Ausonius are the same kinds of buildings found in Constantinople that were lauded by fifth-century authors. In his orations on Antioch and Nicomedia, Libanius similarly celebrates the porticoes, the temples, the baths, the harbour, the streets, and the imperial palace.[56] Indeed, all of these cities were imperial seats. The buildings that writers are wont to include in their encomia are undoubtedly the most characteristically beautiful, the elements that appeal to the eye and make these urban centres superior to all the other cities.

Moreover, the images evoked by written sources are corroborated by historical evidence. The centres that between the third and the fourth centuries became tetrarchic capitals or those that were used as such by the western and eastern courts until the middle of the fifth century – though all only temporary seats of the empire – share common structures of particular grandeur. This is the case, for instance, of the tetrarchic capitals of Augusta Treverorum (Trier), Mediolanum, Sirmium (Sremska Mitrovica), Thessalonica (Thessaloniki), Nicomedia (İzmit), Nicaea (İznik), and Antiochia (Antakya). Also Aquileia, Arelatum (Arles), and Eboracum (York), where emperors occasionally stayed, were equipped with large-scale and expensive buildings that were becoming associated with the ruler. More than monuments, they were indexes of imperial presence. In the fourth century, the imperial authority impacted the cities of Serdica (Sofia) and Naissus (Niš) as centres linked to Constantine and his family,[57] and Ravenna when it became the seat of the western court of Honorius (395–423) at the beginning of the fifth century.[58] While for major urban centres such as Thessaloniki, Trier, and Antioch, the imposing dimensions of the urban expanse surely added monumental value to it, smaller centres such as Naissus, Sirmium, Nicomedia, Nicaea, and even Ravenna owed their monumental character to the presence of these important buildings. Around 358, Libanius clearly states this about the city of Nicomedia, which was much smaller than other major cities of the time, writing that because of its geographical location and buildings, Nicomedia surpassed Rome, Constantinople, Antioch, and Alexandria in splendour.[59]

These urban centres – just as other centres of the empire that never came to be imperial cities but were large provincial capitals, such as Ephesus or Sardis – offered enjoyment to the public by means of constructing large public baths, theatres, major porticoed streets and squares, temples, and, in the course of Late Antiquity, churches. The architecture and decoration of main urban structures are often praised in written sources: for instance, the presence of statues or columns in squares and the exterior of public buildings are particularly appreciated. Columns and statues concurred in transforming major urban roads into pleasant public spaces, indeed they were perceived as adding to the *decus* of the city:[60] they were not only suited to decorate the urban setting but also with their imagery and, in some cases, antiquity, they augmented the value of the space itself, thereby becoming identifying features of Roman civilization. A long tradition of epigrams on statues is testimony to the value of these elements as bearers of meaning and magnificence for common people.[61] After the riot of 378, the destruction of statues in the public spaces of Antioch made the city appear unadorned and empty.[62] The legends of the *Patria* often attach magical powers to ancient statuary of Constantinople and, in the tenth century, Constantine of Rhodes still praises the "statues by which, like stars, the city is adorned and turns its bright gaze everywhere".[63] Libanius recalls the temples of Antioch clad in marble, Procopius of Gaza the imperial statues adorning the cities newly restored by Anastasius' munificence.[64]

The geographical location is also often praised, adding to the concept of the city's monumentality: in particular the presence of water – such as rivers, water sources, or the sea – or of hills and a mountainous setting seem to augment the value of the city, an urban spectacle described as a vision seen from afar.[65] This is evidenced in Ausonius, Libanius, Procopius of Gaza, even in the epic of Nonnus of Panopolis, and in saintly lives.[66] Far from being a literary trope derived from the classic *locus amoenus*, a pleasant natural location appears as a greatly admired setting for its respective marvellous urban centre, something that enhanced the city's monumentality.

Also smaller provincial cities had a certain monumental character expressed by their major buildings. The paucity of written sources describing smaller cities between the fourth and seventh/eighth centuries is counterbalanced by the extant visual and archaeological evidence. Between the third and the sixth centuries, the cities were provided by massive fortifications, the most defining feature of monumentality even among the smaller towns. Ausonius' attentive praise of towns highlights the importance of the urban walls not only in imperial cities such as Milan but also in smaller centres, among which are Tolosa (Toulouse) and Burdigala (Bordeaux), his home town.[67] City walls were perhaps the major urban feature from Late Antiquity to the end of Byzantium, the element that stands out in every visual representation from the imaginary cities of Jerusalem and Bethlehem of church apses to miniature painting.[68] As stated above, fortifications were a central need of cities, and not only on the frontiers in a period of constant threat of invasions such as Late Antiquity. This is well evidenced everywhere in the empire, from the building of a walled enceinte in

Galerius' palace-city at Romuliana (Gamzigrad) at the beginning of the fourth century,[69] to the extant massive fifth-century walls of Thessaloniki,[70] to the walled enceintes of the cities on the Euphrates promoted by Anastasius (491–518) and Justinian.[71] Procopius clarifies the importance of urban walls. After naming all the fortifications restored or built anew by the emperor in the Danube area, he states that the urban renovation and the strong fortification made Singidunum (Belgrade) "a famous and important city",[72] as if the walls magnified the city itself. Later he adds that large defences and a number of houses give settlements the rank of cities.[73] Procopius' view equates the visual evidence of the Peutinger Map, where the major cities of the empire which had imperial palaces and/or were of particular strategic importance – namely Ravenna, Aquileia, Thessalonica, Nicomedia, Nicaea, and Ancyra – are all marked by the stylized image of an urban wall with towers, a symbol communicating the great value the city itself to the viewer.[74] Therefore, in the common mentality of the time – and in the following centuries of Byzantium – urban walls were understood as monumental features and considered iconic elements of the cities themselves: in the reality as well as in the imagery, such imposing and massive structures impacted viewers, epitomizing representations of the cities. Their iconic, representative value went beyond their practical function of providing defence into declaration of strength and power for the inhabitants of the city and for the authority who erected the urban walls.

One of the major characteristics of the Roman city was its typical orthogonal grid with two major axes (*cardo* and *decumanus*) that, in large and medium size centres, were monumentalized by columns, statues, nymphaea, or fountains and, often, a celebrative structure at their crossing, which in Late Antiquity often was a *tetrapylon*.[75] Between the third and the sixth centuries, colonnaded porticoes were a constant feature lining the main avenues, which responded to both practical and aesthetical needs. While they could provide cover for pedestrians during hot Mediterranean summers or rainy days, and adjunct spaces for shops, they could also become shelters for poor people at night. The porticoes were paved and, in some cases, even decorated with mosaics.[76] As it has been suggested on the bases of very narrow porticoed ways on the main streets of fourth-century Ephesus and sixth-century Salona, sometimes these architectural structures were purely ornamental rather than practical. It was the colonnaded road and not necessarily the usability of the porticoes, therefore, that added monumentality to the city.[77] The importance of column-lined roads, and, in general, of columnar architecture, is perhaps best evidenced by the mosaic floor of the Syro-Palestinian churches from the six through eighth centuries, like the Church of Madaba. There, the representation of the cities of the Holy Land suggests the iconographer's conception of different urban centres.[78] Jerusalem, the heart of the region and of Christianity, features as the largest city. Its renowned monuments, although rendered in a quite schematic way, are all recognizable and, above all, well visible are the *cardo* with its porticoes and a parallel columned road to the west. Indeed, the major characteristic of the city seems to be the porticoed *cardo*.[79]

Similarly, apart from the frequent towered walls, porticoes, which may be one of the most important visual elements testifying to the importance of the Late-Antique city, feature in the vignettes of Gaza, Neapolis, Diospolis, Kyriakopolis, and Ascalon. Indeed, in the sixth century, the major buildings showed in the Madaba map were the same ones encountered in written sources.

Apart from columned roads and walls in the Madaba Map's image of Jerusalem, special attention is given to the representation of sacred places. This is not surprising in a church such as that of Madaba, the floor of which was possibly designed as a cartographic

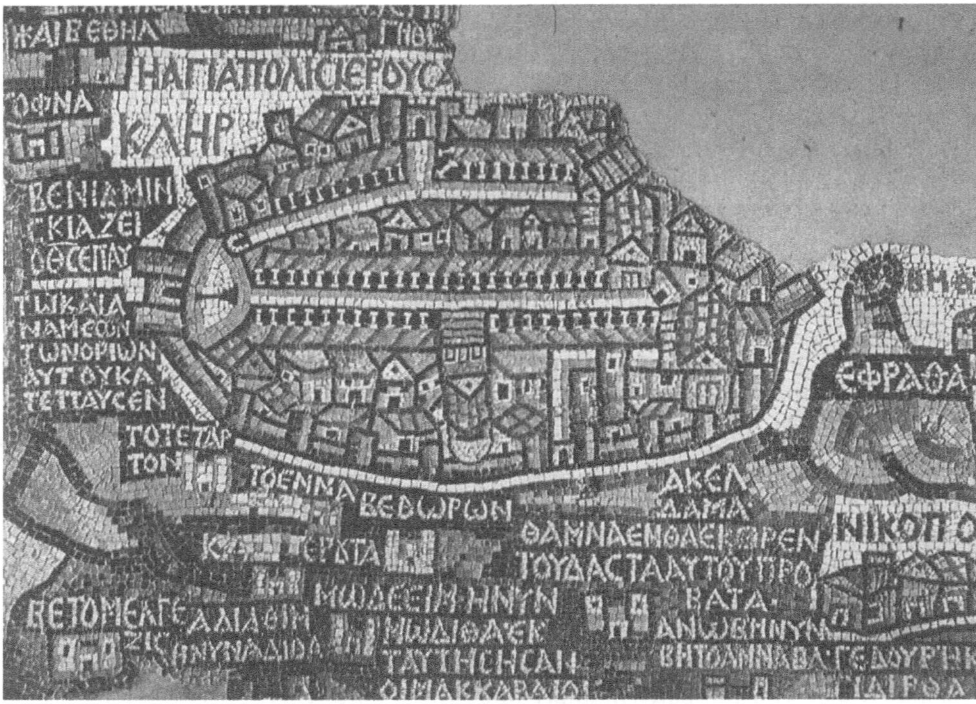

Figure 13.3 Madaba [Jordan] – Madaba Map (sixth century)

map to orient Christians through the sacred geography of the area.[80] Apart for the Anastasis, well visible thanks to the golden dome of the Rotunda and the basilica, other churches with a longitudinal plan and gabled roofs have been identified. Among those near the southern gate was the large structure of the Nea, the New Church of Mary built by Justinian in 542–543, one of the biggest ecclesiastical buildings in antiquity.[81] Indeed, from Late Antiquity onwards, churches are among the main features of the city, and the great expense and building effort spent for their architecture and decoration insure those to acquire a certain monumentality. Even in the case of provincial churches, such as the fourth-century cathedral of Tyre described by Eusebius, although the building materials were largely in wood and did not include the great variety of colourful marbles that adorned other major Constantinian churches, it is clear that the building reached a certain monumentality.[82] However, if, as it has recently been suggested, the Madaba map mosaic was in fact set into a civic hall,[83] the inclusion of such a high number of churches in the representation of Jerusalem would reflect the contemporary perception of the city and of its monumentality, which was conveyed by the presence of ecclesiastical buildings and sanctuaries. Although architectural representations in Late Antiquity and Byzantium were never exact reproductions of reality – and in fact the complex of the Anastasis here is represented at the centre of the *cardo* when it could not actually be located there – clearly, when depicting a specific city, the mosaicist took care to portray its major monuments, those which best characterised the urban centre and retained certain importance for people. This was not only to make that city recognizable – the captions would have served this task – but also to express the character of the city by means of its impressive and distinguishing monuments.

The Byzantine City as a Christian City: Ecclesiastical Monumentality

That the church is a fundamental element – a real bearer of monumentality – of the Late-Antique and Byzantine city is well attested both in written and visual sources. In chronicles of the empire as well as church chronicles, authors do not neglect to mention the building of churches. In the seventh-century *Chronicon Paschale*, which largely draws on the sixth-century *Chronographia* by John Malalas, the building of churches appears as one of the emperor's greatest accomplishments. In the tenth century, in addition to the new constructions in the palace, the *Vita Basilii* lists a number of churches built by Constantine and repaired or renewed by Basil I (867–886) and carefully describes the *Nea*, the new church which arose within the premises of the Great Palace.[84] The latter demonstrated "the emperor's piety towards the Godhead and the wondrous magnificence of his undertakings"[85] and was designed to celebrate the "everlasting memory" of Christ, Archangel Michael, Elijah the Tishbite, the Virgin, and Nicholas. Churches, with their dedications and the relics enshrined within their walls, were conceived as holy shrines and memorials, as is well attested by the accounts of Russian travelers between the fourteenth and fifteenth centuries, who visited Constantinople in pilgrimage.[86] The words of Constantine of Rhodes are perhaps the most revealing to understand the impact of churches on the monumentality of the city in the tenth century. In his poem, he introduces the description of the Holy Apostles mentioning the church along with Hagia Sophia, as the two buildings that made the city overcome all nature and sweep away everyone into utter astonishment.[87] These buildings, the church dedicated to the Apostles for its beauty and the Great Church for its tall and imposing dimensions, had an extraordinary effect on the appearance of Constantinople: by their presence "it inhibits the speech of everyone, this city, the envy of the whole world".[88] Certainly, in line with the architecture patronized by Justinian, these churches were enormous and their appearance impressive for the volumes of domes and semidomes clad in bright metals of their exteriors.[89]

Outside Constantinople, the church appears to be one of the most characteristic elements of towns during Late Antiquity and well after the age of Justinian. As attested by church mosaic floors in the areas of Syria, Palestine, and Egypt, images of walled cities often centred around basilicas, as if the church was the most representative element of the city itself.[90] The surviving mosaic depicting Alexandria from the Church of St. John at Gerasa (531) shows several churches inside a towered wall with the Pharos: their roofs are decorated with crosses, following a convention for depicting ecclesiastical buildings. The eighth-century mosaics of the Church of St. Stephen at Kastron Mefaa (Umm Ar-Rasas, Jordan) demonstrate that in the former Byzantine territories the urban imagery did not change after the Muslim conquest: apart from the walls, almost all the representations of cities lining the nave floor have churches at their centre, while a simple basilica just serves as a vignette for several cities on the Nilotic frieze of the nave.[91] In a similar fashion appeared the representations of cities on the mosaic floor of the Church of Belemous (Ma'in, near Madaba), dating to the years 719/720. Such imagery was quite spread in the East[92] and demonstrates the important role of churches in expressing the monumentality of a city.

Figure 13.4 Church of St. Stephen at Kastron Mefaa (Umm Ar-Rasas) [Jordan], mosaic floor (eighth century)

Conclusion

Late-Antique Constantinople met all the criteria of monumentality as it has been defined in recent scholarship. Authors provide further evidence about how it was perceived at the time as a mighty and grand city filled with buildings and structures that beautified it and created spaces for inhabitants and visitors to experience grandeur of scale. For instance, in 361, Himerius celebrated the huge size and beauty of the city, as big as a continent.[93] Authors, such as Zosimus and Sozomenus often expand on the great extension covered by single structures, or the city itself, and on the great effort to build such a marvellous enterprise.[94] The location of the city is always praised, from Himerius to Ibn Battuta in the fourteenth century, and so is its ancient history.[95] The large investments and the manpower employed in the construction of Constantine city as well as on the single and most iconic monuments of Constantinople are exalted: this sometimes leads to exaggerations and hyperboles like those we read in the seventh-century legendary account of the construction of Justinian's Hagia Sophia.[96] Even from a distance, its great walls rose in the landscape and, once inside, there were colonnaded streets, fountains, *fora*, great freestanding columns, golden-domed palaces, and marbled churches built to impress people with the power and wealth of the capital and the emperor. Indeed, Constantinople – and not only its buildings – appears to embody the very concept of monumentality, even according to the most recent theories.

Between the sixth and the ninth centuries, Byzantine architecture changed, progressively decreasing in size. Apart from a few cases of reconstruction of old churches, such as that of Hagia Eirene at Constantinople after the earthquake of 740, in the capital the expression of monumentality stopped relying so heavily on building dimensions. The scale of Hagia Sophia was never repeated as churches became much smaller in scale adopting centralized plans and reduced volumes that developed around a central dome.[97] This phenomenon is typical of the Empire at large and scholars have often connected it to a period of crisis and decay of the city, of ruralization that only recently have been scaled down and understood as a typical feature of a changing society.[98] In fact, the medieval Byzantine city changed in its basic structures, reflecting its social transformations. For instance, it abandoned great public baths for a number smaller local baths[99] and acquired numerous churches and monasteries that – apart from rare instances – would have been characterised by smaller dimensions, a multiplication of domes, and exterior volumes. However, as I tried to show above, the megastructures of antiquity and the décor of the ancient city still had a considerable impact on inhabitants and travelers, who left traces of their impressions in their accounts. Even if some ancient buildings did not survive and were replaced by new ones, they were still considered the most prominent features of Constantinople well into the Middle Ages. Furthermore, the idea of city monumentality does not seem to have changed much if, after the ninth century, urban representations continued to show towered walls surrounding churches.

In short, if columns, churches, and walls continued to be mentioned by authors and represented in urban depictions, the monumentality of the capital still largely relied on its ancient structures. The particular attention to *spolia*, often used in an evocative and meaningful way in middle and late Byzantine structures,[100] betrays an attention to the past and its conscious exhibition by Byzantines. The very fact that these structures have survived until now, continuously reused and transformed in function, and that the twentieth century has seen destruction of more than fifteen centuries of previous history, in Late-Antique capitals such as Thessaloniki, show that those antique buildings have been perceived as bearers of meaning – monuments of the city – creating a sense of monumentality for generations of people through the time. Indeed if, as I have tried to show, the monumentality of the Byzantine city can be understood in the framework of the modern discourse on monumentality, not only did the Byzantines have a sense of monumentality and felt it, but built cities were also indeed monumental and continue to be still today.

Notes

1 N. Westbrook, K. R. Dark, and R. van Meeuwen, "Constructing Melchior Lorichs' Panorama of Constantinople," *Journal of the Society of Architectural Historians* 69, no. 1 (2010): 62–87, https://doi.org/10.1525/jsah.2010.69.1.62.

2 K. Wulzinger, "Melchior Lorichs Ansicht von Konstantinopel Als topographische Quelle," in *Festschrift Georg Jacob*, ed. T. Menzel (Leipzig: Harrassowitz, 1932), 355–368; C. Mango and S. Yerasimov, *Melchior Lorichs' Panorama of Constantinople* (Istanbul: Ertug and Kokabiyik, 1999); Westbrook, Dark, and Meeuwen, "Constructing Melchior Lorichs' Panorama of Constantinople."

3 G. E. Meyers, "The Experience of Monumentality in Etruscan and Early Roman Architecture," in *Monumentality in Etruscan and Early Roman Architecture: Ideology and Innovation*, ed. M. L. Thomas, G. E. Meyers, and I. E. M. Edlund-Berry (Austin: University of Texas Press, 2012), 1–20; M. Furholt, M. Hinz, and D. Mischka, "'As Time Goes by'. Meanings, Memories and Monuments," in *"As Time Goes by?" Monumentality, Landscapes and the Temporal Perspective. Proceedings of the International Workshop "Socio-Environmental Dynamics over the Last 12,000 Years: The Creation of Landscapes II (14th–18th March 2011)" in Kiel*, ed. M. Furholt, M. Hinz, and D. Mischka (Bonn: Habelt, 2012), 13–20.

4 F. Levenson, "Monuments and Monumentality – Different Perspectives," in *Size Matters – Understanding Monumentality across Ancient Civilizations*, ed. F. Buccellati et al. (Bielefeld: Transcript Verlag, 2019), 17–39.

5 See for example: C. T. Lewis, Charles Short, *A Latin Dictionary* (New York: Harper & Brothers, 1879), 1161.

6 Lewis, Short, *A Latin Dictionary*, 1163. On the relationship between monument and memorial in a contemporary perspective, see most recently: A. Pinotti, *Nonumento. Un paradosso della memoria* (Varese: Johan & Levi, 2023).

7 H. Brunke et al., "Thinking Big. Research in Monumental Constructions in Antiquity," *ETopoi. Journal for Ancient Studies* 6 (2016): 250–305.

8 A. Bravi, "Ornamenta, Monumenta, Exempla. Greek Images of Gods in the Public Spaces of Constantinople," in *Divine Images and Human Imaginations in Ancient Greece and Rome*, ed. J. Mylonopoulos (Leiden: Brill, 2010), 289–301.

9 This is Cicero's use of this term (L. Van Hoof and P. Van Nuffelen, eds., *The Fragmentary Latin Histories of Late Antiquity (AD 300–620): Edition, Translation and Commentary* (Cambridge: Cambridge University Press, 2020), 74 n. 2).

10 Procopius, *De aedificiis* I.1.1–I.1.20, ed. and trans. H. B. Dewing (New York: Loeb Classical Library, 1940), 1–9. Similarly, in the fourth century, Gregory of Nazianzus mentions images of major cities bringing gifts to the emperor, as if cities were an expression of the imperial power while, at the same time, represented the populace honouring the emperor: Gregorius Nazianzenus, *Or.* IV.80, ed. J. Bernardi, Sources Chrétiennes 309 (Paris: Les éditions du Cerf, 1983), 204.

11 F. Buccellati, "Monumentality: Research Approaches and Methodology," in *Size Matters – Understanding Monumentality Across Ancient Civilizations*, ed. F. Buccellati et al. (Bielefeld: Transcript Verlag, 2019), 41–64; M. Furholt, M. Hinz, and D. Mischka, eds., *"As Time Goes by?" Monumentality, Landscapes and the Temporal Perspective. Proceedings of the International Workshop "Socio-Environmental Dynamics over the Last 12,000 Years: The Creation of Landscapes II (14th–18th March 2011)" in Kiel* (Bonn: Habelt, 2012).

12 Meyers, "The Experience of Monumentality in Etruscan and Early Roman Architecture."

13 J. F. Osborne, ed., *Approaching Monumentality in Archaeology* (Albany: SUNY Press, 2014).

14 Approaching the subject of early medieval monumentality: M. O. H. Carver, "Why That? Why There? Why Then? The Politics of Early Medieval Monumentality," in *Image and Power in the*

Archaeology of Early Medieval Britain: Essays in Honour of Rosemary Cramp, ed. H. F. Hamerow and A. MacGregor (Oxford: Oxbow Books, 2001), 1–22.

15 Brunke et al., "Thinking Big. Research in Monumental Constructions in Antiquity," 254–255.

16 Levenson, "Monuments and Monumentality – Different Perspectives," 23–25. On the connection between the concept of monumentality and a social system: Furholt, Hinz, and Mischka, "'As Time Goes by'. Meanings, Memories and Monuments."

17 Brunke et al., "Thinking Big. Research in Monumental Constructions in Antiquity," 255.

18 Socrates, *Historia Ecclesiastica* I.16.1, ed. G. C. Hansen, trans. P. Maraval and P. Périchon, Sources Chrétiennes 477 (Paris: Éditions du Cerf, 2004), 172–173; Sozomenus, *Historia Ecclesiastica* II.3.1, ed. J. Bidez, trans. A.-J. Festugière, Sources Chrétiennes 306 (Paris: Éditions du Cerf, 1983), 236–237.

19 The trope that Constantinople was even shaped on and around seven hills, like Rome, appeared only later: *Patria Constantinoupoleos*, III.19, trans. A. Berger (Washington: Dumbarton Oaks Medieval Library, 2013), 146–147. For discussion: A. Berger, "Das apokalyptische Konstantinopel. Topographisches in apokalyptischen Schriften der mittelbyzantinischen Zeit," in *Endzeiten: Eschatologie in Den Monotheistischen Weltreligionen*, ed. W. Brandes and F. Schmieder (Berlin: De Gruyter, 2008), 139–146.

20 Sozomenus, *Hist. Eccl.* II.3, ed. Bidez, trans. Festugière, 236–245; Zosimus, *Historia Nova* II.30–31, ed. F. Paschoud (Paris: Les Belles Lettres, 2000), I.101–103.

21 Malalas, *Chronographia* XIII.7–8, ed. H. Thurn, *Corpus Fontium Historiae Byzantinae. Series Berolinensis* 35 (Berlin - New York: De Gruyter, 2000), 245–247; followed by the seventh-century *Chronicon Paschale*, s.a. 328, ed. L. A. Dindorf, *Corpus scriptorum historiae Byzantinae* (Bonn: Weber, 1832), 527–529; trans. M. Whitby and M. Whitby, 2nd ed. (Liverpool: Liverpool University Press, 2007), 15–16.

22 G. Vespignani, *Il circo di Costantinopoli Nuova Roma* (Spoleto: Centro Italiano di Studi sull'Alto Medioevo, 2001); G. Vespignani, *ΙΠΠΟΔΡΟΜΟΣ: Il circo di Costantinopoli Nuova Roma dalla realtà alla storiografia* (Spoleto: Fondazione Centro italiano di studi sull'alto Medioevo, 2010).

23 M. Moser, *Emperor and Senators in the Reign of Constantius II: Maintaining Imperial Rule between Rome and Constantinople in the Fourth Century AD* (Cambridge: Cambridge University Press, 2018), 258–263.

24 C. Mango, "Antique Statuary and the Byzantine Beholder," *Dumbarton Oaks Papers* 17 (1963): 53–75; S. Basset, *The Urban Image of Late Antique Constantinople* (Oxford: Oxford University Press, 2004); A. Berger, *The Statues of Constantinople* (Cambridge: Cambridge University Press, 2021) P. Chatterjee, *Between the Pagan Past and Christian Present in Byzantine Visual Culture: Statues in Constantinople, 4th-13th Centuries CE* (Cambridge: Cambridge University Press, 2022).

25 J. Crow, J. Bardill, and R. Bayliss, *The Water Supply of Byzantine Constantinople* (Oxford: Oxbow Books, 2008).

26 For the social value of Roman baths: Inge Nielsen, *Thermae et Balnea: The Architecture and Cultural History of Roman Public Baths*, 2 Vols. (Aarhus: Aarhus University Press, 1990); for baths in Byzantium and the development of their architecture: F. Yegül, "Baths of Constantinople: An Urban Symbol in a Changing World," in *Archaeology and History in Roman, Medieval and Post-Medieval Greece Studies on Method and Meaning in Honor of Timothy E. Gregory*, ed. William R. Caraher, L. J. Hall, and S. R. Moore (Farnham – Burlington: Ashgate, 2008), 169–196; for the baths of Zeuxippos and the fountains of Constantinople: Paul Stephenson and Ragnar Hedlund, "Monumental Waterworks in Late Antique Constantinople," in *Fountains and Water Culture in Byzantium*, ed. B. Shilling and P. Stephenson (Cambridge: Cambridge University Press, 2016), 36–54 with references.

27 G. Dagron, *Naissance d'une capitale: Constantinople et ses institutions de 330 à 451* (Paris: Presses Universitaires de France, 1974), 388–409; C. Mango, *Le Développement Urbain de Constantinople (IVe-VIIe Siècles)*, 2nd ed. (Paris: De Boccard, 1990), 34–36.

28 Socrates, *Hist. Eccl.* I.16.2 and II.16.16, ed. Hansen, trans. Maraval and Périchon, I.172–I.175 and II.64–II.65.

29 A. Kazhdan, "'Constantin Imaginaire'. Byzantine Legends of the Ninth Century about Constantine the Great," *Byzantion* 57 (1987): 196–250; P. Magdalino, "Introduction," in *New Constantines. The Rhythm of Imperial Renewal in Byzantium, 4th–13th Centuries, Papers from the*

Twenty-Sixth Spring Symposium of Byzantine Studies (St. Andrews, March 1992), ed. P. Magdalino (Aldershot: Ashgate, 1994), 1–9 and various contributions in the same volume.

30 C. Mango, "The Triumphal Way of Constantinople and the Golden Gate," *Dumbarton Oaks Papers* 54 (2000): 173–188.

31 J. Bardill, "The Golden Gate in Constantinople. A Triumphal Arch of Theodosius I," *American Journal of Archaeology* 103, no. 4 (1999): 671–696.

32 P. Yoncaci-Arslan, "Registrars of Urban Movement in Constantinople: Monumental Columns and the Mese," *Annual of Istanbul Studies* 7 (2018): 6–29, especially 16.

33 Hagia Eirene served as the cathedral until the consecration of Hagia Sophia in 360. For the patriarchate: C. Rapp, "The Early Patriarchate (325–726)," in *A Companion to the Patriarchate of Constantinople*, ed. C. Gastgeber et al. (Leiden: Brill, 2021), 1–23. For imperial urban liturgies: F. A. Bauer, "Urban Space and Ritual: Constantinople in Late Antiquity," *Acta Ad Archaeologiam et Artium Historiam Pertinentia, n.s. 1* 15 (2001): 27–62.

34 *Parastaseis Syntomoi Chronikai* 70, trans. A. Cameron and J. Herrin, eds., *Costantinople in the Early Eight Century: The "Parastaseis Syntomoi Chronikai"* (Leiden: Brill, 1984), 150–153. Discussing the passage: A. Berger, "Constantine's City: The Early Days of a Christian Capital," *Studia Ceranea. Journal of the Waldemar Ceran Research Centre for the History and Culture of the Mediterranean Area and South-East Europe* 10 (2020): 11–29.

35 A. Berger, "Das Haus des Manns aus Amastris: Zu einem Gebäudekomplex im byzantinischen Konstantinopel," *Acta Antiqua Academiae Scientiarum Hungaricae* 51, no. 2 (2011): 87–97.

36 Cecil L. Striker, *The Myrelaion (Bodrum Camii) in Istanbul* (Princeton: Princeton University Press, 1982); R. Naumann, "Der antike Rundbau beim Myrelaion und der Palast Romanos I. Lekapenos," *Istanbuler Mitteilungen* 16 (1966): 199–216; P. Niewöhner, "The Rotunda at the Myrelaion in Constantinople. Pilaster Capitals, Mosaics, and Brick Stamps," in *The Byzantine Court: Source of Power and Culture. Papers from the Second International Sevgi Gönül Byzantine Studies Symposium (Istanbul, 21–23 June 2010)*, ed. A. Ödekan, N. Necipoğlu, and E. Akyürek (Istanbul: Vehbi Koç Vakfı Yayınları, 2013), 41–52.

37 Berger, "Constantine's City: The Early Days of a Christian Capital," 21–22.

38 A. Berger, "Tauros e Sigma. Due piazze di Costantinopoli," in *Bisanzio e l'Occidente. Arte, archeologia, storia. Studi in onore di Fernanda de' Maffei*, ed. C. Barsanti (Roma: Viella, 1996), 17–31.

39 R. Naumann, "Neue Beobachtungen am Theodosiusbogen und Forum Tauri in Istanbul," *Istanbuler Mitteilungen* 26 (1976): 117–147.

40 F. A. Bauer, *Stadt, Platz und Denkmal in der Spätantike: Untersuchungen zur Ausstattung des öffentlichen Raums in den spätantiken Städten Rom, Kostantinopel und Ephesos* (Mainz am Rhein: Philipp von Zabern, 1996), I.203–212. On the column: C. B. Konrad, "Beobachtungen zur Architektur und Stellung des Säulenmonumentes in Istanbul-Cerrahpasa – 'Arkadiossäule," *Istanbuler Mitteilungen* 51 (1975): 319–401; A. Taddei, "La Colonna di Arcadio a Costantinopoli: profilo storico di un monumento attraverso le fonti documentarie dalle origini all'età moderna," *Νέα Ῥώμη* 6 (2009): 37–102 with references.

41 U. Peschlow, "Eine wiedergewonnene byzantinische Ehrensäule in Istanbul," in *Studien zur spätantiken und byzantinischen Kunst, Friedrich Wilhelm Deichmann Gewidmet, Teil 1. Monographien*, ed. O. Feld and U. Peschlow (Bonn: Habelt, 1986), 21–34; Bauer, *Stadt, Platz und Denkmal in der Spätantike: Untersuchungen zur Ausstattung des öffentlichen Raums in den spätantiken Städten Rom, Kostantinopel und Ephesos*, I.215–217.

42 For Justinian's column and statue, most recently: E. Boeck, *The Bronze Horseman of Justinian in Constantinople: The Cross-Cultural Biography of a Mediterranean Monument* (Cambridge: Cambridge, 2021), with references.

43 Discussing the appearance of the original complex: C. Mango, "Constantine's Mausoleum and the Translation of Relics," *Byzantinische Zeitschrift* 83, no. 1 (1990): 51–62; C. Mango, "Constantine's Mausoleum: Addendum," *Byzantinische Zeitschrift* 83, no. 2 (1990): 434. Most recently: M. Mullet and R. Ousterhout, eds., *The Holy Apostles. A Lost Monument, a Forgotten Project, and the Presentness of the Past* (Washington: Dumbarton Oaks Research Library and Collection, 2020).

44 A. Frazer, "The Iconography of the Emperor Maxentius' Buildings in Via Appia," *The Art Bulletin* 48, no. 3–4 (1966): 385–392.

45 See for instance: K. N. Ciggaar, "Une description de Constantinople dans le Tarragonensis 55," *Revue des Études Byzantines* 53, no. 1 (1995): 117–140 in particular 119–120 (anonymous description of the eleventh century). See also T. Beg, *The History of Mehmed the Conqueror*, ed. H. Inalcik and R. Murphy (Minneapolis – Chicago: Bibliotheca Islamica, 1978).

46 Even if the statue on the column of Constantine represented a pagan deity, in fact it was regarded as the emperor. For Constantine's column: J. Bardill, *Constantine, Divine Emperor of the Christian Golden Age* (Cambridge: Cambridge University Press, 2012), 28–42; R. Ousterhout, "The Life and Afterlife of Constantine's Column," *Journal of Roman Archaeology* 27 (2014): 304–326; P. Yoncaci-Arslan, "Towards a New Honorific Column: the Column of Constantine in Early Byzantine Urban Landscape," *METU Journal of the Faculty of Architecture* 33, no. 1 (2016): 121–145.

47 *Ibidem*, 137.

48 Although Albrecht Berger notices that most of the *fora* were not so large (A. Berger, "Streets and Public Spaces in Constantinople," *Dumbarton Oaks Papers* 54 [2000]: 161–172), their location and imposing architecture seem to have had a considerable impact on the viewers.

49 Socrates, *Hist. Eccl.* VII.22.17, ed. G. C. Hansen, trans. P. Maraval and P. Périchon, Sources Chrétiennes 506 (Paris: Éditions du Cerf, 2004), 86–87.

50 J. F. Baldovin, *The Urban Character of Christian Worship: The Origins, Development and Meaning of Stational Liturgy* (Roma: Pontificium Institutum Studiorum Orientalium, 1987), 167–225.

51 J. Crow, "Water and Late Antique Constantinople," in *Two Romes: Rome and Constantinople in Late Antiquity*, ed. L. Grig and G. Kelley (Oxford: Oxford University Press, 2012), 116–135; J. Crow, "Ruling the Waters: Managing the Water Supply of Constantinople, AD 330–1204," *Water History* 4, no. 1 (2012): 35–55.

52 For the walls of Constantinople and their inscriptions: N. Asutay-Effenberger, *Die Landmauer von Konstantinopel-Istanbul: Historisch-topographische und baugeschichtliche Untersuchungen* (Berlin – New York: De Gruyter, 2008); C. Mango, "The Byzantine Inscriptions of Canstantinople: A Bibliographical Survey," *American Journal of Archaeology* 55 (1951): 52–66; C. Foss, "Anomalous Imperial Inscriptions of the Walls of Constantinople," in *Studies Presented to Sterling Dow on His Eightieth Birthday*, ed. S. Dow and A. L. Boegehold (Durham: Duke University, 1984), 77–87.

53 C. Mango, M. Vickers, and E. D. Francis, "The Palace of Lausus at Constantinople and Its Collection of Ancient Statues," *Journal of the History of Collections* 4, no. 1 (January 1, 1992): 89–92; J. Bardill, "The Palace of Lausus and Nearby Monuments in Constantinople: A Topographical Study," *American Journal of Archaeology* 101, no. 1 (1997): 67–95.

54 For Anicia Juliana's palace and church: M. Harrison, *A Temple for Byzantium: The Discovery and Excavation of Anicia Juliana's Palace-Church in Istanbul* (London: Harvey Miller, 1989); J. Bardill, "A New Temple for Byzantium: Anicia Juliana, King Solomon, and the Gilded Ceiling of the Church of St. Polyeuktos in Constantinople," in *Social and Political Life in Late Antiquity*, ed. W. Bowden, A. Gutteridge, and C. Machado (Leiden – Boston: Brill, 2006), 339–370; J. Bardill, "Église de Saint-Polyeucte à Constantinople: nouvelle solution pour l'énigme de sa reconstitution," in *Architecture paléochrétienne*, ed. J.-M. Spieser (Gollion: Infolio, 2011), 77–103.

55 Ausonius, *Ordo urbium nobilium* 7, ed. S. Prete (Leipzig: Teubner, 1978), 195.

56 Libanius, *Oratio* XI.196–XI.229 and LXI.7–LXI.10, ed. R. Foerster (Leipzig: Teubner, 1903 and 1908), I.504–I.517 and IV.332–IV.335.

57 P. Petrović, "Naissus. Foundation of Emperor Constantine," in *Roman Imperial Towns and Palaces in Serbia: Sirmium, Romuliana, Naissus*, ed. D. Srejović (Beograd: Serbian Academy of Sciences and Arts, 1993), 55–81; S. Ćurčić, *Architecture in the Balkans. From Diocletian to Suleyman the Magnificent, c. 300–1550* (New Haven – London: Yale University Press, 2010), 50, 147–148.

58 For the late antique and medieval city: E. Cirelli, *Ravenna: archeologia di una città* (Firenze: All'Insegna del Giglio, 2008); D. M. Deliyannis, *Ravenna in Late Antiquity* (Cambridge: Cambridge University Press, 2010); J. Herrin, *Ravenna: Capital of Empire, Crucible of Europe* (Princeton: Princeton University Press, 2019).

59 Libanius, *Oratio* LXI.7, ed. Foerster, IV.332–IV.333. For Libanius' special attachment to Nicomedia: R. Cribiore, *Between City and School: Selected Orations of Libanius* (Liverpool: Liverpool University Press, 2015), 29–30. In the life of St. Thecla, Seleucia is said to be so splendid and charming to surpass most of the cities: *Vita S. Theclae* 27, ed. G. Dagron, *Subsidia Hagiographica* 62 (Bruxelles: Société des Bollandistes, 1978), 276-279. Similarly, writing at the turn of the sixth century, Choricios of Gaza praised Caesarea, for it was beautiful, large, and flourishing: Choricius Gazaeus, XXXII (= *Or.* 8).95, ed. R. Foerster and E. Richtsteig, *Choricii Gazaei opera* (Leipzig: Teubner, 1929), 365–366.

60 On this concept: Bravi, "Ornamenta, Monumenta, Exempla. Greek Images of Gods in the Public Spaces of Constantinople"; see also: A. Bravi, *Ornamenta Urbis. Opere d'arte greche negli spazi romani* (Bari: Edipuglia, 2012).

61 See for instance: *Anthologia Graeca* II, ed. and trans. W. R. Paton, revised by M. A. Tueller, *Loeb Classical Library* 67 (Cambridge – London: Harvard University Press, 2014), 86–145 on the statues of the gymnasium of Zeuxippos.

62 I. Chrysostomus, *Hom. ad pop. Ant.* 17.2, ed. J.-P. Migne, *PG* 49 (Paris: J.-P. Migne, 1862), 173–180. See, with discussion: L. Lavan, "The Agorai of Antioch and Constantinople as Seen by John Chrysostom," *Bulletin of the Institute of Classical Studies* 50 (2007): 157–167.

63 οἷς ὥσπερ ἄστροις ἀγλαΐζεται πόλις / καὶ τὄμμα φαιδρὸν πανταχοῦ περιστρέφει. Constantinus Rhodius, *Ekphrasis* 261–262, trans. V. Dimitropoulou, L. James, and R. Jordan, in: Constantine of Rhodes, *On Constantinople and the Church of the Holy Apostles, with a New Edition of the Greek Text by Ioannis Vassis*, ed. L. James (Burlington: Ashgate, 2012), 37.

64 P. Gazaeus, *Op.* XI (= *Or.* II, *Panegyricus Anastasii*), 29, ed. E. Amato, trans. P. Maréchaux (Paris: Les Belles Lettres, 2014), 305.

65 H. Saradi, "Beholding the City and the Church: The Early Byzantine Ekphraseis and Correspoding Archaeological Evidence," *Δελτίον Τῆς Χριστιανικῆς Ἀρχαιολογικῆς Ἑταιρείας* 24 (2003): 31–36 especially 31–33.

66 For Procopius of Gaza's *ekphraseis*: P. Gazaeus, *Ep.* 119.9–119.12 (on Alexandria), ed. A. Garzya and R.-J. Loenertz, *Studia patristica et Byzantina* 9 (Ettal: Buch-Kunstverlag, 1963), 61; P. Gazaeus, *Op.* XI (= *Or.* II, *Panegyricus Anastasii*), 2 (passage on Epidamnon/Dyrrachium, modern Durres), ed. Amato, trans. Maréchaux, 284. For Choricius of Gaza's: Choricius Gazaeus, I (= *Or.* I).83–85 (on Gaza), XXXII (= *Or.* 8).95 (on Caesarea), ed. Foerster and Richtsteig, 23–24, 365–366. For Nonnus' praise to Tyre's and Berytus' geographical location: Nonnus, *Dionysiaca* 40.338–40.355 and 41.14–49, ed. B. Simon, F. Vian (Paris: Les Belles Lettres, 1999), XIV; P. Chuvin, M.-C. Fayant (Paris: Les Belles Lettres, 2006), XV.31–XV.34. In the *Life of St. Thecla*, Seleucia competes with Tarsus for its location, the abundance of fruits, and the good supply of water (*Vita S. Theclae* 27, ed. Dagron, 276–279).

67 Ausonius, *Ordo urbium nobilium* 6, 18, 20, ed. Prete, 194, 198, 200.

68 This is evidenced across the time, see for instance the manuscript illumination of the sixth-century *Codex Purpureus Rossanensis* or the fourteenth-century Slavonic version of Constantine Manasses' *Chronicon* now at the Vatican (Cod. Vat. Slav. 2). For the walls as a major urban character of all times: I. Ehrensperger-Katz, "Les représentations de villes fortifiées dans l'art paléochrétien et leurs dérivées byzantines," *Cahiers Archéologiques* 19 (1969): 1–27; C. Bertelli, "Visual Images of the Town in Late Antiquity and the Early Middle Ages," in *The Idea and Ideal of Town between Late Antiquity and the Early Middle Ages*, ed. G. P. Brogiolo and B. Ward-Perkins (Leiden: Brill, 1999), 99–126; A. M. Orselli, "Imagines urbium alla fine del tardoantico," in *Imago urbis: l'immagine della città nella storia d'Italia. Atti del Convegno internazionale (Bologna, 5–7 settembre 2001)*, ed. F. Bocchi and R. Smurra (Roma: Viella, 2003), 233–250.

69 D. Srejović, "Imperial Palace," in *Felix Romuliana – Gamzigrad*, ed. I. Popović (Belgrade: Institute of Archaeology, 2011), 43–48.

70 J. Crow, "Fortifications and Urbanism in Late Antiquity: Thessaloniki and Other Eastern Cities," in *Recent Research in Late-Antique Urbanism (Journal of Roman Archaeology Supplementary Series 42)* (Portsmouth, 2001), 89–105.

71 J. Crow, "Fortification and the Late Roman East: From Urban Walls to Long Walls," in *War and Warfare in Late Antiquity (Late Antique Archaeology 8)*, ed. A. Sarantis and N. Christie (Leiden: Brill, 2013), 397–432; J. Crow, "Fortifications," in *The Archaeology of Byzantine Anatolia: From*

the End of Late Antiquity Until the Coming of the Turks, ed. P. Niewöhner (Oxford – New York: Oxford University Press, 2017), 90–108.

72 Πόλιν περιφανῆ τε καὶ λόγου πολλοῦ ἀξίαν πεποίηκεν αὖθις. Procopius, *De aed.* IV.5.15–IV.5.16, ed. and trans. Dewing, 268–269.

73 Procopius, *De aed.* IV.6.2, ed. and trans. Dewing, 268–269.

74 For the Peutinger Map, see with references: R. J. A. Talbert, *Rome's World. The Peutinger Map Reconsidered* (Cambridge: Cambridge University Press, 2010); M. Rathmann, *Die Tabula Peutingeriana*, 3rd ed. (Darmstadt: Philipp von Zabern, 2018), 30–31 (for the vignettes).

75 L. Lavan, "The Monumental Streets of Sagalassos in Late Antiquity: An Interpretative Study," in *La rue dans l'Antiquité. Définition, aménagement et devenir de l'Orient méditerranéen à la Gaule*, ed. P. Ballet, N. Dieudonné-Glad, and C. Saliou (Rennes: Presses Universitaires de Rennes, 2008), 201–214.

76 Between the fourth and the seventh centuries, porticoes with mosaic floors are found at Sardis, Ephesus, Laodicea ad Lykum, Stratonicea in Caria, Side, Perge, Antioch, Apamea, Beritus, Sepphoris, Scythopolis, Caesarea Palestianae, Gerasa (Luke Lavan, *Public Space in the Late Antique City*, 2 Vols. [Leiden: Brill, 2020], I.48-51).

77 *Ivi*, 35.

78 For architectural representations in the Madaba map: N. Duval, "Essai sur la signification des vignettes topographiques," in *The Madaba Map Centenary 1897–1997. Travelling through the Byzantine Umayyad Period. Proceedings of the International Conference Held in Amman (7–9 April 1997) (Studium Biblicum Franciscanum. Collectio Maior 40)*, ed. M. Piccirillo and E. Alliata (Jerusalem: Studium Biblicum Franciscanum, 1999), 134–146.

79 Wendy Pullan, "Representation of the Late Antique City in the Madaba Map," in *The Madaba Map Centenary 1897–1997. Travelling through the Byzantine Umayyad Period. Proceedings of the International Conference Held in Amman (7–9 April 1997) (Studium Biblicum Franciscanum. Collectio Maior 40)*, ed. Michele Piccirillo and Eugenio Alliata (Jerusalem: Studium Biblicum Franciscanum, 1999), 165–171.

80 Discussing the purpose of the Madaba map and suggestion a new and intriguing hypothesis: B. Leal, "A Reconsideration of the Madaba Map," *Gesta* 57, no. 2 (2018): 123–143. P. Arad, "Another reconsideration of the Madaba map," in *Byzantine and Modern Greek Studies* 47, no. 2 (2023), 149–167.

81 Y. Tzafrir, "The Holy City of Jerusalem in the Madaba Map," in *The Madaba Map Centenary 1897–1997. Travelling through the Byzantine Umayyad Period. Proceedings of the International Conference Held in Amman (7–9 April 1997) (Studium Biblicum Franciscanum. Collectio Maior 40)*, ed. M. Piccirillo and E. Alliata (Jerusalem: Studium Biblicum Franciscanum, 1999), 155–163.

82 Eusebius, *Historia Ecclesiastica* X.4.37–X.4.45, ed. G. Bardy, Sources Chrétiennes 55 (Paris: Les éditions du Cerf, 1958), 93–96.

83 Leal, "A Reconsideration of the Madaba Map."

84 The text mentions at least 25 churches in Constantinople and 6 in the suburbs. For the *Nea*: *Vita Basilii*, 83–86, ed. I. Ševčenko, *Corpus Fontium Historiae Byzantinae* 42 (Berlin – Boston: De Gruyter, 2011), 273–279.

85 Ὅπερ ἀρκεῖ καὶ μόνον τήν τε περὶ τὸ θεῖον αὐτοῦ δηλοῦν ὁσιότητα καὶ τὸ πρὸς τὰ ἐπιβαλλόμενα μεγαλουργόν τε καὶ θαύματος ἄξιον. *Ibidem.*

86 G. P. Majeska, *Russian Travelers to Constantinople in the Fourteenth and Fifteenth Centuries* (Washington: Dumbarton Oaks Research Library and Collection, 1984).

87 C. Rhodius, *Ekphrasis* 264–271, trans. Dimitropoulou, James and Jordan, 36–38.

88 Γλώττας τε πάντων τοῦ λαλεῖν ἀποτρέπει / ἡ κοσμοπαμπόθητος αὕτη πως πόλις. Constantinus Rhodius, *Ekphrasis* 264–271, trans. Dimitropoulou, James and Jordan, 36.

89 For the aesthetics of metal roofs: M. C. Carile, "The Imperial Palace Glittering with Light: The Material and Immaterial in the Sacrum Palatium," in *Hierotopy of Light and Fire in the Culture of the Byzantine World*, ed. A. Lidov (Moscow: Theoria, 2013), 105–135.

90 For a recent discussion on the urban imagery of the mosaic floors of Syria, Palestina, and Egypt: H. G. Saradi, *The Byzantine City in the 6th Century: Literary Images and Historical Reality* (Athens: Society of Messenian Archaeological Studies, 2006), 119–135.

91 N. Duval, "Le rappresentazioni architettoniche," in *Umm Al-Rasas Mayfa'ah*, I, *Gli scavi del complesso di Santo Stefano (Studium Biblicum Franciscanum. Collectio Maior 28)*, ed. M. Piccirillo and E. Alliata (Jerusalem: Studium Biblicum Franciscanum, 1994), 165–204.

92 Bertelli, "Visual Images of the Town in Late Antiquity and the Early Middle Ages."
93 Himerius, *Or.* XLI.4–XLI.6, ed. A. Colonna (Rome: Polygraphica, 1951); trans. R. J. Penella, *Man and the Word. The Orations of Himerius* (Los Angeles: University of California Press, 2007), 60–61.
94 For the dimensions of Constantine city: Zosimus, *Hist. Nova* II.30, ed. Paschoud, I.101–I.102; Sozomenus, *Hist. Eccl.* II.3.6, ed. Bidez, trans. Festugière, 240–241.
95 Himerius, *Or.* 41.5–41.6, ed. Colonna, and trans. Penella, 61; Ibn-Battuta, *Travels* VIII, trans. H. A. R. Gibb, *The Travels of Ibn Battuta, A.D. 1325–1354* (Cambridge: The Hakluyt Society, 1962), 506–507.
96 *Patria Constantinoupoleos*, IV.1–IV.31, trans. Berger, 231–275.
97 R. Krautheimer, *Early Christian and Byzantine Architecture*, ed. S. Ćurčić, 6th ed. (New Haven – London: Yale University Press, 1986); R. Ousterhout, *Master Builders of Byzantium* (Philadelphia: University of Pennsylvania Museum of Archaeology and Anthropology, 1999), 86–128.
98 On this point see other contributions in this volume and Luca Zavagno's forthcoming book.
99 Robert Ousterhout, "Houses, Markets, and Baths: Secular Architecture in Byzantium," in *Heaven & Earth: Cities and Countryside in Byzantine Greece*, ed. A. Drandaki, D. Papanikola-Bakirtzi, and A. Tourta (Athens: Benaki Museum, 2013), II.211–II.213; Yegül, "Baths of Constantinople: An Urban Symbol in a Changing World."
100 For instance in the walls of so-called Little Metropolis at Athens. Most recently, B. Kiilerich, "Making Sense of the Spolia in the Little Metropolis in Athens," *Arte Medievale, n. s.* 4, no. 2 (2015): 95–114 with references.

14

MAINTAINED, STORED AND PROTECTED

Water and the Byzantine City

Elisabetta Giorgi

The management and use of water resources are not features specific to the Byzantine city – whatever this expression could mean – but are rather an element of continuity with the urban water culture inherited from classical Antiquity.

In the Roman Empire, the urban water supply relied quite completely on spring water: the aqueducts of the Greco-Roman cities drew water from sources far away from the city, to ensure a water supply of good quality and unlimited in quantity. Inside the city, running water was visible in quantity and quality, and its strong ideological value overshadowed "other possible waters" (water from wells, rainwater from reservoirs). Spring water was reputedly the only kind suitable for drinking, and for this reason, the aqueducts became essential components in the Roman city tool-kit.[1]

The Byzantine water culture was decidedly less monolithic: the Roman legacy of water use culture and its related structures were ideally managed not only in continuity but also through adaptations and pragmatic solutions; the common need to have good quality water – and the willingness to display such a resource – was translated into water-related structures of varying degrees of scale and complexity all over the empire.[2]

A Short Typology of Water Use in the Byzantine City

Different levels of complexity characterize the interaction between a city and its water resources, ranging from the simple exploitation of water naturally available within the urban perimeter to the construction of complex systems drawing water from distant springs, and this increase in systemic complexity is paralleled by the increase in the level of well-being that water can provide to an urban community.

The exploitation of natural springs and water courses located inside a single urban area – together with the excavation of wells – marks the most basic level of interaction. At a higher level, we can mention the collection of rainwater[3] through the construction of cisterns. Although subject to seasonal rainfall variations, the use of cisterns represents an easier solution to conveniently make water available city without interfering with the natural landscape.

By contrast, the construction of an aqueduct that captures the spring water of a specific territory and drives it towards a distant city marks a significant alteration in the water

DOI: 10.4324/9780429203923-18

balance of a landscape, diverting a water flow in a direction other than the natural one and connecting a city to a spring that would be otherwise unavailable and thereby making water available wherever it is needed in the city with its squares, thermal baths, fountains and private buildings. This is therefore a complex operation that is the result of a political decision involving both an initial construction cost and ongoing maintenance.

Yet such a schematic typology of interaction between water and human communities clashes with the reality of archaeological evidence, which presents a much more complex picture. In many urban contexts, in fact, different water systems – aqueducts carrying spring water, wells capturing vein water, cisterns storing rainwater – in reality worked together. This was done either to optimize the exploitation of different water resources or to progressively adapt an existing water system to new needs.

The difficulty in dating structures such as wells and the general lack of archaeological data on urban distribution both make it difficult to establish whether the various elements were used concurrently or whether they date to different periods. We can summarize the three hypotheses as follows:

a Different structures not in use in the same period, typically when the construction of an aqueduct coincides with the abandonment of wells and cisterns.
b Different structures functioning together but related to different uses, with the aqueduct intended to feed public fountains and baths, and wells and cisterns intended to serve private users.
c Different structures working together as parts of an organic and integrated system[4]: the aqueducts connect perennial sources both to the urban distribution network and reservoirs and/or cisterns intended to store a certain amount of water within the city, as in the case of Constantinople, Ephesus Apamea and Gortyn. These systems are normally the result of a series of additions to the original core: Constantinople[5] and Gortyn[6] – at a different scale – provide clear examples, with Roman and Late Antique aqueducts that were connected to a network of cisterns in the Byzantine period.

Such a complex water system frees the city from the seasonal variability of the springs and from interruptions in supply due to lack of maintenance, sieges in wartime or seasonal droughts. This is because the use of different forms of supply creates an artificial balance that remains stable as long as the city can ensure control and maintenance.

Continuity, Limits and Discontinuity of Water Legacy

The Byzantine cities inherited water structures, ideology and material culture from the Greco-Roman tradition. According to J. Pickett, this legacy had some limits, namely[7]: (a) the ideological value of the city's control over the spring waters; (b) the high maintenance costs of the aqueducts; (c) the total dependence of cities on aqueducts. The aqueducts in fact had introduced a hierarchy of drinking water, in which the highest position was occupied by spring water, considered superior to any other source. Yet in the Byzantine age, the fragility of a water supply system based almost exclusively on the aqueducts is evident both in written sources and in archaeological remains.

In general, the Roman aqueducts were maintained, though sometimes with significant transformations, while rainwater collection increased in importance, as indicated by the proliferation of cisterns. These structures are perhaps the most visible archaeological indicator of a simplified but extremely pragmatic approach to the problem of water supply.

Even when the ideological value of controlling spring water ostensibly failed, the water inside the city retained its aesthetic value, as recorded by written sources[8] and manifested in the building of new monumental fountains or the transformation of existing ones.[9] Moreover, the use of water as a means of self-representation continued in private and domestic contexts.[10] The position and the decorative apparatus of these structures seem to indicate that they continued to serve much as they had during the Greco-Roman era, albeit with different formal characteristics, as is attested in many cities, including Ephesus and Sagalassos.[11]

The legacy of water management also entails a legacy of engineering knowledge. The continuity of the water culture is particularly evident in the construction of new water supply systems, including those of the cities founded by Justinian. These were built with spring water collection structures, underground or suspended channels connected to water towers, pipelines and basins, as in Iustiniana Prima (see below). The same technical continuity can be witnessed by the transformation of preexisting water structures, as in the siphon of the Justinianic aqueduct at the basilica of St. John in Ephesus.[12]

The material persistence of water culture is also recorded in two cities "outside" of the Byzantine Empire: Ravenna and Recopolis. In Ravenna, some stamped *fistulae* testify to the Theoderician restoration of the aqueduct originally constructed during the reign of Trajan, still through an underground distribution system.[13] In the newly built city of Recopolis in the late 6th century, the aqueduct was built according to the principles of Roman hydraulics, probably also as an act of propaganda aggrandizing the Gothic monarchy.[14]

The spread continuity of ancient water culture[15] means also the continuity of different water supply systems, resulting from the interaction between a community's needs with some particular environmental conditions. In desert and semi-arid regions, the lack of water requires different solutions than the traditional supply system based on spring water,[16] as in the cities born in Roman times along the *limes arabicus*, such as Umm el Jemal or Resafa. For these settlements, connected to their fortresses, rainwater is in fact the only feasible source, but since rain falls only in some periods of the year, it must be collected and stored in covered cisterns to prevent evaporation.

The archaeological indicators of these water supply systems are almost exclusively the remains of their cisterns; the example at Umm el-Jimal can store about 20,000 cubic meters of water, enough not only to satisfy the needs of the community but also to irrigate the crops and raise the animals.[17] The success of this system, based on the conservation of a seasonal water resource, is evident from their long period of use[18] and from the economic prosperity of a site like Umm el-Jimal between the 5th and 6th centuries, when the Hauran region was dotted with towns and villages dedicated to agricultural production.[19] In an ongoing project,[20] the structures of the ancient water system have been restored to allow the inhabitants to again use a natural resource in a sustainable way[21] (Figure 14.1). The combination of old and new water harvesting systems has made possible the agricultural exploitation of a region where the average annual rainfall is around 150 mm/year and never exceeds 300 mm/year.

In Resafa, the rainwater collected through a dam is channeled towards a system of cisterns within the city walls, thus guaranteeing the water supply of the fortified site (see below).

There are also Byzantine cities which survived without a structured water system.[22] The four Roman aqueducts of Nicopolis ad Istrum were destroyed during the sack of the city in 450 and seem not to have been restored even when the city became the capital of Moesia in the 6th century. It is therefore possible that the water supply was provided by the rivers.

Figure 14.1 The still in use main reservoir in Umm el-Jimal
Source: Photo Credit – Conor Whately.

Some other cities with administrative status such as Amorium, Larissa and Mokissos do not seem to rely on aqueducts either.[23]

The absence of aqueducts in cities with administrative status became more pronounced in the thematic age, when the essential requirement for a city capital seems to have been an effective defensive system rather than access to good quality water. The analysis of the relationship between aqueducts and thematic capitals indicates that only one-third of the cities, usually ports, kept their aqueducts in operation. Another third let their aqueducts gradually decay, while the rest had no aqueducts at all and got water from rivers or lakes or through the collection of rainwater.[24] This evidence seems to indicate that the diversification of the water systems which began in the Byzantine age as a response to the unsustainability of the spring-based Roman water system became increasingly pronounced in the Middle Byzantine era.[25]

From an Archaeology of Structures to an Archaeology of Water

In the Byzantine age, the transformations of water supply systems often resulted in the addition of structures or segments to preexisting systems; these mainly concern the water distribution network rather than the extra-urban supply network.

The water routes to the city are marked in the landscape at the time of their construction and the water technology is consolidated[26]; except for extraordinary events, aqueducts are not subject to excessive wear. On the other hand, the urban distribution system is much more subject to wear, being the final segment of the water system; it is by nature built with "light structures" (pipes), and so is both more "fragile" and more flexible in how it can be to the people needs. Due to this dynamism, the distribution system is of the greatest interest in an analysis of urban transformation, because it works in a very close connection to the daily life of the urban community.

The best way to analyze the transformations of the distribution network is through stratigraphic analysis, which naturally requires very different, more intensive, methods when compared to an investigation aimed at reconstructing the route of an aqueduct, which is faster and is often now supported by low-cost technology (use of drones, photogrammetry, LIDAR).[27] Moreover, the urban water distribution system must necessarily be investigated within a city that has often been continuously occupied even until today; this means that the sequence of multi-layered interventions may be difficult to read or even impossible to investigate precisely due to this continuity of use.

The case most emblematic of the difficulty of being able to bring together so much different information is represented by the project researching the water system of Constantinople,[28] a contemporary, multi-layered city, with a complex water system that is the result of a series of additions and transformations, with well-known monumental structures, such as large cisterns. The water system of the city is of exceptional technical interest, and the project has been carried out with adequate technological tools, by highly qualified researchers, and has yielded a very large dataset. Thanks to this project, we can now reconstruct the very long path that the water traveled to reach the city; we can now relate some stretches of urban canalizations to cisterns or fountains, but it is not yet possible to fully and clearly map the distribution network which had to have been very branched and multi-layered.

On the contrary, archaeological investigations in abandoned cities have often focused on monuments and structures such as aqueducts, but with an interest above all in the technical aspects rather than in their anthropological implications. In addition to the obvious exception of Constantinople, we have a fairly defined image of the water supply systems of some Early Byzantine cities, including both cities of the eastern Mediterranean with an older tradition (Antioch, Apamea, Jerusalem) and the new "Justinianic" cities (Iustiniana Prima, Dara).

On the other hand, research projects on the residential and productive contexts of Byzantine cities have been increasing, examples include Gortyn, Sagalassos and Ephesus[29]; in these works, the water supply systems are studied in a diachronic perspective to read the transformation of the urban history and to focus on their ecological impact on the natural environment. In such projects, scholars can experiment with ecological and economic approaches to analyze the changes that a water system can cause to an ecosystem, influencing the agricultural productivity and the economic potential of a city; this is the case of North African region and Palmyra.[30]

From this perspective, water supply systems can be seen as mechanisms for regulating seasonal cycles, which are able to provide a perennial supply even in areas where rainfall is not uniformly distributed throughout the year. The artificial balance that the aqueducts are able to create allows the city to intensively exploit its lands and produce an agricultural surplus to be sold on the medium- and long-range market.[31]

The archaeology of water can prove to be an effective analysis tool even at sites where it is not possible to carry out extensive archaeological excavations. An analysis of the localization of the water-related structures can also be useful for tracing the geography of the urban population in the Byzantine city and better understanding the dynamics of transformation of ancient cities in their last stages of life, as in the case of Gortyn.[32]

Written Sources for the Archaeology of Water

In the study of water in Byzantine cities, written sources have not yet yielded their full potential; we are in fact aware that written sources constitute an ostensibly inexhaustible mine of information, but a collection of texts to be read from an archaeological and anthropological perspective remains a desideratum.

A summary of the written sources dealing with water in relation to the 6th-century city has been offered by Helen Saradi, who discusses many passages from literary, legislative and epigraphic sources.[33] From the analysis of these texts, we can obtain information on the cleaning of canals and cisterns, on the interventions of private citizens and the role played by bishops, as well as on the initiatives of the emperors in favor of several cities. The work of L. Di Segni on the literary and epigraphic sources relevant to the study of the water supply systems of Byzantine Palestine is an example of texts compiled on a regional basis.[34] The discussion of the texts presented provides information on the construction of the aqueducts, the role of the provincial governors in the care of the aqueducts, the municipal management of maintenance works and on their execution of such work by private citizens. Both works show the usefulness of legislative sources to reconstruct the administrative framework of water structures, their management and maintenance. In the aforementioned project on Constantinople's water system, great attention has been paid to the collection and study of the written sources in all these aspects.[35] These three works, although particular case studies, give an idea of the information potential offered by analysis of written sources.

In the Justinianic legislation from 530, the local bishop is indicated as the supervisor of all works carried out with public funds (baths, aqueducts, walls, roads, towers),[36] and this authority is also borne out by some cases recorded by inscriptions (i.e. Bosra,[37] Gortyn[38]). The bishop's authority over public works is well established in the 7th century, as indicated by the role played by the bishops Plutarch and Arcadius in the construction of the Salamis aqueduct of Cyprus, still attested by epigraphy.[39]

Although major interventions such as the construction of an aqueduct or a cistern are attested by epigraphic sources, much less information is available concerning ordinary processes, such as the granting of permits or the calibration of the amount of water allotted for individual buildings in the cities of the Empire.

Such information may in fact hidden in the most diverse written sources, including private texts, as evidenced by a letter addressed to Emperor Constantine Porphyrogenitus from the bishop of Cyzicus Theodore,[40] which contains the last mention of a *comes hydaton*.[41] The letter therefore testifies to the continuity of function of a figure in charge of water management still in the 10th century; though in other urban contexts, the disintegration of the urban curiae raises doubts about the continuity of control over water by a civic authority.[42]

Urban scenarios connected to water emerge from the texts of some ancient authors. Libanius in the *Antiochikos*[43] emphatically describes the water system of Antioch in the 5th century, magnifying the grace and purity of the water distributed to the nymphaea and the houses within the city by the aqueduct. In his Anastasius Panegyric, Procopius of Gaza considers the construction of an aqueduct an honor paid by the emperor to the city of Jerusalem, which previously could only rely on the collection of rainwater.[44] In a completely different situation only a few decades later, Cyril of Scythopolis refers to a prolonged drought that would have afflicted Jerusalem, so much so as to push the poor of the city to beg for water.[45] The aforementioned examples can give an idea of the extreme variety of the written sources (prayers, panegyrics, chronicles) in which the topic of water is addressed within the tradition of the specific literary genre. The different contexts in which water is mentioned therefore increase the information potential of the texts, ranging from technical-structural details to anthropological and social aspects.

Procopius of Caesarea is an exception for the quantity and quality of the water references that are recorded in his works. Since hydraulic interventions were one of the main goals of Justinian's action on the cities of the empire, water is in fact one of the main themes of the *De Aedificiis*.[46]

Numerous passages record meeting the water needs as the basic element in the planning of a restoration or in the foundation of a new city[47]: in 14 cities, Procopius says that Justinian has had an aqueduct restored or built, though archaeological investigations do not always agree with the chronology of the written source.[48] The text as a whole offers an internal point of view about the redefinition of the water management priorities by the State. The traditional aqueducts no longer represent the only structures for supplying a city; their functioning is part of a wider, diversified, but easier system, in which the water storage becomes, or perhaps returns to being, the dominant method, based on the criteria of not wasting water and creating structures of water storage that can replace extra-urban water sources.[49] The water supplies of new cities have a particular importance. Dara, with its water system made up of aqueduct, cisterns, river dam and river gates,[50] and Iustiniana Prima, built near a river and equipped with a traditional aqueduct,[51] are both described in detail.

References to aqueducts are also not lacking in *De Bellis*, as an element of the urban scenarios in which war actions took place and where Procopius highlights the danger represented by the surface ducts as potential access routes to besieged cities.[52] Even in the Secret History Procopius sketches, a scene of daily life connected to water, speaking of Justinian's reluctance to have a section of the Constantinople aqueduct repaired, although it caused severe inconvenience to the population.[53]

Water in the Byzantine Cities

The state of our knowledge and the very nature of the Byzantine city make it quite difficult to identify some typical characteristics of Byzantine water systems. In most cases, our knowledge is almost always limited to certain types of buildings (monumental, such as large cisterns) or to specific historical periods (the era of Justinian). We have also to take into account that each city was dealing with a water system inherited from its past, more or less functioning, that was maintained or adapted to new needs. Furthermore, we yet know very little about the urban scenarios in which the transformations of the water systems occurred, and we do not fully understand the dynamics of evolution of many cities. Rather, when we observe urban and peri-urban spaces changing without knowing the surrounding context, we too often analyze isolated monumental complexes or residential quarters without any connection with the rest of the urban fabric.[54]

At a larger scale, the discontinuity and partiality of our knowledge are a common feature in the Mediterranean context, in which the study of the late antique and Byzantine water systems has developed only for some areas – such as the cities of the Eastern Mediterranean – and very little in others: only recently has a volume collected evidences from the Roman period of mainland Greece.[55]

Nevertheless, starting from the most significant case studies, we can summarize some topics briefly: the regulation of the rivers, the building of cisterns, the restoring of urban and suburban water networks, the transformations of the preexisting installations in more complex systems and the building of completely new systems.

Rivers

The exploitation of a river's waters has always served as the primary water supply for a city that rises near one. In addition to the supply of drinking water, river waters can be used for animal breeding, land cultivation, craft activities and to transport goods. In all environmental contexts, but particularly in semi-desert areas, rivers are a fundamental water resource; at the same time, they are potentially dangerous for the cities[56] that can be exposed to floods and overflows, especially in the case of seasonal and torrential waterways.

The attractiveness of proximity to a river is evidenced by the case of Iustiniana Prima that was not in fact built exactly on the birthplace of Justinian, but rather near the Caričinska River. The river played a decisive role in the selection of the site, because it was considered necessary to find a place to which it would be possible to convey water from distant abundant springs that also had a natural water resource in a region known for its shortage during the summer months. A moon-shaped dam to better resist the force of the current was built outside the city, to control the river and ensure an adequate water reserve.[57]

The ambivalent role of the river is very evident in Dara, where from the foundation of the city, the Cordes River was included within the perimeter of the walls,[58] to be used as the main water resource (Figure 14.2). In the Justinianic age, the course of the river was regulated through the construction of a dam and sluice gates provided with systems for controlling the water flow.[59]

Figure 14.2 The eastern fluvial gate at Dara (Photo Credits: Enrico Zanini - Centro di Documentazione di Storia dell'Arte Bizantina, Sapienza, Università di Roma)

A similar dam was also built in Antioch,[60] where it ensured a supply system based on river water, replacing the spring waters brought by the previous Roman aqueduct.[61]

Structures aimed at stemming the waterways are often the only archaeological evidence of the interaction between the city and the rivers; although river environments were important workspaces, the traces of the citizens' daily activities are in fact much less visible. We can suppose that the urban community used the river through mobile structures (rafts or floating barges) that leave no archaeological traces; the floating mills of Rome, mentioned for the first time by Procopius during the Gothic siege,[62] have left no archaeological evidence, although they were a feature of the river landscape until the 19th century, as testified by modern iconographic sources.[63]

Cisterns

In his *De Aedificiis*, Procopius seems to highlight a new imperial water policy, aimed not at providing the cities with plenty of water, but at storing rain or spring water that would otherwise be wasted.[64] The most evident archaeological trace of this new trend is the proliferation of cisterns that collected rainwater or that were filled by the aqueducts. The cisterns became public structures like city walls and churches, being released from their former functional connection with isolated sites (military outposts, fortresses, monasteries).[65]

For the first time, in Procopius' text, the cisterns are elevated to the rank of structures subject to the intervention of the emperor, whereas previously their construction was a prerogative of the civil or ecclesiastical elites.[66] The most salient example of this new trend is Justinian's patronage of the construction of the Basilica Cistern[67] in Constantinople. A monumental inscription also testifies to the direct involvement of Justinian in the building of the cistern under the Nea Ecclesia in Jerusalem, this being one of the best known cases of an imperial patronage in favor of a cistern outside Constantinople.[68]

In modern Istanbul, the cisterns represent the most numerous Byzantine surviving structures (Figure 14.3); 209 structures have been identified to date,[69] varying in size from the large open-air reservoirs located between the Constantinian and Theodosian land walls (the cisterns of Aetius, Aspar and Mocius, with a total water capacity of more than 600,000 cubic meters), to small cisterns providing water for individual dwellings. The three large open reservoirs have been dated to the 5th century and were related to the construction of the Valens aqueduct,[70] while from the reign of Anastasius, large covered cisterns were built in the very center of the city (Birbindirek, Cold Cistern in the Sphendone of the Circus), culminating with the Justinianic Basilica Cistern.[71]

A large number of cisterns recorded in Constantinople testify to the development of a water supply system that seems to be very different from the typical Roman one and more similar to the water storage system used in Roman North Africa, Mesopotamia and Syria.[72]

Also in Alexandria, the second largest city in the Eastern Mediterranean, archaeological investigations by the Centre d'Études Alexandrines have to date identified 144 surviving cisterns with a total capacity of 38,000 cubic meters. This network of cisterns was built starting from the 5th century onwards, to provide the city with drinkable water after the tsunami/earthquake of 365 AD that increased the salinity of the Nile water so that it was no longer usable. It is not known whether they were for public or private use, although some of them can be related to Christian foundations. The network was expanded in the 9th and 10th centuries with the construction of new cisterns, a number of which were multistory including the three-story el-Nabih.[73]

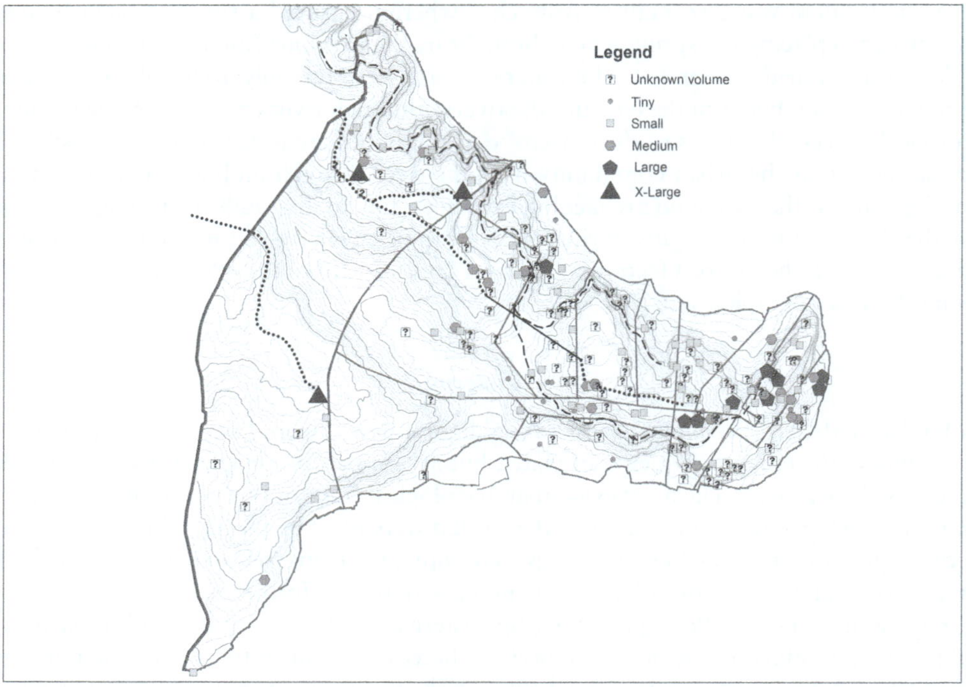

Figure 14.3 The distribution of more than 200 Byzantine Cisterns in Constantinople (Crow, "The Imagined Water Supply of Byzantine Constantinople, New Approaches", 226, Fig. 9)

Cisterns are also a typical feature of the water systems adopted in the cities and military outposts of the arid regions along the eastern boundary of the Byzantine Empire. Due to its geographical position and climatic conditions, Dara had from its foundation some cisterns within the walls that ensured the city a good water supply to withstand prolonged sieges. The largest one was divided into ten barrel-vaulted naves and was filled by a covered channel drawing spring water from the mountain northeast of the city; a second cistern, smaller in dimensions, was squared in plan and covered with cross vaults on pillars[74]; a third large cistern can perhaps be identified in the basement of a public building.[75]

In Resafa, the water supply system was based on three cisterns located within the city walls that collected rainwater.[76] The cisterns were fed by a sophisticated system of channels and settling tanks that purified the water of a large extra-urban artificial basin created by a dam.[77] Written sources, along with archaeological and epigraphic evidence, indicate that the system was built together with the walls in the 6th century and that after the Arab conquest, it was not only maintained but also buttressed by the construction of the largest cistern.[78] These cisterns closely resemble both those of Dara and, especially in the brick vaults, the great underground cisterns of Justinian in Constantinople, constituting an interesting piece of evidence pointing to the circulation of specific aspects of material culture between center and periphery.[79]

The cisterns also played a very important role in the supply of Bosra, which also relied on an aqueduct fed by natural springs; the tanks, dating back to the 1st century BC, were in fact filled by the aqueduct that was partially restored in the Justinianic period.[80]

Aqueducts

Between the 5th and 6th centuries, the interventions on aqueducts seem to be in contrast with the other urban transformation that are recorded in many Byzantine cities.[81] The pre-existing aqueducts were maintained, with more or less significant transformations or new additions, and therefore, they must have continued to perform their structural function for the daily life of the urban community. The observed modifications tend to have been grafted onto preexisting water systems and are marked by pragmatism.[82] It is therefore difficult to identify some typical trends of the Byzantine aqueducts; these can only be analyzed in the new aqueducts built in the cities founded by Justinian (see below).

Nevertheless, a general feature of aqueducts in the Early Byzantine age is the preference for underground channels; these are both easier to build and are safer, because they do not constitute a potential access route into the city during a siege.[83] Several passages by Procopius testify as to how an aqueduct could be used to grant besiegers access; one of the best known episodes records that an Armenian soldier, curious to know how the aqueduct was made, entered it from the point where Belisarius had had it cut and discovers the way to enter the city of Naples, at the time controlled by the Ostrogoths.[84]

Many of the aqueducts maintained or restored in Byzantine times continued to function until the Islamic era, as in Palmira[85] and Bosra.[86] Furthermore, maintenance works on individual structures are recorded in various cities of the empire, as in Gerasa[87] and Thessaloniki, where in the Byzantine age, the water system was renewed through some significant transformations.[88]

Procopius records a wide Justinian program of urban renovation in Antioch,[89] with the restoration of the existing water supply system proceeding without evident alterations of its various elements.

The reconstruction of sewers and channels and the building of fountains and thermal baths was also accompanied by the construction of an imposing dam on the Orontes (see above). The functioning of the water system is attested by written sources from the end of the 6th century and again in the 12th. It thus remained one of the distinctive features of the city even into the Crusader era.[90]

In Caesarea Maritima in Palestine, the aqueduct was restored and new fountains were built in the middle of the 6th century. Some wells were also dug in different parts of the city.[91] This restructuring seems to have integrated the functions of a traditional distribution system (channels feeding fountains) with a series of more elementary systems (wells).

In the same period in Carthage, we see a different transformation of the water system after the cut of the aqueduct in 533. Some springs are fortified, while the large complexes of cisterns do not seem to be integrated into the asset of the new water system; they rather seem to function for the collection of rainwater and to serve the productive structures that have arisen all around in the meantime.[92]

Complex Water Systems

Among the water systems transformed in the Byzantine age, we can distinguish some case studies that can be defined as complex water systems, in which different means of collection and use of water are functionally integrated. The perception complexity derives from a series of factors: (a) the multi-layering of the Byzantine cities; (b) our level of knowledge; (c) their objective complexity.

The long continuity of life in some cities such as Rome or Constantinople is itself an index of complexity; in these cities, the water supply systems are by their very nature comprised a basic framework to which functional segments are constantly being added or removed. In archaeological analysis, such a water supply system appears structured in its general layout, yet is subject to pragmatic adaptations and functional changes that are not necessarily regulated by precise rules. Our perception of the complexity of a water system may also depend on our difficulty in analyzing a system in a diachronic perspective, which leads us to define as an articulated image what actually derives from the superimposition of structures dating to several periods. Finally, some water systems really are complex, especially if in their last stage of life, they are structured as systems in which different ways of collecting, storing and using water are well and fully integrated.

As multi-layered cities, Rome and Constantinople constitute two particular case studies. The water system of Constantinople[93] has recently been studied through the multidisciplinary project "Engineering the water supply of Constantinople", which made it possible to model the main distribution lines of the aqueducts and to analyze water distribution within the city.[94] A new aqueduct was added (to supplement those built by the emperors Hadrian and Valens) in the 5th century, drawing spring water from the city of Bizye (modern Vize), over 240 km away, and thus being the longest aqueduct so far known in the ancient world. Within the city, more than 200 cisterns have been recorded and mapped; they were built starting from the 4th century, varying in size from small basins for individual settlements, also fed by rainwater, to large open or covered reservoirs dating back to 5th and 6th century (Birbindirek, Cold Cistern, Basilica Cistern).[95]

The mapping of the cisterns highlights a concentration of collected water in the eastern end of the peninsula, perhaps as a response to increasing insecurity in the eastern Balkans that threatened the city. In fact, during the Avar siege of 626, the long-distance supply line was cut and was restored only in 766 by Constantine V. Urban cisterns continued to function and to be built; from the 9th century onwards, they are often inserted in preexisting elite buildings or connected to monastic churches (Studios, Chora, Pantokrator-Zeyrek Camii), which seem to have become important nodes of the water distribution network in the Middle Byzantine age.[96]

On the contrary, the water supply system of Byzantine Rome is not attested by archaeological evidence and we can only hypothesize a complexity that cannot have failed to exist. Written sources attest that until the Gothic War, the city maintained an efficient water supply system feeding thermal baths, private houses and other structures mostly under the control of the Church (baptisteries, *balnea* and fountains). The cutting of the aqueducts during the siege of 537 marked an interruption in the continuity of the system as a whole; written sources attest that the Byzantine civil administration at the beginning of the 7th century had repaired the damage of the siege for almost 4 of the 11 aqueducts[97] and that it continued to take care of the repairs up to the pontificate of Hadrian I.[98] After a restoration of the aqueducts under Hadrian, an urban-scale water system continued to function at least until the 11th century.[99]

Although on a very different scale, other cities did have complex water systems in which the total or partial functioning of a preexisting system was integrated with more traditional systems for collecting and storing spring water and rainwater. At Gortyn, during the 6th century, the Roman aqueduct was connected to a new network of over 50 cisterns that consisted of accumulation tanks of different sizes with one or more fountains (Figure 14.4).

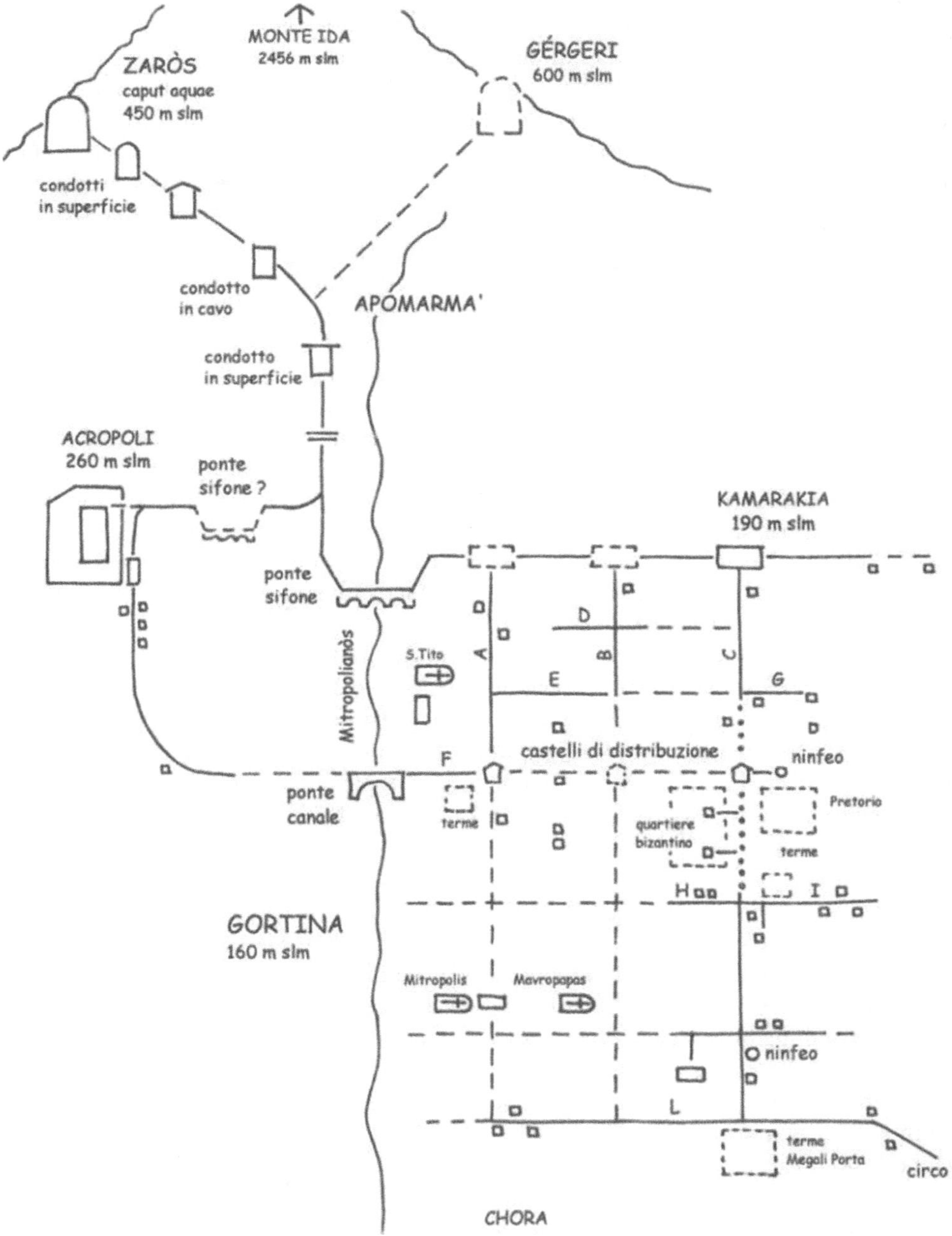

Figure 14.4 Schematic drawing of the early Byzantine water system in Gortyn (Giorgi, *Archeologia dell'acqua a Gortina di Creta*, 72, Fig. 39)

Archaeological investigations have indicated that some of these structures were located inside courtyards connected to one or more buildings. For some larger cisterns standing near important monuments such as thermal complexes, churches or acropolis, it cannot be excluded that they could also collect rainwater. We have also uncovered traces of the functioning of some underground channels built with reused amphorae and tubules and connected to prestigious buildings, some also with drains that collected rainwater to store in underground cisterns. The decision to provision the city with stored water even though the aqueduct drew from perennial sources can be explained either by a possible reduction in the water flow or by the need to have a water reserve in case of interruptions due to maintenance or natural disasters. The water system of Gortyn thus seems emblematic of some trends of Byzantine water policy: releasing the city from a total dependence on flowing water, re-evaluating the use and quality of stored water and using more practical solutions in the transformation/integration of preexisting water structures.

At Apamea, Ephesus and Elaiussa Sebaste, we observe the connection of a preexisting aqueduct with a network of new cisterns, homogeneous in their construction aspects, though probably built privately. In Apamea at the end of the 5th century, the aqueduct was restored with the construction of an underground conduit which seems to have functioned well into the 7th century.[100] The analysis of fluid mechanics and archaeological evidence seems to indicate that the Byzantine cisterns placed in the courtyards of some urban residences may have been supplied by the new aqueduct rather than being simple tanks for collecting rainwater, as was previously believed.[101]

The existence of a public supply for most of the late monumental fountains also attests to the continuity of the decorative and symbolic value of water, seen as an expression of the wealth of the landlord who intended to demonstrate that he had a link with the network of urban supply.[102] In Ephesus, from the beginning of the 5th century, the aqueduct was reconfigured and connected to a network of large cisterns that also served to store rainwater,[103] as also seen in Elaiussa Sebaste, where cisterns for the collection of rainwater helped keep the water potential of the city stable.[104]

Water in the New Cities

The urban water systems of newly founded cities are the only ones that can be defined as truly Byzantine; these systems concretize the typical characteristics of the Byzantine *water policy* that combined the legacy of Roman water culture with pragmatic solutions in the historical and geographical conditions of the new cities.

Iustiniana Prima[105] was founded near the Caričinska River in a particularly favorable place to collect as much water as possible[106]; the city (Figure 14.5) was also served by an aqueduct[107] that captured the spring waters of Mount Radan about 20 km away from the city, crossing a completely non-urbanised area.

The extra-urban route of the aqueduct was identified using LidarScan technologies[108]: it consisted of an underground channel that was raised on some bridges just before its entrance into the city. This elevation was necessary so that the water could fill the reservoir of the distribution tower located at the junction between the ramparts of the upper and lower cities. The position of the *castellum aquae* appears to have been perfectly functional to supply the two known thermal baths. From the distribution tower, a network of pressurized pipes supplied the two parts of the city, feeding fountains and storage tanks such as the large cistern in the lower city. A tank in the atrium of the episcopal basilica on the acropolis

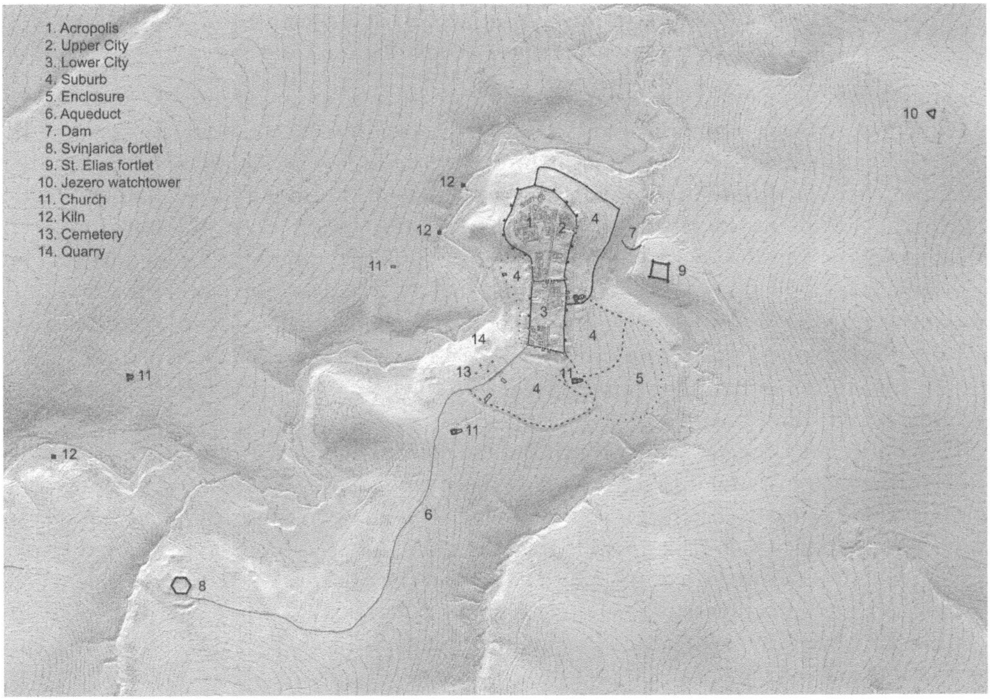

Figure 14.5 LiDAR and plan of the city of Iustiniana Prima (Ivanišević, "Caričin Grad Justiniana Prima", 111, Fig. 2)

collected rainwater. Some wells also functioned within the city, as well as an efficient sewage system running below the main roads.[109]

Dara, on the border between the Byzantine and Persian empires, was provided with a water supply system[110] that allowed the city to withstand prolonged sieges.[111] The city is crossed by the Cordes River, so river waters are a primary resource, being regulated through a dam just outside the city walls and through two fluvial gates (see above). Dara is also fed by an aqueduct that captures the spring waters from the mountains to the northeast of the city; the aqueduct consists of a rock-cut channel and a series of canalizations that distribute water within the city.[112] To the spring and fluvial waters were added the rainwater collected through the cisterns (see above).

The two new cities clearly had a very close relationship with water. They were both designed and built close to two rivers and great care was taken in the management of river water; they both had a dam that allowed for the creation of a water reserve – in Dara, this was even diverted to an area protected by the walls – so that the city would not run out of water even in the event of a siege or the cutting of the aqueduct. They were both supplied by an aqueduct that ran from the springs to the city by means of an underground channel that was better protected and less subject to damage. The existence of a traditional aqueduct with underground supply channels, distribution towers and channels indicates the continuity of a water culture that attributes an important but no longer exclusive primacy to spring water; both cities can also rely on urban cisterns, which make clear the new attitude of the Byzantine city towards stored water.

Using Water in the Byzantine City: Perspectives on Everyday Life from Archaeological Data

The way water was used in the Byzantine city is another key topic of interest. If the ancient aqueducts were being maintained and indeed even continued to be built, it is evident that the water was used not only for its primary uses (drinking and cooking) and bathing (thermal baths) but also for a series of daily economic activities. Among these, craft production is of particular interest because it provides useful information about the transformations of urban spaces and the social composition of the urban community. From a certain moment onwards, some productive activities that had previously occurred on the edges of the monumental areas[113] resettled in the centers of the cities; the archaeological record indicates that the production of objects for everyday life (pottery and glass kilns, structures for dyeing fabrics), to the grinding of cereals (mills), to the care of animals (watering places) all began to occur there.

The connection of water structures with these daily activities is evident at Gortyn, where some of the cistern-fountains seem to have been intended to be used by both men and animals; some of these structures were provided with a system that conveyed waste water into a basin, from which it is possible that the animals could have been watered while a protective slab prevented them from drinking from the tap; the waste water could also be channeled into the courtyards (including a small pottery kiln), while the overflow water could be conveyed into side basins for different activities (perhaps a washhouse or a basin for treading grapes).[114]

Among the productive activities related to water, the grinding of cereals is one of the most evident.

According to Medieval written sources, mills for the production of flour were a constant presence on the river landscape of Rome; this image was anticipated by Cassiodorus[115] and Procopius, who records the working of floating mills along the Tiber during the Gothic War.[116] We do not know if these floating mills replaced or integrated the functions of the imperial and late antique mill complexes connected to the organization of the Annona. Some structures of these complexes have been identified on the slopes of the Janiculum and on the Palatine Hill, in connection with the aqueducts that fed these urban quarters.[117] Both complexes seem to have functioned at least until the siege of the Gothic War, while the mill in the eastern hemicycle of the Circus Maximus is of uncertain date.[118] The need to grind wheat seems to have been one of the main reasons that led Pope Adrian I to restore the Roman aqueducts at the end of the 8th century.[119]

The existence of mills within the monumental areas of the cities is also attested in Athens, in the area of the ancient agora, where some mills have been dated to 5th–6th century,[120] as in other cities of mainland Greece (Eleusi, Messene, Tebe) and at the monastic sites on Mount Athos.[121] We can observe the same phenomenon in Ephesus, where starting from the 5th century, some water mills were installed in the monumental center of the city,[122] while in the same period in Jerash, a watermill was working in the cryptoporticus of the temple of Artemis, to power a stone saw for cutting spolia.[123]

At Iustiniana Prima, it is assumed that some mills, together with several craft activities, could have been operated through the river dam located immediately outside the city.[124] The functioning of mills related to aqueducts is recorded at Bosra[125] and Tiberias, where some structures for the processing of cane sugar have been identified and dated to the Byzantine and Arab periods. A complex of basins, perhaps for the dyeing of fabrics, has also been related to the aqueduct. At Tiberias, we have also evidence of an irrigation network originating from a cistern and flowing towards the countryside.[126]

This evidence in particular introduces the issue of agricultural uses of urban water, which are often complex to identify, but particularly interesting for evaluating the relationship between water and land productivity, in the perspective of the economic utility of the use of water.[127] The existence of rural aqueducts and water offtakes for agricultural uses is also recorded in Aphrodisias, where a recent survey has mapped the suburban water network[128] and the possible connection with olive oil production and mining activities. Archaeological evidences, including some cisterns and structures for the olive oil production dating back to the Ottoman era, attest that agricultural investments in the area around the city increased over time.[129] An agricultural water system is also known in Bosra, where the aqueduct was also used for the irrigation network that consisted of channels provided with a control system for the rational use of water in case of a lower water flow.[130]

At Gortyn, we have no archaeological evidences of an irrigation system starting from the terminal tanks of the aqueduct towards the Messarà plain; on the base of the relationship between the water flow and the estimated urban population, it is possible to imagine that the maintenance of the water supply in the Early Byzantine age could also have been motivated by the need to increase the agricultural yield of otherwise arid lands.[131] The expansion of an irrigation network can also be related to urban development, as in Palmyra, where the increase in the agricultural potential of the city seems to have been translated into an expansion of the urban structure.[132]

Final Remarks

To conclude, we can surmise that in the Byzantine age, there was a general tendency to maintain and restore the preexisting aqueducts and to build new water systems in accordance with Greco-Roman hydraulic technology, though with a preference for underground and safer channels. Within the city, a very pragmatic system of water management seems to prevail, which led to the connection of existing water networks to new cisterns and reservoirs; these structures are the main archaeological indicators of any new *water policy* of the Byzantine state that encouraged the use of stored water and which removed the primacy of running water as the only suitable drinking water. Great attention was paid to the management of river waters in their dual role as a resource and at the same time a potential danger to the city. Urban fountains continued to make evident the ideological and aesthetic value of water within the city, but in a new urban context in which water was not only exhibited but also used for the development of productive activities that arose in central areas.

Notes

1 J. Pickett, "Water in Byzantium: Food, Environment and Landscape Round Table," in *Proceedings of the 23rd International Congress of Byzantine Studies*, Belgrade 22–27 August 2016, Round Tables, eds. B. Krsmanović and L. Milanović (Belgrade: The Serbian National Committee of AIEB, 2016), 835–839.

2 D. K. Rogers, *Water Culture in Roman Society* (Leiden – Boston: Brill, 2018), 86.

3 A general overview in B. Haut et al., "Evolution of Rainwater Harvesting in Urban Areas through the Millenia. A Sustainable Technology for Increasing Water Availability," in *Water and Heritage, Material, Conceptual and Spiritual Connections*, eds. H. van Schaik, W. Willems, and M. van der Valk, Sidestone (Leiden: Sidestone Press, 2015), 37–57.

4 An overview of the integrated management of the water resources in E. Hermon, ed., *Vers une gestion intégrée de l'eau dans l'Empire Romain: Actes du Colloque International, Université Laval, Octobre 2006*, Atlante Tematico di Topografia Antica. Supplemento 16 (Roma: L'Erma di Bretschneider, 2008). E. Hermon, "La gestion intégrée de l'eau entre l'adaptation et la résilience aux variations et changements climatiques dans l'Empire Romain," in *Riparia, un patrimoine culturel: la gestion intégrée des bords de l'eau. Proceedings of the Sudbury Workshop, April 12–14, 2012*, eds. E. Hermon and A. Watelet (Oxford: Archaeopress, 2014), 271–286.

5 J. Crow et al., *The Water Supply of Byzantine Constantinople*, 1st ed., Journal of Roman Studies Monographs 11 (London: Society for the Promotion of Roman Studies, 2008); J. Crow, "Waters for the Capital: Hydraulic Infrastructure and Use in Byzantine Constantinople," in The *Cambridge Companion to Constantinople* (Cambridge: Cambridge University Press, 2022), 67-86.

6 E. Giorgi, *Archeologia dell'acqua a Gortina di Creta in età protobizantina* (Oxford: Archaeopress Access Archaeology, 2016).

7 Pickett, "Water in Byzantium," 835–836.

8 Gregorius Nazianzus, *Orationes*, 33, 6.

9 B. Shilling and P. Stephenson, eds., *Fountains and Water Culture in Byzantium* (Cambridge: Cambridge University Press, 2016).

10 I. Uytterhoeven, "Running Water: Acqueducts as Suppliers of Private Water Facilities in (Late) Roman Asia Minor," *Bulletin Antieke Beschaving (BABesch) Supplement* 24 (2013): 139–160.

11 I. Jacobs and J. Richard, "'We Surpass the Beautiful Waters of Other Cities by the Abundance of Ours': Reconciling Function and Decoration in Late Antique Fountains," in *Journal of Late Antiquity, 5.2012* (Baltimore, MD: Johns Hopkins University Press, 2012), 3–71.

12 G. Wiplinger, *De Aquaeductu Urbis Ephesi: Water for Roman Ephesus* (Leiden: The Babesch Foundation, 2019).

13 E. Cirelli, *Ravenna: Archeologia di una città* (Firenze: All'Insegna del Giglio, 2008). Y. A. Marano,"'Watered... with the Life-Giving Wave'. Aqueducts and Water Management in Ostrogothic Italy," in *Ownership and Exploitation of Land and Natural Resources in the Roman World*, eds. P. Erdkamp, K. Verboven, and A. Zuiderhoek, Oxford Studies on the Roman Economy (Oxford: Routledge, 2015), 150–169.

14 J. Martínez Jiménez, "A Preliminary Study of the Aqueduct of Reccopolis," *Oxford Journal of Archaeology* 34, no. 3 (2015): 301–320; A. Wilson, "Water, Power and Culture in the Roman and Byzantine Worlds: An Introduction," *Water History* 4, no. 1 (April 1, 2012), 1–9.

15 For water culture as a broad concept see Rogers, *Water Culture,* 3.

16 A. Chevalier, J. M. Dentzer, and J. Leblanc, "Techniques et systèmes d'acquisition de l'eau à Bosra: initiatives de groupes et pouvoirs politiques," in *Stratégies d'acquisition de l'eau et société au Moyen-Orient depuis l'Antiquité*, eds. M. Al-Dbiyat and M. Mouton, Bibliothèque Archéologique et Historique (Beyrouth: Presses de l'Ifpo, 2010), 107–132.

17 D. Kennedy, "Water Supply and Use in the Southern Hauran, Jordan," *Journal of Field Archaeology* 22 (1995): 275–290.

18 L. Mays, "Use of Cisterns during Antiquity in the Mediterranean Region for Water Resources Sustainability," Water Science & Technology: Water Supply 14 (2014): 38–47.

19 C. Dumond-Maridat, "Les Systèmes Publics d'alimentation En Eau Dans Le Hauran Aux Époque Classique et Byzantine," *Syria* 85 (2008): 71–86.

20 http://www.ummeljimal.org.

21 For the rehabilitation of ancient irrigation systems in modern times in the arid territories of central Syria see M. Al-Dbiyat, "Eau et peuplement dans les marges arides: le cas de la région de Salamya en Syrie centrale," in *Stratégies d'acquisition de l'eau et société au Moyen-Orient depuis l'Antiquité, "Archéologie et histoire de l'Antiquité,"* BAH 186), eds. M. Dbiyat and M. Mouton (Beyrouth: Presses de l'Ifpo, 2009): 179–187.

22 J. Pickett, "Hydraulic Landscapes of Roman and Byzantine Cities," in *Landscapes of Preindustrial Urbanism*, ed. G. Farhart, vol. 41, Dumbarton Oaks, Colloquium on the History of Landscape Architecture (Washington, D.C, 2020), 115–142.

23 See Pickett, "Hydraulic Landscapes," n. 101–104 for specific bibliographical references.

24 Pickett, "Hydraulic Landscapes," 130.

25 Pickett, "Hydraulic Landscapes," 133.

26 M. J. T. Lewis, "Antique Engineering in the Byzantine World," in *Technology in Transition A.D. 300-650*, eds. L. Lavan, E. Zanini, and A. Sarantis (Leiden – Boston: Brill, 2007), 367–378.

27 V. M. Ivanišević, "Caričin Grad (Justiniana Prima): A New-Discovered City for a 'New' Society," in *Proceedings of the 23rd International Congress of Byzantine Studies*, Belgrade, 22–27 August 2016, Plenary Papers, ed. S. Marjanović-Dušanić (Belgrade, 2016), 107–126.

28 The project "Engineering the Byzantine water supply: procurement, construction and operation" is a transdisciplinary programme involving civil engineers, archaeologists and historians to realize many of the water features lost or concealed by the modern city of Istanbul and their expansion into its hinterland: see J. Crow, "The Imagined Water Supply of Byzantine Constantinople, New Approaches," *Constantinople Réelle et Imaginaire: Autour de l'œuvre de Gilbert Dagron*, Travaux et Mémoires, 22, no. 1 (2018): 211–235.

29 Giorgi, *Archeologia dell'acqua a Gortina di Creta*. F. Martens, "The Diachronic Research of Urban Water Management at Sagalassos, Southwest Turkey," in *Cura Aquarum in Ephesus* (Dudley, MA: Peeters, 2006), 165–174; F. Martens, "Urban Water Management at Sagalassos. Studying Urban Development from an Hydrological Perspective," in *The Greek City from Antiquity to the Present. Historical Reality, Ideological Construction, Literary Representation*, ed. K. Demoen (Louvain: Peeters, 2001), 49–86.

30 A. Leone, "Water Management in Late Antique North Africa: Agricultural Irrigation," *Water History* 4, no. 1 (April 1, 2012): 119–133. A. Wilson, "Rivers, Wadis and Climate in North Africa: Torrents and Drought," in *Fluvial Landscapes in the Roman World*, ed. T. Franconi, Journal of Roman Archaeology supplement 104 (Portsmouth, Rhode Island: Journal of Roman Archaeology, 2017), 111–125. M. Hammad, *Palmyre: Transformations Urbaines; Développement d'une Ville Antique de La Marge Aride Syrienne*, Librairie de l'Architecture et de La Ville (Paris: Geuthner, 2010).

31 Giorgi, *Archeologia dell'acqua a Gortina di Creta*, 107.

32 Giorgi, *Archeologia dell'acqua a Gortina di Creta*, 96–100.

33 H. Saradi, *The Byzantine City in the Sixth Century. Literary Images and Historical Reality* (Athens: Society of Messenian Archaeological Studies, 2006), 343–352.

34 L. Di Segni, "The Water Supply of Roman and Byzantine Palestine in Literary and Epigraphical Sources," in *The Aqueducts of Israel*, eds. D. Amit, J. Patrich, and Y. Hirschfeld, Journal of Roman Archaeology Supplement 46 (Portsmouth, Rhode Island: Journal of Roman Archaeology, 2002), 37–67.

35 See Appendix 1 in J. Crow et al., *The Water Supply of Byzantine Constantinople*. J. Crow, "Ruling the Waters: Managing the Water Supply of Constantinople, Ad 330–1204," *Water History* 4, no. 1 (2012): 35–55.

36 *Corpus Juris Civilis* I, 4, 26; previously, the bishops' interventions on water structures seem to have been the result of private initiatives. In the first half of the 5th century Theodoret of Cyr (Ep., 81, ed. Azéma 1964, II, 196, 15–19) had two bridges, arcades and an aqueduct built in his diocese with the funds of the Church, without asking for the intervention of the emperor (see D. Feissel, "L'évêque, titres et fonctions d'après les inscriptions grecques jusqu'au VIIe siècle," in *Actes du Xie congrès international d'archéologie chrétienne*, vol. 123 (Rome: Publications de l'École Française de Rome, 1989), 801–828). At the end of the same century the bishop *Firminianus* had an aqueduct built in Zenonopolis (see J. Kubińska, "L'évêque Firminianos de Zénonopolis et Son Aqueduc," *Les Études Classiques* 62 (1994): 169–175).

37 *Inscriptiones Grecae et Latinae Selectae*, XIII, 1 9128–9134.

38 *Inscripiones Creticae* IV, 465; A. C. Bandy, *The Greek Christian Inscriptions of Crete* (Athens: Christian Archaeological Society - Athens, 1970), 63–64. N. 33; the inscription records an intervention on the water network related to a certain George, whom many recognize as bishop, although no ecclesiastical title is indicated, as frequently happens in the epigraphy of this period. Also see Saradi, *The Byzantine City*, 183.

39 J. P. Sodini, "Les inscriptions de l'aqueduc de Kythrea à Salamine de Chypre," in *Ευψυχια. Mélanges offerts à Hélène Ahrweiler*, Byzantina Sorbonensia 16 (Paris: Publications de la Sorbonne, 1998), 619–633.

40 A new edition of the letter in M. Tziatzi-Papagianni, *Theodori metropolitae Cyzici epistulae accedunt epistulae mutuae Constantini Porphyrogeniti*, Corpus fontium historiae byzantinae. Series Berolinensis 48 (Berlin – Boston: De Gruyter, 2012).

41 A. P. Kazhdan, "S.v. Komes Ydaton," in The Oxford Dictionary of Byzantium, eds. A. P. Kazhdan et al., vol. 2 (Oxford, 1991), 1139.
42 Giorgi *Archeologia dell'acqua*, 116–117.
43 Libanius, *Orationes* XI, 240–248.
44 *Panegyricus Anastasii* c. 18. C. Jones, "Procopius of Gaza and the Water of Holy City," *Greek, Roman and Byzantine Studies* 47 (2007): 455–467.
45 *Cyril of Scythopolis, Vita S. Sabae*. 67, cited by L. Di Segni, "The Water Supply of Roman and Byzantine Palestine in Literary and Epigraphical Sources."
46 J. Pickett, "Water and Empire in the De Aedificiis of Procopius," in *Dumbarton Oaks Papers* (Washington, DC Dumbarton Oaks Research Library and Collection, 2017): 95–125.
47 Procopius, *De Aedificiis*, 2.5.11.
48 Pickett, "Water and Empire," 111.
49 Pickett, *Water in Byzantium*, 838.
50 Procopius, *De Aedificiis*, 2.2.2–9
51 Procopius, *De Aedificiis*, 4.1.19.
52 Procopius, *Bella* 1.9
53 Procopius, *Historia Arcana*, 26. 23–24.
54 Giorgi, *Archeologia dell'acqua a Gortina di Creta*, 11
55 G. A. Aristodemou and T. P. Tasios, eds., *Great Waterworks in Roman Greece: Aqueducts and Monumental Fountain Structures: Function in Context*, Archaeopress Roman Archaeology 35 (Summertown, Oxford: Archaeopress, 2018).
56 T. Franconi et al., "Fluvial Landscapes in the Roman World," *Journal of Roman Archaeology Supplement* 104 (Portsmouth, Rhode Island: Journal of Roman Archaeology, 2017).
A theoretical approach to the management of flood risk in ancient world in C. Allinne, "La Place Des Sources Archéologiques Dans La Construction de Modèles de Gestion Des Risques Naturels Dans l'Empire Romain: L'exemple Du Risque d'inondation," *Riparia* 1 (2015): 193–228.
57 V. M. Ivanišević, "Caričin Grad (Justiniana Prima)," 110.
58 E. Zanini, "La cinta muraria di Dara. Materiali per un'analisi stratigrafica," in *Costantinopoli e l'arte delle Province Orientali*, eds. F. de' Maffei, C. Barsanti, and A. Guiglia Guidobaldi, Milion 2 (Roma: Edizioni Rari Nantes,, 1990), 229–264: 245.
59 Procopius, *De Aedificiis* 2.3.1–23. I. Furlan, *Accertamenti a Dara*, Studi Sull'arte Bizantina (Padova, 1984). G. Garbrecht, "Procopius und die Wasserbauten von Dara," in *Wasserbauten im Königreich Urartu und weitere Beiträge zur Hydrotechnik in der Antike*, ed. C. Ohlig, Schriften der Deutschen Wasserhistorischen Gesellschaft 5 (Norderstedt: BoD – Books on Demand, 2004), 105–132.
60 Procopius, *De Aedificiis* 2.11.15–20.
61 M. Döring, "The Roman Hydraulic Engineering Buildings of Antioch, Turkey," in *Cura Aquarum in Israel II. Proceedings of the 15th International Conference on the History of Water Management and Hydraulic Engineering in the Mediterranean Region*, eds. C. Ohlig and T. Tsuk, vol. 21, Schriften Der Deutschen Wasserhistorischen Gesellschaft (Siegburg: DWhG, 2014), 149–164.
62 Procopius, *Bella*, 1.19.
63 R. Krautheimer, *Roma: profilo di una città, 312-1308* (Roma: Edizioni dell'Elefante, 1981), 302–304. M. M. Segarra Lagunes, "Le attività produttive del Tevere nelle dinamiche di trasformazione urbana : i mulini fluviali," *Mélanges de l'école française de Rome* 118, no. 1 (2006): 45–52.
64 Pickett, "Water and Empire," 121.
65 Pickett, "Water and Empire," 118–120.
66 Pickett, "Water and Empire," 105.
67 Procopius, *De Aedificiis* 1.11.12–15.
68 Procopius, *De Aedificiis* 5.6.1–26; SEG 27.1015.
69 K. Ward et al., "The Byzantine Cisterns of Constantinople," *Water Science and Technology: Water Supply* 17, no. 6 (2017): 1499–1505. K. Ward, J. Crow, and M. Crapper, "Water-Supply Infrastructure of Byzantine Constantinople," *Journal of Roman Archaeology* 30 (2017): 175–195.
70 Crow et al., *The Water Supply of Byzantine Constantinople*.
71 J. Crow, "'Still Waters Run Deep': Cisterns and the Hydraulic Infrastructure of Constantinople and Alexandria," *Antiquité Tardive* 28 (2021): 113–125.
72 J. Crow, "Ruling the Waters: Managing the Water Supply of Constantinople, Ad 330–1204," *Water History* 4, no. 1 (2012): 35–55; 41.

73 Crow, "'Still Waters Run Deep'."
74 I. Furlan, "Cisterne a Dara," in *Arte Profana e Arte Sacra a Bisanzio*, vol. 3 (Roma: Argos, 1995), 51–63.
75 I. Furlan, "Oikema Katagheion. Una Problematica Struttura a Dara," in *Storia dell'arte e della cultura artistica bizantina. Atti della giornata di Studio*, Roma 4 Dicembre 1986, a cura di C. Barsanti, A. Guiglia Guidobaldi, A. Iacobini(Roma: Biblioteca di Storia Patria 1988), 105–129.
76 C. Hof, "The Monumental Late Antique Cisterns of Resafa, Syria as Refined Capacity and Water-Quality Regulation System," in *Size Matters – Understanding Monumentality Across Ancient Civilizations*, by Cluster of Excellence TOPOI, eds. F. Buccellati et al. (Bielefeld: transcript-Verlag, 2019), 223–240.
77 W. Brinker, "Zur Wasserversorgung von Resafa-Sergiupolis," *Damaszener Mitteilungen* 5 (1991): 119–146.
78 S. Westphalen and P. Knötzele, "Water Supply of Resafa, Syria – Remarks on the Chronology of the Big Cisterns," in *Men of Dikes and Canals*, eds. H. D. Bienert and J. Haser (Rahden/Westf: M. L. Leidorf, 2004), 345–354.
79 E. Zanini, "The Urban Ideal and Urban Planning in Byzantine New Cities of the Sixth Century A.D.," in *Theory and Practice in Late Antique Archaeology*, eds. L. Lavan and W. Bowden (Leiden – Boston: Brill, 2003), 196–223; 213.
80 IGLSyr 13/1.9134; M. Sartre, *Bostra. Des origines à l'Islam*, Bibliothèque Archéologique et Historique, CXVII (Paris: Geuthner, 1985), 137; P. M. Blanc, D. Gazagne, and P. Wech, "L'eau à Bosra: approche diachronique, nouvelles données sur la question," in *L'eau. Enjeux, Usages et Représentations, Colloques de La Maison René-Ginouvès*, 4 (France: De Boccard, 2008), 29–41.
81 J. López Quiroga and E. Zanini, "Early Byzantine Urban Landscapes in the Southwest and Southeast Mediterranean," in *Proceedings of the 23rd International Congress of Byzantine Studies*, ed. S. Marjanović-Dušanić, 2016, 69–106.
82 Pickett, "Water in Byzantium," 838.
83 Pickett, "Water and Empire," 113.
84 Procopius, *Bella* 1.9.
85 M. Żuchowska and H. Juchniewicz, "Remarks on Water Supply in Palmyra. Results of a Survey in 2010," *Polish Archaeology in the Mediterranean* 22 (2013): 341–350.
86 Blanc et alii "L'eau à Bosra"; J. M. Dentzer, "Le Développement Urbain de Bosra de l'époque Nabatéenne à l'époque Byzantine: Bilan Des Recherches Françaises 1981–2002," *Syria* 79 (2002): 75–154.
87 A. Lichtenberger et al., "Radiocarbon Analysis of Mortar from Roman and Byzantine Water Management Installations in the Northwest Quarter of Jerash," *Journal of Archaeological Science: Reports* 2 (2015): 114–127.
88 M. Manoledakis, "The Water Supply of Roman Thessaloniki," in *Great Waterworks in Roman Greece*, eds. G. A. Aristodemou and T. P. Tassios, Archaeopress Roman Archaeology 35 (Oxford: Archaeopress, 2018), 50–69.
89 Procopius, *De Aedificiis* 2.10.1–25.
90 H. Kennedy, "Antioch: From Byzantium to Islam and Back Again," in *The City in Late Antiquity*, ed. J. Rich (London: Routledge, 1992), 181–198.
91 P. Mayerson, "Choricius of Gaza on the Watersupply System of Caesarea," *Israel Exploration Journal* 36 (1986): 269–272. Y. Porath, "The Water-Supply to Caesarea: A Re-Assessment," in *The Aqueducts of Israel*, eds. D. Amit, J. Patrich, and Y. Hirschfeld, Journal of Roman Archaeology Supplement 46 (Portsmouth, Rhode Island: Journal of Roman Archaeology, 2002), 104–129.
92 A. Wilson, "Water Supply in Ancient Chartage," in Carthage Papers : The Early Colony's Economy, Water Supply, a Public Bath, and the Mobilization of State Olive Oil, ed. T. J. Peña, Journal of Roman Archaeology Supplementary Series 28 (Portsmouth, Rhode Island: Journal of Roman Archaeology, 1998), 65–102.
93 Crow et al., *The Water Supply of Byzantine Constantinople*. James Crow, "Water and the Creation of a New Capital," in *Istanbul and Water*, eds. N. Ergin and P. Magdalino, Ancient Near Eastern Studies, Supplement 47 (Leuven: Peeters, 2015), 115–128.
94 Crow "The Imagined Water Supply of Byzantine Constantinople."
95 Ward et al., "The Byzantine Cisterns of Constantinople." Ward, Crow, and Crapper, "Water-Supply Infrastructure of Byzantine Constantinople."

96 J. Crow, "Waters for a Capital."
97 A. Wilson, "Hydraulic Engineering and Water Supply," in *The Oxford Handbook of Engineering and Technology in the Classical World*, ed. J. P. Oleson (Oxford: Oxford University Press, 2009), 285–318.
98 R. Coates-Stephens, "La committenza edilizia bizantina a Roma dopo la riconquista," in *Le città italiane tra la Tarda Antichità e l'Alto Medioevo* (Firenze: All'Insegna del Giglio, 2006), 299–316.
99 R. Coates-Stephens, "The Walls and Aqueducts of Rome in the Early Middle Ages, A. D. 500-1000," *The Journal of Roman Studies* 88 (1998): 166–178; R. Coates-Stephens, "The Water-Supply of Rome from Late Antiquity to the Early Middle Ages," *Acta Ad Archaeologiam et Artium Historiam Pertinentia*, N.S. 3, 17 (2003): 165–186.
100 M. Vannesse et al., "Analysis of Three Private Hydraulic Systems Operated in Apamea during the Byzantine Period," *Journal of Archaeological Science* 46 (2014): 245–254. B. Haut and D. Viviers, "Water Supply in the Middle East during Roman and Byzantine Periods," in *Evolution of the Water Supply through the Millennia*, ed. A. N. Angelakis et al. (Londra: IWA Publishing, 2012), 319–350.
101 B. Haut and D. Viviers, "Analysis of the Water Supply System of the City of Apamea, Using Computational Fluid Dynamics. Hydraulic System in the North-Eastern Area of the City, in the Byzantine Period," *Journal of Archaeological Science* 34, no. 3 (2007): 415–427.
102 M. Vannesse, "Les Nymphées Tardifs de l'architecture Domestique d'Apamée de Syrie: Mise En Scène de l'eau et Expression d'un 'Status Symbol'," in *Mediterraneo Antico. Economie*, Società, Culture, 17 (2014) (Pisa: Istituti editoriali e poligrafici internazionali, 2014), 487–518; 504.
103 Pickett, "Hydraulic Landscapes of Roman and Byzantine Cities," 126–127.
104 A. Falcone and V. Iacomi, "Archeologia dell'acqua ad Elaiussa Sebaste, Cilicia (Turchia): un contesto di scavo di età protobizantina nel quartiere residenziale presso il porto Sud," *Bollettino di Archeologia Online* XI, no. 1 (2018): 43–75.
105 V. Ivanišević, "Main Patterns of Urbanism in Caričin Grad (Justiniana Prima)," in *New Cities Late Antiquity : Documents and Archaeology*, ed. E. Rizos, Bibliothèque de l'Antiquité Tardive 35 (Turnhout: Brepols, 2017), 221–232.
106 Ivanišević, "Caričin Grad (Justiniana Prima)," 110.
107 Procopius, *De Aedificiis* 4.1.21–25.
108 V. Ivanišević, "Akvedukt Caričinog grada – Justinijane Prime (Aqueduct of Caričin Grad – Justiniana Prima)," *Saopštenja* XLIV (2012): 13–31.
109 V. M. Ivanišević, "Caričin Grad (Justiniana Prima)."
110 *Procopius, De Aedificiis* 2.1.4–2.3.26.
111 E. Zanini, *Introduzione all'archeologia bizantina*, Studi superiori NIS. Archeologia 228 (Roma: Nuova Italia Scientifica, 1994), 153.
112 E. Keser-Kayaalp, N. Erdogan, and A. Palmer, "Recent Research on Dara/Anastasiopolis," in *New Cities in Late Antiquity. Documents and Archaeology*, ed. E. Rizos, Biblothéque de l'Antiquité Tardive 35 (Turnhout: Brepols, 2017), 153–175.
113 Julian of Ascalon, 11.1; 14.1 (ed. Saliou 1996, 40; 42).
114 Giorgi, *Archeologia dell'acqua a Gortina di Creta*, 120.
115 Cassiodore, *Variae*, 11.39.
116 Procopius, *Bella* 1.19
117 M. Bell, "An Imperial Flour Mill on the Janiculum," in Le Ravitaillement En Blé de Rome et Des Centres Urbains Des Débuts de La République Jusqu'au Haut Empire. Actes Du Colloque International Org. Par Le Centre Jean Bérard et L'URA 994 du CNRS, Naples, 14–16 Février 1991 (Naples/Rome: École Française de Rome, 1994), 73–89. A. Wilson, "The Water-Mills on the Janiculum," *Memoirs of the American Academy in Rome* 45 (2000): 219–246. Marano, "'Watered... with the Life-Giving Wave'. Aqueducts and Water Management in Ostrogothic Italy," 161–164.
118 R. Coates-Stephens, "Gli impianti ad acqua e la rete idrica urbana," *Mededelingen van Het Nederlands Instituut Te Rome* LX/LXI (2001): 135–153; 143, n. 17. Coates-Stephens, "The Water-Supply of Rome from Late Antiquity to the Early Middle Ages," 175.
119 On the restoring of the aqueducts and city walls in the 8th century see Coates-Stephens, "The Walls and Aqueducts of Rome in the Early Middle Ages, A. D. 500-1000"; R. Coates-Stephens,

"Le Ricostruzioni Altomedievali Delle Mura Aureliane e Degli Acquedotti" 111 (1999): 209–225. Coates-Stephens, "The Water-Supply of Rome from Late Antiquity to the Early Middle Ages."

120 M. Christaki et al., "Water Supply Associated with the Development of the City of Athens from the Hellenistic Era until the End of the 19th Century," *Water History* 9, no. 4 (December 1, 2017): 389–410.

121 An overview in K. T. Raptis, "Water as Power. Early Christian and Byzantine Watermills in Greece: Typology and Distribution," in *1st IWA International Symposium on Water and Wastewater Technologies in Ancient Civilizations* (Iraklio: National Agricultural Research Foundation, 2006), 109–117. S. Germanidou, "Watermills in Byzantine Greece (5th-6th Centuries): A Preliminary Approach to the Archaeology of Byzantine Hydraulic Milling Technology," *Byzantion* 84 (2014): 185–201.

122 Pickett, "Hydraulic Landscapes of Roman and Byzantine Cities," 126.

123 J. Seigne and T. Morin, "Une Scierie Hydraulique Du VIe Siècle à Gerasa (Jerash, Jordanie). Remarques Sur Les Prémices de La Mécanisation Du Travail," in *Énergie Hydraulique et Machines Élévatrices d'eau Durant l'antiqué*, eds. J. Brun and J. Fiches (Naples: Centre Jean Bérard, 2007), 243–257.

124 Ivanišević, "Caričin Grad (Justiniana Prima)," 123–124. Ivanišević, "Main Patterns of Urbanism in Caričin Grad (Justiniana Prima)," 230.

125 P. M. Blanc and D. Genequand, "Le Développement Du Moulin Hydraulique à Roue Horizontale à l'époque Omeyyade : À Propos d'un Moulin Sur l'aqueduc de Bosra (Syrie Du Sud)," *Syria* 84 (2007): 299–310. P. M. Blanc and D. Genequand, "Un moulin hydraulique omeyyade sur l'aqueduc de Bosra (article en arabe traduit du français par Hassan Hatoum)," in *Hauran V, la Syrie du Sud du Néolithique à l'Antiquité tardive, Recherches récentes, Actes du colloque de Damas 2007*, vol. II, Bibliotheque Archeologique et Historique (BAH) (Beyrouth: Institut français du Proche-Orient (IFPO), 2013), 87–96.

126 Z. S. Winogradov, "The Aqueduct of Tiberias," in *The Aqueducts of Israel*, eds. D. Amit, J. Patrich, and Y. Hirschfeld, Journal of Roman Archaeology Supplement 46 (Portsmouth, Rhode Island: Journal of Roman Archaeology, 2002), 295–304.

127 B. D. Shaw, "The Noblest Monuments and the Smallest Things. Wells, Walls and Aqueducts in the Making of Roman Africa," in Future Currents in Aqueduct Studies, ed. A. Trevor Hodge (Leeds: Francis Cairns, 1991), 63–91. A. Wilson, "Deliveries Extra Urbem: Aqueducts and the Countryside," *Journal of Roman Archaeology* 12, no. 1 (1999): 314–332.

128 A. Commito, "The Aqueducts of Aphrodisias: A Regional Approach," *De Aquaeductu Atque Aqua Urbium Lyciae Pamphyliae Pisidiae: The Legacy of Sextus Julius Frontinus. Tagungsband Des Internationalen Frontinus-Symposiums, Antalya, 31. Oktober–9. November 2014*, Babesh Supplementa, 2016, 65–73.

129 F. Rojas and A. Commito, "The Aqueducts of Aphrodisias," in *Aphrodisias V. The Aphrodisias Regional Survey*, eds. C. Ratté and P. D. De Staebler (Zabern, Darmstadt/Mainz: Verlag Philipp von Zabern, 2012), 239–308.

130 K. Mukdad, "L'approvisionnement Hydrique de La Ville de Bosra," in *XXXV Corso Di Cultura Sull'Arte Ravennate e Bizantina* (Ravenna: Edizioni del Girasole, 1988), 171–203.

131 Giorgi, *Archeologia dell'acqua a Gortina di Creta*, 105–107.

132 Hammad, *Palmyre*.

15

ISLAMIC CITY, OTTOMAN CITY

Byzantine Prousa to Ottoman Bursa

Suna Çağaptay

For my ImpAncCity gang with much appreciation

From the rise of the Seljuks in Anatolia to the era of the Turkish principalities (1308–1453), including the Ottomans, archaeological evidence usually focuses on an urban life confined within the city walls.[1] The textual evidence, meanwhile, offers an idealised view of urban life and the role of the city's walls in survival and the creation of an urban identity.[2] But was there urban survival beyond city walls at times of relative peace and stability in the late Byzantine cities? What role did cultivated and uncultivated lands play in the agrarian and urban life outside the city walls? How did urban life move beyond the city and extend into the hinterland through the process of Ottomanisation? What is the interplay between an 'Islamic city', an 'Ottoman city' and a classical city? Herein I discuss how the early Ottoman city of Bursa grew out of the late Byzantine Prousa, which had itself grown out of classical Prousa. Through these transitions, I focus on the changing boundaries and focal points of the city and how its rulers manipulated the urban fabric to announce their legitimacy and cement their legacy as well as examining what it means to be an 'Islamic city' or an 'Ottoman city' and the process of colonisation.

In a recently published work examining urbanism in Byzantine Anatolia, Philipp Niewöhner discusses how ruralisation was a widespread phenomenon from the ninth century to the arrival of the Seljuks in Anatolia in the late eleventh century, resulting in a steady deurbanisation process and the abandonment of cities. This abandonment process in the eleventh century gave an impetus to securing the walls of the Byzantine cities, Cotyaeum (Kütahya), Doryleaion (Şarhöyük) and Pegea (Karabiga) being a few examples.[3] Another such example is the restoration of the walls in the western Anatolian city of Tralles (Aydın) by Andronikos II Palaiologos (r. 1282–1328), who added a new line of fortifications and sought to beautify the city, which he renamed after himself.[4] In other places, as displayed in Prousa and Nicaea, the interventions to secure the walls were varied and minimal, including immuring reused blocks into the wall plane and building anew towers to strengthen the walls.[5] It is sensible to agree that around the time of the sieges by the Turkish principalities, its inhabitants became confined within the city walls,

DOI: 10.4324/9780429203923-19

which were situated on hilltops as a means of protecting the people against invasions. But what did securing the walls mean in the medieval urban context of Anatolia and how did this change during the Byzantine to Ottoman transition? By looking at the transition of Prousa into Bursa, we can see how the pre-existing urban fabric of the city was revived and repurposed by the Ottomans.

Founded by Prusias I in the third century BC and set in the foothills of Mount Olympus, Prousa's vertiginous natural and man-made acropolis was praised by the fifth-century historian Paulus Orosius as the 'most fortified city' ('munitissima civitas').[6]

Its walls were originally built in the Hellenistic period (late third to early second century BC) and were constantly rebuilt thereafter, as indicated by inscriptions dating to the first or second century AD as well as the seventh and thirteenth centuries (Figure 15.1). Throughout the Byzantine and classical periods, the city exhibited a thriving urban life in and outside the city walls before eventually becoming confined within the walls of the acropolis due to the rising incursions of the Ottomans in the early fourteenth century.[7] Perhaps as a result of the sturdy walls, the city was able to withstand the Ottomans for a ten-year-long siege before falling in 1326.

Soon after this conquest, the city became the first capital of the burgeoning Ottoman state, and the Turkish conquerors began appropriating and reworking the urban fabric to signal their inheritance of Seljuk and Byzantine pedigrees. However, this change in the political regime did not fully reshape the attributes for which the city is famous. The Byzantine city of Prousa had four major functions: agrarian, devotional, hydraulic and therapeutic. It remained and even thrived as a centre of agricultural production, a commercial hub and a spa city with a profusion of devotional and imperial complexes. Once housing devout Christians and monastic foundations,[8] under the Ottomans, the city began to accommodate Sufi dervishes and saintly figures[9] and its skyline was shaped by the construction of *külliyes*, or socio-religious complexes, that visibly commemorated the sultanic power. In this moment of transition, the classical and Byzantine past was acknowledged and reused

Figure 15.1 Aerial view of the Walled City from north

while at the same time a range of new architectural campaigns were conducted to further complement the transition.

Beyond the Walls: Reuse and Revival of the Urban Framework and Imagery

We can begin by viewing the urban framework of the old city of Prousa (Figure 15.2). The ancient *decumanus maximus* running from east to west, known as Ortapazar Street, has survived moderately well to the present day.[10] Salvage excavations conducted on this street have revealed a set of female and male busts and fragments of sculptures, which have been stylistically dated from the first century BC to the first century AD, as well as sealed floors complemented by large terracotta water pipes. This evidence supports the imagining of this street as the main east-west axis.[11] For the *cardo maximus*, cutting the *decumanus* at a 90-degree angle, there are two possibilities: Engin Yenal suggests Kavaklı Street leading into the Yerkapı (Ground gate), while Mustafa Şahin argues for the modern-day Oruçbey Street leading into Sukapı (Water gate). I favour the latter suggestion, made by Şahin, which indicates an axis that cut the walled city into two halves.[12] The archaeological evidence for

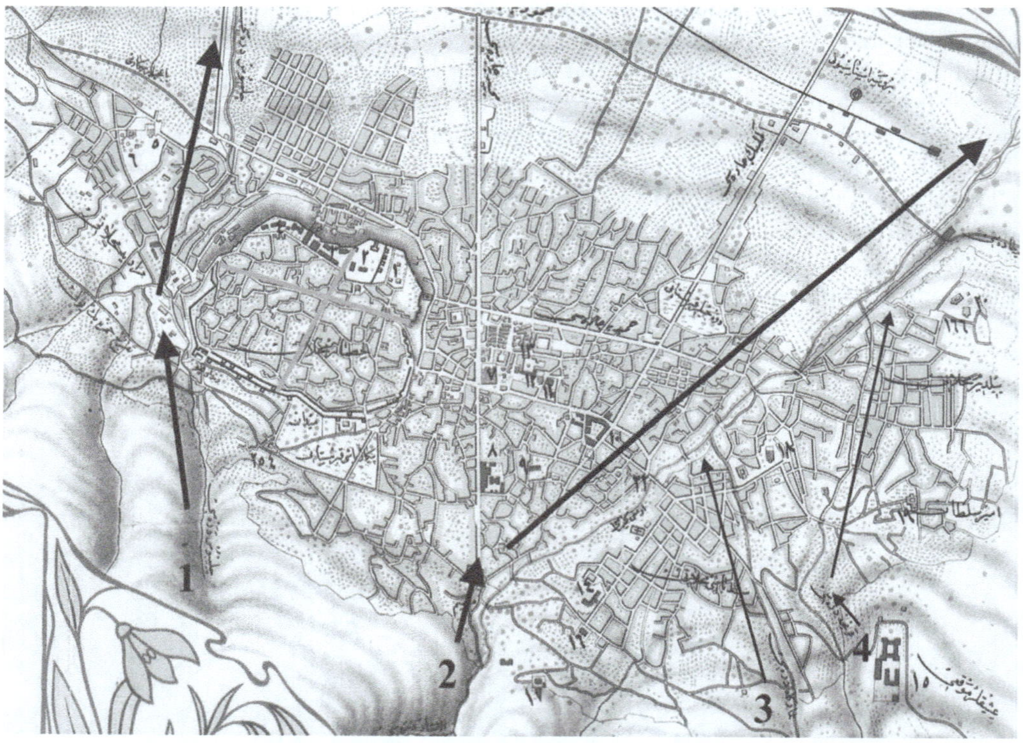

Figure 15.2 Map of Bursa, 1908. Taken from Hüdâvendigâr Vilâyeti Sâlnâmesi, Def'a 34, Matbaa-i Vilâyet, Bursa, Hg.1325. (Numbers 1-4 indicate the rivers running through the city. The cross pattern in the old city indicate the main streets: the *decumanus* running east to west and *cardo* running north to south). (The lines for the main streets in the walled city are added by the author on the map published by İsmail Yaşayanlar, "Su, Çevre, Sanayi ve Devlet: Modernleşme Sürecinde Bursa Kentinin Suyunu Sıhhileştirmek." *Toplumsal Tarih Akademi* 2 (2023), Figure 1)

an evidence for one or both of these streets being colonnaded resonates with the words of Dio, an orator and philosopher native to Prousa (c. AD 40–115) who wished to construct a colonnaded street to enhance the city and rival Antioch in the Roman east. This created tensions around supplanting the old urban fabric. Elsewhere, I have discussed Dio's description of his residence in the city and the row of workshops he rented out near the natural hot springs (*epi tôn thermôn*).[13] Were his attempts to bring a colonnaded street to Prousa limited to his neighbourhood, located towards the west where the *külliye* of Murad I was later built, or was he keen to commission another one in the walled city? His council speeches give us insight into how he was interested in conducting broader urban interventions. For example, he requested that the cenotaph of Prusias I, as well as other tombs, be transferred to other locations in the city to create new space for urban development projects within the walls.[14]

In this period, we also note the exchanges of letters between Pliny the Younger, the governor of Bithynia and Pontus from AD 113 to 115, and Emperor Trajan (r. AD 98–117) about restoring and refurbishing temples in the city.[15] Further epigraphic evidence indicates the presence of *agoranomos* and *gymnasiarch*, or people in charge of organising festivals and sports events.[16] Due to the size of the walled city, 800 metres by 500 metres, evidence of buildings associated with the abovementioned personnel, such as temples, *gymnasion* or *stadion*, must be looked for outside the walled city, hinting at a range of activities not just inside the walls but also beyond them.

Beginning with Orhan's reign (r. 1324–1361), much of the classical and Byzantine urban fabric situated within the walled city of Prousa was repurposed. Orhan also began utilising the area outside the city walls to further his architectural patronage, including building a *külliye*, a complex that comprised sultanic socio-religious and commercial functions centred around a convent-masjid (Figure 15.3). Moving outside the citadel a decade after the conquest, this decision is often seen as a civilising mission in an area supposed to be barren and uninhabited, as reported in an account by the fifteenth-century Ottoman historian, Neşri. However, this phrasing seems to be mistranslated by V. L.

Figure 15.3 Aerial view of Orhan's lower town from south with his Convent-Masjid and Bayezid I's Ulu Cami and the commercial quarters

Menage, who did the initial translation of the text, and has been repeated verbatim by the other editions of the same source, perpetuating the idea that the site Orhan chose was barren.[17] Indeed, photographs and travellers' accounts from the fourteenth century until the 1950s provide evidence for how the land around the walled town was ample and relatively unoccupied and was likely arranged in concentric rings.[18] But while this might have been the case during the reign of Orhan, it was not surely the case in the classical period. In the aftermath of the 1958 fire in this area, which demolished much of the commercial quarters, a team of archaeologists involved in the clean-up found a cemetery with dozens of burials with grave goods dating to the Hellenistic period, as well as some remains belonging to dwellings possibly dating to the Roman period.[19] This hints at inhabitation and use in the pre-Ottoman period. Judging from its location, 800 metres to the east of the walled city, this section might have functioned as the lower city in the late classical and Byzantine periods.

Within the walled city, Orhan converted a Byzantine complex, possibly the *katholikon* of Saint John Prodromos, to a Friday mosque, in accordance with the Ottoman practice of conquest, as well as reusing parts of the same complex for an eternal resting place for himself and his father, Osman.[20] Discussed elsewhere, I have used a set of travellers' accounts and visual depictions as well as archaeological evidence to elucidate the nature and context of this Ottoman conversion process.[21] These accounts are especially valuable given the 1855 earthquake obliterated much of pre-Ottoman and early Ottoman Bursa, which has made reconstructing the city a challenge for historians today. The archaeological evidence includes data from salvage excavations of Roman or Late Antique villa mosaics, a sixth-century church with a basilica plan,[22] and remnants of residential and bathing complexes in the area of the so-called Byzantine/Ottoman Palace.[23] In my own work, through the use of ground-penetrating radar (GPR), I have aimed to identify the buried remains of fortification walls, towers, water channels, chapels, and churches.[24] Within the same round of Ottoman conversion, the complex within the inner citadel corresponding to the palace or administrative quarters of a typical late Byzantine city was reused.[25] In the walled city, earlier buildings were repurposed to function as a *madrasa* and a bathhouse and new mosques were constructed, such as the one his brother Alaeddin built in 1331.

Murad I (r. 1361–1389) moved west of the urban centre on a prominent hilltop, to where the hot springs of the Old Bath (known as the *Basilika Thermae*) and Kükürtlü Bath (famous for its sulphur waters) abounded, famed since the classical period (Figure 15.4). His complex centred around a two-storey edifice, a plan that was never repeated in its entirety in Ottoman architecture, with the first floor reserved for praying as well as lodging, while the second floor functioned as a madrasa, accompanied by an *imaret*, a bathhouse, latrines and what would later be his own tomb.[26] This part of the town housed many spas, the water sourced from the same thermal springs used for the Roman- and Byzantine-period bathing complexes. Several travellers talked about the rich and therapeutic waters in the city. For Evliya Çelebi, 'In sum, Bursa consists of water'.[27] Murad I, in a way, brought back to life the classical-era efforts of Dio and Pliny the Younger in the first and second centuries AD to beautify this suburb renowned for its flowing waters.

From the third century onwards, Prousa's therapeutic waters within the walled city and outside of it were often visited by the Byzantine emperors.[28] The nineteenth-century traveller von Hammer talks about how five different streams originating from the foothills of Mount Olympus, around the area of the convent belonging to Abdal Murad, were collected at the Su kapı (Water gate) and Zindan kapı (Dungeon gate) on the south side of the city walls and pumped into the city via a conduit system, and from there the water was distributed into the walled city.[29] During his rulership, Murad I made sure the walled city's water needs would be met by reusing the pre-existing water infrastructure that fed water into the old city.[30] A team of specialists from the Bursa Metropolitan Municipality has developed a map for the water channels, fountains and bathhouses by tracing archival, written and archaeological evidence.[31] This proves there was an impressive hydraulic infrastructure in the walled city—and is an indication of how little we know about the nature of the agrarian and hydraulic practices in Bursa. Only with the help of further archaeological surveys would we be able to better understand how dramatic the changes the Ottomans brought were and how much they simply revived the landscape of Prousa.

Either way, Murad I's complex is visual testimony to his royal, devotional and sacerdotal personalities,[32] and the siting of his complex and the reuse of the bathing complexes allowed him to display ownership over a piece of valuable land and its resources. By reviving and adding new wings to the Old Bath as can be seen in the lower right-hand corner of Figure 15.4, this complex became an important source of income for the *waqfs*. He also remodelled the Kükürtlü Bath complex for a men's section, and his son Bayezid I later added a women's section. His complex elevated the status of the bathing complexes while also fulfilling the functions of a sultanic complex, providing a venue for education and ritual practices. After his assassination at the Battle of Kosovo in 1389, Murad I transformed from being an Ottoman sultan to being a saintly figure and martyr.[33] A Friday mosque known as *Şehadet* (Martyrdom), which probably began to be constructed while Murad I was alive, was completed and named as such to commemorate his martyr identity. With the addition of the Friday Mosque in the old city, the walled city's role as a focal and sacred point was strengthened.[34]

Figure 15.4 A nineteenth-century by Sebah and Joaillier and comes from the author's archive

Figure 15.5 Aerial view of Bayezid's complex from north

Bayezid I (r. 1389–1402) moved east of the city to make his personal and dynastic imprint on Bursa's landscape by building his *külliye* in an area that previously had large plots of gardens and orchards (Figure 15.5). Bayezid I's site largely corresponds to the Küşteri or Şüşteri *bağçe* (garden) listed in Orhan's *waqfiyya* as the site of his *külliye*. As compensation, Bayezid I bequeathed a larger tract of agricultural land to Orhan's *waqf*.[35] Just like his father, Murad I, he was keen on maintaining the water resources for the complex. Following his father's footsteps, he was instrumental in bringing water into his complex with the help of an aqueduct that was built at the site. He also gifted the five aforementioned streams originating from Mount Olympus to Gülçiçek Hatun, his mother and Murad I's wife.[36] As with Murad I's hydraulic efforts, Bayezid I might have used the pre-existing infrastructure to draw water into his complex.

Two more *külliye* complexes were built in the aftermath of the Timurid sack in 1402: Mehmed I (r. 1413–1421) built the Green Complex (also known as Yeşil in the Turkish scholarship) in the eastern part of the city, occupying a hilltop, and Murad II (r. 1421–1444; 1446–1451) built a complex, named after him, situated on the plain to the northwest of the acropolis. Built after the interregnum period (1402–1413), the *külliye* of Mehmed I evokes a sense of continuity and new beginnings (Figure 15.6). The construction and the siting represented a sultanic comeback affirming the dynastic continuity, albeit after a short break. It conforms to the practice of using ashlar as the predominant construction material, as in his father Bayezid I's complex. But it also introduces the use of *cuerda seca* turquoise tiles, which are linked to the impact of the Rum Seljuk and Timurid artistic production.[37] It is these turquoise tiles that gave the complex its name.

The complex of Murad II is situated immediately to the northwest of the old city.

On a low plain, like Orhan's *külliye*, it offers a snapshot of the Ottoman imperial family, housing the tombs of princes, who died untimely deaths, died in exile, or were killed by

Figure 15.6 Aerial view of Mehmed I's complex from north

their reigning brothers or fathers, as well as the tombs of princesses, the sultans' wives and favourite consorts, and midwives (Figure 15.7). The siting of this complex and its immediate function as the eternal resting place for the sultan himself as well as his immediate family members help us to understand how the notion of dynastic mausolea was transformed from being familial to 'ancestral' and is reminiscent of creating a necropolis outside the city walls.[38]

Figure 15.7 Aerial view of Murad II's complex from northwest

Just as early Ottoman Bursa arose around the reused fabric of Byzantine Prousa, the new sultanic neighbourhoods made use of the immediate surroundings of the Byzantine city to present the past in the present. It can be seen, then, that the loss of the Greco-Roman city from the fabric of the early Ottoman city (and from more recent city versions) was a result of centuries-old urban accumulation, transformation and intervention. Hence the walled city of Bursa can be seen as the original Ottoman city, wherein Bursa's reinventors Ottomanised the pre-existing urban fabric as they built their capital city and moved in different directions of the city to mimic the urban imagery of the walled city and its urban and rural surroundings.

Colonisation, Ottomanisation, and the Classical City

Under the Ottomans, Bursa's urban transformation was bound to the practices of reuse, recycling, rebranding and building anew. Upon conquering the city, both confessional and non-confessional loci went through the processes of reuse and accommodation.[39] This was the first of three steps in the Ottomanisation process. In the second step, the Ottomans claimed, settled and reinhabited the land by moving outside the city walls and building new structures and complexes. Topographical reality required promoting urban development on an east-west axis, and each sultan exploited this topography to leave their sultanic and dynastic legacy on the landscape, while also emphasising the historical connection between the acropolis surrounded by the walls and the plain. With the siting of the complexes on hilltops and slightly elevated areas, each created a version of Prousa's acropolis with its siting and urban framework. The ones built on a low plain, such as those of Orhan or Murad II, aimed to revive commercial quarters, still creating a focus for a dynastic claim (Figure 15.8).[40]

The second step of colonisation is often portrayed as the quintessential Ottoman way of colonising. Discussed by Ömer Lütfi Barkan in 1942, the theory of colonisation

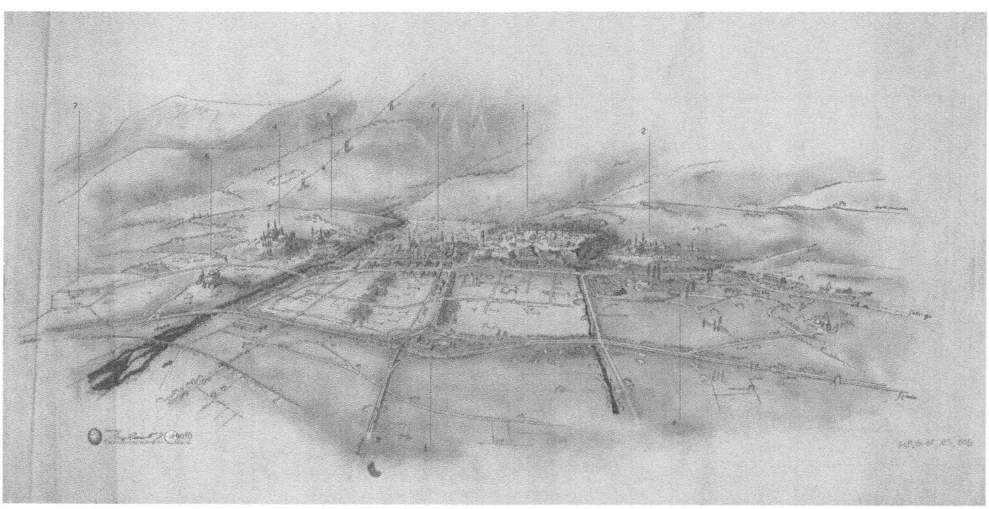

Figure 15.8 Panorama of Bursa by Piccinato (Credit: L'Archivio Luigi Piccinato (ALP), La Sapienza University, Rome). Legends: (1) Old City; (2) Muradiye; (3) Green Mosque; (4) Emir Sultan; (5) Bayezid; (6) Commercial Quarters; (7) New Residential Area; (8) New Commercial Area; (9) Public Parks and Sports Complex (N.B. This Unfortunately omits the Complex of Murad I)

encompasses how the Ottomans deliberately intervened in the spatial and urban fabric of Byzantine cities and the role of dervishes in this transformation.[41] Barkan's theory has been revisited by a series of scholars but suffice it to say that the so-called Ottoman colonisation transcended the work of dervishes alone. A more intricate reading is necessary to appreciate the emergence of different audiences and alliances in the Ottoman urban context, including examining references to the travelling dervishes or sheikhs, scholars known as *baba*s, converts, *akıncı*s (warlords) and *ahi*s (fraternities). If we refrain from the assumption that these areas were uninhabited and barren in the classical and Byzantine periods and prior to the construction of the Ottoman *külliyes*, this is more of a re-inhabiting and reviving of pre-existing areas of the city than a colonising act.

Furthermore, the model of Ottoman spatial configuration exemplified in the Bursa *külliyes* has been compared to the Rum Seljuk practice of constructing dervish convents and mausolea in peripheral areas away from the urban core.[42] Attributing this spatial configuration to the Rum Seljuk model, several scholars have argued that the Ottomans similarly aspired to move away from the old city, while transforming the urban scene through the construction of complexes. In Bursa, as in other Ottoman cities, this spatial intervention was meant to establish new neighbourhoods or revive the ones with pre-existing remains.[43] While each of these complexes stimulated an urban rejuvenation and resettlement, the reasons for the Ottomans to build on outlying lands differed from those of the Rum Seljuks. This is supported in part by the Bursa cadastral registers, the earliest being compiled in 1487.[44]

In examining the siting of the *külliyes* and their urban choreography, I would like to suggest that the Ottoman urban intervention in the areas outside the walled city follows the strategies of classical city-making. I have reached this conclusion for three main reasons. First, the *külliyes* were not always constructed in uninhabited areas. For example, Murad I's complex was hardly in an untouched place—there were still bathing complexes and colonnaded road systems in the area from Roman and Byzantine times.[45] Those built-in previously uninhabited spots, such as Orhan's complex, were commissioned not just to civilise an area considered 'unsafe' but rather, and mainly, to stimulate commercial and economic activity.[46]

Second, in the *külliyes* sponsored by Orhan, Murad I and Bayezid I, the architectural-spatial references point more towards the aspirations of classical cities than to the Rum Seljuk model. As discussed earlier, the siting of each complex exploited the landscape in a way that recalls the siting strategies of classical and late antique cities. Being perched on hilltops, both the Murad I and Bayezid I complexes offered panoramic views overlooking the city and the plains. Orhan's complex, just outside the acropolis, functioned as the heart of the lower city. Here, an imperial core was promoted, mimicking that of the Hellenistic cities; it is perhaps even comparable to a Roman imperial forum, serving as the nucleus for commercial, social and judicial activity. One further archaising pattern can be offered: overall, the focal point of these sultanic complexes was their inverted-T-type convent-*masjid*s, surrounded by subsidiary structures into which the posthumously built mausolea of the Ottoman sultans were incorporated.[47] An important detail to highlight is the funerary function acquired by Ottoman *külliyes* from the time of Murad I onwards. An example is Orhan's mausoleum, situated in the heart of the Byzantine monastic complex that was converted into a Friday Mosque and mausolea.[48]

Unlike the rationally designed külliye complexes of the later Ottoman architecture in Istanbul, where modular units and symmetry were applied, the *külliyes* in Bursa exemplified a kind of urban 'choreography' wherein builders created irregularly designed complexes for the sultans not because they lacked training in geometric order but rather as an act of deliberate planning wherein both the sultans and the builders wanted to ensure prominently placed landmarks signifying a sultanic presence and power would not be missed. They also emphasised the connection between the walled city and its suburbs by monumentally acknowledging the landscape. In Bursa, the *külliyes* followed the organic spatial configuration, and their lack of geometric order is comparable to the classical, medieval and early modern periods.[49] As Diane Favro has argued in the case of the Roman *fora*, the organic construction of the *külliyes* and their prominence in the landscape suggest that the builders were aware of optical strategies that underscored visibility and monumentalisation.[50] This is how Bursa assumed its eventual spatial forms under the Ottomans: by building new and also reviving the pre-existing siting ideals.

Third, each of these complexes functioned almost as a city within the larger urban framework of Bursa. This radically differed from the Rum Seljuk model wherein the dervish convents did not constitute discrete 'cities'. Orhan's complex was the first Ottoman urban intervention beyond the city walls, and the projects in this area helped him symbolically frame the old city. During the reign of Bayezid I, the area inhabited by Orhan's *külliye* became a new centre for establishing the *Ulu Cami* (Grand Mosque), or Friday mosque. In other words, while previously a place for locals to live and get their various needs met, it became, under Bayezid I, a site of sovereignty, where the Friday *khutbas* were offered.

Thus, we see that within the Ottoman colonisation process, classical strategies of city-making may be a more apt comparison than the Rum Seljuk model.

A Comparative Perspective: The Cases of Bursa, Ayasoluk and Miletos

Under the Ottomans, Bursa became a multifunctional metropolis, presaging the rise of a series of urban survival and choreography ideas in different cities that can be only partially compared to what was done in Bursa. Following the conversion of the major cathedral in the city, the rest of the urban interventions are more haphazard, happening both within and beyond the walls. For instance, Nicaea's Hagia Sophia was converted into a mosque and *imaret*s and tombs were constructed *ex novo* around the time of the Ottoman conquest in 1331, but later another *imaret* and a mosque were built within the city walls. In Adrianople, the second capital of the Ottomans (present-day Edirne), the church of Hagia Sophia was converted into a mosque and a royal palace was constructed to the east of the walled city. In addition, Byzantine commercial areas and dwelling quarters were reused by the Ottomans, as much as what remained of the buildings allowed,[51] beginning when they first occupied the city in the 1360s and continuing for the next forty years. Later, in the fifteenth century, the increasing construction of mosques, marketplaces and soup kitchens was intended to feed the indigent outside the walled city.[52] In Constantinople, Mehmed II constructed his second palace in the vicinity of the ruins of the Byzantine palace and converted the Hagia Sophia into a mosque. However, he constructed his *külliye* (begun in 1463) away from the centre but still within the city walls, over the ruins of the site of the Church of the Holy Apostles.[53]

The Ottomanisation of cities in the Balkans such as Didymoteichon and Komotini, because of their non-imperial status, largely entailed new construction commissioned by the warlords as well as the sultans outside the citadel. Thessaloniki, on the other hand, was enclosed by triangular city walls, and significant Ottomanisation took place in the inner fortress on the northern end of the acropolis. In this transformation, the foundations of an early Christian fort were reused to build a new one to accommodate the Ottoman conquerors. Meanwhile, within the city walls, new buildings, mosques, bathhouses and marketplaces were constructed.[54]

In order to examine how Prousa became Bursa, maintaining much of its urban, devotional and hydraulic character, we can look at one more comparison: an examination of the patterns of reuse, conversion and urban maintenance in the late Byzantine cities of Ayasoluk and Miletus. The former was the urban centre of the Aydinids and the latter held a similar function for the Menteshids during the period of the Turkish principalities. This period has been studied from a longstanding, narrow-minded perspective focused primarily on ethnic stratifications and rigid borders, locating the Ottomans to Bursa in Bithynia, the Saruhanid to Manisa in Lydia, the Menteshids to Miletos in Caria and the Aydinids to Ayasoluk in Ionia. By offering a comparative reading of the transformation of the late Byzantine cities into Islamic ones, I intend to examine the built environment based on synchronic parallels instead of the diachronic-sequence approach favoured in previous scholarship. Examining the transformation of Prousa into Bursa and comparing it to the better-studied cities of Ayasoluk and Miletos helps us to appreciate how each of these three cities was flexible and multi-referential in their transformation from a Christian city to an Islamic one. Furthermore, these three cities each display a different urban, dynastic and sociocultural encounter, which has been viewed by previous scholarship as if they followed similar artistic and architectural paradigms.[55] While the case of conversion and reuse is evident due to the change in the political regime, each city's urban transformation was bound by the realities of topography as well as the pre-existing sacred and natural elements.

The ancient city of Ephesos and its Byzantine counterpart Ayasoluk were conquered by the Aydinids in 1304, a princedom rivalling that of the Ottomans (Figure 15.9). Throughout the Byzantine period, the walled city of Ephesos existed more as a superstructure, a medieval cityscape slowly abandoned, whereas Ayasoluk and its Gate of Persecutions literally had the area's sacred history engraved within it. For example, both the walls of Ayasoluk

Figure 15.9 Ancient, Byzantine and Aydinid Ephesos/Ayasoluk (Courtesy of Çağla Caner Yüksel, "A Tale of Two Port Cities: Ayasuluk (Ephesus) and Balat (Miletus) during the Beyliks Period." *Al-Masāq* 31, no. 3 (2019), Figure 3)

and the church of Saint John were built from reused pieces of the Artemision, reinforcing its role as cultic heir.[56]

Ayasoluk comprised two rings of fortifications, one encompassing the Gate of Persecutions and the tomb and church of Saint John, and the second surrounding the acropolis, where the oratory of Saint John was located. While these were major attractions, the site could only be inhabited for brief periods by visitors due to lack of water, as evidenced by the presence of the pithoi remains and cisterns. The area in its entirety was eventually labelled Saint Theologos (Hagios/Ayos Theologos/Ayo Thologo or Alto Luogo) for its association with the cult of the saint, and finally the Turkish version *Ayasoluk* (lit. 'holy breath') emerged.[57] The same name with variations was retained by the Aydinids, and later by the Ottomans, who embraced the sacrality associated with the site.

In the aftermath of the conquest, the Church of Saint John was turned into a mosque. This church was originally built in the fourth century and was subsequently expanded into a major basilica under the emperor Justinian in the sixth century. The Aydinids built their palace around the ruins of the oratory of Saint John and the cisterns, and they also built a modest masjid accompanying the palace. Outside the city walls of Ayasoluk, the Isa Bey Mosque was constructed in 1374–1375 in an area that formerly included Byzantine monastic remains and overlooked modern Selçuk. This was just below Ayasoluk Castle, which was reused by the Aydinids. Built by a Damascene builder from the Mamluk realm, the Isa Bey Mosque's domed-basilical layout fronted by an atrium-like courtyard echoes the Great Mosque of Damascus built by al-Walid I in 715. The newly claimed urban core of the Aydinids included a madrasa, a palace and a bathhouse that were built in close proximity to the classical and Hellenistic Artemision.[58]

The city of Miletos shows a similar urban narrative, albeit there is no physical or textual evidence of a church being converted into a Friday mosque (Figure 15.10). The late Byzantine city was developed in the fortified settlement of Palatia, now known as Kaletepe, as a result of the Turkish threat, and from there it expanded into the nearby fortified Theatre Hill. The extension onto Theatre Hill became the focus of the Menteshid settlement when they conquered Miletos in 1262. It was here that the so-called Hisar Mosque was built, with later expansion south towards the Lion Harbour, where another masjid and a bathhouse were built.[59] Next to the bathhouse was the first Menteshid Palace. The second Menteshid Palace was built in Humeytepe, to the east. The Menteshid urban claim was finalised with the construction of the İlyas Bey Complex in 1404, which included a Friday Mosque, a madrasa, two public baths, a soup kitchen and a market as well as a row of workshops. The Greek Orthodox inhabitants were relocated to Theatre Harbour where they had their own church, known as the Church of Paraskevi, postdating the Menteshid conquest. Next to the Greek Orthodox neighbourhood was an Italian quarter, which reportedly had its own council building, bakery and chapel.[60]

In each of these cities, we observe the Islamisation of the city within a span of several decades. Of the three, Bursa represents a case of urban maintenance and reviving the agrarian, devotional, hydraulic and therapeutic spaces that I argue were the major functions of Byzantine Prousa. Ayasoluk acknowledges the changing functions and fortunes in the urban fabric while embracing its classical and Christian sacred connotations and transports an Islamic trope into the city. Miletos is strictly confined within the Byzantine city wherein reuse is emphasised to some extent, and the lines among the Greek, Italian and Turkish neighbourhoods are not as blurry. These cities differed in many ways, but each was a testimony to the changes in Anatolia's urban landscape. The urban interventions we note are

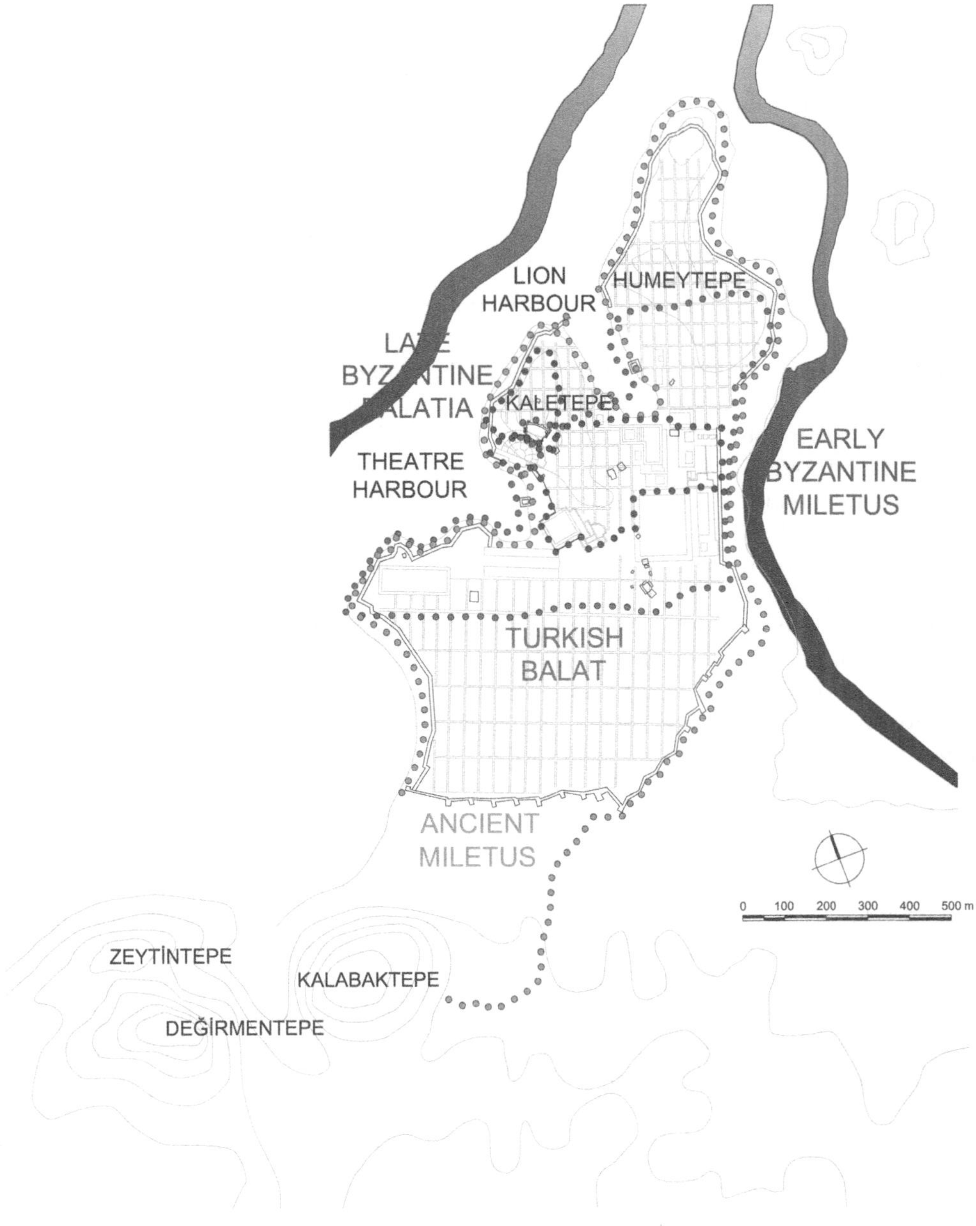

Figure 15.10 Ancient, Byzantine and Menteshid Miletos (Courtesy of Çağla Caner Yüksel, "A Tale of Two Port Cities: Ayasuluk (Ephesus) and Balat (Miletus) during the Beyliks Period." *Al-Masāq* 31, no. 3 (2019), Figure 10)

diverse, and they could hardly be collated under a single heading of the triangulation of a central mosque, commercial quarters and a bath that Orientalist scholars unabashedly attribute to the notion of the Islamic city.[61] Similarly, a series of other cities in Bithynia and the Balkans conquered by the Ottomans were studied from a similar perspective, leading to a narrative underscoring urban survival within the city walls in the late Byzantine cities and how the conquerors moved beyond the city walls after conquest to inhabit, maintain a civic identity and expand.[62] We see from a comparative perspective that Bursa is completely different from its Ottoman or principality counterparts in Anatolia. Bursa is a living city, as opposed to the ruined and deserted cities of Ayasoluk and Miletos. Irrespective of this difference, while Ayasoluk and Miletos' survival is paired with ruination, Bursa's survival is linked to the resilient forms of adaptation, both material and ritual.

How Islamic Was Bursa?: The Islamic City Paradigm

The Islamic city paradigm promoted by Orientalist scholars focuses on the spatial articulation of ethnic, religious and functional divisions within such cities, the triangulation of a central mosque, marketplace and the public bath, coupled with social institutions, and the emergence of the *umma*, a community of 'believers'.[63] Following this ideology, the case of spontaneous or irregular city planning is often linked with the Islamic city paradigm, in contrast to orthogonal planning, a characteristic of the classical world.[64] However, there has been an overemphasis on the orthogonal planning of classical cities (after all, not all the classical cities had it), and its abandonment in the medieval period in Europe and Byzantium has often been ignored. In fact, orientalists denigrated the so-called Islamic city by focusing negatively on its maze-like streets and narrow alleys—implying these attributes did not rise to the level of constituting true cities and, indeed, calling them 'non-cities'. They thus defined the Islamic cities by what they lacked rather than the richness they offered.[65] Rejecting the orientalist view, scholarship on the Islamic city now acknowledges how such cities borrowed from the classical world, such as in the social role of bathing practices and in *suqs* or bazaars occupying central locations.

This type of scholarly debate has surrounded not only the term 'Islamic city' but also the character and context of an Ottoman city.[66] In the discussions on identifying what constitutes the Islamic or Ottoman city, the cases of cities going through similar transformations under the Turkish principalities are often ignored. Nowadays, thankfully, a more diversified view prevails.[67] On the Ottoman front specifically, I believe there is room for a middle ground to appreciate the continuity from the classical and Christian past to the accommodation of the new religion and its urban constituents. This could easily be said for all the cities, not just for Ayasoluk or Miletos, that once housed the princely, commercial and administrative quarters for the Turkish principalities before they all succumbed to Ottoman rule in the late fourteenth and early fifteenth centuries.

Conclusion

I hope I have shown how architectural culture in fourteenth-century Bursa offers a solid foundation on which to explore the spatio-visual strategies of Ottoman city-making, which was largely shaped by pre-existing urban and spatial configurations. The early fourteenth-century Bursa—with its classical Byzantine forerunner in the walled city—fashioned the blueprint of architectural enterprise, a palpable construct closely tied to physical locale and fabric. It was this Bursa that was born within the walled city and the hinterland out of Byzantine Prousa that underscored what an Ottoman city should look like. It was also the same Bursa that survived through the change in the political regime and its resilient visual connotations gave birth to the new Bursas in its hinterland.

Notes

1 Author's note: Funding for the final research for this chapter was provided by the European Research Council Grant/ERC Advanced Grant Agreement n693418, "The Impact of the Ancient City," in the Faculty of Classics at the University of Cambridge. This chapter spins off from my book monograph titled: *The First Capital of the Ottoman Empire: The Religious, Social and Architectural History of Bursa* (IB Tauris, 2020), henceforth, *The First Ottoman Capital.* In this chapter, I not only repeat some of the conclusions appeared in my monograph, but also I especially elaborate on the character and context of the Ottoman city-making practices. Hence, I would like to kindly request readers to refer to the sections in my monograph for further bibliography. I must thank the members of my research team in Cambridge, led by Andrew Wallace-Hadrill (PI), Elizabeth Key Fowden (Senior Researcher), Edward Zychowicz-Coghill, Louise Blanke, Javier Martínez-Jiménez, Sam Ottewill-Soulsby, Sofia Greaves, Thomas Langley and Beth Clark whose though-provoking questions and comments encouraged me to peel back the layers of Prousa and Bursa. As a token of my gratitude, I dedicate this piece to them. I would also like to thank the Metropolitan Municipality of Bursa for providing me with the aerial views of the complexes examined here. My heartfelt thanks go to Prof. Figen Kıvılcım Çorakbaş of Uludağ University whose stimulating enquiry on the *limes* of the Classical Prousa has led me to draft this piece and to Assoc. Prof. İsmail Yaşayanlar of Düzce University for discussing Bursa's impressive hyradulic fabric and its maintenance in the nineteenth century. I am grateful to Dr. Çağla Caner Yüksel of Başkent University for sharing her maps appeared in "A Tale of Two Port Cities," Figures 3 and 10.

Crow, "Walls," 104–106; Çağaptay, "A Brief Survey of Byzantine Architecture and Urbanism," 269–274.

2 For a survey of the sources of this period, Saradi, "Byzantine Urban Imagination," 273–282; for site-specific discussions on Nicaea, Thessaloniki and Trebizond, see Akışık, "Praising a City," 7–10.

3 Niewöhner, "Urbanism," 59; Crow, "Walls," 104–106.

4 For a discussion of this strategy, Thonemann, *The Maeander Valley*, 1.

5 Kiourtzian, "L'Époque protobyzantine," 59–60; Çağaptay, *The First Ottoman Capital*, 26–28.

6 P. Orosius, *Historiae adversum Paganos*, 6.2.23.

7 For a discussion on the ten-year siege and the surrender of the city, Lowry, *Nature of the Early Ottoman*, 56–57, 77, 195–196.

8 For an overview of the Byzantine period in the city, Çağaptay, *The First Ottoman Capital*, 14–15.

9 Kafadar, *Between Two Worlds*, 19–28, 149–150. For a case study on the transformation of those identities, Lowry, *Ottoman Bursa*, 85–98.

10 Originally cited in Bekker-Nielsen, *Urban Life and Local Politics*, 53. For an analysis of the city walls and their transformations and remodellings as well as the pre-Ottoman urban fabric, Çağaptay, *The First Ottoman Capital*, 25–46.

11 Özkan and Ünal, *Hisarkeoloji*, 2009, 36, 144 Inv. 1960; 37, 144 Inv. 2092 and 2096, 147 Inv. 5691; 113 Inv. 10.3.2001, 167.

12 Yenal, *Osmanlı (Baş)Kenti Bursa*, 38–45, especially 45; Şahin, "Hisar Kazıları ve Bey Sarayı," 46, 51, 58.

13 Çağaptay, *The First Ottoman Capital*, 31–32.

14 As discussed Yenal, *Osmanlı (Baş)Kenti Bursa*, 38. For a wide range of temples, theatres and stadiums. Şahin, "Hisar Kazıları ve Bey Sarayı," 49–52 and Yenal, *Osmanlı (Baş)Kenti Bursa*, 38–45.

15 Walsh, *Pliny the Younger*, Book X, 23–26, 70–72.

16 For a discussion on the epigraphic attestations of those figures, Pitt, "Cities on the Periphery," 29–30, 125.

17 Unat and Köymen, *Kitab-ı Cihannüma: Neşri Tarihi*, 187. I thank Prof. Rudi Paul Lindner for bringing this important analysis to my attention.

18 Borrowing from J. H. von Thünen, *Der isolierte Staat in Beziehung*, 2–5, 171–195, 219–223, 228–245. An example of this theory applied to the Hispano-Umayyad Spain, Ruggles, *Gardens, Landscape and Vision*, 11.

19 Mert et al., "Prusa ad Olympum'dan (Bursa) Bir Oda Mezar," 203–205; Özkan and Ünal, *Hisarkeoloji*, 6; Çağaptay, "Prousa to Bursa," 160–184.

20 Çağaptay, *The First Ottoman Capital*, 34–46.

21 Çağaptay, *The First Ottoman Capital, passim.*

22 For a description of the excavation results in Turkish and accompanying photos: http://www.bursadakultur.org/tophanede_kilise.htm.

23 For studies on the mosaics, Okçu, "Prusia ad Olympum Mozaikleri," 31–51; Çıtakoğlu, "Bursa/Hisar Bölgesi Mozaikleri," 1–32. For an overview of the salvage excavations conducted by the Bursa Archaeological Museum, Özkan and Ünal, *Hisarkeoloji, passim* and more recently, Şahin, "Hisar Kazıları ve Bey Sarayı," 54–60.

24 Çağaptay, "Tophane Area GPR Surveys," 387–404; Çağaptay, *The First Ottoman Capital*, 20–21, 45–46. I am grateful to the Turkish Ministry of Culture and Tourism (for the area of the tombs and parks) as well as the Ministry of Defense (for the Byzantine/Ottoman Palace) for granting me a permit to carry out the GPR survey with the collaboration of Larry Conyers (University of Denver) and April Kamp-Whittaker (Arizona State University).

25 Çağaptay, *The First Ottoman Capital*, 30–33.

26 Çağaptay, *The First Ottoman Capital*, 88–90 for an overview and earlier bibliography.

27 E. Çelebi, *Seyahatname*, 2: 20.

28 Ubicini, *La Turquie actuelle*, 30; Kandes, *Προύσα*, 47; Sevim, "1. Murad'ın Vakıfları ve Temlikleri," 377; Çağaptay, *The First Ottoman Capital*, 32–33, 89. I would like to thank Dr. Eser Çalıkuşu for providing me with a copy of the second source cited in this footnote.

29 Von Hammer, *Hammer Seyahatnamesi*, 38.

30 Yalılı and Akal Solmaz, "Su Temini Tesislerinin," 173; Karataş, "Bursa Suları ve Su Vakıfları," 380. Both sources base their arguments on the archival documents. While there is not as yet a ground-penetrating radar survey to peel back the pre-Ottoman and Ottoman waterwork system in Bursa, judging from evidence from the Roman and Byzantine periods, we may assume that there might have been pre-existing water infrastructure in the city. For a brilliant reading of the archival evidence on the anatomy of the Ottoman-period waterworks and their maintenance, see Yaşayanlar, "Su, Çevre, Sanayi ve Devlet," 72–89. I thank Assoc. Prof. İsmail Yaşayanlar for sharing his thoughts on the hydraulic qualities of Bursa.

31 As discussed by Çobanoğlu and Özgökçe, "Bursa Bey Sarayının," 332–349; Yaşayanlar, "Su, Çevre, Sanayi ve Devlet," 75–77.

32 O. Kursar, "Sultans as Saintly Figures," 85–86 with n. 65–68; Yürekli, "Architecture and Hagiography," 67–68.

33 For a detailed description of Murad I's shifting identity from being a sultan into a saintly figure and the impact of the hot therapeutic waters in the formation of the latter, O. Kursar, "Sultans as Saintly Figures," 85–86 with notes 65–68.

34 Çağaptay, *The First Ottoman Capital*, 84–85.

35 Ayverdi, "Yıldırım Bayezid'in Bursa Vakfiyesi," 33–34; Çağaptay, *The First Ottoman Capital*, 90–92.

36 As discussed by Karataş, "Bursa Suları ve Su Vakıfları," 387, based on the archival document in the Bursa Court Registers, numbered B.Ş.S., A25/239a; Yalılı and Akal Solmaz, "Su Temini Tesislerinin," 173.

37 For the impact of this period on the urban interventions and dynastic claims, Kastritsis, "Ottoman Urbanism and Capitals," 287–306; Çağaptay, *The First Ottoman Capital*, 92–95.

38 Çağaptay, *The First Ottoman Capital*, 93–95. I would like to extend my heartfelt thanks to Prof. Figen Kıvılcım Çorakbaş whose enquiry on the whereabouts of the ancient necropolis in Bursa helped me to reframe my thoughts on the relationship between the city walls and cemeteries.

39 Further discussions on framing this cultural transition under the banner of accommodation as opposed to the triumphalist appropriation favoured by previous scholarship, see Çağaptay, *The First Ottoman Capital*, 7–8, 23–47, 107–108.

40 An inspirational work examining the role of the landscape and water, Pancaroğlu, "Architecture, Landscape, and Patronage," 40–55. Elaborating on Pancaroğlu as well as other scholars, I examined this process in length, Çağaptay, *The First Ottoman Capital*, especially 23–47 and 92–94 for more details and bibliography.

41 Barkan, "İstila Devirlerinin Kolonizatör Türk Dervişleri ve Zaviyeler," *Vakıflar Dergisi* 2 (1942): 279–365.

42 Wolper, Cities and Saints, 42–72; Blessing, "Urban Space Beyond Walls," 25–43.

43 More recently viewing the scholarship, Boykov, "T-shaped Zaviye/İmarets of Edirne," 33–44; Çağaptay, The *First Ottoman Capital*, 82–86.

44 For a reading of the archival sources to interpret the urban development, Ergenç, *XVI. Yüzyılın Sonlarında Bursa.*
45 Çağaptay, *The First Ottoman Capital*, 30–34; Bekker-Nielsen, *Urban Life and Local Politics*, 20–25, 268–269, Mundell-Mango, "Thermae, Balnea/Loutra, Hammams," 145, 151, 153.
46 See note 16 in this piece.
47 Necipoğlu, *The Age of Sinan*, 77.
48 Kafescioğlu, *Constantinople/Istanbul*, 79; Çağaptay, *The First Ottoman Capital*, 85.
49 For an overview and further bibliography, Çağaptay, *The First Ottoman Capital*, 91–92.
50 Favro, "Meaning and Experience," 368.
51 According to the fourteenth-century *vita* of John Vatatzes, the majority of the thirteenth-century Laskarid urban interventions were in ruins around the time of the Ottoman conquest, Heisenberg, "Kaiser Johannes Batatzes," 197–201.
52 Kuran, "Three Ottoman Capitals," 118–122, especially 122; Ousterhout and Bakirtzis, *The Byzantine Monuments of Evros/Meriç*, 169.
53 Necipoğlu, *Architecture, Ceremonial, and Power*, 12–13, and as noted by Pancaroğlu, "Architecture, Landscape, and Patronage," 48; Kafescioğlu, *Constantinopolis/Istanbul*, 28–53.
54 Lowry, *Shaping of the Ottoman Balkans*, 154–160; Bakirtzis, "The Urban Continuity and Size of Late Byzantine Thessaloniki," 35–64.
55 As aptly discussed by Pancaroğlu, "Formalism and the Academic Foundation of Turkish Art," 67–78.
56 Çağaptay, "Into the Sacred Space," 197–198, for an overview of the dating and interpretations of the excavated remains and further bibliography.
57 Foss, *Ephesus*, 120–122, 141–181, 174–175; Çağaptay, "Into the Sacred Space," 197–198; Çağaptay, "Yeniden İnşa Edilen Geçmiş," 56–63. Pahlitzsch, "The Greek Orthodox communities of Nicaea and Ephesus," 147–153.
58 Foss, *Ephesus*, 157–161; Ladstätter, "The Türbe in the Artemision," 538–540; Dalanay, "Ephesos During the Beylik and Ottoman Periods," 13–14; Acar, "Architecture of the Islamic Frontier," 58–66, as well as recent review by Caner Yüksel, "A Tale of Two Port Cities," 340–351; Çağaptay, "Sacred Dimishq: From Early Islam to the Anatolian Principalities."
59 Niewöhner, "Miletos," 255–263; Niewöhner, "The End of the Byzantine City," 63–70; Caner Yüksel, "A Tale of Two Port Cities," 352–362, fig. 3.
60 C. Yüksel, "A Tale of Two Port Cities," 352–365, fig. 10; Arel, "The Architecture of the Menteşe,"62–63; Tanman, "Some Reflections on the İlyas Bey Mosque," 87–92.
61 For the Islamic City paradigm, my summary derives from Eldem, Goffmann, and Masters, "Introduction," *The Ottoman City between East and West—Aleppo, Izmir, and Istanbul*, 1–18. For a review of earlier scholarship, Çağaptay, *The First Ottoman Capital*, 17–18; Boykov, "T-Shaped Imarets," 29–31.
62 Constantinople: Kafescioğlu, *Constantinopolis/Istanbul*; Edirne: Singer, "Enter, Riding on an Elephant," 89–109; Kontolaimos, "A Landscape for the Sultan," 19–33. Bursa: Kastritsis, "Ottoman Urbanism and Capitals," 287–306; Pancaroğlu, "Architecture, Landscape, and Patronage," 40–55; Kuran, "Three Ottoman Capitals," 114–131. For the Balkans: Bessi, "The Topographic Reconstruction of Ottoman Dimetoka," 44–85; Riedler, "Communal Boundaries and Confessional Policies," 726–756; Ćurčić and Hadjitryphonos, *Secular Medieval Architecture in the Balkans*, 19–39; Lowry, *The Shaping of the Ottoman Balkans*, 154–160; Bakirtzis, "The Urban Continuity and Size of Late Byzantine Thessaloniki," 35–64.
63 See note 61 above.
64 Sauvaget, "L'enceinte primitive de La Ville d'Alep," 131–159; Sauvaget, "Le Plan Antique de Damas," 314–358.
65 Raymond, "Islamic City, Arab City: Orientalist Myths and Recent Views," 7.
66 Overview and earlier scholarship, Çağaptay, *The First Ottoman Capital*, 17–18; Boykov, "T-Shaped Imarets," 29–30. For challenges to the idea that the spatial interventions were simply based on the Islamic city model, see Kafescioğlu, *Constantinopolis/Istanbul*.
67 Lapidus, "Evolution of Muslim Urban Society," 21–50; Boykov, "T-Shaped Imarets," 29–30.

16

TWO VIEWS OF PORTS AND MARITIME COMMUNITIES IN THE BYZANTINE MEDITERRANEAN

Constantinople and Amalfi

Michael Jones and Matthew Harpster

Introduction

Access to the sea and viable harbors was essential for medieval Mediterranean coastal cities and settlements. Although the importance of local agricultural resources should not be underestimated,[1] most ancient cities of any size required food imports for larger populations, in addition to other raw materials and manufactured goods. Urban harbors dating from the Classical to Roman Imperial periods have tended to receive the most scholarly attention, often due to the scale and sophistication of artificial harbor works and other infrastructure; the applications of hydraulic concrete in port construction in the late Republic and Early Empire have been a particular focus of research.[2] This tradition of centrally planned artificial harbor construction – whether by provincial or imperial governments – continued well into the Byzantine era, even as it disappeared or was vastly reduced in other regions of the Mediterranean, due in large part to the state-subsidized *annona* trade used to feed much of Constantinople's population into the early 7th century AD.[3]

However, small and apparently insignificant harbors and landing places played an essential role in Mediterranean maritime trade throughout history. According to Horden and Purcell, "The informal harbor – for which the Venetian label *skala*, literally a flight of steps, has become widespread in the Mediterranean – is of greater overall significance than the great naturally endowed port, a Piraeus or a Marseille."[4] The importance of small harbors and landing places is supported by archaeological surveys of coastal settlements such as the late antique town of Aperlae on the southern coast of Asia Minor, which displays signs of significant economic activity without any clear evidence for constructed port facilities or even particularly favorable environmental conditions for mooring vessels.[5]

It is important to note that 'informal' harbors were not isolated but integrated into the urban infrastructure and topography of medieval Mediterranean cities and towns. Constantinople and the Amalfitan port towns illustrate some of the ways that urban port communities operated in the early medieval period, under quite different circumstances from

DOI: 10.4324/9780429203923-20

those of the early Roman Empire. Constantinople not only retained and used much of its late antique harbor infrastructure for centuries but also adapted it to the economic, demographic, and political conditions of the medieval period and made extensive use of 'informal' harbors as well. In contrast, the Amalfitan ports lacked built infrastructure or a single urban center. They share characteristics with earlier mercantile communities, but in some ways, the Amalfitans success could be considered a 'medieval' phenomenon. These small, Italian settlements played an outsized role in re-establishing long-distance trade links in the Mediterranean between different cultural groups after the collapse of the Western Roman Empire, despite having relatively little in the way of population or military forces to do so.

The Harbors, Waterfront, and Hinterland of Constantinople, c. 330–1200

As the capital of the Eastern Roman Empire and one of its largest port cities, Constantinople developed an extensive urban maritime infrastructure. Unlike many ancient Mediterranean coastal cities,[6] Constantinople continued as a major port on the same site until modern times due to its strategic position and excellent natural harbor on the Golden Horn. By the 5th century AD, these natural features were augmented by the construction of artificial harbors and other installations, a formidable defense system, and an extensive water supply infrastructure, all of which were maintained to varying degrees for centuries.[7] Constantinople's built maritime infrastructure ranged from wooden piers and other landing places within and outside of the city and infilling of marshy areas along the waterfront to four massive artificial harbors. All of these features were necessary to sustain an exceptionally large population by ancient and medieval standards: up to 500,000 people may have lived in the city just before the Justinianic Plague, and likely up to several hundred thousand again by 1200.[8] Even the minimum estimates by modern scholars of 40,000–70,000 inhabitants for the later 7th century represent a large urban center for the period.[9]

Although Constantinople's harbors have been studied since the 16th century, most research has focused on textual evidence and existing architectural remains, partly due to the difficulties of conducting archaeological investigations in an inhabited modern city. However, recent archaeological research, particularly from the Marmaray Project excavations (2004–2013) of the Theodosian Harbor by the Istanbul Archaeological Museums, provides new information and interpretations of Constantinople's Byzantine waterfront and larger maritime network.[10]

Byzantium's location and unique environmental conditions naturally influenced the development of its commercial harbors. Herodotus and Polybius note that the city's location was ideal for controlling north-south sailing traffic between the Black Sea and the Sea of Marmara, and the winds and currents favor Byzantium over Chalcedon on the Asian side of the Bosporus.[11] Prevailing winds on the Bosporus and Sea of Marmara blow from northeast to southwest, while southwestern-flowing currents average at least three knots annually and can run as much as five to six knots in the summer when rivers emptying into the Black Sea flow at their highest.[12] Southwesterly winds in the area of Constantinople could sometimes aid ships approaching the city (eight days per month on average), but at other times, the frequent tacking into the wind to reach the city made the approach difficult for square-rigged vessels.[13] Although the lateen rig used in the Byzantine period is generally considered to be more suitable on modern vessels for sailing into the wind, voyage accounts and shipwreck finds suggest that medieval ships were less effective at such maneuvers due to their hull shapes and other factors.[14]

These conditions, along with pre-existing natural bays that were artificially enlarged, apparently influenced the placement of the Theodosian and Julian or Sophian harbors on the southern Sea of Marmara shore of the city, which were easier for ships to enter from the southwest.[15] Similarly, Procopius reports that state-owned warehouses on the island of Tenedos (Bozcaada) were constructed during the reign of Justinian in order to shorten the voyages of Alexandrian grain ships faced with contrary winds on the Sea of Marmara; grain cargoes could later be loaded into smaller ships and brought to the capital.[16] Constantinople's overall harbor capacity also included subsidiary ports in its hinterland, some with breakwaters and other harbor construction such as those mentioned by Procopius at Heraeum and Eutropius or documented by archaeologists in the region.[17] These elements were all part of a larger port infrastructure network created for the government-subsidized *annona* trade, used to feed the citizens of the Roman capital as well as the military and civil servants of the emperor from 330 to the early 7th century AD.[18] Although ancient Byzantium's harbors were located on the eastern end of the peninsula and older 'informal' harbors were part of the network,[19] the scale of *annona* shipments required larger harbor facilities; these also doubtless played an important symbolic role "as a place of public presentation of communities and individuals," displaying monuments and sculptures glorifying the city's imperial status.[20]

The four major commercial harbors constructed in Constantinople in the 4th or early 5th century provided an estimated 4–5 km of wharf space for thecity's waterfront.. [21] *Annona* grain was shipped from as far as Egypt, North Africa, and Sicily, although other regions closer to the capital were exploited as well, particularly after the early 7th century.[22] The *Notitia Urbis Constantinopolitanae* (c. AD 425) mentions state and private bakeries as well as 20 stated owned *horrea* (warehouses) for grain, olive oil, and wine situated near the harbors.[23] Mango estimates that the capital received between 2,400 and 3,600 grain ships (given 8–10 m of docking space per vessel) annually based on a 6th-century grain import figure.[24] *Annona* ships were apparently larger than the typical Roman and early medieval seagoing vessels, which, based on shipwreck finds, were typically only 15 m long, with drafts of 1–1.5 m and cargo capacities of under 30–60 tons or even less.[25] The emperor Claudius required a 70 ton minimum cargo capacity for *annona* ships, and much larger vessels, up to 40 m and 600 tons cargo capacity, were used for a portion of the long-distance *annona* voyages.[26] Such ships required deeper harbors, such as the 5–7 m deep harbor basins at Portus, which in turn encouraged a boom in harbor construction along *annona* routes.[27] Although the largest classes of ships were in use until at least the early 7th century when the *annona* transports ended for Constantinople's civilian population, they probably represented only a fraction of overall harbor traffic and likely became even less common in the early medieval period; most of the 28 post-7th-century Yenikapı cargo ships were only 8–15 m long and therefore required less elaborate harbor facilities than larger ships.[28] Constantinople's steep population decline in the 7th and 8th centuries also must have decreased the city's maritime traffic and the need for larger ships and deeper harbors and the need for larger ships and deep harbors.[29]

Large artificial harbors often presented significant maintenance challenges after construction, however, so the end of their construction was not necessarily a symptom of a larger 'decline.' Many experienced siltation problems, due in part to the short tidal range in the Mediterranean.[30] Construction of sluice gates and openings in breakwaters tended to only mitigate the problem, and many Roman harbors seem to have required regular dredging and often silted up in spite of such efforts.[31] Possible evidence for dredging activity was recently identified from 6th-century deposits from the Yenikapı excavations, while dredging operations in some of Constantinople's harbors are also documented in Byzantine textual sources.[32] The stratigraphic record of the Theodosian Harbor includes sediments deposited by the River Lykos, in addition to occasional deposits from storms or other 'high-energy' geological events, which left layers of marine sand that was occasionally thick enough to conceal valuable shipwreck cargoes from salvage.[33] The Theodosian Harbor also served as a garbage dump for material ranging from broken amphorae and animal bones, plant remains, and even derelict ship hulls.[34] Yalçin et al. reconstruct the sedimentation rate in the harbor between the 6th and 8th centuries as 0.8 cm/year on average, a result comparable to estimated siltation rates of other ancient harbors.[35] The Theodosian Harbor presumably became less suitable for larger vessels as it decreased in depth and area. Structures were eventually built on some filled-in sections of the harbor, while other areas were converted into gardens and orchards.[36]

Each of the city's main harbors and waterfront areas was gradually adapted to new roles in the medieval period. Although their exact locations are unknown today,[37] the Neorion and Prosphorion harbors were commercial harbors constructed along the city's northeastern shore in the city's Fifth and Sixth Regions (Istanbul's modern Sirkeci and Eminönü neighborhoods) described in the *Notitia Urbis Constantinopolitanae*, which also included state-owned *horrea*, the Strategion forum, a shipyard, and the Sycae *skala* (quay or landing place).[38] The Prosphorion Harbor was likely silted up and abandoned by the 7th century.[39] The Neorion was apparently converted to naval use during the reign of Justinian; it was dredged in 698 to accommodate warships during the reign of Leontios and used as a naval shipyard until at least the 13th century.[40] Venetian and Amalfitan sailors serving in the Byzantine navy were reported as living in the area in the 10th century, and oars were still produced for the war fleet's galleys in the area in the 12th century.[41] Records of land grants to foreign merchants in the old city survive from the 11th century, coinciding with evidence for the increased importance of maritime commerce along the Golden Horn in the later medieval period.[42] While they were eventually eclipsed by the Venetians, Amalfitan merchants and craftsmen are attested from the early 10th to 12th centuries and were prominent early in this period, being the first Italian community to found a monastery and church in the city.[43]

The larger artificial harbors on the Marmara shore operated for longer periods. The Julian Harbor, named after the 4th-century emperor, was an estimated 600 m in diameter, appears to have been the more active of the two in the first millennium AD based on the number of textual references to its use, perhaps due to its proximity to the imperial palace and aristocratic residential areas and its location on the less windy southern side of the peninsula.[44] After a fire in Justinian's reign, the harbor was dredged (one of several recorded dredging episodes), renovated by Justin II (565–578), and renamed the Sophian Harbor after his wife.[45] This area likely handled some grain imports to the city – the *Horrea Alexandrina* and the *Horreum Theodosianum* were located between the Julian and Theodosian Harbors – and remained in use as a commercial harbor until at least the Fourth Crusade.[46] It later served as a harbor for naval galleys from the Byzantine re-conquest in 1265 through the early Ottoman occupation of the city (the Kontoskalion), finally falling out of use by the mid-16th century.[47]

While information on the Julian Harbor derives almost exclusively from textual sources, a large part of the Theodosian Harbor has been recently excavated.[48] Constructed in the late 4th or early 5th century in a natural bay at the mouth of the Lykos River,[49] it/the Theodosian Harbor was the largest commercial harbour of the city, perhaps 700 m long from east to west and up to 200 m from north to south; recent excavations have uncovered extensive stone and concrete quays and waterfront structures.[50] In the mid-16th century, Pierre Gilles observed a tower and a stone pier at the site, but this feature has not been located[51]; however, the contours of modern streets in the area and surviving remnants of the sea walls delineate parts of the medieval harbor's boundaries.[52] A state-owned grain warehouse known as the *Lamia* (likely one of the 5th-century *horrea*) still operated near the Theodosian Harbor in the 10th century, along with a number of bakeries and the *Forum Taurii* used to sell pigs and Easter lambs.[53] Although the state continued to play a significant role in regulating the city's food supply and some other types of commerce (as shown by documentary sources such as the *Book of the Eparch*), by the 10th century this was achieved more through regulation of non-state commerce rather than the regular organization of large-scale bulk shipments of commodities by the state itself.[54]

The Theodosian Harbor was gradually filled with a combination of river silt, marine sand, and refuse dumped from the city, but the recent Yenikapı excavations show that a significant harbour basin survived on the eastern end of the excavation area until at least the late 10th century.[55] Stone and concrete piers built for mooring ships and unloading cargo were discovered along the northern and western edges of the excavation; many of these structures almost certainly not only date to the late antique phases at the site but also include a pier at the excavation's northeastern end built of ashlar blocks (including many *spolia* pieces) and marine concrete, with a foundation timber cut around AD 800.[56]

Studies of structural timbers from the Theodosian harbor provide more detailed information on the functioning of the Byzantine harbour. An estimated 4,000 wooden piles, mostly of oak, were used to construct wooden piers and other structures at the site, at least 295 of which have been dated using dendrochronology.[57] A chronology for the years AD 398–610 was assembled in one study of sampled oak piles from four wooden piers at the site. Some of these structures were surprisingly long-lived: one was used an estimated 83 years (Marmaray Iskele 1), while another was used at least 45 years (Metro Iskele 3). Moreover, evidence of repairs and expansion of the piers have been identified, and pier locations likely give some indication of the shoreline's contours.[58] Much of this timber was imported from the same source that supplied the Byzantine fort at Capidava (Romania), on the Danube in the late 6th century, perhaps from a Black Sea source.[59] Preliminary results date other wooden piers to the 5th–9th centuries (with a number pre-dating the 7th century); several were damaged or destroyed by a 'high-energy event' (i.e., a storm or tsunami) probably in the early 7th century.[60] In a more recent study (Yalçin et al., 2019), detailed dendrochronological sequences were assembled for three wooden piers constructed in c. AD 524, 582, and 594, with further repairs dating into the 8th century.[61]

Documentary sources also suggest that wooden piers were common sites along the city's waterfront and in the immediate hinterland. Magdalino noted (well before the Yenikapı excavations) a description of Michael Attaleiates of the wooden piers or jetties (*proteichismata*), "called *skalai* in the common dialect" that "girdle the Queen of Cities" and belonged to "various masters," including "sacred houses" and monasteries; these owners also had rights to the foreshore "according to ancestral custom and the imperial decrees, which grant the access to the sea and who are the owners of adjoining land."[62] In this passage, Attaleiates is praising Nicephorus Botaneiates for rescinding imperial attempts to regulate this trade along the foreshore of the city and also at the *phoundax* (or state grain warehouse) at Raidestos.[63] Since this system privileged the property rights of the institutions owning *skalai*, it may have made it easier for merchants from Amalfi and other foreign states to establish themselves in the commercial activities of the capital.[64]

In choosing Constantinople as his imperial capital, Constantine I combined a favorable geographic location with new infrastructure improvements essential for a large city, much of which continued to operate into the medieval period. However, once the fragmentation of the Roman Empire "broke the tax spine" between the capitals of Rome and Constantinople and their *annona* suppliers of bulk goods, the old system for provisioning the city was no longer a viable option[65]; instead, later Byzantine emperors imported grain and other supplies from a variety of sources closer to the capital using state, ecclesiastical, and private or commercial resources.[66] These developments are likely reflected in some of the changes seen in Constantinople's main harbors. Maintenance operations such as dredging occurred less often, and new harbor structures were more often of wood rather than stone or hydraulic concrete.[67] New harbor construction was at a smaller scale than in earlier centuries and less often directed by central authorities, with many state-run harbor maintenance projects being related to naval rather than commercial facilities, and parts of the main harbors were gradually repurposed as they silted up. Textual evidence from the post-7th century period also suggests some resistance by elites to centralized control over aspects of the city's provisioning and maritime commerce in general; they preferred to maintain the trading rights of existing private institutions rather than surrender control to a central authority, encouraging a more dispersed harbor network within and around the city.[68] Although larger cargo ships were sometimes built in the Byzantine Empire, an increased reliance on smaller ships such as those found at the Yenikapı excavations was a sensible response to these economic circumstances. Shallow-draft vessels were well suited for mooring at the numerous wooden *skalai* along the waterfront of the city, examples of which were discovered in the Theodosian Harbor basin itself. The small size of many cargo ships of the period was not necessarily an obstacle to long-distance voyages, as some Middle Byzantine and early Islamic shipwrecks show, but reliance on such technology would have placed some limits on the volume of long-distance maritime trade.[69] When larger cargo ships again became more common and economically viable in the later Middle Ages, the Golden Horn provided good protection and anchorage space into recent times, not least to the Italian merchants who came to play such a significant role in later medieval trade.

Port Cities of the Amalfi Coastline in the Byzantine Era, c. 600–1100

Stretching approximately 53 km between Salerno to the east and Punta Campanella to the west, the Amalfi coastline is a coarse and rugged collection of cliffs, terraced hills, small inlets, and compact, dense settlements at the conjunction of river valleys and the coastline. Immediately south of the Bay of Naples and jutting into the Tyrrhenian Sea, this region is adjacent to sailing routes from the Strait of Messina to the ancient and medieval settlements at Salerno, Naples, Rome, Pisa, and Genoa. Depending upon winds and currents, ships may also pass by while traveling to Sardinia, Corsica, and Marseille. Today, the permanent population of these settlements is approximately 34,000 people so, while past population estimates are always imprecise, the density in the Late Antique and Medieval eras was likely lower.[70]

Despite differences in size and demographics during the Late Antique and Medieval eras, however, the Amalfi coastline embodies a few similarities to the harbors of Constantinople. In addition to the formal and informal political connections between the two cities, which will be discussed, both also had a long history of occupation from the prehistoric era to the first millennium. Moreover, the modern urban densities of Istanbul and the Amalfitan port towns hamper archaeological research. Instead, textual data dominates the historical narrative of both areas, and most archaeological data is the result of accidental finds arising during urban development.[71]

It is this final characteristic that prompted a series of diachronic studies of the Amalfi coastline beginning in 2016.[72] Combined with geo-morphological, archival, textual, and ethnographic research, a series of systematic archaeological investigations on land and under water are modeling and understanding changes in this maritime cultural landscape.[73] The broad goal of this work is to understand how the relationship between the local community and the sea changes over time – the Bay of Salerno may always be a source of sustenance and communication, but for whom does it contain wealth, or embody the untamed environment? Who values the sea, how do people attempt to control it, and who fears what the sea may bring?

The Late Antique and Medieval eras of the Amalfi coastline have been a key component of this project because the region's history from the 2nd to the 9th century AD seems peripheral to surrounding events and political powers. Other than a few textual references in this period, there seems to be little evidence to illuminate if and how life within these small population centers continued for almost 800 years. Integral to modeling change within this maritime landscape, therefore, is attempting to fill this historical lacuna with archaeological information, and data from previous projects on land and under water are beginning to do so. Among the 78 coins found during the excavations of Minori's *villa maritima*, 97 percent were minted between the 1st and 4th centuries AD; 39 percent of the collection are from the 4th century alone.[74] In nearby Salerno, excavations have uncovered a sub-urban *villa* in use during the 3rd century AD, as well as continuity at the Trotula de Ruggiero site in the 4th or 5th centuries.[75] Equally, in 2004, the Archeomar Project documented two deep-water sites near the island of Capri dating to the Roman or Late-Roman eras.[76] Our ongoing research is adding to this corpus of information. Within the collection of 44 amphorae in the *villa maritima* museum in Minori, 20 have been tentatively identified. Among them, examples of Almagro 54 and Beltran 2A types suggest ongoing trade and communication with Spain in the Imperial and Late Antique eras. Possible examples of Keay type 36, 39, 55, or 57 amphorae, and Africana Grande 2A types, suggest similar connections with North Africa from the 2nd to 6th centuries. A Late Roman type I amphora dating from the 5th to 7th centuries, which may be a local variant from the Bay of Naples, hints at the continuity of regional activity and production.[77]

Our systematic archaeological surveys under water are generating much less information, however, which is an unexpected contrast to the present collection of terrestrial data. Even though the small collection of information on land cannot replicate accurately the scale or nature of maritime activity, these data nevertheless suggest that life along the southern side of the peninsula continued after the 1st century AD.[78] After surveying approximately 21 km of the seabed for three seasons, however, a total of three ceramic body sherds tentatively dated to the Medieval era have been found. These remain *in situ*, and so require further study, but this apparent dearth of archaeological material under water has generated a parallel investigation – if Amalfi was traditionally a maritime power, why is there so little material on the seafloor demonstrating this, or any activity at all?[79]

To identify more material data from the first millennium AD and to understand the present lack of material on the seafloor, systematic archaeological surveys continue. Presently, however, much of the region's narrative from Late Antiquity to the Medieval period is still fashioned from textual sources supplemented by material data and built heritage, unlike the wealth of archaeological information emerging from the Marmaray Project excavations. The story they convey is one of rapid economic growth and influence prior to the turn of the millennium, concluded by a rapid downfall in the 12th century AD. In the late 6th or early 7th centuries, for example, Amalfi emerges in letters from Pope Gregory who seems to characterize the settlement as a *civitas* or a *castrum*.[80] The *Codex epistolaris Carolinus* also portrays the Amalfitan community as having a growing social presence in southern Italy during the 8th and early 9th centuries.[81] Indeed, the small port town's emerging strategic importance warranted an attack by the Lombards in 786, whereas by the 9th century, the small town's entanglement in the awkward relations between the Muslim and Byzantine Empires, and the Catholic Church, is manifest. In 812, a Byzantine regional governor in Italy asked Amalfi, Gaeta, and Naples for ships, apparently to fight Muslim naval forces.[82] Papal letters in the 830s, and a treaty between Naples and Benevento from 836, reiterate Amalfi's growing activity although its role in this triumvirate shifted – as their vassalage under Byzantium waned, their ships traveled to the Lipari islands and, soon, to Taranto, both of which were under Muslim control.[83] They became independent from the Byzantine duchy in Naples by 840 and may no longer be considered a formal Byzantine port city, although they sustained relations. For Byzantium, this may have been a political change, but not a change in substance; Amalfi remained a useful ally, and local rulers were still recognised as *praefecturii* and *duces* afterward.[84] For the Church, however, they were a fickle ally. Between 872 and 882, Pope John VIII promised Amalfi substantial annual contributions and commercial advantages for ships to fight the Muslim forces – a contract the Amalfitans apparently never fulfilled.[85] But this growth was not limited only to the port town of Amalfi itself. The adjacent settlement of Atrani increased in size and importance during this time, and the prosperity of these and other small urban settlements nearby grew with Amalfi's independence.[86] Indeed, it may be argued that the elements commonly coalescing within a large port like the Theodosian harbour were instead distributed among the small settlements on this coastline. Cetara, founded by the end of the 9th century, was a fishing community that could support its neighbors.[87] Amalfi was the administrative center, and Atrani contained housing for the local nobility and the palace for the Duchal assembly.[88] Minori embodied the religious heart of the area, purportedly containing the relics of their patron Saint Trophimena, and Maiori remained an agricultural zone until the 12th century and its increased urbanization.[89] During this era, the cities' defensive walls were erected, enclosing key structures in *intra-moenia* zones and relegating agricultural terraces and beaches to *extra-moenia* areas. Elements of these walls are still evident today. In Maiori, the remains of the 12th-century wall still extend approximately 200 meters from the modern Corso Reginna to the steep hill demarcating the town's eastern border and still integrate at least one cylindrical tower and an adjacent *fossato*, or defensive ditch. In Minori, a possible *fossato* and associated tower are extant along the Via Antonio Mancini, although the wall itself appears to be lost. Each city reportedly built their own arsenals during this period of development, although only that in Amalfi is still surviving.[90] Other remnants of built heritage embody this small region's wealth and scope during this period. The bronze doors of Amalfi's Duomo were cast in Constantinople in the 11th century, and Urso Castellomata, a wealthy merchant, built a private family church in nearby Pogerola in the 12th century.[91]

As a community, Amalfi's presence also grew internationally, which was likely key to its wealth and impact. In Constantinople, there was an apparently Amalfitan coastal neighborhood and *skalai* by the 10th century – an eastern manifestation of their strip of port towns in Italy – as well as a possible *ecclesia mercatorum* associated with Saint Mary of the

Latins.[92] Similar relations grew within Antioch, before the Crusaders' conquest in 1098; as the Genoese arrived, they found an Amalfitan hospital and 'street of the Amalfitans' already established.[93] There were strong relations with the Fatimid Caliphate as well. Amalfitan traders established another monastery of Saint Mary of the Latins in the tiny 'Muristan' neighborhood of Jerusalem, and an Amalfitan colony of merchants was also known in Alexandria.[94] Indeed, Amalfi joined naval forces from Rome, Pisa, and Genoa to besiege Mahdia, Tunisia, in 1087, and attacked the local dynastic rivals to the Fatimids in Egypt.[95] As scholars have written, the Amalfitan community gained power through their distribution and redistribution of items through the Mediterranean: They carried mastic from Chios and medicinal plants from Greece to Egypt, and sacred and secular Byzantine fine arts to the west.[96] Spices often came in their craft from the Muslim community and, in particular, the remains of Saint Bartholomew in 838 as the Arabs were attacking the Lipari islands where the relics were kept.[97]

As a political element of the Byzantine Empire, Amalfi had a peripheral role until its dramatic decline in the 12th century after annexation by Roger II of Sicily and the attacks by Pisa. But, this may be because Amalfi was never an integral part of the Byzantine Empire, or another empire before that. Despite the political connections with Constantinople, Jerusalem, and Alexandria, the small polities of the Amalfitan community had economic autonomy. Their local resources made them self-sustaining, but their outlook and fleets made them essential to others – Rome, Constantinople, and Alexandria, or Muslims and Christians. By maintaining a careful balance between their own independence and indispensability to others, the Amalfitan community expressed power in a way uncommon centuries earlier. Unlike Constantinople's harbours, which sustained a concentration of political and religious power, a massive bureaucracy, and military and naval strength, Amalfitan power emerged through a need for economic networks across empires' borders. Amalfi's neighborhoods, hospitals, and fleets were built on an economic rubric, and their power was expressed not though military conquest but mercantile connections. This was not unique. The other maritime republics of Venice, Pisa, Gaeta, and Genoa did the same, and the rapid growth of their influence embodies the needs they fulfilled. Indeed, the diminution of Amalfi in the 12th century under the Normans may be an unfortunate corollary to its specialization. Unlike micro-regions that survived from one century to another through the flexibility of their agricultural and economic practices, the Amalfi port towns were dramatically constrained.[98] Unlike Venice, Pisa, or Gaeta, Amalfi had little space for increased agriculture or industry; even the river valleys in Genoa were expansive in comparison. The small port towns could sustain themselves, but harvesting timber from the hills, agriculture in Maiori, and fishing in Cetara were not enough to replace the wealth and power generated by their economic networks. Combined with an apparent disinterest by the Norman kings for risky commercial ventures, the other maritime republics could flourish whilst the Amalfi port cities retreated, losing their influence abroad.[99]

Conclusions

As discussed in the Introduction, the Theodosian harbour at Constantinople and the Amalfitan ports represent two different but related maritime and mercantile phenomena within the early-Medieval period.

Constantinople's strategic location and the monumental investment in infrastructure projects made by Byzantine emperors of the 4th–6th centuries ensured its lasting importance as an urban center into the Middle Ages. However, the city's harbors were built for an economic and political system that had collapsed by the 7th century. While the Golden Horn remained an excellent natural harbor for large ships, the two main harbors on the Marmara shore were unable to maintain their original depth or capacity due to natural siltation and anthropogenic deposition. As a result, the city's existing port infrastructure was adapted to a less centralized system, used mainly by smaller and more adaptable ships controlled by a variety of interest groups. By the Middle Byzantine period, Constantinople was relying on a combination of modified Roman port infrastructure and a variety of small-scale or 'informal' harbors to sustain one of the biggest urban populations in the Mediterranean.

In contrast, Amalfi and its networks were very much a creation of a more streamlined and sparse approach to harnessing the economic potential of the surrounding communities. As mentioned, their power was not manifested in an emphasis on size and centralization, but in a different utility – the networks and carriage they could provide to others. Their eventual decline, unlike Pisa or Genoa, may reflect not only the parochial interests of the Norman rulers but perhaps also the inflexibility of their base of influence; unlike other growing medieval city-states, Amalfi was either an international mercantile network or it was a rural collection of small ports. It lacked the flexibility to be anything else.

Notes

1 P. Horden & N. Purcell, *The Corrupting Sea: A Study of Mediterranean History* (Oxford: Blackwell, 2000), 113–114.

2 A. J. Blackman,, "Ancient Harbors in the Mediterranean. Part 1", *International Journal of* Nautical Archaeology 11:2 (1982a), 79–104; A. J. Blackman,, "Ancient Harbors in the Mediterranean. Part 2.", *International Journal of Nautical Archaeology* 11:3 (1982b), 185–211. C. J. Brandon, R. L. Hohfelder, M. D. Jackson, & J. P. Oleson, *Building for Eternity: The History and Technology of Roman Concrete Engineering in the Sea* (Oxford: Oxbow Books, 2014).

3 R. Hohfelder, "Procopius, de aedificiis, 1.11.18–20: Caesarea maritima and the building of harbours in late antiquity", *Mediterranean Historical Review* 3:1 (1988), 54–62; R. Hohfelder, "Building Harbours in the Early Byzantine Era: The Persistence of Roman Technology", *Byzantinische Forschungen* 24 (1997), 367–380; J. Preiser-Kapeller, "Harbours and Maritime Networks as Complex Adaptive Systems – A Thematic Introduction.", in J. Preiser-Kapeller & F. Daim (eds), *Harbours and Maritime Networks as Complex Adaptive Systems* (Mainz: Verlag des Römisch-Germanischen Zentralmuseums, 2015), 1–22.

4 Horden and Purcell 2000: 142.

5 R. Hohfelder & R. L. Vann, "Cabotage at Aperlae in Ancient Lycia", *International Journal of Nautical Archaeology* 29:1 (2000), 126–135; Hohfelder, R. 2011. "Maritime connectivity in Late Antique Lycia: A Tale of Two Cities, Aperlae and Andriake", in D. Robinson & A. Wilson (eds), *Maritime Archaeology and Ancient Trade in the Mediterranean*, 211–222. (Oxford: Preiser-Kapeller, 2015), 2–4; M. Veikou, "Mediterranean Byzantine Ports and Harbours in the Complex Interplay between Environment and Society. Spatial, Socio-Economic and Cultural Considerations Based on Archaeological Evidence from Greece, Cyprus and Asia Minor", in J. Preiser-Kapeller & F. Daim (eds), *Harbours and Maritime Networks as Complex Adaptive Systems* (Mainz: Verlag des Römisch-Germanischen Zentralmuseums, 2015), 41–51.

6 Ephesos is one well-studied example: see F. Stock, A. Pint, B. Horejs, S. Ladstätter, & H. Brückner, "In search of the harbours: New evidence of Roman and Byzantine harbours of Ephesus", *Quaternary International* 312 (2013), 57–69; H. Delile, J. Blichert-Toft, J.-P. Goiran, F. Stock, F. Arnaut-Godet, J.-P. Bravard, H. Brückner, & F. Albarède, "Demise of a Harbor: Geochemical Chronicle from Ephesus", *Journal of Archaeological Science* 53 (2015), 202–213. For other examples, see Blackman 1982b: 186–187.

7 B. C. P. Tsangadas. *The Fortifications and Defense of Constantinople* (New York: Columbia University Press, 1980); J. Crow, J. Bardill, & R. Bayliss, *The Water Supply of Byzantine Constantinople,*

Journal of Roman Studies Monograph 11 (London: Society for the Promotion of Roman Studies, 2008), 262–268; K. Ward, J. Crow, and M. Crapper, "Water-Supply Infrastructure of Byzantine Constantinople", *Journal of Roman Archaeology* 30 (2017), 175–195; E. Kislinger, "On Better and Worse Sites: The Changing Importance of the Harbours of Constantinople", in F. Daim & E. Kislinger (eds), *The Byzantine Harbours of Constantinople* (Mainz: Römisch-Germanischen Zentralmuseums, 2022).

8 Magdalino, "Medieval Constantinople", in *Studies on the History and Topography of Constantinople*, 1–111 (Aldershot: Ashgate/Variorum Reprints, 2007), 61–65.

9 C. Mango, *Le développement urbain de Constantinople (IVe-VIIe siècles)*. Travaux et Memoires du Centre de Recherche D'Histoire et Civilisation de Byzance Collège de France Monographies 2 (Paris: Diffusion de Boccard, 1985), 54; C. Mango, "The Shoreline of Constantinople in the Fourth Century", in N. Necipoğlu (ed), *Byzantine Constantinople: Monuments, Topography, and Everyday Life* (Leiden: Brill, Mango, 2001), 17–28; Magdalino 2007: 18–19.

10 For recent studies of Constantinople's harbors and shoreline topography, see F. Daim & E. Kislinger (eds.), *The Byzantine Harbours of Constantinople* (Mainz: Römisch-Germanischen Zentralmuseums, 2022), and Semiz, N., & Z. Ahunbay, "Yenikapı'daki Tarihi Liman Surlarının Durumlarının Değerlendirilmesi ve Korunmaları için Öneriler", *Arkeoloji ve Sanat* 145, Ocak-Nisan (2014), 1–30, 24.

11 See Polybius 4.38 (E. S. Shuckburgh [trans.] *Polybius: Histories* [London: MacMillan, 1962]); Hdt. IV.144 (Godley ed. and trans.) *Herodotus: The Histories* (Cambridge: Loeb, 1938).

12 B. J. Labaree, 1957. "How the Greeks Sailed into the Black Sea", *American Journal Archaeology* 61:1 (1957), 31; J. H. Pryor, *Geography, Technology, and War: Studies in the Maritime History of the Mediterranean, 649–1571* (New York: Cambridge University Press, 2000): 13.

13 Labaree, B. J. 1957: 32–33.

14 Based on textual accounts of sea voyages, Pryor estimates that most medieval ships that sailed against prevailing winds for the majority of a voyage took twice as long as those sailing downwind (Pryor 2000: 32–36). Whitewright (2011) argues that the lateen rig was widely adopted in the late antique and medieval Mediterranean due to economic considerations rather than superior sailing performance to ancient square rigs (see J. Whitewright, 2011. "Efficiency or Economics? Sail Development in the Ancient Mediterranean", in W. V. Harris and K. Iara (eds), *Maritime Technology in the Ancient Economy: Ship-Design and Navigation*, 89–102. Journal of Roman Archaeology Supplementary Series No. 84. Portsmouth, RI: Journal of Roman Archaeology).

15 P. Magdalino, "The Maritime Neighborhoods of Constantinople: Commercial and Residential Functions, Sixth to Twelfth Centuries", *Dumbarton Oaks Papers* 54 (2000), 215; Mango 2001, 17–21.

16 Procop. *Aed.* V.i.8–10 (H. B. Dewing, [trans.] *Procopius: Buildings* [Cambridge, MA: Harvard University Press, 1996]).

17 Hohfelder 1988, 55/Procopius, *De Aedificiis* 1(Cambridge, MA: Harvard University Press): 11 (1988), 18–20; Ş. Aydingün, "Küçükçekmece Gölü Havzası (Bathonea?) Kazıları (2009–2012)", *İstanbul Araştırmaları Yıllığı* 2 (2013), 41–53; O.Tekin, "Bathonea: A Site that Never Existed", *Anadolu Araştırmaları* 20 (2017), 105–114; G. Simeonov, "The Harbours and Landing Stages of Hebdomon", in F. Daim & E. Kislinger (eds), *The Byzantine Harbours of Constantinople* (Mainz: Römisch-Germanischen Zentralmuseums, 2022), 181–198; P. Magdalino, 2002. "Medieval Constantinople: Built Environment and Urban Development", in A. E. Laiou (ed), *The Economic History of Byzantium from the Seventh to the Fifteenth Century*, 529–537. Dumbarton Oaks Studies 39. Washington, DC; K. Belke, 2022. "Gates to Asia Minor: The Harbours of Chalcedon, Chrysopolis, Hiereia and Eutropiu Limen Opposite Constantinople", in F. Daim & E. Kislinger (eds), *The Byzantine Harbours of Constantinople* (Mainz: Römisch-Germanischen Zentralmuseums), 223–233.

18 A. H. M. Jones, *The Later Roman Empire 284–602: A Social Economic and Administrative Survey*, Vols. 1–2 (Norman, OK: University of Oklahoma Press, 1964), 688, 697; Mango 1985, 37.

19 Mango 2001, 17–21; A. Külzer, "The Harbour of Theodosius in Yenikapı, İstanbul: A Harbour Area Through the Ages", in F. Daim and E. Kislinger (eds), *The Byzantine Harbours of Constantinople* (Mainz: Römisch-Germanischen Zentralmuseums, 2022), 75–91; E. Kislinger, 2022. "Neorion and Prosphorion: The Old Harbours on the Golden Horn", in F. Daim and E. Kislinger

(eds), *The Byzantine Harbours of Constantinople* (Mainz: Römisch-Germanischen Zentralmuseums), 133–139. Heher (2022: 133) notes a reference in Cassius Dio (LXXV 10, 5) to two enclosed harbors within the Roman city walls in this area (D. Heher, "Harbour of Julian – Harbour of Sophia – Kontoskalion", in F. Daim and E. Kislinger (eds), *The Byzantine Harbours of Constantinople* (Mainz: Römisch-Germanischen Zentralmuseums, 2022), 133.

20 P. Arnaud, "Maritime Infrastructure: Between Public and Private Initiative", in A. Kolb (ed), *Infrastruktur und Herrschaftsorganisation im Imperum Romanum* 161–179 (Berlin: de Gruyter, 2014), 167–168.

21 C. Mango, "The Development of Constantinople as an Urban Center", in *Studies on Constantinople* (Aldershot: Ashgate/Variorum Reprints, 1993): 120.

22 J. L. Teall, "The Grain Supply of the Byzantine Empire, 330–1025", *Dumbarton Oaks Papers* 13 (1959), 87–139, 119–126.

23 M. M. Mango, "The Commercial Map of Constantinople", *Dumbarton Oaks Papers* 54 (2000), 189–190, 192; Magdalino 2000, 212.

24 Mango 1993: 120. A law from the reign of Justinian I mentions an annual importation of 8,000,000 *artabae* of grain from Alexandria to Constantinople annually; according to one estimate, this is enough grain to feed 600,000 in a year, although some of this amount was certainly stockpiled in case of famine (Mango 1985: 37).

25 G. W. Houston, "Ports in Perspective: Some Comparative Materials on Roman Ships and Ports", *American Journal of Archaeology* 92:4 (1988), 553–564, 553–554, 556; and Parker 1992, A. J. Parker, *Ancient Shipwrecks of the Mediterranean and the Roman Provinces* (BAR-IS 580). (Oxford: Hadrian Books, 1992), 26 for general statements on the sizes of most Roman-period ships, which can also be applied to many Byzantine shipwrecks: see, for example, J. R. Steffy, "Construction and Analysis of the Vessel", in G. F. Bass, S. D. Matthews, J. R. Steffy & F. H. van Doorninck (eds), *Serçe Limanı: An Eleventh-Century Shipwreck*, Vols. 1, 153–170 (College Station: Texas A&M University Press, 2004), 169; C. Pulak, R. Ingram, and M. Jones, "Eight Shipwrecks from the Theodosian Harbour Excavations at Yenikapı in Istanbul, Turkey: An Introduction", *International Journal of Nautical Archaeology* 44:1 (2015), 39–73, 43; Özsait-Kocabaş, İ. "The Yenikapı 12 Shipwreck, a 9th-Century Merchantman from the Theodosian Harbour in Istanbul, Turkey: Construction and Reconstruction", *International Journal of Nautical Archaeology* 47:2 (2018), 357–390, 387.

26 Houston 1988: 556, 559; L. Casson, *Ships and Seamanship in the Ancient World* (Baltimore, MD: Johns Hopkins University Press, 1995), 172, n. 23; H. Khalilieh, "Capacity and Regulations against Overloading of Commercial Ships in Byzantine and Islamic Maritime Practices", *Journal of Medieval History* 31 (2005), 243–263, 246; A. Wilson, "Developments in Mediterranean shipping and trade from the Hellenistic period to AD 1000", in D. Robinson and A. Wilson (eds), *Maritime Archaeology and Ancient Trade in the Mediterranean*, 33–60 (Oxford: Oxford University Press, 2001), 39–40.

27 Keay 2012: 46. Wilson 2011: 47. Wilson (2011: 49) describes 2–3 m of depth as "sufficient for medium to large cargo ships" of the Roman Imperial period.

28 Wilson 2011: 54–55. At least a few of the Yenikapı shipwrecks excavated, such as YK 22 and YK 35 (5th–6th c. AD), could be classified as particularly large ships. U. Kocabaş & I. Özsait-Kocabaş, "A New Milestone in Ship Archaeology: The Yenikapı Shipwrecks Project", in Z. Kızıltan (ed), *Stories of the Hidden Harbor: Shipwrecks of Yenikapı*, 35–46 (Istanbul: Istanbul Archaeological Museums Press, 2013), 41, 42, figs.8–9; Kocabaş 2015: 12, 29, figs. 24, 31, fig. 26. Kocabaş classifies 5 of the 27 shipwrecks under study by Istanbul University as 'large', seven as 'medium' [sized], and ten as 'small' in a preliminary report; only lengths of the small vessels (7–12 m) in this classification are specified (see U. Kocabaş, "The Yenikapı Byzantine-Era Shipwrecks, Istanbul, Turkey: a preliminary report and inventory of the 27 wrecks studied by Istanbul University", *International Journal of Nautical Archaeology* 44:1 (2015), 5–38, 11–12). The roundships studied by Pulak et al. (2015: 43) are also within the 8–15 m range and date from the 7th to 10th centuries.

29 Teall 1959: 102–105, 133; Preiser-Kapeller 2015: 5.

30 J. Morton, *The Role of the Physical Environment in Ancient Greek Seafaring* (Leiden: Brill Morton 2001), 45; Preiser-Kapeller 2015: 4–5.

31 Blackman 1982b: 186–187; C. Morhange and N. Marriner, "Mind the (Stratigraphic) Gap: Roman Dredging in Ancient Mediterranean Harbours", *Bollettino di Archeologia Online Volume Speciale* B/B7 4 (2010), 25–30; Wilson 2011: 51.

32 Morhange and Marriner, 2010: 25–27, 29; M. N. Yalçin, M. Sezerer-Bulut, C. Pearson, P. Kuniholm, O. Algan & T. Wazny, "Establishing a High-Resolution Stratigraphy in the Holocene Marine Sequence of the Ancient Theodosian Harbor of Istanbul with the Help of Dendrochronology", *Geoarchaeology* 34 (2019), 360–374, 372.
33 D. Perinçek, "Geoarchaeology of the Excavation Site for the Last 8,000 Years and Traces of Natural Catastrophes in the Geologic Profile", in U. Kocabaş (ed), *Istanbul Archaeological Museums Proceedings of the 1st Symposium on Marmaray-Metro Salvage Excavations, 5–6 May 2008*, 191–218, (Istanbul: Istanbul Archaeological Museums/Epsilon; Pulak et al. 2015), 59–60; Özsait-Kocabaş 2018, 357–359; C. L. Pearson, C. B. Griggs, P. I. Kuniholm, P. W. Brewer, T. Wazny & L. Canady, "Dendroarchaeology of the Mid-First Millennium AD in Constantinople", *Journal of Archaeological Science* 39 (2012), 3402–3414, 3410). Yalçin et al.'s results revise Perincek's dating of the 'high-energy event' to the early 7th century rather than the 557 earthquake (G. Bony, N. Marriner, C. Morhange, D. Kaniewski & D. Perinçek, "A High-Energy Deposit in the Byzantine Harbor of Yenikapı, Istanbul", *Quaternary International* 266 (2012), 117–230, 128–129; Yalçin et al. 2019, 371).
34 Perinçek 2010: 199–202, 204–215; V. Onar, G. Pazvant, A. Armutak, H. Alpak, İ. Karamut & M. Gökçay, "Preliminary Report on the Animal Remains Uncovered at Yenikapı Metro and Marmaray Excavations", in U. Kocabaş (ed), *Istanbul Archaeological Museums Proceedings of the 1st Symposium on Marmaray-Metro Salvage Excavations, 5–6 May 2008* (Istanbul: Istanbul Archaeological Museums/Epsilon, 2010), 223–232; E. Oybak- Dönmez, "Archaeobotanical Studies at the Marmaray and Metro Excavations in Istanbul", in U. Kocabaş (ed), *Istanbul Archaeological Museums Proceedings of the 1st Symposium on Marmaray-Metro Salvage Excavations, 5–6 May 2008* (Istanbul: Istanbul Archaeological Museums/Epsilon, 2010), 233–249.
35 Yalçin et al. 2019: 372.
36 O. Algan, M. N. Yalçin, İç Yılmaz, E. Kırcı-Elmas, E. Sarı, D. Ongan, Ö. Bulkan Yeşiladalı, D. Perinçek, M. Özdoğan, Y. Yılmaz & İ. Karamut, "Geo-Archaeology of the Theodosian Harbor at Yenikapı", in U. Kocabaş (ed), *Istanbul Archaeological Museums Proceedings of the 1st[st] Symposium on Marmaray-Metro Salvage Excavations, 5–6 May 2008*, 175–180. (Istanbul: Istanbul Archaeological Museums/Epsilon, 2010), 180; M. Gökçay, "Architectural Finds from the Yenikapı Excavations", in Z. Kızıltan (ed), *Istanbul: 8,000 Years Brought to Daylight: Marmaray, Metro, Sultanahmet Excavations* (İstanbul: Vehbi Koç Vakfı 2007), 175; P. Magdalino, "The Harbours of Byzantine Constantinople", in Z. Kızıltan, R. Asal & G. Baran-Çelik (eds), *Stories from the Hidden Harbor: Shipwrecks of Yenikapı* (İstanbul: İstanbul Archaeological Museums Press, 2013), 14; A. A. Ginalis & A. Ercan-Kydonakis, 2022. "Some Reflections on the Archaeology of the Late Antique and Byzantine Harbours of Constantinople", in F. Daim & E. Kislinger (eds), *The Byzantine Harbours of Constantinople*, 37–39, 41 (Mainz: Römisch-Germanischen Zentralmuseums; Külzer 2022), 82.
37 Sections of one of the harbors may have been exposed in the early 20th century (K. Dark, 2005. "The Eastern Harbours of Early Byzantine Constantinople", *Byzantion* 75,151–154).
38 W. Müller-Wiener, *Die Häfen von Byzantion Konstantinupolis Istanbul* (Tübingen: Ernst Wasmuth Verlag, 1994), 6–7, fig. 1; J. Matthews, "The *Notitia Urbis Constantinopolitanae*", in ed. L. Grig & G. Kelly (eds), *Two Romes: Rome and Constantinople in Late Antiquity* (New York: Oxford University Press, 2012), 90. Kislinger, 2022: 133–136, 133 fig. 1, 137, fig. 2. Mango (1993: 120) estimates a combined width of around 700 m for both harbors.
39 Mango 1993: 120–121.
40 C. Mango & R. Scott, (trans.) *The Chronicle of Theophanes Confessor. Byzantine and Near Eastern History AD 284–813* (Oxford, United Kingdom: Clarendon Press, 1997), 517; P. Magdalino, 2007: 20, 94–95; Magdalino 2013: 14; Kislinger 2022: 134–135.
41 Magdalino 2007: 94.
42 Magdalino 2007: 95–102.
43 Magdalino 2007: 95–99.
44 Mango 1993: 121; Magdalino 2000: 215–216; Magdalino 2007: 20, 23; Byrd, K. (trans.) *Pierre Gilles' Constantinople: A Modern English Translation* (New York: Italica Press 2008, 81–82; D. Heher, D. 2022. "Harbour of Julian- Harbour of Sophia- Kontoskalion", in F. Daim & E. Kislinger (eds), *The Byzantine Harbours of Constantinople* (Mainz: Römisch-Germanischen Zentralmuseums, 2022), 93–94.

45 A. Cameron, "Notes on the Sophiae, the Sophianae, and the Harbour of Sophia", *Byzantion* 37 (1968), 14–16; Mango, 1993: 121; Heher 2022: 95–97.
46 Magdalino 2000: 211–213. P. Magdalino 2007: 21–22, 103–104.
47 W. Müller-Wiener, 1994: 27; Byrd 2008: 83; Heher 2022: 101–106.
48 The Theodosian Harbor is also called the Harbor of Kaisarios by Theophanes after the toponym of a nearby neighborhood. He records that warships were assembled in the harbor in 673 to repel an attacking Arab fleet (See A. Berger, "Der Langa Bostani in Istanbul", *Istanbuler Mitteilungen* 43 (1993), 468–469; Scott & Mango 1997: 493; Külzer 2022: 79–80.
49 Müller-Wiener 1994: 9.
50 A. Ercan, 2010. "Yenikapı, A Late Antique and Byzantine Harbor in Constantinople: A Historical, Archaeological and Architectural Study of the Newly Discovered Remains" (Unpublished MA Thesis, Koç Unıversıty, İstanbul); Ginalis & Ercan-Kydonakis 2022: 33–40. Sections of the sea walls preserved today in the Yenikapı area almost certainly date to the Late Byzantine or early Ottoman period, although it is possible they were constructed on much older foundations. See Mango 2001: 24–28; Berger 1993: 473; Semiz & Ahunbay 2014: 22; Külzer 2022: 80–82.
51 Tsangadas 1980: 53–54, 56–58; Berger 1993: 470–472; I. R. Manners, "Constructing the Image of a City: The Representation of Constantinople in Christopher Buondelmonti's *Liber Insularum Archipelagi*", *Annals of the Association of American Geographers* 87:1 (1997), 72–102; Byrd 2008: 201.
52 A. van Millingen, *Byzantine Constantinople. The Walls of the City and Adjoining Historical Sites* (London: John Murray, 1899), 268; Mango 1993: 121; A. Berger, 1993: 469–471; Gökçay 2007: 166, 175; Pearson et al. 2012: 3404, Fig. 2); Semiz & Ahunbay, 2014: 24.
53 Magdalino 2000: 213; Mango 2000: 193; Magdalino 2007: 23–27.
54 Wilson 2011: 51–54. According to Wickham (2004: 717–719), one consequence of this development is likely less long-distance trade and less integration between different regions of the Mediterranean over time; this in turn would affect maritime technology, resulting in fewer large ships, less reliance on large, deepwater harbors and the artificial harbour construction and maintenance seen under the Romans, and a greater reliance on regional shipping routes for urban provisioning (C. Wickham, *Framing the Early Middle Ages: Europe and the Mediterranean, 400–800* [Oxford: Oxford University Press]).
55 Magdalino 2007, 20; Magdalino 2013, 14; C. Pulak, "Yenikapı Byzantine Shipwrecks", in Z. Kızıltan (ed), *Istanbul: 8,000 Years Brought to Daylight: Marmaray, Metro, Sultanahmet Excavations*, 202–215 (Istanbul: Vehbi Koç Vakfı, 2007), 202–203; D. Perinçek, "Geoarchaeology of the Excavation Site for the Last 8,000 Years and Traces of Natural Catastrophes in the Geologic Profile", in U. Kocabaş (ed), *Istanbul Archaeological Museums Proceedings of the 1st Symposium on Marmaray-Metro Salvage Excavations, 5–6 May 2008*, 191–218 (Istanbul: Istanbul Archaeological Museums/Epsilon, 2010), 210–211, 215–216.
56 Gökçay 2007, 175, 177; P. I. Kuniholm, C. L. Pearson, T. Wazny, & C. B. Griggs, 2015. "Of Harbors and Trees: The Marmaray Contribution to a 2367-Year-Old Oak-Tree Ring Chronology from 97 Sites for the Aegean, East Mediterranean, and Black Sea", in P. Magdalino & N. Ergin (eds), *Istanbul and Water*, Ancient Near Eastern Studies: Supplement 20 (Leuven: Peeters, 2015), 63; Ginalis and Ercan-Kydonakis 2022: 41–42.
57 Kuniholm et al. 2015: 47–48.
58 Pearson et al. 2012: 3403, 3407–3408.
59 Pearson et al. 2012: 3412, T. Wazny, P. I. Kuniholm & C. L. Pearson. 2017. "Dendrochronology of the Early Byzantine Fort at Capidava", in I. C. Opriş & A. Raţiu (eds), *Capidava II: Building C1 – Contributions to the History of Annona Militaris in the 6th Century*, 175–182 (Cluj-Napoca: Mega Publishing House, 2017), 178–180.
60 Kuniholm et al. 2015: 58–79.
61 Yalçin et al. 2019: 366–367.
62 P. Magdalino, "The Grain Supply of Constantinople, Ninth-Twelfth Centuries", in C. Mango & G. Dagron (eds), *Constantinople and Its Hinterland*,35–47 (Aldershot: Ashgate Publishing, Ltd., 1995), 42.
63 Magdalino 1995: 42–43.
64 Magdalino 1995: 45–46.
65 Wickham 2004: 711, 716–717; Wilson 2011: 51–54.
66 Magdalino 1995: 38–47.

67 Hohfelder 1988: 59–60.
68 Magdalino 2002: 531.
69 F. H. van Doorninck, 2002. "The Byzantine Ship at Serçe Limanı: An Example of Small-Scale Maritime Commerce with Fatimid Syria in the Early Eleventh Century", in R. Macrides (ed), *Travel in the Byzantine World*, 137–148 (Ashgate: Society for the Promotion of Byzantine Studies, 2002), 140–141; O. Barkai, Y. Kahanov & M. Avissar, 2010, "The Tantura F Shipwreck: The Ceramic Material", *Levant* 42:1 (2010), 81–101, 99–100.
70 G. Iovino, "Transformazioni del paesaggio costiero e aree protette in una regione del Mediterraneo/Transformation of the coastal landscape and protected areas in a Mediterranean region." *Bollettino della Associazione Italiana di Cartografia* 164 (2018), 83–99.
71 C. Albore Livadie (ed.), *Archeologia a Piano di Sorrento: Ricerche di Preistoria e di Protohistoria nella Penisola Sorrentina: catalogo della mostra* (Comune di Piano di Sorrento: Naples, 1990).
72 Matthew Harpster thanks everyone that has been an invaluable part of this ongoing research program, and has contributed to other studies that form the basis of this essay as well: Athena Trakadas, Elif Denel, Vincenzo Capriglione, Carlotta Lucarini, Marie Meranda, Mattia Morselli, Robyn Pelling, Iain Bennett, Chiara Zazzaro, Özge Demirci, Carlo Donadio, Luigi Ferranti, Corrado Stanislao, Luca Zavagno, and Paolo Pecci.
73 For the preliminary results of these surveys, see M. Harpster, A. Trakadas, E. Denel, V. Capriglione, C. Lucarini, M. Meranda, M. Morselli, R. Pelling, I. Bennett, C. Zazzaro, Ö. Demirci, C. Donadio, L. Ferranti, C. Stanislao, L. Zavagno, & P. Pecci, "Risultati Preliminari della Ricerca sul Paesaggio Marittimo della Costiera Amalfitana", *Rassegna del Centro di Cultura e Storia Amalfitana* 59–60 (2020), 247–264; M. Harpster, A. Trakadas, E. Denel, V. Capriglione, C. Lucarini, M. Meranda, M. Morselli, R. Pelling, I. Bennett, C. Zazzaro, Ö. Demirci, C. Donadio, L. Ferranti, C. Stanislao, L. Zavagno, & P. Pecci, "Modeling the Maritime Cultural Landscape of the Costiera Amalfitana: The First Three Seasons of Research (2016–2018)", *The International Journal of Nautical Archaeology* 50 (2021), 63–75.
74 G. L. Mangieri, "La villa romana di Minori: il dato numismatico", *Apollo, Bollettino del Musei Provinciali del Salernitano* 6 (1988), 169–185.
75 M. Iannelli, "Salerno Centro storico", in A. Campanelli (ed), *Dopo lo Tsunami Salerno Antica* (Arte'm: Naples, 2011); M. Iannelli "Via Mercanti, 70", in A. Campanelli (ed), *Dopo lo Tsunami Salerno Antica* (Arte'm: Naples, 2011).
76 P. Recchia "Il progetto Archeomar", *Notiziario a cura dell'Ufficio Studi, Ministerio dei beni e delle attivita culturali, Instituto Poligrafico e Zecca Dello Stato* 19 (2004), 134–137; Anonymous, *Progretto archeomar. Censimento dei beni archeologici sommersi delle regioni Campania, Basilicata, Calabria e Puglia* (Ministero per I Beni e le Attivita Culturali: Rome, 2006), 9.
77 P. Arthur, "Early Medieval Amphorae, the Dutchy of Naples and the Food Supply of Rome", *Papers of the British School at Rome* 61 (1993), 231–244.
78 Archaeological studies around the Bay of Naples reinforce this presumed continuity by demonstrating the ongoing occupation of certain structures, the continuation of agricultural practices on the slopes of Vesuvius, and continued wine production. See G. Mastrolorenzo, D. Palladino, G. Vecchio, and J. Taddeucci, "The 472 AD Pollena eruption of Somma-Vesuvius (Italy) and Its Environmental Impact at the End of the Roman Empire", *Journal of Volcanology and Geothermal Research* 113 (2002), 22; Y. Inoue, J. Baasansuren, M. Watanabe, H. Kamei and D. Lowe, "Interpretation of pre-AD 479 Roman Soils from Physiochemical and Mineralogical Properties of Buried Tephric Paleosoils at Somma Vesuviana Ruin, Southwest Italy", *Geoderma* 152 (2009), 51; E. Allevato, M. Buonincontri, M. Vairo, A Pecci, M. A. Cau, M. Yoneda, G. F. De Simone, M. Aoyagi, C. Angelelli, S. Matsuyama, K. Takeuchi, and G. Di Pasquale, "Persistence of the Cultural Landscape in Campania (Southern Italy) before the AD 472 Vesuvius Eruption: Archaeoenvironmental Data", *Journal of Archaeological Science* 39 (2012), 405; D. Camardo, G. Irollo & M. Notomista (eds.), *Carta del Potenziale Archeologico e del Patrimonio Edilizio Storico del Commune di Dragano (NA)* (Centro di Cultura e Storia Amalfitana: Amalfi, 2016), sites 9, 35, 44 and 49.
79 For preliminary theories regarding the virtual absence of underwater data, see Harpster et al. (2021).
80 J. P. Migne, *Patrologia Latina. LXXVII. Sancti Gregori Magni registrum Epistolarum* (1849), 3, 6, XXIII.
81 D. Espelo, *A Testimony of Carolingian Rule? The Codex epistolaris Carolinus as a product of its time* (Utrecht University: Utrecht, 2014).

82 W. Wattenbach, E. Dümmler & P. Jaffé (eds), *Monumenta Carolina: Codex Carolinus* and *Leonis epistolae* eds. (1864) Vols. 4: 2, 82, 323.
83 A. O. Citarella, "Patterns in Medieval Trade: The Commerce of Amalfi before the Crusades", *Journal of Economic History* 28 (1968), 536; B. M. Kreutz, "The Ecology of Maritime Success: The Puzzling Case of Amalfi", *Mediterranean Historical Review* 3 (1988), 110.
84 V. von Falkenhausen and D. Kinney, 1991. "Amalfi" in A. P. Kazhdan, A. M. Talbot, A. Cutler, T. E. Gregory, & N. Sevcenko (eds), *The Oxford Dictionary of Byzantium,* Vol. I (Oxford University Press: Oxford, 1991), 73–74. See also M. Balard, "Amalfi et Byzance (Xe – XIIx siècles)", *Travaux et Mémoires. Centre de recherche d'histoire et civilization de Byzance* 6 (1976), 86, who writes of the *spatharokandidatos* Manso Fusilis in the 10th century.
85 F. Engreen, "Pope John the Eighth and the Arabs", *Speculum* 20 (1945), 318–330.
86 P. Arthur, "Naples: A Case of Urban Survival in the Early Middle Ages?", *Mélanges de l'École francaise de Rome, Moyen-Age* 103:2 (1991), 762; B. M. Kreutz, *Before the Normans: Southern Italy in the Ninth and Tenth Centuries* (University of Pennsylvania: Philadelphia, PA, 1996), 80–81.
87 M. Camera, *Memorie storico-diplomatiche dell'antica città e ducato di Amalfi,* Vol. I (Libreria antiquaria: Salerno, 1876), 122.
88 Camera, Memorie, 56; G. Sangermano, *Minori. Rheginna Minor. Storia, arte, cultura* (Centro di Cultura e Storia Amalfitana: Salerno, 1981), 60–61; G. Gargano, *La città davanti al Mare. Aree urbane e storie sommerse di Amalfi nel Medioevo* (1992), 22; G. Gargano, "La Topografia di Atrani Medievale", *Rassegna del Centro di Cultura e Storia Amalfitana* 10 (1995), 110; P. Skinner, *Medieval Amalfi and its diaspora 800–1250* (Cambridge University Press: Cambridge, 2017), 86.
89 M. Oldoni, "Agiografia longobarda fra secolo IX e X. La Leggenda di Santa Trofimena", *Studi Medievali* 3:XII (1971), 583-636; A. Braca, "Indagini sul patrimonio artistico di Minori", *Rassegna del Centro di Cultura e Storia Amalfitana* (1996), 181–182; G. Gargano, "L'abitato e il territorio" *Minori. Rheginna Minor. Storia, Arte e Cultura* (Salerno, 2001), 15–16; P. Skinner, *Medieval Amalfi*, 99–100.
90 G. Gargano, "Arsenale e scaria di Amalfi nel contest del Meridione medievale", in D. Blackman & M. Costanza Letini (eds), *Ricoveri per Nai Militari nei Porti del Mediterraneo Antico e Medievale* (Edipuglia: Bari, 2010), 134.
91 Balard, "Amalfi et Byzance (Xe – XIIx siècles)", 87, 95; R. Bergman "Byzantine Influence and Private Patronage in a Newly Discovered Medieval Church in Amalfi: S. Michele Arcangelo in Pogerola", *Journal of the Society of Architectural Historians* 50 (1991), 430; D. Jacoby "Commercio e Navigazione degli Amalfitani nel Mediterraneo Orientale. Sviluppo e Declino", in B. Figiuolo & P. Simbula (eds), *Interscambi Socio Culturali ed Economici fra le Città Marinare d'Italia e l'Occidentale dagli Osservatori Mediterranei* (Centro di Cultura e Storia Amalfitana: Amalfi, 2014), 91.
92 V. Slessarev, "Ecclesiae Mercatorum and the Rise of Merchant Colonies", *The Business History Review* 41 (1967), 187; P. Magdalino, "The Maritime Neighborhoods of Constantinople: Commercial and Residential Functions, Sixth to Twelfth Centuries", *Dumbarton Oaks Papers* 54 (2001), 209–226; P. Schreiner, "The Western Landing Stages (σκαλαι) in the Golden Horn: Some Remarks Relating to the Eleventh and Twelfth Centuries", in F. Daim & E. Kislinger (eds), *The Byzantine Harbours of Constantinople* (Mainz/Frankfurt: Byzanz zwischen Orient und Okzident, 2022), 151–160.
93 Slessarev, "Ecclesiae Mercatorum", 191.
94 Citarella, "Patterns in Medieval Trade", 546–547; T. Miller, "The Knights of Saint John and the Hospitals of the Latin West", *Speculum* (1978), 709–733. For recent research on the monastery in Jerusalem, see J. Krüger, "Il Muristan. Nuovi Metodi del Progetto di Ricerce in Corso", *Rassegna del Centro di Cultura e Storia Amalfitana* 47/48 (2014), 7–19.
95 Balard, "Amalfi et Byzance (Xe – XIIx siècles)", 88; H. E. J. Cowdrey, "The Mahdia Campaign of 1087", *The English Historical Review* 92 (1977), 1–29.
96 Balard, "Amalfi et Byzance (Xe – XIIx siècles)", 91, 93.
97 A. O. Citarella, "The Relations of Amalfi with the Arab World before the Crusades", *Speculum* 42 (1967), 306.
98 Horden & Purcell 2000, 54–80.
99 D. Abulafia, "The Crown and the Economy under Roger II and His Successors", *Dumbarton Oaks Papers* 37 (1983), 13–14.

17

ALEXANDRIA AFTER ANTIQUITY[1]

A City in Transition

Athanasios Koutoupas

Following its celebrated foundation by Alexander the Great in 331 BC, Alexandria evolved into the second most important urban metropolis of the Mediterranean after Rome, and later Constantinople. Alexander's architect, Deinocrates of Rhodes, laid out the city's plan on the location of the Egyptian town of Rakotis, while Cleomenes was assigned to continue its expansion after the king's departure.

Alexandria flourished under the Ptolemaic dynasty to become a major center of commerce and culture. Even if it ceased to be an imperial capital after the death of the last Ptolemaic queen, Cleopatra VIII, the city maintained its importance as a commercial port and intellectual center until the Arab conquest in 641 AD.[2] The arrival of Arab control is largely understood as a milestone in the city's history signaling its gradual decline over the following centuries. By the end of the seventeenth century, the once great city was described as a small provincial town, only to experience prosperity again during the time of Muhammad Ali in the nineteenth century. This chapter will trace the city's development and presumed decline while identifying aspects of its transformations and transitions, including the city's process of Christianization and its inclusion in the economic and geopolitical reorientation of the Late Roman Empire around the new capital of Constantinople. From 641, the city followed a different path as it came under Arab control and was thus integrated into a different socioeconomic and political sphere. Seen from a broader comparative perspective, Alexandria presents a very interesting example in the study of Mediterranean urbanism at the end of Antiquity and beyond, as its long continuity permits us to consider the history and the transformations of a major urban center whose Byzantine trajectory was never fulfilled.

The Hellenistic and Roman City

It is important to first understand the city's Hellenistic and Roman background. In order to connect Greece with the fertile Nile Valley, Alexandria was meant to take the place of Naukratis as Egypt's main Hellenistic city. There was only one place that such a city could be built on the Egyptian coast: directly across from the island of Faros and west of the "canopic" arm of the Nile. Because of its location, a canal from the Nile might provide

 DOI: 10.4324/9780429203923-21

fresh water. The vast Libyan desert to the west and the Nile Delta to the east provided exceptional defense against possible invaders.

Although Cleomenes was responsible for the continuation of the construction of Alexandria, the Heptastadion (a seven-stage peninsula that connected the land with the island of Faros) and the imposing buildings associated with its history were mainly works of the Ptolemies.[3]

Inheriting the trade of now-devastated Tyre and evolving as the center of the new commerce among Europe, the Eastern Mediterranean, and India, the city grew to less than a generation later than Carthage. In a century, Alexandria had become the largest city globally and for more than a few centuries was second only to Rome. It became the leading Greek city of Egypt, which mainly attracted Greeks from many cities and colonies.[4]

Monumental buildings were erected in Alexandria during the third century BC, the main ones being the Heptastadion, the Mausoleum of Alexander, the Lighthouse, the Museum, the Great Library and the Serapion. The Ptolemies promoted and supported the development of the Library of Alexandria and the associated Museum into a famous center of Hellenistic learning and a pioneering research institute. Famous scholars and researchers associated with the Museum were the geometer and number theorist Euclid, the astronomer Eratosthenes, who also served as a leading librarian, known for calculating the Earth's perimeter and its algorithm. Strabo compared education and research in Alexandria with Tarsus and Athens, also noting that Alexandria also hosted foreign scholars and send its own abroad for further training.[5]

The city officially came under Roman jurisdiction in 80 BC, during the reign of Ptolemy Alexander but was already under Roman influence for more than a hundred years. After the defeat of Marcus Antonius Antonios and Cleopatra VII at the Battle of Actium, Octavian occupied Egypt as the emperor's personal property, appointing a prefect who referred to him personally and not to the Roman Senate.

From the time of annexation onwards, Alexandria seemed to have regained its former prosperity, being the "granary" of Rome. This was one of the main reasons that led Octavian to place it directly under imperial rule. At that time, the city's fortifications walls enclosed an area of 5.34 square km. The total population in Roman times was about 500,000–600,000 inhabitants.[6]

The Jewish-Greek ethnic tensions during the Roman administration led to riots in 38 and 66 AD. Many public buildings were destroyed during the war of Queitus (Tumultus Iudaicus) in 115 AD, allowing Emperor Hadrian and his architect Decriannus to rebuild and renovate many of its older infrastructures.

The Late Antique City

Late antiquity was a period of major socioeconomic and cultural transformations in Alexandria. Although the city is better known for its Hellenistic and Roman past, the archaeological record preserves extensive material from late antique Alexandria pointing to a society in transition.

The city was the second most important urban center of the Mediterranean, following the imperial capitals of Rome and later on, Constantinople. It played a key role being among the few metropolitan centers in the Eastern Mediterranean enjoying long and uninterrupted continuities evident in their economic and cultural life since the Hellenistic period. Even after it ceased to be an imperial capital since the death of the last Queen of the

Ptolemies, Cleopatra VII, Alexandria retained its importance as a commercial harbor and cultural center until its Arab conquest in 641.

Our understanding of late antique Alexandria is largely due to the pioneering work of Mahmoud Bey el-Falaki, whose research work from the nineteenth century allows a comprehensive understanding of the city's ancient layout, which would otherwise have vanished in the rapid growth of modern urbanization. His cartographic efforts to map the city serve as the foundation for later maps as well the archaeological research today, which aims to put together the limited surviving material evidence into a reasonably coherent picture of Alexandria at the time (Figure 17.1).

Perhaps the most eloquent ancient testimony for late antique Alexandria dates from the beginning of this era in the work of Ammianus Marcellinus. He declared Alexandria to be the pinnacle of all cities in its nobility and magnificence.[7] Alexandria seems to have retained its importance as a major metropolis under Roman rule. The city continued to play a decisive role in the late Roman Empire's political life, while philosophical and religious ferment turned Alexandria into a hotbed of intellectual development. From the late third century until the sixth century, Alexandria was one of the main Christian centers of the Roman Empire. Nevertheless, the legacy of the Graeco-Roman period was still visible in the city's topography and monumental environment as well as in various aspects of the city during late antiquity, such as the art, the architecture, the religious, civic, intellectual, and everyday life.

The historical roots of Christianity in Egypt are often linked to Alexandria in the first century. Later tradition identifies St. Mark the Evangelist as the first Bishop of Alexandria attributed him with the introduction of the new religion to the city. It's worth mentioning that the first fully developed account of Egypt's transition to Christianity does not appear until the fourth-century history of Eusebius, Bishop of Caesarea, who tells the story about Mark the Apostle establishing churches in Alexandria and the later episcopal successors to Mark.[8]

The spread of the new religion in Alexandria happened over time. As the number of its followers grew, they were persecuted by the emperors Septimius Severus, Decius, Valerian, and Diocletian. Despite persecutions recorded in sources, the Christian Church was firmly founded by the beginning of the fourth century. The number of pagans and the followers of the new religion were still roughly equal.

The late antique city preserved the grid pattern of its layout and street configuration dating from its Hellenistic foundation. Prominent sites were transformed and appropriated for new uses as they were integrated into the city's evolving urbanscape in the fourth century. The Caesarion, which dominated the waterfront of the Great Harbor, was transformed into the patriarchal cathedral (or Great Church) during the mid-fourth century AD. Likewise, near the Great Harbor, the Ptolemaic Temple of Kronos became the church of St. Michael during 320. The Serapeum, the massive temple of the city's patron deity, was converted into the church of St. John by the patriarch Theophilus in 391.[9]

Alexandria was a major pilgrimage hub throughout late antiquity. One of the sites that was well connected with the rise of Christianity and the development of pilgrimage during the period of late antiquity was the town of St. Menas, located approximately 45 km south-west of Alexandria. St. Menas, who was an Egyptian-born Roman legionary, martyred in Phrygia in Asia Minor in 296 after refusing to renounce Christ. His ashes were brought back from Phrygia by camel and were buried where the animal refused to walk any further.[10] The town developed gradually around the tomb of St. Menas, while the place became known for its miraculous events. St. Menas was traditionally depicted between two camels as in the depictions on the distinctive flasks which pilgrims took home as a token of their sacred visit.[11] The

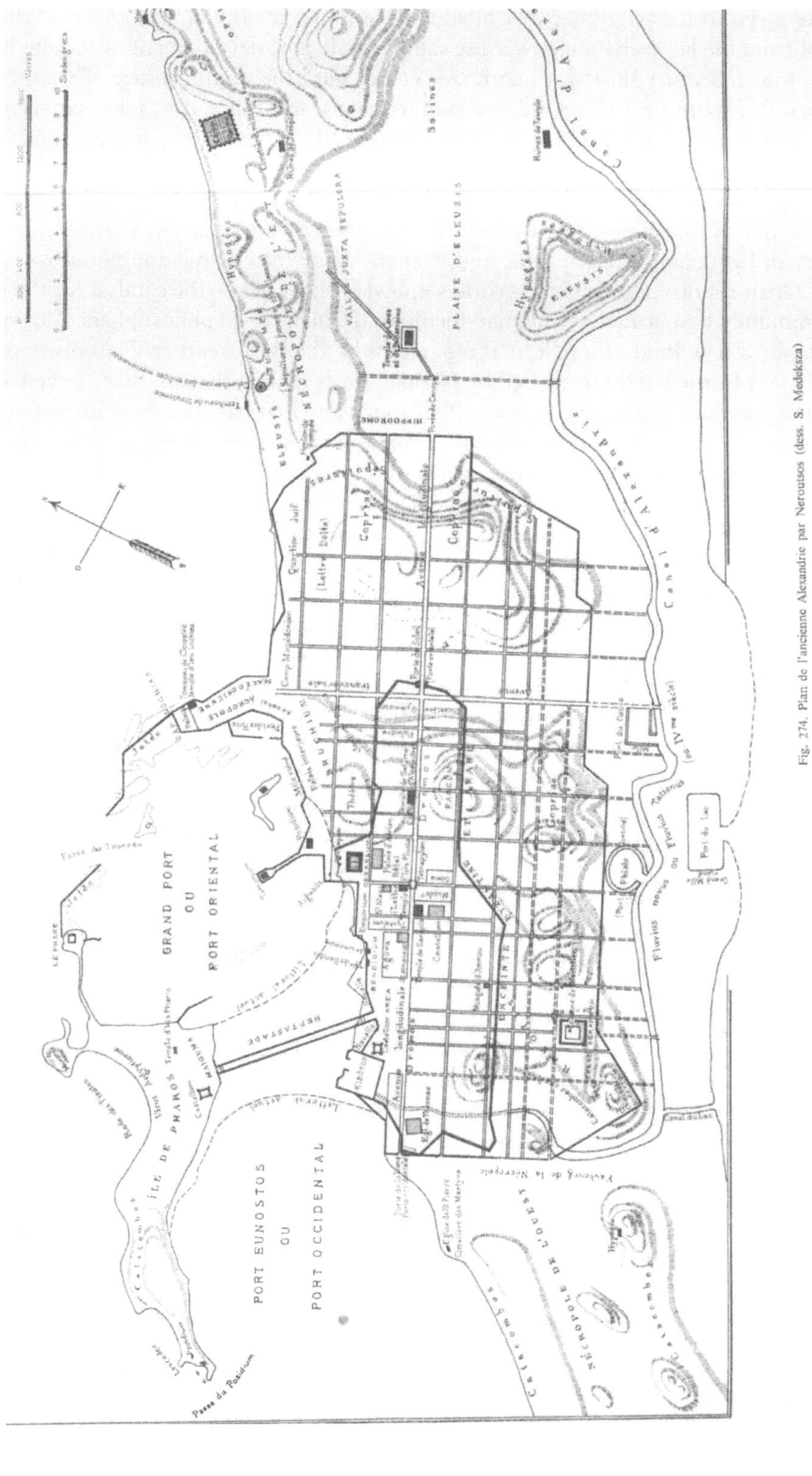

Figure 17.1 The layout of the city, from the late antiquity to the Arab era

flasks were given to the pilgrims either filled with holy water blessed in St. Menas' church, or with oil from the lamps hanging over the saint's tomb. The development of the site began in the late fourth century. It was a pilgrimage center until the ninth century. The extensive archaeological remains provide an indication of its townscape, especially in the sixth century. The main church complex of St. Menas consisted of the Martyr's Church, over the tomb, with the Great Basilica added to its east, and a baptistery at its western end.[12]

Throughout late antiquity, Alexandrian cultural life thrived maintaining the city's status and fame as one of the empire's greatest intellectual and religious centers. The multi-colored community of Egyptians, Greeks, Jews, and Romans made the city religiously diverse, while the legacy Great Library, the center of world's knowledge, would be the catalyst for the intellectual community that attracted Christian theological teachers and philosophers. Alexandria had developed a new kind of intellectual reputation by the third century. Platonism, whose philosophy was learned and interpreted by Neoplatonists and Christians alike, served as the unifying denominator. The city's schools of philosophy and mathematics drew many students to the lectures of Olympius, Theon, Hypatia, Ammonius, Asclepiodotus, and Horapollon. The activity of Christian orators and philosophers, such as Aphthonius, Theodore, and John Philoponus demonstrate that Alexandria's intellectual achievement also spread across communal boundaries. In addition, the successive heads of the Catechetical school – Origen, Pierius, and Didymus the Blind, for example – contributed to the city's rich legacy of patristic exegesis and theology, exemplified by the works of Athanasius and Cyril.[13]

The contours of urban life in late antique Alexandria have become better known through the archaeological work carried out at Kom el-Dikka in the heart of the city (Figure 17.2). A portion of the excavated site consists of an inhabited quarter dated to the fourth through the seventh centuries. The archaeological findings in the area suggest that the Graeco-Roman tradition of the city co-existed with the new social environment rising in Alexandria.

The quarter grew up on either side of a broad colonnaded street that ran in from an elegant Odeon-like structure that seated up to 600 spectators. This Odeon, apart from entertainment, could be used also as bouleuterion (the council house). It has been also suggested that it served also as a lecture theater, since there are many lecture rooms nearby. The consoles and some of the capitals used in the Odeon were decorated with crosses. Twenty lecture rooms (auditoria) have been discovered. The interior of the rooms had stone benches for the students, as well as a central dais for the educator. The presence of the Odeon and the auditoria provides unprecedented archaeological testimony of the city's intellectual life.[14] The imperial baths-building uncovered to the north is also a witness to the co-existence of the different cultural environments of the city during late antiquity. The function of an imperial bath during a period, when the city faces a shift in terms of social behavior and a turn from public expressions to more private, is a testimony of cultural continuity in the city. The biggest part of the quarter was residential. The best preserved residence is the so-called Villa of Birds, named after a mosaic featuring a colorful variety of birds which adorns the floor of one of its rooms.

Fascinating discoveries from Kom el-Dikka, including Christian wall-paintings of the Theotokos and Child, dated to the first half of the sixth century,[15] inscribed crosses, as well as an inscribed monk on a column in front of the theater, serve as clear evidence of the presence of the new religion in an area where a diverse group of students and teachers could meet.[16]

There are over 50 Roman, Byzantine, and Coptic historical and ecclesiastical sources with references to churches in Alexandria. These sources range from the testimony of contemporary Alexandrian church writers, such as Athanasius, to later stories based on earlier

Figure 17.2 Colonnaded street and lecture halls at Kom el Dikka

sources, which have been lost. The present research relies mainly on the works of Eusebius and Epiphanius, the Acts of Mark, and the Syriac Notitia of Michael, Patriarch of Antioch, which provides detailed information on the churches of Alexandria during the first christian centuries.[17] From the churches included in the sources, I will mention those that are mentioned by more than one source, or there are some archaeological evidences to support their existence.

- The Angelion, in honor of Saint John the Baptist in the area of Sarapeion.
- The church of Archangel Michael, in the area of Caesarion.
- The church of Dionysos.
- The Church of Theon, the earliest church for which we have sufficient documentation. After the Arab conquest, it was transformed into the Mosque of a Thousand Columns. In 1798 it was severely damaged by the French and its ruins were destroyed in 1829.
- The church of Mendidion. A church near the temple called either "Mendidion" or "Vendidion". In the fourth century, it was renamed the church of Saint Athanasios. After the Arab conquest, it was turned into the mosque of Souk el-Attarine.
- The church of Alexander, near the Paneion, east of the church of Caesarion.
- The church of Saint Mithras, near the eastern gate, also called the "Gate of the Sun".
- The church of Saint Sophia, where the temple of Isis Faria used to be.

The Christianization of Alexandria's urban space was not accompanied by a fundamental shift in city planning, which might have reoriented public consciousness to new sites such as rural churches and martyrdoms. However, the placement of churches in the strategic locations in the city's topography ensured that the non-Christian inhabitants of the city would constantly engage Christian presence in their daily life. And as if this was not enough, religious processions between these churches and the main streets of the city further enhanced Christian ritual manifestations in the post-Constantine period.

According to John of Nikiu, it was with the support of Constantine that the first conversion of a pagan temple into a church took place in Alexandria; namely when the main imperial temple, the Caesarium, was transformed into a church in honor of Archangel Michael.[18] The conversion of the church not only gave the city's Christians a much-needed larger gathering place but also resulted in the Episcopal Cathedral being moved from the periphery to the center of the city. The transformation of Caesarion even led to the Christianization of an essential part of the city. From that moment, there was a strong declaration of the growing hegemony of the church in the city.

As for the Sarapeion, we have the works of Socrates Scholasticus,[19] Sozomenos,[20] Theodoritos[21] and Rufinus,[22] which describe the events of one of the most important incidents connected with the important changes that Alexandria experienced at that time. Only four months after the publication of his first edict, forbidding pagan worship, in February 391, Theodosius I was obliged to further highlight the prohibition of pagan worship, this time in an edict addressed to the prefect and military commander of Egypt. Encouraged by the imperial edict addressed to the prefect of Rome prohibiting pagan worship,[23] Theophilus, the patriarch of Alexandria, took the cult objects that had been found during the conversion of a pagan temple and contemptuously paraded them in the street, holding them up to ridicule. A riot was provoked and Christians killed. Taking refuge in the Serapeum, the pagans of Alexandria fortified it against attack, forcing Christians who had been captured to sacrifice there and torturing them if they refused.[24] Following this event, the Serapeum was destroyed, and in the site, Theophilus built the martyrdom of Saint John. The conversion of the Sarapeion into a church led to the gradual decline of paganism in Alexandria. Theophilus instituted a building program designed to Christianize the very infrastructure of Alexandria and its surroundings. In this endeavor Theophilus reflected the growing sense in late antique Mediterranean culture that was distinguished a Christian city and what gave a city prestige was its saints, its protectors and axes to heaven.[25]

The image that Alexandria presented during the fifth, sixth, and even the beginning of the seventh century is known to us both from various Byzantine mosaics and from travelers of the time who visited the city. The most important example of a mosaic depicting sixth-century Alexandria with some of its most important churches and buildings is that from the Church of St. John the Baptist in the city of Gerasa, Jordan, which dates to about 531. Another depiction of the city comes from the floor of the nearby Church of the Apostles Peter and Paul with a date between 533 to 540. The mosaic shows colonnaded streets, a staple of urban life in late antique cities, and at least four key Alexandrian buildings, all within the represented fortification walls. The Lighthouse is depicted to the right of the city, having only the first level and part of the second. Unfortunately, the rest of the mosaic has not been preserved. Besides developments in the city's cultural and religious life, it is also significant to highlight that Alexandria had assumed a key maritime role in the grain supply of the new Roman capital of Constantinople with the *Annona Civica* being the backbone of this economic supply system.[26]

The Pharos, the Nilometer (which existed in the Sarapeion and was moved by patriarch Theophilos after the destruction of the temple at 391), and the city itself are also depicted in other mosaics. The Lighthouse is found in a mosaic of 539–540 from the Eastern Church in the city of Theodorias (today's Qasr Libya) in the area of Cyrenaica. In the mosaic, to the right of the Lighthouse, the walls of Alexandria are depicted. In a residence in Diocaesarea (today's Sepphoris) dating from the fifth to the sixth century we find a mosaic depicting Alexandria with a simplicity.

Visitors to the city provide first-hand information about Alexandria in the second half of the sixth and early seventh centuries. These accounts include Agathias, who studied law there and described the severe earthquake of 554 in the "great metropolis of Alexandria", although it was less destructive than in some other areas. The pilgrim of Piacenza in 570 observes: "Alexandria is a well-known city ... full of heresies. Saint Athanasios is buried there and also Saint Faustas, Saints Epimachus, Saint Antonios, Saint Markos and many other saints". An impression of the city in the years before the Persian invasion in 619 was given by John Moschus and Sophronius of Jerusalem, who visited Alexandria, while Saint John the Merciful was patriarch.[27]

An indication of the defensive walls of the city is given by John of Nikiu. His description shows that although the entire area occupied by the city in previous centuries was uninhabited, the city still had two sets of defensive walls on its eastern side. Today only a section of the walls survives to the north of the Shallalat Gardens (Figure 17.3).[28]

Figure 17.3 Section of the walls survives to the north of the Shallalat Gardens

The Arab Conquest and Its Aftermath

The conquest of Egypt by the Arabs under Amr ibn al-As (c. 573–663) began in 641 and was gradually completed by 646. At this time, Alexandria was still one of the major urban centers of the Mediterranean as exemplified by an inventory attributed to the commander Amr ibn al-As who entered the city and reported to Caliph Umar ibn al-Khattab (581–644) that he found "4000 palaces, 4000 baths, 12,000 oil merchants, 12,000 gardeners, 40,000 Jews and 400 theatres and places for entertainment".[29]

During this major geopolitical transition, Alexandria retained its strategic geographical position. The harbor, position, and proximity to other significant Mediterranean ports were still among its natural assets, just as they were when the city was first founded in the particular site in 332 BC. The emergence of Fustat, however, and the new, centralized administration and organizational schemes of the Arabs had a direct impact on the prosperity of the great Mediterranean port-city. Since its foundation, Alexandria had always been a capital city whether the center of a cosmopolitan Mediterranean empire, a region, or, at the very least, the hub of an administrative entity of a province, namely Egypt. Upon its Arab conquest, the capital of Egypt was established in Fustat - Cairo. This momentous change in the location of political and military authority in Egypt and the expansion of Arab power and rule shaped Alexandria's fate and trajectory away from developments in the Byzantine sphere of influence and control.[30] Yet, it's less known history after antiquity provides a useful case study and comparison to Byzantine examples.[31]

Similar claims can be made concerning its contribution to Mediterranean trade, which, while not entirely disappearing as Henri Pirenne argued in his renowned thesis, did undoubtedly undergo a phase of contraction in the seventh and eighth centuries.[32] Following the Arab conquests, Alexandria's role was altered and to a certain extent decreased, although this was not unique to Alexandria alone; most pre-Islamic coastal towns in the Eastern and Southern Mediterranean experienced the same fate. No significant political or administrative center was situated on a coastline throughout the Middle Ages, according to research on the dispersion of urban centers in the region. Furthermore, despite the fact that there were a large number of economically and commercially significant Islamic coastal cities, the main hubs of commerce and economic activity were generally situated at some distance inland. Antioch and Caesarea gave way to Damascus and Ramleh on the Mediterranean coast that came under Islamic rule in the seventh and eighth centuries; Alexandria yielded to Fustat-Cairo, and Carthage to Qairawan.[33]

The Hellenistic city's canonical orthogonal grid plan and layout were preserved in medieval Alexandria.[34] The city continued to have long, straight and broad avenues which was noticed by foreign travelers noting this peculiar appearance and wrote about it in their travelogues. Benjamin of Tudela, who visited Alexandria in the sixth/twelfth century, noted that "the streets are wide and straight, so that a man can look along them for a mile from gate to gate, from the Rashid Gate to the Sea Gate".[35] The colossal stone buildings, still preserved from ancient times, gave the city a primeval splendour, which left an unforgettable impression on its medieval visitors.[36]

The inner division of the city is difficult to reconstruct. Geniza documents refer to terms such as na¯hiyya, ha¯ra, zuqa¯q, and khutt, but there is hardly a way to determine their precise location.[37]

The city substantially shrunk during the Middle Ages as the medieval wall barely encircled about half of Alexandria's urban space during the Hellenistic and Roman eras.[38] Kom el-Dikka which was once the center of the old city was now located at the south-western corner of the medieval city thus offering a clear indication of the smaller perimeter of the medieval city. After the Muslim conquest, the area was used as a cemetery until the end of the Fatimid era and then as a landfill under the Ayyubids. Pointing to the shrinking boundaries of the inhabited space, the mere presence of graves in this historically central space and its later conversion into trash dumps shows that it had become a peripheral zone of the medieval city.[39]

During that period the city's enclosure had four gates[40]:

- Bab al-Sidra, to the south, was the city's main entrance by land.
- Bab Rashıd, on the eastern side of the Alexandrian wall, was the passage towards Rashid and Fuwwa.
- Bab al-Bahr (the sea gate), to the north, led to the port.
- Al-Babal-Akhdar (the green gate) led to the city's big cemeteries and was open only on Fridays.

The city was still split along ethnic lines at the end of the eleventh century. Immigrants were grouped together in various other locations based on their nationality. Towards the end of the eleventh century such spatial distinctions seem to have been completely muddled as attested in the limited available sources on the period. For example, a Jewish woman who resided in an Arab district received a family letter which offers valuable testimony to these developments. The letter mentions that residence was located close to the Babylonian synagogue with another remark in Arabic letters emphasizing "the 'church' of the Jews," perhaps a clarification effort for the Muslim letter-bearer, which may also point to the existence of other Christian churches in the same neighborhood.[41] Based on the above, we can posit that, although the Jewish quarter of Alexandria was often mentioned in Geniza documents,[42] it was actually a multi-ethnic quarter, which had retained this name since antiquity.

In discussing the status of Alexandria under the Arabs, Goitein has written that "the unmistakable testimony of hundreds of Geniza letters proves that Fustat, the inland city, was also the commercial and financial capital of the country on which Alexandria, the originally Greek maritime town, was economically dependent in every respect".[43] This extensive communication suggests that Alexandria was largely rural, with the exception of its significant port facilities. Fustat was Alexandria's go-to source for administrative and technical issues pertaining to commerce and exchange.

Egypt's financial and economic hub was Fustat. It was the main location for purchasing foreign currency, especially from nations with which Alexandria maintained marine relations. Alexandrians were forced to send currencies in their possession to Fustat in order to exchange them for coins that were recognised as legal money in Egypt. A paragraph from a letter sent from Alexandria to Fustat in or around 1050 provides an instructive example: "I sent you two purses containing 205 Nizariyya dinars, coined in al-Mahdiyya. Kindly work to exchange them into local tender and hold the money thus obtained until my arrival".[44]

Although some banking and exchange activity must have certainly occurred in medieval Alexandria's marketplace and port, yet the above mentioned testimony and many others like it[45] found in business letters sent from Alexandria, make it abundantly clear that the center of banking activities and financial transactions relating to international commerce concentrated in Fustat rather than in Alexandria.

The organization and circulation of key commodities (textiles, luxury goods and spices) supplying international trade were also regulated through Fustat, which served as the region's entrance and emporium. There, goods from all over the world were gathered, kept, and then delivered to various destinations. Its markets were wealthy, well-stocked, and international. In comparison, Alexandria's markets had a far smaller selection of goods and were significantly less well-stocked. Even supplies from Mediterranean regions that were imported through Alexandria had to be procured through Fustat when Alexandria ran out of them.[46]

Alexandria served as a point of arrival and departure for persons and goods involved in Mediterranean trade, but it was hardly a hub of exchange and distribution. Additionally, compared to Fustat, its marketplaces had significantly less in stock of the main goods from long-distance marine trade in stock.[47] Beyond the basic commodities of Mediterranean trade, the Alexandrian markets offered a limited selection of goods with limited availability. Alexandrians frequently purchased everyday items from the bazaars of Fustat, including shoes, specific types of clothes, parchment, ink, and tools of various kinds. Evidently, the Fustat market was better than what was available in Alexandria. A common pattern in many Genizah letters is a negative perception and experience of Alexandrian markets: "Nothing is worthwhile buying here".[48] This phrase often prefaces requests to friends in Fustat to send various supplies to Alexandria. In a letter from about 1060, Ibrahim b. Farah, the representative of the merchants in Alexandria, ordered two ounces of ink to be bought in Fustat "from the Persian at the gate of the mosque".[49]

It seems that Alexandrian merchants did not have a big inventory of products on hand. One Genizah letter claims that the community was devoid of any nice attire during a Muslim holiday because everything had been consumed.[50] In effect, compared to Fustat, Alexandria was a location of transit. People from other countries only stayed for a brief time to conduct business before departing. Foreign traders frequently stayed in Fustat for a significant portion of the trading season and occasionally throughout the entire winter. The Genizah documents occasionally mention rowdiness, drunkenness, and other similar activities, which suggest that the foreign presence in eleventh- and twelfth-century Alexandria was consistent with transit and the daily activities of a port-town. The general populace of Alexandria including its Jewish community appear to experience turmoil and disorder on a regular basis.[51]

It is particularly interesting to consider the impact of the Arab conquest in 641 on the Christian Church which was already facing significant challenges. Upon their arrival, the Arabs found two distinct Churches, the Chalcedonian and the anti-Chalcedonian. Both were named in relation to the Council of Chalcedon, where their schism had been finalized two centuries earlier. Upon the Arabs arrival, both churches had leaders in Alexandria who were in charge of two parallel networks of bishop sees. However, in the eighth century, the anti-Chalcedonian patriarch moved his seat to Fustat, though the process was not officially completed until the 1130s.[52] In 641, the Chalcedonian Church had been already actively supported by the imperial power structure of Constantinople for over a century, often pushing the non-Chalcedonian hierarchy to flee city centers and retreat to monasteries from which they controlled their parishes.[53] The geopolitical break of Alexandria with Constantinople caused by the Arab conquest eventually reduced the Chalcedonian Church's position. Reflecting the lingering animosity between the two Churches it is interesting to note that in the first decades after the conquest, the anti-Chalcedonian Church focused much of their polemics on their fellow Christians, the Chalcedonians, rather than Islam.[54] Of course,

Arab rule provided anti-Chalcedonias with a break from the oppression of the Chalcedonians who were supported by Constantinnople. As a result of the Arab conquest and the disputes between the two churches, the Chalcedonian patriarchate remained vacant from after the conquest until 727, and moved to Cairo under the Fatimids, while from the thirteenth century onward the patriarchs frequently resided in Constantinople, though never entirely losing touch with their reduced flock.[55] It is also important to note that at this period the division between the two Churches also took an ethnic dimension. The anti-Chalcedonian authors came to identify their church as the"native one" or, the Coptic Church, while the Chalcedonian Church became known as the "church of the foreigners".[56]

However, despite the differences Christians had, the Arabs generally allowed in Egypt Christians of all denominations to worship freely in Egypt as long as they followed the country's laws and paid their taxes. Westerners were frequently perplexed by Eastern Christian cults whose languages they were unfamiliar with. The Copts, also known as Jacobites, were referred to as "Christians of the Girdle" at times. They were also members of the Nestorian, Maronite, Syrian, and Ethiopian churches, as well as Greek Orthodox Christians. There were also many "renegade Christians" in Egypt at the period, meaning Europeans who had renounced the Latin faith and who, in certain circumstances, held high positions in the sultan's court and had Muslim families.[57]

The transformation of Alexandria under Arab rule was also affected by the related shift in its role along established maritime routes of economic as well as cultural flows of exchange and communication. Upon the arrival of the Arabs the city lost its key position in the momentous system of the *Annona Civica* which supplied the population of Constantinople with grain. Yet, it gained a role in the increasingly important pilgrimage routes to Mecca but also to the Holy Land. From the first decades of the Umayyad Caliphate Alexandria became one of the most important stops for pilgrims to Mecca from Morocco and Arab-controlled Andalusia. In the following centuries, the increasingly strong presence of Venice in the Eastern Mediterranean helped the city become a key point of transit for European pilgrims. Venice had actually arranged an efficient and profitable travel service for pilgrims visiting the Holy Land or taking extended tours of holy sites in Egypt, routes that evolved into staple pilgrimage experiences during and in the aftermath of the Crusades.[58] In this context, it is important to note that Alexandria retained an active religious and intellectual life as it attracted well-known sheikhs, such as Abu al-Abbas al-Mursi (1219–1287) and Abu al-Hasan al-Shadhili (1196–1258), founders of notable Sufi schools.[59]

Under the Mamluk Sultanate the city provided appropriate amenities for European merchants and visitors. In the fifteenth century, increasing concerns about the Ottomans led to efforts to strengthen the city's defense and of course secure control of its strategic coastal location. The construction of the famed citadel of Mamluk ruler Qait Bey, which survives to the present, at the eastern side of the northern tip of Pharos island at the mouth of the eastern harbor provides an iconic example of efforts to protect Alexandria.[60]

Following the conquest of Egypt by the Ottomans in 1517 and during the first three centuries under their control, Alexandria declined further into a fishing town with a few thousand residents.[61] During the early Ottoman period, the people of the walled medieval city had mostly abandoned it in favor of the area adjacent to the harbor along the peninsula's neck. Building activity was thus limited, both regarding religious and secular structures, responding to the needs of its shrinking population. When Napoleon's expedition landed in Alexandria in 1798, they found a stagnating Ottoman port town whose connection to the rest of Egypt was maintained by sea via Rosetta.[62]

The arrival of the French is a milestone in the history of Egypt as well as for the city of Alexandria. It marks the end of a long period of relative obscurity, which in effect summarizes the trajectory of the ancient metropolis into an obscure port town. The city's fate changed after the Ottoman Sultan Selim III selected the ambitious Turkish-Albanian Pasha Mohamed Ali to become his viceroy in Egypt following the French withdrawal after their brief occupation at the turn of the eighteenth century. Mohamed Ali, who ruled Egypt from 1805 to 1849, progressively consolidated his control over Egypt, establishing his own governing dynasty that lasted until the mid-twentieth century. Ali is credited with the refortification, development, and modernization of Alexandria. As viceroy, he commissioned the construction of the Mahmudiyya canal (completed in 1820), which, despite setbacks and a high human toll, provided the city with an ample and continuous supply of fresh water and connected it to the Nile valley.[63] In the context of rapidly growing commerce networks across the Mediterranean, Mohamed Ali developed the city's port as a transit hub from which Egyptian cotton was exported, as well as commissioning a train connection to Cairo and the inland. He was able to reinvent Alexandria's position in modern European economic life in the early nineteenth century. While never a formal colony of France or Great Britain like Algeria or India, Egypt was subject to a quasi-colonial administration, where legal justifications for the occupation demanded the retention of Ottoman institutions and shaped administration practices.[64] The growth of modern Alexandria is inextricably linked to the interests of European powers in Egypt. As Reimer writes: "The city's history [...] dynamically illustrates the complexities and ambiguities of the country's modern orientation toward the West. Alexandria was [...] both a bridgehead of European colonialism and a crucible of Egyptian national integration and identity".[65]

The momentous changes and growth brought to the city by Mohamed Ali's efforts to reposition Alexandria as a cosmopolitan urban center at the nexus of Mediterranean commerce, effectively ended a long cycle of decline and missed opportunities. After the Arab conquest, the city was deprived of its vital economic role and strategic position in the networks of the broader Mediterranean. As Fustat became the political, economic, and cultural center of Egypt, Alexandria faded into the background, following a path that is not dissimilar to the fate of numerous Byzantine and Medieval cities whose decline and changing direction was caused by the end of the ancient economic and political systems that sustained them for centuries. Of course, the city found new socioeconomic roles, functions and geopolitical orientation, this time in the context of Arab and then Ottoman rule. The study of these developments in the context of Alexandria's urbanism provides instructive comparative evidence to the historical trajectory of a Byzantine city that never was.

Notes

1 I want to thank Prof. Luca Zavagno and Prof. Nikolas Bakirtzis their invitation to participate in this volume, as well as, for all their advice in the writing of my essay. I would also like to express my appreciation to Prof. Ioli Kalavrezou, Prof. Mona Hagga, and Dr. Kyriakos Savvopoulos for the valuable comments and suggestions.

2 Bowman, A., *Egypt after the Pharaohs,* (1986), p. 204.

3 Bowersock, G. W., "Late Antique Alexandria", in K. Hamma (ed.), *Alexandria and Alexandrianism* (1996), pp. 263–272.

4 Scheidel, W., "Creating a Metropolis: A Comparative Demographic Perspective", in *Ancient Alexandria between Egypt and Greece* (2004), pp. 1–31.

5 Polyzoides, A. J., *Alexandria: City of Gifts and Sorrows: From Hellenistic Civilization to Multiethnic Metropolis* (2014).
6 Delia, D., *The Population of Roman Alexandria* (Transactions of the American Philological Association (1974-) 118, (1988), pp. 275–292.
7 Amm. Marc. 22.16.7.
8 Eusebius Hist. Eccl. 2.16.
9 Martin, A., "Alexandria a l'epoque romaine tardive: l'impact du christianisme sur la topographie et les institutions", in C. Decobert (ed.), *Alexandrie Medievale* 1 (1998), pp. 9–21; About Temple of Kronos transformation see John of Nikiu Eccl. Hist. 7.13. About Serapeum's transformation see Sozomen Eccl. Hist. 7.15.3–7.15.10.
10 Krause, M., "Menas the Miracle Worker, Saint", in A. S. Atiya (ed.), *The Coptic Encyclopedia* vol.5 (1991).
11 Kiss, Z., *Les ampoules de saint Menas découvertes à Kôm el- Dikka (1961–1981)* (1989), pp. 14–18.
12 Grossman, P., *Abu Mina I. Die Gruftkirche und die Gruft, 1989; Grossman, P., Abu Mina II. Das Baptisterium* (2004).
13 Haas, C., *Alexandria in Late Antiquity: Topography and Social Conflict* (1997); Watts, E., *Riot in Alexandria* (2010).
14 Majcherek, G., "The Auditoria on Kom el-Dikka: A Glimpse of Late Antique Education in Alexandria", in E. T. Gagos (ed.), *Proceedings of the Twenty-Fifth International Congress of Papyrology* (2010), pp. 471–484.
15 McKenzie, J., *The architecture of Alexandria and Egypt, c. 300 B.C. to A.D. 700* (2007), no. 406, p. 238.
16 Haas, C., *Alexandria in Late Antiquity: Topography and Social Conflict* (1997).
17 About the churches of Alexandria see H. Leqlerq, "Alexandrie (Archeologie)", in F. Cabrol (ed.), *Dictionnaire d'archeologie chretienne et de liturgie* (1907), pp. 1.1098–1.1182, esp. 1107–1125; Calderini, A., *Dizionario dei nomi geografici e topografici dell'Egitto greco-romano, vol. 1* (1935); Adriani, A., *Repertorio d'arte dell'Egitto Greco-Romano, series C* (1966).
18 John of Nikiu, Chronicle 84. 87–103.
19 S. Scholasticus, *The Ecclesiastical History of Socrates Scholasticus: Comprising a history of the church from AD 323 to AD 425*, A.C. Zenos (transl), (1891).
20 Sozomen, Church History (trans. C. D. Hartranft), in P. Schaff and H. Wace (eds.), *Nicene and Post-Nicene Fathers: Second Series*, vol. 2, (1890).
21 Theodoret, Church History (trans. B. Jackson), in P.S chaff and H. Wace (eds.), *Nicene and Post-Nicene Fathers: Second Series*, vol. 3, (1892).
22 Rufinus, Church History (trans. P. R. Amidon) (1997).
23 Codex Theodosius XVI.10.10.
24 Rufinus Eccl. Hist. XI.23.
25 Frankfurter, D., "Urban Shrine and Rural Saint in fith-century Alexandria", in J. Elsner et al. (eds.), *Pilgrimage in Graeco-Roman & Early Christian Antiquity* (2005), pp. 437-438.
26 For the 'Annona Civica' during the byzantine period see Segre, A., "Essays on Byzantine Economic History, I. The Annova Civica and the Anna Militaris," *Byzantion* 16 (1942-1943), pp. 393-444.
27 McKenzie, J., *The architecture of Alexandria and Egypt, c. 300 B.C. to A.D. 700* (2007), p. 253.
28 McKenzie, J., *The architecture of Alexandria and Egypt, c. 300 B.C. to A.D. 700* (2007), p. 254.
29 Haag, M., *An Alexandria Anthology: Travel Writing through the Centuries* (2014), p. 17.
30 It is also important to note that the Arab conquest of Alexandria, affected, as it was expected, the free-trade relationship between Constantinople and Alexandria, and especially the import of grains from the last (*Annona Civica*). For the 'Annona Civica' during the byzantine period see Segre, A., "Essays on Byzantine Economic History, I. The Annova Civica and the Anna Militaris," *Byzantion* 16 (1942-1943), pp. 393-444.
31 Such examples are, among others, cities like Antioch (see De Giorgi, U. & Asa Eger, A., *Antioch, A History* (2021), Carthage (see Bockmann, R., "Late Byzantine and Early Islamic Carthage and the Transition of Power to Tunis and Kairouan", in *Africa – Ifrīqyia. Continuity and Change in North Africa from the Byzantine to the Early Islamic Age. Papers of a Conference held in Rome, Museo Nazionale Romano – Terme di Diocleziano, 28 February – 2 March 2013* (2019), pp. 77-89) and Jerusalem (see Avni, G., *The Byzantine-Islamic Transition in Palestine* (2014). In general for the

changes the Byzantine cities went after their Arab conquest see Zavagno, L., *The Byzantine City from Heraclitus to the Fourth Crusade, 610-1204* (2021).

32 Pirenne, H., *Mohammed and Charlemagne* (1958).

33 Goitein, S. D., “Cairo: An Islamic City in the Light of the Geniza Documents”, in I. M. Lapidus (ed.), *Middle Eastern Cities* (1969), pp. 6–10; Udovitch, A. L., “A Tale of Two Cities”, in H. A. Miskimin, David Herlihy, Abraham L. Udovitch (eds.), *The Medieval City* (1977), pp. 144–148.

34 The Christian-Muslim transformation of the city did not alter significant its existing components. The same appears also in other byzantine cities which share similar path with Alexandria. Such a case is Jerusalem, see Avni, G., “Between wars and peace: Some archaeological and historiographical aspects to studying urban transformations in Jerusalem”, in E. K. Fowden et al. (eds.), Cities as Palimpsests? (2022), pp. 37-43.

35 *The Itinerary of Benjamin of Tudela*, ed. and trans. M. N. Adler (1907), p. 104.

36 Muhammad Ibn Jubayr, Rihlat Ibn Jubayr (1964), p. 14; Abu¯ ʿAbdalla¯h al-ʿAbdar¯ı, Rihlat al-ʿAbdari¯ al-musamma¯ al-rihla al-maghribiyya (1968), p. 90.

37 Goitein, S. D., *A Mediterranean Society: The Jewish Communities of the Arab World as Portrayed in the Documents of the Cairo Geniza*, volumes I–V (1967–1988), IV: 13.

38 M. Rodziewicz, “Le debat sur la topographie de la ville antique”, *Révue de l’Occident Musulman et de la Méditerrannée* 46 (1987), pp. 38–48. For Alexandria’s wall during the Islamic era see Husam al-Dın Ismaıl, M., “The˙ Fortification of Alexandria during the Islamic Period,” in N. Swelim (ed.), *Alexandrian Studies in Memoriam Daoud Abdu Daoud* (1993), pp. 153-161.

39 François, V. “Les céramiques médievales d’Alexandrie: un témoinage archéologique dʿimportance”, in *Alexandrie médiévale*, I (1999), pp. 57–64.

40 Melton, E., *Eduward Meltons, Engelsch Edelmans, Zeldzaame en Gedenkwaardige Zee-en Land-Reizen ; door Egypten, West-Indien, Perzien, Turkyen, Oost-Indien* (1681), pp. 62-68; P. Kahle, “Die Katastrophe des Mittelalterichen Alexandria”, in *Mélange Maspero III: Orient Islamique* (1940), pp. 137–154; Charles-Dominique, P., *Voyageurs arabes, Ibn Fadlan, Ibn Jubayr, Ibn Battuta et un auteur anonyme* (1995).

41 ENA 154 (2588); A bill of repudiation from the thirteenth century, given by the Jewish court of Alexandria, refers to a house in the same quarter owned by a Jew, which bordered the house of a Christian priest. The bill frees the house owner from the obligation to grant his neighbors preemptive rights, which suggests that he intended to sell it to non-Jews (TS AS 150.1).

42 TS 12.254; ENA 2738.6.

43 Goitein, S.D., *A Mediterranean Society*, p. 7.

44 MS. Heb. d68, fol. 108,1. 11; Goitein, S. D., *A Mediterranean Society*, p. 234.

45 T.S. 8J18, fol. 27,11. 5–10; Goitein, S. D., *A Mediterranean Society*, p. 238.

46 T.S. 12, fol. 369V, 11. 9–16; Goitein, S. D., *A Mediterranean Society*, p. 44.

47 Palm fiber reference is to T.S. 10J16, fol. 2,1. 18.

48 ENA 1822, fol. 47,1.23. This letter, dating from the latter half of the eleventh century, was sent from Alexandria to Fustat in midwinter. Goitein, S. D., *Letters of Medieval Jewish Traders* (1973), p. 244.

49 Goitein, S. D., *A Mediterranean Society*, p. 349, n. 22; T.S. 13J17, fol. 15V, 11. 8–9.

50 Goitein, S. D., *A Mediterranean Society*, p. 195.

51 Goitein, S. D., *A Mediterranean Society*, vol. 1, p. 17.

52 den Heijer, J., Le patriarcat copte d’Alexandrie à l’époque fatimide, in C. Décobert (ed.), *Alexandrie médiévale* 2 (2002), pp. 84-87; Mikhail, M. S. A., *From Byzantine to Islamic Egypt: Religion, Identity and Politics after the Arab Conquest* (2016), pp. 204-213.

53 See Wipszycka, E., “The Institutional Church”, in R. S. Bagnall (ed.), *Egypt in the Byzantine World, 450–700* (2007), pp. 331–349.

54 Evetts, B. (ed. and transl.), “History of the Patriarchs of the Coptic Church of Alexandria, III, Agathon to Michael I (766)”, in *Patrologia Orientalis* vol. V (1910), pp. 5-6; 13-14.

55 Παπαδόπουλος, Χ., Ἱστορία τῆς Ἐκκλησίας Ἀλεξανδρείας (62-1934) (1935), pp. 502-789; Christides, V., “The decline of the Melkite Church in Islamic Egypt and its revival by Patriarch Cosmas I (ca 727-768)”, *Pharos journal of theology* 98 (2017).

56 Papaconstantinou, A., “Historiography, Hagiography, and the Making of the Coptic ‘Church of the Martyrs’ in Early Islamic Egypt”, *Dumbarton Oaks Papers* 60 (2006), pp. 65–86.

57 Wolff, A., "Merchants, Pilgrims, Naturalists: Alexandria through European Eyes from the Fourteenth to the Sixteenth Century", in A. Hirst and M. Silk (eds.), *Alexandria, Real and Imagined* (2004), p. 204.
58 Wolff, A., "Merchants, Pilgrims, Naturalists," p. 204; Jacoby, D., "Ports of Pilgrimage to the Holy Land, Eleventh-Fourteenth Century: Jaffa, Acre, Alexandria," in M. Baci et al. (eds.), The Holy Portolano. The Sacred Geography of Navigation in the Middle Ages (2014), pp. 66-71.
59 Wolff, A., "Merchants, Pilgrims, Naturalists," p. 204; Koutoupas, A., "Rebirth of a Cosmopolis: Migration and the Nineteenth-Century Renaissance of Alexandria", in. S. Irakleous et al., (eds.), *Cultural Exchanges in the Eastern Mediterranean* (2022), pp. 7-8.
60 Pradines, S., "The Mamluk Fortifications of Egypt", *Mamluk Studies Review* XIX (2016), pp. 65-67.
61 Reimer, M. J., "Ottoman Alexandria: The Paradox of Decline and the Reconfiguration of Power in Eighteenth-Century Arab Provinces," *Journal of the Economic and Social History of the Orient* 37: 2 (1994), pp. 107–146.
62 Mitchell, T., *Colonising Egypt* (1988); Reimer, M. J., *Colonial Bridgehead: Government and Society in Alexandria 1807–1882* (1998), p. 36.
63 Fahmy, K., "Towards a Social History of Modern Alexandria", in A. Hirst & M. Silk (eds.), *Alexandria, Real and Imagined* (2004), pp. 283–284.
64 Cole, J. R., *Colonialism and Revolution in the Middle East: Social and Cultural Origins of Egypt's Urabi Movement* (1993), p. 3.
65 Reimer, M. J., *Colonial Bridgehead: Government and Society in Alexandria 1807–1882*, p. 3.

PART IV

Daily Life, Visual and Material Culture

18
THE ARTS AND THE BYZANTINE CITY

Ioli Kalavrezou

In this chapter, I would like to address the question of what possibly the Byzantines saw as art in their urban environment and how we consider what art was for them in their surroundings.

What constitutes art, τέχνη, *ars* in a society is a most complex and often a very personal concept or better said a social definition. Over the centuries and in different societies, art was diversely perceived and has had a variety of definitions. We can observe over the centuries how collections in museums have been formed and what was chosen to be considered an "art" object to be included. Many objects today in museums were in previous generations not accepted or not recognised as works of art.

In my discussion of the role, experience and even production of art in the Byzantine city, I will take a broad view of what can be recognised as art. Specifically in the urban environment, we think most often of architectural structures, of colonnaded streets with sculptural capitals, of decorated public buildings with possible exterior paintings or of monuments and statues that honor or commemorate an event or person. In the Late Antique period, it is important to point out that works of art from the past were prized and sought after. Although we hear of the destruction of many pagan temples during the Late Antique Christianization of society, we also have voices that express the importance of saving the artistic decoration of such structures.[1]

A clear and most famous case is Constantine's move to enhance his new capital. He removed a great number of antique statuary from the principal cities and other sites of the ancient world and had them brought to Constantinople. He chose to bring the most illustrious ones, statues as, for example, that of the bronze statue of Athena possibly from Lindos erected in front of the Senate house together with the statue of Zeus from Dodona. Others like the bronze tripods from Delphi as well as the statues of the Dioscuri were erected in the Hippodrome. In the Senate house, Constantine set up also statues of the Muses taken from Mt. Helicon. Among other famous works of art that embellished the Senate house was, according to Constantine Rhodius, a bronze door depicting the Gigantomachia in relief brought from the Temple of Artemis at Ephesus.[2] Some references are made to the original place from where these monuments and statues were moved from, as for example the horses now on San Marco's facade, which were originally brought from the island of

DOI: 10.4324/9780429203923-23

Chios, or the works of art removed from the temple of Ephesus. But for most of the monuments, we do have specific information.

The city was filled with statues mainly of bronze, probably over 300 can be estimated to exist across Constantinople.[3] Constantine's decision to assemble famous works of art from the past is evidence that a city, especially a capital, demanded the presence of monuments that provided an aesthetic experience to those who lived within. Constantine's embellishing the city should in addition be seen as a political move toward a self-presentation, which he sealed with the porphyry column in his own Forum topped with a bronze statue of Apollo-Helios as himself.

Therefore, public spaces were considered spaces that were to provide an environment of some aesthetic experience in the Byzantine urban life. This should not be considered unusual or special. Constantine's concern was to create an urban environment in his capital very much in the Greco-Roman tradition.[4] He gave priority to urban facilities, like public monuments and ceremonial places over the establishment of churches. This was made apparent also through the physical presence of the assemblage of historical statuary from the classical, Hellenistic and Roman past as was practiced in embellishing a city. This practice seems to have continued during the Theodosian period up to the Justinianic age. In this period, we hear only of two horses brought from Ephesus to Constantinople under Justinian.[5] Interestingly, at the same time, Justinian began a program of constructing the grand basilica dedicated to St. John the Theologian in Ephesus and an additional aqueduct to provide water for the area. Procopius informs us that for the new church, Justinian had marbles sent from Constantinople for its interior decoration.[6]

We know that for the greater part of the medieval period, a significant number of the statues that were brought to Constantinople by Constantine and his successors still remained present in the streets and squares of Constantinople, although in ever deteriorating condition. Already the frequent revolts of the fifth and sixth centuries, especially the Nika riot against Justinian, took a heavy toll on these ancient statues, especially the bronze ones which were melted down reducing thus their numbers.

I began my discussion with Constantinople of the early period because it is in this time that we have textual sources which provide valuable information on the role that works of art played in the urban space. The works of art that were brought together for the new city of Constantinople were what was then expected a city to have: not only the necessary public buildings, like the Senate or the Hippodrome, but also open spaces like the various Fora built over time. In these, the displayed works of art included monumental columns, fountains, bronze and marble statues and decorative reliefs on the buildings surrounding the open spaces.

This model of urban environment replicates what was the practice in most important cities of the Mediterranean world from antiquity. Alexandria, for example, the second most important center of the Mediterranean after Rome, was accordingly outfitted with works of art, architecture, from all the different religious and cultural transitions from its long history. However, despite its particular importance, the architectural and artistic evidence of its past, from the Hellenistic to the late Roman and Byzantine era, is quite sparse. The late Roman early Byzantine topography and organization of the city are barely recognizable today. Natural disasters, struggles among pagans and Christians, reuse of materials and the decline of the city following the Arab conquest, all have contributed to the lack of physical evidence of the Byzantine city.[7]

This problem exists unfortunately not only for Alexandria but also for numerous cities of the ancient and medieval world of the eastern Mediterranean. Almost all buildings, those we consider the classical and late antique architecture have disappeared. Especially the buildings that visually shaped a city giving it the appropriate sense of an urban space are lost. They are the structures, which with their presence defined the secular core, the administrative edifices that made visible the governing role of the state. In the capital especially beyond the expected houses of the inhabitants, one could recognise all those buildings representing the large bureaucracy needed to govern the empire such as the palace, the Senate, the fora and even baths. For example, from the Byzantine palace complex in Constantinople, we have only a few structural remains but hardly any evidence of its great artistic decorative programs. Only the large peristyle floor of the late sixth century embellished with a mosaic floor depicting scenes from country life has survived.[8] Interesting is also to point out that scenes and vignettes of country life, far from the lifestyle of emperors and aristocrats, were chosen to decorate an imperial courtyard.

There are two most intriguing texts, *The Parastaseis syntomoi chronikai* of the eighth century and a second *The Patria* of the tenth which incorporates sections of the earlier one, that provide references to monuments in the city. However, more interesting are the listings of numerous ancient statues that in these periods were still present in the city.[9] These texts have been variously interpreted, from seeing in them a complete disinterest on the part of the Byzantines for these ancient statues since they do not say much about them, to seeing them as naïve containers of demons and magic. More recently, however, attempts were made to try to recognise the Byzantine point of view from which these texts were assembled and not apply the western Renaissance ideal toward ancient sculpture and then be disappointed. These studies have brought interesting observations. Liz James, for example, sees the accounts of the statues in the *Parastaseis* as texts that present the phenomenon of the power of images in general, pagan or Christian, and so this text fits the period when the nature and role of art and representation was in dispute, that is Iconoclasm.[10] This is not however the focus of my discussion. I am mentioning them however, because it is important to realize that many of the monuments, especially the tremendous numbers of statuary that was brought to the city from the time of its foundation by Constantine, were still very much present. By the middle Byzantine period, we know that over 100, mostly pagan statues, still remained in Constantinople and had a continuous and significant presence, although many had been damaged by frequent fires.[11] These represented a wide range of subjects from ancient gods, mythological figures, philosophers, poets, emperors and also animals.[12] They were set up in numerous places around the city decorating buildings, galleries, gardens, tall columns and so on. The two texts the *Parastaseis* and the *Patria* offer insights into the cultural world of an age from which very little other literary evidence on this material has survived. These texts are however limited to works of art in the city of Constantinople, but what we read there about sculptures and statues we have to assume was present in the other great cities of the Late Antique and early Byzantine period, possibly with a smaller number specifically of statues. In Constantinople, of all these hundreds of pieces we hear that were brought for the embellishment of the new capital only a handful have survived. The most famous are the Hellenistic horses that were set over the gate to the Hippodrome, now in the façade of San Marco in Venice, and the serpentine bronze tripod brought from Delphi still in the Hippodrome today in its original position and in line with the Egyptian Obelisk which was erected in the end of the fourth century.

In the early Byzantine period, Antioch was a thriving city until it was lost to the Arabs in 637 despite Heraclius' attempt to reconquer it, and for the next 350 years, the city fell into a fast decline. In 969, Nikephoros Phokas succeeded with the help of two generals to take the city. It remained in Byzantine hands until the 11th century when Suleiman ibn Qutalmish captured it in 1084. I bring up the reconquest of the city by the Byzantines in the middle Byzantine period because in the historical texts, we read something hardly ever mentioned before. Nikephoros Phokas explicitly forbade Bourtzes, his general, from taking Antioch by force because he insisted that the structural integrity of the city must remain intact.[13] This expresses on the part of the emperor a recognition and respect toward the physical urban environment of the city and in particular its structures. The center of Antioch had all the appropriate Roman and Late Antiquity buildings and spaces that defined it as a metropolis: a palace, a hippodrome, thermae, a large forum, an agora, all these shaped and embellished the city. However, hardly any of these monuments survives today from that city which until the middle Byzantine period most likely were still present. Repeated earthquakes and the capture of the city in 1086 by the Seljuks, followed by the crusaders in 1098 with continuous battles during the 12th century, not much survived of the medieval monuments of Antioch.

Some famous works of art have come to light from Antioch, as for example the sixth century "so-called" Antioch chalice now at the Metropolitan museum in New York[14] or the many mosaics floors excavated that have ended up in a number of American museums.[15] All however are from the early Byzantine period or earlier. What this material provides is evidence for a flourishing city with a high cultural consciousness that in the tenth century, Nikephoros Phokas wanted to make sure it survived.

Ephesos was another great city with an important harbor connecting it with the Aegean sea. It was famous for its numerous magnificent and notable buildings. The most famous was the temple of Artemis, considered one of the seven wonders of the ancient world. Another was the now partially reconstructed great Library of Celsus with a facade which displayed numerous statues and other sculptures. In addition, in the sixth century, while the temple of Artemis was falling into a ruinous state and was being robbed of its treasures and embellishments, the large basilica dedicated to St. John the Theologian was being constructed by Justinian.[16] The city had also a large theatre, famous for its seating capacity of about 20,000. Its remains still dominate the side of the hill toward the old harbor and an impressive collection of its decorated architectural parts are now on the ground in front of it.[17] We have to realize that some of these buildings recognizable today were also very much present during the medieval period and in much better shape than today. Interesting evidence concerning paintings beyond sculptural works of art that were visible in public as much as in private buildings came up in excavations on the hills of a suburb of Ephesus. Several private houses were uncovered with wall paintings. In one of the terrace houses on the hillslope a room, which had one large wall painting of the first century with a representation of Achilles, had on an adjacent wall a painting with a different subject painted when the house underwent restorations in the fourth century.[18] We know that these houses were still inhabited at least until the seventh century and possibly later. This excavation revealed to us the kind of appreciation that was given to a works of art, in this case a wall painting, which was preserved in a house for centuries. This is another example, where we see that attempts were made to preserve architectural and other works of art from earlier periods most likely because of their artistic or historical value. Unfortunately, not many of these works of art have survived.[19] Continuous attacks by the Arabs on Ephesos and the sacking of the city several times from the second half of the seventh century until the early eighth caused the city to fall into a continuous decline. When in the 1090 the Seljuk Turks conquered Ephesos, it had lost much of its population and the harbor, no longer an important trade center, was slowly silted up by the river. Although the Byzantines reestablished control until 1308 the city never recovered.

From these few examples of notable early Byzantine cities, especially in the territories lost to the Arabs invasion, we could conclude that from the later part of the eighth century, there is not much that can be identified to have been constructed or produced. The middle or late Byzantine art production is not represented in the physical remains in these cities. However of the buildings from the Late antique and early Byzantine period continued to exist and much of their sculptural ornamentation was also reused in structures of the later Islamic period. For example, some water fountains have been decorated using early Byzantine marble reliefs with animal and plant imagery.

From the cities where the Byzantines had a continues presence through the middle and later centuries, as for example Constantinople or Thessaloniki, we should expect to have plenty of evidence of the arts in their city. Unfortunately, in these cases too, there is a limited corpus of medieval Byzantine monuments beyond the church buildings that have survived through the centuries until today. The churches that have survived with many still having their original adornments and interior ornamentation range from the fifth century through the Palaiologan period. They represent the creative process in architectural design and construction and are evidence for the type of brick, stone and mortar formations/creations that Byzantine architecture is known for. However, these structures are limited to church architecture. The churches as isolated buildings and dispersed within the modern urban environment, together with the surviving defense walls, are the only representatives of the Byzantine visual city culture. Examples of this phenomenon can be seen in Thessaloniki, Nicaea or Constantinople.

Byzantinists are well acquainted with the splendid art and architecture of the surviving churches, their wall painting and mosaic programs which cover their interior spaces. But in an attempt to locate and identify other buildings, those that defined the city, from the simple houses of the citizens or aristocratic structures with works of art, we have to turn to other sources that provide this information. These are texts and images, which jointly analyzed, give us a reliable understanding of these structures and a visual record and aesthetic perception of their physical presence in the city. Almost all the material is from the centuries after Iconoclasm, when artistic production began to reassert itself and a kind of freedom of expression and creativity in works of art can be seen again. The tenth-century Book of the Eparch in its xxii chapter, while mentioning the government regulations concerning contractors of all kinds, lists specifically under artisans, plasterers, joiners, marble workers, locksmiths and painters among other occupations.[20] This might relate to or is the result of the vigorous artistic activity beginning with the reign of Basil I of the late ninth century. From the Vita Basilii, it becomes clear that it is a period of renewal with much construction and restauration of buildings, which continues for at least through the reign of Constantine Porphyrogennetos, his grandson. Almost all activities were in Constantinople and were church buildings which needed to be strengthened with various reinforcements and their interior surfaces covered with renewed mosaic iconographic programs. Most seem to have had suffered from earthquakes (the latest in 869) and in general of neglect over the centuries.[21] The number is extraordinary, and it is sad to realize how extensive the loss is of so many structures and their decorations. Basil undertook also to add new residences in the palace. This building complex became the famous new structure, which was also called the Kainourgion, meaning the new one. It was a building

> supported on sixteen columns standing in a row, eight of them being of green Thessalian stone while the other six are of onychites (white onyx) decorated by the stone

> carver with the shape of a vine and within the latter, the forms of various animals. The remaining two columns are likewise of onychites, but they have been carved into a different configuration in that the smoothness of their surface has been furrowed by twisted lines. In this way did the craftsman choose to decorate them, seeking, as he did, beauty and delight through variety.[22]

Although the text refers to a palace structure and not a building of the city, it is important in many ways. First, it provides evidence for a structure being built in this period on columns or colonnades. We also hear how the carver provided "beauty and delight" through his work, a comment of aesthetic appreciation especially pointing out the variety. However, the question arises if "variety" was added to the aesthetic experience by the commentator as a cover up for the reuse of pre-existing columns. The motif of the inhabited vine scroll was popular in Late Antiquity and the question, also raised by Mango, is: was it carved anew in this period or were the columns reused?[23] It would not be unusual since appreciation for the antiquities and their reuse was quite common throughout the earlier centuries. We know from Prokopios that Justinian added an open colonnaded court to the Baths of Arkadios where he used columns and marbles "of surpassing beauty" and adorned it "with great numbers of statues, some of bronze, some of polished stone."[24] In this case, not only columns and other marbles were reused but also a great number of statues most likely of the numerous ones brought by Constantine.[25]

From Theophanes Continuatus, we hear also of statues being used on a project that Constantine Porphyrogennetos undertook. He "embellished the Bucoleon" (a complex of buildings within the Great Palace that reached down to the sea) "with statues which he gathered from different places, and he also installed there a fishpond."[26] This short reference is quite specific about the reuse of older statues in the tenth century and a statement about the value that was placed in the works of art of the past. We also have to realize that by the tenth century, three-dimensional sculpture was no longer produced in Byzantium. To choose to use antique sculptures for the Bucoleon speaks probably also to the personal character of Constantine Porphyrogennetos famous for his great love and devotion to the arts.[27]

These were examples of architectural works of art produced for the emperors' more private environments. However, it is mainly emperors and high officials who are responsible for the construction of the public works and buildings in the cities. To know of specific individuals who were active in the restoration of buildings, the decoration of churches and other structures is evidence for our understanding of the urban development of the Byzantine cities at specific historical times.

I selected to discuss these two more private examples and not present the many churches that Basil restored and built or those by Constantine Porphyrogennetos. Both these texts attest to the important question Byzantinists would like to know more about: how much of the architectural and artistic environment of Late Antiquity or the Greco-Roman world was still present in the cities of the Middle and Late Byzantine period? I see these vignettes as examples of the evidence that the Byzantines were for many centuries surrounded by architectural and sculptural works of art of the Greco-Roman past. They were part of the urban environment of their medieval world. To show how much this architectural environment was present in the urban spaces is to turn to the visual evidence of the middle and later Byzantine periods.

Most of the visual record that has survived is in the art of religious materials and artifacts, a more conservative iconographic language. Much can be seen in the illustrations of manuscripts or other works of art with figural representations like wall paintings. It becomes clear that this urban environment is being often referenced in these representations.

I have chosen works of different types to show through the variety how the historical past of their environment in the middle Byzantine period still formed a living present. I am beginning my discussion with a visual example from the pre-Iconoclastic period because it is unique. It is the side panel of a container made of ivory most likely for a relic.[28] The scene carved depicts its arrival in Constantinople suggested by the two clerics on the chariot holding a reliquary box (Figure 18.1). The procession is shown before a colonnaded street that led from the Chalke gate on the left, recognizable from the image of Christ on its tympanum, to the location where a church was being built on the right.[29] This scene is interesting because it allows us to have a sense of how colonnaded streets which transversed cities might have looked like.[30] In Palmyra, an otherwise much destroyed city, the impressive main colonnaded street with an arch on one of its crossings was still standing until its recent demolition.[31] Similar colonnaded streets were in many of the Late Antique urban centers around the Mediterranean, as for example in Djemila (Roman Cuicul) in Algeria, or in Thessaloniki where the famous colonnaded Egnatia crossed the city from east to west. In the recent excavations, a section of the Egnatia was uncovered. Numerous columns and other marble architectural parts were still in situ showing the location of shops and other structures that existed along that street.[32] These streets often had also sculptural decorations. Not only elaborately carved capitals but also other relief and statuary placed in the upper sections of the colonnade. In Constantinople, the most famous colonnaded main thoroughfare was the Mese (the Middle or Main street) which also traversed the city in a generally east–west direction.

A great source for representations of architecture and sculptural remains can be detected in manuscript illustrations that quite often have buildings, citadels or city walls as backgrounds in a variety of scenes in the portrayals of individual figures. Actual buildings or remains of older structures with their architectural decoration can be seen, for example, in the portraits of the Evangelists in the full-page illustrations of the Stavronikita manuscript on Mt Athos.[33]

Figure 18.1 Trier Ivory, scene depicting the arrival and procession of a relic in Constantinople, fourth century

Figure 18.2 Evangelist Marc, Stavronikita, ms. gr. 43, tenth century

Marc is seated in front of an exedra foregrounding him with a loggia connecting two tower-like tall buildings in the background (Figure 18.2). From this kind of elevated terrace, one had a view over a garden where tall trees can be seen reaching up to the level of loggia and possibly beyond to the sea. We can imagine his kind of structure, a villa, to be at an elevated area at the edge of a city. On the other hand, the portrait of Matthew contemplating is placed in front of a series of buildings that are very much the type of architecture that can be recognised as official administrative structures (Figure 18.3). Impressive entrances, columns and pediments are part of the iconography of government urban city centers.

Figure 18.3 Evangelist Matthew, Stavronikita, ms. gr. 43, tenth century

One type of manuscript that has the greatest variety of architectural and sculptural imagery that can give us a sense of what the Byzantines were familiar with in their urban environment are the Menologia, especially the richly illustrated Menologion of Basil II of ca. 1000.[34] On each folio saints commemorated are depicted and depending on his or her life often architectural details are added in the image. Although many of the martyred saints were executed outside the walls of the cities, there are buildings of a great variety that have been added to the compositions, shown either from a distance or they become the

Figure 18.4 Martyrdom of the Bishop Simeon of Jerusalem, Menologion of Basil II, ms. Vat. gr. 1613, ca. 1000

setting of the presentation of the figure. An interesting case is the image of the martyrdom of the Bishop Simeon of Jerusalem who was crucified (Figure 18.4). He is depicted in front of a colonnade that seems to be part of a long building with many openings. Between the columns, there are two statues of naked military figures, the type well-known of Sol or other heroes typical of the ancient world. The columns support an entablature composed of crenellations interspersed by larger plaques with different heads in relief. This is a most unusual combination of columns, statuary and carved figural heads. A combination of these elements can be seen in the Roman Forum of Merida in Spain. There, a colonnaded section of a monument survives where on top of a series of columns there are rectangular marble panels with heads in relief of a variety of figures (Figure 18.5).[35] The same manuscript contains representations of all kinds of structures that could be still found in middle Byzantine cities and their surroundings. Clearly, in the manuscript illustrations, they are artistic renditions of architecture arranged so to enhance the composition. However, I do believe that the architectural units used to construct these painted buildings follow known identifiable types of structures drawn from their contemporary environment.

Another example typical of numerous compositions is the illustration of St Gregory the bishop of Great Armenia (Figure 18.6). He stands in front of a courtyard-like arrangement of two-storied buildings. At each corner in the front double columns support the upper level where two Atlas figures carry on the shoulders the entablature decorated with a continuous acanthus relief and other plants. Here we have a variety of elements put together to enhance the grand architectural structure framing the saint.

In one of the most famous images from the tenth century Paris psalter, which accompanies the canticle of Isaiah, two personifications that of the Night and of Dawn flank the praying

Figure 18.5 Roman Forum of Merida

Figure 18.6 St Gregory, Bishop of Great Armenia, Menologion of Basil II, ms. Vat. gr. 1613, ca. 1000

Figure 18.7 Representations of night and dawn flanking the praying prophet, Paris psalter, Paris, Bibliothèque Nationale, ms. gr. 139, tenth century

prophet (Figure 18.7). From the text, we know that Isaiah was praying during the whole night until dawn arrived. The image makes this temporal description visible through the device of the personification. The personification of Night stands with her torch turned downwards which is extinguished. On the other side, the youthful Dawn with a lit torch enters the scene. In the courtyard of Hagia Sophia in Constantinople, where numerous fragmentary sculptures are assembled, there is among them a large block of stone with a relief.[36] It is not known where it was found and brought to the collection (Figure18.8). It is very likely to be from the fourth to the sixth century.[37] Carved in high relief, a running naked youthful Dawn with his lit torch has just passed by the figure of Night who holds her torch downwards in an attempt to extinguish it. I believe that the creator of the Paris Psalter composition must have known this ancient visual language of using personifications, and here specifically the

Figure 18.8 Marble relief depicting the figures of dawn and night, Hagia Sophia museum, ca. fourth-sixth century

female figure of the night and the youthful dawn and their specific iconographic types. They are not the invention of the tenth-century artist and it is a happy coincidence that this relief has survived until today. What I am arguing with this example is to state one more time that much of the ancient Greek, Roman and Late Antique works of art, sculptures or other were visible and present in the life of the Byzantine and often were a source of inspiration or direct appropriation of figures and styles. These works were surrounding them: they were on columns, in niches on buildings, in the Hippodrome where many of the animal and other statues were set up and in many other places. I believe we should not speak of a renaissance phenomenon, which is quite common in the art historical literature every time we see a classicizing composition or style as found for example in this psalter.[38]

In a late eleventh century manuscript of the Octateuch in the Vatican (ms. gr. 747) in a scene where two merchants are approaching a seated king, we see in the background just behind them a stone monument with a relief representing a dancing maenad (Figure 18.9). The monument does not relate to the story represented but is an addition of the illustrator. This little detail is suggestive of the presence of this kind of works of art known to the Byzantine artist who could use it to embellish the architectural background environment of the city.[39]

Another small object but most interesting for the questions raised in this chapter is a silver guilt ink pot in Padua dating possibly from the ninth to tenth century.[40] The decorative system of the inkpot on its outer surface has the repeating motif of the snake column and in-between are individual naked male figures in different positions (Figure 18.10). The repeated snake column serves as ornamental divider in the presentation of the figures, which

Figure 18.9 Detail from scene depicting two merchants approaching a seated king, Vatican Octateuch, ms. Vat. gr. 747), eleventh century

Figure 18.10 Silver guilt ink pot, Diocesan Museum of Padua, ca. ninth-tenth century

are suggestive of ancient statues. We no longer have the actual statues, except the serpent column in the Hippodrome, but we can gain an idea of what the Byzantines at least of the Middle Byzantine period still could see in their cities. One of them the seated figure might be Ares and the young boy possibly a putto next to a column with a lyre.[41] The inscription along the top identifies the owner as the calligrapher Leon and the object as a container of color or ink. It seems to be the personal inkpot of this scribe Leon. On the lid is a clearly identifiable beautiful head of the Gorgon Medusa. Here the memory of the Medusa head as an apotropaic symbol seems to be retained. On the lid of the inkpot, it serves as a guardian and protector of the ink inside and in general of the calligrapher's talent since at the bottom of the inkpot, not visible to others he claims to be the best. Interesting is also the fact that in Constantinople, there were several locations that had in stone the face of the Gorgon. Excavations in the Constantinian Forum revealed the head of the Medusa depicted inside a medallion, which there too like a shield was part of a decorative program warding off and frightening any enemy and protecting probably a structure.[42] It is striking to see the close similarities between the Constantinian marble head and the small head of the silver inkpot lid when placed next to each other. Where the Medusa heads in Constantine's Forum still in place when the inkpot was made?

From the surviving textual and visual evidence, I believe we can conclude that probably up to the sack of Constantinople by the Crusaders in 1204 ancient and early Byzantine works of art and architecture were in some form still recognizable. It is difficult to know what the Byzantines of the centuries after Iconoclasm thought or believed were these buildings and structures that surrounded them in their city. Much was from the Constantinian and Theodosian building activities and a lot was Justinianic, not only in Constantinople. Justinian extended his construction projects in several ancient Greek and Roman cities as we saw for example in Ephesus.[43] Then, in the ninth and tenth centuries beginning with Basil I, the capital was "renewed." Many older structures and their decoration were restored, respecting their place and importance, and new more contemporary buildings built, and this continued for several centuries. The elite most likely was aware that many of their "contemporary" monuments were from earlier periods recognizing the Greco-Roman past of these works brought to the new capital. Additional structures continued to be built in the following centuries which then included many architectural elements, columns, capitals and so on reused from the older buildings.

The surviving churches, in contrast to the secular buildings, testify to this reuse of columns and capitals. It is however very difficult to locate and discuss works of art that were considered not appropriate to be reused in an ecclesiastical environment and these, unfortunately, have disappeared with the passing of time. This loss of the secular urban environment in the major Byzantine cities is what made it necessary to turn to the visual evidence to assist in detecting what was still present in their everyday environment and how the Byzantines perceived that world.

In this chapter, I discussed only a few examples from numerous other medieval works of art that can be brought into the discussion to address the question of what the Byzantines considered their cultural heritage. When they depicted for example a variety of buildings in manuscript illustrations of the Middle Byzantine period, or statues and landscapes, we need to ask which world were they representing? The broader topic remains an open question needing further study and exploration.

Notes

1 H. Saradi-Mendelovici, "Christian Attitudes toward Pagan Monuments in Late Antiquity and Their Legacy in Later Byzantine Centuries," *Dumbarton Oaks Papers* 44 (1990) 46–61, esp. 50–52.

2 C. Mango, "Antique Statuary and the Byzantine Beholder," *Dumbarton Oaks Papers* 17 (1963), 55–75, 68.

3 Mango, "Antique Statuary," 57–58.

4 C. Mango, *Le développement urbain de Constantinople*. Paris, 1985. S. Bassett, *The Urban Image of Late Antique Constantinople* (Cambridge, 2004); S. Bassett, "Sculpture and the Rhetorical Imagination in Late Antique Constantinople," *Archaeology and the Cities of Asia Minor in Late Antiquity*, eds. O. Dally and C. Ratté, Kelsey Museum Publications 6 (Ann Arbor, 2011), 27 – 41.

5 We do however hear from Procopius that Justinian ordered Narses the destruction of certain pagan temples in Egypt but save their statues and send them to Constantinople. Procopius, *History of the Wars, Pers*., ed. H. B. Dewing (London and Cambridge, *MA, 1940*) 1.19.35.

6 C. Foss, Ephesus after Antiquity: A Late Antique, Byzantine and Turkish City (Cambridge, 1979), 89–91.

7 On the destruction of the Serapeum, see N. Q. Kong, *The Emperor Theodosius and the Establishment of Christianity* (London, 1961), 78–82; G. Fowden, "Bishops and Temples in the Easter Roman Empire, A.D. 320–435," *JTS* 29.1 (1978), 69–70

8 J. Trilling, "The Soul of the Empire: Style and Meaning in the Mosaic Pavement of the Byzantine Imperial Palace in Constantinople" *Dumbarton Oaks Papers* 43 (1989), 27–72; H. Maguire, "The Medieval Floors of the Great Palace," *Byzantine Constantinople: Monuments, Topography and Everyday Life*, ed. Nevra Necipoğlu, *The Medieval Mediterranean* 33 (1999), 153–74 W. Jobst and H. Vetters, *Mosaikenforschung im Kaiserpalast von Konstantinopel*, Österreichische Akademie der Wissenschaften, Phil.-Hist. Kl., Denkschriften 228 (Vienna, 1992).

9 J. Herrin and A. Cameron, *Constantinople in the Early Eighth Century. The Parastaseis Syntomoi Chronikai* (Leiden, 1984); T. M. Muhammad, Can Παραστάσεις σύντομοι χρονικαί be considered a real guide to the sculptures of Constantinople during the Isaurian period? *Byzantinoslavica* 64 (2006), 77–98. B. Anderson, "Classified Knowledge: The Epistemology of Statuary in the *Parastaseis Syntomoi Chronikai*," *BMGS* 35 (2011), 1–19; A. Berger, *Untersuchungen zu den Patria Konstantinupoleos, Ποικίλα Βυζαντινά* 8 (Bonn, 1988); A. Berger, trans., *Accounts of Medieval Constantinople: The Patria* [Dumbarton Oaks Medieval Library, 24] (Cambridge, MA and London, 2013); P. Magdalino, "The Patria of Constantinople: scholarship or literature?" in *Bibliophilos, Byzantinisches Archiv* 39 (2021), 259–272.

10 L. James, "'Pray Not to Fall into Temptation and Be on Your Guard': Pagan Statues in Christian Constantinople" *Gesta* 35 (1996), 12–20.

11 Mango, "Antique Statuary," 58.

12 Mango, "Antique Statuary, 57.

13 A. Kaldellis, *Streams of Gold, Rivers of Blood: The Rise and Fall of Byzantium, 955 A.D. to the First Crusade*. (Oxford, 2017), p. 63; J. Romane, *Byzantium Triumphant: Byzantium Triumphant: The Military History of the Byzantines, 959–1025* (Barnsley, South Yorkshire, 2015), 36.

14 On the Antioch chalice see: Ch. Kondoleon, *Antioch. The Lost Ancient City*, (Princeton, 2000), 214–215. It is important also to consider that the various archaeological schools that undertook archaeological excavations were interested mainly to find remains and works of art of the ancient world. Not much attention was given to the medieval remains except to religious structures, eg. churches and religious objects.

15 L. Becker and Ch. Kondoleon, *The Arts of Antioch: Art Historical and Scientific Approaches to Roman Mosaics and a Catalogue of the Worcester Art Museum Antioch collection* (Worcester, MA, 2005).

16 Two horses were brought by Justinian from Ephesus from the temple of Artemis. They were placed in the Chalke gate entrance. This is mentioned in the *Patria* II, 28.

17 In the Seljuk Museum which contains the finds from Ephesus there are numerous works of art from the sixth century BC all the way to the Late Antique period. The collection of statues in marble, one of Artemis, represent mainly ancient Greek mythological figures and gods.

18 H. Vetters, *Ephesos, Jahreshefte des Österreichischen Archäologischen Instituts* (Grabungen 1969), 7–22.

19 In the Seljuk museum mentioned in the footnote above among the ancient Greek and Roman material there is for example the statue of the Proconsul Stephanos, a son of the island Naxos. of the sixth century. However, more interesting for our search of evidence from the middle and later Byzantine period, among the small objects found are two small steatite icons from the eleventh to twelfth centuries. Both depict a bust of the Hodegetria, one of higher quality than the other, but both show much ware, probably from either carrying or better wearing them against the body.

20 J. Koder, *Das Eparchenbuch Leons des Weisen, Corpus Fontium Historiae Byzantinae 33* (1991), Regulation 22, 139. The book is a work of Basil's son Leo VI and it seems that regulations on the various guilds and professions had to be legislated.

21 *Vita Basilli*, 78–90. Also see translation by C. Mango, *The Art of the Byzantine Empire 312–1453*, Sources and Documents in the History of Art Series, ed. H. W. Hanson (Englewood Cliffs, NJ, 1972), 192–199.

22 Mango, *The Art of Byzantium*, 197.

23 Mango, *The Art of Byzantium*, 197, ftn. 67.

24 Procopius, *De aedificiis I.1.1–I.1.20, ed. and trans. H. B. Dewing (New York: Loeb Classical Library, 1940)*, I, xi 6–7.
25 Justinian also refashioned the Chalke gate by assembling statues from different locations and setting them in front of the entrance. Among them were also statues of earlier emperors. Bassett, *The Urban Image*, 125–26.
26 Theophanes Continuatus, *Chronicle*, ed. I. Bekker, CSHB, # 15.
27 Theophanes Continuatus, *Chronicle*, # 20 We learn also in # 21 that he had a silver eagle made placed on top of a water pipe in a water basin. The eagle had his head proudly turned to the side and with his feet was stifling a serpent. Actually, a three-dimensional statue made of silver.
28 K. Holum and G. Vikan, "The Trier Ivory, Adventus Ceremonial, and the Relics of St Stephen," *Dumbarton Oaks Papers* 33 (1979), 115–33. I. Kalavrezou, "Helping Hands for an Empire: Imperial Ceremonies and the Cult of Relics at the Byzantine Court," *Byzantine Court Culture from 829 to 1204*, ed. H. Maguire (Washington, DC, 1997), 53–79.
29 If the relic which is being carried by the two priests on the chariot is that of St Stephen brought in Constantinople in the fifth century, then the church being built is the one that was going to house it. See, Kalavrezou, "Helping Hands," 57.
30 We cannot reconstruct the street from this representation, but we see that people are shown on the story above the colonnade. Residences were built on top of the row of column and often shops were located at the lower level with their facades visible between the columns.
31 It was destroyed in 2015 together with sculptures that had survived all these centuries.
32 Sections of the Egnatia were uncovered in the recent excavations undertaken for the installation of a Metro line. Unfortunately, this important Byzantine site is going to be covered and only some elements displaced in a different location.
33 *Οι Θησαυροί του Αγίου Όρους. Εικονογραφημένα Χειρόγραφα*, ed. P. Christou,vol. 4 (Athens, 1991). Stavronikita ms. gr. 43, 334–337, figs 348, 349.
34 *l Menologio di Basilio II (cod. Vaticano Greco 1613)*. Facsimile edition (Turin 1907).
35 Merida, a Roman city, was conquered in 713 by the Arabs. In 1230 it was reconquered and Christianized by Alfonso IX of Leon. Of the Forum structure only two of the marble panels with the heads survive in situ. The remaining are now in the museum together with the statues that were in the walls behind.
36 I came across the stone relief with the personifications of Night and Dawn while studying the outdoor collection of sculptural pieces at the Hagia Sophia Museum. Knowing the images of the Paris Psalter, I was immediately struck by the resemblance of the relief's figures and the overall composition.
37 The representation of the personifications of the two figures, the Night and Dawn, suggests a late antique period.
38 This is specifically directed to the question of the so-called "Macedonian Renaissance".
39 K. Weitzmann and M. Bernabo *The Illustrations in the Manuscripts of the Septuagint II, The Byzantine Octateuchs*, (Princeton 1999) Vat. ms. gr. 747, 331–334.
40 H. Maguire, "Epigrams, Art, and the 'Macedonian Renaissance,'" *Dumbarton Oaks Papers* 48 (1994), 105–115. Also, P. Chatterjee, "The Gifts of the Gorgon: A Close Look at a Byzantine Inkpot," Res 65–66 (2015), 212–223.
41 The same decorative system also with ancient figures representing statues is found on the glass cup in the treasury of San Marco. See I. Kalavrezou, "The Cup of San Marco and the 'Classical' in Byzantium", *Late Antique and Medieval Art of the Mediterranean World*, ed. E. R. Hoffman (Oxford, 2007), 273–284.
42 Also, four gigantic Medusa heads survive in Constantinople from a late antique monument. Two are reused as bases supporting columns in the Justinianic cistern along the Mese and two more in the collection of sculptures in the courtyard of Hagia Sophia. In the Forum in Merida the panels with the series of heads on top of the columns have in several of them the head of the Medusa.
43 Procopius, *De aed*, V, 1.6.

19

ON EARLY BYZANTINE IMAGES OF *POLEIS*

Meanings and Messages

Jenny P. Albani

In his seminal 1945 article "Plotin et les origines de l'esthétique médiévale," André Grabar pointed out the relationship of medieval/Byzantine art to Neo-Platonic thought, particularly Plotinus' concepts, which for the first time presaged medieval approaches to artworks. According to Plotinus (205–70 AD), works of art should provide a representation of the Νοῦς (Intellect), a spiritual vision, seen through the "inner eyes."[1] The arts "οὐχ ἁπλῶς τὸ ὁρώμενον μιμοῦνται, ἀλλὰ ἀνατρέχουσιν ἐπὶ τοὺς λόγους" (give no bare reproduction of the thing seen but go back to the Reason-Principles).[2] In what follows, given the polyvalence of Byzantine images, I will attempt to explore some of the potential messages that late antique representations of cities conveyed to the beholder.[3] My main tools will be remarks on the structure, imagery, and meanings of compositions with cityscapes and the accompanying inscriptions. Besides, early Byzantine written sources, religious and secular, will provide the clues for exploring modes of perception of the visual language in their age.[4]

Post-iconoclastic art—anthropocentric *par excellence*—regularly used cityscapes as complementary components of religious or historical narratives, thus yielding topographic indications. On the other hand, late antique representations of cities were not only background features but also significant elements of the compositions and their overlapping layers of meaning. Topographic motifs were part of the iconographic repertory of mosaic pavements in mansions and churches of the early Byzantine world. Remarkable assemblages depicting cities, dated to the sixth to eighth century, are those found in churches of *Provincia Arabia* (modern Jordan and Syria).[5] These cityscapes, arranged in friezes or in loose connection with other motifs, belonged to compositions containing an ample variety of subject matter: donor portraits, dedicatory inscriptions, geometric patterns, Nilotic scenes, personifications, inhabited vine or acanthus scrolls, fruit-laden trees, and other motifs from nature. Thus, topographic mosaics, as parts of these images of the earth, revealing humanity's mastery over nature, gave rise to the idea that cities were an essential component of this prosperous world and its culture—material and spiritual.[6]

Cities were represented "in sum" as polychrome compact vignettes, either in the reverse perspective or in bird's eye view, accompanied by toponyms in Greek.[7] That is, they were usually rendered either as elaborate buildings or as walled ensembles drawing on Hellenistic and Roman models of polygonal walled cities.[8] In some cases, the walled-city

DOI: 10.4324/9780429203923-24

motif appears in association with a real landmark, for example, Jerusalem with Holy Sepulchre, Alexandria with the Pharos, and Kastron Mefaa (modern Umm ar-Rasas, Jordan) with a column—probably associated with a Stylite—combining convention with reality (Figure 19.1).[9]

The most profuse of the assemblages of cityscapes is that on the early eighth-century mosaic pavement (717/18) in the church of Saint Stephen in Kastron Mefaa, which reveals the persistence of Byzantine visual tradition in a region that had passed from Byzantium to the Muslims.[10] This church, an eighth-century three-aisled basilica (*ca* 24.0 m long by 13.5 m wide) built upon the ruins of a probably sixth-century church, belonged to a large ecclesiastical complex (2.500 m^2) *extra muros*, with a sepulchral character (Figure 19.2).[11] It included, in its last phase, three more churches, namely the church of the Niche (sixth century?), the church of Bishop Sergius (second half of the sixth century), furnished with a baptistery and a funerary chapel dated to the Umayyad period, the church of the Courtyard (seventh to eighth century), the chapel of the Column (Umayyad period), various annexes and four courtyards.[12] The apse of the north chapel of Saint Stephen featured a polygonal niche, which could have accommodated a reliquary, and the north aisle was aligned with and opened to the south aisle of Saint Sergius for direct communication between them.[13] This arrangement seems appropriate for the veneration of relics, a fragment of a marble reliquary in the shape of a small coffin from the south courtyard being a find of particular relevance.[14] On the other hand, two pit graves beneath the floor of the south chamber of Saint Stephen, which probably belonged to its sixth-century predecessor, and one more burial, discovered through a spot dig at the north aisle, attest to the funerary character of the church.[15] Moreover, two mosaic panels with donor portraits on the floor appear in eschatological contexts: close to the martyrial chapel and the funerary chamber, associated with two architectural images of Diblaton and Limbon, two towns of *Provincia Arabia*, and probably their home places, and votive inscriptions asking for salvation (See Figure 19.3–1,2). Six more on the mosaic floor of the side aisles ask the Lord to remember several donors. The dedicatory inscription on the mosaic floor of the nave also displays an eschatological dimension (See Figure 19.3-3).[16] Therefore, we may suggest that the whole church was home to commemorative services. Thus, it is tempting to explore the impact of Saint Stephen's function—that of a pilgrimage and funerary church—on the iconography of its mosaic pavement and its perception by the viewers.

The central carpet of the nave's pavement depicts an inhabited vine scroll with hunting, agricultural, and pastoral scenes within its curls (See Figure 19.3-4), whose figures were deliberately damaged.[17] Although the vine tree and the relevant agricultural activities may have reflected an economic reality at Kastron Mefaa,[18] as recently proposed, the faithful were undoubtedly familiar with the several symbolic meanings of the vine tree, which appear in the Bible, including the Eucharistic one with its salvific messages.[19] The plethoric vine-scroll composition is framed on all sides by a continuous frieze with images of ten Egyptian cities and towns at the Nile Delta (See Figure 19.3-5): Alexandria, Kasin, Thenesos, Tamiathis (Damietta), Kynopolis, Panau, Pelusin (Pelusium) (see Figure 19.1), Antinau (See Figure 19.1), Heraclion, and Pseudostomon. They are dispersed within an aquatic environment (See Figure 19.1), among putti, fishing from boats or riding a goose, or a fish, octopuses, jellyfish, crocodiles, fishes, shells, waterbirds, storks, and lotus plants.[20] This Nilotic panorama, a composition of pagan origin, highly estimated in Late Antiquity for its aesthetic value, evoked, moreover, the idea of fertility.[21] However, the frequent inclusion of flora, fauna, and towns of the Nile in church iconographic programs also calls for

Figure 19.1 Pelusin, Antinau, Kastron Mefaa, Philadelphia, and Nilotic Motifs. Detail of the floor mosaic in the church of Saint Stephen, 717/18. Umm ar-Rasas, Jordan

Source: Photo Credit–Public Domain.

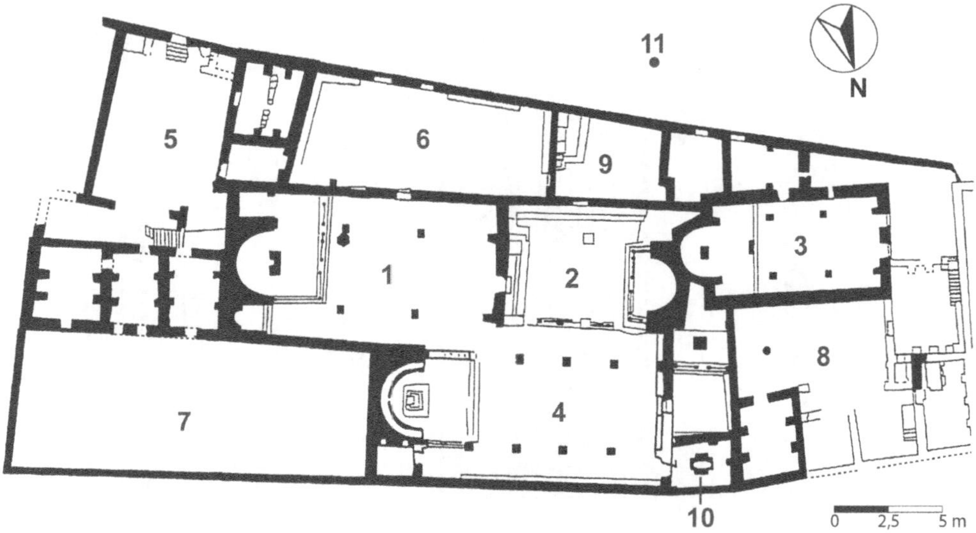

Figure 19.2 Plan of the Ecclesiastical complex, including Saint Stephen, Umm ar-Rasas, Jordan. 1. Church of Saint Stephen. 2. Church of the Courtyard. 3. Church of the Niche. 4 Church of Bishop Sergius. 5. East courtyard. 6. South courtyard. 7. Northeast courtyard. 8. West courtyard. 9. Chapel of the column. 10. Baptistery. 11. Cistern. Based on Leal, "Christians," Plan 11

an *Interpretatio Christiana*.[22] A pertinent source is the *Hexaemeron* by Anastasius of Sinai, an exegesis of Genesis datable to the second half of the seventh century, which refers to the redemption of Egypt by Christ. According to Anastasius, when the Holy Infant arrived in Egypt, he found it darkened and choked by evil for a very long time. In his authority as God, Christ cried out: "Let the water be gathered into their congregations, and let the dry land be seen." Then, at once, the waters of the Nile withdrew, and the earth became beautiful and irrigated, the grooves filled, the fields sprouted, the towns emerged, as they arose from the bottom of the waters. And this happens every year since then. After the inundation of the Nile, Christ chases away the waters to remind us that he is the creator of the world and had freed Egypt from darkness and deceit.[23] Moreover, a hymn in a sixth-century papyrus from Antinoë, Egypt, cited and commented by Henry Maguire, praises the Nile for the benefits he brings to the land and humans and appeals to Christ—the real source of the river's power—for the salvation of the human soul.[24] It seems, therefore, probable that the Nilotic landscape with its cities, on the mosaic in question, evoked connotations of redemption.

Next to the border with the Nilotic scenes, on the north and south intercolumniations, a series of rectangular panels with representations of 15 cities are arranged in linear sequence. The north frieze depicts eight urban centers of *Provincia Palaestina Prima* (See Figure 19.3-6): Jerusalem, Gaza, Ascalon, Eleutheropolis (Beit Guvrin), Diospolis (Lydda), Caesarea, Sebastis (Sebaste or Sebastia), and Neapolis (Nablus). The south border depicts seven cities and towns of *Provincia Arabia* (See Figure 19.3-7): Kastron Mefaa (See Figure 19.1), Philadelphia (Amman) (See Figure 19.1), Madaba, Esbous (Hesban), Belemounta (Ma'in), Areopolis (Rabba), Charachmoba (Kerak).[25] Notwithstanding their stylized

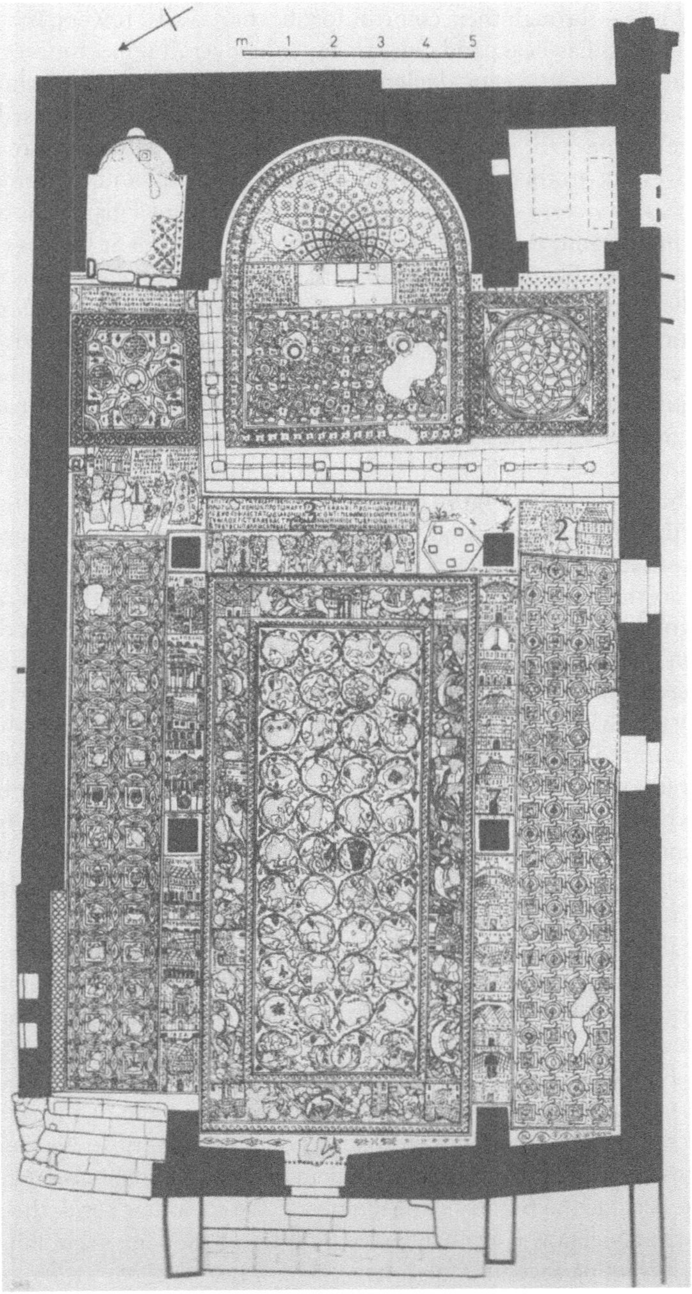

Figure 19.3 Drawing of the floor mosaic in the church of Saint Stephen, 717/18. Umm ar-Rasas, Jordan. 1. Panel with the representation of four donors and the Village Diblaton. 2. Panel with the representation of a donor and the village of Limbon. 3. Dedicatory inscription. 4. Panel depicting an inhabited vine scroll with hunting, agricultural, and pastoral scenes. 5. Frieze illustrating ten Egyptian cities and Nilotic scenes. 6. Frieze with eight cities of Provincia Palestina Prima. 7. Frieze showing seven cities of provincia Arabia. Based on Piccirillo, Jordan, Fig. 383

rendering, they give—through their colorful fortification walls, towers, monumental gates, multi-story buildings, basilicas, and colonnades—the overall impression of thriving urban settlements. The cities and towns depicted on the mosaic floor of the church were main stations along actual roadways, on both sides of the River Jordan, also used by devotees in their pilgrimage journeys for spiritual benefits. Besides, some of them were also pilgrimage targets themselves due to their religious sites. Gaza, a cultural and economic hub, was the city of Samson's last victory and home to the church of Saint Porphyrius above the tomb of the homonymous saint. Religious sites, including the tomb of St Cosmas and St Damian and that of the Three Egyptian Martyrs, were, according to pilgrims' accounts, located in Ascalon. The tomb of St George in Lydda developed into the saint's primary shrine, a significant supra-local pilgrimage center. Mentions and depictions of Lydda and Gaza in Greek sixteenth- to eighteenth-century illustrated *Proskynetaria* imply their enduring popularity as pilgrims' goals. Caesarea possessed a sanctuary of Saint Procopius. Sebaste was a pilgrimage site due to the tomb of Prophet Elisha, which tradition associates with this city.[26] Madaba attracted worshippers because of its proximity to the Memorial of Moses on Mount Nebo—a famous pilgrimage place where, according to tradition, Moses was buried—while the city was a pilgrims' destination in its own right exhibiting holy relics and icons for veneration.[27] Probably Mefaa was also a pilgrimage site with the church of priest Wa'il and the north chapel of Saint Stephen dedicated to martyrial cults and the Stylite's monument a worshippers' destination.[28] Thus, topographic motifs in Saint Stephen, related to itineraries on both sides of the River Jordan, possibly, highlighted spiritual associations of the pilgrimage journey to the holy city of Jerusalem, through *Provincia Palaestina Prima*, with that to Kastron Mefaa, through *Provincia Arabia*. Given that the worshippers' journey to Jerusalem appeared in medieval thought as "the pilgrimage of pilgrimages," other religious travels were of significance only if presented as an imitation of the pilgrimage to the holy city.[29] Therefore, in a period unfavorable for visiting holy places due to the Umayyad rule,[30] Jerusalem and Kastron Mefaa depicted on the mosaic floor symmetrically as to its axis and very close to the altar, the focus of Eucharist, appeared as the destinations of a virtual and an actual pilgrimage, respectively, equal in spiritual and salvific merit.

An additional connection between Jerusalem and Mefaa may have derived from the association of both cities with the cult of St Stephen. From 415, the commemoration feast of the protomartyr, very popular in Jerusalem, took place at the church of Hagia Sion, which hosted his relics.[31] Some decades later, during her retirement in the holy city (443–60), Empress Aelia Eudocia, the wife of Theodosius II (r. 402–50), founded as a new Helena a church dedicated to Saint Stephen, where she translated some of the saint's relics. This shrine, located *extra muros* on the main road, leading northward to Neapolis and Damascus, enhanced the cult of St Stephen in Jerusalem, enriched the memorial landscape of the sacred city, and became the burial site of Eudocia.[32] On the other hand, the church of Saint Stephen at Kastron Mefaa was probably also a center of the saint's worship on the eastern side of Jordan, attracting several donations.

Topographic mosaic representations in Saint Stephen depend on the cartographic tradition as to their rendering—with elements of realistic topography—and their relationship with actual roads.[33] This tradition is best represented in *Provincia Arabia* by the unique composition of the so-called Madaba map dated around 557 (Figure 19.4).[34] It is the fragment (10.5 × 5.6 m.) of a mosaic pavement at the homonymous city, situated 30 km northwest of Umm ar-Rasas. The mosaic, unearthed in 1896 during the construction of a church dedicated to Saint James (nowadays known as the church of Saint George) over the remains

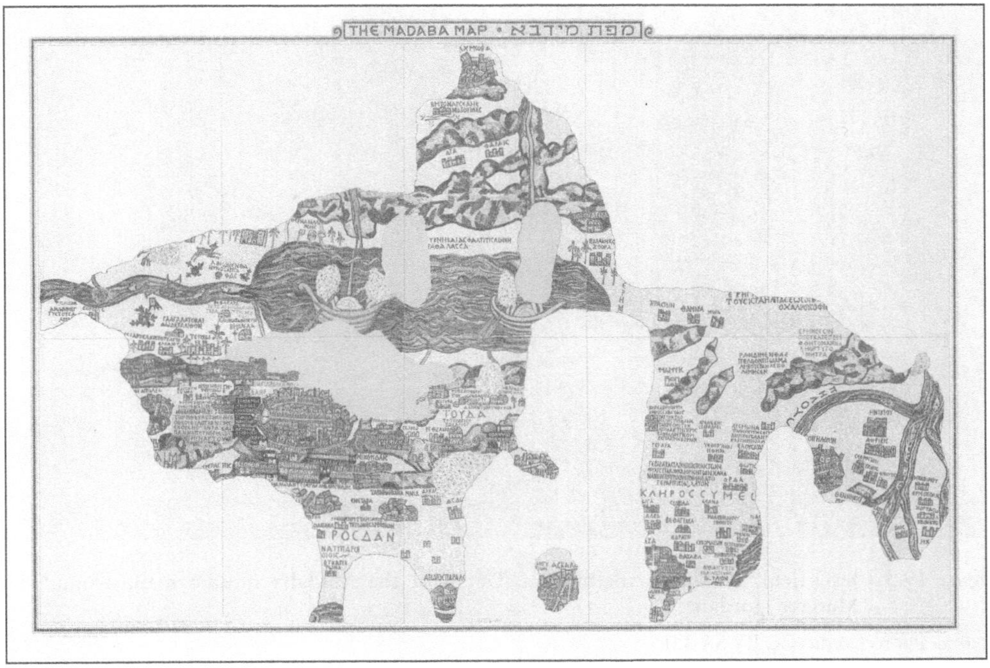

Figure 19.4 Drawing of the Madaba mosaic map by Bernard Gagnon
Source: Photo Credit–CC BY-SA 3.0.

of a Byzantine building—perhaps a basilica—has been the subject of numerous studies.[35] It spans the nave and the south aisle of the modern church. Parts of a mosaic in the north aisle imply that the map continued to the north, with a total length originally of *ca* 15.70 m. Scholars believe that, in its original form, the Madaba mosaic map was a large-scale cartographical depiction of the entire Holy Land, from Sidon in the north to the Nile Delta in the south and from the Mediterranean coast in the west to the Arabian Desert in the east.[36] The sites on the map are ordered according to road networks and annotated, suggesting a pilgrimage map as one of its sources.[37] Setting up a "monumental" map depiction in a public space is a well-documented Roman practice used for commemorative or instructive purposes.[38] Contribution to the building of shared identity—that of the chosen people–inhabitants of the Holy Land—and construction of collective memory for the future were probably two of the Madaba map's purposes.[39]

The map mosaic depicts—in the form of vignettes—more than 120 cities, towns, and villages, along with monuments and places of pilgrimage in the Holy Land, identified by numerous detailed Greek inscriptions. Greek labels also name landscape elements, such as mountains, rivers, deserts, and a lake, the Dead Sea, as well as places related to the Bible. Notable are the inscriptions that define the boundaries of areas as well as the land allotments of Judah, Simeon, Benjamin, Dan, and Ephraim—probably those of the seven more tribes of Israel also appeared once on the map.[40] Many scholars supposed that the principal source of the map was the *Onomasticon* by Eusebius of Caesarea, a fourth-century Greek "gazetteer" with entries based on the Bible.[41] However, recent re-examinations of this issue suggest additional sources for the map.[42]

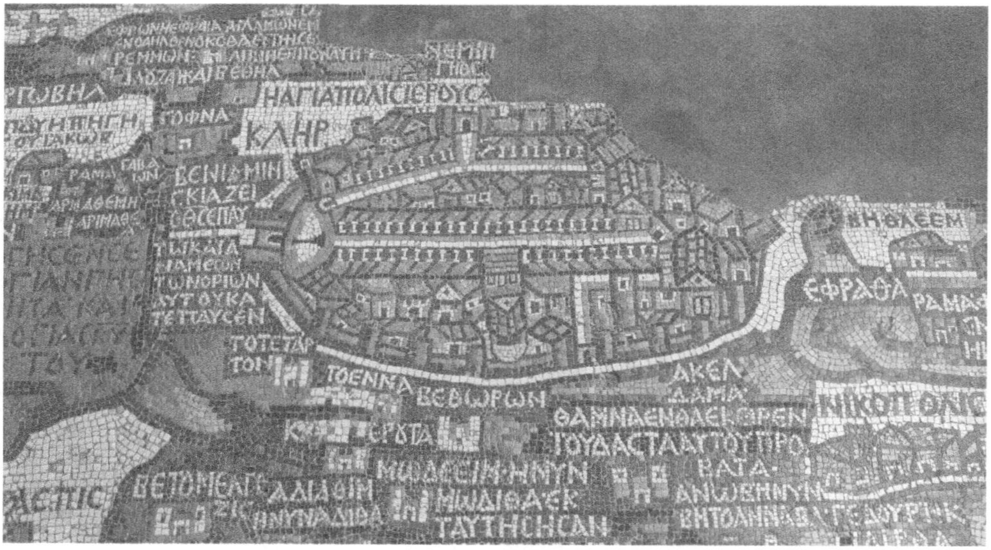

Figure 19.5 Jerusalem, Nicopolis, Bethlehem. Detail of the Madaba mosaic map, around 557. Madaba, Jordan

Source: Photo Credit–CC BY-SA 3.0.

Though the rendering of the geographical area on the Madaba map lacks uniformity in scale and coordinates,[43] the images of the various human settlements—cities, towns, and villages—and individual buildings/monuments provide evidence of their character and size through their execution conforming to a meticulous visual typology.[44] Cities are shown in bird's eye view, walled, with a dense but orderly urban organization and the main road(s) accentuated by colonnaded arcades. Jerusalem, Ascalon, Pelusium, Gaza, Neapolis, Eleutheropolis, and Charach Moba belong to this category (Figure 19.5).[45] Large towns, such as Nicopolis (See Figure 19.5), Bethzachar(ia), Jabneel ("or Jamnia"), Beersheba ("now Berosabba"), Bethlehem (See Figure 19.5), and others, are also depicted in bird's eye view, as compact assemblages of buildings (churches, towers, parts of curtain walls, and buildings with gable roofs or terraces). Their vignettes, smaller than those of cities, display, occasionally, a colonnaded street, as in Lod ("also Lydea, also called Diospolis") and Azotus Paralus.[46] Probably less populated towns, like Jericho, Archelais (See Figure 19.6), Accaron ("now Accara"), Ashdod ("also Azotus"), Thamara, Elusa, Tharais, Orda, Hermupolis, Chortaso, Balak ("or Segor, now Zoora"), and others, are rendered smaller, in a frontal view, walled, with several square towers in a linear sequence (Figure 19.6).[47] Typified images of villages, such as Anob ("now Betoannaba"), Geth ("now Gitta"), Thamna, Modeim ("now Moditha"), Koreae Praesidium, Arad, Iethor ("also called Iethera"), and others, are more numerous, composed of two towers arranged symmetrically to the right and left of a gate.[48] Buildings in the form of Basilicas with a gable roof or small buildings denote pilgrimage places, such as Jacob's Well, Bethabara—the site of Baptism of St John—(See Figure 19.6) the shrine of Saint Lot as well as the church of Saint Philip.[49] With the central and dominant image of Jerusalem, the See of the fifth patriarchate since 451, on the axis of the church, and the above hierarchic visual typology in the network of cities, towns, villages, and monuments, this landscape composition of the Madaba map acquires a salient spatial organization.

Figure 19.6 Jericho, Archelais, Bethabara, the place of baptism of St John. Detail of the Madaba mosaic map, around 557. Madaba, Jordan

Source: Photo Credit–CC BY-SA 3.0.

The numerous and, in some cases, too lengthy labels on the map,[50] creating the feeling of *horror vacui* (See Figures 19.4 and 19.5), were not only informative but also essential elements of the composition since letters of the alphabet were—and still are—especially attractive to beholders.[51] However, above all, the script and particularly the Greek script, an essential tool of Byzantine administration, probably evoked in viewers, especially the illiterate ones—who would have been the majority—the notion of the state's presence. In other words, it enhanced the confidence in the governmental control upon the depicted regions.[52] Moreover, to literate beholders acquainted with the Greek language, the concepts of boundaries and the division of land into properties, which were also related to the legal distribution of land and taxes, created connotations regarding well-functioning administration.[53] Order (*τάξις*) and economy (*οἰκονομία*), two key concepts predominant in Byzantine political ideology,[54] were visualised on the Madaba map depicting the regions related to the Plan of the Divine Dispensation (*θεία Οικονομία*).[55] Pursuant to the two former concepts, every creature should acquire, in the church organization, the state, and the society, a stable position/function (*τάξις–ἱεραρχία*), prudently determined (*κατ' οἰκονομίαν*).[56] According to the comment by Theodore Balsamon on the 34th Apostolic Canon, order unifies everything, both heavenly and earthly.[57] This notion epitomises significant concepts from the *Corpus Donysiacum* (*ca* 500) by Pseudo-Dionysius the Areopagite,[58] which probably stimulated the perception of the earthy order/hierarchy from the Madaba map as a mirror image of heavenly order.[59] Sixth-century proems of Novels by Justinian I (r. 527–65), mentioning the proper order,[60] old order,[61] former order,[62] advocated the permanent imposition of order for its beneficial effects. Thus, blending religious and political ideas, the Madaba map, depicted in a period of affluence, as well as political and social harmony in Byzantine Palestine and Arabia, invited the local congregation to pray for the everlasting good order throughout the depicted area during the Divine Liturgy.[63] On the other hand, it conveyed pilgrims a sense of security in traveling all over the *Terra Sancta*.

The connection of good order (εὐταξία—the combination of order and economy) with cities also appears in a Greek narrative, the tenth miracle of St Demetrius "On the Lady Eutaxia" (*Περὶ τῆς κυρίας Εὐταξίας*), included in the *First Book of Miracles of Saint Demetrius*, compiled by Archbishop of Thessalonike John I, probably in the first years of the reign of Heraclius (r. 610–41).[64] This story begins with the civil unrest, during the reign of Phocas (r. 602–10), throughout the Orient, and in cities of Cilicia, Asia, and Palestine, up to Constantinople. Accounts of those events and civil uprisings also spread in Illyricum, and disorder was about to affect the society of Thessalonike. However, nothing happened on account of the divine intervention of St Demetrius as the dream of a decent man revealed, a relative of the eparch, who visited the city for the first time: This man dreamt of himself entering the church of Hagios Demetrios in Thessalonike and noticing that inside the sacred ciborium in the middle of the nave, to the left, St Demetrius, the patron saint of the city, sat upon a golden throne placed at the head of a couch. A seemly woman, in modest garments, sat on a throne of silver at the feet of the couch, gazing at the saint. The visitor thought that St Demetrius had a private conversation with that lady, but at that moment, the woman rose from her throne and proceeded toward the ciborium's door. The saint pulled her at once and seated her on her throne again. Then he asked her not to abandon the city, which always needed her—even more so because of the developing situation. The stranger asked an attendant at the gates of the church about the identity of that woman and was informed that she was the lady Eutaxia (i.e., good order), whom everyone in Thessalonike knew since she permanently lived in the city. God had placed her long ago next to St Demetrius, and the saint did not allow her to leave her position. At that point, the narrator woke up and later spoke of his dream to his relative, the eparch. They both visited a pious monk and narrated that dream, asking him to interpret it. The monk answered them that Thessalonike would escape the civil conflict since the glorious St Demetrius had held Eutaxia in the city. And that came true: Thessalonike escaped the danger.[65]

Scholars have ingeniously related Lady Eutaxia to early Christian representations of Tyche (goddess of fortune) of Thessalonike.[66] Images of Goddess Tyche of cities, frequent in antiquity, also appeared in the early Byzantine period representing the city itself. Personifications of cities expressed ideas relevant to their prosperity and thereby to that of the Empire. The personification of its capital, paired with that of Roma, appeared on late antique artifacts, including coins, medallions, and ivory diptychs, conveying political messages of state unity, stability, concord, and well-being.[67] Significant among them is the ivory diptych with the personifications of Roma and Constantinopolis in the Kunsthistorisches Museum, Vienna,[68] widely considered a fifth- to sixth-century work (Figures 19.7 and 19.8).[69] Anthony Cutler, though, based on technical, stylistic, and iconographic details of the representations on both of its leaves, has convincingly attributed it to Carolingian artists, faithfully copying a late antique diptych within the artistic climate of the *Renovatio Imperii Romani*.[70] Nevertheless, it is significant for our study that the iconography of the Vienna ivory diptych still reveals the cluster of ideas emanated by its now lost late antique model. I will advance the idea that its manufacture falls in the late Justinian era celebrating an exceptional event in the capital associated with the emperor.

Each one of the two personifications on the Vienna diptych stands within an *aedicula* composed of columns with Corinthian capitals, architrave adorned with a *rinceau*, and pediment bordered by an Ionian frieze. On the left leaf (See Figure 19.7), Roma is clad

Figure 19.7 Roma. Left leaf of an ivory diptych, early ninth century. Vienna, Kunsthistorisches Museum, inv. no X37

Source: Photo Credit–Public Domain

in *peplos*, girdled below the breasts, and *paludamentum*, fastened over the right shoulder with a jeweled fibula, and bears a helmet quite typical of her iconography. In the left hand, she grasps a thyrsus-like scepter with pinecone finials at either end, a symbol of authority associated with Dionysus' gifts, victory, and welfare.[71] In her right hand, she holds an orb, a symbol of imperial dominance over the *oekoumene* and a frequent emblem of Roma's imagery.[72] A Victory on globe, holding a stylized palm frond, an imperial symbol of victory,[73] offers her a wreath. Roma is the mother of the Roman Empire, which she glorified on the battlefields, providing prosperity. Constantinopolis (See Figure 19.8), in a frontal stance on the right leaf, differs from her warlike counterpart, rendered as an attractive noble lady. She wears a tunic with a jeweled collar and an elegant girdle similar to that worn by Roma, a turreted crown adorned with precious stones, an emblem of sovereignty, and a veil held on her shoulder by a cupid, symbolic bearer of fecundity and happiness.[74] She holds a cornucopia in the left hand, a symbol of abundance and a typical attribute in her iconography.[75] With the right hand, she raises a flaming torch whose light can be related to Christ, the "Light of the World" (John 8:12).[76] Constantinopolis ensures with her walls a peaceful and prosperous life for the Empire, illuminating the world through Christianity.

Roma's iconography reveals the admiration for the sublime of this city still vivid in the early Byzantine imperial milieu.[77] However, Constantinopolis is the real protagonist in the diptych, given that Roma turns slightly toward her partner. In the sixth century, Constantinople was the *urbs regia*, the indisputably most important intellectual and artistic center of the Empire and, according to written sources, a city of exceptional urban beauty.[78] The composition of the two Romas is a visual expression of Byzantine unswerving aspirations of ecumenicity, especially prevailing in Justinian's policy.[79]

On December 24, 562, Hagia Sophia was re-consecrated after Justinian I rebuilt its dome, which had collapsed on May 7, 558, after a major earthquake on December 14, 557. The completion of this project was presented as an achievement of the 80-year-old emperor and celebrated in the capital. On this occasion, Paul the Silentiary, a well-educated poet and courtier of Justinian, wrote a descriptive poem of the church (*Ἔκφρασις τοῦ ναοῦ τῆς Ἁγίας Σοφίας*), commissioned by the emperor. He recited it in a special ceremony, probably at the Feast of Epiphany (January 6), in 563, to a select audience of dignitaries.[80] In this notable work,[81] the poet accurately describes Hagia Sophia, emphasizing its lighting, and praises the emperor, the patriarch (Eutychius), and the personified Constantinople, which he calls Roma. He refers to her relation to Old Roma (daughter–mother) and presents her dialogue with the emperor, pointing to her obeisance to him and his affection for her. It is also noteworthy that Paul the Silentiary regards Hagia Sophia as a source of Divine Light (Divine torch—θεουδέα λαμπὰς) and likens the emperor to light for West and East (ll. 895–922).[82]

In the panegyrist's words, if the emperor had not built Hagia Sophia, the city of Constantinople would not have proceeded to such good cheer and happy indulgence (ll. 116–20).[83] Addressing fruitful (personified) Constantinopolis, the poet asks her to praise the emperor not because he subjugated the peoples on earth under her yoke and extended the enormous size of her throne to the outermost boundaries on the ocean shores. The emperor is praiseworthy because he built the infinite church (Hagia Sophia) in her arm, making her more brilliant than her mother on the Tiber. Hymns in honor of Capitoline Roma should be set aside. So much the emperor surpassed that wonder, as God is superior to any idol. Therefore, the poet wants the gold-clad Anthousa (Constantinopolis) to

Figure 19.8 Constantinopolis. Right leaf of an ivory diptych, early ninth century. Vienna, Kunsthistorisches Museum, inv. no X38

Source: (Photo Credit: Public Domain)

praise her lord with melodic songs (ll. 145–56).[84] A little further below, the poet addresses first-born Latin Roma, inviting her to sing in harmony with fresh-budding Roma (Constantinopolis), rejoicing to see that her daughter has outshone her, for this is the delight of parents (ll. 164–67).[85] The author then refers to the earthquake that struck the city, as a result of which the dome of Hagia Sophia collapsed. Shield-brandishing Constantinopolis approaches the emperor complaining that human envy despoiled her. But it is a sign of grace in Megaera that the damage to her beauty happened during the emperor's lifetime. She suffers from a gaping wound in her breast, which the emperor can heal. After mentioning the goods she enjoys thanks to his achievements, she begs him in *proskynesis* not to neglect the restoration of Hagia Sophia, the most brilliant symbol of his throne. The emperor reassures her that he will reconstruct the church, thus making her even more celebrated (ll. 219–54).[86]

After a bleak five-year time, marked by the collapse of the Great Church's vaulting, the second attack of bubonic plague to Constantinople, the threat of Kutrigur Bulgars to capture the capital, social unrest, and also a plot against Justinian in 562, the reconstruction of the dome of Hagia Sophia appeared as a glory of the Empire.[87] This imperial achievement may have been celebrated—along with hymns, sermons, and Paul the Silentiary's panegyric—with a luxurious commemorative object, visualizing the welfare and civilizing power of Constantinople and the *reconquista* of Roman West. The poem, highlighting the relationship between Justinian, Hagia Sophia, and the personification of Constantinopolis on the one side, and that of the personified Constantinopolis and Roma on the other side, provides evidence of the spiritual and artistic milieu in which the sixth-century model of the Vienna diptych could have appeared.[88]

This brief discussion of early Byzantine images of cities, as topographic motifs or personifications, in public and private contexts, reveals the wealth of meanings and messages they could convey to their contemporary viewers in various conditions. In the case of the profuse assemblage of cityscapes depicted on the mosaic pavement of Saint Stephen at Kastron Mefaa, the eschatological ideas of salvation relate to pilgrimage networks in *Provincia Arabia*, compared to that in the Holy Land. These sacred sites, which were home to the Plan of the Divine Dispensation, are visually connected on the Madaba mosaic map with the ideas of "order" and "economy," two key concepts of Byzantine political thought, ensuring a good life for the inhabitants and safe pilgrimage routes for the faithful. The notion of good administration, contributing to social well-being, also appears in association with city personifications. The combination of their images in numerous artifacts, including the model of the—probably—Carolingian ivory diptych with Roma and Constantinopolis, in Vienna, also highlights Byzantium's political ideology of ecumenicity and Constantinople's civilizing mission in the age of Justinian.

Acknowledgments

Many thanks to Professors Nikolas Bakirtzis, The Cyprus Institute, and Luca Zavagno, Bilkent University, for inviting me to participate in this edited volume. I am grateful to Dr Eugenia Chalkia, Ephor Emerita of Antiquities, and the anonymous reviewer for kindly commenting on this article, Dr Dimitrios Doumas, translator, for editing it, and Mr Spilios Pistas, graphic designer at the Hellenic Ministry of Culture and Sports, for elaborating the drawing of Figure 19.2.

Notes

1 A. Grabar, "Plotin et les origines de l'esthétique medieval," *Cahiers archéologiques* 1 (1945): 15–34, esp. 22.

2 "Εννιάς V 8, 1–2: Περὶ τοῦ νοητοῦ κάλλους," in Plotinus, *Εννεάδων βιβλία 30–33 (Το «Μεγάλο Βιβλίο»)*, Introduction, Translation, Commentary by J. Tzavaras (Athens: Δωδώνη 1995), 110–11; Plotinus, *The Enneads*, trans. S. MacKenna. Second Edition Revised by Bertram Samuel Page. With a Forward by E. R. Dodds and an Introduction by P. Henry (London: Faber and Faber, 1956; 1st ed. by the Medici Society, 1917–30), 422–23.

3 On the polyvalence of images, see H. Maguire, *Earth and Ocean: The Terrestrial World in Early Byzantine Art* (University Park, PA: The Pennsylvania State University Press, 1987), 8–15.

4 Henry Maguire aptly indicates that a medieval text, even if not known to the artist, helps modern art historians understand the ideological context of a medieval work of art by revealing the way of thinking in its time. Maguire, *Earth and Ocean*, 1–3.

5 In Jerash (Gerasa), Madaba, Umm ar-Rasas (Kastron Mefaa), Ma'in, Khirbat al-Mukhayyat (village of Nebo), Khirbat al-Samra. From the large bibliography on the subject, see R. de Vaux, "Une mosaïque byzantine à Ma'in (Transjordanie)," *Revue Biblique* 47, no. 2 (Avril 1938): 227–58, especially 240–55; M. Piccirillo, *The Mosaics of Jordan*, American Center of Oriental Research Publications 1, ed. P. M. Bikai and T. A. Dailey (Amman: American Center of Oriental Research, 1993), 26, 34–37; J. M. Turner, "The Relation between the Topographical Mosaics of Provincia Arabia and the Madaba Mosaic Map" (Master Thesis, University of Adelaida, 2010), https://digital.library.adelaide.edu.au/dspace/bitstream/2440/65145/8/02main.pdf; H. Dey, "Urban Armatures, Urban Vignettes: The Interpermeation of the Reality and the Ideal of the Late Antique Metropolis," in *Using Images in Late Antiquity*, ed. S. Birk, T. M. Kristensen, and B. Poulsen (Oxford: Oxbow Books, 2014), 190–208; T. E. Eckersley, "Putting Christians on the Map: Topographic Mosaics from Late Antique Jordan as Representations of Authority and Status" (PhD diss., University of Louisville, 2016), https://doi.org/10.18297/etd/2484.

6 cf. H. G. Saradi, "Space in Byzantine Thought," in *Architecture as Icon: Perception and Representation of Architecture in Byzantine Art*, ed. S. Ćurčić and E. Hatjitryphonos (Princeton, NJ: Princeton University Art Museum, 2010), 73; eadem, *The Byzantine City in the Sixth Century: Literary Images and Historical Reality* (Athens: Society of Messenian Archaeological Studies, 2006), 72; Turner, "Relation," 78, 85–86; A. Cameron, *The Mediterranean World in Late Antiquity AD 395–600* (London: Routledge, 1993), 129.

7 In the multilingual milieu of *Palaestina* and *Arabia*, from the fifth to the seventh century, Greek was the principal language of business and bureaucracy and preferred by the Hellenized middle and upper classes. L. di Segni, "Late Antique Inscriptions in the Provinces of *Palaestina* and *Arabia*: Realities and Change," in *The Epigraphic Cultures of Late Antiquity*, Heidelberger Althistorische Beiträge 60, ed. K. Bolle, C. Machado, and C. Witschel (Stuttgart: Franz Steiner Verlag, 2017), 298.

8 cf. I. Ehrensperger-Katz, "Les représentations de villes fortifiées dans l'art paléochrétien et leurs dérivées byzantines," *Cahiers archéologiques* 19 (1969): 1–27, esp. 14; N. Duval, "Architekturdarstellungen in jordanischen Mosaiken," in *Byzantinische Mosaiken aus Jordanien*, ed. H. Buschhausen (Vienna: Amt der Nö. Landesregierung, 1986), 175–80; Turner, "Relation," 21–28.

9 cf. G. W. Bowersock, *Mosaics as History: The Near East from Late Antiquity to Islam*, Revealing Antiquity 16 (Cambridge, MA: The Belknap Press of Harvard University, 2006), 66–69; Duval, "Architekturdarstellungen," 176–77; Dey, "Urban Armatures," 203; Piccirillo, *Jordan*, 37; Turner, "Relation," 19–20. On the association of the column depicted in the vignette of Kastron Mefaa with a Stylite's place, see D. Kennedy, "Christianity in the Hinterland of Roman and Umayyad Philadelphia: Evidence and Inference in the Belqa," in *Text and the Material World: Essays in Honour of Graeme Clarke*, Studies in Mediterranean Archaeology and Literature 185, ed. E. Minchin and H. Jackson (Uppsala: Astrom Editions, 2017), 235–40.

10 Originally a site of the Iron Age and a Roman military camp, mentioned in the *Onomasticon* by Eusebius (128.21) and the *Notitia Dignitaum* (Dux Arabiae XXXVII.8: Mefa Equites promote indigenae), Kastron Mefaa (Mefa'a in Arabic sources) developed, from the fifth century, as a late

antique fortified settlement with 16 churches infra and extra muros. M. Piccirillo, "Les églises paléochrétiennes d'Umm er-Rasas (Jordanie): cinq campagnes de fouilles." *Comptes rendus des séances de l'Académie des Inscriptions et Belles-Lettres* 135, no. 2 (1991): 281; Piccirillo, *Jordan*, 232; A. Michel, *Les églises d'époque byzantine et umayyade de Jordanie (Provinces d'Arabie et de Palestine), Ve–VIIIe siècle: Typologie architecturale et aménagements liturgiques (avec catalogue des monuments)*, Bibliothèque de l'Antiquité tardive 2 (Turnhout: Brepols Publishers, 2001), 379, 381; Bowersock, *Mosaics*, 66; A. Walmsley, "Byzantine Palestine and Arabia: Urban Prosperity in Late Antiquity," in *Towns in Transition: Urban Evolution in Late Antiquity and the Early Middle Ages*, ed. N. Christie and S. T. Loseby (Aldershot: Scolar Press, 1996), 150; Eckerslay,"Christians," 136, 176, 205.

11 The church of the Niche was built upon a tomb with multiple burials and the courtyard southwest of the church of Saint Sergius had a sepulchral use. Michel, *Églises*, 383, 387, 396. On the tombs excavated inside the church of Saint Stephen, see below.

12 Piccirillo, "Églises paléochrétiennes," 278–81; M. Sartre and T. Waliszewski, "Umm al-Rasas." *Syria* 72, nos 3–4 (1995): 428; Michel, *Églises*, 381–83, Fig. 358; Eckerslay,"Christians," 291.

13 A fragment of a marble reliquary was found at the courtyard south of the church. Michel, *Églises*, 76, 79, 391.

14 Michel, *Églises*, 389, 104, Fig. 369. On the relationship of annex chapels with relics to the liturgy, see Gordana Babić, *Les chapelles annexes des églises byzantines: Fonction liturgique et programmes iconographiques*, Bibliothèque des Cahiers Archéologiques publiée sous la direction d'André Grabar et de Jean Hubert 3 (Paris: Éditions Klincksieck, 1969), 9–14, 67–74. Robert Ousterhout believes that through the possession of holy relics, every church could acquire the status of a martyrium. R. G. Ousterhout, *Eastern Medieval Architecture: The Building Traditions of Byzantium and Neighboring Lands* (New York, NY: Oxford University Press, 2019), 64.

15 M. Piccirillo, "Les mosaïques d'époque omeyyade des églises de la Jordanie," *Syria* 75 (1998): 268; Peter Baumann, *Spätantike Stifter im Heiligen Land: Darstellungen und Inschriften auf Bodenmosaiken in Kirchen, Synagogen und Privathäusern* (Wiesbaden: Reichert Verlag, 1999), 146–48 (Peter Baumann considers the south chamber a memorial chapel and the earliest building of the church complex).

16 The dedicatory inscription in the nave of Saint Stephen reads: "Under the most holy bishop Sergius, the mosaic of the holy and famous (church of) Protodeacon and Protomartyr Stephen was completed, through the zeal of John, son of Isakios, son of Lexus, the most godly deacon and archon of Mefaa (and) oikonomos, and of all of the Christ-loving people of Kastron Mefaa, in the month of October, second indiction, in the year of the Province of Arabia 680; and in memory and eternal rest for Christ-loving Phidonos, son of Aeias." According to mainstream scholarship, this inscription dates the mosaics to 717/18. Baumann, *Spätantike Stifter*, 179; J. Pahlitzsch, "Christliche Stiftungen in Syrien und im Irak im 7. und 8. Jahrhundert als ein Element der Kontinuität zwischen Spätantike und Frühislam," in *Islamische Stiftungen zwischen juristischer Norm und sozialer Praxis*, ed. by A. Meier, J. Pahlitzsch, and L. Reinfandt (Berlin: De Gruyter, 2009), 48–49; J. Balty, "Les mosaïques d'Umm al-Rasas et la date de 718," *Journal of Roman Archaeology* 11 (1998): 701–2; Michel, *Églises*, 392.

17 On the issue of the deliberate destruction of human and animal figures on mosaics in regions under Islamic rule, see B. Caseau, "Sacred Landscapes," in *Interpreting Late Antiquity. Essays on the Postclassical World*, ed. G. W. Bowersock, P. Brown, and O. Grabar, 2nd ed. (Cambridge, MA: The Belknap Press of Harvard University Press, 2001), 50; Piccirillo, "Églises paléochrétiennes," 283; Piccirillo, *Jordan*, 238; R. Schick, "Christian Life in Palestine during the Early Islamic Period," *The Biblical Archaeologist* 51, no. 4 (December 1988): 218–21, 239–40.

18 Eckerslay,"Christians," 146, 174–76.

19 cf. Maguire, *Earth and Ocean*, 32, 35–38.

20 M. Piccirillo, "The Mosaics at Um er-Rasas in Jordan," *Biblical Archaeologist* 51, no 4 (December 1988): 227; idem, "Recenti scoperte di archeologia cristiana in Giordania," in *Actes du XIe congrès international d'archéologie chrétienne. Lyon, Vienne, Grenoble, Genève, Aoste, 21–28 septembre 1986*, Publications de l'École française de Rome 123 (Rome: École Française de Rome, 1989), 1723; idem, "Églises paléochrétiennes," 285; B. Hamarneh, "The River Nile and Egypt in the Mosaics of Middle East," in *The Madaba Map Centenary, 1897–1997: Travelling through*

the Byzantine Umayyad Period. Proceedings of the International Conference Held in Amman, 7–9 April 1997, Collectio Maior 40, ed. M. Piccirillo and E. Alliata (Jerusalem: Studium Biblicum Franciscanum, 1999), 187.

21 Maguire, *Earth and Ocean*, 43.

22 Michele Piccirillo points to the association of the Nile, as one of the four rivers of Paradise, with the Christian sacred geography. Piccirillo, *Jordan*, 37. For the topic of the Nile in early Byzantine writings and the meanings of its depictions in floor and mural mosaics, see A. Hermann, "Der Nil und die Christen," *Jahrbuch für Antike und Christentum* 2 (1959): 30–69; Maguire, *Earth and Ocean*, 17–18, 23, 26, 29, 42–44, 51; H. Maguire, "The Good Life," in *Interpreting Late Antiquity. Essays on the Postclassical World*, ed. G. W. Bowersock, P. Brown, and O. Grabar, 2nd ed (Cambridge, MA: The Belknap Press of Harvard University Press, 2001), 245–46; T. Polański, "The Nilotic Mosaic in Saint Stephen's Church of Gaza in Choricius' Description." *Studies in Ancient Art and Civilization* 13 (2009): 169–81; H. Maguire, "The Nile and the Rivers of Paradise," in *The Madaba Map Centenary, 1897–1997: Travelling through the Byzantine Umayyad Period. Proceedings of the International Conference Held in Amman, 7–9 April 1997*, Collectio Maior 40, ed. M. Piccirillo and E. Alliata (Jerusalem: Studium Biblicum Franciscanum, 1999), 179–84; J. Chick, "*Okeanus* and the Nile: The Imagery of Sacred Waters in the East Church Complex at Qasr el-Lebia in Cyrenaica, Lybia," in *Holy Water in the Hierotopy and Iconography of the Christian World*, ed. A. Lidov (Moscow: Theoria, 2017), 210–29.

23 Εἰς τὴν τρίτην ἡμέραν τῆς ἑξαημέρου κτίσεως, λόγος τρίτος, IX, 4. Anastasius of Sinai. *Hexaemeron*, Orientalia Christiana Analecta, 278, ed. and trans. C. A. Kuehn and J. D. Baggarly, with a foreword by Joseph A. Munitiz (Rome: Pontificio Istituto Orientale, 2007), 84–85.

24 Maguire, "Good Life," 250; Henry Maguire, *Nectar and Illusion: Nature in Byzantine Art and Literature* (New York, NY: Oxford University Press, 2012), 21.

25 Piccirillo, "Mosaics at Um er-Rasas," 227; idem, "Recenti scoperte," 1723; idem, "Églises paléochrétiennes," 283, 285; idem, *Jordan*, 238.

26 Eckerslay,"Christians," 147–48, 158, 166, 172–73, 185–86, especially 189–97; Turner, "Relation," 34–45; C. Walter, *The Warrior Saints in Byzantine Art and Tradition*, 2nd ed. (New York, NY: Routledge, 2016), 119–21, 268; P. Maraval, *Lieux saints et pèlerinages d'Orient: Histoire et géographie des origines à la conquête arabe*. Preface by Gilbert Dagron (Paris: Les Éditions du Cerf, 1985), 72; J. L. Hevelone-Harper, *Disciples of the Desert: Monks, Laity, and Spiritual Authority in Sixth-Century Gaza* (Baltimore, MD: The Johns Hopkins University Press, 2005), 3; S. N. Kadas, *Οι Άγιοι Τόποι: Εικονογραφημένα προσκυνητάρια 17ου–18ου αι.* (Athens: Εκδόσεις Καπόν, 1998), 38, 60, 67, 71, 79, 91, 94, 113, 137; A. Külzer, *Peregrinatio graeca in Terram Sanctam. Studien zu Pilgerführern und Reisebeschreibungen über Syrien, Palästina und den Sinai aus byzantinischer und metabyzantinischer Zeit*, Studien und Texte zur Byzantinistik 2 (Frankfurt am Mein: Peter Lang 1994), 52, 143, 154–55, 157–58; L. di Segni, "On the Development of Christian Cult Sites on Tombs of the Second Temple Period," *ARAM* 18–19 (2006–07): 383, 388. For the concept of pilgrimage and the motives and expectations of the pilgrims, see Maraval, *Lieux saints*, 137–51, especially 148; Külzer, *Peregrinatio graeca*, 72–76; idem, "Byzantine and early post-Byzantine pilgrimage to the Holy Land and to Mount Sinai", in *Travel in the Byzantine World. Papers from the Thirty-fourth Spring Symposium of Byzantine Studies, Birmingham, April 2000*, Society for the Promotion of Byzantine Studies. Publications 10, ed. R. Macrides (Aldershot: Ashgate Variorum, 2002), 151–53; J. Wilkinson, *Egeria's Travels*, 3rd ed. (Warminster: Aris and Phillips, 1999), 4–8; idem, "Jewish Holy Places and the Origins of Christian Pilgrimage", in *The Blessings of Pilgrimage*, ed. Robert Ousterhout (Urbana, IL: University of Illinois Press, 1990), 41–53; A. Demsky, "Holy City and Holy Land as Viewed by Jews and Christians in the Byzantine Period: A Conceptual Approach to Sacred Space," in *Sanctity of Time and Space in Tradition and Modernity*, Jewish and Christian Perspective Series 1, ed. A. Houtman, M. J. H. M. Poorthuis, and J. Schwartz, 285–96, 361–68 (Leiden: Brill, 1998), 289; R. Ousterhout, "Pilgrimage Architecture," in *Egeria: Monuments of Faith in the Medieval Mediterranean*, ed. M. Kazakou and V. Skoulas (Athens: Hellenic Ministry of Culture, 2008), 47; idem, *Eastern Medieval Architecture*, 61–63.

27 E. Alliata, "The Pilgrimage Routes during the Byzantine Period in Transjordan," in *The Madaba Map Centenary, 1897–1997: Travelling through the Byzantine Umayyad Period. Proceedings of*

the International Conference Held in Amman, 7–9 April 1997, Collectio Maior 40, ed. M. Piccirillo and E. Alliata (Jerusalem: Studium Biblicum Franciscanum, 1999), 123; Kennedy, "Christianity," 232, 234–35.

28 B. Hamarneh, "Geography of Devotion in Byzantine Arabia and Palaestina: The Epigraphic Evidence," in *Knowledge and Wisdom: Archaeological and Historical Essays in Honour of Leah Di Segni*, Studium Biblicum Franciscanum. Collectio Maior 54, ed. G. C. Bottini, L. D. Chrupcala, and J. Patrich (Milan: Edizioni Terra Santa, 2014), 121; E. Alliata, "The Pilgrimage Routes during the Byzantine Period in Transjordan," in *The Madaba Map Centenary, 1897–1997: Travelling through the Byzantine Umayyad Period. Proceedings of the International Conference Held in Amman, 7–9 April 1997*, Collectio Maior 40, ed. M. Piccirillo and E. Alliata (Jerusalem: Studium Biblicum Franciscanum, 1999), 123.

29 S. M. Yeager, *Jerusalem in Medieval Narrative* (Cambridge: Cambridge University Press, 2008), 3; D. R. Howard, *Writers and Pilgrims: Medieval Pilgrimage Narratives and Their Posterity* (Berkeley, CA: University of California Press, 1980), 12.

30 Christian pilgrims faced the risk of imprisonment or harassment by the Muslims. Schick, "Palestine," 239.

31 Babić, *Chapelles annexes*, 13.

32 K. K. Klein, "*Do good in thy good pleasure unto Zion*: The Patronage of Aelia Eudokia in Jerusalem," in *Female Founders in Byzantium and Beyond*, ed. Lioba Theis, Margaret Mullett, and M. Grünbart; with Galina Fingarova and Matthew Savage, *Wiener Jahrbuch für Kunstgeschichte* 60–61 (2011–12): 89–95. Returning to Constantinople after her pilgrimage to Jerusalem—probably in 439—Eudocia brought relics of the saint. Her husband and the citizens received the empress and the holy relics in an *adventus*. K. G. Holum, *Theodosian Empresses: Women and Imperial Dominion in Late Antiquity* (Berkeley, CA: University of California Press, 1982), 189. Kenneth Holum believes that the church of Saint Stephen in Jerusalem was consecrated by Cyril of Alexandria in 438, in the presence of Eudocia, and that later the empress rebuilt this church on a larger scale. Holum, *Theodosian* Empresses, 186, 219.

33 For a detailed examination of this topic, see Turner, "Relation."

34 A. M. Madden, "A New Form of Evidence to Date the Madaba Map Mosaic," *Liber Annuus* 62 (2012): 495–513. For a detailed discussion on the map's dating by mainstream scholarship, see Turner, "Relation," 50–52.

35 See, among others, M. Avi-Yonah, *The Madaba Mosaic Map* (Jerusalem: Israel Exploration Society, 1954); M. Piccirillo, "Die Mosaiken von Justinian bis Jazid II," in *Byzantinische Mosaiken aus Jordanien*, Katalog des Nö. Landesmuseums, Neue Folge, Nr. 178, ed. H. Buschhausen (Vienna: Amt der Nö. Landesregierung, 1986), 55–60; Piccirillo, *Jordan*, 26–34; G. Ortolani, "Cartografia e architettura nella 'carta di Madaba'," *Palladio. Rivista di Storia dell' Architettura e Restauro* 14 (Luglio – Dicembre 1994): 55–68; M., Piccirillo, and E. Alliata, eds, *The Madaba Map Centenary, 1897–1997: Travelling through the Byzantine Umayyad Period. Proceedings of the International Conference Held in Amman, 7–9 April 1997*. Collectio Maior 40 (Jerusalem: Studium Biblicum Franciscanum, 1999); K. M. D. Dunbabin, *Mosaics of the Greek and Roman World*. 4th ed. (Cambridge: Cambridge University Press, 1999), 199–202; P. Donceel-Voûte, "La carte de Madaba: Cosmographie, anachronism et propaganda," *Revue Biblique* 95, no. 4 (Octobre 1988): 519–42; Turner, "Relation." Beatrice Leal has recently suggested that the Madaba mosaic map decorated the audience room in the mansion of a wealthy merchant or local official—alternatively a public institutional structure such as a hall for judicial hearings. B. Leal, "A Reconsideration of the Madaba Map," *Gesta* 57, no. 2 (Fall 2018): 123–43.

36 cf. Dunbabin, *Mosaics*, 200.

37 cf. Y. Tsafrir, "The Maps Used by Theodosius: On the Pilgrim Maps of the Holy Land and Jerusalem in the Sixth Century C. E.," *Dumbarton Oaks Papers* 40 (1986): 136–40; Dunbabin, *Mosaics*, 202; Turner, "Relation," 43–44.

38 A case in point is Agrippa's world map drawn up by Marcus Vipsanius Agrippa, general, statesman, and architect (*ca* 63–12 BC), known to have been set up and publicly displayed in the colonnade Porticus Vipsania (modern Via del Corso area) in Rome. J. J. Tierney, "The Map of Agrippa," *Proceedings of the Royal Irish Academy: Archaeology, Culture, History, Literature* 63 (1962–64): 151–52; O. A. W. Dilke, "Maps in the Service of the State: Roman Cartography to the End of the Augustan Era," in *The History of Cartography. Volume One: Cartography in*

Prehistoric, Ancient, and Medieval Europe and the Mediterranean, ed. J. B. Harley and D. Woodward (Chicago, IL: University of Chicago Press, 1987), 207–8.

39 cf. Alliata, "Pilgrimage Routes," 124. Scholars point also to the instructive/informative/allegoric character of the map. See, for example, O. A. W. Dilke, "Cartography in the Byzantine Empire." With Additional Material Supplied by the Editors. In *The History of Cartography. Volume One: Cartography in Prehistoric, Ancient, and Medieval Europe and the Mediterranean*, ed. J. B. Harley and D. Woodward (Chicago, IL: University of Chicago Press, 1987), 265; H. G. Thümmel, "Zur Deutung der Mosaikkarte von Madeba," *Zeitschrift des Deutschen Palästina-Vereins* 89, no 1 (1973): 66–79; Demsky, "Sacred Space," 289. On the key role of inscriptions in the construction of memory, see A. Chaniotis, "Mnemopoetik: die epigraphische Konstruktion von Erinnerung in den griechischen Poleis," in *Medien der Geschichte – Antikes Griechenland und Rom*, ed. O. Dally, T. Hölscher, S. Muth, and R. M. Schneider (Berlin: De Gruyter, 2014), 132–69.

40 ΟΡΟΙ ΑΙΓΥΠΤΟΥ/ Κ(αὶ) ΠΑΛΑΙCΤΙΝΗC (Borders of Egypt and Palestine). ΒΗΡCΑΒΕ Η ΝΥΝ/ ΒΗΡΟCCΑΒΑ. ΕΩC/ ΤΑΥΤΗC ΤΑ Ο/ΡΙΑ ΤΗΣ ΙΟΥΔΑΙΑC/ ΤΑ ΠΡΟC ΝΟΤΟΝ/ ΑΠΟ ΔΑΝ. ΤΗC ΠΡΟC/ ΠΑΝΕΑΔΙ ΗΤΙC ΟΡΙ/ΖΕΙ ΤΑ ΠΡΟC ΒΟΡΡΑΝ (Beersheba, present-day Borosabba. The boundaries of Judaea to the South from Dan close to Paneas, which defines the boundary to the North). ΓΕΡΑΡΑ. ΒΑCΙΛΙΚΗ ΠΟΤΕ ΠΟΛΙC ΤΩΝ/ ΦΥΛΙCΤΙΑΙΩΝ ΚΑΙ ΟΡΙΟΝ ΤΩΝ ΧΑΝΑ/ΝΑΙΩΝ ΕΝΘΑ ΤΟ/ ΓΕΡΑΡΙΤΙΚΟΝ [C]ΑΛΤΟΝ (Gerara, once a royal city of Philistines and boundary of Canaanites where is the Saltus Gerariticus). ΑCΕΜΩΝΑ/ ΠΟΛΙC ΕΠΙ ΤΗC ΕΡ[ΗΜΟΥ]/ΔΙΟΡΙΖΟΥCΑ ΑΙΓ[ΥΠΤΟΝ]/ ΚΑΙ ΤΗΝ ΕΙC ΘΑΛ[ΑΣΣΑΝ] (Asemona, a city by the desert bordering Egypt and the [way] to the Sea). Cf. E. Alliata, "The Legends of the Madaba Map," in *The Madaba Map Centenary, 1897–1997: Travelling through the Byzantine Umayyad Period. Proceedings of the International Conference Held in Amman, 7–9 April 1997*, Collectio Maior 40, ed. M. Piccirillo and E. Alliata (Jerusalem: Studium Biblicum Franciscanum, 1999), 86, 88, 93.

41 On this question, see Piccirillo, *Jordan*, 28–29; Leal, "Reconsideration," 129.

42 L. Di Segni, "The 'Onomasticon' by Eusebius and the Madaba Map," in *The Madaba Map Centenary, 1897–1997: Travelling through the Byzantine Umayyad Period. Proceedings of the International Conference Held in Amman, 7–9 April 1997*, Collectio Maior 40, ed. M. Piccirillo and E. Alliata (Jerusalem: Studium Biblicum Franciscanum, 1999), 115–20; Bowersock, *Mosaics*, 17–19, 25–26.

43 The scale ranges from *ca* 1:15,000 for the area of central Judaea to *ca* 1:1,600 for the city of Jerusalem. Dilke, "Cartography," 265. According to Aaron Demsky, 1:16,000 for central Judaea and 1:1,613 for Jerusalem (Demsky, "Sacred Space," 287).

44 cf. Bowersock, *Mosaics*, 13, 28; Leal, "Reconsideration," 140–41; Demsky, "Sacred Space," 288.

45 For the rendering of the vignettes of this group, see Noël Duval, "Essai sur la signification des vignettes topographiques," in *The Madaba Map Centenary, 1897–1997: Travelling through the Byzantine Umayyad Period. Proceedings of the International Conference Held in Amman, 7–9 April 1997*, Collectio Maior 40, ed. M. Piccirillo and E. Alliata (Jerusalem: Studium Biblicum Franciscanum, 1999), 135–39.

46 For more details on the depiction of these towns, see Duval, "Vignettes," 139–40.

47 On this group, see Duval, "Vignettes," 140–42.

48 On the representation of villages, see Duval, "Vignettes," 142–43.

49 cf. Piccirillo, *Jordan*, 28; Duval, "Vignettes," 134–44; Turner, "Relation," 17–18.

50 Scrutiny of the legends in Alliata, "Legends," 47–101.

51 H. Hunger, "Die Herrschaft des 'Buchstabens.' Das Verhältnis der Byzantiner zu Schrift- und Kanzleiwesen." *Δελτίον της Χριστιανικής Αρχαιολογικής Εταιρείας*, 4th ser., 12 (1984): 17. On the decorative and magical dimensions of inscriptions, see M. D. Lauxtermann, *Byzantine Poetry from Pisides to Geometres: Texts and Contexts. Volume One*, Wiener byzantinische Studien 24.1 (Vienna: Verlag der Österreichischen Akademie der Wissenschaften, 2003), 272–73; L. James, "'And Shall These Mute Stones Speak?' Text as Art," in *Art and Text in Byzantine Culture*, ed. Liz James (Cambridge: Cambridge University Press, 2007), 188–206; A. Rhoby, "Text as Art? Byzantine Inscriptions and Their Display," in *Writing Matters: Presenting and Perceiving Monumental Inscriptions in Antiquity and the Middle Ages*, Materiale Textkulturen 14, ed. I. Berti, K. Bolle, F. Opdenhoff, and F. Stroth (Berlin: De Gruyter, 2017), 265–83; idem, "Interactive Inscriptions: Byzantine Works of Art and Their Beholders," in *Spatial Icons: Performativity in Byzantium and Medieval Russia*, ed. A. Lidov (Moscow: Indrik, 2011), 319, 325–26.

52 Hunger, "Herrschaft," 17–38, especially 30.
53 cf. Hunger, "Herrschaft," 21–22; A. H. M. Jones, *The Greek City from Alexander to Justinian* (Oxford: At the Clarendon Press, 1940), 291–94.
54 Order (a synonym of hierarchy in Byzantium), with a political and social background, and economy (prudent management), with spiritual and intellectual connotation, were two fundamental and permanent concepts of the organization and worldview of both the Byzantine state and the Church. Hélène Ahrweiler, *L'idéologie politique de l'Empire byzantin*, L'historien. Section dirigée par Roland Mouslier 20 (Paris: Presses Universitaires de France, 1975), 129–47, esp. 132–33.
55 In the *Notitia Dignitatum* manuscript, information on hierarchy and administrative geography associated with topographic motifs (walled cities, *burgi*, and *castella*) also highlighted the idea of the well-governed and safe Roman territory with fortified frontier lines. Cf. J. Arce, "Civitates et castella in the Notitia Dignitatum," in *Ruling an Empire in a Changing World: Studies on Origin, Impact, and Reception of the Notitia Dignitatum. Conference Booklet. 20–23 November 2019* (Freiburg: Albrecht-Ludwigs-Universität-Freiburg, 2019), 13.
56 Good order in Christian worship is inspired by Apostle Paul: Πάντα εὐσχημόνως καὶ κατὰ τάξιν γινέσθω (Everything should be done in a fitting and orderly way) (1 Cor. 14:40). On the significance of good order in the Christian Church, see Ioannikios Koulianopoulos, "Η έννοια της τάξεως και της ευσχημοσύνης στη Λατρεία των τεσσάρων πρώτων αιώνων" (Post-graduate Diplomatic Thesis, National and Kapodistrian University of Athens. 2017). On the governmental principles of order (*taxis*) and management (*oikonomia*) in the Byzantine political ideology, see. Ahrweiler, *L'idéologie politique*, 132–47.
57 Τάξις συνέχει πάντα καὶ τὰ οὐράνια, ἀλλὰ καὶ τὰ ἐπίγεια. *Σύνταγμα τῶν θείων καὶ ἱερῶν κανόνων τῶν τε ἁγίων καὶ πανευφήμων ἀποστόλων, καὶ τῶν ἱερῶν οἰκουμενικῶν καὶ τοπικῶν συνόδων, καὶ τῶν κατὰ μέρος ἁγίων πατέρων, σὺν πλήσταις ἄλλαις τὴν ἐκκλησιαστικὴν κατάστασιν διεπούσαις διατάξεσι, μετὰ τῶν ἀρχαίων ἐξηγητῶν, καὶ διαφόρων ἀναγνωσμάτων*, ed. George A. Ralles and Michael Potles, vol. 2 (Athens: Ἐκ τῆς Τυπογραφίας Γ. Χαρτοφύλακος, 1852), 46.
58 Koulianopoulos, "Λατρεία," 7.
59 V. Ivanovici, "Pseudo-Dionysius and the Staging of Divine Order in Sixth-Century Architecture," in *Pseudo-Dionysius and Christian Visual Culture, c. 500–900*, ed. F. Dell'Acqua and E. Sergio Mainoldi (Cham: Palgrave Macmillan, 2020), 180–81.
60 προσήκουσα τάξις (Nov. 10, Nov. 15, Nov. 22, and Nov. 31 by J. I. Herbert Hunger, *Prooimion. Elemente der byzantinischen Kaiseridee in den Arengen der Urkunden*, Wiener byzantinische Studien 1 (Vienna: Österreichische Akademie der Wissenschaften, 1964), 87, 110, 177, 181, 188).
61 ἀρχαία τάξις (Nov. 59 by Justinian I. Hunger, *Prooimion*, 104).
62 προτέρα τάξις (Nov. 145 by Justinian I. Hunger, *Prooimion*, 132).
63 cf. Turner, "Relation," 94–95. On the well-being in late antique Palestine and Arabia, see Walmsley, "Prosperity," 126–58.
64 On the author and date of the text, see P. Lemerle, *Les plus anciens recueils des miracles de saint Démétrius et la pénétration des Slaves dans les Balkans. II. Commentaire* (Paris: Centre National de la Recherche Scientifique, 1981), 27–34, 44–50; R. Cormack, *Writing in Gold: Byzantine Society and Its Icons* (London: George Philip, 1985), 60; C. Bakirtzis, ed., *Ἁγίου Δημητρίου θαύματα: Οἱ Συλλογὲς Ἀρχιεπισκόπου Ἰωάννου καὶ Ἀνωνύμου. Ὁ βίος, τὰ θαύματα καὶ ἡ Θεσσαλονίκη τοῦ Ἁγίου Δημητρίου*, trans. A. Sideri (Athens: Ἐκδόσεις Ἄγρα – Σταῦρος Πετσόπουλος, 1997), 11–12, 439–40.
65 *Les plus anciens recueils des miracles de saint Démétrius et la pénétration des Slaves dans les Balkans. I. Le texte*, ed. and trans. Paul Lemerle (Paris: Centre National de la Recherche Scientifique, 1979), 109–16; idem, *Commantaire*, 76, 78, 212; Bakirtzis, *Θαύματα*, 148–59; Cormack, *Writing in Gold*, 69–70; C. Bakirtzis, "Η κυρία Ευταξία της Θεσσαλονίκης / Lady Eutaxia of Thessaloniki / Dame Eutaxia de Thessalonique." *Μουσείο Βυζαντινού Πολιτισμού / Museum of Byzantine Culture / Musée de la civilization byzantine* 6 (1999): 23–26; J. C. Skedros, *Saint Demetrios of Thessaloniki: Civic Patron and Divine Protector 4th–7th Centuries CE*, Harvard Theological Studies 47 (Harrisburg, PA: Trinity Press International, 1999), 125–27; T. Papamastorakis, "Ιστορίες και ιστορήσεις βυζαντινών παλληκαριών." *Δελτίον της Χριστιανικής Αρχαιολογικής Εταιρείας*, 4th ser., 20 (1998): 223.
66 Bakirtzis, "Eutaxia," 25–26; Skedros, *Saint Demetrios*, 127.
67 C. Olovsdotter, *The Consular Image: An Iconological Study of the Consular Diptychs*, BAR International Series 1376 (Oxford: John and Erica Hedges, 2005), 97; J. M. C. Toynbee, "Roma and Constantinopolis in Late-Antique Art from 312 to 365," *The Journal of Roman Studies* 37 (1947):

135–44; G. Bühl, *Constantinopolis und Roma: Stadtpersonifikationen der Spätantike*. (Zurich: Akanthus, 1995).

68 Antikensammlung, inv. no X37 (Roma) and X38 (Constantinopolis).

69 See, among others, R. Delbrueck, *Die Konsulardiptychen und verwandte Denkmäler*. Vol. 1, *Text*. Vol. 2, *Tafeln* (Berlin: Verlag von Walter De Gruyter & Co, 1929), no. 38; W. F. Volbach, *Elfenbeinarbeiten der Spätantike und des frühen Mittelalters*, Kataloge vor- und frühgeschichtlicher Altertümer 7, 3rd ed. (Mainz am Rhein: Verlag Philipp von Zabern, 1976), no 38; S. R. Zwirn, "Diptych with Roma and Constantinopolis," in *Age of Spirituality: Late Antique and Early Christian Art, Third to Seventh Century*, ed. K. Weitzmann (New York, NY: The Metropolitan Museum of Art, 1979), no 153; M. Laubenberger, "Diptych with Personifications of Rome and Constantinople," in *Byzantium: An Oecumenical Empire. Byzantine Hours. Works and Days in Byzantium*, ed. M. Evangelatou, H. Papastavrou, and T.-P. Skotti (Athens: Hellenic Ministry of Culture, 2002), no 6; S. R. Zwirn, "The Late Antique Style and Context of the Roma and Constantinopolis Ivory Diptych in Vienna," in *Ninth Annual Byzantine Studies Conference. 4–6 November 1983. Duke University, Durham, North Carolina. Abstracts of Papers*, https://bsana.net/conference/archives/1983/abstracts_1983.php; L. Grig, "Competing Capitals, Competing Representations: Late Antique Cityscapes in Words and Pictures," in *Two Romes: Rome and Constantinople in Late Antiquity*, ed. L. Grig and G. Kelly (New York, NY: Oxford University Press, 2012), 44–48.

70 A. Cutler, "'Roma' and 'Constantinopolis' in Vienna," in *Byzanz und der Westen: Studien zur Kunst des europäischen Mittelalters*, Österreichische Akademie der Wissenschaften. Philosophisch-Historische Klasse. Sitzungsberichte, 432. Band, ed. I. Hutter (Vienna: Verlag der Österreichischen Akademie der Wissenschaften, 1984), 43–64.

71 Toynbee, "Roma and Constantinopolis," 140. For a similar thyrsus and girdle, see the early-sixth century ivory relief with Ariadne at the Musée de Cluny, Paris, inv. no Cl. 455. Volbach, *Elfenbeinarbeiten*, no 78; W. A. P. Childs, "Relief with Ariadne", in *Age of Spirituality: Late Antique and Early Christian Art, Third to Seventh Century*, ed. K. Weitzmann (New York, NY: The Metropolitan Museum of Art, 1979), no 127.

72 G. Ferguson, *Signs and Symbols in Christian Art* (London: Oxford University Press, 1961), 175; C. Olovsdotter, *Consular Image*, 99; Toynbee, "Roma and Constantinopolis," 140. For a similar *victoriola*, see the Barberini ivory (2nd quarter sixth century), at the Louvre, inv. no OA. 9063. J. D. Breckenridge, "Diptych Leaf with Justinian as Defender of the Faith," in *Age of Spirituality: Late Antique and Early Christian Art, Third to Seventh Century*, ed. K. Weitzmann (New York, NY: The Metropolitan Museum of Art, 1979), no. 28.

73 Ferguson, *Signs and Symbols*, 36; C. Olovsdotter, "Representing Consulship: On the Concept and Meanings of the Consular Diptychs," *Opuscula. Annual of the Swedish Institutes at Athens and Rome* 4 (2011): 115.

74 On the symbolism of *erotes* in late antique art, see Olovsdotter, *Consular Image*, 134–37; Olovsdotter, "Consulship," 114.

75 Toynbee, "Roma and Constantinopolis," 139.

76 J. Gazé, "Fackel (Kerze)," in *Reallexikon für Antike und Christentum*, ed. T. Klause, vol. 7 (Stuttgart: Anton Hierseman, 1969), col. 155. Constantinopolis holds a torch in two more sixth-century artworks, the imperial diptychon at the Castello Sforzesco, Milan (Delbrueck, *Konsulardiptychen*, no. 49; Volbach, *Elfenbeinarbeiten*, no 49. Bühl, *Constantinopolis und Roma*, 182–93) and the ivory comb at the Benaki Museum, Athens, inv. no 10287 (Yannis D. Varalis, "Ελεφαντοστέινο κτένι με τις προσωποποιήσεις της Ρώμης και της Κωνσταντινούπολης," *Μουσείο Μπενάκη* 2 (2002): 78). A steelyard-weight, based on representations of Tyche (of Constantinople?), at the British Museum (inv. no 1907,1022.1), which bears a mural crown and holds a torch and a cornucopia, also dates from the sixth to seventh century (https://www.britishmuseum.org/collection/object/G_1907-1022-1).

77 E. Fenster, *Laudes Constantinopolitanae*, Miscellanea Byzantina Monacensia 9 (Munich: Institut für Byzantinistik und neugriechische Philologie, 1968), 89.

78 Fenster, *Laudes*, 89–91.

79 On Justinian's program of *reconquista*, see G. Ostrogorsky, *History of the Byzantine State*, trans. Joan Hussey. Revised Edition (New Brunswick: Rutgers University Press, 1969), 69–71; Cameron, *Mediterranean World*, 104–27.

80 Fenster, *Laudes*, 87–89; M. Whitby, "The Occasion of Paul the Silentiary's Ekphrasis of S. Sophia," *The Classical Quarterly* 35, no 1 (1985): 216–17; R. Macrides and P. Magdalino, "The Architecture of Ekphrasis: Construction and Context of Paul the Silentiary's Poem on Hagia Sophia," *Byzantine and Modern Greek Studies* 12 (1988): 62–64, 77; *Three Political Voices from the Age of Justinian. Agapetus, Advice to the Emperor; Dialogue on Political Science; Paul the Silentiary, Description of Hagia Sophia*, Translated Texts for Historians 52, trans. with notes and an introduction by P. N. Bell (Liverpool: Liverpool University Press, 2009), 17–18.

81 The writer Agathias (*ca* 532 to *ca* 580) recommended that those who had not visited Hagia Sophia could read Paul's description to gain a full picture of the church. Macrides and Magdalino, "Ekphrasis," 49; *Political Voices*, 79–80. For the Greek text, its German translation, and a commentary, see *Prokop, Bauten; Pavlos Silentiarios, Beschreibung der Hagia Sophia*, ed. O. Veh. Archaeological Commentary by Wolfgang Pülhorn (Munich: Heimeran Verlag, 1977), 306–80, 475–510. Parts of the *ekphrasis* appear in Eugenios M. Antoniades, Ἔκφρασις τῆς Ἁγίας Σοφίας, vol. 2 (Athens: Τύποις Π. Δ. Σακελλαρίου, 1908), 4–5, 14–15, 19, 24, 31, 52–57, 65–66, 81, 85–86, 103–4, 112–13,115–17, 127, 188–89, 216, 257, 260–62, 266. For an English translation, see *Political Voices*, 189–212; C. Mango, *The Art of the Byzantine Empire, 312–1453: Sources and Documents*, Medieval Academy Reprints for Teaching 16 (Toronto: Toronto University Press, 1986), 80–96.

82 *Silentiarios, Beschreibung*, 350–53; *Political Voices*, 207; P. N. Bell, *Social Conflict in the Age of Justinian: Its Nature, Management, and Mediation* (Oxford: Oxford University Press, 2013), 330; Macrides and Magdalino, "Ekphrasis," 64, 73.

83 *Silentiarios, Beschreibung*, 312–13; *Political Voices*, 195.

84 *Silentiarios, Beschreibung*, 312–15. For comments on the personifications of both cities in the *ekphrasis* by Paul the Silentiary and their Latin models, see M. Whitby, "Paul the Silentiary and Claudian," *The Classical Quarterly* 35, no. 2 (1985): 507–16.

85 *Silentiarios, Beschreibung*, 314–15; *Political Voices*, 197.

86 *Silentiarios, Beschreibung*, 316–19.

87 Bell, *Social Conflict*, 325; *Political Voices*, 81, 87–88; J. A. S. Evans, *The Age of Justinian: The Circumstances of Imperial Power* (New York, NY: Routledge, 2000), 253–60; Macrides and Magdalino, "Ekphrasis," 67–68.

88 For comments on this milieu, see Macrides and Magdalino, "Ekphrasis," 70–71, 76–78.

20

THE CONSUMPTIVE CAPITAL

Commercial Activities and Ceramic Finds at Constantinople (ca. 500–1000)

Joanita Vroom

Introduction

The archaeology of the Byzantine city is, although developing rapidly, a field of study which is in some respects – at least from a ceramic perspective – still in its infancy. Ceramic finds of the Byzantine period in the eastern Mediterranean, though ubiquitous in most urban and rural sites, have rarely been studied to their full extent. If these 'later' wares were investigated at all, their great significance to yield valuable information about urban activities of production, trade, consumption and cultural interaction in Byzantine cities and towns remained often underrated. Nevertheless, the relevance of pottery as object of study is clear: it is the most widespread, most commonly used and most mobile material product of the past and an indicator of broader patterns of economic as well as cultural changes and interactions in Byzantium.

But what kind of Byzantine pottery was moving to which harbour or city along local, regional or interregional networks by sea? Can such patterns be documented by archaeology in the first place? And more specific: what happened with maritime exchange systems of ceramics within and outside the eastern Mediterranean basin between the 4th and the 7th centuries in general, and in the subsequent period of the 8th and 9th centuries in particular? This last period is still considered by many to be a sort of black hole, literally 'Dark Ages' or 'transition era', not in the least because not much is yet known about trade during these centuries.[1] In fact, well-documented synthetic studies of 8th- and 9th-century material culture are generally still scarce.

It is my intention to search for answers to some of these questions by presenting here a general overview of the distribution of Late Antique-Early Byzantine and Middle Byzantine ceramic finds within the eastern Mediterranean extent of the Byzantine Empire.[2] The focus is initially on local/regional systems of pottery distribution to and from Constantinople (the Capital of the Byzantine Empire, present-day Istanbul), and on interregional ceramic distribution in the Aegean basin and in the eastern Mediterranean in general (the core area of Byzantium). Furthermore, I present in particular 8th- and 9th-century ceramics found at Constantinople, and I mention occasionally those of the 10th and 11th centuries.

Thus, the story is told from the perspective of the political, administrative, commercial and economic heart of the Byzantine Empire, and from the centripetal role played by its

DOI: 10.4324/9780429203923-25

Capital Constantinople. In order to understand the rational of this perspective, as well as of these local/regional and interregional ceramic exchange systems, it is my aim to start with a short introduction to the social and economic organisation of the Byzantine Empire (also known as the Eastern Roman Empire), which was one of the Medieval superpowers in the eastern Mediterranean from ca. 330 to 1453.[3] Thereafter, a survey is presented of Late Antique-Early Byzantine and Middle Byzantine pottery finds from main structures (among which palaces and church complexes) in Constantinople, followed by the distribution of some local ceramic products from the Capital to other areas within the Byzantine Empire.

The Byzantine Empire and Its Capital Constantinople

The emergence of the Byzantine Empire as the independently surviving eastern part of the Roman Empire was a rather drawn-out affair. Some take as starting point the reign of Emperor Constantine I (*r.* 324–337), who reorganised the Roman Empire, made Constantinople the new Capital and legalised Christianity, but in reality the Byzantine Empire was the result of a long period of transition during the 4th to 6th centuries in which the eastern Empire oriented towards Greek rather than Latin culture and became characterised by Eastern Orthodox Christianity. During its lengthy existence (roughly 11 centuries), the Byzantine Empire was the most powerful economic, cultural and military force in Europe. Still, its history is one of a gradual diminishing size of political and economic territory since its western extension in land during the reign of Emperor Justinian I (*r.* 518–527).

The organisation of the Empire rested on the dominance of one powerful ruler, one court, one central government and one state religion (in short, one god, one empire, one emperor).[4] The Byzantine Empire was thus a highly centralised state ruled from an overpowering Capital, with an all-pervasive strong administration, religious and military organisation, consisting of ministers (and their bureaucrats), the clergy and the army. The Byzantines not only maintained Roman core institutions (such as officials and a standing army) but also continued the taxation practices of the Romans by paying bureaucrats and soldiers through the centralised tax system of the Roman Empire.

The Byzantine state drew revenues from diverse fertile regions (Egypt, Sicily and Aegean) in order to feed its administration and its army (in time composed of mercenaries). An important tax mechanism was the *annona*, the tax in kind, which was levied in the provinces under state supervision. Tenant farmers in the countryside (*coloni*), who were tied to their farms, provided the necessary agricultural surplus to sustain the Empire's network of taxes.[5] Tax collecting was efficient and carried out by trustworthy state officials who were prudently supervised in order to prevent corruption.

Furthermore, the Byzantine Empire affected the economic life of its citizens by issuing laws and commercial regulations. One of its economic foundations was trade: both internal and international exchange systems were strictly controlled by the state. There was definitely a central regulated state control of the production of luxury goods in the Capital, of which the most important ones were the silk industry (placed within the imperial palace), and the making of armaments (another state monopoly), followed by the manufacture of objects by master artisans from prized materials: gold and silver plate or jewellery, the carving of ivory objects and the construction of mosaic glass *tesserae*. Some industries were run by the state (with the Byzantine Emperor acting as a kind of captain-of-industry), others by gilds or by individual magnates in the provinces. The production of certain commodities by craftsmen in specific city quarters certainly facilitated the state's supervision.[6] On the other hand, we know from written documents that also commercial consumer-orientated activities must have taken place in a market-driven, free enterprise system.[7]

The issuing and the circulation of coins were surely centrally controlled, which provided a reasonable stable coinage for ca. 700 years and the possibility of keeping fixed prizes (specifically for Byzantine manufactured products). The gold coinage consisted in general of three denominations: *solidus*, *semissis* (1/2 *solidus*) and *tremissis* (1/3 *solidus*); the imperial copper coinage included the *nummus*; and after the late 5th century the *follis* for smaller transactions. The golden *solidus* (*nomisma* in Greek), a coin first issued in 312 by Emperor Constantine I (*r.* 306–337), kept its theoretical value of 4,55 grams of 24 carats of gold in Byzantium until the mid-11th century and was therefore considered to be the Dollar of the Middle Ages. Mints were based in important urban hubs, such as Constantinople, Thessaloniki, Carthage, Rome, Ravenna and Antioch (in the last case the mint was strategically located close to mines).[8] The *solidus* became standard for weighing gold wherever coins were used and continued to be imitated by various neighbouring states during Medieval times. The stable value of the Byzantine coinage also ensured capacity to build monuments or aqueducts and to maintain a good infrastructure in and around main cities.

Urban and Commercial Patterns in Constantinople

The undisputable imperial Capital, Constantinople, was a well-fortified, large and complex urban centre. This metropolis had a strong strategic position on a peninsula, surrounded by water and on the landside by huge fortification walls, which made this city both easily defensible and easily accessible. Furthermore, it was located on a nodal point connecting Europe with Asia and the Black Sea with the Mediterranean.[9] The city was provided with several harbours: two main ones (Neorion, Prosphorion) stretching out towards the Golden Horn on the northern shore and two other ones (Theodosius/Kaisarios, Julianus/Sophia/Kontoskalion) towards the Sea of Marmara on the southern one.[10]

A large palace complex, known as the Great Palace, and a hippodrome (next to it) were located in the heart of Constantinople, on the south-eastern end of this peninsula next to the Bosporus.[11] An imperial and religious ideology was evidently present in the city's development, among which the glorification of the Byzantine Emperor in the Great Palace and in statues on commemorative columns in vital squares, as well as the veneration of Christian monotheism in large churches.

Nevertheless, the urban landscape of Constantinople underwent a metamorphosis from the 5th century onwards. Its ever-changing infrastructure started to display not only a more organic street grid but also an architectural reuse of earlier monuments. Abandoned temples, theatres and baths turned into churches, chapels, monasteries or even into coach houses and gambling halls.[12] Imperial wealth was from now on invested in the construction of churches, monasteries, palaces and philanthropic establishments, although chariot racing continued inside the Hippodrome as a major source of entertainment until Middle Byzantine times. Besides games, it was also essential for the government to keep the Capital's population satisfied and well-fed by safeguarding a steady flow of low-priced food and other necessary articles.[13]

A commercial outline of Constantinople (in particular of wholesale food distribution) can be drawn from written texts, ranging from the *Notitia Urbis Constantinopolitanae* of ca. 425 to the *Book of the Prefect* of 912, of which the last source provides useful information about the regulation of trade guilds in the Capital.[14] Between the 5th and 7th centuries, there was a concentration of warehouses for grain (*horrea*) as well as an oil-, a fish- and a meat-market (*macellae*) near the city's north-eastern (Prosphorion) harbour (see encircled areas in Figure 20.1). Furthermore, the two southern harbours each had a grain warehouse as well, and a nearby square (the so-known Theodosian Forum) had a fish- and a meat-market. Bakeries and distribution centres of bread (*gradus*) were spread all over Constantinople, whereas columned streets (*stoai*) with shops (*ergasteria*) were concentrated along one of the most important ancient streets (the *decamus*), also known as the Mese.[15]

The control on food provisions to Constantinople was a vital necessity for the Byzantine state.[16] The distribution of foodstuffs included maritime grain transports, which were carried to the Capital through the *annona* system from North Africa, Egypt and Anatolia.[17] Wine and olive oil came as bulk goods in ceramic transport containers (amphorae) from various regions within the Byzantine Empire, whereas fresh vegetables, fruits and herbs were provided by city gardens (within the walls) and by Constantinople's immediate hinterland.[18] Fish was caught in the Bosporus, and meat came mostly from herds of sheep and goats driven from western and central Anatolia.[19] A recent archaeozoological study, in which 65,535 excavated animal remains from Constantinople's southern harbour were analysed, shows that ovicaprids or sheep/goat (40.49%), cattle (25.68%), equids (20.14%)

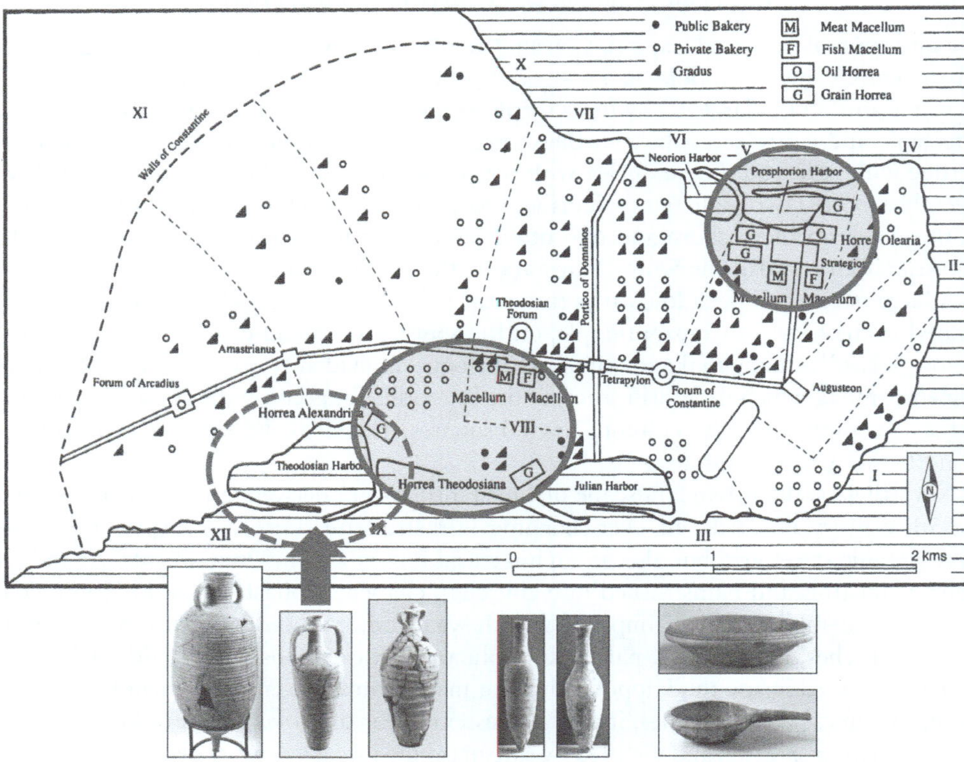

Figure 20.1 Commercial outline of 5th- to 7th-century Constantinople with the concentration of warehouses (see encircled areas) in the north-eastern harbour and the southern harbours. The images below show imported amphorae and ceramics arriving in the city from the south (map after Mundell-Mango, 'The commercial map', Fig. 20.4; Images after *Stories from the Hidden Harbour*, Nos. 132, 135, 144, 159, 161, 163, 165)

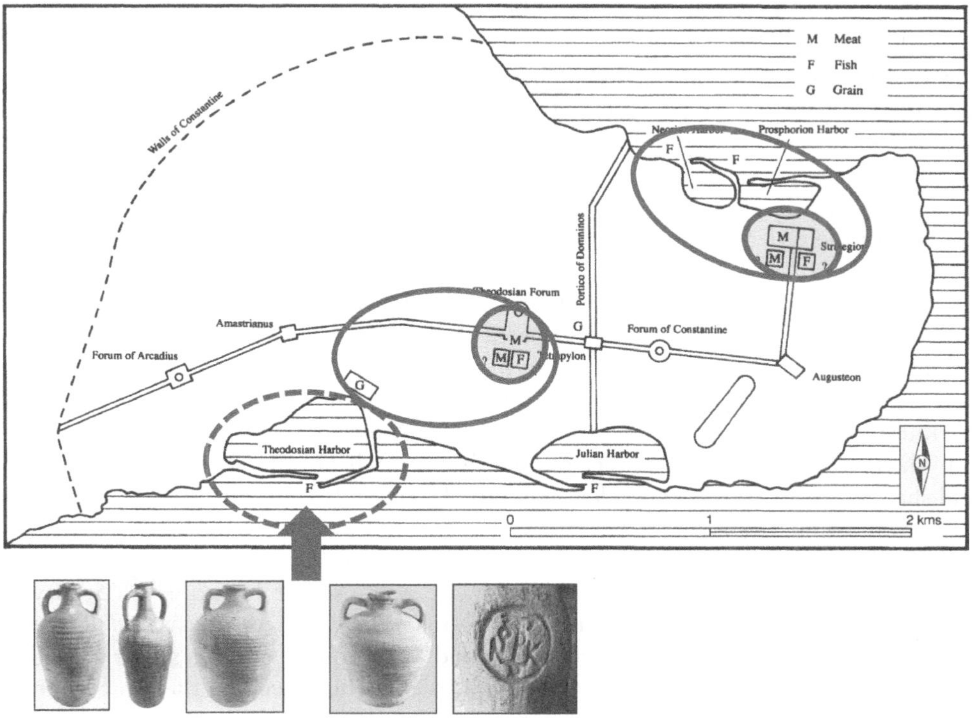

Figure 20.2 Commercial outline of 10th- to 12th-century constantinople with the Concentration of warehouses (see encircled areas) in the north-eastern harbour and the southern harbours. The images below show imported amphorae arriving in the city from the south (map after Mundell-Mango, 'The commercial map', Fig. 22; Images after *Stories from the Hidden Harbor*, Nos. 237, 240, 255, 265, 269)

and pig (6.75%) were the most frequently consumed species related to meat consumption in the Capital.[20] Of these, sheep and goat remains had the largest number of butchering marks on the bone surfaces, with evidence of cutting and chopping of the skulls showing the practice of brain removal for the consumption of offal.[21] Other (more exotic but less used) species included camels, game, hare, dolphins, sea turtles, chicken and fish (e.g., tuna, swordfish, catfish).[22]

The grouping of commercial enterprise in two key areas (around the north-eastern harbour and the two southern harbours) in the 5th to 7th centuries seems to continue into later times, between the 10th and 12th centuries (see encircled areas in Figure 20.2). This continuation occurred with the addition of marketplaces for wine, bazaars for non-food commodities, and inns (*xenodocheia, metata*) for the housing of visiting merchants coming from abroad.[23]

Ceramic Finds at Constantinople

Since 1912, excavations and cleaning have been taking place in various parts of the city on the peninsula. These projects included work at the Akataleptos Monastery (Kalenderhane Camii),[24] Blakernai Palace (Tekfur Palace),[25] Boukoleon Palace,[26] Euphemia Church,[27]

Great Palace,[28] Hagia Eirene Church,[29] Hagia Sophia Church,[30] Hippodrome and Zeuxippus Baths,[31] Mangana Palace,[32] Myrelaion Church (Bodrum Camii),[33] Palace of Antiochos,[34] Palace of Botaneiates[35] and Polyeuktos Church (Saraçhane),[36] which were sometimes supplemented with (more or less detailed) publications of the pottery finds. More recently, large-scale excavations were undertaken not only at the Great Palace in the garden of the old Sultanahmet jail (now the Four Seasons Hotel) but also near the so-known Theodosius Harbour (at Yenikapi) and behind the 19th-century railway station at Sirkeçi (the eastern terminus of the Orient Express) – the last two due to the construction of a modern metro line.[37]

Let us focus on the archaeological basics of these projects: what did archaeologists find so far of 8th- to 9th-century material (particularly ceramics) within the Capital and thus within the core of the Byzantine Empire in a stratigraphical context, and what was the character of this material? This is easier said than done. In contrast to the production and distribution of the Late Roman tablewares and transport amphorae dated between the 4th and 7th centuries, Byzantine pottery of the 8th century is not quite well-known and much published in great detail.[38] Even identifying published finds from this period (and beyond) is sometimes a puzzle.

An earlier archaeological perspective for 8th-century Constantinople and Byzantium was presented by the author during a conference organised at Trento in 2005, of which the proceedings were published in the 2011 book *When Did Antiquity End?*[39] The emphasis in my contribution in this volume, titled 'The other Dark Ages: Early Medieval pottery finds in the Aegean as an archaeological challenge', was on the most important studies relating to excavations in Constantinople (modern Istanbul), on Mainland Greece (showing evidence from sites such as Athens, Corinth, Argos), on Crete and on the other Greek islands.[40] Furthermore, it was my intention to discuss some general ideas on the production and distribution as well as on the transport and patterns of use of 8th-century pottery in the Aegean.

Presently, I set out to take my earlier observations in this 2011 article as a starting point and to move forward from there. But before doing so, it is indispensable to take a first inventory of which kind of 8th-century pottery finds have been excavated in the Capital of the Byzantine Empire. The study by John Hayes of the 8th-century pottery finds from the Polyeuktos church excavation in the Saraçhane district is still the most detailed and adequate for dating finds in present-day Istanbul.[41] The bulk of the Late Roman/Early Medieval finds from this excavation was essentially made up by transport amphorae. These last ones, for instance, accounted for some 85% of the total sherd finds.[42] Hayes classified the amphorae into ca. 60 types, ranging in date from the 4th to the 13th centuries.[43]

A map shows the distribution of Hayes' types of 4th- to 7th-century amphorae coming from production areas in the Mediterranean to Constantinople (Figure 20.3a). It is clear that major bulk goods (such as wine and olive oil) can be associated with distinct agricultural zones in the Byzantine provinces, which exported food provisions in ceramic containers to the Capital. Constantinople surely maintained commercial ties with North Africa, the Near East, Egypt, Palestine, Israel, south-eastern Turkey, Cyprus, the (eastern) Aegean and the southern Black Sea coast in this period.

The Saraçhane excavations yielded, amongst others, fragments of the Tunisian spatheion and mini-spatheion, of the LRA 7 and bag-shaped amphora from northern and middle Egypt, of the LRA 4, LRA 5/6 and Agora M334 from Akko and Palestine, of the LRA1 from Cilicia and/or western Cyprus, of the Agora M273 and LRA 3 of the

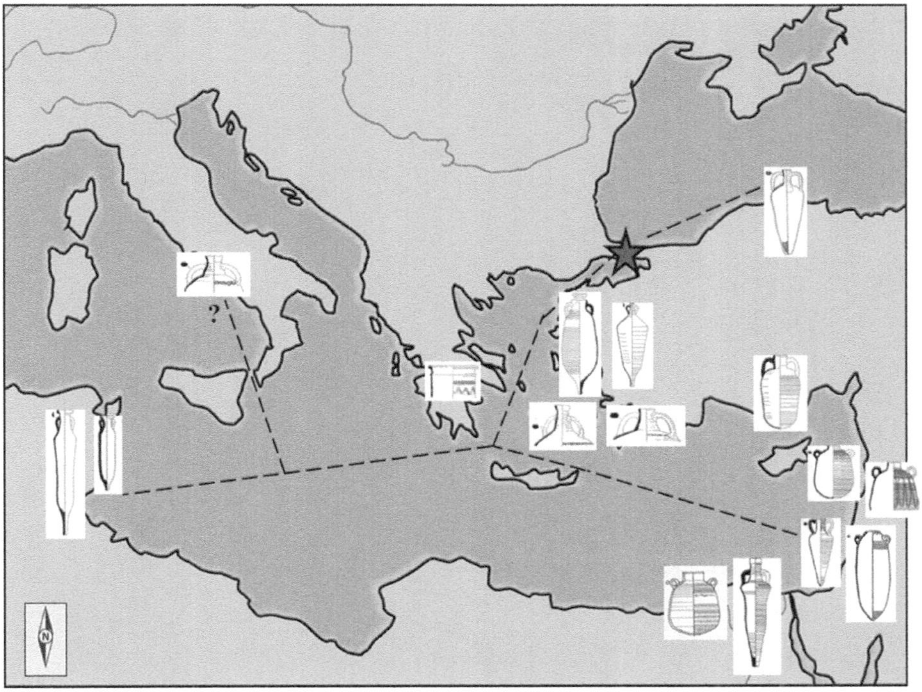

Figure 20.3a Map of the Mediterranean showing the distribution of 4th- to 7th-Century amphora types to Constantinople (Images after Hayes, *Excavations at Saraçhane*, 61–71)

Samos-Ephesus region and the Sinope amphora (see Figures 20.3a and 20.3b for their shapes).[44] Most of these amphora types were also recovered during excavations of Constantinople's southern harbour at Yenikapı, so they must have been transported into the city and to the area of St. Polyeuktos Church from the South, evidently from the Sea of Marmara (Figure 20.1).[45]

The most dominant amphora types in the Saraçhane assemblage of the late 7th to 8th centuries were globular-ovoid-shaped amphorae, which were mostly produced and used in the eastern Mediterranean and in particular in the Aegean. This broad and miscellaneous group, often coined in previous literature as 'globular amphorae', included types that we can now better differentiate due to the recent location of their production centres. The Polyeuktos church excavation yielded, for instance, several variants of the so-called Late Roman amphora 2/13 from Cyprus and the Aegean (Figure 20.4b). These included the earlier amphora type 'Saraçhane 29' (similar to amphora finds on the so-called Yassi Ada 2 shipwreck),[46] as well as the 8th-century amphora types 'Saraçhane 35-43' which were probably of an eastern Aegean origin.[47]

Apart from transport amphorae, the 8th-century ceramic finds from this excavation showed wares in a whitish fabric covered with a lead glaze, known as Glazed White Ware I, the locally made fine ware *par excellence* from Constantinople (Figure 20.4a).[48] The earliest examples have a whitish to pink-orange kaolin clay, often with a thin, reddish-orange slip over the whole surface of the vessel and even under the glaze. This makes this pottery type essentially a 'Late Antique' Red Slip Ware with a glaze component on top. The lead glaze was indeed initially not used for decorative reasons but was put on the interior of vessels for use as a sealant.

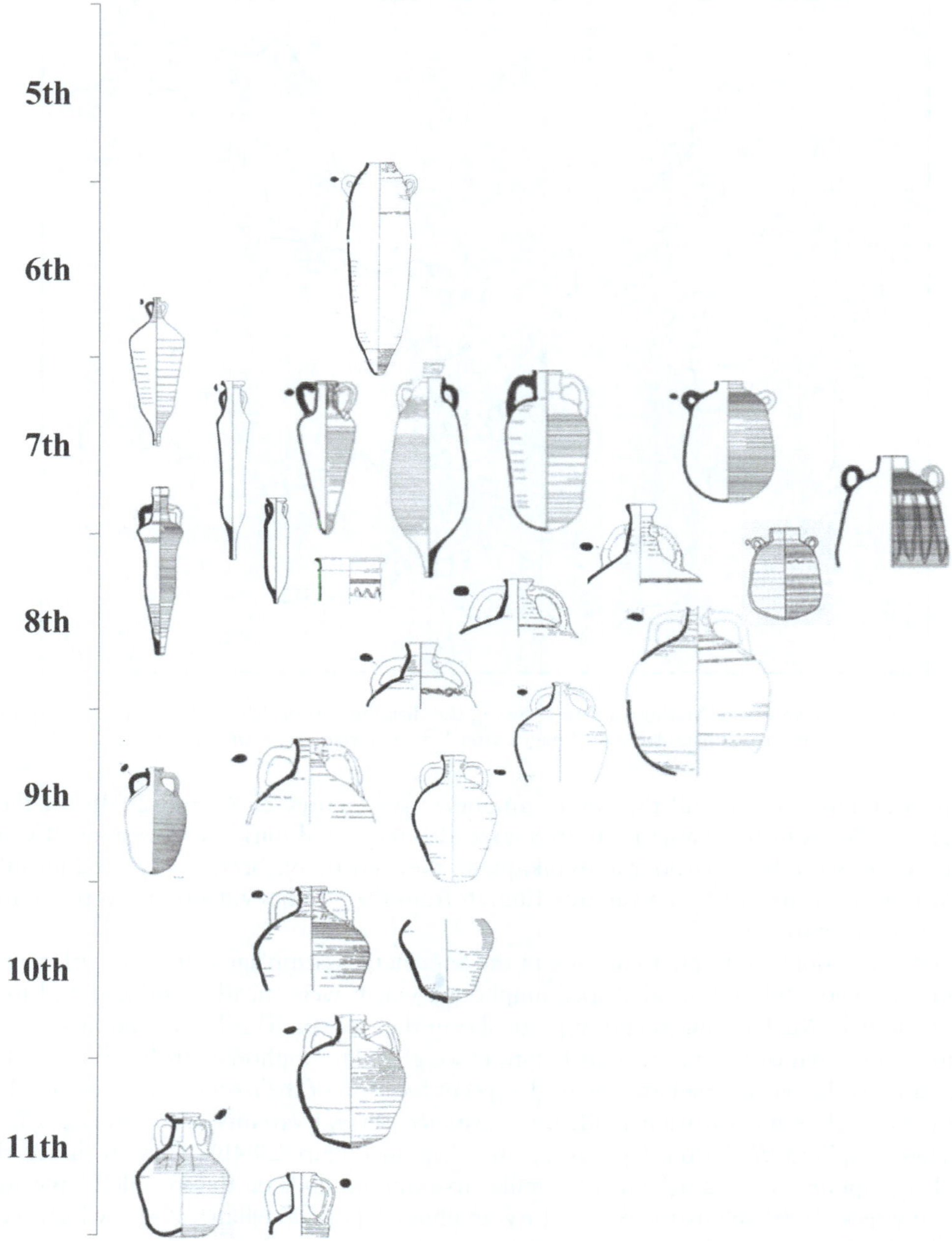

Figure 20.3b Overview of amphora types found at the St. Polyeuktos Church excavations at Saraçhane (Images after Hayes, *Excavations at Saraçhane*, 61–75)

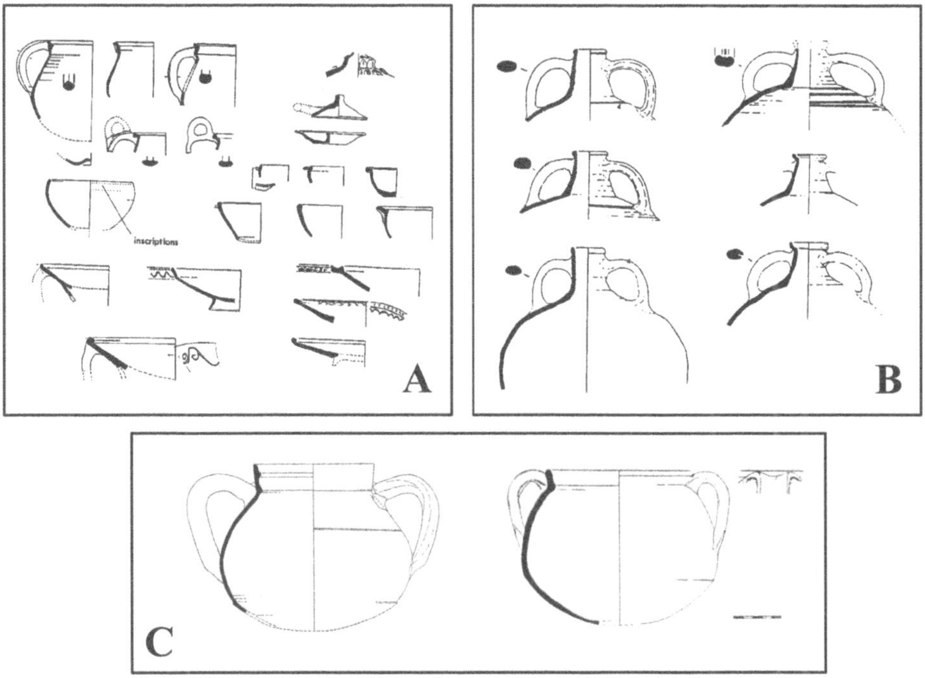

Figure 20.4 Pottery finds from the St. Polyeuktos Church excavations at Saraçhane (Images after Hayes, *Excavations at Saraçhane*, Figs. 4, 23, 38, 45, 56; Vroom, 'Ceramics', Figs. 13.6–13.7)

The first examples were undecorated cooking pots of a utilitarian character, followed by glazed dishes and chafing dishes, which were incised with scrollwork, wavy lines, crosses, fishes and inscriptions in Greek letters. Nice examples of this last group are Glazed White Ware I chafing dishes from Constantinople found on the island of Samos, dated to the 8th century, as well as in the Byzantine quarter at Gortyna on Crete.[49]

Furthermore, Early Medieval coarse wares of the 8th century found at the Saraçhane excavation were represented by baggy cooking pots. In Figure 20.4c, we can distinguish two types: first, the locally produced type of a brown-grey fabric and black slip with a slightly everted rim and two strap-like heavy handles (Saraçhane 'CW3', also known as 'Constantinopolitan cooking pot'), which can be dated to the late 7th to 8th centuries (Figure 20.4c on the left),[50] and second, the imported type with a different fabric (Saraçhane 'CW 4'), which can be dated between the late 7th and early 9th centuries (Figure 20.4c on the right).[51] These last ones were made in a micaceous brown fabric, which included a substantial amount of golden mica. Archaeometrical research on samples from Ephesus has proven that these pots probably originated from the Phocaea area in western Turkey, which makes them regional products with respect to Constantinople.[52]

When looking at ceramic finds of ca. the 7th and 8th/early 9th centuries found at imperial palaces in Constantinople we may distinguish examples of the locally made Constantinopolitan cooking pots with a black slip (Saraçhane 'CW3') at excavations of the Great Palace and of the Palace of Antiochos in the heart of the city centre (Figure 20.5).[53] This last palace also generated another unglazed kitchen utensil (a mortarium with a spouted rim

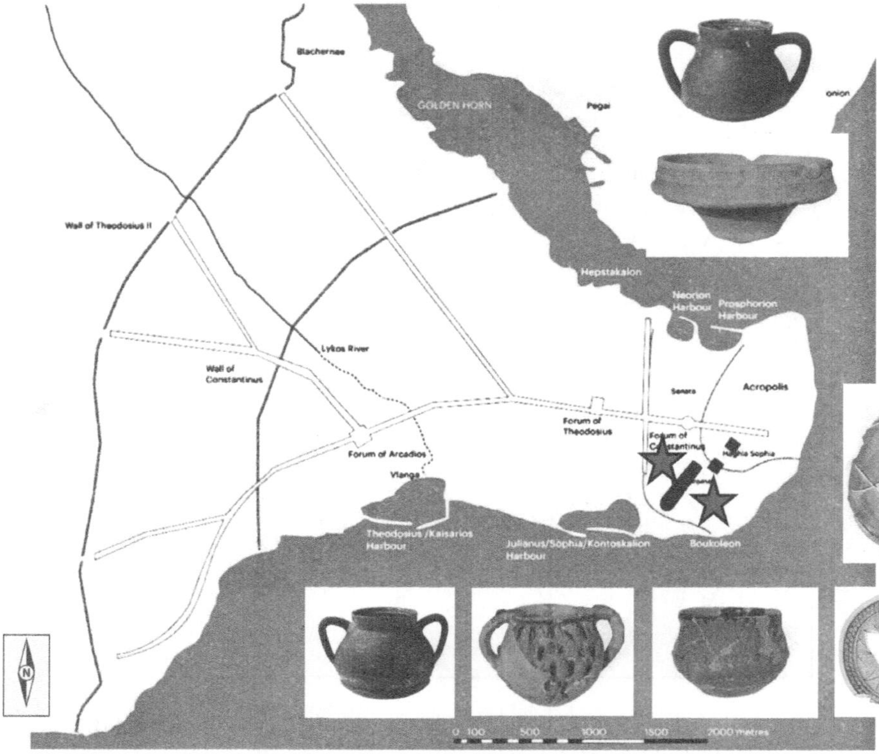

Figure 20.5 Map of Constantinople showing pottery finds (ca. 6th to 8th century) in Constantinopolitan palaces (map after Magdalino, 'The harbors',13; Images after Stevenson, 'Chapter II: The pottery', Colour Plate Stages I–III; *Byzantine Palaces*, Nos. 31, 48-49, 149–150)

and traces of yellowish brown glaze on the interior),[54] whereas the Great Palace excavations yielded unglazed earthenware oil lamps as well as some dishes, bowls and a double handled pot of Glazed White Ware I (sometimes with an incised or petal decoration).[55]

Ceramic finds of ca. the 9th to 11th centuries from excavations at imperial palaces in Constantinople show, on the other hand, a larger repertoire of glazed pottery shapes (mostly of the Glazed White Ware II repertoire) which were probably used on or next to the table. Excavated finds from the Great Palace, the Palace of Antiochos and the Blachernae Palace included large shallow dishes, broad serving bowls and wide-rimmed drinking vessels, as well as beakers/chalices, cups/mugs, chafing dishes and footed lamps (Figure 20.6).[56]

Ceramic Distribution within the Byzantine Empire

From the 7th century onwards, locally made glazed wares began to dominate production in the Byzantine Capital. For the first time, Constantinople was manufacturing its own products (Glazed White Ware I) for export. This urban manufacture reached at first a modest level, but it made a difference from the 7th century, when various unglazed Red Slip Wares from various provincial workshops were still imported into Constantinople as

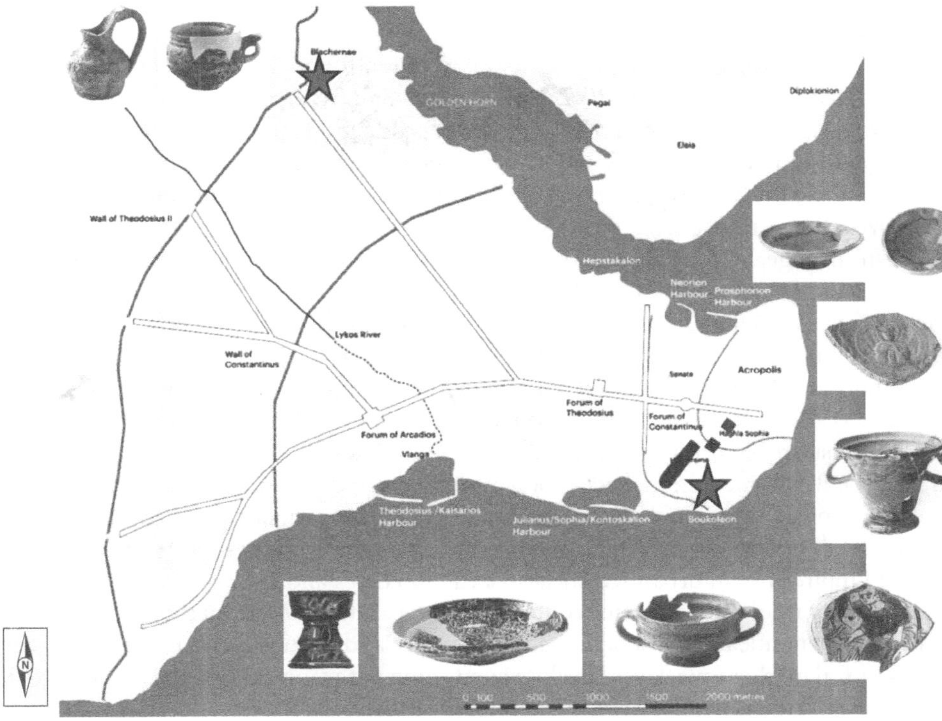

Figure 20.6 Map of Constantinople showing pottery finds (ca. 9th to 11th Century) in Constantinopolitan palaces (map after Magdalino, 'The harbors',13; Images after Stevenson, 'Chapter II: The pottery', Colour Plate Stages I–IV *Byzantine Palaces*, Nos. 41–43, 166, 196–197)

tableware. Due to a large consumers market in the Capital, the quality and technology of its local pottery production improved gradually and became stabilised.[57] Besides distribution in the region around Constantinople (specifically the western and south-western Turkish coasts), Glazed White Ware I also reached other parts in the eastern Mediterranean, among which southern Albania, northern Africa, the Aegean, Crete, Cyprus, the Crimea and central Turkey.[58]

The Glazed White Ware I chafing dishes made in Constantinople were soon imitated in the Aegean by lead-glazed examples in reddish coarse and porous fabrics (for instance, in provincial Byzantine cities such as Amorium, Corinth, Butrint and Otranto). These characteristics would make these vessels suitable as cooking or heating utensils. The Glazed Red Ware chafing dishes circulated in Constantinople, Greece, Turkey and in the Black Sea region, as well as in Albania and southern Italy.[59]

Even the local cooking pots made in Constantinople (Saraçhane 'CW 3C') were travelling to other parts within the Byzantine Empire. To date, examples were found at sites in the Black Sea region, Rumania, Turkey, Cyprus, northern Africa, Italy, southern France and Spain.[60] On the other hand, there seems to be a concentration of the regional cooking pots from western Turkey in the eastern part of the Mediterranean. So far, specimens of this second cooking pot type (Saraçhane 'CW4') were found at sites in Rumania, Turkey, Cyprus, the Near East, northern Africa and southern France.[61] Among these were, for instance, eight partial and complete pots from the 9th-century Bozburun shipwreck off the Turkish Coast.[62]

But let us focus on the 'globular amphorae' found in the St. Polyeuktos Church excavation at Constantinople. In Figure 20.7, we see some main types of the 8th- and 9th-century amphora finds from Saraçhane in relation to their production zones in Byzantine territories, where they were made in various smaller workshops. As one may notice, we are dealing here with a diverse group of amphorae with different fabrics and with different shapes in smaller sizes. Some transport vessels (Saraçhane types 35, 37, 39 and 45) were produced in the eastern Aegean (probably in the Samos-Ephesus region or on the island of Kos),[63] others (such as the Saraçhane type 44) came from eastern Sicily (Figure 20.7).[64] But what all these different smaller amphora types do share is that they were a perfect container for interregional and long-distance transport of low-value staple commodities, for instance for the distribution of wine or olive oil. Judging from the archaeological material, an intra-regional, long-distance or cabotage movement of smaller globular amphorae certainly existed in the eastern Mediterranean between the late 7th and 9th centuries.

In fact, the Byzantine Empire had a good infrastructure with cities connected to each other by maritime and road systems. Maritime movement between major ports depended upon a system of smaller harbours, aiding cabotage and tramping from one place to another. The Byzantine Empire was an urbanised society of ca. 900 cities and towns, connected by a good infrastructure of roads and maritime routes which were taken over from the Romans.[65] Cities were self-sufficient nuclei of production and commerce and dependent on interregional transactions. Central market towns were in close connection with Constantinople, and villages had direct links with towns by means of marketplaces for their supplies.[66]

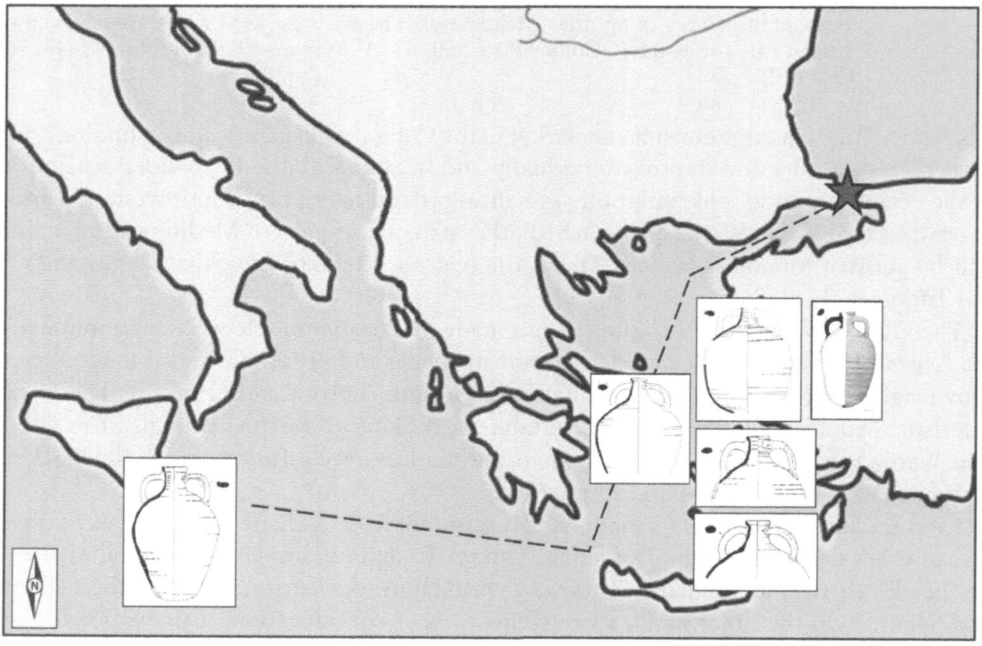

Figure 20.7 Map of the Mediterranean showing the distribution of late 7th- to 9th-century amphora types to Constantinople (Images after Hayes, *Excavations at Saraçhane*, 71–73)

Warehouses (*horrea, apothiki*) stacked with pottery (mostly amphorae) were so far seldom recovered in Byzantine ports and cities in the Mediterranean. The only exceptions were a coastal warehouse excavated at Classe (the harbour of Ravenna) full of imported tablewares, lamps and amphorae grouped together in sets,[67] a military storehouse at the fort of Dichin (along the Danube river) with six amphorae of different types (for instance, LRA 1 and LRA 2) stacked in a row,[68] and another warehouse and anchorage at 'Ard el-Mihjar, south of Ashqelon (Israel), packed with local Gaza-type amphorae ready for inspection and for transport to other Mediterranean harbours.[69] While the last 7th-century warehouse shows the export of a prized wine from a productive viticultural region, the first two ones show how goods were imported (around 500) on their way to consumption sites. Furthermore, we know of shops (often within a *stoa*) in Byzantine cities, which housed potters (Justiniana Prima), or which functioned as grocers (*ergasteria*) where amongst many things pottery was sold (Constantinople).[70]

Several 7th- to 8th-century amphorae made on the island of Kos bear incised *graffiti* in Greek characters (apparently, abbreviated names), as well as different types of control stamps depicting busts of emperors or cross-like monograms with inscriptions (mentioning 'exceedingly glorious') which can be connected with state officers. At least 24 stamps of an official nature were found on 20 amphorae, showing that these were controlled and approved as a cargo with an official stamp on 1 or 2 of them (per cargo). According to the Greek archaeologist Charikleia Diamanti, these stamped amphorae were proof of a state control mechanism upon the commercial activities of Kos, performed by authorised officers such as commercial inspectors (the *kommerkiaroi*) who were charged with the collection of the imperial sales tax (*kommerkion*) and with inspecting the transactions of warehouses on the island.[71]

The smaller sized amphorae of the 8th century had commercial advantages: they had for example less carrying capacity, which facilitated easy handling during short-, medium- and long-distance transport on various means of transfer in the Aegean and in the Mediterranean. In addition, they enabled easy handling during loading and unloading of cargoes in minor and less sophisticated coastal harbours, perhaps by smaller sized merchant ships of ca. 10–15 metres in length as the ones from the Yenikapı excavations in Constantinople. Most Byzantine ships involved in commerce seem to be fairly small, often up to 20 metres long and around 8 metres wide.[72]

A substantial percentage of most ship cargoes contained amphorae (sometimes up to 1500 specimens in a load), which were good indicators of the circulation of staple goods from the Mediterranean (such as olive oil, wine and grain) to other regions within and outside the Byzantine Empire. Through their circulation, we can detect regional, interregional and extra-regional movements of basic food supplies in the Mediterranean and beyond. Furthermore, these ceramic containers often mirrored the distribution of other archaeologically invisible and lighter weighted merchandises in ships, such as high-value textiles, metalware, spices, drugs and aromatics.[73]

Ceramic Finds at Yenikapı

At Constantinople's southern Theodosius harbour (the present-day Yenikapı area in Istanbul), at least 37 shipwrecks were fully excavated between 2004 and 2013. They dated between the late 6th/early 7th and 10th/11th centuries.[74] Some of the Yenikapı shipwrecks even contained their cargo, among which the so-called YK 35 that carried at least 29 specimens of the Agora M273 amphora from the Samos-Ephesus region, 14 examples of the Sinop amphora from the southern Black Sea coast and one vessel of the LRA 3 amphora from the western coast of Turkey on board (Figure 20.1 images below map).[75] In addition, the shipwreck yielded personal ceramic items of the crew, such as unglazed oil lamps, Late Roman *unguentaria*, a one-handled pot, Red Slip Ware dishes (among which a Cypriot Red slip Ware dish form 9C, dated to 580/600 to late 7th century) and an Unglazed White Ware frying pan with solid handle, showing that the wreck should be dated in the 7th century.[76] Apparently, organic residue analysis of the Sinop amphorae from this shipwreck indicate that they were carrying anchovies remains, showing thus a trade in pickled/salted fish (or even *garum)* to the Capital.[77] It is clear that these ceramic vessels and transport containers entered Constantinople through the Theodosius harbour at Yenikapı (see for their shapes, Figure 20.1 beneath the broken encircled zone).

Other shipwrecks at Yenikapı contained amphorae of a later date in their cargo. The 'YK12' transported, for instance, 9th-century prototypes of the so-called Ganos amphora (with a narrower body shape) and an 'LRA 1 survival/derivative' of the same date (see Figure 20.2 on the left below beneath the broken encircled zone).[78] Furthermore, objects from the boat's pantry were found in this shipwreck, such as an earthenware brazier (which was probably used like a *tannur* on board for food preparation), a one-handled jug, a small cooking pot, two mugs and a small jug with a trefoil rim.[79] Most of the recovered amphorae have Greek *graffiti* on their shoulder. One amphora not only has a painted *dipinto* on the shoulder mentioning 'wine measure' but also has a resin residue on the interior body that appears to refer to the transport of wine.[80]

More to the east in the excavated area at Yenikapı, the 'YK 1' shipwreck mostly revealed 10th/11th-century wine amphorae of the more classical type from Ganos (a region south of Constantinople), displaying thus regional transactions between the Capital and the Sea of Marmara (Figure 20.2 on the right below beneath the broken encircled zone).[81] The role of Constantinople as a large consumer centre and as a regional and interregional transit hub is shown by the thousands of pieces of these Ganos amphorae (also known as 'Günsenin 1/ Saraçhane 54 amphorae'), which were arriving the Capital through the Theodosius harbour at Yenikapı.[82] Some of these amphorae have Greek graffiti on their shoulder; others are stamped on the handles with monograms showing Greek letters such as 'ΚΩΣΤ' or 'made in Constantinople' (Figure 20.2 on the right below beneath the broken encircled zone).[83]

Ceramic containers with food supplies from Constantinople's hinterland and from its neighbouring provinces must have entered the Capital from its southern harbour by sea, while they were marked with the city's trademark stamp. The manufacture of such amphorae and their content undoubtedly was still strictly controlled by the central administration in the Capital. According to the *Book of the Prefect*, all the producers and merchants of goods in Constantinople were paying taxes to the prefect of the city (or Eparch), whose task was to supervise if such commercial activities were following the correct rules.[84] As there are no potters mentioned in this 10th-century written document, it is likely that the imperial administration was controlling amphora production as well as the quantity of their contents (wine, oil and cereals) in Middle Byzantine times.

It seems clear that between the 7th and 10th/11th centuries, long-distance voyages on small, low-status merchant ships (such as the ones found at the recent Yenikapı excavations) were more prevalent in the eastern Mediterranean and in the Aegean than previously known. Coastal cities (and specifically the Capital) were in the 11th century provided with ceramic containers full of agricultural products from other parts of the Mediterranean. This

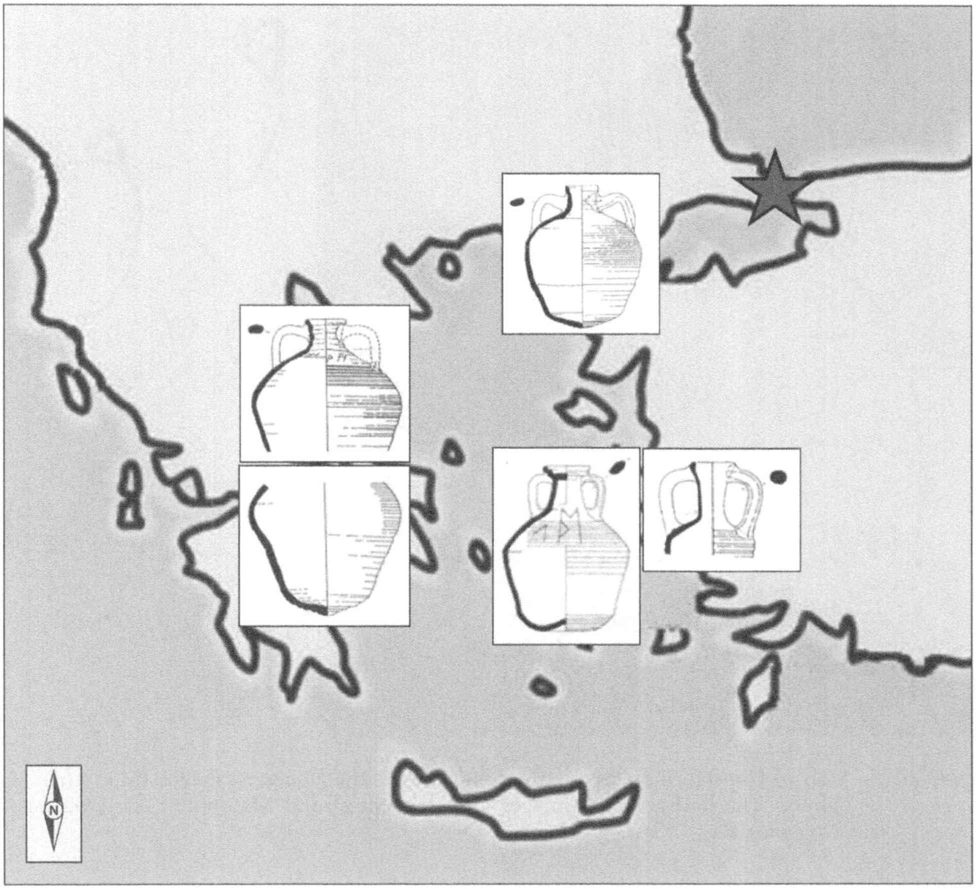

Figure 20.8 Map of the Aegean showing distribution of 10th- and 11th-century amphora types to Constantinople (Image after Hayes, *Excavations at Saraçhane*, 73–75)

is evident from the excavations at the Polyeuktos Church in the Saraçhane area (Figure 20.8). One of the most common of all Middle Byzantine amphorae here is the Günsenin 1/ Saraçhane 54 or the wine amphora from Ganos that reached between 30% and 50% of all amphora fragments in late 10th- to early 12th-century contexts (Figure 20.8). Other Middle Byzantine amphorae reaching the Capital in this period were for instance the so-called Saraçhane types 55 and 58 from the Aegean, originating from Ephesus and Chalcis (Figure 20.8).[85] These last two provincial cities were not only connected to a rich agricultural hinterland but also important industrial zones during Middle Byzantine times.[86]

In addition, one may notice the amphora type from Ganos back in the 1921–1922 excavations by a French mission in the Mangana quarter of Constantinople, where such containers probably were used during the 11th century in the vaulted constructions of an imperial palace, of the monastery of St. George and along the seafront fortification walls.[87] In the substructures of the Mangana Palace, they were found together with four other Middle Byzantine amphora types of the same date, which seem to be imported from different production areas (e.g., Ganos, Chalcis, Ephesus) in the Aegean (see Figure 20.9 and

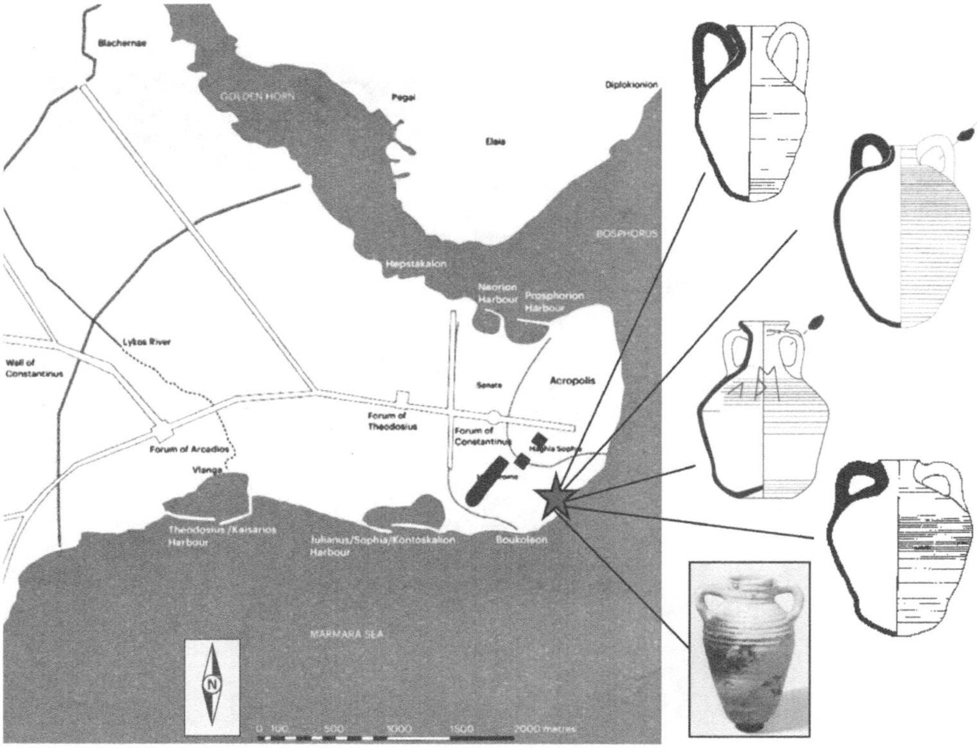

Figure 20.9 Map of Constantinople with amphora finds at the Mangana Palace (Map after Magdalino, 'The harbors', 13; Images after Demangel and Mamboury, *Le Quartier des Manganes*, Fig. 198)

Table 20.1).[88] Apparently, the weight of the amphorae from the Mangana Palace was up to 5 kilo, and some had *dipinti* and *graffiti* on the exterior shoulder.[89]

Looking at imports of amphorae in the Capital, one may notice the continuity of an interregional overlapping system of production and distribution, which was essentially Aegean-centred. At first, between the 4th and 7th centuries, this organisation stretched beyond the Aegean basin to the West (Italy, North Africa) and the East (Levant, Egypt) in the Mediterranean (Figure 20.3a). Afterwards, one can distinguish the shrinking of commercial zones to a more regional distribution providing Constantinople with wine and olive oil eventually between the late 7th and 9th centuries and even more in the 10th and 11th centuries (Figures 20.7 and 20.8).

Conclusion

The aim of this chapter is to present a first overview of local/regional and interregional movements of pottery and related finds from other parts of the Mediterranean basin to Constantinople and vice versa. Considering the Empire's highly centralised economic organisation, it is extremely likely that the production and distribution of highly crafted goods were controlled by the Byzantine state. It is known from written sources that there was indeed centrally regulated state control in the Capital of specialised export products

Table 20.1 Middle Byzantine amphora types (ca. 11th century) from the 1921 to 1922 excavations in the Mangana Quarter at Constantinople with an updated interpretation (after Demangel and Mamboury, *Le Quartier des Manganes*, fig. 198).

Amphora Type	Old Drawing	Recent Drawing	Height	Rim Diameter	Body Diameter	Handle Width	Surface	Provenance
Mangana **No. 1** (also known as Günsenin IIa / Saraçhane 60)	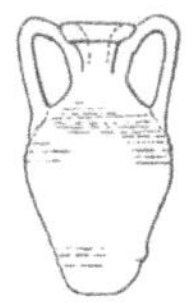	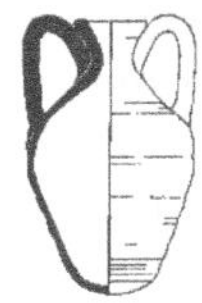	43.5	11	25	27	*Dipinti* in black and red	Probably from Chalkis
Mangana **No. 2** (also known as Günsenin VI?)	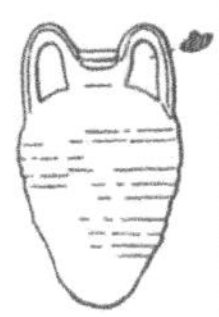	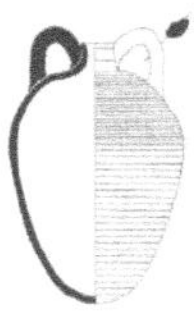	41.5	6	26	22		?
Mangana **No. 3** (also known as Günsenin XXIII / Saraçhane 58)		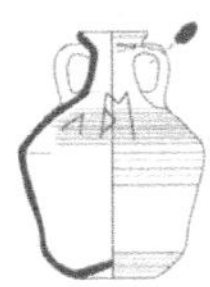	38	8.5	28	18		Probably from Ephesus
Mangana **No. 4** (also known as Günsenin I / Saraçhane 54)		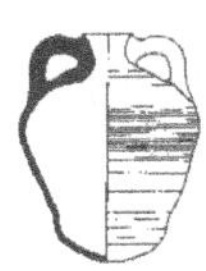	31-46	7-9	24-40	22-51	*Graffiti*	Probably from Ganos
Mangana **No. 5** (also known as Günsenin XVIII)	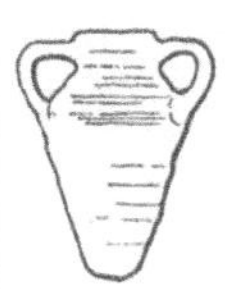		30	10	19	23		?

made of high-valued materials (including silk textiles, coins, jewellery, ivory objects, weapons, gold and silver utensils). Furthermore, the collecting of taxes in the provinces and the issuing of coinage were centrally controlled, which guaranteed the payment of the Empire's administration and army, as well as the constant value of money during various centuries. Even the distribution of bulk goods in amphorae (such as wine, olive oil and grain) seems to have been regulated (if not organised) by commercial inspectors of the state (*kommerkiaroi*) through a system of control stamps on these ceramic containers. This system was certainly helped by the easy availability of amphorae which were stored in warehouses of coastal cities within the Byzantine Empire and seemed to exist up to the 11th century.

Constantinople remained, both as a consumer centre of enormous magnitude and as a transit hub of proto-global importance, one of the most important commercial centres of

Europe and the Near East during the Late Antique-Early Byzantine and Middle Byzantine periods. The Capital was easily accessible through several harbours, where goods (among which regionally manufactured amphorae filled with bulk goods from the provinces) arrived by ship in order to bring these to concentrated clusters of warehouses and regulated marketplaces in two districts near the city's waterfronts. Between the 4th and 7th centuries, amphorae and tablewares (known as Red Slip wares) were manufactured in large quantities in restricted geographical parts of the Empire and exported in mass to other Byzantine cities. In the case of amphorae, this happened near rich wine- or oil-producing zones in the Mediterranean, from which these containers were exported, filled with bulk goods to the Capital.

From the 7th century onwards, Constantinople started to produce its own ceramic products, among which unglazed utilitarian vessels (cooking pots, the first products of Glazed White Ware I) and eventually the fancier looking glazed tablewares (such as Glazed White Ware II–V, Polychrome Ware). These locally made ceramics were distributed to provincial cities and towns in the Aegean, in the eastern Mediterranean – and eventually sometimes ended up in more faraway places.

The Capital was thus a prime consumptive hub in an interregional ceramic network of production and distribution, which was essentially Aegean-centred but could stretch at various times beyond this area to the West and the East in the Mediterranean. The question of whether these interregional Byzantine exchange systems functioned in a direct way between locations of demand and supply, or rather in an indirect way along various intermediate stations, is not easy to answer on the basis of the archaeological record. The availability and desirability of some commodities probably changed with the formation of each new political and socio-economic arrangement and structure in the eastern Mediterranean and beyond. These tantalising questions are beyond the scope of this chapter but should certainly be asked in the limelight of future research.

Notes

1 All centuries in this chapter are of the Christian era, unless otherwise stated.
2 In this chapter, the terms 'Late Roman' or 'Late Antique' are used for the period of ca. 4th to 7th centuries.
3 The term 'trade' is broadly described here as commercial transaction (the buying and selling of goods and transactions), although other distribution possibilities (diplomatic gifts, pilgrimages, raids) are discussed as well; cf. M. Mundell Mango, "Byzantine trade: Local, regional, interregional and international," in M. Mundell Mango (ed.), *Byzantine Trade, 4th-12th Centuries. The Archaeology of Local, Regional and International Exchange* (*Society for the Promotion of Byzantine Studies Publications* 14) (Farnham & Burlington: Ashgate, 2009), 3. See also for Byzantine trade and economy in general, D. Jacoby, *Trade, Commodities and Shipping in the Medieval Mediterranean* (London: Taylor & Francis Ltd, 1997); D. Jacoby, *Medieval Trade in the Eastern Mediterranean and Beyond* (London: Taylor & Francis Ltd, 2017); A. E. Laiou and C. Morrisson, *The Byzantine Economy* (Cambridge: Cambridge University Press, 2007); C. Morrisson (ed.), *Trade and Markets in Byzantium* (Washington, DC: Dumbarton Oaks Research Library and Collection, 2012).
4 J. Burbank and F. Cooper, *Empires in World History. Power and the Politics of Difference* (Princeton, NJ & Oxford: Princeton University Press, 2010), 65.
5 Burbank and Cooper, *Empires in World History*, 68.
6 S. Runciman, "Byzantine trade and industry," in M. M. Postan and E. Miller (eds.), *The Cambridge Economic History of Europe from the Decline of the Roman Empire, Vol. 2* (Cambridge: Cambridge University Press, 1987), 132–167.

7 P. Sarris, "Merchants, trade, and commerce in Byzantine law from Justinian I to Basil II," in P. Magdalino and N. Necipoğlu (eds.), *Trade in Byzantium. Papers from the Third International Sevgi Gönül Byzantine Studies Symposium* (Istanbul: ANAMED, 2016), 11–23.
8 See J. Haldon, *The Palgrave Atlas of Byzantine History* (Basingstoke: Palgrave MacMillan, 2005), 46 and map 3.6.
9 J. Vroom, "From Xi'an to Birka and back: Constantinople as a nodal point in long-distance contacts during the Early Middle Ages," in H. Nol (ed.), *Riches beyond the Horizon: Long Distance Trade in Early Medieval Landscapes* (*Medieval and Post-Medieval Mediterranean Archaeology Series* IV) (Turnhout: Brepols, 2021), 149–200.
10 P. Magdalino, "The harbors of Byzantine Constantinople," in *Stories from the Hidden Harbor. Shipwrecks of Yenikapı* (museum catalogue Istanbul Archaeological Museums) (Istanbul: Vehbi Koç Vakfı, 2013), 13–15.
11 Nowadays it is difficult to trace the Byzantine remains of the Great Palace with a modern city on top, but the size and shape of the ancient Hippodrome are still visible in the modern street layout.
12 J. Blid, "What Scandinavians may have seen and experienced in Miklagarõr: The urban fabric of Constantinople during the Middle Ages," in L. Holmquist, S. Kalmring and Ch. Hedenstierna-Jonson (eds.), *New Aspects on Viking-Age Urbanism c. 750–110* (*Theses and Papers in Archaeology* B:12) (Stockholm: Archaeological Research Laboratory, Stockholm University, 2016), 205.
13 Runciman, "Byzantine trade," 133.
14 See M. Mundell Mango, "The commercial map of Constantinople," *Dumbarton Oaks Papers* 54 (2000): 189–207 for using these written texts for establishing a commercial map of Constantinople.
15 Mundell Mango, "The commercial map," fig. 4; see also E. Kislinger, "Lebensmittel in Konstantinopel: Notizen zu den einschlägigen Marktorten der Stadt," in K. Belke, E. Kislinger, A. Külzer and M.A. Stassinopoulou (eds.), *Byzantina Mediterranea. Festschrift für Johannes Koder zum 65. Geburtstag* (Vienna, Cologne & Weimar: Bohlau Verlag, 2007), 303–325 and fig. 1.
16 Kislinger, "Lebensmittel in Konstantinopel," 304.
17 For example, J. L. Teall, "The grain supply of the Byzantine empire, 330–1025," *Dumbarton Oaks Papers* 13 (1959): 87–139; A. E. Müller, "Getreide für Konstantinopel. Überlegungen zu Justinians Edikt XIII als Grundlage für Aussagen zur Einwohnerzahl Konstantinopels im 6. Jahrhundert," *Jahrbuch für Österreichischen Byzantinistik* 43 (1993): 1–20; E. Kislinger, "Pane e demografia: l' approvigionamenmto di Constantinopoli," in O. Longo and P. Scarpi (eds.), *Nel nome del pane: atti del IV colloquio interuniversitario* (*Homo Edens* IV) (Bolzano/Bozen and Trento: Regione Trentino-Alto Adige, 1995), 279–293.
18 J. Koder, *Gemüse in Byzanz. Die Versorgung Konstantinopels mit Frischgemüse im Lichte der Geoponika* (*Byzantinische Geschichtsschreiber. Ergänzungsband* 3) (Vienna: Fassbaender, 1993); J. Koder, "Fresh vegetables for the capital," in C. Mango and G. Dagron (eds.), *Constantinople and Its Hinterland* (*Society for the Promotion of Byzantine Studies, Publications* 3) (Aldershot: Ashgate, 1995), 49–56; J. Koder, "Maritime trade and the food supply for Constantinople in the middle ages," in R. Macrides (ed.), *Travel in the Byzantine World* (*Society for the Promotion of Byzantine Studies, Publications* 10) (Aldershot: Ashgate, 2002), 109–124.
19 G. Dagron, "Poissons, pěcheurs et poissonniers de Constantinople," in C. Mango and G. Dagron (eds.), *Constantinople and Its Hinterland* (*Society for the Promotion of Byzantine Studies, Publications* 3) (Aldershot: Ashgate, 1995), 57–73; O. Schmitt, "Zur Fleischversorgung Konstantinopels," *Jahrbuch für Österreichischen Byzantinistik* 54 (2004): 135–157; J. Vroom, "The ceramics, agricultural resources and food," in J. Haldon, H. Elton and J. Newhard (eds.), *Archaeology and Urban Settlement in Late Roman and Byzantine Anatolia: Euchaita-Avkat-Beyözü and its Environment* (Cambridge: Cambridge University Press, 2018), 151–176, figs. 6.24–5.25 and tables 6.1–6.3 (with further literature).
20 V. Onar, "Animals in food consumption during the Byzantine period in light of the Yenikapı metro and Marmaray excavations, Istanbul," in S. Y. Waksman (ed.), *Multidisciplinary Approaches to Food and Foodways in the Medieval Eastern Mediterranean* (Lyon: Mom Editions, 2020), 333 and fig. 2. Noteworthy is the fact that the *Book of the Prefect* (912) mentions the processing of sheep, pigs and fish, but no cattle and bird species. Apparently, cattle and water buffalos were rather used as beasts of burden or plough animals; cf. J. Koder, "Multidisciplinary approaches to food and foodways in the medieval Eastern Mediterranean," in S. Y. Waksman (ed.), *Multidisciplinary Approaches to Food and Foodways in the Medieval Eastern Mediterranean* (Lyon: Mom Editions, 2020), 497.

21 Onar, "Animals in food consumption," 334.
22 Onar, "Animals in food consumption," 334–340; see also V. Onar, "Animal skeletal remains discovered at the Metro and Marmaray excavations," in *Stories from the Hidden Harbor: Shipwrecks of Yenikapı* (museum catalogue Istanbul Archaeological Museums) (Istanbul: Vehbi Koç Vakfı, 2013), 139–143.
23 M. Mango, "The commercial map," fig. 22.
24 Excavations took place here between 1966 and 1978; cf. C. L. Striker and Y. D. Kuban, *Kalenderhane in Istanbul. The Buildings, Their History, Architecture, and Decoration* (Mainz am Rhein: Verlag Philipp von Zabern, 1998).
25 Cf. G. Baran Çelik and M. Kiraz, "Blakhernai Palace," in G. Baran Çelik (ed.), *Istanbul'Daki Bizans Sarayları/Byzantine Palaces in Istanbul* (Istanbul: Istanbul Archaeological Museums, 2011), 124–130.
26 Excavations started by R. Mesguich, T. Wiegand and K. Wulzinger in 1912, later followed by cleaning in 1995 and 2009 by the Istanbul Archaeological Museums; cf. G. Kongaz, "Boukoleon Palace," in G. Baran Çelik (ed.), *Istanbul'Daki Bizans Sarayları/Byzantine Palaces in Istanbul* (Istanbul: Istanbul Archaeological Museums, 2011), 74–84.
27 The first excavations took place since 1942, then afterwards between 1950 and 1952; cf. R. Naumann and H. Belting, *Die Euphemia-Kirche am Hippodrom zu Istanbul und ihre Fresken* (*Istanbuler Forschungen* 25) (Berlin: Gebr. Mann, 1966); R. Durukan, "First report on excavations on the site of the new Palace of Justice at Istanbul," *Istanbul Arkeoloji Müzeleri Yıllığı* 5 (1952): 23–38; R. Durukan, "Second report on excavations on the site of the new Palace of Justice at Istanbul," *Istanbul Arkeoloji Müzeleri Yıllığı* 6 (1953): 74–80.
28 The first excavations started after a fire in 1912, followed by those between 1935 and 1938, and between 1952 and 1958; cf. E. Mamboury and Th. Wiegand, *Die Kaiserpaläste von Konstantinopel zwischen Hippodrom und Marmara-meer* (Berlin: W. De Gruyter & Co, 1934); G. Brett, W.J. Macaulay and R.B.K. Stevenson (eds.), *The Great Palace of the Byzantine Emperors* (Oxford: Oxford University Press, 1949); R. B. K. Stevenson, "Chapter II: The pottery, 1936–7," in G. Brett, W.J. Macaulay and R. B. K. Stevenson (eds.), *The Great Palace of the Byzantine Emperors* (Oxford: Oxford University Press, 1949), 31–63; D. Talbot Rice, *The Great Palace of the Byzantine Emperors. Second Report* (Edinburgh: The University Press, 1958) and A. Denker, "The Great Palace (Palatium Magnum)," in G. Baran Çelik (ed.), *Istanbul'Daki Bizans Sarayları/Byzantine Palaces in Istanbul* (Istanbul: Istanbul Archaeological Museums, 2011), 14–69.
29 Excavations stated here in 1946–1947, followed by those between 1958 and 1960 and cleaning in 1973–1974; cf. F. Dirimtekin, "Les fouilles faites en 1946–1947 et en 1958–1960 entre Ste-Sophie et Ste-Irène à Istanbul," *Cahiers Archéologiques* 13 (1962): 161–185; U. Peschlow, "Byzantinische Keramik aus Istanbul – Ein Fundkomplex bei der Irenenkirche," *Istanbuler Mitteilungen* 27–28 (1977–1978): 363–414.
30 The first excavations started here in 1935, after the mosque became a museum; cf. A. M. Schneider, *Die Grabung im Westhof der Sophienkirche zu Istanbul* (*Istanbuler Forschungen* 12) (Berlin: Deutsches Archäologiches Institut, 1941).
31 Excavations took place in 1927–1928; cf. S. Casson, 1928. *Preliminary Report Upon the Excavations Carried Out in the Hippodrome of Constantinople in 1927* (London: Pub. for the British Academy by H. Milford, Oxford University Press, 1928); S. Casson and D. Talbot Rice, *Second Report Upon the Excavations Carried Out in the Hippodrome of Constantinople in 1928* (London: Pub. for the British Academy by H. Milford, Oxford University Press, 1929).
32 The first excavations took place in 1921–1922; cf. R. Demangel and E. Mamboury, *Le Quartier des Manganes et la première région de Constantinople* (Paris: E. De Boccard, 1939); S. Öztopbaş, "Mangana Palace," in G. Baran Çelik (ed.), *Istanbul'Daki Bizans Sarayları / Byzantine Palaces in Istanbul* (Istanbul: Istanbul Archaeological Museums, 2011), 98–104.
33 The first excavations took place in 1930–1931, followed by those in 1965–1966 and in the 1970s; cf. D. Talbot Rice, "Excavations at Bodrum Camii 1930: The Messel expedition," *Byzantion* 8 (1933): 151–174; R. Naumann, "Ausgrabungen bei der Bodrum Camii (Myrelaion)," *Istanbul Arkeoloji Müzeleri Yıllığı* 13–14 (1966): 135–142; C. L. Striker, *The Myrelaion (Bodrum Camii) in Istanbul* (Princeton, NJ: Princeton University Press, 1981); Ş. Karagöz, "Myrelaion Palace," in G. Baran Çelik (ed.), *Istanbul'Daki Bizans Sarayları/Byzantine Palaces in Istanbul* (Istanbul: Istanbul Archaeological Museums, 2011), 114–121.

34 Cf. Ş. Karagöz, "Palace of Antiokhos," in G. Baran Çelik (ed.), *Istanbul'Daki Bizans Sarayları/ Byzantine Palaces in Istanbul* (Istanbul: Istanbul Archaeological Museums, 2011), 86–95.

35 Cf. Ş. Karagöz, "Palace of Botaneiates," in G. Baran Çelik (ed.), *Istanbul'Daki Bizans Sarayları/ Byzantine Palaces in Istanbul* (Istanbul: Istanbul Archaeological Museums, 2011), 106–109.

36 Excavations took place in Istanbul between 1964 and 1968; cf. R. M. Harrison, *Excavations at Saraçhane in Istanbul, Vol. I: The Excavations* (New Jersey & Washington, DC: Princeton University Press, 1989); R. M. Harrison and N. Fıratlı, "Excavations at Saraçhane in Istanbul: Fifth preliminary report," *Dumbarton Oaks Papers* 22 (1968), 195–216.

37 A. Denker, "Excavations at the Byzantine Great Palace (Palatium Magnum) in the area of the old Sultanahmet jail," in A. Ödekan, N. Necipoğlu and E. Akyürek (eds.), *The Byzantine Court. Source of Power and Culture. Papers from the Second International Sevgi Gönül Byzantine Studies Symposium, Istanbul, 21–23 June 2010* (Istanbul: Koç University Press, 2010), 13–18; Denker, "The Great Palace"; see also J. Vroom, "Het oude Constantinopel onder het moderne Istanbul: Archeologische sensaties dankzij een nieuwe metrolijn," in D. Burgersdijk and W. Waal (eds.), *Constantinopel. Een mozaïek van de Byzantijnse metropool (Mededelingen en Verhandelingen van het Vooraziatisch-Egyptisch Genootschap "Ex Oriente Lux"/Mémoires de la Société d'Études Orientales "Ex Oriente Lux"* 36) (Leuven: Ex Oriente Lux/Peeters, 2009), 229–239.

38 See for Late Roman tablewares, J. W. Hayes, *Late Roman Pottery* (London: The British School at Rome, 1972); S. Costa, P. Reynolds and J. Vroom, "Pottery, Roman and post-Roman," in O. Nicholson (ed.), *The Oxford Dictionary of Late Antiquity* (Oxford: Oxford University Press, 2018), 1217–1220. Late Roman amphorae were produced in huge quantities in restricted geographical areas, often near rich agricultural regions, and exported in mass; cf. J. A. Riley, "Typology of the Hellenistic and Roman coarse pottery of Berenice," in J. A. Lloyd (ed.), *Excavations at Sidi Khrebish Benghazi (Berenice) (Supplements to Libya Antiqua* 6.2) (Tripoli: Dept. of Antiquities, Ministry of Teaching and Education, People's Socialist Libyan Arab Jamahiriya, 1979), 112–236; J. A. Riley, "The pottery from cisterns 1977.1, 1977.2 and 1977.3," in J. A. Humphrey (ed.), *Excavations at Carthage Conducted by the University of Michigan, vol. VI* (Ann Arbor, MI: University of Michigan, 1981), 85–124; D. P. S. Peacock and D. F. Williams, *Amphorae and the Roman Economy. An Introductory Guide* (London & New York: Longman, 1986); P. Reynolds, *Hispania and the Roman Mediterranean, AD 100–700. Ceramics and Trade* (London: Duckworth, 2010); P. Reynolds and J. Vroom, "Amphorae," in O. Nicholson (ed.), *The Oxford Dictionary of Late Antiquity* (Oxford: Oxford University Press, 2018), 65–66.

39 J. Vroom, "The other Dark Ages: Early Medieval pottery finds in the Aegean as an archaeological challenge," in R. Attoui (ed.), *When did Antiquity End? Archaeological Case Studies in Three Continents (BAR I.S.* 2268) (Oxford: Archaeopress, 2011), 137–158 (the text was already submitted in 2005 and has not been revised since); see also J. Vroom, *After Antiquity. Ceramics and Society in the Aegean from the 7th to the 20th Century A.C.: A Case Study from Boeotia, Central Greece (Archaeological Studies Leiden University* 10) (Leiden: Leiden University Press, 2003); J. Vroom, "Late Antique pottery, settlement and trade in the east Mediterranean: A preliminary comparison of ceramics from Limyra (Lycia) and Boeotia," in W. Bowden, L. Lavan and C. Machado (eds.), *Recent Research on the Late Antique Countryside (Late Antique Archaeology* 2) (Leiden & Boston, MA: Brill, 2004), 281–331; J. Vroom, "New light on 'Dark Age' pottery: A note on finds from south-western Turkey," *Rei Cretariae Romanae Fautorum Acta* 39 (2005): 249–255.

40 Vroom, "The other Dark Ages", 137–145.

41 J. W. Hayes, *Excavations at Saraçhane in Istanbul, Vol. II: The Pottery* (Princeton, NJ: Princeton University Press, 1992).

42 Hayes, *Excavations at Saraçhane*, 3.

43 Hayes, *Excavations at Saraçhane*, 61.

44 Hayes, *Excavations at Saraçhane*, 61–71 and fig. 22.

45 Cf. Ö. E. Öncü and S. Çölmekçi, "Yenikapı kazıları ve Bizans dönemi amphora buluntuları," in F. Yenişehirlioğlu (ed.), *XIth Congress AIECM3 on Medieval and Modern Period Mediterranean Ceramics Proceedings, Vol. I* (Ankara: Koç University VEKAM, 2018), 15–29.

46 This last amphora type is also known as an LRA 2C, Yassi Ada 2 or Kuzmanov XX, and is distributed in the Aegean, the Black Sea region and North Africa; see also G. F. Bass, "The pottery," in G. F. Bass and F. H. van Doorninck, Jr. (eds.), *Yassi Ada I: A Seventh-Century Byzantine Shipwreck* (College Station, Texas: Institute of Nautical Archaeology, 1982), 157–161.

47 Hayes, *Excavations at Saraçhane*, fig. 23.
48 Glazed White Wares were first described in D. Talbot Rice, *Byzantine Glazed Pottery* (Oxford: Clarendon Press, 1930), 19–28 (his groups A 2–5 and B4); see also Hayes, *Excavations at Saraçhane*, 12–34; J. Vroom, "Some Byzantine pottery finds from Kaman – Kalehöyük: A first observation," *Anatolian Archaeological Studies* 15 (2006): 163–169; J. Vroom, "From one coast to another: Early Medieval ceramics in the southern Adriatic region," in S. Gelichi and R. Hodges (eds.), *From One Sea to Another. Trading Places in the European and Mediterranean Early Middle Ages, Proceedings of the International Conference Comacchio, 27–29 March 2009* (Turnhout: Brepols, 2012), 355–359; J. Vroom, *Byzantine to Modern Pottery in the Aegean. An Introduction and Field Guide. Second & Revised Edition* (Turnhout: Brepols, 2014^2), 62–63, 74–77.
49 E. Gerousi, "Early Christian ceramics from the area of 'Episkopi' on Samos (in Modern Greek)," *Archaiologikon Deltion* 47–48 (1992–1993): (A), 258–259, no. 8050, figs. 7–8, pl. 50; S. Costa, "An archaeology of domestic life in Early Byzantine Gortyna: Stratigraphy, pots and contexts," in D. Dixneuf (ed.), *LRCW 5-2. Late Roman Coarse Wares, Cooking Wares and Amphorae in the Mediterranean. Archaeology and Archaeometry* (*Études Alexandrines* 43) (Alexandria: Centre d'Études Alexandrines, 2017), fig. 4, no. GQB–CER 1032.17+18.
50 Hayes, *Excavations at Saraçhane*, 55 (his 'Grey gritty ware type c').
51 Hayes, *Excavations at Saraçhane*, 55–57.
52 S. Ladstätter, "Funde," in M. Steskal and M. La Torre (eds.), *Das Vediusgymnasium in Ephesos. Archölogie und Baubefund* (*Forschungen in Ephesos* XIV.1) (Vienna: Austrian Academy of Sciences Press, 2008), 184–186, 189.
53 Denker, "The Great Palace," 37, no. 31 (2001 excavation at the Former Sultanahmet Prison); Karagöz, "Palace of Antiokhos," 91, no. 149 (1950 excavation at the Courthouse, the southern part of the palace complex).
54 See for similar looking examples from Constantinople, Hayes, *Excavations at Saraçhane*, 9–10, fig. 3, nos. 1, 2 and 8 and specifically fig. 39, nos. 23–25 from deposit 30 dated 655–670 (described by him as 'Mortaria of Lead-Glazed Type'), which according to him were not locally made.
55 Karagöz, "Palace of Antiokhos," 92, no. 150 (1950 excavation at the Courthouse); Denker, "The Great Palace," 38–39, nos. 32–34 (2001 and 2003 excavations at the Former Sultanahmet Prison) and 44, nos. 48–49 (1936–1937 excavations at the Great Palace); see also Stevenson, "Chapter II: The pottery," stages I–II, nos. 1–16.
56 Denker, "The Great Palace," 41–42, nos. 41–43 (2000–2001 excavations at the Former Sultanahmet Prison), 45–47, nos. 50–52, 55–56, nos. 80–83 (2000, 2003, 2005 and 2007 excavations at the Former Sultanahmet prison; 1936–1937 excavations at the Great Palace); see also Stevenson, "Chapter II: The pottery," stage III.
57 J. Vroom, "Production, exchange and consumption of ceramics in the Byzantine Mediterranean (ca. 7th–14th c.)," in J. Vroom (ed.), *Feeding the Byzantine City. The Archaeology of Consumption in the Eastern Mediterranean (ca. 500–1500)* (Turnhout: Brepols, 2023), 283-338.
58 Vroom, "From one coast to another," 357; J. Vroom, "Ceramics," in P. Niewöhner (ed.), *The Archaeology of Byzantine Anatolia. From the End of Late Antiquity until the Coming of the Turks* (Oxford: Oxford University Press, 2017), 176–178 and fig. 13.1.
59 Vroom, *Byzantine to Modern Pottery*, 74–75.
60 J. Vroom, "Ceramics," 187 and fig. 13.6.
61 Vroom, "Ceramics," 188 and fig. 13.7.
62 F. M. Hocker, "A ninth-century shipwreck near Bozburun, Turkey," *INA Quarterly* 22.1 (1995): 12–14.
63 Hayes, *Excavations at Saraçhane*, 71, 73 and fig. 23, nos.6, 10; see also fig. 57, deposit 35, nos. 26, 36, 43 and fig. 58, deposit 36, no. 16.
64 Hayes, *Excavations at Saraçhane*, 73, fig. 58, deposit 36, no. 17.
65 See Haldon, *The Palgrave Atlas*, map 3.2.
66 Runciman, "Byzantine trade," 133.
67 E. Cirelli, *Ravenna. Archeologia di una cittá* (Florence: All'Insegna del Giglio, 2008), 133, figs. 113, 334; E. Cirelli, "Typology and diffusion of amphorae in Ravenna and Classe between the 5th and the 8th centuries AD," in N. Poulou-Papadimitriou, E. Nodarou and V. Kilikoglou (eds.), *LRCW 4. Late Roman Coarse Wares, Cooking Wares and Amphorae in the Mediterranean. Archaeology and Archaeometry* (*BAR I.S.* 2616.I) (Oxford: Archaeopress, 2014), 541–552, figs.

2–3; see also A. Augenti and E. Cirelli, "Classe: Un observatorio privilegiato per il commercio della tarda antichità," in S. Menchelli, S. Santoro, M. Pasquinucci and G. Guiducci (eds.), *LRCW 3. Late Roman Coarse Wares, Cooking Wares and Amphorae in the Mediterranean. Archaeology and Archaeometry* (*BAR I.S.* 2185.II) (Oxford: Archaeopress, 2010), 605–615, figs. 5, 10, 11; M. McCormick, "Movements and markets in the first millennium: Information, containers, and shipwrecks," in C. Morrisson (ed.), *Trade and Markets in Byzantium* (Washington, DC: Dumbarton Oaks, 2012), 51–98, figs. 3.4–3.5.

68 V. G. Swan, "Dichin (Bulgaria): The fifth- and sixth-century destruction deposits, and their implications for ceramic chronology," in M. Bonifay and J.-C. Tréglia (eds.), *LRCW 4. Late Roman Coarse Wares, Cooking Wares and Amphorae in the Mediterranean. Archaeology and Archaeometry* (*BAR. I.S.* 1662, II) (Oxford: Archaeopress, 2007), 835–844.

69 P. Fabian and Y. Goren, "A Byzantine warehouse and anchorage site of Ashqelon," *'Atiqot* 42 (2001): 211–219.

70 M. Mango, "The commercial map," 195.

71 Ch. Diamanti, "Stamped Late Roman/Proto-Byzantine amphoras from Halasarna of Kos," *Rei Cretariae Romanae Fautorum Acta* 41 (2010): 1–8; Ch. Diamanti, "Byzantine emperors on stamped Late Roman/Early Byzantine amphoras," *Rei Cretariae Romanae Fautorum Acta* 42 (2012): 1–5.

72 S. Kingsley, "Great voyages, great ocean-going ships?," in M. Mundell Mango (ed.), *Byzantine Trade, 4th–12th Centuries. The Archaeology of Local, Regional and International Exchange* (*Society for the Promotion of Byzantine Studies Publications* 14) (Farnham & Burlington: Ashgate, 2009), 324.

73 J. Vroom, "Byzantine sea trade in ceramics: Some case studies in the eastern Mediterranean (ca. seventh - fourteenth centuries)," in P. Magdalino and N. Necipoğlu (eds.), *Trade in Byzantium. Papers from the Third International Sevgi Gönül Byzantine Studies Symposium* (Istanbul: Koç University's Research Center for Anatolian Civilizations, 2016), 157–177.

74 For example, C. Pulak,"Yenikapı Bizans batıkları," in *Gün Işığında. Istanbul'un 8000 yılı: Marmaray, Metro, Sultanahmet kazıları* (Istanbul:Vehbi Koç Vakfı, 2007), 202–215; C. Pulak, R. Ingram, M. Jones and S. Matthews, "The shipwrecks of Yenikapı and their contribution to the study of ship construction," in *Stories from the Hidden Harbor. Shipwrecks of Yenikapı* (museum catalogue Istanbul Archaeological Museums) (Istanbul: Vehbi Koç Vakfı, 2013), 22–34; A. Denker, F. Demirkök, G. Kongaz, M. Kiraz, Ö. K. Kömörcü and T. Akbaytogan, "YK 12," in *Stories from the Hidden Harbor.Shipwrecks of Yenikapı* (museum catalogue Istanbul Archaeological Museums) (Istanbul: Vehbi Koç Vakfı, 2013), 198–209; I. Özsait Kocabaş, "The centuries-long voyage of ship Yenikapı 12," in *Stories from the Hidden Harbor. Shipwrecks of Yenikapı* (museum catalogue Istanbul Archaeological Museums) (Istanbul: Vehbi Koç Vakfı, 2013), 47–55; see also F. Daim and E. Kislinger (eds.), *The Byzantine Harbours of Constantinople* (Mainz: Verlag der Römisch-Germanischen Zentralmuseum, 2021).

75 Öncü and Çölmekçi, "Yenikapı kazıları," 25–27, figs. 10–12; M.A. Polat, "YK 35," in *Stories from the Hidden Harbor.Shipwrecks of Yenikapı* (museum catalogue Istanbul Archaeological Museums) (Istanbul: Vehbi Koç Vakfı, 2013), 155–170, nos. 102–146.

76 Due to these pottery finds, shipwreck 'YK 35' should not be dated in the 5th but rather in the 7th century; the finds are shown in Polat, "YK 35," 175–177, nos. 159–165 but with different dating.

77 Onar, "Animals in food consumption," 340.

78 Denker et al., "YK 12," 204–209, nos. 237–255.

79 Denker et al., "YK 12," 202–204 and 206, nos. 232, 236 and 245.

80 Denker et al., "YK 12," 209, no. 254.

81 A. Denker, F. Demirkök, M. Kiraz and T. Akbaytogan, "YK 1," in *Stories from the Hidden Harbor. Shipwrecks of Yenikapı* (museum catalogue Istanbul Archaeological Museums) (Istanbul: Vehbi Koç Vakfı, 2013), 211–215, nos. 256–274.

82 For example, Öncü and S. Çölmekçi, "Yenikapı kazıları," 27 with graph showing a large percentage of Günsenin 1 / Saraçhane 54 amphorae from Ganos (43.14%) within the total of amphora finds at the Yenikapı excavations.

83 Denker et al., "YK 1," 213, no. 265; see also E. Todorova, "Timbres amphoriques médievaux du musée de Silistra, Bulgarie de nord-est," in *Culture and Civilization at Lower Danube, vol. XXIV* (Călărași, 2008), 303–304.

84 Todorova, "Timbres amphoriques médievaux," 303.
85 Hayes, *Excavations at Saraçhane*, 73–, 75, fig. 24, nos. 1–11 and 14. Furthermore, a Günsenin 1/ Saraçhane 54 type amphora with a small round stamp on the handle has also been found during excavations at the St. Irene church of Constantinople; cf. U. Peschlow, "Byzantinische Keramik aus Istanbul. Ein Fundcomplex bei der Irenenkirche," *Istanbuler Mitteilungen* 27/28 (1977–1978), 413, no. 125, fig. 19.
86 Hayes, *Excavations at Saraçhane*, 75, fig. 25, nos. 11 and 15; see for the provenance of Ephesus for the amphora type Saraçhane 58, J. Vroom, "On the trail of the enigma amphora: Following the flow of Middle Byzantine ceramic containers," *Archeologia Medievale* 45, 77–90.
87 Vroom, "On the trail of the enigma amphora," 78–83; J. Vroom, E. Tzavella and G. Vaxevanis, "Exploring daily life in the Byzantine Empire: Pottery from Chalkis (Euboea, Greece), ca. 10th/11th–13th c.", in P. Petridis, A. G. Yangaki, N. Liaros and E.-E. Bia (eds.), *12th Congress on Medieval and Modern Period Mediterranean Ceramics, Athens, October 21-27, 2018, vol. I* (Athens: National Hellenic Research Foundation & Hellenic Republic National and Kapodistrian University of Athens, 2021), 449–458.
88 Demangel and E. Mamboury, *Le Quartier des Manganes*, 148–149, fig. 198, no. 4 and fig. 199.
89 Demangel and E. Mamboury, *Le Quartier des Manganes*, 149 and figs. 200–201.

21

PERA IANUENSIUM PULCHERRIMA CIVITAS EST

Creating a Genoese Identity on the Golden Horn (1261–1453)[1]

Mabi Angar

Introduction

This chapter considers Genoese Pera, with a focus on the perception of the outpost on the Golden Horn by Westerners passing through the Eastern Aegean during the 14th and the first half of the 15th century. Some enjoyed week-long visits to Pera, where communication with the Latin population, and concomitantly any social, commercial, diplomatic, ecclesiastic, or other activity could be pursued easily. Known as Galata to the Byzantines, Turks and Arabs, Pera (*Peyra, Peira*) offered visitors a first-hand impression of a Genoese merchant city governed by a Podestà and serving, with its excellent harbor, as a major transfer point in the lucrative long-distance trade between the Black Sea and the Mediterranean.

The Genoese, backed by trade privileges given to them by Byzantine emperors since the Treaty of Nymphaion (1261), excelled in commercial ventures with their many cargo-ships and a fully developed network of Genoese ports along the main sea routes. Pera had been a Western stronghold since the late 13th century; its location directly across from the capital of the Byzantine Empire facilitated political and economic contact, even as Constantinople was under attack by the Ottomans, with whom in turn the Genoese of Pera conducted separate negotiations, while benefiting from the overlordship of the Byzantine emperor.

Foreign Merchants in Constantinople

Byzantine Constantinople had always been a commercial hub with merchants of different ethnic and cultural backgrounds trading in the city for a certain period of the year. Specific harbors and landing stages, guest houses, commercial streets, and houses of prayer were reserved for the various foreign communities (Arabs, Bulgars, Kievan Rus, etc.) who stood under the scrutiny of the city prefect. Modern Beşiktaş (St. Mamas) was traditionally the base of Russian and Bulgarian merchants active in the Byzantine capital, whereas Muslim merchants seem to have had a quarter with houses and a mosque near the Church

DOI: 10.4324/9780429203923-26

of St. Eirene in Perama (today Eminönü), probably located outside the sea wall. While this mosque was destroyed during the fires of the siege of Constantinople by Latin armies in 1203/1204, Michael VIII Palaiologos (1259–1282) built a new mosque in 1261/1262 which was equipped with furnishings by the Mamlūk sultan Baybars (1260–1277) according to Arab sources.[2] Already by the middle of the 12th century, Genoese merchants had been admitted to Constantinople and possessed a distinct quarter with landing stages,[3] following hereby a model established in the 10th and 11th centuries with the Amalfitans, the Venetians, and the Pisans who enjoyed favorable taxations and were granted by the Byzantine emperor their own quarters at the southern shore of the Golden Horn, in modern Sirkeci and Eminönü.[4]

As such, the Genoese were not at all newcomers to the Byzantine capital after the successful Byzantine reconquest in 1261, but they had suffered from marginalization by their major rivals in commerce, the Venetians, during the preceding so-called Latin Empire of Constantinople (1204–1261).[5] While the Genoese and the Venetians should become the most potent groups of Late Byzantine Constantinople, further Latin communities – Anconitans, Catalans, Florentines, and Provençals to mention some – were admitted to Constantinople in the course of the 14th and 15th centuries.[6] The Genoese, however, favored by the relative spatial isolation were especially able to establish a distinguishable civic entity marked by surrounding walls on the other side of the Golden Horn.

Questions and Sources

How did the Genoese create a specifically Genoese identity in Pera? What exactly might have reminded visitors of Genoa? This and other questions around identity, self-fashioning, propaganda, external perception, and the scarcely acknowledged but important role of emblems and insignia in the medieval Mediterranean will be addressed in the following pages. Written and pictorial travel accounts that shape our understanding of Genoese Pera will be complemented by references in Byzantine sources that reveal interesting aspects when re-assessed in broader contexts. Byzantine-Genoese contracts and archival notes provide relevant information that collectively cast a spotlight on Genoese Pera, a topic, that has received substantial attention since the 19th century.[7]

Like Byzantine Constantinople, Genoese Pera must be reconstructed mainly on the basis of written sources: Except for the lower part of the Galata Tower (Figure 21.1),[8] scattered fragments of the city walls partly incorporated into modern structures (Figure 21.2), the Arap Camii (the former *ecclesia Sancti Dominici*),[9] St. Benoît built in 1427,[10] and the Bereket Han (the former Podestà Palace) in a deplorable state of decay since many years (Figure 21.3), not much of medieval Pera has survived in modern-day Beyoğlu.[11] Yet, it is mainly the material remains and their protection as a shared cultural heritage within a broader framework of the study of Genoese colonies that has more recently gained increased attention.[12]

Buondelmonti's View of Pera and Constantinople

In pictorial terms, various Ottoman and Western cityscapes of Constantinople dating to the 16th century include Pera.[13] The earliest representation, however, is Cristoforo Buondelmonti's bird's eye view of Constantinople and Pera in his *Liber insularum archipelagi* (*Lia*), a very popular book on the Aegean islands made around 1420, of which some

Figure 21.1 Istanbul [Turkey], Galata Tower. Viewed from the north, 1348 (photo: author, 2017)

Figure 21.2 Istanbul [Turkey], Genoese Wall. Section built in connection with the Galata Tower; today incorporated into a modern restaurant (photo: author, 2017)

70 manuscripts (mostly from the late 15th and 16th century) have survived (Figure 21.4).[14] This work, a combination of geographic information and references to the classical and mythological past, also had a political dimension.[15] At a time when crusading ideas were powerful at European courts, references in the *Lia* to Turkish raids, the mentioning of destroyed churches, as well as its bias against Byzantines, and the positive image of the Genoese and other Western groups can be seen as propaganda with a clear sympathy for Catholic compatriots in the region.[16]

Well-aware of the inconsistency of including Constantinople in a book dedicated to islands, Buondelmonti nevertheless provides a description because of the city's ancient glory. In fact, the entry on Constantinople is the most extensive in the *Lia* and includes a full-page depiction of it and Pera. The latter is defined as a very beautiful city of the Genoese (*Pera Ianuensium pulcherrima civitas est*) lying north of the Golden Horn (*sinus*) opposite the *City* (Constantinople) and only 18 miles away from the Black Sea, waters traditionally perceived as unknown and dangerous. However, Buondelmonti's readers were surely aware of the strategic and economic importance of the Genoese colony on the Bosphorus.

Almost all depictions of the City in Buondelmonti's manuscripts emphasize Pera: the Genoese outpost is represented in a disproportionally large manner which cannot be explained by compositional and perspective reasons alone but seems to allude to the significance and vitality ascribed to the relatively new *civitas* in contrast to Constantinople's storied, but fading splendor. The discrepancy in the dimensions between the walled peninsula and Pera becomes apparent when modern maps of the region are juxtaposed to Buondelmonti's spatial concept (Figure 21.5).

The bias becomes fully visible in an early Buondelmonti manuscript kept in Holkham Hall Library in Norfolk (Ms. 475, fol. 42v) that dates to 1429 (Figure 21.6).[17] Unfortunately, the commissioner of this manuscript is unknown but, significantly, its production is attributed to a Genoese scribe on a Doria ship (*in naue de Auria*) in the harbor-city of Chios[18] – another Genoese dominion.[19] In this case, Pera is depicted as a densely populated and thriving

Figure 21.3 Istanbul [Turkey], Bereket Han. Rear side of the former Podestà Palace built after 1315 (photo: author, 2015)

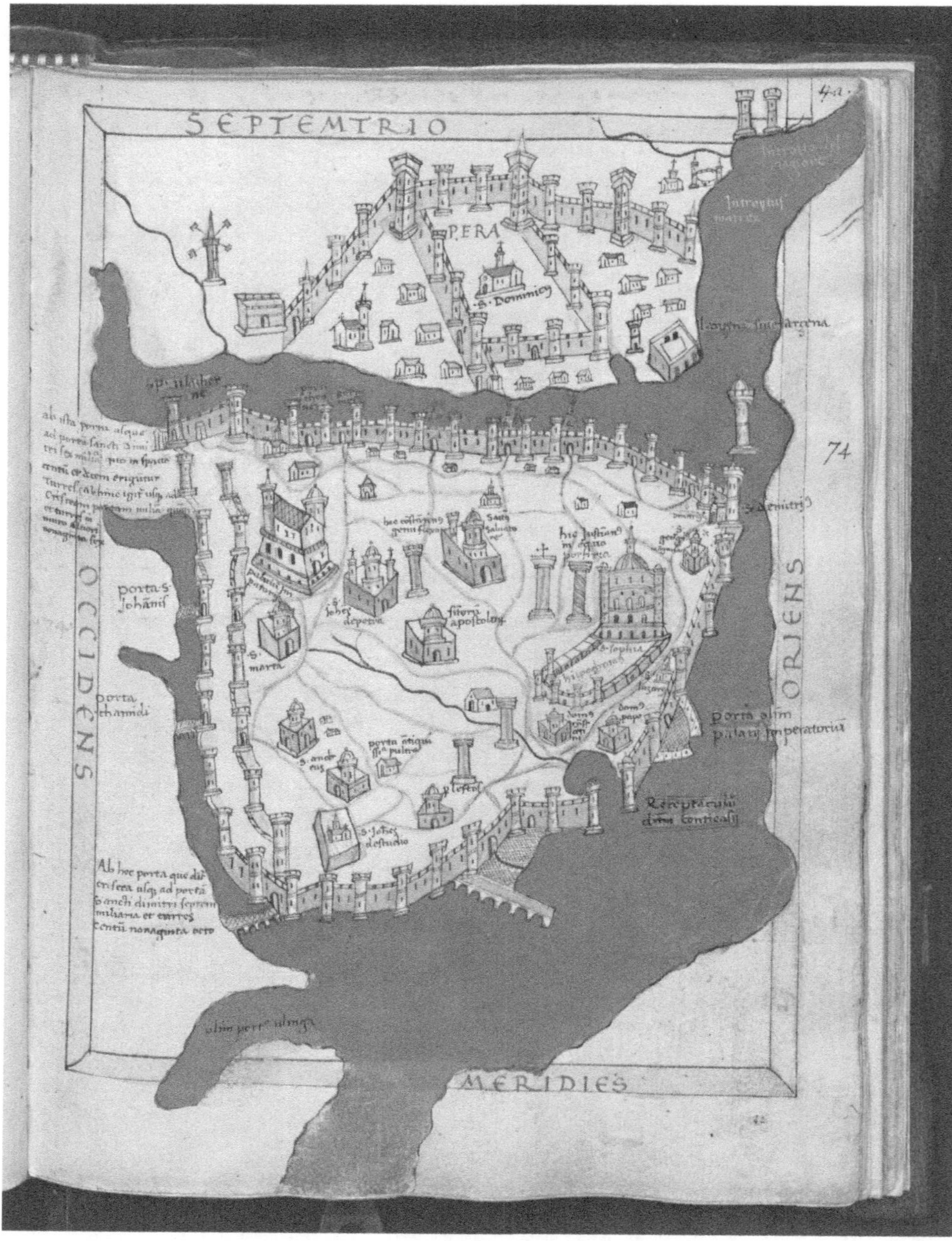

Figure 21.4 Pera and Constantinople as represented in Buondelmonti's *Liber insularum archipelagi*, Ms. Plut. 25.29, fol. 42.r, 15th century. Florence, Biblioteca Medicea Laurenziana (Reproduced with kind permission of MiBACT)

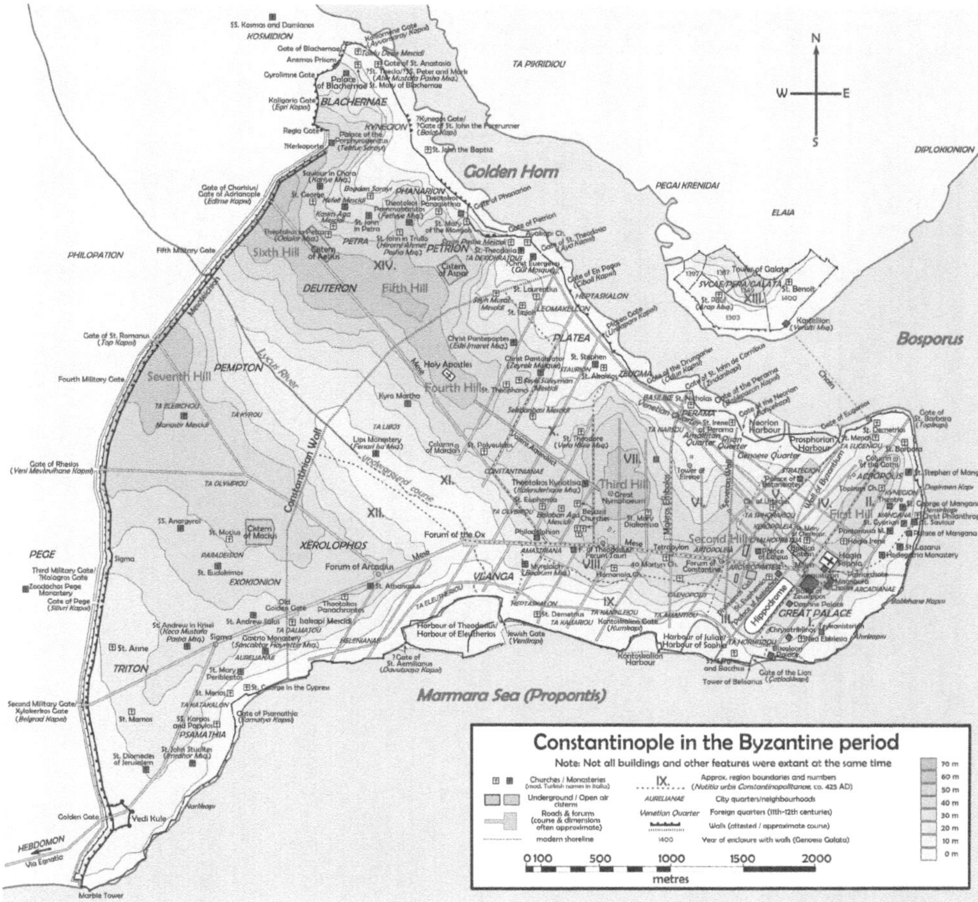

Figure 21.5 Modern map of Constantinople and Sykai/Galata/Pera (CC BY-SA 3.0, https://de.wikipedia.org/wiki/Konstantinopel#/media/Datei:Byzantine_Constantinople-de.svg)

tripartite city surrounded by turreted walls. A massive Genoese banner – the red cross on a white field – highlights ownership and glory. In contrast, Constantinople, marked by a stiff red flag bearing in yellow the tetragrammatic cross with four "Beta" at the location of the emperor's seat, the Blachernae Palace in the northwest of the peninsula, is literally deserted with the exception of a church labeled as Sancta Sophia and a nearby honorific column that lacks its top. The striking emptiness of Constantinople, or rather its reduction to architectural symbols epitomizing "Christianity" and "Empire," is explicable neither by a lack of information on the topography nor by aesthetic considerations. Indeed, the void seems programmatic in nature and could be seen as an allusion to Byzantine decline in the first half of the 15th century with John VIII Palaiologos (1425–1448) desperately pursuing a church union that would entail joint military efforts against the Turks.[20] While the Holkham Hall image of Constantinople and Pera is, admittedly, a rare example,[21] Buondelmonti's famous view of Constantinople is equally or even more so a representation of Genoese Pera.

Since the Genoese fortifications of Pera were documented prior to their almost complete demolition in 1864 for road expansion, the courses of the walls of the Genoese settlement

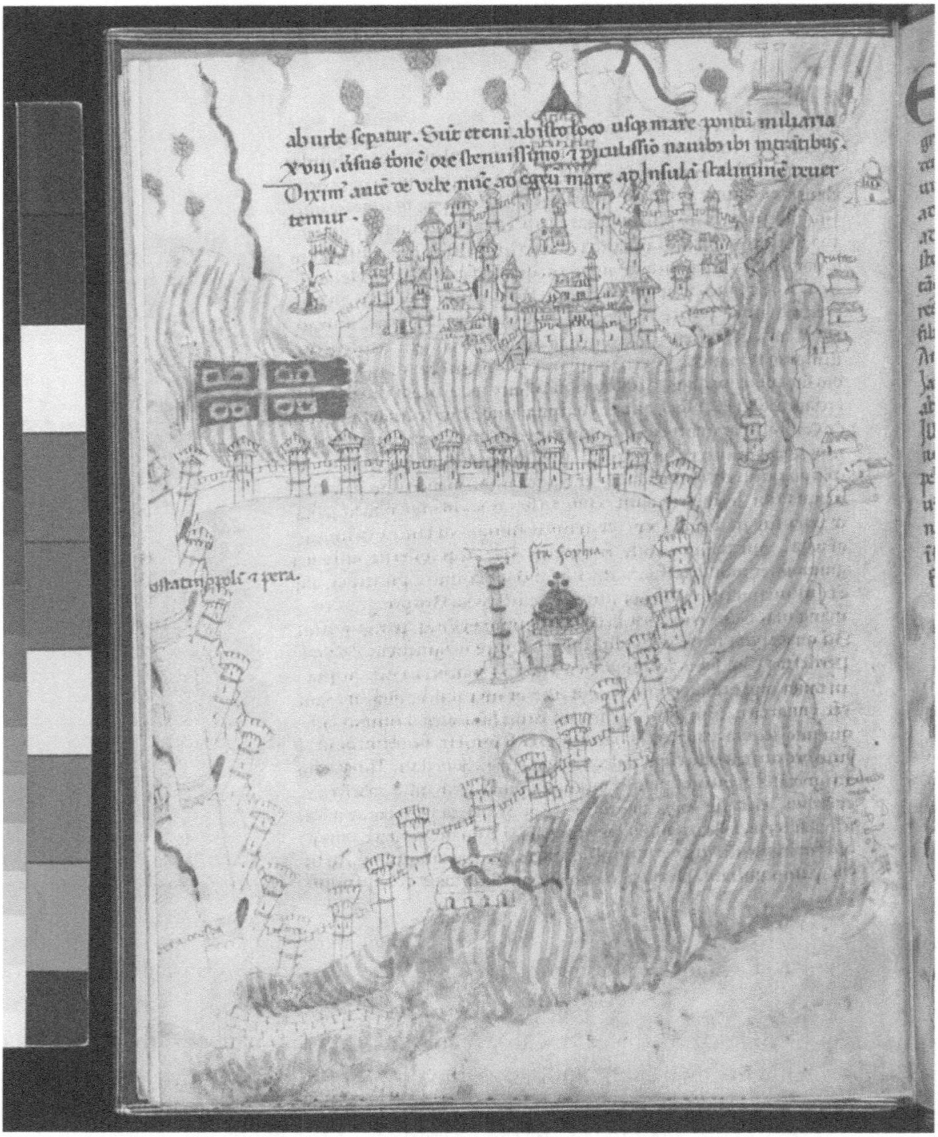

Figure 21.6 Pera and Constantinople as represented in Buondelmonti's *Liber insularum archipelagi*, Ms. 475, fol. 42v, Chios, 1429. Norfolk, Holkham Hall Library (by permission of the Earl of Leicester and the Trustees of the Holkham Estate)

that grew after 1315 onward are well known (Figure 21.7).[22] Marble slabs from the walls and towers of Pera, now in the Archaeological Museum in Istanbul – bearing the construction year, the name of the Podestà, his personal coat of arms and those of Genoa (and Byzantium) –, help to establish a rough chronology.[23] Yet given the patchy evidence, it remains difficult to precisely assess the various instances of land acquisition and building activity (Figure 21.8). What impact depictions like the Buondelmonti view might have had on the perception of the particular area in general terms still remains to be studied, but

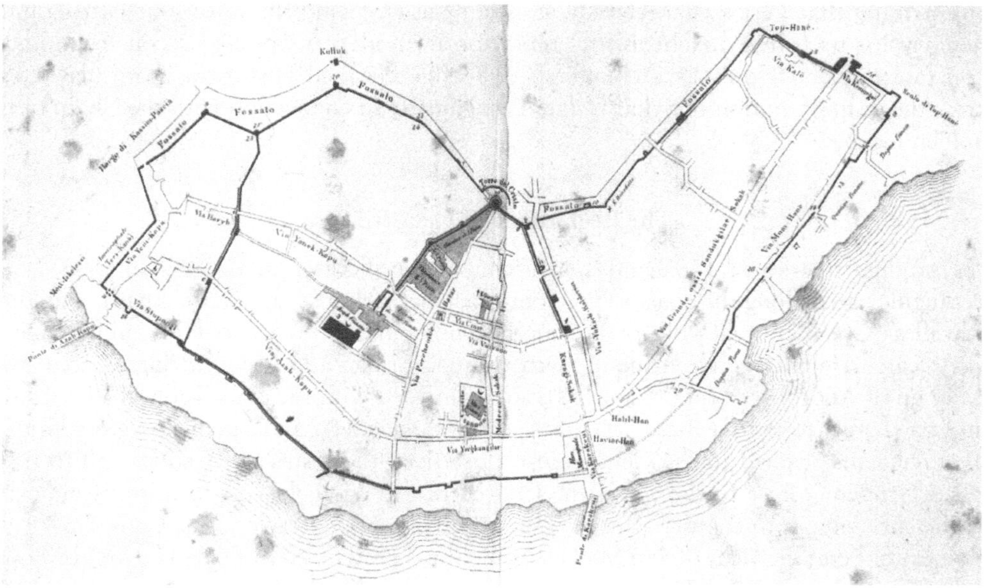

Figure 21.7 Map with courses of the city walls of Pera by M. De Launay, 1864 (as reproduced in Belgrano, Documenti riguardanti la colonia genovese di Pera, 1877–1884, Tav. 1)

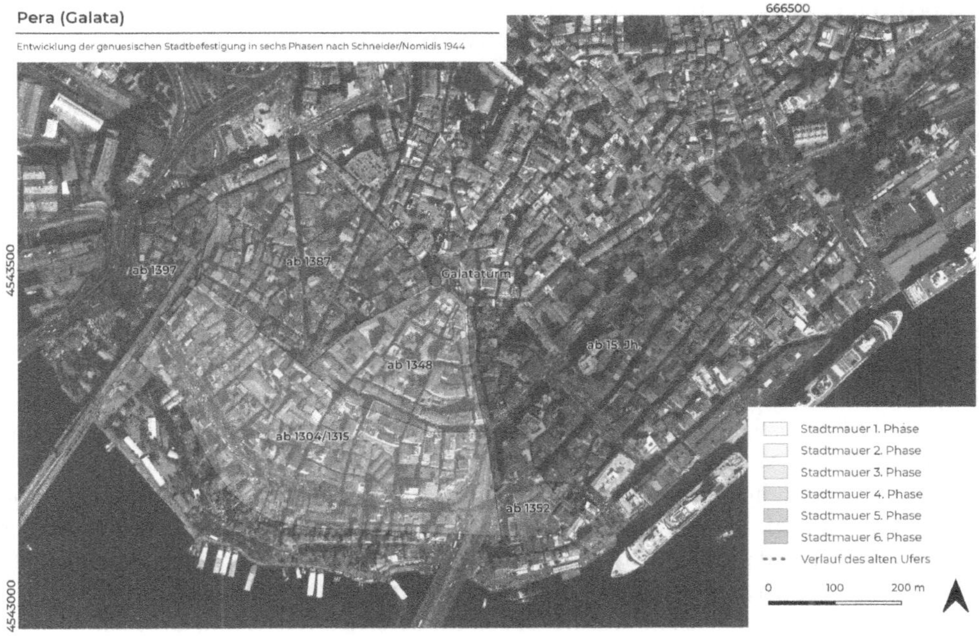

Figure 21.8 Subsequent expansion of Pera (Galata) in six phases after Schneider/Nomidis, Galata, 1944. Remodeled on a modern satellite image (copyright: author, 2021)

it is striking that Pera's characteristic contour has been imprinted on our cartographic memory for its (often anachronistic) rendition in modern maps and reconstructions of Constantinople – if only as a counterspace to the so-called Historical Peninsula and to stress the military notion of Sykai/Galata/Pera, mostly in connection with the Chain of the Golden Horn.[24]

The Beginnings of Genoese Pera

The original treaties of 1303 and 1304 define a specific area in Galata,[25] a transversely rectangular area along the coast with a logia, a slaughterhouse, a bakery, a bath, and Latin as well as Greek churches plus a surrounding uninhabited buffer zone 60 cubits wide. It was located roughly between the modern Atatürk Bridge and Galata Bridge, dated from the reign of Andronikos II (1282–1328), and coincided with the concession of a quarter in Smyrna (Izmir) to the Genoese.[26] Genoese scribes, weighers, and butchers were admitted; all agreements applied to the Genoese, to those from the district of Genoa, and to those called Genoese. Close to the coast, the Church of San Michele – its location is indicated by the surviving 16th-century Rüstem Paşa Caravanserai – served as the Cathedral of the Genoese of Pera, the vicar of San Michele being the representative of Genoa's Archbishop.[27]

However, the origins of Pera as a Genoa-run entity in the late 1260s under Michael VIII Palaiologos are more difficult to grasp. The emergence of a concession in Pera is generally seen as the result of the Treaty of Nymphaion drawn in March 1261 at Nymphaion (modern Kemalpaşa near Izmir), and ratified on 10 July 1261 in Genoa. This treaty was meant to facilitate the Byzantine reconquest of Constantinople that was accomplished only 15 days later, but without any Genoese aid.[28] The treaty, set up at the Byzantine exile court of Nicaea, provided the Genoese with tax exemptions, commercial outposts, and exclusive access to the Black Sea, in exchange for naval support. The agreements were also meant to curtail the Venetians who were identified as a common enemy.[29] Yet, the treaty does not specifically pinpoint any site within Constantinople, leaving one to believe that the Genoese were to return to their pre-1204 quarter *Koparion*, on the southern coast of the Golden Horn, in modern Sirkeci, next to the former quarters of the Pisans and the Venetians (Figure 21.9).[30]

Or did they want to resettle *in Orcu* (conceded in 1169), a Genoese interim settlement that is commonly believed to have been on the other side of the Golden Horn: *ultra, trans* or *apud Constantinopolim*,[31] and in use by Genoese and other Latins from 1204 to 1261?[32]

Pera, or Galata as the Byzantines would call it, had been fortified as early as the 5th–6th century. According to the *Notitia urbis Constantinopolitanae* (5th century), the former 13th region of Constantinople was mainly referred to as Sykai (*regio Sycena*), i.e. "fig trees," and after some restoration work of its city walls and theatre by Justinian I in 528, it was also called Iustinianoupolis or Iustinianae.[33] The many different names assigned over time to the coastal suburb opposite Constantinople do not make things easier. That part of the city, literally the other side of the Golden Horn – πέραν means "beyond" in Greek – remains little known.[34] Prior to the Genoese period, it was above all an important strategic point.[35] The role Galata played in Constantinople's defense becomes fully evident by the early 8th century, when the Chain of the Golden Horn, with which one could close the inlet, is first mentioned. The chain was housed in the so-called Kastellion, a secular structure from the so-called Byzantine Dark Ages (7th/8th century), of which only the substructions have survived and that is known today as the Yeraltı Camii (Underground Mosque) in the vicinity of the modern Galata Bridge (Figure 21.10).[36]

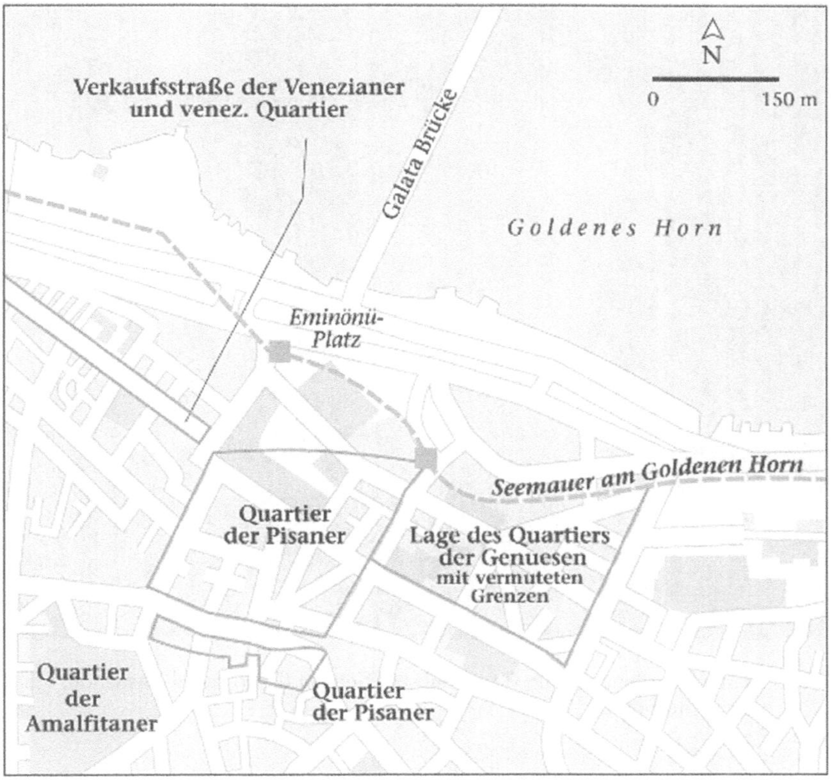

Figure 21.9 Italian settlements on the southern shore of the Golden Horn (as reproduced in Schreiner, Konstantinopel, 2007)

Before the late 13th century, Pera was not a preferred spot for Italian merchants: It was the least favored option for the Genoese diplomats negotiating over a new quarter in 1155 with Manuel I Komnenos (1143–1180). By all means, the Genoese then tried to remain on the peninsula.[37] Whatever the destructions of the 4th Crusade and the following decades of Latin rule brought to Constantinople as a whole,[38] Pera was still sufficiently fortified and defended in 1261 – significantly by Italians, as Georgios Pachymeres attests in his account.[39]

Only in 1267, following some rather difficult years of Byzantine-Genoese relations, in part due to a fraud by Guglielmo Guercio, Podestà of Pera in 1264, that prompted Michael to expel the Genoese and allow their settlement only in remote Herakleia on the Sea of Marmara, the emperor finally conceded Galata to the Genoese, fulfilling his earlier promises.[40] The Genoese, the largest foreign community, Pachymeres tells us, were settled across the Golden Horn in order to avoid conflicts and conspiracies between the various Italian groups who had their own governors known as Bailo to the Venetians, Consul to the Pisans, and Podestà to the Genoese.[41] As a further safety measure, Pachymeres continues, the walls of Galata were torn down.[42]

This was certainly not the full story. To prevent violent conflicts among the various groups (with strident fleets at hand) was almost impossible – the Venetians severely attacked the Genoese settlement in 1296 – nor could the various groups be strictly divided.[43] Furthermore, Constantinople had since long been a multiethnic city; suffice it to remember the many mixed

Figure 21.10 Istanbul [Turkey], Yeraltı Camii/Substructions of the so-called Kastellion, 7th/8th century (photo: author, 2017)

marriages, mainly between Latin men and Byzantine women, and their descendants known as *Gasmouloi*, and the resulting mixed identities and interests of a rather multicultural population that often counteracts conceptions of nation implicit in written accounts.[44]

Late medieval Pera was indeed attractive in the eyes of the Genoese. Among the already existing buildings, the old shipyard (*palaia exartysis, vetus tersana*) at Pegai, west of Pera/Galata, that was not used by the Byzantines any longer, must have been compelling.[45] In 1265, while the Genoese were exiled to Herakleia, the emperor had offered this area to the Venetians, but the negotiations failed eventually.[46] With those shipyards, where ships could be stored during winter season, repaired and built, it was possible for the Genoese to turn the coast north of the Golden Horn into a harbor in its own right, since the coastal conditions on this side were just as advantageous as on the northern peninsular coast. In fact, the geographic features of Pera were similar to the conditions in Genoa – an important prerequisite given the size of their cargo ships and the intensified long-distance trade. Here as there the waters were especially deep close to the coastal line, here as there a flat stretch along the coast and a steeply rising landscape marked the view from the sea.[47] Even for the largest ships, it was possible to land along the entire coastal area stretching from Pegai on the Golden Horn, west of Galata, to Argyropolis on the Bosphorus.

Impressions of Pera

In 1332, the Muslim judge and world traveler Ibn Battuta from Morocco stayed in Constantinople and was dazzled by Pera's floating city – namely its harbor. He stated that the Frankish settlement inhabited by Genoese and other Latins was cramped and dirty, while he admired the manifold merchandise and the harbor right in front of the settlement that was one of the largest he had ever seen with hundreds of ships and uncountable boats of different size and type.[48]

Further information is provided by a trading handbook (*Pratica della Mercatura*) written in the 1340s by Francesco Pegolotti. An accountant working for the Bardi, a Florentine banking and entrepreneur family, he was well-acquainted with long-distance trade matters in the Aegean and the North Sea.[49] While Pegolotti treats the harbors of Pera and Constantinople together, mentioning commodities available in different packaging ranging from soap, oil, and wine of different provenance, dried meat, rice, and sugar to silk fabrics, wool, mastix, madder, amber, and gold wire, he stresses that Pera was indeed the place of all relevant transactions. He furthermore states that the general control-station for animal skins, where one could negotiate new prizes, if the wares were wet and damaged, was located in Pera.[50] Interestingly, he also advocates bribery: being polite and keeping ready little gifts and money sums for the *kommerkiarioi* of the Byzantine emperor and the weighers of Constantinople and Pera would affect the tariffs levied.[51]

Another Arab source, the account of al-ʿUmarī of Damascus from approximately the same time, knows a great deal about Genoa's form of government, and also of Galata and Caffa as important ports of the Genoese.[52] Some 500 ships, all in the possession of aristocratic Genoese families, sailed the Mediterranean and Black Sea, al-ʿUmarī continues. While the number of ships might be exaggerated, it was in fact the many vessels, often but not exclusively in the possession of mighty families (he mentions the Doria, Spinola, Grimaldi, De Mari, and others)[53] that linked the scattered Genoese colonies and created the wealth and almost global prestige of the maritime republic.[54]

The Genoese Insignia and Questions of Genoese Nationality

The Genoese ships and their flagging bring us to the aspect of national and communal identity in the medieval Mediterranean by virtue of the ubiquitous use of emblems and insignia, often in perishable media such as textiles and wood, and thus rarely preserved.[55] This colorful sign language was a cross-culturally understood phenomenon as implied by a 14th-century Castilian handbook on the insignia of the various kingdoms.[56] Written by an anonymous Franciscan author, we learn that Genoa was represented by a red cross on a white (or silver) ground.[57] Also later known as the Cross of St. George, it was visible in the form of flags waving from towers of Genoese colonies, as in some of Buondelmonti's views.[58] Public buildings in particular were marked by these insignia, while also every ship was equipped with the appropriate signs (*vexilla*) (Figure 21.11).[59] In addition to the red cross on a white field, the Genoese used further iconographies that were conceived, promoted, and recognised as Genoese symbols: e.g. the griffin, saints like the Roman deacon St. Lawrence, St. John the Baptist, and St. George (Genoa's three city patrons), or the Virgin Mary with the Child.[60] Scarcely noticed, but quite remarkable, is the fact that from 1198 onward the Genoese at sea and in their colonies did not use primarily representations of Genoa's main patron saint, Lawrence, but instead of the Cappadocian dragon slayer George – who happened to be a highly popular saint among the Byzantines, and was moreover closely linked to the Byzantine emperors.[61]

Such visual manifestations of identity, by land and by sea, mattered; the flag of a medieval community (or nation) represented it fully; accordingly disregarding or violating such symbols was deemed disrespectful or even an attack.[62] For example, upon entering

Figure 21.11 The Fall of Acre. Leaf from the Cocharelli Codex (Inv. 2065), Genoa, 14th century. Florence, Museo Nazionale del Bargello (su concessione del Ministero della Cultura – Museo Nazionale del Bargello)

the Golden Horn, each Genoese ship first had to hoist the imperial flag – the Tetragrammaton – in front of the Blachernae Palace as a sign of recognition of Byzantine sovereignty. The suspension of such regulations could result in a noticeable deterioration of Byzantine-Genoese relations.[63]

The nationality of a person was furthermore relevant for legal jurisdiction and taxation, and closely connected to the latter were tax fraud and tax evasion. A notarial deed from Kilia on the Black Sea, from 1360, probably implies the latter: a grain-loaded Byzantine ship which belonged half to an inhabitant (*habitator*) of Constantinople and half to an inhabitant (*habitator*) of Genoese Pera was to sail only under the Genoese flag during the upcoming voyage to Constantinople (*debeant in dicto ligno portare et levare insigna Comunis Ianue et non alicuius alterius in dicto viagio*).[64] The decision to sail under the Genoese flag might have been dictated by privileged tax conditions the Genoese enjoyed in contrast to others. Thus, in multiethnic contexts such as the Eastern Mediterranean and the Black Sea region with different forms of taxation for distinct groups, the nationality was a relevant, and often, disputed issue. Adopting the nationality of a privileged group facilitated tax evasion and this remained a huge problem for the Late Byzantine economy.[65] The generous granting of Genoese citizenship by Genoese authorities in the colonies was repeatedly a bone of contention; the Byzantine treasury justifiably feared to lose tax revenues since naturalized Genoese (or naturalized Venetians) could expect comparable tax benefits granted to those originating from Genoa (or Venice).[66]

The Podestà Palace

In Pera, especially around the Podestà Palace (*palatium communis*), which together with the *logia*, formed the administrative and commercial center, specifically Genoese iconographies were in use. This was the most important building complex in the words of Michel Balard, to whom we owe much of our understanding of medieval Genoese colonization.[67] Pero Tafur, the Castilian merchant traveler who in 1437 spent several weeks on the Golden Horn staying with compatriots in Pera, states that there was also "*a fine exchange, well-built and enclosed.*"[68] How this area was protected by walls is difficult to say, but the overall impression among the visitors from afar, already by the end of the 14th century, was that Pera was a solidly fortified and well-built city with stone in wide use.[69]

From the Annals of Genoa (*Annales Ianuenses*), we learn that, after a fire devastated Pera in 1315, Podestà Montano de Marini rebuilt the *palatium communis*, the *pondus communis* (city scales), the *platea* (an open space), the *logia* (commercial center), and landward walls.[70] Since the most representative parts of Pera – the spatial nucleus where Genoese authority was in effect, Genoese law was administered, Genoese measures were valid, and Genoese customs were kept up – had to be rebuilt anew, one might presume a deliberate orientation towards the mother-city, but it is difficult to discern any architectural alignments with surviving medieval structures in Genoa. The badly damaged building in Istanbul, Bereket Han, as the former Podestà Palace is now called, at the crossroads of Bankalar Caddesi and Galata Kulesi Sokaği,[71] does not allow any comparisons to the heavily restored Palazzo San Giorgio in Genoa, the former *palatium Communis*, that was built in the early 1260s and could have served as a prototype for newly built communal structures in the colonies.[72]

From the accounts of artisanal services in the registers of the Massaria of Pera, we learn that the Podestà Palace was a white-washed, two-storey building with a balcony, a representative stairway, and glass windows. The façade of the palace bore a representation of St. George on horseback (akin to the presumed imagery at the *palatium Communis* in Genoa) that was solemnly illuminated by torches during religious feasts.[73]

Interesting in this regard is a miniature of the Fall of Acre in 1291 (Inv. 2065) in the so-called Cocharelli Codex, a beautifully illuminated edifying booklet on virtues and vices from the early 14th century commissioned by a member of the Cocharelli, a Genoese merchant family that acquired its wealth in the Levant and in France (Figure 21.11).[74] In the representation of the historical battle, each of the armed forces can be identified by its symbol (such as the "Lion of Baybars" of the Mamlūks), while the main Latin churches and the most important public buildings of Acre are characterised by specific imagery. The crenelated building at the center bears an image of St. George on horseback in a tympanon, while the building next to it displays the winged lion, the symbol of the Evangelist Mark.

According to Chiara Concina, these buildings represent the *logiae*, that means the commercial headquarters, of the Genoese and the Venetians in Acre, as indicated by iconographies closely associated with the two maritime republics.[75]

Again, visual manifestations of a particular identity were also important expressions of authority. The emblem of a place represented the place itself and marked its representatives,[76] especially in the context of official interactions of the Genoese elite with the emperor – for example at the Blachernae Palace where much emphasis was put on ceremonies, dress codes and hierarchies. Communication with the imperial court was a highly ritualized matter; according to Pseudo-Kodinos' book on imperial ceremonies and offices dating to the 14th century, it was expected that the Podestà of Pera and his retinue would be present each Sunday. If such a frequency of encounters can be presumed is difficult to say, but at least on the occasion of secular and religious feasts, the presence of the Podestà was obligatory.[77] One may speculate whether the high-ranking representatives of the Genoese and the Venetians, described by Bishop Ignatius of Smolensk who, during his stay in Constantinople, attended the coronation ceremony of Manuel II (1391–1425) in Hagia Sophia, had representations of St. George, and St. Mark's lion, respectively, embroidered on their costumes. At least, Ignatius states that the various Frankish groups wearing varicolored velvet robes were recognizable by their "*own emblems*" executed in pearl embroidery on the chest.[78]

The Podestà's Duties

The duties of the annually appointed Podestà of Pera were manifold, ranging from communicating with the imperial court, receiving ambassadors, and reporting to Genoa to dispensing justice, keeping trade and civic life in order, granting citizenship, and protecting the settlement.[79] By the early 15th century, Pera was inhabited by Genoese, Greeks, Turks, Armenians, Venetians, Catalans, and others, while a specific Genoese identity in Pera was constituted and performed by virtue of the daily routines, formal actions and rituals based on the statutes promulgated by the mother-city Genoa, and meticulously implemented in the colonies.[80] The office of the Podestà was demanding – accordingly, it was a well-paid post and assisted by professional staff. Notaries, treasurers, and translators supported the highest representative of the Commune on the Golden Horn.[81] Additionally, specialised officers (*masarii*) for overlooking the expenses of the colonies were in charge. Sent from Genoa early in fall, the new Podestà had to first pay homage to the emperor and then present himself to the Genoese community. Among his first actions was to constitute a small council (6 members) and a large council (24 members) from among the male inhabitants of Pera to assist him. Both the Podestà and his legally trained vicar lived in private apartments within the Podestà Palace, respectively, whereas a large hall and further rooms were used for gatherings and hearings, and the basement as an arsenal.[82]

Not only was the Genoese administrative center visually remarkable by specifically Genoese iconographies like St. George on horseback, Genoa's heraldic colors, and the coats of arms of respected Genoese families, but there must also have been an acoustic facet to the creation of identity (*Identitätsstiftung*). Pera's soundscape, in contrast to Constantinople's, was e.g. distinctly marked by bell-ringing of the Latin churches and monasteries as stressed by Alex Rodriguez Suarez,[83] and one might add music played in public contexts as well as the Podestà's exclamations to the community that contributed to a genuinely Genoese or Latin soundscape.[84]

The Genoese Expansion in Pera and The Height of Galata Tower

Although accusations by the Byzantine writer Alexios Makrembolites that the Barbarians from "Gehenna" (a Biblical place of wicked people, as he calls the Genoese) first had only wooden huts covered with grass must be taken with a grain of salt, the expansion of Pera provoked controversy, given the building regulations and restrictions on land acquisition imposed by Byzantine-Genoese treaties.[85] Even Ruy González de Clavijo, the leader of a Castilian embassy to Samarkand in 1403, who conveys a positive image of Pera in his travel account, can't hold back when it comes to the subsequent enlargement of the settlement which he compares to Dido's cunning as conveyed in Carthage's founding legend.[86]

From the beginning, according to the Byzantine historian Nikephoros Gregoras, the Genoese wanted to expand their original settlement in all three landward directions (west, north, east), an aim the colonists achieved within the first six decades of the 14th century.[87] The attack of the Venetians in 1296 and several skirmishes with the Byzantines had proven the vulnerability of the insufficiently fortified settlement. Once the sea wall was erected,[88] the Genoese focused on securing the rear side. Especially the nearby heights (Şişhane and Taksim) served as potential bases for launching military assaults on Pera, as Clavijo specifies regarding the long Ottoman siege of Bayezid I in the 1390s.[89] Thus, the subsequent expansion of the fortifications northward was very much dictated by the specific topography of Pera, while the sideways expansion incorporating parts of Spiga (Pegai), and Lagirio (Argyropolis), relieved the increasing population of Pera and in turn contributed to securing the settlement as a whole.[90]

In the words of Emperor John VI Kantakuzenos (1341, 1347–1354), the hill on which the Genoese built the Galata Tower "[...] *was so steep, that it hung above their* [the Genoese'] *heads.*"[91] No wonder that the Genoese, fearing (revenge) attacks by the Byzantines, wanted to incorporate the hill in their settlement.[92] Clandestinely, while Kantakuzenos was confined to bed in Didymotichon due to an illness in fall 1348, they "[...] *fortified the hill, raising a tower on its summit.*"[93]

Galata Tower's actual height of 67 m is a result of the 19th century, and then of restoration measures undertaken in 1965–1967 prior to its opening as a tourist attraction that still provides a breathtaking panorama of modern Istanbul.[94] However, the original height of Galata Tower, known as *Christea turris* to the Genoese, probably did not exceed the average height of the defensive towers in the region (ca. 20 m) by more than 10 m. The spiral stairs inside the tower end at about 24 m and seem to indicate the original stone tower's height, while wooden constructions set on top of the tower might have added more meters, but it was above all the position of the tower on the summit of a hill of ca. 40 m above sea level,[95] plus the massiveness of the structure (16 m in diameter) that suggested a commanding height.

A viewshed analysis, based on a hypothetical height of 30 m for the original Galata Tower, demonstrates that especially the area around Şişhane and the slope towards Taksim as well as the southern shore of the Golden Horn could be well monitored (Figure 21.12). An originally lower altitude of the tower and the adjacent walls that together formed an ascending triangle towards the north is furthermore implied by the mentioning of a stone shortage in the course of the building project. Once the piles of unhewn stones and spoliated building material that the Genoese had stocked were all spent, Gregoras reports that they used great amounts of wooden beams for the construction of palisades. The defensive

Galataturm | Sichtbereichsanalyse 2021 | Konzept und wiss. Analyse: Mabi Angar | Grafikdesign und Geodatenverarbeitung: Jan Hubert

Figure 21.12 Viewshed analysis with a hypothetical height of 30 m for the Galata Tower (copyright: author, 2021 The map is reproduced in colour, available at: https://www.geistes-und-sozialwissenschaften-bmbf.de/de/Genua-am-Bosporus-Interview-mit-Byzantinistin-Dr-Mabi-Angar-uber-die-spatmittelalterliche-2324.html.)

stronghold that helped to monitor the hinterland, the settlement, and the surrounding waters was additionally secured by a very deep moat dug quickly by a collective effort of the commune.[96]

Were these actions really conducted secretly? At least in part, such accusations belong to the rhetorical arsenal of the Byzantine writers. Of course, they preferred to downplay any wrong decisions, failures and consent by the contemporary Byzantine emperors, and rather described the Genoese as notoriously mendacious and in the end ungrateful foreign subjects.

However, Gregoras does not deny the conflict-ridden situation – the first half of the 14th century was marked by civil wars – and concomitant dependencies of certain imperial and aristocratic circles on Genoese money, military aid, and other favors. The various deals between Andronikos III (1328–1341) and the Genoese – he had friends among the elite of Pera and needed them as allies and financiers in his war with his grandfather[97] – certainly facilitated the expansion of the settlement.

There cannot be any doubt that the emperors were always sooner or later informed about what was going on in Pera – the relations were too close, while spying added to the court's knowledge about the various foreign groups in the capital. It is striking that the emperors only rarely intervened against the expansionist politics in Pera. In most cases, they sanctioned what the Genoese had carried out. Significantly in this context, Gregoras mentions not only corrupt Byzantine officials selling land outside the Genoese quarter to the

Genoese,[98] but also the transfer of spolia – columns and other building components made of marble – from the Great Palace and other structures in Constantinople that had been sold and were taken to Galata.[99] While the latter reproach might be a rhetorical exaggeration, another symbol of the rise and fall of empires, there were in fact many dilapidated high-quality structures in Constantinople and Pera, areas that had suffered in the sieges of the Fourth Crusade and the neglect of 1204–1261, that could have served as building material for new building projects of the Genoese.[100]

Genoa – A Republic of Towers and Conflicts

The various contemporary texts at hand remain our most valuable source of evidence for the reconstruction of Genoese urbanity on the Golden Horn and yet it remains difficult to judge to what extent any statements reflect urban realities and what might be of topic character. For example, Pero Tafur provides a concise description of the houses in Genoa and Pera. Prior to his stay on the Golden Horn, he had visited Genoa and described the houses there as "*towers of four or five storeys or more.*" He then states for Pera that "*the buildings are notably and lofty, as in Genoa.*"[101]

A scarcely known but important aspect of Genoa itself is indeed interesting in our search for structural alignments of the various Genoese colonies to the mother-city: Genoa was a turreted city in the Middle Ages,[102] comparable to Bologna and San Gimignano, with the major difference of having the sea on one side. Some 70 tower-houses of noble families once formed a unique skyline of medieval Genoa that, together with the rising landscape, made an impression on visitors arriving at the harbor (Figure 21.13).[103] Our Byzantine sources ponder about Genoese houses of two and three storeys in Pera and of high towers, although these structures were in all likelihood nowhere near the average height of the tower-houses in the mother-city. Pero Tafur was nevertheless reminded of Genoa – maybe by virtue of the aforementioned Genoese insignia with which especially the well-visible structures of the Genoese settlement on the Golden Horn were decorated in the same manner as in Genoa.[104]

As so often, the surviving historical layers in Istanbul do not allow any definite conclusions, nor are the pictorial sources reliable when it comes to such details. What seems more interesting anyway is that inherent to such accusations by Byzantine authors might have been a general critique of the Genoese and their distinct political system as a medieval republic.[105] According to the Genoese self-image conveyed in the *Annales Ianuenses*, a textual corpus that served above all as an important tool for the self-assurance and the collective memory function of the Community,[106] the Genoese tower-houses became a symbol of factionalism and violent disputes that had disturbed the public order of Genoa time and again. A miniature in a 12th/13th-century manuscript of the *Annales Ianuenses* kept in the Bibliothèque nationale in Paris (Ms. lat. 1036, fol. 111v) displays two fighting knights in front of their heavily armed tower-houses in Genoa and thereby vividly conveys this disruptive notion (Figure 21.14).[107] The Genoese conditions were not unknown in Byzantium. On the other hand, especially since the Crusades, a more general Byzantine concept of Westerners who were perceived as an easy-to-provoke, on the whole aggressive force, had come into being. It would be interesting to know whether any (self-)descriptions and attributions of the Genoese were taken up and deliberately used by Byzantine authors who often knew much more about the Other than they revealed in the framework of their literary works.[108]

Figure 21.13 Genoa [Italy], Torre dei Morchi, 12th–14th century (photo: author, 2016)

Figure 21.14 Knights fighting in front of tower houses in Genoa. Detail from the *Annales Ianuenses* (Ms.lat.10136), fol. 111v, Genoa, late 12th century. Paris, Bibliothèque nationale de France (photo: Bibliothèque nationale de France)

Conclusion

To sum up: Pera was surely a special example of the ability of the Genoese to efficiently create "another Genoa" (*un'atra Zenoa*) in foreign territories, as an often quoted anonymous Genoese poet enthusiastically described Genoese migration in the 13th century.[109] The systematic use of the specific colors, signs, and saints of Genoa was especially important for the 'branding' process outside the home region. As outlined in this chapter, establishing a distinctive communal identity in a multiethnic hub like Constantinople, mainly by visual means that allow immediate recognition, was a common cultural practice in the Mediterranean worth further comparative study.

Rarely were the foreign groups given undeveloped land by the emperor. The challenge was to turn a specific urban, often litoral, zone into a distinguishable quarter of its own right, sometimes only for a short period. In conflicted times with always changing political and economic alliances, the sudden expulsion from (or the voluntary abandonment of) a conceded merchant settlement was a perfectly possible scenario. Performative acts, rules, and attire mattered as did language and sound, protective walls marking one's territory were important features as were structures and public spaces modeled after prototypes of the mother-city. However, the use of colorful emblematic large-format representations – visible from afar and yet also mobile – was probably the most effective means to create a distinctive identity.

Notes

1 I thank the Federal Ministry of Education and Research (BMBF) for generously supporting my Pera project at the University of Cologne (12/2018–11/2022). I am grateful to Albrecht Berger, Anthony Kaldellis, Antonio Musarra, Claudia Sode and Christina Stancioiu for their interest in this paper and their valuable comments. Mistakes are mine.

2 On the quarters of foreign communities in Constantinople, see R. Janin, *Constantinople byzantine. Développement urbain et répertoire topographique. Deuxième édition* (Paris, 1964), pp. 245–260. See also S. Reinert, "The Muslim Presence in Constantinople, 9th–15th Centuries: Some Preliminary Observations," in *Studies on the Internal Diaspora of the Byzantine Empire*, eds. H. Ahrweiler and A. E. Laiou (Washington, 1998), pp. 125–150.

3 P. Schreiner, "The Western Landing Stages in the Golden Horn. Some Remarks Related to the Eleventh and Twelfth Centuries," in *The Byzantine Harbours of Constantinople*, eds. F. Daim et al. (Mainz, in print).

4 See Fig. 21.9.

5 M. Balard, "Les Génois en Romanie entre 1204 et 1261. Recherches dans les minutiers notariaux génois," in *Mélanges d'archéologie et d'histoire* 78 (1966), pp. 467–502, at p. 471.

6 N. Oikonomides, *Hommes d'affaires grecs et latins à Constantinople (XIIIe-XVe siècles)* (Montreal-Paris, 1979), pp. 43–45.

7 L. Sauli, *Della colonia dei Genovesi in Galata* (2 vols.) (Turin, 1831); C. Desimoni, "I Genovesi ed i loro quartieri nel secolo XIII," in *Giornale Ligustico di Archeologia, Storia e Belle Arti* 3 (1886), pp. 217–274; L. T. Belgrano, "Prima serie di documenti riguardanti la colonia di Pera," in *Atti della Società Ligure di Storia Patria* 8 (1877/1884), pp. 97–336; T. Belgrano, "Seconda serie di documenti riguardanti la colonia di Pera," in *Atti della Società Ligure di Storia Patria* 8 (1884), pp. 932–1003.

F. A. Belin, *Histoire de la Latinité de Constantinople* (Paris, 1894); J. Sauvaget, "Notes sur la colonie génoise de Péra," in *Syria* 8 (1934), pp. 252–275; E. Dallegio D'Alessio, "*Galata et ses environs dans l'antiquité*," in *Revue des études byzantines* 4 (1946), pp. 218–238; E. Dallegio D'Alessio, "*Galata et la souveraineté de Byzance*," in *Revue des études byzantines* 19 (1961), pp. 315–327.

8 S. Eyice, *Galata ve kulesi – Galata and Its Tower* (Istanbul, 1969); K. Anadol/E. Arioğlu, "Galata Tower Restoration Project," in *IABSE Congress Report* 11 (1980), pp. 952–956.

9 H. Çetinkaya, "Arap Camii in Istanbul: Its Architecture and Frescoes," in *Anatolia Antiqua. Eski Anadolu* 18 (2010), pp. 169–188; S. Westphalen, "Die Dominikanerkirche der Genuesen von Pera (Arap Camii). Griechische Maler – Lateinische Auftraggeber," in *Austausch und Inspiration. Kulturkontakt als Impuls architektonischer Innovation, Diskussionen zur Archäologischen Bauforschung*, eds. U. Wulff-Rheidt and F. Pirson (Mainz, 2008), pp. 276–291.

10 P. Niewöhner, "*Saint Benoît in Galata. Der byzantinische Ursprungsbau,*" in *Jahrbuch des Deutschen Archäologischen Instituts* 125 (2010), pp. 155–241.

11 A. M. Schneider/M. Nomidis, *Galata. Topographisch-Archäologischer Plan. Mit erläuterndem Text* (Istanbul, 1944), pp. 5–6.

12 R. Quirini-Popławski, *Sztuka kolonii genueńskich w Basenie Morza Czarnego (1261–1475)* (Cracow, 2018); R. Quirini-Popławski, "Art in the Genoese Colonies in the Black Sea (in the 13th-15th c.). Present State of Knowledge and Selected Research Problems," in *Biuletyn Historii Sztuki* 3–4 (2012), pp. 425–471; S. Sağlam, *Urban Palimpsest at Galata and an Architectural Inventory Study for the Genoese Colonial Territories in Asia Minor* (Ph.D., Milan, 2018); L. Orlando, "Prospettive per la valorizzazione del patrimonio architettonico genovese nel quartiere di Galata a Iştanbul," in *Atti della Società Ligure di Storia Patria* 60 (2020), pp. 127–156.

For a *Cologne Summer School* and a preceding workshop on Pera's urban fabric through the centuries held in Istanbul in 2019, see (https://www.academia.edu/39018796/Summer_School_in_Istanbul_28_June_4_July_2019_On_the_Other_Side_Exploring_the_Urban_Fabric_of_Pera_during_the_Byzantine_Genoese_and_Ottoman_Period).

13 Ç. Kafescioğlu, "Viewing, Walking, Mapping Istanbul, ca. 1580," in *Mitteilungen des Kunsthistorischen Instituts in Florenz* 56 (2014), pp. 17–35.

14 G. Ragone, "'Membrana Maxima': Cristoforo dei Buondelmonti, Vytuautas of Lithuania and the First Modern Map of Constantinople," in *Lietuva ir jos kaimynai nuo normanu iki Napoleono: Broniaus Dundolio Atminimui*, eds. I. Valikonyte et al. (Vilnius, 2001), pp. 150–187; C. Barsanti, "Il panorama di Cristoforo Buondelmonti," in *Domenicani a Costantinopoli prima e dopo l'impero ottomano. Storie, immagini e documenti d'archivio*, eds. C. Monge and S. Pedone (Florence, 2017), pp. 51–67; A. Effenberger, "Die Illustrationen – Topographische Untersuchungen: Konstantinopel/İstanbul und ägäische Örtlichkeiten," in *Cristoforo Buondelmonti. Liber insularum archipelagi. Universitäts- und Landesbibliothek Düsseldorf Ms. G. 13 Faksimile*, eds. I. Seibert and M. Plassmann (Wiesbaden, 2005), pp. 13–89.

15 Buondelmonti dedicated the *Lia* to his patron, Cardinal Giordano Orsini.

16 M. Balard, "Buondelmonti and the Holy War," in *Shipping, Trade and Crusade in the Medieval Mediterranean*. Studies in Honour of John Pryor, eds. R. Gertwagen and E. Jeffreys (Aldershot, 2012), pp. 387–395.

17 Barsanti, *Panorama*, p. 54.

18 I thank Laura Nuvoloni (Holkham Hall Library) for sharing information on Ms. 475.

19 On Genoese Chios, see P. P. Argenti, *The Occupation of Chios by the Genoese and Their Administration of the Island 1346-1566* (Cambridge, 1958).

20 S. Kolditz, *Johannes VIII. Palaiologos und das Konzil von Ferrara-Florenz (1438/39)* (Stuttgart, 2013–2014), pp. 44-70.

21 The 15th-century Ms. W 309, fol. 35v (The Walters Art Museum, Baltimore) displays Constantinople and Pera in the same manner as Ms. 475, fol. 42v (Holkham Hall Library, Norfolk). (https://thedigitalwalters.org/Data/WaltersManuscripts/W309/data/W.309/sap/W309_000074_sap.jpg).

22 M. De Launay, *Notice sur les fortifications de Galata* (Constantinople, 1864); J. Gottwald, *Die Stadtmauern von Galata* (Constantinople, 1907).

23 On the donor inscriptions of which many got lost in the course of time, see De Launay, *Notice*; E. Rossi, "Le lapidi genovesi delle mura di Galata," in *Atti della Società Ligure di Storia Patria 56* (1928), pp. 143–164. For a more recent assessment, see Sağlam, *Urban Palimpsest*, pp. 381–421. An ongoing European Research Council project (*GRAPH-EAST, Latin as an Alien Script in the Medieval 'Latin East'*, 2021-2026) by Estelle Ingrand Varenne will consider the Genoese material of Pera in detail.

24 See Fig. 21.5. On the Chain of the Golden Horn, see further below. It is unknown whether the area of Pera defined by its Genoese walls corresponded one-to-one to the space defined as late antique Sykai.

Since the topographic disposition of the area in question remained relatively constant over the centuries, it has become common practice to presume a certain degree of consistency of its spatial configuration, see A. Berger, "Regionen und Straßen im frühen Konstantinopel," in *Istanbuler Mitteilungen* 47 (1997), pp. 349–414, at p. 373; A. Külzer, *Tabula Imperii Byzantini 12. Ostthrakien (Eurōpē)* (Vienna, 2008), pp. 361–367 (Galata), pp. 576–577 (Pera); pp. 664–665 (Sykai).

25 See Fig. 21.8.

26 For these treaties, which have only survived in Latin translations, see *I Libri Iurium della Repubblica di Genova, vol. I/8 a cura di* Eleonora Pallavicino (Genoa, 2002), nos. 1266, 1267, pp. 69–78; F. Dölger, *Regesten der Kaiserurkunden des Oströmischen Reiches, 4. Teil: Regesten von 1282-1341* (Munich, 1960), nos. 2256, 2261, pp. 40–42.

27 The *ecclesia Sancti Michaelis de Peira* is mentioned in notarial deeds dating to 1281, see M. Balard, *La Romanie génoise (XIIe-début du XVe siècle)* (2 vols.) (Paris, 1978), I, p. 183.

28 On the Treaty of Nymphaion, see F. Dölger, *Regesten der Kaiserurkunden des Oströmischen Reiches von 565-1453, 3. Teil: Regesten von 1204-1282* (Munich, 1932), no. 1890, pp. 73–75; D. J. Geanakoplos, *Emperor Michael VIII Palaeologus and the West 1258-1282. A Study in Byzantine-Latin Relations* (Cambridge, MA, 1959), pp. 81–91; M. Balard, "1261. Genova nel mondo: il tratatto di Ninfeo," in *Gli anni di Genova* (Rome, 2010), pp. 39–68.

29 The contract even allowed the Genoese to obtain a palace and a church with surrounding houses that originally belonged to the Venetians [...] *quod dabit dicto communi ecclesiam Sancte Marie quam modo tenant Venetici cum logiis que sunt circa ipsam ecclesiam et cimiterio ipsius atque solum castri Veneticorum quod est in ipsa civitate* [...]. Quoted from *I Libri Iurium della Repubblica di Genova, vol. I/4 a cura di* Sabina Dellacasa (Genoa, 1988), no. 749, p. 275. According to the *Annales Ianuenses*, the Genoese destroyed the palace of the Venetians in Constantinople and sent selected stones (*lapides*) as spolia to Genoa. The lion protoms at the Palazzo San Giorgio in Genoa, the former *palatium Communis*, are commonly identified with these stones, see R. Müller, *Sic hostes Ianua frangit. Spolien und Trophäen im mittelalterlichen Genua* (Weimar, 2002), pp. 72–73.

30 C. Desimoni, "Memoria sui quartieri dei Genovesi a Costantinopoli nel XII," in *Giornale Ligustico di Archeologia, Storia e Belle Arti* 1 (1874), pp. 137–180; Schreiner, *Landing Stages*.

31 Balard, *Romanie génoise*, I, pp. 107–109; F. Dölger, *Regesten der Kaiserurkunden des Oströmischen Reiches von 565-1453, 2. Teil: Regesten von 1025-1204* (Munich, 1925), no. 1488, p. 82. It is telling that as early as by the late 1180, the Genoese merchant Guglielmo Arnaldo (who brought the news of Manuel I Komnenos' death) returned from Pera (*Peyra*), and not from Constantinople, according to the Genoese Annals, see *Codice Diplomatico della Repubblica di Genova dal MCLXIIII al MCLXXXX a cura di* Cesare Imperiale di Sant'Angelo (Rome, 1938), II, no. 126, p. 261.

32 After all, severe fires had devastated large parts of the Italian merchant settlements along the southern coast of the Golden Horn during the siege of Constantinople. On the fires, see T. F. Madden, "The Fires of the Fourth Crusade in Constantinople, 1203-1204: A Damage Assessment," in *Byzantinische Zeitschrift* 84/85 (1993/94), pp. 72–93.

33 Külzer, *Ostthrakien*, p. 419 (Iustinianai).

34 Balard, *Romanie génoise*, I, p. 182; A. Failler, "De l'appelation de Péra dans les textes byzantins," in *Revue des études byzantines* 56 (1998), pp. 239–247.

35 Berger, *Regionen*, p. 373.

36 On the Kastellion, see N. Erkal, "The Corner of the Horn: An Architectural Review of the Leaded Magazine in Galata İstanbul," in *METU. JFA* 28/1 (2011), pp. 197–227. The peninsular fixing point of the chain, the Tower of Eugenios, has not survived. Although the chain was rarely in use, it has attracted great attention, see J. H. Pryor, "The Chain of the Golden Horn, 5-7 July 1203," in *In Laudem Hierosolymitani. Studies in Crusades and Medieval Culture in Honour of Benjamin Z. Kedar*, eds. I. Shagrir et al. (Farnham, 2007), pp. 369–384.

37 P. Magdalino, "The maritime neighborhoods of Constantinople: commercial and residential functions, sixth to twelfth centuries," in *Dumbarton Oaks Papers* 54 (2001), pp. 209–226, at pp. 221–222. Settlement on the other side of the Golden Horn was even conceived as a punishment. After some conflicts, the Pisans were obliged to intermittently settle in Pera. They were only allowed to return to the peninsula in July 1155, see Dölger, *Regesten, 2. Teil*, no. 1400, p. 71.

38 The troops of the Fourth Crusade established their main camp in Pera in 1203. The camp became a major access point for the fleeing Latin inhabitants of Constantinople, see D. E. Queller/T. F. Madden, *The Fourth Crusade. The Conquest of Constantinople (Second Edition)* (Philadelphia, 2000), p. 144.

A strong Latin presence in Pera prior to 1261 is also implied by the existence of the newly established center of the Dominicans with a church dedicated to St. Dominic and St. Paul (today's Arap Camii) built between 1225 and 1230, see Schneider-Nomidis, *Galata*, p. 25; N. Melvani, "Dominicans in Byzantium and Byzantine Dominicans: Religious Dialogue and Cultural Interaction," in *Domenicani a Costantinopoli prima e dopo l'impero ottomano. Storia, immagini e documenti d'archivio*, eds. C. Monge and S. Pedone (Florence, 2017), pp. 33–50.

39 G. Pachymeres, *Relations historiques* (5 vols), ed. A. Failler, trans. V. Laurent (Paris, 1984–2000), I, 2, chap. 20, pp. 170–175.

40 Pachymeres, *Relations historiques*, I, 2, chap. 35, pp. 224–226.

41 Pachymeres, *Relations historiques*, I, 2, chap, 32, pp. 218–221.

42 Pachymeres, *Relations historiques*, I, 2, chap. 35, pp. 226–227.

43 A. Laiou, *Constantinople and the Latins. The Foreign Policy of Andronicus II 1282-1328* (Cambridge, MA, 1972), pp. 104–106, pp. 301–302.

44 S. A. Epstein, *Purity Lost. Transgressing Boundaries in the Eastern Mediterranean 1000-1400* (Baltimore, 2006); A. Kaldellis, *Ethnography after Antiquity. Foreign Lands and Peoples in Byzantine Literature* (Philadelphia, 2013), pp. 175–176.

45 The Byzantines reduced their fleet substantially in 1284, see G. Makris, *Studien zur spätbyzantinischen Schiffahrt* (Genoa, 1988), p. 108.

46 G. I. Bratianu, *Recherches sur le commerce génois dans la mer noire au XIIIe siècle* (Paris, 1929), pp. 88–89; M. Pozza / G. Ravegnani (eds.), *I tratatti con Bisanzio 1265-1285* (Venice, 1996), no. 2, pp. 26–47, here at p. 34. The shipyards are known as *navarchio di Pera* by the 15th century, see W. Heyd, *Histoire du Commerce du Levant au Moyen-Âge* (2 vols.) (Amsterdam, 1959), I, p. 454; Balard, *Romanie génoise*, I, p. 195. A second shipyard of the Genoese was located in Lagirio (Argyropolis).

47 S. A. Epstein, *Genoa and the Genoese. 958-1528* (Chapel Hill-London, 1996), p. 13; Berger, *Regionen*, p. 373.

48 Ibn Battuta, *Travels in Asia and Africa 1325-1354. Translated and selected by* H. A. R. Gibb *with an Introduction and Notes* (New York, 1969), p. 160.

49 F. Pegolotti, *La Pratica della Mercatura. Book of Descriptions of Countries and of Measures of Merchandise*, ed. A. Evans (Cambridge, MA, 1936), pp. ix–xlix (introduction).

50 Pegolotti, *Pratica*, pp. 32–54, esp. pp. 32–33.

51 Pegolotti, *Pratica*, p. 42, p. 44.

52 A. Musarra, "Political Alliance and Conflict," in *A Companion to Medieval Genoa* (Brill's Companions to European History, 18), ed. C. E. Beneš (Leiden-Boston, 2018), pp. 120–143, at p. 131.

53 Musarra, *Alliance*, p. 132. On the presence of branches of several Genoese aristocratic families in Pera and Caffa, see Balard, *Romanie génoise*, I, p. 235, pp. 252–253. On members of the Doria and the Spinola families who served as Podestà of Pera, see Balard, *Romanie génoise*, II, p. 525.

54 That such information circulated in Mamlūk Cairo where al-ʿUmarī was active, is not surprising. Genoese merchants are recorded in Egypt since the 11th century, see M. Balard, "Le commerce génois à Alexandrie (XIe-XIVe siècle)," in M. Balard, *Gênes et la mer – Genoa e il mare* (Genoa, 2017), pp. 269–282.

55 For aristocratic identities, see R. Ousterhout, "Byzantium between East and West and the Origins of Heraldry," in *Byzantine Art. Recent Studies*, ed. C. Hourihane (Tempe, 2009), pp. 153–170.

56 *El libro del conoscimiento de todos los reinos (The Book of Knowledge of all Kingdoms). Edition, Translation, and Study by* N. F. Marino (Tempe, 1999); C. F. Weber, *Zeichen der Ordnung und des Aufruhrs. Heraldische Symbolik in italienischen Stadtkommunen des Mittelalters* (Cologne-Weimar-Vienna, 2011).

57 According to the anonymous author, the term *iustitia* (justice) was written onto the Genoese flag. For an overview of all the signs in the *Libro*, see p. 323 in the digitized edition of M. Jiménez de la Espada's edition from 1877 (http://bdh-rd.bne.es/viewer.vm?id=0000079823&page=1).

See also N. Oikonomides, "The Byzantine Overlordship in the Genoese Possessions," in *Porphyrogenita: Essays on the History and Literature of Byzantium and the Latin East in Honour of Julian Chrysostomides*, eds. C. Dendrinos et al. (Aldershot, 2003), pp. 235–238.

58 See Fig. 21.6.

59 R. Pavoni, "I simboli di Genova alle origini del Comune," in *Saggi e documenti* 3 (1983), pp. 31–64, at pp. 31–34 (*il magno Ianuensium vexillo cum figura beati Georgi*). Makris, *Schiffahrt*,

p. 123. The Genoese fleet of 1242 was even painted white with red crosses, thus becoming swimming carriers of the Genoese coat of arms, see Weber, *Zeichen*, pp. 369-370; G. Pistarino, "Les symboles de Gênes dans les établissements d'Outremer," in *Coloniser au Moyen-Âge. Méthodes d'expansion et techniques de domination en Méditeranée du 11e au 16e siècle*, eds. M. Balard and A. Ducellier (Paris, 1995), pp. 299–317, at p. 301.

60 Pavoni, *Simboli di Genoa*. The griffin, a mythological creature popular in many medieval cultures, was probably the least accepted genuinely Genoese symbol in Byzantium.

61 S. Origone, "San Giorgio nel mondo bizantino," in *Rivista di storia, arte, archeologia per le province di Alessandria e Asti* 109 (2000), pp. 16-29, at p. 28.

62 Pistarino, *Symboles de Gênes*.

63 Makris, *Schiffahrt*, p. 260. Nikephoros Gregoras, *Rhomäische Geschichte – Historia Rhomaïke. Übersetzt und erläutert von* J. L. van Dieten, *Erster Teil (Kapitel I-VII)* (Stuttgart, 1973), p. 259.

64 Makris, *Schiffahrt*, p. 264, p. 304; M. Balard, *Gênes et l'Outre-Mer II. Actes de Kilia du notaire Antonio di Ponzò 1360* (Paris, 1980), p. 69.

65 Gregoras mentions that most of the sailors of the Byzantine fleet adopted the Genoese nationality, see Nikephoros Gregoras, *Byzantina Historia*, ed. L. Schopen (Bonn, 1829), I, 11.1, p. 527; Nikephoros Gregoras, *Rhomäische Geschichte – Historia Romaïke. Übersetzt und erläutert* von J. L. van Dieten, *Zweiter Teil (Kapitel VIII-XI)* (Stuttgart, 1979), p. 275.

66 D. Jacoby, "Between the Imperial Court and the Western Maritime Powers: The Impact of Naturalizations on the Economy of Late Byzantine Constantinople," in *The Byzantine Court: Source of Power and Culture*, eds. A. Ödekan et al. (Istanbul, 2013), pp. 95–103; C. Maltezou, "Venetian 'habitatores', 'burgenses' and merchants in Constantinople and its hinterland (twelfth-thirteenth centuries)," in *Constantinople and Its Hinterland*, eds. C. Mango and G. Dagron (Aldershot, 1995), pp. 233–241. A famous example is Lukas Notaras who seems to have possessed the Byzantine, the Genoese and the Venetian nationality, see Oikonomides, *Hommes d'affaires*, p. 20.

67 Balard, *Romanie génoise*, I, p. 182.

68 *Pero Tafur. Travels and Adventures, 1435-1439. Translated and Edited with an Introduction by* M. Letts (London, 1926), p. 149.

69 *Embassy to Tamerlane, 1403-1406, Ruy González de Clavijo, translated from the Spanish by* G. Le Strange *with a new introduction by* C. Stone (Kilkerran, 2009), p. 64; P. Tafur, *Travels*, p. 149. The sea walls must have been built prior to 1324, see Balard, *Romanie génoise*, I, p. 186.

70 Balard, *Romanie génoise*, I, 186; F. W. Hasluck, "Dr. Covel's Notes on Galata," in *The Annual of the British School at Athens* 11 (1904/1905), pp. 50–62, at pp. 61–62; F. W. Hasluck, "Genoese Heraldry and Inscriptions at Amastra," in *The Annual of the British School at Athens* 17 (1910/1911), pp. 132–144; at pp. 142–144.

71 See Fig. 21.3.

72 On the former *palatium Communis* in Genoa, see L. Cavallaro, *Il Palazzo del Mare. Il nucleo medioevale di Palazzo San Giorgio* (Genoa, 1992).

73 Balard, *Romanie génoise*, I, 193.

74 See Fig. 21.11. On the codex, see C. Concina, "Unfolding the Cocharelli Codex. Some Preliminary Observations about the Text, with a Theory about the Order of the Fragments," in *Medioevi* 2 (2016), pp. 189–265, at p. 190.

75 Concina, *Cocharelli Codex*, pp. 208–217, at p. 216. There is a third building with a tympanon painted in red lacking any figurative imagery. According to Concina, it is "*possible that a third symbol was meant to be painted on it (Pisa's white cross on a red ground?)*." It should be noted that Pisa also operated with a simple red flag, see Weber, *Zeichen*, p. 371.

76 Pistarino, *Symboles de Gênes*.

77 R. Macrides, *Pseudo-Kodinos and the Constantinopolitan Court: Offices and Ceremonies* (Farnham, 2013), pp. 152–153, pp. 182–183, p. 387.

78 G. P. Majeska, *Russian Travelers to Constantinople in the Fourteenth and Fifteenth Centuries* (Washington, 1984), p. 106. On the costume of the Podestà, see Pistarino, *Symboles de Gênes*, p. 302.

79 Balard, *Romanie génoise*, I, pp. 359–368.

80 S. Origone, "Colonies and Colonization," in *A Companion to Medieval Genoa* (Brill's Companions to European History, 18), ed. C. E. Beneš (Leiden-Boston, 2018), pp. 496–520.

81 Epstein, *Genoa*, p. 190; Balard, *Romanie génoise*, I, pp. 359–368; Pistarino, *Symboles de Gênes*.

82 Balard, *Romanie génoise*, I, p. 193.

83 A. Rodriguez Suarez, *The Soundscape of Constantinople and Galata* (Paper given at a workshop on the urban fabric of Pera in Istanbul, 29 June 2019, see no. 11).
84 Pistarino, *Symboles de Gênes*, pp. 302–303.
85 A. Makrembolites, "Logos Istorikos," in *Analekta Hyrosolymitikes Stachyologias*, ed. A. Papadopoulos-Kerameus (St. Petersburg, 1891), I, pp. 144–159, p. 144.
86 Clavijo, *Embassy*, p. 66.
87 N. Gregoras, *Byzantina Historia*, ed. I. Bekker (Bonn, 1855), III, 37, p. 554. Gregoras died around 1360.
88 Prior to 1324, see Balard, *Romanie génoise*, I, p. 186.
89 Gottwald, *Stadtmauern*, pp. 10–11; Clavijo, *Embassy*, p. 65.
90 Schneider-Nomidis, *Galata*, pp. 5–6; Balard, *Romanie génoise*, I, pp. 189–190.
91 Quoted after T. S. Miller, *The History of John Cantacuzenus (Book IV). Text, Translation, and Commentary* (Ph.D., Washington, 1975), chap. 24, p. 203.
92 D. M. Nicol, *The Last Centuries of Byzantium 1261-1453* (Cambridge, 20022), p. 223: "*The plan was for them* [the Byzantines] *to engage the Genoese in a sea battle while an army marched round to lay siege to Galata from behind.*"
93 Quoted after Kantakuzenos (trans. Miller), 24, 209.
94 Eyice, *Galata*, p. 77. See Fig. 21.1. I thank Köksal Anadol for his interest in my research and the generous provision of material on the Galata Tower.
95 For a comparison, the average height of the towers of the Theodosian Wall is ca. 20 m, see N. Asutay-Effenberger, *Die Landmauer von Konstantinopel-İstanbul. Historisch-topographische und baugeschichtliche Untersuchungen* (Berlin-Boston, 2007), p. 3. For the hill, see Eyice, *Galata*, p. 73 (35 m.a.s.l.); See also E. Oberhummer, "Constantinopolis," in *Paulys Realencyclopädie der classischen Altertumswissenschaft. Neue Bearbeitung. Unter Mitwirkung zahlreicher Fachgenossen herausgegeben von* Georg Wissowa, 7. *Halbband* (Stuttgart, 1900), pp. 963–1013, at p. 973 (41 m.a.s.l.).
96 N. Gregoras, *Byzantina Historia*, ed. L. Schopen (Bonn, 1830), II, 17.2, p. 848; N. Gregoras, *Rhomäische Geschichte – Historia Romaïke. Übersetzt und erläutert von* J. L. van Dieten, *Dritter Teil (Kapitel XII-XVII)* (Stuttgart, 1988), p. 204.
97 N. Gregoras, *Byzantina Historia*, I, 8.1, p. 284. The Genoese friends were members of the Doria, Spinola, and De Mari families, see N. Gregoras, *Rhomäische Geschichte – Historia Romaïke. Übersetzt und erläutert von* J. L. van Dieten, *Zweiter Teil (Kapitel VIII-XI) 1. Halbband* (Stuttgart, 1979), II.1, p. 102.
98 N. Gregoras, *Byzantina Historia*, I, 11.1, p. 527; N. Gregoras, *Rhomäische Geschichte – Historia Romaïke. Übersetzt und erläutert von* J. L. van Dieten, *Zweiter Teil (Kapitel VIII-XI)* (Stuttgart, 1979), pp. 275–276.
99 N. Gregoras, *Byzantina Historia*, III, 37.49, p. 556; N. Gregoras, *Rhomäische Geschichte – Historia Rhomaïke in Fortsetzung der Arbeit von Jan Louis van Dieten. Übersetzt und erläutert von* F. Tinnefeld, *Sechster Teil (Kapitel XXX-XXXVII)* (Stuttgart, 2007), p. 167.
100 The sources are silent about what happened to the masses of hewn stone gained from tearing down the late antique fortifications of Pera.
101 Quoted from Pero Tafur, *Travels*, p. 27, p. 149.
102 F. Petrarca, *Itinerarium ad sepulcrum Domini nostri Iesu Christi. Reisebuch zum Grab unseres Herrn Jesus Christus. Lateinisch-Deutsch. Übersetzt und herausgegeben von* Jens Reufsteck (Stuttgart, 1999), p. 12.
103 A. Cagnana / R. Mussardo, "Le torri di Genova fra XII e XIII secolo: caratteri architettonici, committenti, costruttori," in *Archeologia dell'Architettura* 17 (2012), pp. 94–110, at p. 94.
104 Balard, *Romanie génoise*, I, p. 191 ("[...] *la tour de Saint-Michel portand l'étendard de la Commune*"). The tower belonged to or was adjacent to the Church of San Michele on the coast.
105 Kaldellis, *Ethnography*, pp. 179–182.
106 F. Schweppenstette, Die *Politik der Erinnerung. Studien zur Stadtgeschichtsschreibung Genuas im 12. Jahrhundert* (Frankfurt am Main, 2003).
107 H. Haug, *Annales Ianuenses. Orte und Medien des historischen Gedächtnisses im mittelalterlichen Genua* (Göttingen, 2016), pp. 311–312.
108 Kaldellis, *Ethnography*.
109 Epstein, *Genoa*, p. 166.

INDEX

Note: Page references in *italics* denote figures, in **bold** tables and with "n" endnotes.

For Product Safety Concerns and Information please contact our EU representative GPSR@taylorandfrancis.com Taylor & Francis Verlag GmbH, Kaufingerstraße 24, 80331 München, Germany